# SIGMUND FREUD

# The Penguin Freud Reader

*Selected and Introduced by Adam Phillips*

PENGUIN BOOKS

PENGUIN BOOKS

Published by the Penguin Group
Penguin Books Ltd, 80 Strand, London WC2R ORL, England
Penguin Group (USA) Inc., 375 Hudson Street, New York, New York 10014, USA
Penguin Group (Canada), 90 Eglinton Avenue East, Suite 700, Toronto, Ontario, Canada M4P 2Y3
(a division of Pearson Penguin Canada Inc.)
Penguin Ireland, 25 St Stephen's Green, Dublin 2, Ireland
(a division of Penguin Books Ltd)
Penguin Group (Australia), 250 Camberwell Road,
Camberwell, Victoria 3124, Australia (a division of Pearson Australia Group Pty Ltd)
Penguin Books India Pvt Ltd, 11 Community Centre,
Panchsheel Park, New Delhi – 110 017, India
Penguin Group (NZ), cnr Airborne and Rosedale Roads, Albany,
Auckland 1310, New Zealand (a division of Pearson New Zealand Ltd)
Penguin Books (South Africa) (Pty) Ltd, 24 Sturdee Avenue,
Rosebank 2196, South Africa

Penguin Books Ltd, Registered Offices: 80 Strand, London WC2R ORL, England

www.penguin.com

This collection of essays first published in Penguin Classics 2006

017

Introduction copyright © Adam Phillips, 2006
The information on pp. 567–70 constitutes an extension of this copyright page
All rights reserved

The moral rights of the translators and the author of the Introduction have been asserted

Set in 10/12.5 point New Caledonia by
Palimpsest Book Production Limited, Polmont, Stirlingshire
Printed and bound in Great Britain by Clays Ltd, Elcograf S.p.A.

ISBN-13: 978-0-14-118743-3

www.greenpenguin.co.uk

MIX
Paper from
responsible sources
FSC
www.fsc.org   FSC™ C018179

Penguin Books is committed to a sustainable
future for our business, our readers and our planet.
This book is made from Forest Stewardship
Council™ certified paper.

PENGUIN BOOKS
*The Penguin Freud Reader*

Sigmund Freud was born in 1856 in Moravia; between the ages of four and eighty-two his home was in Vienna: in 1938 Hitler's invasion of Austria forced him to seek asylum in London, where he died in the following year. His career began with several years of brilliant work on the anatomy and physiology of the nervous system. He was almost thirty when, after a period of study under Charcot in Paris, his interests first turned to psychology; and after ten years of clinical work in Vienna (at first in collaboration with Breuer, an older colleague) he invented what was to become psychoanalysis. This began simply as a method of treating neurotic patients through talking, but it quickly grew into an accumulation of knowledge about the workings of the mind in general. Freud was thus able to demonstrate the development of the sexual instinct in childhood and, largely on the basis of an examination of dreams, arrived at his fundamental discovery of the unconscious forces that influence our everyday thoughts and actions. Freud's life was uneventful, but his ideas shape not only many specialist disciplines, but also the whole intellectual climate of the twentieth century.

Adam Phillips was formerly Principal Child Psychotherapist at Charing Cross Hospital in London. He is the author of several books on psychoanalysis including *On Kissing, Tickling and Being Bored, Darwin's Worms, Promises, Promises, Houdini's Box* and *Going Sane*.

# Contents

Contents

# Introduction

There is an inducement to say, 'Yes, of course, it must be like that'.
A powerful mythology.        Wittgenstein, *Conversations on Freud*

In the so-called *Standard Edition* of Freud's work – the first official and virtually complete translation of Freud's writing by James
Strachey, published in 1959 – the word 'reader' is used one hundred
and twenty-two times. The reader, whom Freud often addresses
directly in his writing, and reading itself were very important for
Freud, all of whose work as a writer and as a clinician is about the
impact of language on the ever-changing modern individual: the
person who suffers and enjoys more words than ever before in
history; the person who is defined economically, politically and
psychologically by her literacy, or lack of it. Freud is the writer for
people who want to find out what words may have done to them,
and may still be doing. And like the modernist writers who are his
contemporaries – Freud's psychoanalytic writing beginning like
Wilde and Conrad in the 1890s, and ending with his death in 1939,
two years before the deaths of James Joyce and Virginia Woolf –
Freud changes our reading habits. He makes us wonder, among
many other things, what we may be doing when we are reading,
what the desire to read is a desire for? When we read psychoanalysis we are reading about what people do to each other with
words; and words, for Freud, are what we do our wanting with.

And yet psychoanalysis as a therapy, it would seem, is not about
writing at all. It is the talking and listening cure because only spoken
words (and money) are exchanged between the analyst and what
Freud as a doctor called the patient. It is not a reading cure; what,

after all, would reading be a cure for? But in order to become a psychoanalyst one has to have been a Freud reader. The patient, ideally, will be the beneficiary of, among other things, his analyst's reading. And this brings us to a question that is at the heart of psychoanalysis, and that is part of the point of this selection of Freud's writings; how does one find out about psychoanalysis? If the question was asked of any other science, the answer would be, among other things, witness or actually perform the experiments that constitute the science. But no one can witness a psychoanalysis; the experiment cannot be exactly replicated. So if you want to find out what psychoanalysis is there is only the recondite experience of being psychoanalysed oneself, gossip and so-called informed discussion about the subject, and reading. The very first psychoanalysts practised what they had heard and read that Freud did. Much of Freud's voluminous and fascinating correspondence with his most talented followers – Jung, Ferenczi, Abraham, Jones, Binswanger, Groddeck, Pfister, Lou Andreas-Salomé – are responses to Freud's writing. Freud, in other words, was a writer who for some reason inspired passionate reading; which, of course, has continued in the rancour and relish with which he is still read. Normally, when people don't like a writer they simply stop reading him, and there is no fuss about it. When people don't like Freud they can't stop both reading him and not reading him, and pronouncing on him; they can't just let him go. 'Once psychoanalysis has held one in its grip,' his colleague Ludwig Binswanger wrote to Freud in 1924, 'it never lets go again'. It is not that psychoanalysis holds one in its grip, it is that people grip on to it (as a hate-object, as a love-object, but not usually as an irrelevant object).

So it is the aim of *The Penguin Freud Reader* not to introduce people to psychoanalysis as a therapy, which can only be done by trying it out; nor to provide a comprehensive selection of Freud's writing, which would merely reveal more about the selector than the selected; nor to take it for granted that a 'great writer' is here on show, when Freud himself had so much to tell us and did so much to ironize our wishes for greatness. It is, rather, the aim of this *Reader* to enable the curious, who are by definition not the converted, to discover what, if anything, is so haunting about Freud's writing. Why, for some people, Freud's writing was the kind of reading experience that was (and is) more akin to a conversion experience; why Freud's sentences had what might be called a religious effect on people, even, or especially when, they wanted to describe psychoanalysis as a science. 'The analytic revelation,' Thomas Mann wrote in his speech of 1936 on Freud's eightieth birthday, 'is a revolutionary force. With it a blithe scepticism has come into the world, a mistrust that unmasks all the schemes and subterfuges of our own souls. Once roused and on the alert, it cannot be put to sleep again. It infiltrates life, undermines its raw naïveté, takes from it the strain of its own ignorance . . . inculcates the taste for understatement, as the English call it – for the deflated rather than for the inflated word . . .' (published in his *Essays of Three Decades*). It is among the paradoxes of Freud's writing that he inspires us by deflating us; that his blithe scepticism – and scepticism, as Mann knows, is often bitter, resigned and boastful – can make our lives, in their very disillusionments, more amusing, more sexually awakened, more charged with interested and interesting meaning. Understatement reminds us that there is something under our statements. Something at work, and at play. In Freud's description of what we are like, it is our passion for ignorance that animates us; and it is our passion for ignorance about ourselves that is so time-consuming, so life-consuming. What Mann calls mixing the language of politics and of religion, the psychoanalytic revelation that is a revolution suggests, at its most minimal, that there may be a contagious energy about Freud's writing. It can make people excessive in their responses.

Excess is Freud's theme. Our desire, he tells us, is way in excess of any object's capacity to satisfy it; the meanings we make are in excess of the meanings we intend; our desire for death can be in excess of our desire for more life. Freud's influence, many people now think, has itself been excessive. It is as though we can't help but read now through the glasses he has given us. Alerted by him to puns and ambiguities, hesitations and non-sequiturs, slips and over-emphases; wily about the sex under the sentences, the deflected aggressions, the egotism involved in whatever is shied away from, we are all Freud readers now. And yet Freud counsels us to be wary of our knowingness, mindful of our need to know where we are at the cost of seeing where we are. He shows us that we are prone to read and listen – two things that are closer than they at first seem – too wishfully, too fearfully; and that we often deal with what we fear by identifying with it, by trying to be like it (so Freudians, whatever else they are, are people frightened of Freud). Indeed, there is nothing more excessive, in Freud's account of us, than our craving for authority.

If Freud wants us to be attentive by showing us how defensive we are, that in the struggle to be pleased with ourselves we can miss too much, he also wants to persuade us that we are always reading for pleasure. Because it is pleasure that we are always seeking, and never more so than when the nature of that pleasure is obscure. The question, in other words, for the Freud reader, is: what is the pleasure of reading Freud? Can she read Freud – or indeed anyone else now – in her own way rather than in Freud's way?

Contributing to a questionnaire on reading in 1907, Freud was asked simply to name, without explanation, ten good books. As a man with a passion for riddles, a man for whom living a life was always a matter of reading the signs, this simple enough request puzzled him. 'Accustomed to paying attention to small signs,' he wrote, 'I must then trust the wording in which you couch your enigmatical demand.' As a psychoanalyst, of course, it was the couching of demands that Freud was interested in; and, indeed, the sense in which the simplest demand was enigmatic. What is it, after all, that makes us think that any given demand is simple? Freud trusts the wording of the demand for ten good books by unpacking it at some length. There are, he says in his slightly farcical way, at least three other kinds of books, apart from the good ones.

You did not ask, he tells the editors by way of reply, for 'the ten most magnificent works (of world literature)', in which case he would have named Homer, the tragedies of Sophocles, Goethe's *Faust*, Shakespeare's *Hamlet*, *Macbeth* 'etc.'; the etc. referring, presumably, to all the other great books in a certain European canon of the highest literary art. Nor did they ask for the 'ten most significant books'. If they had, Freud would have named what he calls the 'scientific achievements' of Copernicus, Darwin and the rather more obscure Johann Weir ('on the belief in witches') among others. Finally, if they had asked him for his 'favourite books', he would certainly have mentioned Milton's *Paradise Lost* and Heine's *Lazarus*. For Freud it is the 'good' book that he finds the most difficult to define, as though it is the simple adjective that asks the most of us, the ordinary words that read like riddles.

Good books, Freud suggests, must be like good friends, 'to whom one owes a part of one's knowledge of life and view of the world – books which one has enjoyed oneself and gladly commends to others, but in connection with which the element of timid reverence, the feeling of one's own smallness in the face of greatness, is not particularly prominent.'

One's relationship to a 'good' book, like one's relationship to a good friend, is not fearful; the other kinds of books are intimidating. They can even inspire us by diminishing us, by making us feel small. Indeed, the 'element of timid reverence, the feeling of one's own smallness in the face of greatness' are rather more akin to feelings of religious awe. The secular religion of great writing – for Freud, as for so many of his bourgeois contemporaries – had replaced the sacred religions of their forefathers. Freud was someone who had clearly been daunted by literature, someone who had felt traumatized – humiliated, belittled and inspired – by reading. Good books for him are clearly reassuring and useful; the other kinds of books he mentions are overpowering. It would not be overstating the case to say that, for Freud, reading had been the modern equivalent of what, beginning in the eighteenth century, had been called the experience of the sublime. To write and to read was to be close to the source of something, close to the source of the most important something. Freud, in short, did not want to be a writer of good books.

He also didn't particularly want to be a good doctor. He felt, he wrote in his *Autobiographical Study* (1925) 'no particular partiality for the position and activity of a physician in those early years, nor, by the way, later. Rather, I was moved by a sort of greed for knowledge.' What he doesn't tell us, at least there, is what he thought a greed for knowledge was a greed for. Since reading is one form that this greed takes, and since, for Freud, there were three kinds of appetite – the appetite to survive (to eat and be protected), the appetite, that is the desire, for the forbidden object of desire (incest), and the appetite, that is also a desire, for death – it is worth wondering what this greed for knowledge that is so well served by reading might be about. Because Freud as a writer is both acquiring knowledge through the process of writing, and satisfying his reader's appetite for what they are likely to think of as knowledge about something.

In all his writing Freud is very didactic; if you dip into any page of this *Reader* you will find Freud informing you about something, explaining to you how dreams work, how and why memory is memory of desire, how symptoms are forms of sexual satisfaction, why pain is so alluring as a pleasure, and so on. He assumes that the reader wants to know about things. But he also assumes, more paradoxically, that the one thing the reader wants to do more than know, is not to know; that, indeed, the very ways we go about knowing things is the form our greed for ignorance takes. Psychoanalysis is a very elaborate redescription of curiosity.

Freud tells us, as his phrase 'the greed for knowledge' suggests, that what we have been taught to call knowing we should call desiring; knowledge is a way of making desire sound less disreputable. But knowing is really (i.e. in Freud's terms) what another psychoanalyst, D. W. Winnicott, called 'the imaginative elaboration of physical function'. There are not only bodies of knowledge, there are only bodies that want knowledge. Because our desire, when it is not solely the struggle for survival, is essentially, in Freud's view, a desire for something forbidden, it is the very thing we try not to know about, and the only thing that really interests us. Like Freud's magnificent, significant and favourite books, there is always a feeling of one's own smallness in the face of the greatness of one's desires. Like Oedipus, the Freud reader is on a self-blinding quest. And the quest is conducted in language. It is in language that the self is constructed, and it is in language that the self is free to deceive itself. Virtually every page of Freud's writing says something about language, and something about the hiding and the seeking of desire.

Living a life is reading a life, in Freud's view; and since life is composed of its desire for more life, and its desire for less life, and, above all, its desire for the forbidden life, nothing is going to make us more resistant than this reading. The (Freudian) reader and writer are not only partners in crime; they are partners in concealing the crime from themselves. 'The writer enables us,' Freud writes in 'The Creative Writer and Daydreaming', '. . . to enjoy our own fantasies without shame or self-reproach.' Our fantasies, which are the conscious formulation of our unconscious desires, are shameful and guilt-provoking; the writer renders the unacceptable acceptable, and the reader consents. Then Freud provokes us, in his ironically understated way, to wonder whether it is better or worse for us to be aware of just what it is we have consented to. (If pleasure is contraband, is it better for the smuggler to know what he is smuggling?) What is it, Freud wants to know, that can make reading (and writing) so pleasurable; and what do we need to do, and not to do, in order to sustain this pleasure? For Freud, like many of his contemporary modernist writers, reading and writing seems like the best analogy, the most illuminating way of talking about the dramas and melodramas of everyday modern life. Writing about writing was writing about holding on to an appetite for modern life, about what language can sustain in us.

Like anyone with an appetite for reading and writing, for listening and speaking, Freud is mindful not only of the enigmas of language – indeed of language itself as an enigma – but of its limits. Psychoanalysis, in its dependence on words is, by the same token, an inquiry into what language can't do for us, into what we can't change about ourselves by redescribing ourselves (Freud often writes most interestingly about psychoanalysis when he writes about why it doesn't work). In Freud's account of modern people as animals of desire and of language, he is at once struck by both their mobility and their paralysis. Freud's modern individual is staggeringly ingenious in his pleasure-seeking – and his verbal ingenuity is integral to his hedonism; and ineluctably fixated, repetitious, self-frustrating. He is too often defeated by the desires that animate him, and driven by the self-hatred, the hatred and fear of his own desire, that is called guilt. Adulthood, for many people, has become a long hangover created by childhood. The modern individual who claims to want the new, to believe in progress, to want to grow and develop her self, is furtively seeking only the pleasures of the past. The wish to be a child seems to have usurped the point of being an adult.

In Freud's view, we can only look forward now by looking back; our longing is to recreate the past, and the future is the place in which we may be able to rework the satisfactions and frustrations of our childhood. Freud is preoccupied, in other words, by whether it is possible for modern people to have new experiences, to find new objects of desire, to improvise upon their pasts.

We repeat in action what we are unable to remember in words or images, Freud writes in 'Remembering, Repeating, and Working Through'; we experience new people as though they were familiar, inventing them on the basis of our first familial loves and hates, he tells us in his writings on transference; and we revise past experiences and memories on the basis of present desires and impressions, he tells us in the case of the Wolfman, as he begins to describe the essential psychoanalytic notion of 'deferred action'. The dream uses experiences in the day before the dream' – what Freud calls 'the dream day' – to revive and recycle the desires of childhood. 'The direction of time in terms of past/present/future – the foundation of all secure positions of thought which only take conscious experiences into account,' the psychoanalyst André Green writes in 'Time in Psychoanalysis', is 'shattered' by psychoanalysis. The retrospective and the prospective are multiply related and reconfigured in Freud's writing.

So it would not be strange if, in reading Freud, our reading habits also changed. Our traditional sense of a beginning, a middle and an end – the parallel of Green's direction of time in terms of past/present/future – begins to look different, as these discrete categories begin to interfere with each other. The trajectory of Freud's own writing when it is read – as it can be more easily in this *Reader* – from end to beginning can lose that spurious sense of linearity, of an inevitable development, of a necessary direction or momentum in the work. We can see Freud continually reworking, in his ambition to be one of those great daunting unforgettable writers, the nature of memory. It is perhaps not surprising that the man who made wishing so central to our lives – who showed us just how literally we wish our lives away – should have been so ambitious as a writer, so keen and so canny about the magic of words.

Reading Freud back to front, as it were, or dipping in, or jumping around in the book when Freud begins to bore or irritate us, we can relinquish that old-fashioned diligence – the thoroughness, the conscientiousness, the fantasies of rigour – that psychoanalysis has helped us make a mockery of (and helped us see the mockery in). If anything, Freud encourages us to read as we dream, according to our desire, surprised by what may strike us, and unable to predict what will haunt us; and able, if possible, to notice those resistances that Freud found so telling, in our difficulties with his own texts in which he is telling us something, so he tells us, that is the only thing we want to know, and that therefore we don't want to know at all.

# A Note on the Texts

This *Penguin Freud Reader,* unlike the previous *Freud Reader* edited by Peter Gay (London, 1995) and unlike *The Essentials of Psychoanalysis* edited by Anna Freud (London 1986), intersperses texts from the new Penguin Freud translations and some new translations commissioned for this volume, which are not published elsewhere. So the reader of this new *Penguin Freud Reader* will find no house-style Freud; and unlike those who have the misfortune to be able to read Freud only in the original, the reader will find here a more various Freud, less consistent in idiom and terminology than even Freud himself was able to be.

# An Outline of Psychoanalysis

*Part One: The Nature of Things Psychical*

The purpose of this brief essay is to offer as it were a dogmatic conspectus of psychoanalysis by bringing together all its doctrines in the most concentrated and clear-cut form. Obviously, it is not intended to convert or to convince you.

The postulates of psychoanalysis rest on an immeasurable wealth of observations and experiences, and only the person who has repeated these observations on himself and others has set about being able to pass his own judgement on them.

## Chapter 1: the Psychical Apparatus

Psychoanalysis makes a basic assumption, the discussion of which remains the preserve of philosophical thought, and the justification for which lies in its results. We know two things about what we call the psyche (or psychical life). Firstly, we know about the brain (nerve system), the physical organ and scene of the psyche; secondly, we know that there are acts of consciousness that are presented to us in their immediate form and that no description can bring us any closer to. Everything in between is an unknown quantity to us; there is no direct relationship between these two end points of our knowledge. If there were such a relationship, it would at most give us an exact location of the processes of consciousness, and would not in the slightest help us to comprehend them.

Our two hypotheses take these ends or beginnings of our knowledge as their starting point. The first hypothesis concerns localization. We suppose that psychical life is the function of an apparatus which, we say, extends spatially and consists of several pieces – pieces which we, then, imagine to be similar to a telescope, a microscope or suchlike. The logical extension of such a notion is, disregarding certain attempts already made to approach it, a scientific novelty.

We have come to know about this psychical apparatus by studying the individual development of human beings. We call the oldest of these psychical provinces or forces the *Es*; it contains everything that is inherited, everything present at birth, everything constitutionally determined – above all, then, the drives originating from the bodily organization, which here [that is, in the *Es*] find a first psychical expression in forms unknown to us.[1]

Under the influence of the objective external world around us, part of the *Es* has developed in a particular way. In its original capacity as a cortical layer it was equipped both with organs to receive stimuli and with apparatus to protect against them; but, since then, a particular form of organization has developed that mediates between the *Es* and the external world. We have called this zone of our psyche the *Ich*.

## The Main Characteristics of the *Ich*

Due to the relationship formed earlier between sensory perceptions and muscular action, the *Ich* has control over voluntary movement. It has the task of self-assertion, and fulfils it with respect to the *outside* world by getting to know the stimuli there, by storing information about them (in the memory), by avoiding excessively strong stimuli (through flight), by dealing with moderate stimuli (through adaptation), and finally by learning to change to the external world in an expedient way to its own advantage (through activity). It also fulfils its task with respect to the *inner* world, that is, with respect to the *Es*, by gaining mastery over the demands of the drives, by deciding whether they should be allowed gratification, by postponing this gratification until the time and circumstances are favourable in the external world, or by suppressing their excitations altogether. Its actions are directed by observing the tensions that are either already present in it or have been introduced into it. If these tensions increase, this is generally perceived as *unpleasure*, and if they decrease, it is perceived as *pleasure*. However, it is probably not the absolute levels of this tension that are felt as pleasure or unpleasure but, rather, something about the rhythm in which they change. The *Ich* strives for pleasure, wants to avoid unpleasure. An expected, foreseen increase in unpleasure is answered by a *fear signal*; its cause, whether it threatens from without or within, is called a *danger*. From time to time, the *Ich* dissolves its connection with the external world and retreats into the dormant state in which it makes extensive changes to its organization. We can conclude from this dormant state that this organization consists in a particular distribution of psychical energy.

The growing human has a particularly long period of childhood during which he is dependent on his parents. As a residue of this period, a special authority develops in his *Ich*, in which this parental influence continues to exist. We have called this the *Über-Ich*. In so far as the *Über-Ich* is distinguished from the *Ich* or is opposed to it, it is a third authority that the *Ich* has to take into account.

An action of the *Ich* is then fully apt if it simultaneously satisfies the demands of the *Es*, the *Über-Ich* and reality – in other words, if it can reconcile their demands with one another. The details of the relationship between the *Ich* and the *Über-Ich* become altogether comprehensible if we trace them back to the child's relationship with his parents. It is, of course, not only the personality of the individual parents that affects the influence they have over the child, but also the familial, racial and national traditions that they hand down, along with the demands of the particular social milieu they represent. During the course of the individual's development, the *Über-Ich* absorbs in the same way contributions from the later parental substitutes and other people who carry on having an influence, such as educators, public role models and respected social ideals. We see that, for all their fundamental dissimilarity,

3

the *Es* and the *Über-Ich* have one thing in common: they represent the influences of the past. The *Es* represents the influence of what is inherited, and the *Über-Ich* essentially represents the influence of what is taken over from other people; whilst the *Ich* is mainly determined by what we experience ourselves – in other words, by accidental and current events.

This general pattern of a psychical apparatus could also be applied to the higher animals, those that are psychically similar to humans. We can suppose that an *Über-Ich* is always present when there has been a prolonged period of childhood dependency, as with humans. One can't avoid assuming that there is a distinction between the *Ich* and the *Es*.

Animal psychology has not yet started to tackle the interesting problem that raises itself here.

## Chapter 2: the Theory of the Drives

The power of the *Es* expresses the actual purpose of the individual's life. This consists of gratifying his innate needs. We can't attribute to the *Es* an intention to remain alive and to use fear to protect itself from dangers. This is the task of the *Ich*, which also has to discover the most favourable and least dangerous kind of gratification whilst taking the external world into account. The *Über-Ich* may assert new needs, but its main function remains the restriction of gratifications.

*Drives* are what we call the forces that we suppose to lie behind the tensions caused by the needs of the *Es*. They represent the physical demands on the psyche. Although they are the ultimate cause of all activity, they are conservative in nature; whatever state a being has arrived at, an urge emerges to re-establish this state as soon as it has been abandoned. We can, then, distinguish between an indeterminate number of drives; indeed, one does so in common practice. Significant for us, however, is the possibility of being able to trace this multiplicity of drives back to a few basic ones. We have discovered that the drives can change their aim (by displacement), and also that they can replace one another, by the energy from one drive moving over to another. The latter process is still not well understood. After much wavering, we have decided to propose only two basic drives: *Eros* and the *destruction-drive*. (The opposition between the self-preservation and species-preservation drives, along with the other opposition between *Ich*-love and object-love, still falls within Eros.) The aim of the first drive is to establish and maintain ever greater unities, that is, 'binding'; the aim of the second is, by contrast, to dissolve connections, and thus to destroy things. In the case of the destruction-drive, we can also suppose that its ultimate aim is to convert the living into the inorganic state. Because of this, we also call it the *death-drive*. If we assume that the living appeared later than the lifeless and arose from this, then the death-drive fits into the formula I have mentioned, namely that drives strive to restore everything to an earlier state. We can't use this formula for Eros (or the love-drive). This would mean presupposing that living substance was once a unity which was then torn apart and now strives to be reunified.[2]

In the biological functions, the two basic drives work against one another or combine with one another. Thus the act of eating means destroying the object with the ultimate aim of incorporating it; and the sexual act is an act of aggression with the intention of creating the most intimate union. This way in which the two basic drives work with and against each other gives rise to the whole spectrum of life-phenomena. The analogy of our two basic drives leads us beyond the realm of the living to the diametric opposition between the forces of attraction and repulsion that dominates the inorganic world.[3]

Changes to the proportions in which the drives are merged have the most tangible consequences. A strong increase in the proportion of sexual aggression turns the lover into the sex-murderer; a strong reduction in the aggressive factor makes him timid or impotent.

There can be no question of restricting either of the basic drives to one of the psychical provinces. They have to be found everywhere. We imagine an initial state in this manner: all the available energy of Eros, which we shall henceforth call 'libido', is present in the *Ich-Es*, which has not yet been differentiated, and serves to neutralize the destructive tendencies that are present at the same time. (We lack an analogous term to 'libido' for the energy of the destruction-drive.) It is relatively easy for us to trace the fate of the libido later on; it is more difficult to do so in the case of the destruction-drive.

So long as this drive operates within the individual as a death-drive, it remains silent; it only impinges on us when it is turned outwards as a destruction-drive. That this should happen seems to be necessary for the preservation of the individual. The muscle system serves this diverting of energy. When the *Über-Ich* is established, considerable amounts of the aggression drive are fixated within the *Ich* and act self-destructively there. It is one of the dangers to health that humans take upon themselves en route to cultural development. It is wholly unhealthy to withhold aggression; the effect of this is that the person becomes ill. The shift from averted aggression into self-destruction via turning the aggression against one's own person is often demonstrated by someone in a fit of rage in which he tears out his hair or punches his own face, in the process obviously wishing that he were meting out this treatment to somebody else. A degree of self-destruction remains under any circumstances within the individual until it eventually succeeds in killing him, perhaps only once his libido is used up or fixed in a disadvantageous way. Thus one can generally suppose that the individual dies of his inner conflicts – but the species, on the other hand, dies of its unsuccessful struggle against the external world, if this has changed in such a way that the adaptations it has made are not sufficient.

It is difficult to say anything about the behaviour of the libido in the *Es* and in the *Über-Ich*. Everything that we know about it is related to the *Ich*, in which the entire available amount of libido is initially stored. We call this state absolute, primary *narcissism*. It lasts until the *Ich* begins to invest its notions of objects with libido, to transform narcissistic libido into *object-libido*. Throughout the whole of our lives, the *Ich* remains the great reservoir from which libido-investments are sent out to objects and into which they are pulled back again, in the same way that a protoplasm behaves with its pseudopodia. It is only when the individual is totally in love that the main quota of libido is transferred on to the object, and the object to a certain extent take the place of the *Ich*. One characteristic of the *Ich* that is important in life is the libido's *mobility*, the ease with which it passes from one object onto another. In contrast to this is the fixation of the libido on certain objects that often persists throughout one's entire life.

It is an unmistakable fact that the libido has somatic sources; that it streams from various organs and parts of the body to the *Ich*. We can see this most clearly in that portion of the libido that is described according to its drive-aim as 'sexual arousal'. We call the most prominent of these parts of the body from which the libido comes the *erogenous zones* – although, in fact, the whole body is an erogenous zone of this kind. The best information we have about Eros, that is, about its exponent, the libido, has been gleaned by studying the sexual function which, of course, coincides with Eros in the popular view, if not in our theory. We can form a picture of the way in which the sexual urge, which is destined to have a decisive influence on our life, gradually develops from the successive contributions from several partial drives, all of which represent particular zones.


## Chapter 3: the Development of the Sexual Function

According to the popular view, human sexual life essentially consists of the urge to bring our own genitals into contact with those of someone of the opposite sex. Kissing, looking at, and touching this other body appear in the process as concomitant and introductory acts. This urge is supposed to appear at puberty, that is, at the age of sexual maturity, and is supposed to serve reproduction. Nevertheless, we have always known certain facts that don't fit into this narrow purview.

1) It is odd that there are people who are attracted only to individuals of their own sex and with their own type of genitals.
2) It is equally peculiar that there are people – we call them perverts – whose desires behave just like the sexual ones but which ignore the sexual organs or their normal use.
3) And, finally, it is striking that some children demonstrate a very early interest in their genitals and signs of arousal in them. They are said to be degenerate because of this.

It is understandable that psychoanalysis aroused a stir and provoked denials when, partly on the basis of these three disregarded facts, it contradicted all the popular opinions about sexuality. Its main results are as follows:

a) Sexual life doesn't bide its time until puberty, but starts to manifest itself very clearly soon after birth.
b) It isn't necessary to draw a sharp distinction between the terms 'sexual' and 'genital'. The former is the broader term and encompasses many activities that have nothing to do with the genitals.
c) Sexual life encompasses the function of obtaining pleasure from zones of the body, a function which is later put into the service of reproduction. These two functions are often not necessarily mutually inclusive.

We are, of course, mainly interested in the first assertion, the most unexpected of them all. It has been demonstrated that there are signs of physical activity in early childhood to which only an old prejudice could deny the name sexual, and that are connected with the kinds of psychical phenomena that we later find in adult love-life such as, say, the fixation on particular objects, jealousy, or suchlike. Beyond this, however, it is evident that these phenomena are part of a natural and orderly development: they emerge in early childhood and invariably increase, reaching a climax somewhere around the end of the child's fifth year, before taking a break. During this break, everything stands still: much is unlearnt and recedes again. Once this so-called latency period has run its course, sexual life advances into puberty – we could say that it comes into bloom again. Here we come up against the fact that sexual life begins in two phases – something that is only known in humans, and something that is clearly very important for the process of becoming human.[4] It is not a matter of indifference that the events of this early period of sexuality, give or take a few residua, fall victim to infantile amnesia. Our insights into the aetiology of the neuroses and our technique of analytical therapy are derived from these views. Tracing the developmental processes of this early period has also offered evidence for other hypotheses.

The first organ that appears from birth onwards as an erogenous zone and makes a libidinous claim on the psyche is the mouth. All psychical activity is initially directed at obtaining gratification of this zone's needs. Of course the mouth, with its function of providing nourishment, primarily serves self-preservation, but we ought not to confuse physiology with psychology. A need for gratification manifests itself early on, in the child's stubborn and persistent sucking; a need that – although it comes from and is stimulated by the taking in of nourishment – is nevertheless independent of nourishment and strives to gain pleasure. Because of this it can and should be called sexual.

During this oral phase, sadistic impulses already begin to occur sporadically with the cutting of teeth. This happens to a much greater extent in the second phase, which we called the sadistic-anal one, because here gratification is sought in aggression and in the excretory function. We base the right to mention the aggressive urges under the heading 'libido' on the view that sadism is a drive-blending of purely aggressive and purely destructive urges; a blending that will persist from now on for the rest of the person's life.[5]

The third phase is the so-called phallic phase; this is, as it were, a forerunner to the final form taken by sexual life, and is already very similar to it. It is worth noting that it is the male member (phallus) alone that plays a role here, rather than the genitals of both sexes. The female genitals remain unrecognized for a long

9

time to come; in its attempt to understand the sexual processes, the child clings devotedly to the venerable cloacal theory which is, genetically speaking, entirely justified.[6]

With and during the phallic phase, early childhood sexuality reaches its climax – and approaches its decline. From now on, boys and girls have separate fates. Both have begun to place their intellectual activity in the service of sexual investigation; both take as their starting point the assumption that a penis is universally present. Now, though, the paths taken by the sexes diverge from one another. The boy enters the Oedipal phase: he begins to manipulate his penis whilst fantasizing about using it in some sexual way on his mother – until he sees that girls have no penis and this, combined with a castration threat, causes him to experience the greatest trauma of his life, which ushers in the latency period with all its consequences. After a vain attempt to do the same as the boy, the girl comes to recognize her lack of a penis or, rather, the inferiority of her clitoris. This has permanent consequences for her character-development; as a result of this first disappointment in rivalry she often initially rejects sexual life altogether.

It would be a mistake to believe that these three phases are smoothly replaced by each other. The one appears in addition to the other; they overlap; they exist alongside one another. In the early phases, the individual partial drives embark upon their search for pleasure independently of one another; the phallic phase marks the beginnings of an organization that subordinates the other urges to the primacy of the genitals and signifies the beginning of the general striving for pleasure being categorized as belonging to the sexual function. The complete organization of a fourth, genital, phase is only achieved at puberty. Then, we find a state in which

1) some earlier libido investments have remained intact;
2) others are taken up into the sexual function as preparatory, supporting actions, the gratification of which creates so-called fore-pleasure;
3) other urges are excluded from the organization either by being completely suppressed (repressed) or by being used

in some other way in the *Ich*, to create character traits, to undergo sublimation with displaced aims.

This process is not always performed flawlessly. The inhibitions in its development express themselves as the manifold disruptions to sexual life. In these circumstances, fixations of the libido on states from earlier phases are then evident; their urges, which are independent of the normal sexual aim, are called *perversions*. One example of such inhibited development is homosexuality, if it is manifest. Analysis demonstrates that a homosexual object-attachment was present in all cases and, in most cases, has also been *latently* retained. The circumstances are complicated by the fact that the processes necessary to bring about the normal outcome are usually neither, say, fully completed nor entirely lacking, but are *partially* completed so that the final outcome is dependent on these *quantitative* relations. The genital organization is then indeed achieved, but is weakened by the portions of the libido that have not made the transition and have remained fixated on pre-genital objects and aims. This weakening shows itself in the libido's inclination, in cases where it obtains no genital gratification or where it experiences objective difficulties, to return to its early, pre-genital investments (regression).

While studying the sexual functions we were able to come to an initial, provisional conviction or – more correctly speaking, a suspicion – that we had made two discoveries that would turn out to be important in this sphere as a whole. First, we saw that the normal and abnormal phenomena that we were observing (that is, their phenomenology) demand to be described from dynamic and economic points of view (in our case, this means from the point of view of the quantitative distribution of the libido); and second, we say that the aetiology of the sorts of disorder that we study is to be found in the history of the individual's development – that is to say, in his early years.

## *Chapter 4: Psychical Qualities*

We have described the structure of the psychical apparatus, the energies or forces that are at work in it, and we have used a prominent example to trace the ways in which these energies, mainly the libido, organize themselves into a physiological function that serves the preservation of the species. There was nothing in this that represented the quite unique character of what is psychical apart, of course, from the empirical fact that the functions that we call our psyche are based on this apparatus and these energies. We shall now turn to something that is characteristic of the psyche alone, indeed, something that, according to a most widespread belief, coincides with it to the exclusion of all else.

The starting point of this investigation is the unparalleled fact of consciousness, which defies all explanation and description. Undefinable and inexplicable it may be, but if we speak of consciousness then we none the less immediately know from our own most personal experience what is meant by it.[7] Many people, both within and outside science, are content to suppose consciousness alone to be the psychical thing, and in this case there remains nothing for psychology to do other than to distinguish between perceptions, feelings, thought processes and acts of will within the psychical phenomena. However, according to general consensus, these conscious processes don't in fact form a seamless, self-contained sequence – so the only thing that remains for us is to assume that physical or somatic processes accompany the psychical ones, processes which, we must grant, are more complete than those in the psychical sequences, since a few of them have parallel conscious processes, though others don't. Of course, it then seems obvious to place psychological emphasis on these somatic processes, to recognize in them what is really psychical, and to look for another way to evaluate the conscious processes. Most philosophers, along with many others, now resist this, and declare the idea of something being simultaneously unconscious and psychical to be nonsense.

However, it is precisely this that psychoanalysis has to do, and this is its second fundamental assumption. It declares that the allegedly somatic 'accompanying processes' are the really psychical things and, by doing so, initially disregards the quality of consciousness. It is not alone in this. Some thinkers such as Theodore Lipps, for example, have said the same thing in more or less the same words, and the general dissatisfaction with the normal view of things psychical has led to ever more urgent demands for the concept of the unconscious to be adopted by psychological thought – although these demands have been made in such an indefinite and obscure manner that they could have no influence on science.

Now, it would seem that this difference between psychoanalysis and psychology concerned nothing more than a trifling question of definition; a question as to whether the name 'psychical' should be applied to the one or the other sequence. In fact, this step has become highly significant. Whereas in the psychology of consciousness people never got beyond those incomplete sequences that were clearly dependent on something else, the other view – that the psychical is in itself unconscious – has allowed psychology to develop into a natural science like any other. The processes with which it is concerned are in themselves just as unknowable as those of other sciences – of, say, chemistry or physics – but it is possible to establish which laws they obey, to trace their mutual relationships and interdependencies seamlessly over long stretches; in other words, to reach what one calls an 'understanding' of the relevant area of natural phenomena. This can't happen without our making assumptions and creating new terms – but these should not be despised as testifying to any embarrassment on our part. On the contrary, they should be treasured as an enriching of science; they have as much claim to 'approximate value' status as the corresponding working premises have in other sciences; they can expect to be amended, corrected and fine tuned after we have accumulated and sifted through further experiences. It is then also quite in keeping with our expectations that the fundamental terms and principles of the new science (drives, nervous energy et al.) remain for a long time as obscure as those of the older sciences (force, mass, attraction).

All sciences are based on observation and experience that are mediated by our psychical apparatus. However, as our science takes this apparatus itself as an object, the analogy ends here. We make our observations by means of the same perception apparatus, precisely with the help of the gaps in what is psychical, by using the obvious conclusions to elaborate on what is omitted, and by translating these omissions into unconscious material. Thus we construct as it were a sequence of conscious events in addition to the unconscious psychical processes. The relative certainty of our knowledge of the psyche is based on the binding force of these conclusions. Anyone who immerses himself in this work will find that our technique withstands every criticism.

In the course of this work, those distinctions that we call psychical qualities force themselves upon our notice. We don't need to characterize what we call 'conscious': it is the same as the consciousness of philosophy and popular opinion. Everything else that is physical is, for us, the unconscious. We are soon led to postulate an important distinction within this unconscious. Some processes can become conscious easily; they may then cease to be conscious, but can become so again with no trouble; they can, as we say, be reproduced or remembered. This reminds us that consciousness is only ever a very fleeting state. Anything that is conscious is only conscious for a moment. If our perceptions don't confirm this, then that is only an apparent contradiction; it stems from the fact that the stimuli that lead to perception can last for a long time so that, meanwhile, the perceptions may be repeated. The entire state of affairs becomes clear in the conscious perception of our thought processes: they may indeed persist, but they may just as easily disappear in the blink of an eye. Everything unconscious that behaves in this manner, that can so easily exchange the unconscious state for the conscious one, we thus prefer to call 'capable of becoming conscious', or *preconscious*. Experience has taught us that there is hardly any psychical process that is so complicated that it could not occasionally remain preconscious, even if it usually presses, as we say, to become conscious.

Other psychical processes and material don't enter the consciousness so easily, but have to be deduced, guessed at, and translated into conscious expression in the manner described. For these, we reserve the name of the actual unconscious. We have, then, attributed three qualities to the psychical processes: they are either conscious, preconscious, or unconscious. The differentiation between the three categories of material that bear these qualities is neither absolute nor permanent. Something preconscious becomes, as we have seen, conscious without our being involved; and the unconscious can, through our efforts, be made conscious, whereby we may have the sense that we are often overcoming very strong resistances. If we try to do this with another individual, we mustn't forget that the conscious filling of the gaps in his perception, the interpretation that we present to him, doesn't yet mean that we have made the relevant unconscious material conscious in his case. This material is, rather, initially present in him in a two-fold fixation: firstly, in the conscious reconstruction he has heard and, in addition to this, in its original, unconscious state. Our continued efforts mostly succeed in making him conscious of this unconscious material himself, as a result of which both fixations coincide. The degree of effort by which we estimate resistance against the material coming to consciousness differs depending on the individual case. For example, something that is the result of our efforts in analytical treatment can also occur spontaneously; material that is otherwise unconscious can transform itself into something preconscious and can then become conscious, as happens on a large scale in psychotic states. We infer from this that upholding certain inner resistances is a condition of normality. Such a reduction of resistances and the resultant clamouring of unconscious material frequently takes place while we are asleep and thus establishes the conditions under which dreams can be formed. The reverse can also happen: preconscious material can become inaccessible, cut off by resistances – as is the case when we temporarily forget something or when it just escapes our memory. Alternatively, a preconscious thought can even be temporarily transferred back into the unconscious state; this seems to be the pre-condition for jokes. We shall see that a similar transformation of preconscious content (or processes) back into the unconscious state plays a major role in the causation of neurotic disturbances.

Portrayed in this generalized and simplified form, the theory of the three qualities of things psychical seems to be a source of immense confusion rather than a step towards an explanation. But we mustn't forget that it is in fact not a theory at all but a first report on the facts that we have observed; that it sticks as closely as possible to these facts and makes no attempt to explain them. The complications that it reveals may make people understand the particular difficulties that our research has to struggle with. However, this theory will presumably also be made more accessible to us if we trace out the relationships that arise between the psychical qualities and the provinces or forces that we have supposed to be part of the psychical apparatus. These relationships are, though, anything other than simple.

The process of becoming conscious is above all connected to the perceptions that our sense-organs receive from the external world. From a topographical point of view, therefore, it is a phenomenon that occurs in the outermost cortex of the *Ich*. It is true that we also receive conscious information from within the body – the feelings, which have even more of a domineering influence on our psyche than external perceptions; and, moreover, under certain circumstances the sense-organs also deliver feelings and sensations of pain outside their specific perceptions. Since, however, these sensations – as we call them, in order to distinguish them from conscious perceptions – at the same time emanate from the terminal organs, which we regard as extensions or offshoots of the cortical layer, we can still maintain the above assertion [that is, the one at the start of this paragraph]. The sole difference would be that the body itself would replace the external world so far as the terminal organs of sensation and feeling are concerned.

Processes on the periphery of the *Ich* as conscious, and all other processes in the *Ich* as *un*conscious: this would be the most simple idea that we could imagine. It may really be so in the case of animals – but, in the case of humans there is an added complication: the inner processes of the *Ich* can also acquire the quality of consciousness. This is the function of language, which firmly connects the material within the *Ich* with memory traces of visual or, more particularly, acoustic perceptions. From then onwards, the perceiving periphery of the cortical layer can also be excited from within to a far greater extent; inner processes such as those of imagination and thought can become conscious, and a special device is needed in order to distinguish between the two possibilities, namely *reality testing*. It has become invalid to equate perception with reality (the external world). Errors which can now easily occur, and frequently do so in dreams, are called *hallucinations*.

The interior of the *Ich*, which above all encompasses the thought processes, has the quality of precociousness. This is characteristic of the *Ich*; it is its sole prerogative. However, it would not be right to turn the connection with the memory traces of language into a pre-condition of the preconscious state; rather, this state is independent of these memory traces, even though the fact of language allows us to draw confident conclusions as to the preconscious nature of the process. Yet the preconscious state, distinguished on the one hand by its access to consciousness and on the other hand by its link with language traces, is still something special; its nature doesn't simply consist of these two characteristics. The proof for this is that large portions of the *Ich*, and above all of the *Über-Ich*, whose preconscious character can't be denied, still mostly remain unconscious in the phenomenological sense. We don't understand why this should be the case. The real nature of the preconscious is a problem that we shall try to tackle later.

The unconscious is the quality that reigns supreme in the *Es*. *Es* and unconscious belong just as intimately together as *Ich* and preconscious; indeed, the relationship between the former pair is even more exclusive. A review of the developmental history of an individual and his psychical apparatus allows us to establish that there is a significant distinction within the *Es*. Originally, *everything* was *Es*; the *Ich* grew up from the *Es* due to the constant influence of the external world. During the course of this long development, certain things within the *Es* were transformed into the preconscious state and were thus absorbed into the *Ich*. Other things remained unchanged within the *Es* as its barely accessible core. But as things took their course, the young and weak *Ich* dropped certain material that it had already adopted, transferred it back into the unconscious state, and behaved in the same way towards some new impressions that it could have adopted – so that these, finding themselves repulsed, could leave a trace only in the *Es*. Bearing its genesis in mind, we call this last part of the *Es* the *repressed*. It doesn't really matter that we can't always clearly distinguish between the two categories in the *Es*. They more or less coincide with the distinction between what it originally brought with it, and what it acquired while the *Ich* was developing.

If, however, we have decided to undertake a topographical analysis of the psychical apparatus into *Ich* and *Es*, which runs parallel to the distinction between the qualities of preconscious and unconscious, and if we want to take this quality only as a *sign* of a difference rather than as the essence of it – then what is the actual nature of the state that betrays itself in the *Es* through the quality of unconsciousness and in the *Ich* through that of preconsciousness? And wherein lies the difference between the two?

Now, we know nothing about this; and our paltry insights figure very pitifully in comparison with the deeply obscure ignorance that lies behind them. Here, we have approached the actual secret of things psychical, as yet unrevealed. We suppose, as we are accustomed to do in the other sciences, that a kind of energy is at work in the psyche, but we lack anything to go on that will enable us to approach an understanding of it by analogies with other forms of energy. We believe we can see that nervous or psychical energy is present in two forms; one freely flowing and the other, by comparison, bound; we speak of material being invested and hyper-invested with energy; and even venture the supposition that a 'hyper-investment' establishes a kind of synthesis of different processes, in which free energy is converted into bound energy. We have got no further than this. All the same, we remain firmly of the opinion that the difference between the unconscious and conscious states lies in dynamic relationships such as these, from which it would be possible to derive an explanation for the way in which one can be converted into the other either spontaneously or with our being involved in some way.

Behind all this insecurity, however, there lies a new fact; one which was discovered thanks to psychoanalytical research. We have found that the processes in the unconscious or in the *Es* obey different laws from those in the preconscious *Ich*. We call these laws as a whole the *primary process*, as opposed to the *secondary process* which governs the pattern of things in the preconscious, in the *Ich*. Thus the study of the psychical qualities has, it would seem, ultimately proved itself to be fruitful after all.

## Chapter 5: Explanatory Notes Concerning the Interpretation of Dreams

Imagine an investigation of normal, stable states, in which the barriers of the *Ich* against the *Es* have remained secure and unruffled by resistances (opposing investments) and in which there is no difference between the *Ich* and *Über-Ich* because they are working in harmony with one another. Well, such an investigation would not be in the slightest bit enlightening. States of conflict and turbulence alone can further our knowledge, if the material of the unconscious *Es* has the prospect of penetrating the *Ich* and thrusting itself into consciousness – and if the *Ich* renews its stand against this attack. Only under these conditions can we make the observations that confirm or correct our assertions about the two partners. Our nightly sleep, however, is just such a state and because of this, the psychical activity during sleep, which we perceive as dreams, is also our most promising object for study. Moreover, by studying dreams, we will also avoid the oft-repeated accusation that we base our picture of the normal psyche on our findings in pathology; for dreams frequently occur in the lives of normal people, however much their characteristics may also differ from what we produce when we are awake. As is generally known, dreams can be confused, incomprehensible, practically nonsensical; what they say may contradict everything we know about reality; and we behave like insane people so long as we are dreaming, by attributing objective reality to the contents of a dream.

We set about understanding ('interpreting') the dream by supposing whatever we remember of a dream when we wake up not to be the real dream process but just a façade that hides this real process. This is what we mean when we differentiate between the *manifest* dream content and the *latent* dream thoughts. We call the process that allows the former to proceed from the latter the *dream-work*. The study of the dream-work uses an excellent example to teach us how unconscious material from the *Es* – both originally unconscious and repressed unconscious material – forces itself upon the *Ich*, becomes preconscious and, as a result of the *Ich*'s opposition, undergoes that transformation which we know as *dream-distortion*. There are no features of a dream that could not be explained in this way.

It is best to start by saying that dreams are formed for two different reasons. Either a drive-impulse that is otherwise suppressed (that is, an unconscious wish) has found the strength while the individual is asleep to assert itself within the *Ich*; or an urge left over from waking life, a preconscious train of thought with its concomitant conflicting impulses, has been reinforced during sleep by an unconscious element. In other words, dreams originate from the *Es* or the *Ich*. The mechanism for dream-formation is the same in both cases, as is the dynamic pre-condition. The *Ich* proves its later derivation from the *Es* by abandoning its functions from time to time and allowing things to revert to an earlier state. This happens, correctly speaking, by the *Ich* breaking off its relationships to the external world and withdrawing from the sense-organs whatever it has invested in them. We are quite justified in saying that, at birth, a drive arises to return to the intra-uterine life we have given up – a drive to sleep. Sleep is a return to the womb of this kind. As the *Ich* governs motility when it is awake, this function is paralysed during sleep, and a good deal of the inhibitions that were imposed on the unconscious *Es* accordingly becomes superfluous. The withdrawal of these 'opposing investments' allows the *Es* a measure of freedom that is now harmless. There is rich and compelling evidence for the part played by the unconscious *Es* in dream-formation.

a) The dream memory is far more extensive than the memory in waking life. Dreams produce memories that the dreamer has forgotten, which would be inaccessible to him while he was awake.

b) Dreams make unlimited use of linguistic symbols, the meaning of which the dreamer mostly doesn't understand. However, we can draw on our experience to say what they mean. They probably come from earlier phases of language development.

c) The dream memory very often reproduces impressions from the dreamer's early childhood. We can say for certain that these had not only been forgotten but had been made unconscious because of repression. The help – mostly indispensable – that dreams afford us when we try to reconstruct the dreamer's childhood in the analytical treatment of neuroses is based on this.

d) In addition to this, dreams bring material to light which can come neither from the dreamer's mature life nor from his forgotten childhood. We are forced to regard this as part of an *archaic* inheritance that the child, influenced by the experiences of his forebears, brings into the world with him prior to having any experiences of his own. We then find the counterparts to this phylogenetic material in the earliest legends of mankind and in surviving customs. Thus dreams become a source of human prehistory that we should not dismiss out of hand.

However, what makes dreams so invaluable in giving us an insight into the psyche is the circumstance that, if the unconscious material penetrates the *Ich*, it brings its own ways of working along with it. I mean by this that the preconscious thoughts in which this unconscious material has found its expression are treated during the course of dream-work as if they were unconscious parts of the *Es*; and in other cases of dream-formation, the preconscious thoughts, which have garnered strength from the unconscious drive-impulse, are reduced to the unconscious state. Only in this way do we discover which the rules governing the course of events in the unconscious are, and what distinguishes them from the rules we are familiar with in waking life. Dream-work is, then, essentially a case of the unconscious dealing with preconscious thought processes. To take an analogy from history: the invading conquerors don't treat a country according to the laws they find there, but according to their own laws. However, it is unmistakably the case that the result of dream-work represents a compromise. In the distortion imposed on the unconscious material and in the attempts – often inadequate – to give the whole thing a form that is still acceptable to the *Ich* (secondary processing), we can see the influence of the *Ich*-organization that is not yet paralysed. That is, to use our analogy, an expression of the continued resistance of the vanquished.

The laws governing the course of events in the unconscious that come to light in such a way are peculiar enough, and give us an adequate explanation for most of what we find strange about dreams. Above all, there is a striking tendency to *compression*, an inclination to create new unities out of elements that we would certainly have kept separate in waking thought. As a consequence of this, a single element of the manifest dream often represents a whole host of latent dream thoughts, as if it were an allusion common to all of them, and the scope of the manifest dream is as a whole extra-ordinarily condensed compared to the rich material that it came from. Another peculiarity of dream-work, not entirely independent of the earlier one, is the ease with which psychical intensities (investments) are displaced from one element to another, so that in the manifest dream one element that was unimportant in the dream thoughts often appears to be the clearest and, correspond-ingly, the most important; and, vice versa, essential elements of the dream thoughts are represented in the manifest dream merely by slight allusions. Moreover, having quite insignificant points in common is mostly sufficient for the dream-work to be able to replace one element with another in all further operations. It is easy to grasp the extent to which these mechanisms of compression and displacement can make it difficult for us to interpret a dream and to uncover the relationships between the manifest dream and the latent dream thoughts. From the proof that these two tendencies to compress and displace one another do exist, our theory draws the conclusion that energy exists in a state of free movement in the unconscious *Es* and that it matters more than anything else to the *Es* to find a release for quantities of excitation;[8] and it [our theory] uses both of these two peculiarities to characterize the primary processes attributed to the *Es*.

By studying dream-work, we have come to know yet many more characteristics of the processes in the unconscious; characteristics that are as remarkable as they are important. Only a few of these will be mentioned here. The decisive rules of logic don't apply in the unconscious; we could call it the Empire of the Illogical. Urges with opposing aims exist alongside one another in the unconscious, without the need ever arising for them to adjust to one another. They either have no influence whatsoever on one another or, if they have, then what arises is not a decision in favour of one or the other, but a compromise that becomes nonsensical because it includes details that are mutually incompatible. Closely related to this is the fact that oppositions are not kept apart in the unconscious but are treated as if they were identical, so that every element in a manifest dream can also signify its opposite. A few linguistic researchers have recognized that it was just the same in the most ancient languages and that oppositions like 'strong–weak', 'light–dark', or 'high–deep' were originally expressed through the same root until two different modifications of the original word separated the two meanings from one another. Remnants of the original dual meaning are still supposed to be preserved even in a language so highly developed as Latin, in the use of words like *altus* ('high' and 'deep') and *sacer* ('sacred' and 'infamous') among others.

In view of the complications and the ambiguity of the relationships between the manifest dream and the latent content that lies behind it, it is of course justifiable to ask how we can arrive at the very idea of deriving the one from the other and whether we are not solely thrown back on making a lucky guess, supported perhaps by a translation of the symbols appearing in the manifest dream. We may respond by saying that this task can be satisfactorily solved in practically all cases, but only with the help of the associations that the dreamer himself brings to the elements of the manifest content. Every other way of proceeding is arbitrary and provides no surety. However, the dreamer's associations reveal the intermediate links; we can slot these into the gaps between the two [that is, the manifest and the latent] and, with their help, we can reinstate the latent content of the dream, 'interpret' the dream. It is hardly surprising if every now and again this interpretative work, acting in opposition to the dream-work, fails to deliver a secure answer.

It still remains for us to offer a dynamic explanation for why the sleeping *Ich* takes on the task of dream-work at all. Luckily, this explanation is easy to find. With the help of the unconscious, every dream that is in the process of being formed makes a demand on the *Ich* to have a drive gratified (if it comes from the *Es*); or to resolve a conflict, remove a doubt, form an intention (if it comes from a residue of preconscious activity in waking life). However, the sleeping *Ich* is focused on the wish to carry on sleeping; it perceives this demand as a disturbance and thus seeks to get rid of it. The *Ich* succeeds in doing so through an act of apparent indulgence: it meets the demand with a *wish-fulfilment* which is harmless in these circumstances and thus removes it. This replacement of the demand by a wish-fulfilment remains the dream-work's most essential function. It is perhaps not superfluous to elaborate on this with three simple examples: a hunger dream, a comfort dream, and a dream provoked by sexual desire. While he is asleep the dreamer feels a need for food; he dreams of a magnificent meal and carries on sleeping. He had, of course, the choice either to wake up and eat, or to continue sleeping. He decided on the latter and satisfied his hunger through his dream. For a while, at any rate; if his hunger persisted, he would have to wake up after all. Here is the second example: the sleeper, a doctor, is supposed to wake up in order to be at the hospital at a certain time. However, he carries on sleeping and dreams that he is already at the hospital – but as a patient who doesn't need to leave his bed. Or, to take a third example, the dreamer feels a yearning during the night to enjoy a forbidden sexual object, namely a friend's wife. He dreams of sexual intercourse with, it is true, an indifferent person – but one who nevertheless shares his friend's wife's name. Alternatively, his attempt to resist his desire expresses itself by his dream-lover remaining totally anonymous.

Of course, not all cases are so easy. Particularly with dreams that come from the day's undealt-with residua and that have simply undergone an unconscious reinforcement in the sleeping state it is often difficult to uncover the unconscious drive-force and to establish its wish-fulfilment, but we can assume that it is always present. The theory that dreams represent a wish-fulfilment will easily provoke disbelief if one remembers how many dreams have a directly unpleasant content or even cause us to wake up through fear, quite apart from the frequent dreams that have no particular emotional tone. But the objection about fear-dreams doesn't stand up to analysis. One mustn't forget that dreams are always the result of a conflict; they are a type of compromise-formation. Anything that is gratifying to the unconscious *Es* can be a cause for the *Ich* to feel fear – precisely because it *is* gratifying.

As the dream-work proceeds, the unconscious sometimes asserts itself better; at other times, the *Ich* defends itself more energetically. Fear-dreams are mostly the ones in which the content has been least distorted. If the demand of the unconscious becomes so great that the sleeping *Ich* is not in a position to fend it off by the means at its disposal, then it abandons its desire to sleep and returns to waking life. We will be taking all our experiences into account if we say that every dream is an *attempt* to eliminate disturbances to sleep by wish-fulfilment; thus dreams are the guardians of sleep. This attempt can be more or less completely successful;

it can also fail – and then the sleeper awakes, apparently roused from his slumber by precisely this dream. Likewise, the good night-watchman who is supposed to guard the sleep of the little town sometimes has no alternative but to make a commotion and awaken the sleeping townspeople.

To conclude these discussions I shall add a remark that will justify the large amount of time we have spent on the problem of dream interpretation. It has turned out to be the case that the unconscious mechanisms that we have come to know through studying dream-work and that explain dream-formation to us also help us to understand the formation of the puzzling symptoms that make neurosis and psychosis so interesting to us. A correspondence of this kind must invariably awaken great hopes in us.

# Part Two: The Practical Task

## Chapter 6: the Psychoanalytical Technique

Dreams, then, are a psychosis, with all the inconsistencies, delusions, and tricks of the senses that the psychoses demonstrate. Admittedly, they are a short-lived psychosis; a harmless one; one even entrusted with a useful function, introduced with the individual's consent, ended by an act of his will. But, all the same, they are a psychosis; and we learn from them that even such a profound change in the psyche can be reversed and the normal function can take its place. Is it, then, too bold to hope that it must be possible to make the dreaded spontaneous psychical illnesses submit to our influence as well – and that they must be curable?

We already know a number of things that prepare us to undertake this task. According to our premiss, the *Ich* has the job of satisfying the claims of its three dependencies – reality, the *Es*, and the *Über-Ich* – while still retaining its organization and asserting its independence. The condition that brings about the state of illness that we are talking about can only be a relative or total weakening of the *Ich* that makes it impossible for it to fulfil its tasks. The most difficult demand on the *Ich* is probably that of suppressing the drive-claims from the *Es*; for this, it has to maintain large amounts of energy in opposing investments. However, the demands of the *Über-Ich* can also become so powerful and relentless that the *Ich* faces its other tasks as if it were paralysed. We suspect that in the economic conflict that arises here, the *Es* and *Über-Ich* often make common cause against the besieged *Ich*, which wants to cling onto reality in order to retain its normality. If the first two become too powerful, they succeed in breaking up and changing the organization of the *Ich* so that its proper relationship to reality is disturbed or even cancelled out. We saw this in the case of dreams; if the *Ich* becomes detached from the reality of the external world then it sinks, under the influence of the internal world, into psychosis.

We base our plan for a cure on these insights. The *Ich* is weakened by the internal conflict; we have to come to its aid. It is like being in a civil war that is to be decided by the assistance of an ally from outside. The analyst and the patient's weakened *Ich* are, basing themselves on the objective external world, supposed to form a team against the enemies, namely the drive-demands of the *Es* and the conscience-demands of the *Über-Ich*. We make a deal with each other. The ailing *Ich* promises to be fully honest with us, that is, to put at our disposal all the material that its self-perception offers it; in return, we promise it the utmost discretion, and we put at its service our experience in interpreting material influenced by the unconscious. Our knowledge is supposed to compensate for its *lack* of knowledge; it is supposed to return to the *Ich* its dominance over lost zones of the psyche. This deal constitutes the analytical situation.

No sooner have we taken this step than the first disappointment awaits us, the first reminder that we should be more modest. If the patient's *Ich* is to be a valuable ally in our mutual labours, it must have preserved a certain measure of coherence, a modicum of understanding of the demands of reality – despite all the pressure put on it by hostile forces. But this can't be expected of the psychotic's *Ich*; this can't stick to a deal of this kind, indeed it can barely enter into such a deal at all. It will very soon have rejected us and the help that we are offering as belonging to the parts of the external world that no longer signify anything to it. We thus recognize that we have to abandon the idea of trying out our attempts at a cure on psychotics. Perhaps we will have to give up forever; perhaps only temporarily, until we have found another, more suitable, plan for them.

However, there is another class of people with psychical illnesses, who are clearly closely related to the psychotics: the vast number of people suffering from severe neurosis. The conditions that bring about their illness as well as its pathogenic mechanisms have to be the same – or at least very similar – in both cases. But the *Ich* of neurotics has proved itself to be more capable of resistance, has become less disorganized. Many neurotics have been able to hold their own in real life, despite all their complaints and the short-comings that these cause. These neurotics may show themselves prepared to accept our help. We want to restrict our interest to them, and to attempt to see how far and by which methods we can 'cure' them.

With the neurotics, then, we make this deal: total honesty in return for complete discretion. That gives the impression that we were simply aiming to take the place of a secular father confessor. But there is a great difference. For we don't simply want to hear from the patient the things he knows and hides from others: he also has to tell us what he *doesn't* know. With this in mind, we give him a more precise definition of what we mean by honesty. We commit him to the *fundamental rule* of analysis, which is hence-forth to govern his behaviour towards us. He is not simply to tell us what he intends to say, what he is happy to say, the things that would give him the kind of relief he would get after a confession: he has to tell us everything that his self-observation yields to him; everything that comes into his mind, even if it is unpleasant for him to say it, even if it seems to him to be unimportant or even ridiculous. If he succeeds in switching off his self-critical mecha-nism after being instructed thus, he will give us a wealth of material – thoughts, associations, memories – that are already under the influence of the unconscious, indeed are often directly derived from it, and that thus put us in a position to deduce his repressed unconscious material and to extend the knowledge his *Ich* has of his unconscious by sharing this with him.

However, this by no means suggests that the role of the *Ich* would be restricted to one of passive obedience, whereby it would deliver us the material we demand, and would trustingly accept our translation of this. A number of other things happen, a few of which we might have foreseen and others which are bound to surprise us. The most remarkable thing is that the patient doesn't continue to see the analyst in a realistic light, as a helper and advisor who, moreover, is paid for his efforts and who would himself be quite happy to play the role of, say, a mountain-guide on a difficult mountain climb. Rather, he sees in the analyst the return – the reincarnation – of an important person from his childhood, his past; and, because of this, transfers feelings and reactions onto him that undoubtedly applied to this role model. This fact of transference soon proves to be a factor of undreamt-of significance: on the one hand, it is an aid of irreplaceable value; on the other hand, it is a source of serious dangers. This transference is *ambivalent*: it encompasses positive and tender attitudes as well as negative, hostile ones towards the analyst, who is as a rule put in the place of one or other of the patient's parents, his father or his mother. So long as it is positive, it serves us admirably. It changes the whole analytical situation; it forces aside the patient's rational intention of becoming healthy and free from suffering. In its place appears the intention of pleasing the analyst, of gaining his approval and love. This becomes the actual motivating force of the patient's co-operation; the weak *Ich* becomes strong and, under its influence, the patient achieves things that he would normally find impossible; the symptoms cease and he appears to become healthy – but only for the sake of the analyst. The analyst may admit rather shamefacedly that he had embarked upon a difficult task without having the faintest idea as to the extraordinary powers that would put themselves at his disposal.

Moreover, the transference relationship brings two further advantages with it. If the patient puts the analyst in the place of his father (or his mother), then he also grants him the power that his *Über-Ich* exercises over his *Ich*, as these parents were, of course, the origins of the *Über-Ich*. The new *Über-Ich* now has the opportunity to, so to speak, re-educate the neurotic: it can correct mistakes for which his parents were responsible in his upbringing. Admittedly, we must at this point insert a warning against misusing our new influence. However much the analyst may be tempted to become teacher, role model and ideal for others, to create humans in his own image, he mustn't forget that this is not his task in the analytical relationship; indeed, that he would be betraying his task if he allowed himself to be swept away by his inclinations. He would then simply be repeating one of the mistakes of the parents, who crushed their child's independence by their influence. He would be merely replacing the earlier dependence by a newer one. In all his efforts to improve and educate the patient, though, the analyst should respect his individuality. The degree of influence that he can legitimately allow himself will be determined by the degree of developmental inhibition that the patient exhibits. Some neurotics have remained so infantile that in analysis, too, they can only be treated like children.

Yet another advantage of transference is that it allows the patient to present us with an important part of his life story in all its plastic clarity – a part about which he would probably otherwise have given us insufficient information. He as it were acts it out for us instead of telling us about it.

Now let us turn to the other side of the relationship. As transference reproduces the patient's relationship to his parents, it also takes over the ambivalence of this relationship. It is almost impossible to avoid the positive attitude towards the analyst ultimately changing into the negative, hostile one. This, too, is usually a repetition of the past. The patient's tractability vis-à-vis his father (if the father was the person in question) and his courting of his father's favour were rooted in an erotic desire directed towards the latter individual. At some time or another, this demand presses its

way forward in transference as well, and will insist on being gratified. In the analytical situation, it can only meet with a refusal.
Actual sexual relations between patient and analyst are ruled out;
even the more subtle means of gratification such as showing preference to someone or being intimate with them are granted only
very sparingly by the analyst. A spurning of this kind is taken by
the patient as a reason to change his attitude; the same probably
happened during his childhood.

It is suspected that the successful cures that were brought about
while the positive transference was dominant might be of a *suggestive* nature. If negative transference gains the upper hand they are
blown away like chaff in the wind. We are horrified to see that all
our efforts, all our work, have been in vain thus far. Indeed, even
that which we might take to be a permanent intellectual gain on
the patient's part – his understanding of psychoanalysis and his faith
in its effectiveness – suddenly disappears. He behaves like a child
who has no faculty to judge for himself, who blindly believes
whoever he loves – and no outsider. The danger of these transference states obviously consists in the patient misunderstanding
their nature and taking them to be new, real experiences, rather
than reflections of the past. If he (or she) feels the strong erotic
desire hidden behind positive transference, then he believes that
he has fallen passionately in love; if the transference then veers in
the opposite direction, he considers himself to be insulted and
neglected; he hates the analyst, his enemy, and is quite prepared
to give up analysis. In both extreme cases, he has forgotten the
deal he made at the start of the treatment and has become no use
for further work together. The analyst's task is always to tear the
patient away from the threatening illusion; to show him again and
again that what he takes to be a new, real life is actually a reflection of the past. And, in order that the patient doesn't get into a
state that makes him inaccessible to all evidence, we have to take
care that neither his love nor his hostility reaches an extreme level.
We do this by being prepared early on for these possibilities, and
by paying due regard to their early signs. Such care when managing transference tends to be very worthwhile. If we succeed, as we

mostly do, in enlightening the patient about the true nature of the phenomena of transference, then we shall have deprived his resistance of a powerful weapon and shall have converted dangers into gains, for the patient will never forget what he has experienced in the forms of transference; it has more power to convince him than anything he has acquired in any other way.

We find it most undesirable if the patient *acts out* his experiences outside transference rather than remembering them. For our purposes, the ideal conduct would be for him to behave as normally as possible outside treatment and to express his abnormal reactions only in transference.

Our method of strengthening the weakened *Ich* takes an increase in its self-knowledge as its starting point. We know that there is more to it than this – but it is a first step. The loss of such knowledge means that the *Ich* forfeits power and influence; it is the first tangible sign that it is being hemmed in and hampered by the demands of the *Es* and the *Über-Ich*. Thus the first part of the assistance we offer is an intellectual exertion on our part and a summons to the patient to collaborate in it. We know that this initial activity is supposed to prepare the way for us to undertake another, more difficult task. We shall not lose sight of the dynamic elements of this task even during its introductory phase. We acquire the material for our work from various sources: from whatever the patient's communications and free associations allude to; from what he demonstrates in his transferences; from whatever we draw from the interpretation of his dreams; from whatever is betrayed by his 'slips'. All this material helps us to make suppositions about what has happened to him and what he has forgotten, as well as about what is currently happening inside him without his understanding it. However, we never forget in the process to keep a strict distinction between our knowledge and his knowledge. We avoid plunging in and telling him things that we have deduced often very early on in the piece, and we avoid telling him *everything* that we believe we have deduced. We consider very carefully at what point we should make him privy to one of our suppositions; we wait for a moment that seems the most suitable – something that is not always easy to decide. Normally we postpone sharing a supposition with him, enlightening him, until he has himself come so close to it that all that remains is for him to take one more step – albeit the step representing the decisive synthesis. If we proceeded differently, if we were to bombard him with our interpretations before he was prepared for them, then what we said would either have no effect or it would provoke a violent attack of *resistance* that would make it difficult to continue with our work, or could even jeopardize it altogether. If, however, we have prepared the ground correctly then we often achieve a situation in which the patient immediately confirms our interpretation and himself remembers the forgotten internal or external processes. The more precisely our interpretation coincides with the details of what the patient has forgotten, the easier it is for him to agree with it. Our knowledge on that particular matter has in this case become his knowledge, too.

Mentioning resistance brings us to the second, more important part of our task. We have already heard that the *Ich* protects itself against being invaded by undesired elements from the unconscious and repressed *Es* by means of opposing investments that must remain intact if it is to function normally. The more oppressed the *Ich* now feels, the more desperately it persists – terrified, as it were – with these opposing investments, in order to protect what remains of it against further encroachment. This defensive tendency, however, doesn't in the slightest accord with the intentions of our treatment. On the contrary, what we want is for the *Ich*, emboldened by the security that our help affords it, to venture an attack in order to recapture what it has lost. In the process we come to sense the force of this opposing investment as *resistance* to our work. The *Ich* recoils from apparently dangerous undertakings of this kind that threaten unpleasure. It has constantly to be spurred on and pacified in order for it not to refuse to cooperate with us. This resistance, which persists throughout the entire course of treatment and which renews itself with every new piece of work, is what we somewhat incorrectly call *repression-resistance*. We shall hear that this resistance is not the only one we have to face. It is interesting to see that in this situation the party divisions are to a certain extent reversed: the *Ich* resists our suggestions, but the unconscious, normally our opponent, comes to our aid, for it has a natural 'impetus' and desires nothing more than to advance beyond the barriers the *Ich* sets up against it and into consciousness. The battle that develops if we achieve what we intend to achieve – namely to incite the *Ich* to overcome its resistances – is carried out under our direction and with our assistance. It doesn't matter what its outcome is, whether it leads to the *Ich* adopting a rejected drive-demand after submitting to fresh examination, or if it dismisses it again, this time for good. In both cases, a constant danger has been eliminated, the scope of the *Ich* has been broadened, and a wasteful expenditure of energy has been made unnecessary.

Overcoming resistances is the part of our work that takes up the most time and the greatest trouble. However, it is also worth it, for it brings about an advantageous transformation in the *Ich*; a transformation that will be maintained and will stand the test of life quite regardless of the outcome of transference. At the same time, we have also worked to remove the change within the *Ich* that had come about under the influence of the unconscious, for whenever we were able to demonstrate the existence of such progeny within the *Ich*, we pointed out their illegitimate origins and incited the *Ich* to reject them. We will recall that one of the conditions we attached to our assistance when we did our deal was that a change of this type within the *Ich* caused by an unconscious element storming it was not to exceed a certain measure.

The further our work progresses, and the more deeply we come to understand the psyche of neurotics, the more clearly are we pressed to recognize two new factors that demand the closest attention as sources of resistance. Both are completely unknown to the patient, and neither could be taken into account when we made our deal; moreover, they don't come from the patient's *Ich*. Whilst we can draw them together under the single phrase 'the need to be ill or to suffer', their origins differ, although there is an affinity between them as regards their nature. The first of these two factors is the feeling of guilt, or consciousness of guilt, as it is called, disregarding the fact that the patient neither feels nor recognizes it. It is evidently the contribution to resistance made by an *Über-Ich* that has become particularly harsh and cruel. The individual shall not become healthy: he shall remain ill, for he deserves nothing better. This resistance doesn't actually disrupt our intellectual work but it does render it ineffectual; indeed, it often allows us to dispose of one form of neurotic suffering, but is immediately ready to replace it by another illness – a somatic one, if it comes to it. This consciousness of guilt also explains the phenomenon that we see every now and again whereby severe neurosis is cured or improved by real misfortunes; for the only thing that matters is that the individual is wretched, irrespective of how. The uncomplaining resignation with which such people often bear their hard fate is most remarkable, but is also revealing. In defending ourselves against this resistance, we have to restrict ourselves to making it conscious and to the attempt to slowly dismantle the hostile *Über-Ich*.

It is less easy to prove the existence of another form of resistance, a form that we find ourselves particularly ill-equipped to fight against. Among the neurotics, there are people in whom, to judge from all their reactions, the self-preservation drive has undergone a reversal. They seem to be set on nothing other than self-harm and self-destruction. The individuals who really do ultimately commit suicide perhaps belong to this group of people, too. We suppose that in their case, extensive drive de-mergences have taken place, which have resulted in the liberation of excessive quantities of the destruction-drive that are turned inwards. Such patients can't endure being restored to health by our treatment, and resist it with every means at their disposal. But we do have to admit that this is a case that we have not entirely succeeded in explaining yet.

Let us now survey the situation that we have put ourselves into by trying to help the neurotic *Ich*. This *Ich* can no longer fulfil the tasks set for it by the external world, including human society. It doesn't have all its experiences at its disposal; a large portion of its memory bank has gone astray. Its activity is arrested by the strict prohibitions of the *Über-Ich*; its energy is eaten up by vain attempts to defend itself against the demands of the *Es*. Moreover, as a result of the continuing incursions of the *Es*, its organization is damaged;

it is split; it can no longer create any kind of orderly synthesis; it is torn apart by mutually opposing urges, unresolved conflicts, and unrelieved doubts. The first thing we do is allow the patient's weakened *Ich* to take part in the purely intellectual work of interpretation, which strives provisionally to fill the gaps in his psyche; we have the authority of his *Über-Ich* transferred onto us – and then we incite it to take up the cudgels over every single demand made by the *Es* and to conquer the resistances that arise in the process. At the same time, we reinstate the order in his *Ich* by tracking down the material and urges that have penetrated it from the unconscious and by exposing them to criticism by tracing them back to their origins. We serve the patient in various functions: as authority and parent substitute; as teacher and educator; we will have served him best if we manage in our capacity as analysts to raise the psychical processes in his *Ich* onto a normal level, transform material that has become unconscious, repressed, into *preconscious* material and thus give it back to the *Ich*. So far as the patient is concerned, we find a few of his rational factors work in our favour, such as his need (motivated by his suffering) to get better and the intellectual interest that we can awaken in him for what psychoanalysis can teach and reveal to us all. Of far greater force, however, is the positive transference with which he meets us. Fighting against us, on the other hand, are the negative transference, the repression-resistance of the *Ich* (its unpleasure at having to expose itself to the hard work imposed on it), the feelings of guilt provoked by its relationship with the *Über-Ich*, and the need to be ill, resulting from far-reaching changes to its drive-economy. Whether we can describe the patient's particular case as a mild or severe one depends on the degree to which the two latter factors are involved. Apart from these, we can recognize a few other factors that can be considered to have a favourable or unfavourable effect. A certain psychical lethargy or a sluggishness of the libido that doesn't want to abandon its fixations can't be welcome to us; the person's capacity to sublimate his drives plays a large role, as does his capacity to raise himself above the crude life of the drives and the relative power of his intellectual functions.

Rather than being disappointed by this, we find it entirely understandable if we come to the conclusion that the final outcome of the battle that we have entered into depends on quantitative relations – on the amount of energy that we can mobilize in the patient to our advantage, as compared to the sum of energy of the forces operating against us. Here, again, God is with the stronger battalions. It is true that we don't always emerge victorious, but we can at least mostly see why the victory was not ours. Anyone who has followed our explanations only out of therapeutic interest will probably turn away contemptuously after this admission. But here we are concerned with the therapy only in so far as it works with psychological means; at the moment we have no others. The future may tell us how we can use particular chemicals to directly influence the amounts of energy and their distribution in the psychical apparatus. Perhaps other therapeutic possibilities, as yet unimagined, will also present themselves. But for the time being we have nothing better at our disposal than the psychoanalytical technique – and for that reason, despite its limitations, we ought not to despise it.

## Chapter 7: a Sample of Psychoanalytical Work

We have obtained for ourselves a generalized knowledge of the psychical apparatus, of the parts, organs and authorities that it consists of, of the forces that operate within it, and of the functions entrusted to its parts. Neurosis and psychosis are the states that express disturbances to the function of the apparatus. We have chosen the neuroses as an object for study, for they alone seem to be accessible to the psychological methods of our interference. While we are making an effort to influence them, we gather the observations that will give us a picture of where and how they arise.

We want to mention one of our main findings in advance of our portrayal. Unlike infectious diseases, for example, the neuroses are not caused by some specific thing. It would be quite pointless to go looking for pathogens in their case. For one thing, they merge imperceptibly with the so-called norm; and, on the other hand, there is barely a single supposedly 'normal' state in which we could not point out indications of neurotic traits. Neurotics are equipped with pretty much the same innate constitution as everyone else; they experience the same things; they have no different tasks to perform. So why are their lives so much worse, so much more difficult? Why do they suffer more unpleasurable feelings, more fear and pain in the process?

We need not leave this question unanswered. What are responsible for the shortcomings and sufferings of neurotics are quantitative *disharmonies*. Indeed, the causation of *all* the forms of the human psyche is to be sought in the reciprocal action between innate dispositions and adventitious experiences. At one point, the disposition of a particular drive may be too strong or weak; a particular capacity may be stunted or may not have developed sufficiently during the individual's life. On the other hand, external impressions and experiences can make demands of varying strength on different individuals, and what one person's constitution can deal with may present an impossible task for another's. These quantitative differences will determine the variety of possible outcomes.

However, we shall very soon realize that this is not a satisfactory explanation. It is too general; it explains too much. Our specified aetiology does apply to all cases of psychical suffering, misery and paralysis – but not all these states can be called neurotic. The neuroses have specific characteristics; they are a special type of misery. Thus we must expect that we will after all be able to find specific causes for them; or we can come up with the notion that, of all the tasks that the psyche has to deal with, there are some that defeat it particularly easily – which means that we could say, without having to retract our previous remarks, that the peculiarity of neurotic phenomena, often so remarkable, would be derived from this. If it remains the case that the neuroses are essentially no different from the norm, then the study of them promises to deliver us valuable contributions to our knowledge of this norm. In the process, we shall perhaps discover the 'weak spots' of a normal organization.

The above supposition is confirmed. Analytical experiences teach us that there really is one drive-demand that tends to be dealt with either unsuccessfully or with only partial success; and that there is a particular period of life that exclusively or predominantly merits consideration so far as the formation of neurosis is concerned. Both the nature of the drive and the period of life are factors that demand to be considered separately, although they have much to do with one another.

We can comment with some degree of certainty on the role played by the period of life. It appears that neuroses are acquired only in early childhood (up until the age of six), although the symptoms may not appear until much later. Childhood neurosis may manifest itself for a short time, or may even be overlooked. In all cases, later neurotic illness links up with this prelude in childhood. So-called traumatic neurosis (caused by extreme terror or severe somatic shocks such as railway collisions, being buried alive, and such like) is perhaps an exception to this; its relationship to the determining factors of infancy has thus far eluded investigation. It is easy to account for the aetiological preference for the first period of childhood. The neuroses, as we know, are disorders of the *Ich*, and it is hardly surprising that the *Ich*, so long as it is weak, unformed, and incapable of resistance, fails to master tasks that it could deal with later on with its eyes shut, so to speak. (In these cases, the drive-demands from within, like the excitations from the external world, act as 'traumas' – especially if they encounter certain tendencies.) The helpless *Ich* defends itself against them by making attempts to flee (repressions), which later turn out to be inexpedient and mean permanent restrictions on its further development. The damage done to the *Ich* by its first experiences seems to us to be disproportionately large, but if we want an analogy, we need only think of the differences between the effect of a needle being stuck into a mass of cells that are in the process of cell-division (as in the experiments of Roux) and that of it being stuck into the finished animal that the cells have later turned into. No human individual is spared traumatic experiences of this kind; none is absolved from the repressions that they give rise to. These dubious reactions of the *Ich* are perhaps indispensable for it to achieve another goal that it sets for itself for the same period of life. Within the space of only a few years, the little primitive is supposed to have turned into a civilized human child; is supposed to have completed an immensely long stretch of human civilized development in an almost uncannily abbreviated form. This is made possible by whatever predispositions it inherits but it can, moreover, almost never do without the assistance of its upbringing, of the parents' influence that is a precursor of the *Über-Ich* in that it circumscribes the activity of the *Ich* through rules and punishments, and encourages or enforces repressions to be carried out. Nor ought we to forget, therefore, the influence of civilization when it comes to the factors conditioning neurosis. We recognize that it is easy for the barbarian to be healthy, whereas it is a difficult task for the civilized human. We may find the yearning for a strong, uninhibited *Ich* perfectly comprehensible; but, as our current age shows us, it is in the most profound sense inimical to civilization. And, since the demands of civilization are represented by the upbringing in the family, we must also bear in mind this biological characteristic of the human species, the extended period of childhood dependency, when we are considering the aetiology of neurosis.

So far as the other point, the specific drive-factor, is concerned, we discover an interesting dissonance between theory and practice. Theoretically speaking, there is no reason not to suppose that any old drive-demand could give rise to the same repressions with all their consequences; but our observations frequently show us, so far as we can judge, that the excitations that play this pathogenic role arise from the partial drives of sexual life. The symptoms of neurosis are always, so one might argue, either substitute gratifications for some sexual urge or another, or measures to prevent them being gratified; they are as a rule compromises between the two, of the kind that come about according to the laws of oppositions that apply to the unconscious. At this moment in time the gap in our theory can't be filled; the decision is made all the more difficult by the fact that most sexual urges are not purely erotic in nature, but are the product of erotic drives and elements of the destruction-drive being combined with one another. However, there can be no doubt that the drives that manifest themselves in a physiological sense as sexuality play a prominent, unexpectedly large role in the causation of neurosis – though it remains to be seen whether it is an exclusive one. We also have to bear in mind that no other function has been so energetically and comprehensively rejected over the course of cultural development as precisely the sexual one. Our theory will have to make do with a few hints that point to a more profound connection: the fact that the first period of childhood, when the *Ich* begins to differentiate itself from the *Es*, is also the period of early sexual blossoming, which the latency period puts an end to; that it can hardly happen by chance that this momentous 'prehistory' is later subject to infantile amnesia; and, finally, that biological changes in the sexual life – such as precisely this two-phased onset of the function, the loss of the periodicity of sexual arousal and the transformation in the relationship between female menstruation and male excitation – must have been highly significant for man's evolution from animals. It remains for the science of the future to put these isolated pieces of data together to come to a new view. It is not psychology but biology that shows a gap here. It would perhaps not be unjustified to say that the weak spot in the organization of the *Ich* lay in the way it related to the sexual function, as if the biological opposition between self-preservation and species-preservation had here managed to create for itself a form of psychological expression. If analytical experience has convinced us that the assertion we hear so often – that the child is, psychologically speaking, the father of the man, and that the experiences of his early years are of unsurpassable significance for his entire later life – is totally correct, then it will be of particular interest to us if there is one special thing that we can take to be the central experience of this period of childhood. Our attention is firstly attracted by the effects of certain influences that don't apply to all children, although they appear often enough – such as the sexual abuse of children by adults; their being seduced by other, slightly older, children (brothers or sisters);

and, unexpectedly enough, their being deeply affected by taking part (as visual or aural witnesses) in adults' (their parents') sexual deeds, mostly at a time when we would not believe them either to be interested in or to understand such processes, nor to be able to remember them later on. It is easy to establish the extent to which the child's sexual receptiveness is awakened by such experiences and the extent to which his own sexual urges are forced down certain paths that he can never leave again. Since these impressions are subjected to repression either immediately or as soon as they try to return as memories, they set up the conditions for the neurotic obsessions that will later make it impossible for the *Ich* to master the sexual function and will probably make it turn away from it permanently. The latter reaction will result in a neurosis; if it fails to appear, then manifold perversions develop – or the function, so immeasurably important both for reproduction and for the entire shaping of life, will become totally insubordinate.

Instructive though such cases may be, the influence of another situation commands an even greater degree of interest. This is a situation that all children are destined to experience and that is necessarily derived from the factor of the extended period during which the child is looked after and during which it lives together with its parents. By this, I mean the *Oedipus complex*, so called because its essential content recurs in the Greek legend of King Oedipus, which has, luckily, been preserved for us by a great dramatist. The Greek hero kills his father and takes his mother as his wife. The fact that he does this unawares – by not recognizing them as his parents – is a divergence from the analytical facts of the matter, which we can easily understand and which, indeed, we can even recognize as inevitable.

Here, we have to depict the development of boys and girls – males and females – separately, for it is now that the difference between the sexes expresses itself psychologically for the first time. The biological fact of the duality of the sexes presents itself to us as a great enigma; this represents one of the ultimate facts of our knowledge, defying all attempts to trace it back to anything else. Psychoanalysis has contributed nothing to explaining this problem;

it clearly belongs entirely to biology. In the psyche we find only reflections of that great opposition, which are made difficult to interpret by a fact we have long suspected, namely that no individual being is restricted to one sex's ways of reacting but always allows a certain amount of room for those of the opposite sex too – in just the same way that the body bears the atrophied and often useless rudiments of the opposite sex's organs alongside the developed organs of its own. An empirical and conventional equation that is quite clearly inadequate serves to distinguish the male from the female in the psyche. We call everything that is strong and active 'male' and everything that is weak and passive 'female'. This fact that there is also *psychological* bisexuality weighs upon all our investigations, making it difficult for us to describe them.

The child's first erotic object is the maternal breast that feeds it; love arises on the pattern of the gratified need for nourishment. At first, the child certainly doesn't distinguish between the breast and its own body; when the breast then has to be separated from the child's own body, transferred 'outwards' because he so often finds it absent, it takes part of the originally narcissistic libido-investment with it as an 'object'. Later on, the whole person of the mother comes to constitute this initial object; she not only nourishes the child but also cares for it and thus awakens a number of other physical sensations within it – both pleasurable and unpleasurable. In taking care of the child's bodily needs, she becomes its first seductress. The significance of the mother – unique, incomparable, unalterable throughout the whole of the individual's life – is rooted in these two relations; she is the first and strongest love-object, the paradigm for all later love-relationships – for both sexes. In all this, phylogeny has the upper hand over the individual's personal, accidental experiences to such an extent that it makes no difference whether the child really did suck at the breast or whether it was in fact bottle-fed and thus never enjoyed the tenderness of maternal care. In both cases, the individual's development takes the same course; indeed, in the latter case, the later yearning may become all the more intense. And, regardless of how long the child was nourished by its mother's breast, it will always remain convinced once it has been weaned that it was not long enough, and that she did not give it enough food.

This introduction is not superfluous; it can enhance our understanding of the intensity of the Oedipus complex. Once the boy has entered the phallic phase of his libido development (from two to three years old), has obtained pleasurable sensations from his sexual organ, and has learned how to create these for himself whenever he feels like it through manual stimulation, he becomes the mother's lover. He desires to possess her physically in the ways he has divined from his observations and notions of sexual life; he tries to seduce her by showing her his male member, his pride and joy. In short, his early awakened maleness tries to replace his father in her affections – the father who has already been his envied role model up to this point due to the physical strength which he perceives in him and due to the authority in which he sees him clothed. Now the father is the rival who stands in his way, and whom he wishes to get rid of. If his father happened to be away and he was allowed to share his mother's bed, only to find himself banished from it again on his father's return, then it comes to make a profound impression on him that his father's disappearance means gratification, and his re-emergence means disappointment. This is the content of the Oedipus complex, which the Greek legend has translated from the child's fantasy world into supposed reality. In our particular cultural circumstances, a terrible end normally awaits it.

The mother understands perfectly well that the boy's sexual arousal relates to her own person. At some point, she reflects that it is wrong to allow it to continue, and she believes she is doing the right thing if she forbids him to manipulate his member. This ban, though, is of little use; at the most, it brings about a modification in the *method* of self-gratification. Eventually, the mother resorts to the severest measure: she threatens to take the thing away from him which he is using to defy her. She usually attributes the responsibility for carrying out this threat to the father, in order to make it more terrifying and believable. She, so she says, will tell Father, and he will chop the organ off. Strangely enough, this threat is only effective if another condition is fulfilled both beforehand and afterwards.[9] In itself, it seems all too unimaginable to the boy that such a thing could happen. But if, when he is threatened, he can recall what female genitals look like, or if he encounters such genitals shortly afterwards – where this part of the body, prized above all else, really is absent – then he believes in the gravity of what he has heard and, becoming enmired in the *castration complex*, experiences the most severe trauma of his young life.[10]

The effects of the castration threat are manifold and quite enormous; they affect all the boy's dealings with his parents and, later, with men and women as a whole. Mostly, the child's maleness can't stand up to this initial shock. In order to rescue his sexual organ, he more or less entirely renounces all ownership of the mother; his sexual life frequently remains burdened by this ban for ever more. If a strong female component – as we put it – is present in him, then it gains strength from his maleness being intimidated. He gets into a passive attitude vis-à-vis his father such as he ascribes to his mother. As a result of the threat he has indeed given up masturbating – but he has not abandoned the flights of fantasy that accompany it. On the contrary, as they are now the sole form of sexual gratification remaining for him, they are nurtured more than ever before – and in these fantasies he does indeed still identify with his father but at the same time, perhaps even predominantly, he identifies with the mother. Offshoots and modified products of these early onanistic fantasies tend to find their way into his later *Ich* and play a role in his character-formation. Fear and hatred of his father will become hugely increased, quite apart from such furtherance of his femaleness. The boy's maleness as it were withdraws and turns into a defiant attitude towards his father, one that will obsessively dictate his later conduct in the human community. As a left-over of his erotic fixation on his mother, an excessively large dependence on her sets in, which will persist in later life as servitude towards women. He no longer dares to love his mother – but nor can he risk not being loved by her, for this would put him in danger of her betraying him to his father and of being delivered up to castration. The whole experience with all its pre-conditions and consequences, of which our account could give only a selection, falls victim to the most energetic repression; and, as is permitted by the laws of the unconscious *Es*, all the competing emotional impulses and reactions that were activated then remain preserved in the unconscious, ready to disrupt the later development of the *Ich* after puberty. If the somatic process of sexual maturity gives a new lease of life to libido fixations that have apparently been overcome, then sexual life will prove to be inhibited; it will lack unity, and will collapse into conflicting urges.

To be sure, the incursion of the castration threat in the boy's burgeoning sexual life doesn't always have these dreaded consequences. Again, the amount of damage done and the amount of damage avoided will depend on quantitative relations. The entire occurrence, which we may very probably regard as the central experience of childhood, the greatest problem of early life and the most powerful source of later inadequacy, is so fundamentally forgotten that when we try to reconstruct it in the analysis of adults, it meets with the most decided disbelief. Indeed, they are so averse to it that they want to silence any mention of this taboo subject and, with peculiar intellectual blindness, fail to recognize the most obvious reminders of it. Thus, for instance, one hears it said that the Oedipus legend doesn't actually have anything to do with the interpretation put upon it by psychoanalysis; that this, so it is claimed, is a quite different case since, after all, Oedipus didn't realize that it was his father he had murdered and his mother that he had married. In putting forward this kind of argument, people fail to recognize that an approach such as the psychoanalytical one is essential to an attempt to give this material poetic form, and that it doesn't introduce anything alien, but simply skilfully brings out the theme's given factors. Oedipus' ignorance is the legitimate representation of the unconsciousness into which the entire experience is sunken for adults. And the compulsion of the oracle that makes – or is supposed to make – the hero innocent is a recognition of the inevitability of the fate that has condemned all sons to live through the Oedipus complex. When on an earlier occasion it was pointed out from psychoanalytical quarters how easily the riddle of another literary hero, Shakespeare's procrastinator Hamlet, could be solved with reference to the Oedipus complex – since of course the prince fails in his task of punishing another person for something that matches up with his own Oedipal desires – then the general lack of understanding from the literary world demonstrated the huge extent to which the mass of humans were prepared to cling to their infantile repressions.[11]

And yet, more than a century before the emergence of psychoanalysis, the Frenchman Diderot testified to the significance of the Oedipus complex, expressing the difference between the primitive age and the civilized one in this sentence: *Si le petit sauvage était abandonné à lui-même, qu'il conservât toute son imbécilité, et qu'il réunît au peu de raison de l'enfant au berceau la violence des passions de l'homme de trente ans, il tordrait le col à son père et coucherait avec sa mère.*[12] Even if psychoanalysis could boast of no other achievement than uncovering the repressed Oedipus complex, I would venture to say that this alone would give it a claim to be classified among the most valuable new acquisitions of mankind.

In the little girl's case, the effects of the castration complex are more uniform and no less profound. The female child doesn't, of course, have to fear losing her penis; however, she does have to react to not having had one in the first place. Right from the start, she envies the boy his possession; indeed, one could say that her whole development takes place under the influence of penis envy. Initially, she makes vain attempts to do the same as boys; and later on she makes more successful attempts to compensate for her defect – attempts that can ultimately lead to a normal female attitude. If during the phallic phase she tries like the boy to create pleasurable sensations in her genitals by manually stimulating them, then she often fails to obtain sufficient gratification, and the judgement she has made about the inferiority of her atrophied penis becomes extended to her whole person. As a rule, she soon abandons masturbation because she doesn't want to be reminded of the superiority of her brother or playmate, and she turns her back on sexuality altogether.

47

If the little woman persists in her first wish – to become a 'little boy' – she will end up being manifestly homosexual (in the most extreme cases) or will otherwise demonstrate pronounced male characteristics in later life: she will choose a 'male' career and suchlike. The alternative path runs via abandoning the beloved mother whom the daughter, influenced by penis envy, can't forgive for having sent her out into the world so ill-equipped. Full of resentment about this, she renounces the mother and substitutes another person for her as a love-object – namely the father. If someone has lost a love-object, then the obvious thing to do is to identify with it, to as it were replace it from within by identification. Here, this mechanism comes to the little girl's aid. The identification with the mother can now dissolve the initial attachment to her. The little daughter puts herself into her mother's place, as she has always done in her games; she wants to replace her in her father's affections, and, having previously loved her mother, she now has double motivation to hate her: she is jealous, as well as hurt by being denied a penis. Her new relationship with her father may initially consist of her desire to have his penis at her disposal; however, it culminates in another desire, namely for him to give her the gift of a baby. Thus the desire for a baby has taken the place of the desire for a penis – or has, at least, separated itself from it.

It is interesting to see that the relationship between the Oedipus and castration complexes takes such a different – even opposing – form in women from the one it takes in men. In the case of the latter, so we have heard, the threat of castration puts an end to the Oedipus complex; whereas in the case of the woman, we discover the opposite: she is forced into the Oedipus complex due to the effect of lacking a penis. It does little damage to the woman if she remains in her female Oedipal attitude (the name 'Electra complex' has been suggested for this). Such a woman will go on to choose her husband for his fatherly characteristics and will be prepared to recognize his authority. Her yearning for a penis, which is in fact insatiable, can only be gratified if she succeeds in rounding out her love for the organ into a love for the person who bears it – just as had happened earlier when she progressed from loving the mother's breast to loving the mother's entire person.

If we ask an analyst about which of his patients' psychical formations have, in his experience, proved themselves least inaccessible to influence, then the answer will be thus: in the woman's case, it is the desire for a penis; in the man's case, it is his female attitude towards his own sex – which, of course, has the loss of his penis as its premiss.

## Part Three: What We Gain For Our Theory

### Chapter 8: The Psychical Apparatus and the External World

Even all the very general insights and premisses that we listed in our first chapter were, of course, obtained through arduous and patient detailed work, of which type the previous chapter gave us an example. We may now find it tempting to assess the ways in which our knowledge has been enriched by such work, and what sorts of paths to further progress we have opened up. In this respect we may be struck by the fact that we were so often compelled to venture beyond the boundaries of psychological science. The phenomena we were dealing with don't only belong to psychology, but also have an organic-biological dimension and, accordingly, we have also made some significant biological discoveries in our attempts to build up psychoanalysis, and we have not been able to avoid coming up with new biological hypotheses too.

However, to stay with psychology for the moment: we have recognized that it is not scientifically feasible to distinguish between what is psychically normal and psychically *abnormal*, so this distinction – despite its practical importance – has only a conventional value attached to it. We have thus established the right to understand the normal life of the psyche from its disruptions – something that would not be permitted if these states of illness, neuroses and psychoses, had specific causes that operated along the lines of foreign bodies.

The key to understanding the psychical ailments that are permanent and life-damaging was put into our hands by studying a psychical disturbance during sleep – one that is fleeting, harmless, indeed serves a useful function. And we can now venture to assert that the psychology of consciousness was no more capable of understanding the normal functions of the psyche than it was of understanding dreams. The data of conscious self-perception, which alone were at its disposal, have proved themselves to be in every respect inadequate to grasp the wealth and complications of the psychical processes, to uncover the connections between them and thus to recognize the conditions under which they are disrupted.

Our postulate of a psychical apparatus that is spatially extended, expediently constructed, and developed according to the needs of life, an apparatus that gives rise to the phenomena of consciousness only in one particular place and under certain conditions, has enabled us to develop the science of psychology on the same sort of basis as any other natural science such as, for example, physics. Here, as there, the task consists of discovering something else behind the characteristics (qualities) of the object of research that are directly given to our perception – something that is more independent of the particular receptive capacity of our sense-organs and that approximates more closely to what we suppose to be the real facts of the matter. We don't hope to be able to approach these themselves, for we see that everything new that we have inferred has after all to be translated back into the language of our perceptions, from which we simply can't now escape. But this just is the nature and limitation of our science. It is as if we were saying in physics: 'if we could see that clearly, we would find that the apparently solid body consists of small parts of such and such a shape, size, and respective position'. In the meantime, we keep trying with artificial means to improve the effectiveness of our sense-organs to the utmost, although we can't really expect all such efforts to make any difference to the eventual outcome: 'reality' will always remain 'unknowable'. The gain brought to light by scientific work on our primary sense-perceptions will consist of insights into connections and dependencies that are present in the external world, that can somehow or another be reliably reproduced or mirrored in the internal world of our thoughts, and the knowledge of which enables us to 'understand' something in the external world, to predict it and, possibly, to change it. We proceed in much the same way in psychoanalysis. We have found the technical means that enable us to fill the gaps in the phenomena of our consciousness and we avail ourselves of these means in the same way as a physicist would experiments. In this way, we deduce a certain number of processes that are in themselves 'unknowable', link them with those we are conscious of, and when we say, for example, that 'an unconscious memory has intervened here', then what that actually means is: 'something has happened here that's totally beyond us – but something that could only have been described in such and such a way if it had ever come to consciousness'.

What right we have to draw such conclusions and interpolations, and the degree of certainty we can attach to them remains, of course, open to criticism in each individual case, and we can't deny that it is often very difficult to decide – this difficulty being expressed in the lack of agreement among analysts. The novelty of the task is to blame for this – that is to say, the lack of training; but there is also a particular factor inherent in the subject, for psychology, unlike physics, doesn't always deal with things that can awaken only a cool, scientific interest. Thus we won't be too surprised if a female analyst, insufficiently convinced as to the intensity of her own desire for a penis, doesn't give this factor its due recognition in the case of her patients either. However, such sources of error from the personal element are ultimately of little significance. If we read old textbooks on the use of microscopes, then we are amazed to discover what extraordinary demands were made on the personality of those observers using the instrument in the days when the technology was still new – something that is not mentioned at all today.

We can't set ourselves the task of outlining a complete picture of the psychical apparatus and what it does; even if we were to do so, we would in any case find ourselves hampered by the fact that psychoanalysis has not yet had time to study all the functions equally. Therefore I shall content myself with a detailed recapitulation of what I told you in the introductory chapter.

The dark *Es*, then, forms the core of our being; it has no direct contact with the external world and is accessible even to our knowledge only as mediated by another entity. The organic *drives* operate in this *Es*; they themselves consist of a fusion between two primal forces (Eros and destruction) that are combined together in varying proportions and are differentiated from one another by their relationship to the organs or organ-systems. The sole thing these drives strive for is gratification, and they expect to arrive at this by way of certain changes in the organs achieved with help from objects in the external world. However, the kind of immediate and heedless gratification of the drives that the *Es* demands would often enough lead to dangerous conflicts with the external world and to extinction. The *Es* is not in the slightest bit solicitous about ensuring the continuation of existence, and it knows no fear – or it would perhaps be more correct to say that it can indeed develop sensory elements of fear, but can't make use of them. The processes that are possible in and between the postulated psychical elements in the *Es* (the *primary process*) differ considerably from those which are known to us through conscious perception in our intellectual and emotional life; moreover, they are not subject to the critical restrictions of logic that rejects some parts of these processes as inadmissible and wants to annul them.

The *Es*, cut off from the external world, has its own world of perception. With extraordinary acuteness, it senses certain changes within itself, especially the fluctuations in the tension of the needs of its drives, which come to consciousness as sensations in the pleasure-unpleasure series. Granted, it is difficult to specify in which ways these perceptions come about and which sensory terminal organs help them to do so. But it is a fact that the self-perceptions – the vital sense, and sensations of pleasure or unpleasure – rule the processes in the *Es* with despotic violence. The *Es* obeys the unrelenting pleasure principle. This, however, doesn't apply to the *Es* alone. It seems that the activity of the other psychical forces is also capable only of modifying the pleasure principle, not of cancelling it out; and when and how the pleasure principle is overcome at all remains, theoretically speaking, a highly significant question, and one that has not been answered so far. The consideration that the pleasure principle demands a reduction – basically, perhaps, an extinction – of the tension of needs (*nirvana*) – leads to the relationships, as yet unassessed, of the pleasure principle to the two primal forces, Eros and the death drive.

The other psychical force which we think we understand best and in which we are most likely to recognize ourselves, the so-called *Ich*, has developed from the cortical layer of the *Es* which is in direct contact with the external world (reality) by its being set up to receive and exclude stimuli. Starting from conscious perception, it has subjected even greater areas and deeper layers of the *Es* to its influence, and shows in its persisting dependency on the external world the ineradicable stamp of its origins (a bit like, for instance, being marked 'made in Germany'). Psychologically speaking, its job consists of raising the processes in the *Es* on to a higher dynamic level (by, say, transforming freely flowing energy into bound energy, as it corresponds with the preconscious state); what it does for the construction of the psyche is that, between a drive-demand and a gratificatory action, it switches on the faculty of thought, which seeks by means of trial actions to calculate the success of the intended undertakings according to its orientation in the present and its evaluation of earlier experiences. In this way, the *Ich* comes to a decision about whether the attempt at gratification should be carried out or postponed, or whether the demand of the drive might not have to be entirely suppressed as something dangerous (this is the *reality principle*). Just as the *Es* sets out exclusively in search of gaining pleasure, so the *Ich* is ruled by a consideration for security. The *Ich* has set itself the task of self-preservation, which the *Es* seems to neglect, and avails itself of the sensations of fear as a signal that heralds dangers threatening its integrity. Since memory traces can become conscious just as much as perceptions, especially through their associations with the remnants of language, the possibility exists here of confusion arising that would lead to a misreading of reality. The *Ich* protects itself against this through the device of *reality-testing*, which is allowed to lapse in dreams because of the conditions prevailing while the individual is asleep. Dangers threaten the *Ich* that wants to assert itself against the excessively powerful mechanical forces that surround it, forces that primarily, though not exclusively, come from external reality. Our own *Es* is a source of similar dangers for two different reasons. First, excessively strong drives can damage the *Ich* in a similar way to the excessively great 'stimuli' of the external world. They can't, it is true, destroy it; however, they *can* probably destroy its unique dynamic organization and can turn the *Ich* back into being part of the *Es*. Second, experience may have taught the *Ich* that gratifying a drive-demand that is in itself not intolerable would bring dangers in the external world with it, so that in this way the drive-demand itself becomes a danger. The *Ich*, then, does battle on two fronts: it has to defend its existence against an external world that threatens to destroy it, as well as against an all-too-demanding internal world. It uses the same methods of defence against both, but the defence against the inner enemy is particularly inadequate. As a result of its original identity with the inner dangers and of having lived with them on the most intimate terms since then, it is very difficult for it to escape them. They remain threats, even if they can be temporarily kept under control. We have heard that the weak and immature *Ich* of the first period of childhood is permanently damaged by the stresses imposed on it by its attempts to defend itself against the dangers that are part of this period of life. The child is protected against the dangers that threaten it from the external world by the solicitude of its parents; it pays for this security through a fear of *loss of love* that would deliver it up, helpless, to the dangers of the external world. This factor expresses its decisive influence on the outcome of the conflict when the little boy gets into the Oedipal situation, in which the threat to his narcissism of castration, reinforced by primeval factors, gets the better of him. Driven by the combination of the two influences – the current, objective danger and the remembered, phylogenetically based, one – the child undertakes his attempts at defence-repressions – that, despite serving a purpose at that moment, none the less prove themselves to be psychologically inadequate if the later revival of the sexual life strengthens the drive-demands that were rebuffed in the past. Viewed in a biological light, the explanation for this would have to be that the *Ich* fails in its task of mastering the excitations of early sexual life – something that it is not qualified to do at this point because of its immaturity. We can see the essential pre-condition for neurosis in the way that the development of the *Ich* lags behind that of the libido, and we can't avoid coming to the conclusion that neurosis could be avoided if the childish *Ich* were spared this task – if, that is, infantile sexual life were granted its freedom as happens in the case of many primitive peoples. The aetiology of neurotic illness is possibly more complicated than is described here; but if that is so, then we have at least chosen to describe an essential thread of the aetiological knot. Nor must we forget the phylogenetic influences that are represented somehow in the *Es* in forms as yet unfathomable to us, and that will certainly have a stronger effect on the *Ich* in that early phase than they will later. On the other hand, it begins to dawn on us that such an early attempt to dam in the sex drive, such a decisively partisan stance on the part of the young *Ich* in favour of the external world as opposed to the internal one as comes about due to the ban on childhood sexuality, can't fail to have an effect on the individual's later cultural adaptability. The drive-demands forced away from direct gratification are compelled to take new routes that lead to substitute gratification and can, whilst taking these diversions, become desexualized and can loosen the connection with their original drive-aims. By saying this, we are anticipating the assertion that much of what our culture possesses and so highly prizes was gained at the expense of sexuality, through restrictions being imposed on sexual driving forces.

If we have had to emphasize repeatedly up to now that the *Ich* has its relationship to the objective external world to thank for its existence as well as for the most important characteristics it has acquired, we have at least prepared ourselves to assume that sickness – the state in which the *Ich* again most clearly approximates to the *Es* – is founded on this relationship to the external world being relaxed or dissolved. This ties in very well with clinical experience telling us that the trigger for an outbreak of psychosis is either reality becoming unbearably painful, or the drives becoming extraordinarily intensified – which, given the rival claims made by the *Es* and the external world on the *Ich*, necessarily has the same effect. The problem of psychosis would be simple and transparent if *Ich* and reality could be completely separated. But that seems to happen only rarely, perhaps never. Even in states that are so far removed from external reality as, for instance, hallucinatory confusion (amentia) we discover from what the sick people tell us once they have recovered that, while they were ill, a normal person was hiding in a corner of their psyche (as they put it) – a person who, like a detached observer, let the whole illness business pass him by. I don't know if we can assume it always to be thus, but I can report similar things about other psychoses that take a less tempestuous course. I have in mind a case of chronic paranoia in which every attack of jealousy was followed by a dream which brought to the analyst's attention a correct, undeluded version of its trigger. Thus this interesting conflict presented itself: while the dreams of neurotics normally allow us to deduce jealousy that is alien to their waking life, in the case of psychotics we find that the dream corrects the delusions that prevail during the day. We may probably take it to be generally true that what we get in all such cases is a psychical *split*. Two psychical perspectives are formed instead of one single one, the one being the normal one that takes reality into account, and the other being the one that, under the influence of the drives, separates the *Ich* from reality. The two exist alongside one another, and the end result depends on their relative strength. If the latter is or becomes the stronger then this provides the pre-condition for psychosis. If this relationship is reversed, then we find that the delusional illness appears to be cured. In truth, though, it has merely retreated into the unconscious; indeed, countless observations force us to infer that the delusion was fully formed and lying in wait for a long time before its manifest eruption.

The view that postulates a *splitting of the Ich* in all psychoses could not claim so much attention if it didn't turn out to be applicable to other states which are more similar to the neuroses – and ultimately to the neuroses themselves. I was first convinced of this in cases of *fetishism*. This abnormality, which may be classed as belonging to the perversions is, as is well known, based on the patient – almost always a male – not acknowledging the female's lack of a penis, this being highly undesirable to him as evidence that his own castration is a possibility. This leads him to deny what his own senses tell him, namely that female genitals lack a penis, and he clings to the opposite conviction. The denied perception does not, however, remain entirely without influence, for he still doesn't have the courage to assert that he did actually see a penis. Rather, he seizes upon something else – a part of the body or an object – and confers on it the role of the penis, which he doesn't want to be without. The thing he seizes on is mostly something which he did genuinely see when looking at the female genitals, or something that is a suitable symbolic substitute for the penis. Now, it would be wrong to call this process of fetish-formation a 'splitting of the *Ich*'; it is a compromise-formation aided by the displacement we have come to know about from dreams. But our observations show us yet more. The fetish was initially created in order to eradicate the evidence of possible castration, in order to avoid the fear of castration: if the female, like other living beings, possesses a penis, then there is no need for the male to be anxious about whether he will continue to possess one himself. However, we then encounter fetishists who have developed the same fear of castration as non-fetishists, and who react to it in the same way. Thus their behaviour simultaneously expresses two contradictory premisses. On the one hand they deny the very fact that they perceived – that they saw no penis in the female genitals – and on the other hand, they acknowledge the female's lack of a penis and draw the right conclusions from this. The two attitudes exist alongside one another for the whole of the individual's life, without influencing one another. *This* is what we can call a *splitting of the Ich*. These facts also allow us to understand why fetishism is so often only partially developed. It does not exclusively dominate the individual's object-choice but leaves space for a greater or lesser degree of normal sexual behaviour; indeed, it sometimes withdraws into a modest role or to a mere allusion. The fetishist has, then, never fully succeeded in detaching the *Ich* from the reality of the external world.

It should not be supposed that fetishism represents an exceptional case with regard to the splitting of the *Ich*: it is simply a particularly suitable object of study for this process. We are returning here to our argument that the childish *Ich*, dominated by the real world, deals with unpleasant drive-demands by means of so-called repression. We can now supplement this with the further remark that, during the same period of life, the *Ich* finds itself often enough in the position of defending itself against a demand of the external world that it experiences as painful; and it does so by *denying* the perceptions that tell it that reality is making this demand. Such denials occur very often – not only in the case of fetishists – and wherever we get into a position to study them, they prove themselves to be half measures, incomplete attempts at detachment from reality. A refusal to accept the perceptions is supplemented every time by an acknowledgement of them; two opposing outlooks, independent of one another, always set themselves up – and this results in the splitting of the *Ich*. The outcome depends once again on which of the two can seize for itself the greater intensity.

The facts of the *Ich* being split, which we have described here, are not as new and strange as they might at first appear. After all, it is a general characteristic of the neuroses that, with respect to some particular behaviour, two different stances, opposed to one another and independent of one another, exist within the person's psyche; the only difference being that the one belongs to the *Ich*, while the opposing one, being repressed, belongs to the *Es*. The difference between the two cases is essentially a topographical or structural one, and it is not always easy to decide which of the two possibilities we are dealing with in any individual case. However, the important thing they both have in common is the following: whatever the *Ich* undertakes in striving to defend itself – whether it wants to deny a part of the real external world, or to reject a drive-demand of the internal world – the outcome is never a total, complete one. On the contrary, it always gives rise to two opposing stances of which the defeated, weaker one also leads to psychical complications. To conclude, we need only point out how little our conscious perception tells us about all these processes.

### Chapter 9: the Internal World

The only way that we can give an account of complex clusters is to describe their various elements one by one. And consequently, all our explanations are initially guilty of being one-sided simplifications, and wait to be filled out, added to and thereby corrected.

The concept of an *Ich* that mediates between the *Es* and the external world, taking over the drive-demands of the one in order to procure their gratification and making perceptions with respect to the other that it uses as memories; the concept of an *Ich* that, in its concern for self-preservation, wards off excessively strong demands from both sides, all its decisions being dictated in the process by the directive of a modified pleasure-principle – this concept actually applies only to the *Ich* as it is until the end of the first period of childhood (around the age of five). At about this time, an important change has taken place. A part of the external world has – partially, at least – been abandoned and has instead been adopted by the *Ich* (through the process of identification); has, that is to say, become part of the internal world. This new psychical authority continues to carry out the functions that those particular abandoned people had performed in the external world: it observes the *Ich*, gives it orders, judges it, and threatens it with punishments – just like the parents whose place it has occupied. We call this authority the *Über-Ich*, and experience it in its judging capacity as our *conscience*. What is striking is that the *Über-Ich* often develops a severity for which the actual parents have provided no pattern; and also that it calls the *Ich* to account not only for what it does, but also because of thoughts and unfulfilled intentions that the *Über-Ich* somehow seems to be familiar with. This reminds us that the hero of the Oedipus legend, too, feels guilty on account of his deeds and submits to a self-inflicted punishment, even though the compulsion that the oracle put him under ought to acquit him of all blame both in our judgement and in his own. The *Über-Ich* is indeed the legacy of the Oedipus complex and is only set in motion once this complex has been dealt with. Thus its excessive severity doesn't follow an actual model, but corresponds to the strength of the defence used against the temptations of the Oedipus complex. The claims of philosophers and believers that man's moral sense isn't instilled into him by his parents or acquired by him as a member of the community but is infused into him from a higher authority are probably based on an inkling of the Oedipal fact.

So long as the *Ich* works in total harmony with the *Über-Ich* it is not easy to distinguish the manifestations of one from those of the other, although tensions and estrangements between them make themselves very clearly apparent. The agony we feel when our conscience reproaches us precisely corresponds to the child's fear of loss of love which was replaced by its moral authority. If, on the other hand, the *Ich* has successfully resisted a temptation to do something that the *Über-Ich* would find objectionable, then its sense of itself is elevated and its pride is strengthened, as if it had made a valuable acquisition. In such a way, the *Über-Ich* continues to play the role of an external world for the *Ich* – although it has become part of the *internal* world. For the whole of later life, it represents the influence of the individual's childhood – the care and upbringing given to him by his parents, his dependency on them – the childhood that has become so very prolonged in humans because of their living together in families. And it is not only the personal characteristics of the parents that come into play in this process but everything else that has had a determining effect on *them*, too: the proclivities and expectations of the social milieu in which they live; the dispositions and traditions of the race they come from. Someone who preferred to make general assertions and sharp distinctions might say that the external world in which the individual finds himself exposed when he has detached himself from his parents, represented the power of the present; the *Es*, with its inherited tendencies, represented the organic past; and the *Über-Ich*, the later addition, represented above all the past of the whole civilization that the child is meant to relive, as it were, in the short span of its early period of life. Such generalizations can't easily be generally correct. Some part of our cultural inheritance has certainly left its traces behind in the *Es*; much of what the *Über-Ich* contributes will awaken an echo in the *Es*; the effect of all kinds of things that the child experiences freshly will be intensified because these things are repetitions of some ancient phylogenetic experience. ('You have to *earn* what you have inherited from your fathers, to make it your own'.[3]) Thus the *Über-Ich* occupies a kind of middle ground between the *Es* and the external world; in it, the influences of past and present are unified. With the inception of the *Über-Ich*, one has as it were a lived experience of the way in which the present is converted into the past.

(1940)

## Notes

1. This oldest part of the psychical apparatus remains the most important throughout one's entire life. Psychoanalytical research also took this as its starting point.

2. Poets have fantasized about similar things, though nothing that corresponds to this is known from the history of living substance.

3. The philosopher Empedocles of Acragas was already familiar with the portrayal of the basic forces or drives, which many analysts still resist.

4. Cf. the supposition that humans are descended from a mammal that became sexually mature at the age of five. According to this view, the straight course of sexual development was disturbed at around that age by some great external influence. Other changes in the sexual life of humans

in comparison to animals could be connected with this, such as, say, the disappearance of the libido's periodicity and the role played by menstruation in the relationships between the sexes.

**5**. The question arises as to whether the gratification of purely destructive drive-impulses can be felt as pleasure; whether pure destruction can occur without the addition of the libido. Gratification of the death-drive that has remained in the *Ich* seems not to provoke sensations of pleasure, although masochism represents a blending quite analogous to sadism.

**6**. Early vaginal excitations are often reported; however, this is very probably a case of *clitoral* excitation – that is, excitation in an organ analogous to the penis. This does not stop us being justified in calling the phase 'phallic'.

**7**. One extreme branch of thought, exemplified by American behaviourism, believes it can found a psychology that ignores this basic fact!

**8**. The analogy would be a non-commissioned officer who has just silently accepted a reprimand from his superior taking out his anger about this on the first unsuspecting private he comes across.

**9**. [The contradiction here (that this condition be fulfilled *both* beforehand *and* afterwards, followed by the remark that the child *either* recalls having seen the female genitals *or* sees them later on) is Freud's own.]

**10**. Castration is not missing from the Oedipus legend, either – for the blindness with which Oedipus punishes himself for his crime is, according to the evidence of dreams, a symbolic substitute for castration. We can't exclude the possibility of a phylogenetic memory-trace being partly responsible for the extraordinarily terrifying effect of the threat – a memory-trace from the prehistory of the primal family, when the jealous father really did rob the son of his genitals if the latter became burdensome for the woman's affections. The ancient custom of circumcision, an alternative symbol for castration, can only be understood as an expression of the son's submission to the father. (Cf. the primitives' puberty rites.) The form taken by the course of events described above in peoples and cultures where childhood masturbation is not suppressed has not yet been investigated.

**11**. The name 'William Shakespeare' is very probably a pseudonym hiding a great unknown. A man who is thought by some to be the author of Shakespeare's plays, Edward de Vere, Earl of Oxford, lost his beloved and admired father when he was still a boy and completely broke off all relations with his mother, who remarried very soon after her husband's death.

**12**. ['If the little savage were left to his own devices, such that he retained all his imbecility, and such that he joined to his childish paucity of reason

the violent passions of a man of thirty, then he would strangle his father and sleep with his mother', Denis Diderot, *Le neveu de Rameau* (1774). I am grateful to John Reddick and Gerry McCarthy for their great 'teamwork' (to coin a good German expression) on this French translation!]
13. [Goethe, *Faust*, Pt. I, Sc. I.]

# The Splitting of the Ego in Defence Processes

I find myself for a moment in the interesting position of not knowing whether what I have to say should be regarded as something long known and self-evident or something completely new and strange. I suspect, however, it is the latter.

It has finally struck me that, in certain adverse situations, the youthful ego of the person we meet decades later as a patient in analysis must have behaved in a remarkable way. We could state in general – if rather vague – terms that the precondition for this behaviour is the influence of a psychic trauma. I would, however, prefer to focus on a clearly defined individual case, which, to be sure, will not cover every possible causal factor. Let us suppose the ego of the child finds itself governed by a powerful drive-demand, which it is in the habit of satisfying; suddenly it has a terrifying experience which lets it know that to carry on satisfying the drive would lead to a real and almost intolerable danger. It now has to decide whether to acknowledge the real danger, submit to it, and refrain from satisfying the drive, or to deny reality, convince itself there is nothing to fear, and so hold on to the satisfaction. It is a conflict, then, between what the drive demands and what reality forbids. But the child does neither thing, or rather it does both simultaneously, which amounts to the same. It responds to the conflict with two contradictory reactions, each one valid and effective. On the one hand, with the help of certain mechanisms, it rejects reality and refuses any prohibition; on the other hand – and in the very same breath – it acknowledges the danger from reality, turns anxiety about it into a pathological symptom, and attempts subsequently to ward this anxiety off. We must admit this is a very neat solution to the problem. Each of the contending parties gets what it wants; the drive can go on being satisfied, and reality is accorded its due respect. But, as we all know, nothing in life is free except death. This success is achieved at the expense of a rift in the ego that will never heal, indeed it will widen as time goes on. The two contradictory reactions to this conflict persist as the focal point of a splitting of the ego. The whole process seems so strange to us because we take it for granted that ego processes tend towards synthesis. Evidently, though, we are wrong here. The – absolutely crucial – synthetic function of the ego has its own particular preconditions and is subject to a whole range of disorders.

Clearly it will be useful to insert the details of a specific case history into this schematic account. One boy became acquainted with female genitals through being seduced by an older girl when aged between three and four. When these relations were broken off, he kept this sexual stimulation going by means of enthusiastic manual masturbation, but he was soon caught by the vigilant nursemaid and threatened with castration, to be carried out, as usual, by the father. All the conditions were right, then, for a massive trauma. By itself, the threat of castration does not necessarily make much of an impression – the child refuses to believe it and can hardly even imagine the loss of such a highly valued part of his body. The sight of female genitals might have been enough to convince the boy in our case of this possibility, but at the time he had not made this deduction because his disinclination had been too strong and there had been no compelling reason to do so. On the contrary, he had silenced any stirrings of unease by declaring that what was missing had not appeared yet, she would grow one – a penis – later. Anyone with enough experience of small boys can remember some such remark being made at the sight of a little sister's genitals. When both factors coincide, however, it is a different matter. Now the memory of the perception, previously considered harmless, is revived by the threat and provides the dreaded corroboration of it. The boy now believed he understood why the girl's genitals were lacking a penis, and he no longer dared doubt that the same thing could happen to his own. From that moment on he had to believe castration was a very real danger.

The usual consequence of castration trauma, the one considered normal, is that the boy, either straight away or after something of a struggle, gives in to the threat with complete or at least partial obedience, in that he no longer touches his genitals. That is to say, he fully or partly renounces satisfaction of the drive. But we are prepared for our patient having found a different solution. He created a substitute for the woman's missing penis – a fetish. By so doing, he may have been denying reality, but he had safeguarded his penis. If he did not have to acknowledge that women had lost their penis, then the threat made against him lost its credibility, he no longer had to fear for his penis, and he could go on masturbating undisturbed. Our patient's action here seems like a clear case of turning away from reality, a process we would prefer to restrict to psychosis. Indeed, it is not very far removed from this, but let us reserve judgement, because closer analysis reveals a not insignificant distinction. The boy did not simply contradict his perception and hallucinate a penis where there was none, he merely carried out a displacement in value, transferring the significance of the penis to another part of the body, a process facilitated – in a way we need not explain here – by the mechanism of regression. Of course, this displacement related only to the female body; as far as his own penis was concerned, nothing had changed.

This – one might almost say crafty – way of dealing with reality determined how the boy behaved in practice. He carried on masturbating as if it involved no danger to his penis, but at the same time, in complete contrast to his apparent bravery or nonchalance, he developed a symptom that showed he had indeed acknowledged the danger. Immediately after having been threatened with castration at his father's hands, and simultaneously with his creation of a fetish, he developed an intense anxiety about being punished by his father. This was to become a lasting preoccupation for him, one he was able to overcome and overcompensate for only by bringing to bear the full force of his masculinity. Even this anxiety about his father bore no trace of anything to do with castration. With the help of regression to an oral phase, it manifested itself as an anxiety about being eaten by his father. It is impossible not to be reminded here of an archaic piece of Greek mythology, which tells how the old father-god Kronos swallowed his children and also wanted to devour his youngest son Zeus, and how Zeus, rescued by his mother's cunning, subsequently emasculated his father. To return to our case history, though, let me add that the patient produced a further, albeit minor symptom, which he retains to this day – an anxious sensitivity about his little toes being touched. It is as if, after all the to-ing and fro-ing between denial and acknowledgement, it was the castration that managed to find the clearer expression . . .

(1940 [1938])

# Letter to Romain Rolland (A Disturbance of Memory on the Acropolis)

My dear friend!

Urgently pressed to contribute a written text to the celebration of your seventieth birthday, I have tried for a long time to find something that would be in some sense worthy of you, something that could express my admiration for your love of truth, your openness, your humanitarianism and your generosity. Or something that would attest to my gratitude to a writer who has given me so much pleasure and delight. I tried in vain; I am a decade older than you, and my work is over. What I finally have to offer you is the gift of an impoverished man who 'has seen better days'.

You are aware that my academic work set itself the goal of illuminating unusual, abnormal and pathological phenomena in the life of the mind, that is, of tracing them back to the psychical forces at work behind them, and revealing the mechanisms in operation. I first attempted this upon my own person, then on others too, and finally, in a bold assault, upon the human race as a whole. One such phenomenon, which I myself experienced a generation ago, in 1904, and had never understood, has come to my mind repeatedly over the past few years; initially I did not know why. I finally resolved to analyse the little experience, and below I shall tell you the result of this study. In doing so, of course, I must ask you to devote greater attention to details from my personal life than they would otherwise deserve.

## A *disturbance of memory on the* Acropolis

In those days, every year in late August or early September, I used to set off with my younger brother on a holiday that lasted several weeks and took us to Rome, some region of Italy or the Mediterranean coast. My brother is ten years younger than I am, and thus the same age as you – a coincidence that strikes me only now. That year my brother explained that his business dealings meant a long absence was impossible, and that he could stay away for a week at most, so our trip would have to be curtailed. Therefore we decided to travel via Trieste to the island of Corfu and to spend our brief holiday there. In Trieste my brother visited a business colleague, and I went with him. The man kindly enquired about our further plans, and, hearing that we were planning on going to Corfu, he urgently advised us against it. 'What are you going to do there at this time of year? It's so hot that you won't be able to do anything at all. You'd be better off going to Athens. The Lloyds steamer sets off this afternoon, it will give you three days to see the city, and pick you up on the way back. That will be more worthwhile and more pleasant for you.'

When we had left the Triestine gentleman, we were both strangely downcast. We discussed the plan that had been suggested to us, found it utterly pointless, seeing nothing but obstacles to its implementation, and also assumed that we would not be allowed into Greece without passports. During the hours before the opening of the Lloyds office, we drifted morosely and irresolutely around the city. But when the time came, we went to the counter and bought tickets to Athens, as though it were quite natural, without worrying about the supposed difficulties, and indeed without even discussing with each other the reasons for our decision. This behaviour was indeed very peculiar. We later acknowledged that we had immediately and readily accepted the suggestion to travel to Athens rather than Corfu. Why then had we spoiled the time leading up to the opening of the counter by being depressed, pretending that we could see only hindrances and difficulties?

Then, when I stood on the Acropolis on the afternoon after our arrival, and my eye took in the landscape, the curious thought suddenly came to me: *So this all really does exist, just as we learned in school!* To describe the situation more precisely, the person delivering the comment was distinguished, much more sharply than would usually have been noticeable, from another who perceived it, and both were amazed, although not by the same thing. One of these persons behaved as though, under the impression of an irrefutable observation, he was obliged to believe in something the reality of which had until then seemed uncertain to him. To exaggerate slightly: it was as though someone walking along Loch Ness were suddenly to see the body of the famous monster washed ashore, and found himself forced to admit: so the sea serpent that we didn't believe in really does exist. But the other person was rightly surprised, because he had not known that the real existence of Athens, the Acropolis and this landscape had ever been a matter of doubt. That person had rather been prepared for an expression of ecstasy and delight.

One might now be inclined to say that the disconcerting thought that came to me on the Acropolis merely emphasized the fact that it is one thing to see something with one's own eyes and quite another only to hear or to read about it. But that would be a strange way of dressing up an uninteresting commonplace. Or else I might go so far as to claim that as a schoolboy I had believed I was convinced of the historical reality of the city of Athens and its history, but had learned from the idea that came to me on the Acropolis that I had not in fact believed in it in my unconscious; only now had I acquired a conviction that 'extended into the unconscious'. Such an explanation sounds very profound, but it is easier to postulate than it is to prove, and will be highly contestable from a theoretical point of view. No, I think that the two phenomena, our depressed state in Trieste and the thought on the Acropolis, are closely linked. The former is the more easily understandable, and may help us to explain the latter.

Furthermore, the experience in Trieste is, it should be noted, nothing but an expression of disbelief. 'We are to see Athens? But that's out of the question, it will be too difficult.' In that case the accompanying depression corresponds to regret that the trip will never happen. It would have been too lovely! And now we understand what we are dealing with. It is one of those instances of 'too good to be true' that we know so well. An example of the kind of disbelief that so frequently occurs when we are surprised by a piece of good news, that we have won the lottery or a prize, or when a girl learns that the man she has loved in secret has presented himself to her parents as a suitor, and so on.

Once we have established that a phenomenon exists, the next question, of course, is to enquire into its cause. This disbelief is clearly an attempt to reject a piece of reality, but there is something strange about it. We would not be at all surprised if such an attempt were directed against a piece of reality that threatened to bring displeasure; our psychical mechanism, we might say, works along those lines. But why such disbelief about something which, on the contrary, promises to deliver a high degree of pleasure? Truly paradoxical behaviour! But I recall that I have in the past dealt with the similar case of those individuals who, as I put it, 'are wrecked by success'. Under normal circumstances one succumbs to failure, the non-fulfilment of a need or desire of great importance to one's life; with these people, however, it is the other way around; they fall ill, they are wrecked by the fulfilment of an overwhelmingly strong desire. But the contradiction between the two situations is not as great as it might at first appear. In the paradoxical case an internal frustration has simply assumed the place of the external one. The subject does not allow himself to be happy; the internal frustration orders him to cling to the external one. But why? Because, the answer runs in many cases, we cannot expect fate to supply anything so good. Hence, once again, 'too good to be true', the expression of a pessimism which many of us seem to harbour within ourselves to a large degree. In some other cases it is just as it is among those wrecked by success, a feeling of guilt or inferiority that may be translated as follows: I am not worthy of such good fortune, I do not deserve it. But these two motivations are essentially the same, the one being merely a projection of the other. For, as has been known for some time, the fate that we expect to treat us so badly is a materialization of our conscience, of the severe super-ego within us, in which the punitive agency of our childhood finds residual expression.

This, I believe, explains our behaviour in Trieste. We could not believe that we were destined for the joy of seeing Athens. The fact that the piece of reality that we wished to reject was at first only a possibility determined the strange qualities of our initial reaction. Then, when we stood on the Acropolis, that possibility had become reality, and the same reaction now found an altered but far clearer expression. In undistorted form, that should have been: 'I would really not have believed that I should ever be granted the chance to see Athens with my own eyes, as is now indubitably the case!' When I recall the passionate yearning to travel and see the world that dominated me during my grammar-school years and beyond, and how long it was before that yearning was fulfilled, I am no longer surprised by its after-effect on the Acropolis; I was forty-eight at the time. I did not ask my younger brother whether he felt anything similar. A certain reticence surrounded the whole experience, and had already prevented us from exchanging our thoughts in Trieste.

But if I have correctly guessed the meaning of the thought that came to me on the Acropolis, and it did indeed express my delighted amazement at now being in that place, the further question arises of why that meaning had, in that thought, been subjected to such a distorted and distorting disguise.

The essential content of the thought has been preserved even in its distortion: it is disbelief. 'According to the evidence of my senses, I am now standing on the Acropolis, but I can't believe it.' But the expression of that disbelief, that doubt about a piece of reality, was doubly displaced, first by being shifted back into the past and secondly by being transferred away from my relation to the Acropolis to the Acropolis's very existence. Thus something came into being which amounted to the assertion that I had in the past doubted the real existence of the Acropolis, although my memory rejected this as incorrect and, indeed, impossible.

The two distortions involve two quite separate problems. We can attempt to penetrate more deeply into the process of transposition. Without for the moment elaborating upon how I reached this idea, I wish to start from the hypothesis that the original factor must have been a feeling at the time that there was something dubious and unreal about the situation. That situation included myself, the Acropolis and my perception of it. I could not account for that doubt, indeed I could not cast doubt upon my sensory impressions of the Acropolis. But I recalled that I did in the past doubt something to do with this locality, and it was here that I found the means required to shift the doubt into the past. But in the process the content of the doubt was lost. I could not just remember doubting, in my early years, whether I myself would ever see the Acropolis, but asserted that at the time I disbelieved in the reality of the Acropolis. It is precisely this result of the distortion that leads me to conclude that the actual situation on the Acropolis contained an element of doubt about reality. I am still a long way from explaining the process, so I shall briefly conclude by saying that the entire psychical situation, apparently confused and difficult to describe, is precisely resolved by the hypothesis that I had – or could have had – the momentary feeling on the Acropolis: '*What I am seeing there is not real.*' This is called a 'feeling of estrangement'. I attempted to ward it off, and succeeded in doing so at the expense of making a false statement about the past.

These estrangements are very curious phenomena that are still very little understood. They are described as 'sensations', but they are clearly complicated processes bound up with particular contents and linked with decisions made concerning those contents. While they occur very frequently in certain mental illnesses, they are also not unknown to normal people, just as healthy individuals have occasional hallucinations. But they are certainly failed actions, and like dreams – which, despite their regular occurrence in healthy people, we see as models of mental disturbance – they are abnormal in their structures. These phenomena can be observed in two different forms; the subject feels that a piece of reality or a piece of his own self has become strange. In the latter case we speak of 'depersonalization'; estrangement and depersonalization are very closely connected. There are other phenomena in which we can recognize what we might call their positive counterparts, so-called *'fausse reconnaissance'* [false recognition], *'déjà vu'*, *'déjà raconté'* [already recounted], illusions in which we seek to assume something as belonging to our own selves, just as, in the case of estrangement, we attempt to exclude something from ourselves. A naïvely mystical, unpsychological attempt at explanation seeks to exploit the phenomena of *déjà vu* as proof of former existences of our psychical self. The path from depersonalization leads to the extremely curious condition of *'double conscience'* [double consciousness], more correctly called 'split personality'. This is all still so obscure, so little mastered by science that I must refrain from talking to you about it any further.

It will be enough for my purposes if I return to two universal characteristics of the phenomena of estrangement. First, they all serve the purposes of defence, they seek to keep something away from the ego, to deny it. Now the ego is approached on two sides by fresh elements that can prompt defensive measures, from the real external world and from the internal world of the thoughts and impulses appearing within the ego. It may be that this alternative coincides with the difference between actual estrangements and depersonalizations. There are an extraordinarily large number of methods, mechanisms, we might say, employed by the ego as it accomplishes its defensive tasks. Very close to myself, a work is now under way which will deal with the study of these defensive methods; my daughter, the child analyst, is writing a book on the subject. Our deeper understanding of psychopathology had its source in the most primitive and thorough of these methods, 'repression'. Between repression and the 'normal' way of defending ourselves against things that are painful and unbearable, through recognition, consideration, judgement and appropriate action, there lies a whole series of modes of behaviour on the part of the ego that are more or less clearly pathological in character. May I stop for a moment to discuss a marginal case of such defence? You are familiar with the famous lament of the Spanish Moors, *'Ay de mi Alhama'* ['Alas for my

Alhama'], which relates how King Boabdil receives the news of the fall of his city of Alhama. He senses that this loss means the end of his rule. But he is not willing to accept it, and decides to treat the news as though it had not come. The verse runs:

> *Cartas le fueron venidas.*
> *de que Alhama era ganada.*
> *Las cartas echó en el fuego*
> *y al mensajero mataba.*

[Letters reached him saying that Alhama was taken. The letters he threw in the fire, and killed the messenger.]

It is easy to guess that this behaviour on the part of the king is in part determined by the need to fight against his feeling of powerlessness. By burning the letters and having the messenger killed, he is still trying to demonstrate his absolute power.

The second general characteristic of estrangements, their dependence upon the past, upon the hoard of memories within the ego and earlier painful experiences that may in the meantime have succumbed to repression, is not accepted without dispute. My experience on the Acropolis, which ends in a disturbance of memory, a falsification of the past, helps us to demonstrate that influence. It is not true to say that I doubted the real existence of Athens during my time as a grammar-school boy. I only doubted that I would ever be able to see Athens. It struck me as utterly beyond the realms of possibility that I would travel such a long way, that I would 'come so far'. That had to do with the strictures and poverty of our living conditions in my youth. The longing to travel was certainly also an expression of the wish to escape that pressure, like the urge that compels so many adolescents to run away from home. I had realized long ago that much of the pleasure in travel consists in the fulfilment of those early desires, and is thus rooted in dissatisfaction with home and family. The first time one sees the sea, crosses the ocean, experiences cities and countries as realities which were for so long remote, inaccessible objects of desire, one feels like a hero who has accomplished incredible feats. Back then, on the Acropolis, I could have asked my brother, 'Do you remember how, in our youth, we made the same journey day after day, from —— Street to school, and then how we went every Sunday to the Prater or on one of those outings to the countryside with which we were already so familiar, and now here we are in Athens standing on the Acropolis! We really have come a long way!' And if one may compare something so small with something larger, did Napoleon I not turn to one of his brothers during his coronation as Emperor in Notre Dame – it was probably the eldest, Joseph – and observe, 'What would *Monsieur notre père* say if he could see us now?'

But here we reach the solution to the little problem of why the pleasure of our trip to Athens was disturbed while we were still in Trieste. There must be a feeling of guilt associated with the satisfaction of having come such a long way; there is something involved in it that is wrong, something that has for a long time been forbidden. It has to do with criticism of our father in childhood, with the undervaluation that had replaced that overvaluation of his character which had prevailed in early childhood. It seems as though the essential aspect of success lies in getting further than one's father, as though wishing to outdo one's father were forbidden.

To this generally valid motive we should add one element particular to our own case: the very subject of Athens and the Acropolis contains a reference to the superiority of sons. Our father had been a businessman, he had no grammar-school education, Athens would not have meant much to him. What disturbed our enjoyment of the trip to Athens, then, was an impulse of *piety*. And now you will no longer be surprised that the memory of the experience on the Acropolis has haunted me so often now that I myself am old and in need of forbearance, and can no longer travel.

Yours very sincerely

Sigmund Freud

*January 1936*

# Constructions in Analysis

## I

A very well-respected researcher, for whom I have a high regard because he treated psychoanalysis fairly at a time when most people did not feel compelled to do so, none the less once made a comment about our analytical technique that was as hurtful as it was unjust. He said that when we present our interpretation to a patient we deal with him according to the infamous principle of *heads I win, tails you lose* [original in English]. That is to say that when he agrees with us, then we are in the right; but when he contradicts us, then that is just a sign of his resistance, so we are still in the right. In this way we are always right *vis-à-vis* the poor helpless person we are analysing, irrespective of his response to whatever ideas we impose on him. As it is quite true that a 'no' from our patient does not generally incline us to abandon our interpretation as incorrect, his exposure of our technique was very welcome to opponents of analysis. So it is worth while setting out in detail how we assess the 'yes' and 'no', the expression of their agreement or protest, of our patients during analytical treatment. Of course, the practising analyst will learn nothing from this justification that he does not know already.

It is well known that the object of analytical work is to bring the patient to the point of removing the repressions – in the widest sense of the term – of his early development, to replace them with reactions more in keeping with a state of psychological maturity. To do this he has to recall certain experiences and the emotional impulses they gave rise to, which he has now forgotten. We know that his present symptoms and inhibitions are the result of such repressions; in other words, they operate as surrogates for what he has forgotten. What kind of material does he make available to us that we can use to put him on the path to recovering his lost memories? A number of things: fragments of those memories in his dreams, of unique value in themselves, but usually badly distorted by all the factors involved in dream-formation; the thoughts that occur to him when he gives himself over to 'free association', from which we can discover allusions to the repressed experiences and derivatives of the repressed emotional impulses, as well as to his reactions against them; and, finally, indications of the recurrence of emotions attached to what has been repressed, in actions trivial or significant taking place both within and outside the situation of analysis. We have found the transference relationship established with the analyst particularly conducive to the recurrence of such emotional connections. From this raw material – so to speak – we have to produce what we want.

What we want is a reliable picture of the forgotten years of the patient's life, complete in all the essentials. But here we have to remember that this analytical work consists of two quite different parts, and that it takes place in two separate sites, involving two different people, each of them allocated a different task. For a moment you ask yourself why your attention was not drawn to this fundamental fact a long time ago, but you immediately tell yourself that nothing was being held back from you, that it is a matter of a universally known, you might say self-evident, fact that we are stressing and privileging here only for a particular purpose. We all know that the analysand is supposed to be induced to remember something he has experienced and suppressed. The dynamic conditions of this process are so interesting that the other part of the work, the analyst's contribution, fades into the background by comparison. The analyst has not experienced and not suppressed the things in question; it cannot be his job to remember anything. So what is his job? On the basis of the signs it has left behind, he has to guess what has been forgotten; or rather, more accurately, to construct it. What produces the link between both parts of the analytical work, between the analyst's share of it and the analysand's, is how and when and with what explanations he conveys his constructions to the analysand.

His work of construction or, if you prefer, of reconstruction, corresponds extensively to that of the archaeologist who excavates a ruined and buried settlement or an ancient building. It is in fact identical to it, except that the analyst works under better conditions, and has more material to help him, because he is dealing with something living, not a ruined object; and perhaps his objectives are different. But as the archaeologist builds up a picture of the shell of a building from remaining masonry, establishes the number and position of columns from depressions in the ground, and reconstructs the former decorations and pictures on the walls from remains found in the rubble, the analyst proceeds in exactly the same way when he draws his conclusions from fragments of memory and associations, and from comments volunteered by the analysand. Both are granted the right to reconstruct by piecing together and completing the existing remains. They also have many difficulties and potential mistakes in common. It is notorious that one of the most awkward tasks for the archaeologist is establishing the relative age of his finds, and when an object emerges at a particular level there is often a decision to be made whether this object belongs to that level or whether it has sunk down to it through some later disturbance of the site. It is not difficult to guess what corresponds to this doubt in the case of analytical construction.

As we have said, the analyst works under more favourable conditions than the archaeologist because he has material available for which there is no equivalent in an excavation; for example, the repetition of reactions dating from the early stage, and everything brought to light about these repetitions by the transference relationship. Moreover, we must consider that an excavation involves objects that have been destroyed, and that large and important fragments of these objects have quite certainly been lost, through mechanical force, fire and looting. No amount of effort can succeed in locating them in order to reunite them with the surviving remains. Interpretation depends simply and solely on reconstruction, which can therefore quite often claim at best only a certain degree of probability. The case is different with the psychological object whose previous history the analyst wants to establish. Something regularly happens here that occurs only as a fortunate exception where archaeological objects are concerned, as with Pompeii and the tomb of Tutankhamun. Everything essential is preserved; even things that seem to have been totally forgotten are present somehow and somewhere, though buried and not accessible at the individual's will. As is well known, we have reason to doubt whether any psychological formation ever suffers really complete destruction. Whether or not we will succeed in bringing the hidden object to light intact is simply a question of analytical technique.

There are only two facts that run counter to the exceptionally favoured situation of analytical work. The psychological object is incomparably more complicated than the material ones of an excavation; and the state of our knowledge insufficiently prepares us for what we will find, since the innermost structure of the psychological object still contains so many mysteries. But this is where our comparison of the two types of work ends, for the main difference between them is that, whereas for the archaeologist reconstruction is the whole aim and the end of his efforts, for the analyst construction is only preparatory work.

## II

The work is preparatory, however, not in the sense that it must be entirely completed before the next stage can begin, as in building a house, where the walls must all be standing and all the windows fitted before one can go on to decorate the rooms. Every analyst knows that things are not like that in analytical treatment; both types of work go on concurrently, one running ahead, the other linking up with it. The analyst completes a piece of reconstruction, communicates it to the analysand so that it can have its effect upon him; then he constructs a further piece from the new material that begins to pour out, proceeds with it as before, and continues alternating in this way to the end. If you hear very little about 'constructions' in descriptions of analytical technique, that is because we talk instead about 'interpretations' and their effect. But I believe that construction is a far more appropriate term. Interpretation relates to some single element of the material, an idea, a mistake, etc., that you are working on. But a construction means that you present the analysand with a part of his forgotten early life-story, perhaps as follows: until your *n*th year you saw yourself as the sole and undisputed proprietor of your mother, then a second child came along, and with him a serious disappointment. Your mother left you for a while, and afterwards she never again devoted herself exclusively to you. Your feelings for your mother became ambivalent, your father acquired a new significance for you, and so forth.

In this paper our attention is exclusively centred upon work in preparation for constructions. And this raises right from the start the question of what guarantee we have, during the work on constructions, that we are not going wrong; are we putting the success of the treatment in jeopardy by upholding an incorrect construction? It may seem to us that there is no general answer to this question, but before going on to discuss it, let us lend an ear to a comforting piece of information gained from our experience of analysis. What it teaches us is that it does no harm if we sometimes go wrong and present the patient with an incorrect construction as the probable historical truth. Naturally, it represents a waste of time; and if somebody invariably relays mistaken constructions to the patient, he will make a poor impression on him and not get far with the treatment: but one such mistake is harmless. What actually happens in such a case is that the patient appears to remain unaffected, and responds with neither a yes nor a no. This might just mean that his reaction is delayed; but if nothing else follows, then we can draw the conclusion that we are wrong, and at some appropriate moment we can tell the patient as much, without loss of authority. The appropriate moment arises when new material comes to light, which permits a better construction and thus the correction of the mistake. The false construction falls away as though it had never been put forward, and indeed in many cases you have the impression that, to quote Polonius, 'your bait of falsehood takes this carp of truth'. The danger of leading the patient astray by the power of suggestion, by 'talking him into' something you yourself believe in, but which he would be wrong to accept, has surely been grossly exaggerated. For some mishap like this to befall him, the analyst must have behaved very incorrectly; above all he would have cause to reproach himself for not letting the patient have his say. Without vainglory, I can state that such an abuse of 'suggestion' has never once occurred throughout my career.

From the foregoing it will already be clear that we are not at all inclined to ignore the signals that are given out by the patient's reaction when we tell him about the construction. This is a point we would like to examine in detail. It is true that we do not accept the patient's 'no' at face value, but we are no more prepared to accept his 'yes', either; it is completely baseless to accuse us of converting his utterance into a confirmation in every case. Things are not so simple in reality, and we do not make the decision that easy for ourselves.

A direct 'yes' from the analysand is ambiguous. It can indeed show that he accepts the truth of the construction he has just heard, but equally it can be meaningless, or it can be what we may call 'hypocritical', in that it suits his resistance to go on covering up the truth he is hiding by agreeing with us. This 'yes' is only valuable if it is followed by indirect confirmations, if he produces new memories directly linked to his 'yes', which supplement and extend the construction. Only in that case do we recognize this 'yes' as fully settling the point in question.

The patient's 'no' is equally ambiguous, and in fact even less usable than his 'yes'. In rare cases it proves to be an expression of justified rejection; far more frequently it expresses a resistance that may be provoked by the content of the construction put forward, but can equally well derive from some other factor in the complex analytical situation. The patient's 'no' therefore proves nothing about the accuracy of the construction, but it is fully consistent with the possibility of accuracy. However, since every such construction is incomplete and contains only a small part of the forgotten events, we are at liberty to assume that the analysand is not actually denying what he has been told, but is basing his resistance on that part of the material that has not yet been revealed. He will usually only express agreement when he has learnt the whole truth, and the truth is often extremely far-reaching. So the only safe way to interpret his 'no' is as an indication of incompleteness; the construction has certainly not told him everything.

So it may turn out that you gain very few clues as to whether your guess is right or not from the direct comments of the patient after the construction has been put to him. It is all the more interesting that there are indirect kinds of confirmation that are completely reliable. One of them is an expression you hear in more or less unchanging form, as though by prior agreement, from the most varied people. It runs: I have never (would never have) thought (of) that. You can quite safely interpret this as: yes, in this case you have rightly identified what was unconscious. Unfortunately this formula, so welcome to the analyst, is heard more often after single, partial interpretations than after the presentation of an extensive construction. An equally valuable confirmation, this time expressed positively, is when the analysand responds with an association that contains something similar or analogous to the contents of the construction.

Instead of giving an example of this from an analysis, which would be easy to find but complicated to explain, I want to relate a little experience of mine that took place outside analysis, and conveys this kind of occurrence with almost comical vividness. It concerns a colleague who had selected me as a consultant – it was a long time ago – in his medical work. One day he brought his young wife to see me; she was upsetting him by using all sorts of excuses to refuse him sexual intercourse. He obviously expected me to explain to her the consequences of her unsuitable behaviour. I agreed to do so, and put it to her that her refusal would probably have unfortunate health consequences for her husband or lead him into temptations that could bring about the demise of their marriage. At this point he interrupted suddenly to say to me: 'The Englishman whom you diagnosed with a brain tumour has now died *as well*.' The comment at first seemed to make no sense, and the '*as well*' in the sentence was puzzling, since there had been no mention of anybody else dying. A little later it came to me. The man obviously wanted to back me up; he wanted to say: 'Yes, you're absolutely right, and your diagnosis of that patient was vindicated.' It was the complete counterpart to the indirect confirmation through associations that we receive in analysis. I will not dispute that quite different thoughts, which he had thrust to one side, played a part in his comment.

Indirect confirmation through associations that fit into the content of the construction, and which bring this kind of 'as well' with them, provides valuable clues when we have to judge whether this construction is likely to be validated as analysis continues. It is particularly impressive when, thanks to a mistake, the confirmation insinuates itself into a direct contradiction on the part of the patient. I published a fine example of this kind of thing earlier in a different place. The name *Jauner*, which is common in Vienna, recurred frequently in the patient's dreams without any proper explanation in his associations. I then explored the interpretation that he must mean *Gauner* when he said *Jauner* [*Gauner*, '(audacious) crook', 'cunning devil'], and the patient promptly replied: 'that seems a little too daring to me'.[1] Or perhaps the patient uses the words 'ten dollars means nothing to me' while trying to refute the imputation that a particular payment seems to him too high, but in place of dollars he substitutes a less valuable currency and says 'ten schillings'.

If the analysis is under pressure from powerful factors that enforce a negative therapeutic reaction, such as a guilty conscience, a masochistic need to suffer, or resistance to the help the analyst is offering, the attitude of the patient after he has been told about the construction often makes the conclusion very easy for us to arrive at. If the construction is false, there is no change in the patient, but if it is correct or brings us nearer to the truth, he reacts with an unmistakable worsening of his symptoms and of his general well-being.

In summary, we can conclude that we do not deserve to be accused of contemptuously ignoring the analysand's attitude to our constructions. We note it and often gain valuable clues from it. But these reactions of the patient are usually ambiguous and permit no final decision. Only by continuing the analysis can we reach a decision about the rightness or uselessness of our construction. We do not claim that an individual construction is any more than a supposition that will eventually be investigated, confirmed or rejected. We do not claim any authority for it, do not demand any direct agreement with it from the patient, and do not discuss it with him if he initially contradicts it. In short, our model is that character in Nestroy, the porter who had one answer ready for every question and objection: 'Everything will become clear in the course of events.'

### III

It is hardly worth relating how this happens in the further course of analysis, and by what means our supposition turns into conviction on the part of the patient; it is known to every analyst from his everyday experience and is not difficult to grasp. There is only one point about it that needs examination and explanation. The route whose point of departure is the analyst's construction should end in the patient's recall; but it does not always take us that far. Often enough it fails to lead the patient to recall what has been repressed. In lieu of that, through the correct conduct of the analysis, we succeed in firmly convincing him of the truth of the construction, and therapeutically this achieves the same result as regaining a memory. Under what circumstances this occurs and how it is possible for an apparently incomplete substitution to have this full effect, is a topic for future research.

I want to close this short paper with a few remarks that open up a wider perspective. I have noticed in a few analyses that being presented with what was obviously an accurate construction had a surprising and at first incomprehensible effect on the analysands. They experienced vivid memories, which they themselves described as 'unusually clear', but what they recalled was not so much the event itself that formed the content of the construction, but details closely related to this content, for example, the unnaturally sharp features of the people who appeared in it, or the rooms in which something of that sort could have happened, or – a little less immediate – the furnishings of these rooms, of which the construction naturally could know nothing. This happened both in dreams immediately after the presentation, and in waking states, in a condition of heightened imagination. Nothing else followed in the wake of these memories; so it seemed reasonable to see them as the result of a compromise. An 'upsurge' of the repressed, activated by the narrating of the construction, wished to bring these important traces of memory up to the level of consciousness, but a resistance had succeeded, if not in blocking this movement, then in diverting it on to nearby, secondary objects.

You might have been able to call these memories hallucinations, if, in addition to their clarity, the patient also believed in their actual reality. But this analogy increased in significance for me when I noticed the occasional occurrence of true hallucinations in other cases that were definitely not psychotic in nature. My chain of ideas continued: perhaps it is a universal characteristic of hallucinations, not yet sufficiently recognized, that in them something returns that has been experienced at an early age and then forgotten, something the child heard or saw at a time when it was still incapable of speech, and that now imposes itself upon consciousness, probably distorted and displaced by the effects of the forces which oppose such a return. And with the close relationship of hallucinations to certain forms of psychosis, our chain of ideas can be extended even further. Perhaps the delusions in which we regularly find these hallucinations embedded are not so independent of the upsurge of the unconscious and the return of the repressed as we commonly assume. In the mechanism of a delusion we generally pick out just two factors; the turning away from the real world and its motives, on the one hand, and on the other the influence of wish-fulfilment on the contents of the delusion. But perhaps the dynamic of the process takes a course rather more like the following: turning away from reality gives the resurgent repression an opportunity to impose its content on consciousness. At the same time, the resistances aroused in this process, and the tendency to wish-fulfilment, are responsible respectively for the distortion and the displacement of what is recalled. This is, after all, what we know to be the mechanism of the dream, long ago equated with madness by the intuition of primitive man.

I do not believe that this conception of delusion is completely new, but it does emphasize a point of view that is not usually foregrounded. The essential thing about it is not just the assertion that madness has method in it, as the poet recognized, but that it also contains a certain historical truth, and we feel it is reasonable to assume that the compulsive conviction that delusions enjoy draws its power precisely from this infantile source. I have no fresh impressions at my command to demonstrate this theory, only reminiscences. It would probably be worth while to try studying relevant cases of illness in the light of the assumptions I have developed here and adapting the treatment accordingly. One would then give up the vain attempt to convince the sufferer of the insanity of his delusion and its contradiction of reality, and instead find common ground upon which therapeutic work can develop by recognizing the core of truth. The work would consist in freeing this piece of historical truth from its distortions and its dependence on the real present and shifting it back to the place in the past to which it belongs.

A shift from the forgotten past into the present or into expectations of the future is of course a regular occurrence with the neurotic, too. Often enough, when a state of anxiety gives him the feeling that something terrible is about to happen, he is simply under the influence of a repressed memory, which wishes to reach the conscious level but cannot, of something terrible really having taken place at that time. I believe that the therapeutic efforts to help psychotics that I have suggested can teach us valuable lessons, even when the therapy does not succeed for them.

I know it is not creditable to deal with such an important topic as casually as I have here. I was tempted into following an analogy. The delusions of the sick seem to me equivalent to the constructions that we build up in analytic treatment. They are attempts at explanation and recuperation, which, admittedly, under the conditions of psychosis, can only lead to our replacing the piece of reality which is being denied in the present, by another piece that the patient has already similarly denied in his early years. It becomes the aim of investigating individual cases to reveal the close relationship between the content of the current denial and that of the earlier one. Just as our construction can only work by retrieving a part of the patient's life-history that was previously lost, so a delusion owes its power of conviction to the segment of historical truth that it substitutes for the rejected reality. In this sense it would be appropriate to apply to delusion something I once said about hysteria: that the patient suffers from his reminiscences. With this brief formulation I had no intention, even at the time, of disputing the complex causes of illness or excluding the impact of so many other factors.

If you take mankind as a whole, and put it in the place of the individual human being, then you find that it too has developed delusions that are inaccessible to logical critique and that contradict reality. If these delusions none the less exert an extraordinary influence over people, investigation leads to the same conclusion as in the case of the single individual. They owe their strength to the measure of historical truth that they have extracted from the repression of forgotten past ages.

(1937)

## Note

1. [In the original German the man says *jewagt* (for bold, audacious, daring) rather than *gewagt*, a form of the past participle that is not implausible, because the substitution of 'j' for 'g' occurs in the famous Berlin

dialect. But the use of 'j' for 'g' unconsciously suggests confirmation of the validity of Freud's interpretation, at the very same time that the patient intends to contradict it. In other words, 'Jauner' really could easily suggest 'Gauner' to the patient, since he is familiar with the 'j'/'g' interchange.]

# Fetishism

Over the last few years I have had the opportunity to study analytically a number of men whose object choices were governed by a fetish. We need not suppose it was because of their fetish that these people came for analysis, for while its devotees recognize it as an abnormality, they rarely feel it to be the symptom of an illness; on the whole, they are perfectly happy with the fetish, and even extol the way it simplifies their love life. As a rule, then, their fetish came to light only incidentally during analysis.

The details of these cases cannot be published for obvious reasons. Nor, therefore, can I demonstrate the role played by accidental circumstances in the choice of fetish. The most remarkable case in this respect was one in which a young man had elevated a certain 'shine on the nose' into a fetishistic prerequisite. The surprising explanation for this was that the child had been brought up in England but had then come to Germany, where he almost completely forgot his native language. The fetish, which stemmed from earliest infancy, needed to be read not in German, but in English; the 'shine [*Glanz*] on the nose' was actually a 'glance at the nose', so the fetish was the nose – which, incidentally, he could endow at will with this particular sheen, invisible to others.

What analysis revealed about the meaning and purpose of these fetishes was the same in every case. It emerged so spontaneously and seemed to me so compelling that I am prepared to anticipate the same general solution for all cases of fetishism. If I now state that a fetish is a penis substitute, this will no doubt come as a disappointment. I hasten to add, then, that it is a substitute not just for any penis, but for a specific and very special one, one which is of great significance in early infancy but which is subsequently lost. That is to say, it should normally be renounced, but it is precisely the purpose of a fetish to prevent this loss from occurring. To put it more plainly, a fetish is a substitute for the woman's (mother's) phallus, which the little boy once believed in and which – for reasons well known to us – he does not want to give up.[1]

What has happened, then, is this: the boy has refused to acknowledge the fact that he has perceived that women have no penis. No, this cannot be true, because if women have been castrated, then his own penis is in danger, and the piece of narcissism, with which nature providently equips this very organ, recoils at the thought. In later life, an adult might experience a similar panic on hearing the cry that king and country are in peril, and it will have similarly illogical consequences. If I am not mistaken, Laforgue would say in this case that the boy 'scotomizes' his perception that women have no penis.[2] A new term is justified if it describes or highlights a new fact, but this is not the case here; the oldest piece of psychoanalytical terminology, the term 'repression', already refers to this pathological process. If, within this process, we wished to distinguish the fate of the idea more sharply from that of the emotion, and to reserve the term 'repression' for the emotion, then the correct term for the fate of the idea would be 'denial'. 'Scotomization' seems to me particularly unsuitable because it implies that the perception has been completely erased, with the same effect as if the visual impression had fallen on the retina's blind spot. On the contrary, though, our case reveals that the perception remains and a very energetic action has been undertaken to maintain the denial. It is not true that the child's belief in the female phallus remains unchanged after he has observed a woman. He both retains this belief and renounces it; in the conflict between the force of the unwelcome perception and the intensity of his aversion to it, a compromise is reached such as is possible only under the laws of unconscious thought, the primary processes. In his psyche, yes, the woman still has a penis, but this penis is no longer the same thing as before. Something else has taken its place, has been appointed its successor, so to speak, and this now inherits all the interest previously devoted to its predecessor. But because the horror of castration has been immortalized in the creation of this substitute, this interest also becomes intensified to an extraordinary degree. The repression that has taken place leaves behind a further *stigma indelebile* in the form of an aversion towards real female genitals, common to all fetishists. Now we have an overview of what the fetish achieves and how it is maintained. It remains a mark of triumph over the threat of castration and a safeguard against it; it also spares the fetishist from becoming homosexual, in that it endows women with a characteristic making them acceptable as sexual objects. In later life, the fetishist believes his genital substitute offers yet another advantage. Other people are unaware of its significance and so do not withhold it from him; the fetish is easily accessible and the sexual satisfaction it provides is readily available. What other men have to pursue and strive for presents no such problems for the fetishist.

Probably no male is spared the horror of castration at the sight of female genitals. Admittedly, we cannot explain why some men become homosexual as a result of this experience, others ward it off by creating a fetish, while the vast majority overcome it. It could be that, of all the various contributory factors, we do not know yet which ones determine the less common pathological outcomes; we shall just have to content ourselves with being able to explain what has happened, without, for the time being, worrying about explaining why something has not.

It seems reasonable to expect that the organs and objects chosen as substitutes for the missing female phallus will be those already used to symbolize the penis. This may well be the case often enough, but it certainly is not the decisive factor. The process involved when a fetish first becomes established seems reminiscent, rather, of the way memories are blocked out in traumatic amnesia. Here, too, the patient's interest stops in its tracks, so to speak, if indeed it is the last impression prior to the uncanny, traumatic one that becomes fixed as the fetish. Thus feet or shoes owe their prominence as fetishes, at least in part, to the fact that the curious boy looked at women's genitals from below, from the legs up; fur and velvet are

– as we have long suspected – fixations on the sight of pubic hair, which should have been followed by the longed-for sight of the female member; pieces of underwear, so commonly adopted as fetishes, capture the moment of undressing, the last point at which the woman could still be regarded as phallic. But I do not wish to claim we know for certain how fetishes are determined in every case. I do, however, strongly recommend the study of fetishism to anyone who still doubts the existence of the castration complex, or anyone who can believe that dread of the female genitals has some other cause and derives from, say, a supposed memory of the trauma of birth. For me, however, the elucidation of fetishes held a further theoretical interest.

Recently I arrived, by pure speculation, at the formula that the essential difference between neurosis and psychosis was that in neurosis the ego, at the behest of reality, suppresses a piece of the id, whereas in psychosis it is impelled by the id to detach itself from a piece of reality; later I returned to this theme once again.[3] Soon afterwards, though, I had cause to regret having been so presumptuous. The analysis of two young men showed me that each of them, at the ages of two and ten respectively, had failed to acknowledge – 'scotomized' – the death of a beloved father, and yet neither had developed a psychosis. Here, then, a patently significant piece of reality had been denied by the ego, just as the fetishist denies the unwelcome fact of female castration. I also began to suspect that analogous occurrences are by no means uncommon in infancy, and I took this to be proof that my characterization of neurosis and psychosis was wrong. Of course, one possible way out remained open; my formula would just need to have been restricted to a more advanced level of differentiation in the psychic apparatus – the child was free to do something which, in an adult, would lead to serious harm. Further investigation, however, led to a different resolution of the contradiction.

As it turned out, the two young men had no more 'scotomized' their father's death than fetishists do female castration. Only one current in their psyche had failed to acknowledge the father's death; there was another that took full account of this fact. The wishful attitude and the realistic attitude existed side by side. In one of the cases, this split formed the basis of a moderately severe compulsion neurosis; in every situation in his life he would waver between two assumptions – one that his father was still alive and was holding him back from doing what he wanted, and the opposite one, that he had the right to consider himself his dead father's successor. Thus I can persist with my expectation that had this been a case of psychosis, one of these two currents – the realistic one – would actually be missing.

To return to my description of fetishism, let me say there are many further substantial pieces of evidence for the fetishist's dual attitude towards the issue of female castration. In particularly ingenious cases both the denial and affirmation of castration are incorporated within the structure of the fetish itself. This was the case with a man whose fetish consisted of a modesty girdle of the kind that can also be worn as a swimming costume. This piece of clothing completely concealed the genitals and the difference between them. According to analysis, it signified both that women were castrated and that they were not, and, furthermore, it allowed for the assumption of male castration, because all these possibilities could equally well be hidden beneath the girdle, the first incarnation of which, in infancy, had been a fig-leaf on a statue. A fetish such as this, doubly determined by an antithesis, naturally proves particularly resilient. In other cases the duality manifests itself in what the fetishist does with the fetish, either actually or in fantasy. To emphasize only that he worships the fetish does not tell the whole story; in many cases his treatment of it clearly amounts to an enactment of castration. Here, if he has developed a strong father-identification, he tends to adopt the role of the father, because it was to him that the child ascribed the act of castrating women. Affection and hostility towards the fetish, corresponding to the denial and acknowledgement of castration, combine in unequal proportions in each different case, so that one or the other is more clearly discernible. In this light, perhaps we can understand, albeit from a distance, the behaviour of men who like to cut off women's plaits and ponytails, where the need to act out the denied castration has pushed its way to the fore. This action fuses together the two incompatible beliefs – that women still have a penis, and that women have been castrated by the father. Another variant of – and ethnopsychological parallel to – fetishism may be seen in the Chinese custom of deforming women's feet and then revering the deformed foot as a fetish. It would seem Chinese men wish to show their gratitude towards women for having submitted to castration.

We can conclude by stating that the normal prototype of a fetish is the man's penis, just as the prototype of an inferior organ is the woman's actual little penis, the clitoris.

(1927)

## Notes

1. This interpretation was published, without substantiation, as early as 1910 in my study *A Childhood Memory of Leonardo da Vinci*.
2. Let me correct myself, however, by adding that I have very good reason to believe Laforgue would say no such thing. We know from his own account that 'scotomization' is a term derived from the description of dementia praecox, not from any attempt to transfer psychoanalytical concepts to the psychoses, and that it is not applicable to processes of development or neurosis formation. He is very careful in his written account to make this incompatibility clear.
3. 'Neurosis and Psychosis' (1924) and 'The Loss of Reality in Neurosis and Psychosis' (1924).

# Negation

The manner in which our patients present their associations during analytical work gives us occasion for some interesting observations. 'Now you'll think I want to insult you, but I really don't mean to.' This, we realize, is a thought being rejected as it emerges, by means of projection. Or: 'You ask who this person in my dream can be. It's *not* my mother.' This we amend: 'So it is your mother.' In our interpretations we take the liberty of disregarding the negation and seizing on the pure content of the thought. It is as if the patient had said: 'My first thought was, it's my mother, but I have no desire to admit this.'

Occasionally we can get sought-after information about unconscious repressed material by a very easy method. We ask: 'So what would you say is absolutely least likely in this situation? What do you think was furthest from your mind at that point?' If the patient walks into the trap and tells us what he would find most incredible, he almost always gives the truth away. Compulsion neurotics who have already been initiated into an understanding of their symptoms often provide a nice counterpart to this experiment. They say: 'I've got a new compulsive idea. My immediate thought was, it could mean such and such. But no, surely that can't be true – otherwise I couldn't have had that thought.' The interpretation of the new compulsive idea that they reject with this argument picked up from the treatment is, of course, the correct one.

The content of a repressed idea or thought can get through to consciousness, then, on condition that it is *negated*. Negation is a way of acknowledging the repressed, indeed it amounts to a lifting of the repression, although not, of course, an acceptance of what is repressed. Here we see how an intellectual function differs from an emotional process. Only one of the consequences of the process of repression – that of the ideational content not being allowed into consciousness – is undone with the help of negation. The result is a kind of intellectual recognition of the repressed while the essential element of the repression remains in place.[1] During analytical work, we often produce a further very important and somewhat strange variant of this situation. We manage to overcome even the negation and bring about a full intellectual acknowledgement of the repressed – but still without lifting the repression itself.

Since it is the task of the intellectual function of judgement to affirm or negate the contents of thoughts, these remarks have led us to the psychological source of this function. To negate something in judgement is basically to say: 'This is something I'd rather repress.' Disapproval is the intellectual substitute for repression – its 'no' is a hallmark of repression, a kind of certificate of origin like 'Made in Germany'. By means of this symbol of negation, thought frees itself from the restrictions imposed by repression and appropriates material without which it could not perform its function.

Essentially, it is the function of judgement to make two kinds of decision. It has to decide whether or not a thing possesses a certain property, and whether or not an imagined thing exists in reality. The property to be decided on might originally have been good or bad, useful or harmful, or, expressed in the language of the most archaic, oral drive impulses: 'I want to eat this, or spit this out.' In more general terms: 'I want to take this into me, or keep it out of me,' that is: 'I want it inside me, or outside me.' As I have explained elsewhere, the primal pleasure-ego wants to introject into itself everything good and expel from itself everything bad. That which is bad, that which is alien to the ego, that which is outside, are initially identical as far as it is concerned.[2]

The other kind of decision that it is the function of judgement to make – whether or not an imagined thing exists in reality (reality-testing) – is a matter for the reality-ego, into which the primal pleasure-ego ultimately evolves. Now the question is no longer whether what is perceived (a thing) should be taken into the ego or not, but whether something already present in the ego, as a mental image, can also be rediscovered in perception (reality). We see that, once again, it is a question of *inside* and *outside*. That which is non-real, merely imagined, subjective, exists only on the *inside*; other things, real things, are also there on the *outside*. In this development, adherence to the pleasure principle has been set aside. Experience has taught that what matters is not only whether a thing (an object of satisfaction) possesses the property of 'goodness', and so merits being taken into the ego, but also whether it is actually there in the outside world, and so can be appropriated whenever the need arises. To understand this development, we have to remember that all mental images stem from – are reproductions of – perceptions. Originally, then, the mere existence of the idea of a thing is a guarantee that the thing actually exists. The opposition between subjective and objective does not exist from the start. It comes about only because thought has the capacity to bring back something once perceived by reproducing it as a mental image, with no need for the external object still to be present. The first and immediate aim of reality-testing, then, is not to discover, in real perception, an object corresponding to the mental image, but to *rediscover* it, to ascertain that it still exists. Another feature of the faculty of thought leads to a further widening of the gap between the subjective and the objective. The reproduction of a perception as a mental image is not always a faithful copy; it can be modified by omissions or by the fusion of various elements. Here the job of reality-testing is to assess the extent of these distortions. Clearly, though, what led to the actual inception of reality-testing was the loss of objects that had once brought real satisfaction.

Judging is the intellectual action which determines the choice of motor action, puts an end to pausing for thought, and leads the way from thought to action. I have discussed pausing for thought elsewhere, too. It should be regarded as a trial run of an action, a 'feeling out' involving a low expenditure of motor discharge. Now let us think: Where has the ego previously employed this kind of feeling out? Where did it learn the technique it now applies in thought processes? It was at the sensory end of the psychic apparatus, in connection with sense perceptions. Perception, according to our hypothesis, is not an entirely passive process, rather the ego periodically invests small amounts of energy in the perceptual system by means of which it samples the external stimuli, withdrawing again after each such exploratory advance.

Studying the phenomenon of judgement gives us perhaps our first insight into the way an intellectual function evolves from the play of primary drive impulses. Judging something is an expedient progression from the primal act, governed by the pleasure principle, of incorporating it into or expelling it from the ego. Its polarity seems to correspond to the opposition we have posited between two basic groups of drives. Affirmation – as a substitute for unification – belongs to Eros; negation – the successor to expulsion – belongs to the destruction-drive. A general desire for negation, the negativism of some psychotics, can probably be regarded as indicating a drive disintegration caused by withdrawal of the libidinal components. But judgement is able to perform its function at all only because the creation of the symbol of negation provides thought with its first measure of independence from the effects of repression and so from the constraints of the pleasure principle.

Fully consonant with this view of negation is the fact that during analysis we never find a 'no' in the unconscious, and recognition of the unconscious by the ego is always expressed in negative formulations. There is no stronger evidence that the unconscious has successfully been uncovered than when the patient reacts with the words: *'That's not what I was thinking,'* or *'I wasn't thinking (have never thought) any such thing.'*

(1925)

### Notes

1. This process is also the basis of the well-known phenomenon of 'tempting fate'. 'How nice that I haven't had one of my migraines for so long!'

This, however, is the first sign of an attack, which we have already sensed approaching, but without wanting to believe it yet.

2. Cf. my comments in 'Drives and Their Fates'.

# Note on the 'Magic Notepad'

If I mistrust my memory – neurotics, as is well known, do this to a striking degree, but normal people have every reason to do it as well – I am able to complement and confirm its function by making a written note. The surface on which this note is preserved, a blackboard or a sheet of paper, is then, so to speak, a materialized part of the apparatus of memory which I otherwise bear invisibly within myself. I need only notice the place where the 'memory' thus captured is stored, and I am able to 'reproduce' it at will at any time, certain that it has remained unchanged, and that it has escaped the distortions that it might have undergone in my memory.

If I wish to make abundant use of this technique in order to improve my memory function, I notice that I have two different procedures at my disposal. First of all I can choose a writing surface which preserves the note entrusted to it intact for an indefinite period of time, which is to say a sheet of paper on which I write in ink. When I do that, I receive a 'lasting trace of memory'. The disadvantage of this procedure lies in the fact that the receptiveness of the writing surface is soon exhausted. The sheet is filled, it has no more room for additional notes, and I find myself obliged to use another sheet that is still blank. The advantage of this procedure, which leaves a 'lasting trace', can also lose its value for me, if my interest in the note has expired after a period of time, and I no longer wish to 'keep it in my memory'. The other procedure is free of both shortcomings. If, for example, I write in chalk on a board, I have a receptive surface which can preserve traces for an unlimited period of time, and I can destroy the notes on it the moment they cease to interest me, without having to throw away the writing surface itself. The disadvantage in this case is that I cannot receive a lasting trace. If I want to write fresh notes on the board, I must wipe away the ones with which it is already covered. So unlimited receptiveness and the preservation of lasting traces thus seem to be ruled out for the devices that we substitute for our memory: either the receptive surface must be renewed, or the note must be destroyed.

The devices that we have invented to improve or reinforce our sensory functions are thus all constructed like the sensory organ itself or parts of it (spectacles, camera, ear trumpet and so on). By this standard, the devices designed to back up our memory seem to be particularly inadequate, because our mental apparatus accomplishes precisely what we are unable to; it is boundlessly receptive to new perceptions, and yet it creates lasting – although not unchangeable – memory traces of them. In my *Interpretation of Dreams* (1900), I expressed the suspicion that this unusual ability was divided between two different systems (organs of the mental apparatus). I suggested that we possess a *Pcpt-Cs* system that absorbs perceptions but preserves no lasting trace of them, so that it can respond as a blank page to each fresh perception. The lasting traces of the received excitations come into being in 'systems of memory' which are left behind them. Later (in *Beyond the Pleasure Principle*) I added the observation that the inexplicable phenomenon of consciousness arises in the system of perception *in place of* the lasting traces.

Some time ago, a small piece of equipment, going by the name of *Wunderblock* or 'magic notepad', was available in the shops, promising to accomplish more than the sheet of paper or the blackboard. It claimed to be nothing more than a board from which one can remove one's notes with a single easy movement. But inspecting it more closely, one discovers in its construction a remarkable agreement with the structure that I suggest in our perceptual apparatus, and one will be convinced that it can really provide both things, a receptive surface that is always ready, and lasting traces of the notes recorded.

The magic notepad is a board consisting of dark-brown resin or wax within a paper frame, with a thin, translucent sheet laid over it, firmly attached to the wax board at the top and lying flat at the bottom. This sheet is the more interesting part of the little apparatus. The sheet itself consists of two layers which may not only be lifted by their two side edges, but also separated from one another. The upper layer is a transparent celluloid plate, the lower a thin and thus translucent piece of wax paper. If the apparatus is unused, the lower surface of the wax paper adheres slightly to the upper surface of the wax board.

This magic notepad is employed by making the note on the celluloid plate of the sheet covering the wax board. To do this one does not need a pencil or chalk, because the writing is not based upon the material being passed on to the receptive surface. It is a return to the way the ancients wrote on boards of clay and wax. A pointed stylus scratches the surface, whose indentations produce the 'writing'. In the magic notepad this scratching does not occur directly, but through the agency of the covering sheet above it. At the points which it touches, the stylus presses the lower surface of the wax paper against the wax pad, and these grooves become visible as dark writing in the otherwise smooth whitish-grey surface of the celluloid. If one wishes to destroy the writing, it is enough to lift the composite covering sheet from the wax pad by its free lower edge. The internal contact between wax paper and wax pad at the scratched points, on which the visibility of the writing was based, is thus broken and is not recreated when the two touch once again. The magic notepad is now free of writing and ready to receive new notes.

The minor imperfections in the apparatus are naturally of no interest to us, as we only wish to pursue the ways in which it resembles the structure of the psychical perceptual apparatus.

If, while the magic notepad is being written upon, one carefully lifts the celluloid plate from the wax paper, one sees the writing just as clearly on the surface of the latter, and can ask the question why the celluloid plate of the covering sheet is at all necessary. Experimentation then shows that the thin paper would very easily be wrinkled or torn if it were written upon directly with the stylus. The celluloid sheet is thus a protective cover for the wax paper, designed to shield against damaging effects from without. The celluloid is a 'stimulus barrier'; the layer that actually receives the stimulus is the paper. I might now point out that in *Beyond the Pleasure Principle* I put forward the idea that our perceptual apparatus consists of two layers, an external stimulus barrier which is supposed to reduce the size of incoming excitations, and the stimulus-receiving surface behind it, the *Pcpt-Cs* system.

There would not be much value to the analogy if it could not be followed further. If one lifts the whole covering sheet – celluloid and wax paper – from the wax tablet, the writing disappears, and cannot, as I have said, be produced again later on. The surface of the magic pad is free of writing and ready to receive once again. But it is easy to establish that the lasting trace of the writing is preserved on the wax tablet itself, and is readable under appropriate lighting. So the pad not only provides a reusable receptive surface like a blackboard, but also lasting traces of writing like a normal paper notepad; it solves the problem of combining both functions by *distributing them between two separate but connected components – systems*. But that is the same as the way in which, according to my hypothesis mentioned above, our psychical apparatus performs the function of perception. The stimulus-absorbing layer – the *Pcpt-Cs* system – does not form lasting traces, and the foundations of memory come into being in other colliding systems.

We need not be disturbed by the fact that the lasting traces of the received notes are not used in the case of the magic notepad; it is enough that they are present. The analogy between an auxiliary apparatus of this kind and the exemplary organ must come to an end somewhere. Neither can the magic notepad 'reproduce' the writing from within; it really would be a magic notepad if it accomplished that, as our memory can. None the less, it does not strike me as excessively audacious to equate the covering sheet consisting of celluloid and wax paper with the *Pcpt-Cs* system and its stimulus barrier, and the wax tablet with the unconscious behind it, the visible appearance of the writing and its disappearance with the flashing and fading of consciousness in perception. But I confess that I am disinclined to take the analogy any further.

With the magic notepad, the writing disappears whenever the close contact between the stimulus-receiving paper and the wax tablet that stores the impression is abolished. This coincides with an idea that I developed a long time ago about the way in which the psychical perceptual apparatus works, but which I have hitherto kept to myself. I have suggested that investment innervations are sent in rapid periodic thrusts from within into the entirely permeable *Pcpt-Cs* system and then withdrawn again. As long as the system is invested in this way, it receives the perceptions accompanied by consciousness and passes the excitation on to the unconscious systems of memory; as soon as the investment is withdrawn, consciousness is extinguished again, and the functioning of the system is interrupted. It is as though the unconscious were extending feelers towards the *Pcpt-Cs* system, and quickly withdrawing them after they had probed its excitations. So I allowed the interruptions that occur from outside in the use of the magic notepad to come into being through the discontinuity in the current of innervation, and according to my hypothesis the place of a real abolition of contact is taken by the periodical immunity of the perceptual system to excitation. I went on to suppose that this discontinuous working method of the *Pcpt-Cs* system underlies the origin of the idea of time.

If we consider that while one hand writes upon the surface of the magic pad, and the other periodically lifts the covering sheet from the wax tablet, then that would provide a symbol for the way in which I wished to imagine the functioning of our psychical perceptual apparatus.

(1925)

105

# 'Psychoanalysis' and 'Libido Theory' (Second Introductory Lecture)

## 1 Psychoanalysis

*Psychoanalysis* is the name 1) of a procedure for the investigation of psychical processes that are otherwise barely accessible; 2) of a method of treating neurotic disorders based on that investigation; 3) of a series of psychological insights acquired in this way, which are gradually growing into a new scientific discipline.

*History*. Psychoanalysis is always best understood by studying its origins and development. In Vienna in 1880 and 1881, Dr Josef Breuer, well known as a houseman and an experimental physiologist, undertook the treatment of a girl who had, while caring for her sick father, begun to suffer badly from hysteria, and whose symptoms consisted of a combination of motor paralyses, inhibitions and disorders of the consciousness. Following a suggestion from this very intelligent patient, he placed her under hypnosis, and in this way always managed to return her, by communicating her dominant moods and thoughts, to a normal mental state. By consistent repetition of the same arduous procedure he managed to free her from all her inhibitions and paralyses, so that his efforts were finally rewarded by great therapeutic success as well as by unexpected insights into the essence of the mysterious neurosis. But Breuer refrained from pursuing his discovery any further, and published nothing on the subject for about a decade, until the personal influence of the author of the present paper (Freud, who had returned from Charcot's school to Vienna in 1886) managed to persuade him to return to the subject and their common work upon it. Then, in 1895, Breuer and Freud published a provisional paper, 'On the psychical mechanism of hysterical phenomena', and in 1895 a book, *Studies in Hysteria* (published in its fourth edition in 1922), in which they described their healing method as 'cathartic'.

*Catharsis*. The investigations upon which Breuer and Freud's studies were based yielded two results above all, which were not disturbed by later experience, first that hysterical symptoms have sense and meaning, in that they are a substitute for normal psychical acts; and secondly that the revelation of this unknown sense coincides with the abolition of the symptoms, and that scientific research and therapeutic effort thus tally with one another. The observations were made on a series of patients who were treated in the same way as Breuer's first patient, which is to say that they were placed under deep hypnosis, and the consequences seemed dazzling, until their weakness later became apparent. The theoretical ideas that Breuer and Freud nurtured in those days were influenced by Charcot's theories concerning traumatic hysteria, and were able to borrow from the findings of his pupil P. Janet, which might have been published earlier than the *Studies*, but which were of a later date than Breuer's first case. From the very beginning the affective element came to the fore in these cases; the hysterical symptoms were supposed to have emerged from a psychical process with a strong affective charge being in some way blocked from balancing itself in the normal way, leading to consciousness and motility (being worked off), whereupon the affect, being in a sense 'jammed', ended up on the wrong path and was discharged into physical innervation (conversion). Breuer and Freud described the occasions on which such pathogenic 'ideas' came about as 'psychical traumas', and as in many cases they belonged to times long past the authors were able to say that for the most part the hysterics suffered from (undealt-with) reminiscences.

'Catharsis' then followed under treatment by opening up the way to consciousness and normal discharge of the affect. The assumption of unconscious psychical processes was, as we see, an indispensable part of this theory. Janet too had worked with unconscious acts in the life of the mind, but, as he stressed in later polemics against psychoanalysis, that was only a phrase drawn from the air as far as he was concerned, *une manière de parler*, with which he did not wish to suggest any fresh insight.

In a theoretical section of the studies, Breuer communicated some speculative thoughts about the processes of excitation in the mind which have continued to point the way towards the future, and have not been fully appreciated even today. Here his contributions to this field of knowledge came to an end, since shortly afterwards he withdrew from the collaboration.

*The Transition to Psychoanalysis.* As early as the *Studies*, oppositions in the views of the two authors had become apparent. Breuer hypothesized that pathogenic ideas express a traumatic effect because they come about in 'hypnoid states' in which the psychical function is subjected to particular restrictions. The present writer rejected this explanation, and believed he recognized that an idea becomes pathogenic when its content resists the predominant tendencies of the life of the mind, in such a way that it provokes the 'defence' of the individual. (Janet had attributed to the hysterics a constitutional inability to hold their psychical contents together; at this point Breuer's and Freud's paths parted from his.) The two innovations with which the present writer left the terrain of catharsis has already been mentioned in the *Studies*. Now, after Breuer's withdrawal, they became the starting point for further developments.

*Abandonment of Hypnosis.* One of these innovations was based on practical experience and led to a change in technique, while the other consisted in an advance in the clinical knowledge of neurosis. It soon became apparent that the therapeutic hopes that had been placed upon hypnosis remained in some ways unfulfilled. The disappearance of symptoms did indeed run parallel to catharsis, but overall success proved to be entirely dependent on the doctor–patient relationship, and thus behaved as though it were the consequence of 'suggestion', and if that particular relationship was destroyed all the symptoms reappeared as though they had never found a solution. Added to this was the fact that the very small number of people who allowed themselves to be placed under deep hypnosis created a restriction in the application of the cathartic procedure, which was very significant from the medical point of view. For these reasons the present writer decided to abandon hypnosis. But at the same time he took from his impressions of hypnosis the means of replacing it.

*Free Association.* The hypnotic state had brought about such an increase in the patient's associative ability that he was immediately able to find the way, inaccessible to his conscious reflection, from the symptom to the thoughts and memories connected with it. The abandonment of hypnosis seemed to create an impasse, but the present writer recalled Bernheim's demonstration that that which was experienced in somnambulism only seemed to have been forgotten, and could always be recalled by the doctor's insistent assurance that one knew it. So he tried to urge his non-hypnotized patients to communicate associations as well, and to find their way through such material to that which had been forgotten or warded off. Later he realized that such insistence was not required, and that an abundance of ideas appeared in almost every case, but that they were kept away from communication, indeed from the consciousness itself, by certain objections that he himself made. The expectation, still unproven at the time but later confirmed by extensive experience, that everything which occurred to the patient from a particular starting point must also have a profound connection with that point, gave rise to the technique of encouraging the patient to abandon all his critical attitudes and the use of the material thus brought to light in order to reveal the connections that one was seeking for. A high level of confidence in the strictness of determination in the sphere of the mind was certainly involved in the application of this technique, which was supposed to replace hypnosis.

*The 'Basic Technical Rule'*, the procedure of 'free association', has been retained in psychoanalytic work. Introduction to the treatment involves persuading the patient to put himself in the position of an attentive and passionate observer of himself, only ever reading the surface of his consciousness and on the one hand imposing upon himself the duty of the most complete honesty, on the other to keep silent no idea that occurs to him, even if 1) he found it too unpleasant, or 2) if he were forced to judge it nonsensical, 3) too unimportant, or 4) it was not what he was looking for. It regularly becomes apparent that the ideas which provoke these latter observations are precisely those which are of special value for the revelation of forgotten material.

*Psychoanalysis as an Art of Interpretation.* The new technique so altered the impression of treatment, it put the doctor in such new relationships with the patient and supplied so many surprising results, that there seemed good reason to distinguish the procedure by name from the cathartic method. For the method of treatment, which could now be extended to many other forms of neurotic disorder, the present writer chose the name *psychoanalysis*. This psychoanalysis was primarily an art of interpretation, and assumed the task of deepening the first of Breuer's great discoveries, that the neurotic symptoms are a meaningful substitute for other psychical acts that had not taken place. Now it was a question of comprehending the material supplied by the ideas that occurred to the patients as though it pointed towards a hidden meaning, and to guess that meaning from it. Experience soon showed that the analysing doctor acted in the most appropriate way if he abandoned himself, *allowing his attention to float evenly*, to his own unconscious mental activity, avoiding reflection and the formation of conscious expectations as much as possible, trying not to fix in his memory anything particular that he had heard, and in this way capturing the patient's unconscious with his own unconscious. Then one became aware, if conditions were not too unfavourable, that the ideas occurring to the patient in a sense felt their way around a particular subject, like allusions, and one did not oneself need to take a step further to be able to guess that which was hidden from the patient and communicate it to him. Certainly strict rules could not be applied to this interpretative work, and the tact and skill of the doctor was given a great deal of latitude, but if impartiality combined with practice one generally achieved dependable results, that is, results that were confirmed by repetition in other, similar cases. At the time, since so little was known about the unconscious, the structure of neuroses and the pathological processes behind them, one had to content oneself with being able to use such a technique despite the fact that it did not have a more secure theoretical foundation. Incidentally, it is also practised in the same way in contemporary analysis, but with a feeling of greater assurance and a better understanding of its limitations.

*The Interpretation of Lapses and Chance Actions.* It was a triumph for the interpretative art of psychoanalysis when it succeeded in proving that certain frequently occurring psychical acts on the part of normal people, for which one had previously not so much as considered a psychological explanation, were to be understood as neurotic symptoms, that is, that they have a meaning that is unknown to the subject and can easily be found through the efforts of analysis. The phenomena in question, the temporary forgetting of otherwise familiar words and names, the forgetting of intentions, slips of the tongue, of reading, of writing, losing and misplacing objects, certain errors, acts of apparently chance self-harm, and finally movements that are habitually performed as though unintentionally, playfully, tunes 'thoughtlessly' hummed, and so on – all of this has been removed from physiological explanation, where such an explanation has even been attempted, demonstrated to be strictly determined, and acknowledged as the expression of suppressed intentions on the part of the person or as a consequence of the interference of two intentions, of which one was unconscious, either lastingly or at that time. The value of this contribution to psychology was manifold. The scope of psychical determination was thus extended in an unsuspected way; the supposed gulf between normal and pathological psychical events was diminished. In many cases a comfortable insight was given into the play of psychical forces that must be suspected to lie behind the phenomena. Finally, in this way, one reached material better suited than any other to awaken a belief in the existence of unconscious psychical acts even among those to whom the hypothesis of a psychic unconscious appears strange or even absurd. The study of one's own lapses and chance actions, for which most people have ample opportunity is, even today, the best preparation for a penetration of psychoanalysis. In analytic treatment, the interpretation of lapses lays claim, as a means of revealing the unconscious, to a place alongside the disproportionately more important interpretation of freely associated ideas.

*The Interpretation of Dreams.* Fresh access to the depths of the life of the psyche was opened up when the technique of free association was applied to dreams, whether the analyst's own or those of analytic patients. In fact, most and the best of what we know of the processes in the unconscious layers of the mind we know from the interpretation of dreams. Psychoanalysis has restored to dream the significance that was once universally attributed to it in times past, but it deals with it in a different way. It does not rely on the wit of the dream-interpreter, but transfers the bulk of the task to the dreamer himself, by asking him about his associations to the individual elements of the dream. By pursuing these associations further one attains a knowledge of thoughts that completely tally with the dream, but which can be recognized – one respect aside – as complete and entirely intelligible parts of waking psychical life. The remembered dream thus confronts, as *manifest dream content*, the *latent dream-thought* found through interpretation. The process which has transposed the latter into the former, the 'dream' itself, and which is reversed by the work of interpretation, may be called *dream-work*.

Because of their relationship to waking life we also call the latent dream-thoughts *the day's residues*. They are *condensed* by the dream-work, to which one would be quite wrong to ascribe a 'creative character', *distorted* by the displacement of psychical intensities, rearranged to be *represented in visual images*, and also, before they are formed into the manifest dream, undergo a *secondary treatment* which seeks to give the new formation something like meaning and context. This last process is no longer part of the dream-work proper.

*Dynamic Theory of Dream Formation.* It has not been too difficult to see through the dynamics of dream-formation. The drive force leading to dream-formation is joined not by the latent dream-thoughts or day's residues, but by an unconscious striving, repressed during the day, with which the day's residues have been able to connect, and which creates a *wish-fulfilment* from the material of the latent thoughts. Consequently every dream is on the one hand a wish-fulfilment of the unconscious, and on the other, in so far as it succeeds in protecting the sleeping state against disturbance, a fulfilment of the normal wish for sleep that has led to sleep. If we leave aside the unconscious contribution and reduce the dream to its latent thoughts, it can represent everything that has preoccupied the waking life, a pondering, a warning, an intention, a preparation for the immediate future or equally the satisfaction of an unfulfilled wish. The indecipherability, the strangeness, the absurdity of the manifest dream on the one hand follows on from the transfer transposition of the dream-thoughts into another mode of expression that might be described as archaic, while on the other hand it is the effect of a restrictive, critically refusing agency that is not entirely abolished even during sleep. One would be led to assume that the '*dream-censorship*' which we hold primarily responsible for the distortion of the dream-thoughts into the manifest dream, is an expression of the same psychical forces that had restrained and repressed the unconscious wish impulse by day.

It was worth going more deeply into the elucidation of dreams, because analytic work has shown that the dynamic of dream-formation is the same as that of symptom-formation. In both cases we can recognize a conflict between two tendencies, an unconscious, otherwise repressed tendency which strives for satisfaction – wish-fulfilment – and a refusing and repressing tendency which probably belongs to the conscious ego, and as the result of this conflict a compromise formation – the dream, the symptom – in which the two tendencies have found imperfect expression. The theoretical significance of this accord is illuminating. Since dreams are not pathological phenomena, it demonstrates that the psychical mechanisms which generate the symptoms of illness are also already present in the normal life of the psyche, that the same laws encompass both the normal and the abnormal, and that the results of research into neurotics or mental patients may not be insignificant for the understanding of the healthy psyche.

*Symbolism.* In the study of the mode of expression created by the dream-work, we encountered the surprising fact that certain objects, activities and relationships are to a certain extent represented indirectly in dreams by 'symbols', which the dreamer uses without knowing their significance, and to which his association usually brings nothing. Their translation must be provided by the analyst, who can himself only find them empirically, by experimentally inserting them into the context. It later turned out that linguistic usage, mythology and folklore contain the most abundant analogies to dream-symbols. The symbols to which the most interesting, still unsolved problems are attached seem to be part of an ancient psychical legacy. The symbolic community extends beyond the linguistic community.

*The Aetiological Significance of the Sexual Life.* The second innovation that arose once the technique of hypnotism had been replaced by free association was clinical in nature, and was found on the continued search for the traumatic experiences from which hysterical symptoms appeared to derive. The more carefully one delved into this area, the more abundant appeared the concatenations of such aetiologically significant impressions, but also the further back they appeared to extend into the puberty or childhood of the neurotic. At the same time they assumed a unified character, and in the end one was obliged to bow to the evidence and acknowledge that traumatic impressions from the sexual life of infancy were to be found at the root of all symptom-formation. Sexual trauma thus took the place of banal trauma, and the latter owed its aetiological significance to its associative or symbolic relationship with the former, which had preceded it. Since the investigation of cases of ordinary nervousness, classified as *neurasthenia* and *anxiety neurosis*, undertaken at the same time, revealed that these disturbances could be traced back to actual abuse in sexual life, and could be removed by putting a stop to that abuse, one was led to conclude that the neuroses in general are the expression of disturbances in the sexual life; the so-called *actual* neuroses are the (chemically conveyed) expression of present, and the *psychoneuroses* the (psychically reworked) expression of long-forgotten, damage to this function, biologically so important but for a long time terribly neglected by science. None of the assertions of psychoanalysis has encountered such stubborn disbelief and such embittered resistance as that of the exceptional aetiological significance of sexual life for neuroses. But we should make a point of observing that even psychoanalysis, in its development to the present day, has found no cause to step back from this assertion.

*Infantile Sexuality*. Its research into aetiology has placed psychoanalysis in the position of dealing with a subject the existence of which was barely suspected before it came into being. In science, one had become accustomed to seeing the sexual life as beginning with puberty, and condemned manifestations of child sexuality as rare indications of abnormal precocity and degeneracy. Now psychoanalysis revealed a wealth of phenomena, both curious and regular, which forced one to see the beginning of the sexual function in the child as almost coinciding with the beginning of extra-uterine life, and one wondered in astonishment how all this could possibly have been ignored. The first insights into child sexuality were admittedly won by the analytic examination of adults, and accordingly marked with all the doubts and sources of error that one might expect from a backward look so long after the fact, but when one later began (from 1908 onwards) to analyse children themselves, and to observe them without inhibition, one gained direct confirmation of all actual content of the new conception of the subject.

In many respects, child sexuality showed a different picture from adult sexuality, and surprised us by displaying numerous characteristics that would have been condemned as 'perversion' in adults.

The concept of the sexual had to be extended until it encompassed more than a striving for the unification of the two sexes in the sexual act or the prompting of certain sensations of pleasure in the genitals. But that extension was rewarded by the fact that it became possible to understand child, normal and perverse sexual life from a single context.

The analytic investigation of the present writer initially succumbed to the error of greatly overestimating seduction as a source of child sexual manifestations and the nucleus of neurotic symptom-formation. He succeeded in overcoming this mistake when the extraordinarily important role of the imagination in the psychical lives of neurotics became apparent, being clearly more crucial for neurosis than external reality. From behind these fantasies the material then emerged that permits us to give the following description of the development of the sexual function.

*The Development of the Libido.* The sexual drive, whose dynamic manifestation in the psychical life we shall call 'libido', is composed of partial drives into which it can also fragment back again, and which only gradually unite into certain organizations. The source of these partial drives is the organs of the body, particularly certain special erogenous zones, but contributions to the libido are also supplied by all the important functional processes in the body. The individual partial drives at first strive independently for satisfaction, but in the course of development they increasingly come together, become centred. The first (pre-genital) stage of organization can be identified as the *oral*, in which, in accordance with the baby's main interest, the mouth zone plays the most important part. This is followed by the *sadistic-anal* organization, in which the partial drive of *sadism* and the *anal zone* come particularly to the fore; here sexual difference is represented by the opposition of active and passive. The third and definitive stage of organization is the coming together of most of the partial drives under the *primacy of the genital zones*. This development generally occurs quickly and inconspicuously, but individual parts of the drives remain at the preliminary stages of the final outcome and thus produce the *fixations* of the libido, which are important as predispositions for later breakthroughs of repressed tendencies, and stand in a particular relationship to the identification of later neuroses and perversions. (See 'Libido Theory'.)

*Object-finding and the Oedipus Complex.* The oral partial drive first finds its satisfaction by borrowing from the satiation of the need for nourishment and its object in the mother's breast. It then breaks away, becomes autonomous and at the same time auto-erotic, that is, it finds its object in the subject's own body. Other partial drives also behave auto-erotically at first and are only later guided to an external object. It is of particular importance that the partial drives of the genital zone regularly pass through a period of intense auto-erotic satisfaction. Not all partial drives are equally usable for the definitive genital organization of the libido; some of them (such as the anal) are for that reason set aside or suppressed, or subject to complicated transformations.

Even in the first years of childhood (from the ages of about two to five) the sexual tendencies come together, their object in the boy being the mother. This object-choice, along with the concomitant attitude of rivalry and hostility towards the father, is the content of the so-called *Oedipus complex*, which is in all people of the greatest importance for the final form of the erotic life. It has been represented as characteristic for the normal person that he learns to overcome the Oedipus complex, while the neurotic remains stuck within it.

*The Dual-phase Commencement of Sexual Development.* This early period of sexual life normally comes to an end around the fifth year, and is supplanted by a period of more or less complete *latency*, during which the ethical restrictions are constructed as protective formations against the wish-impulses of the Oedipus complex. In the subsequent period of puberty, the Oedipus complex is revived in the unconscious, and moves towards its further transformations. It is during puberty that the sexual drives attain their full intensity; the direction of this development and all the predispositions attaching to it are, however, already determined by the early blossoming of sexuality that has already taken place in infancy. This dual-phase development of the sexual function, interrupted by the period of latency, seems to be a biological peculiarity of the human species and to contain the precondition for the origin of neuroses.

*The Theory of Repression.* The cohesiveness of these theoretical findings with the immediate impressions of analytic work leads to a view of neuroses which in its broadest outlines runs more or less as follows: neuroses are the expression of conflicts between the ego and those sexual tendencies that appear to the ego to be contrary to its integrity or its ethical assertions. The ego has *repressed* these non-ego-*compatible* tendencies, that is, it has withdrawn its interest from them and blocked them both from reaching consciousness and from motor discharge to satisfaction. If, in analytic work, one tries to make these repressed impulses conscious, one becomes aware of the *repressive* forces as *resistance*. But the accomplishment of repression may easily be defeated by the sexual drives. The libido that they have built up creates other outlets from the unconscious by *regressing* to earlier phases of development and object-attitudes, and where infantile fixations are found, breaking through the weak spots in the development of the libido to consciousness and discharge. What thus emerges is a *symptom* and hence basically a sexual substitute satisfaction, but the symptom cannot yet fully escape the influence of the repressive forces, and must consequently make do with alterations and displacements – much like dreams – through which its characteristic as sexual satisfaction becomes indecipherable. The symptom thus receives the characteristic of a *compromise formation* between the repressed sexual drives and the repressing ego-drives, a simultaneous but incomplete wish-fulfilment for both partners in the conflict. This applies most strictly to the symptoms of hysteria, while in the symptoms of compulsive neurosis the share of the repressing agency is more strongly expressed through the production of reactive formations (safeguards against sexual satisfaction).

*Transference*. If further proof were required for the proposition that the drive-forces of neurotic symptom-formation are sexual in nature, it would be found in the fact that a particular emotional relationship is formed by the patient towards the doctor, which goes far beyond a rational degree, varying from affectionate devotion to the most stubborn hostility, and borrows all its particular qualities from earlier, now unconscious, attitudes of love on the part of the patient. This *transference*, which enters the service of *resistance* both in the positive and in the negative form, becomes a powerful aid to treatment in the hands of the doctor, and plays a role in the dynamics of the healing process that can scarcely be overestimated.

*The Foundations of Psychoanalytic Theory*. The assumption of unconscious psychical processes, the acknowledgement of the theory of resistance and repression, the assessment of sexuality and the Oedipus complex are the chief contents of psychoanalysis and the foundations of its theory, and anyone who does not accept them all should not be considered as a psychoanalyst.

*Further Destinies of Psychoanalysis*. More or less up to the point indicated above, psychoanalysis developed through the work of the present writer, who was its sole representative. In 1906 the Swiss psychiatrists E. Bleuler and C. G. Jung began to play an active part in analysis; in 1907 a first meeting of their followers was held in Salzburg, and soon the young science found itself the focus of interest both of psychiatrists and of laypeople. The manner of its reception in authoritarian Germany did not exactly bode well for German scientists, and provoked even such a level-headed advocate as Ernst Bleuler to an energetic defence of the discipline. But no official condemnations and discussions at conferences could stop the internal growth and external spread of psychoanalysis, which over the next ten years advanced far beyond the borders of Europe and became especially popular in the United States, not least thanks to the support or collaboration of J. Putnam (Boston), Ernest Jones (Toronto, later London), Flournoy (Geneva), Ferenczi (Budapest), Abraham (Berlin) and many others. The anathema placed upon psychoanalysis led its followers to form an international organization which this year (1922) is holding its eighth private conference in Berlin, and currently includes the following local groups: Vienna, Budapest, Berlin, Holland, Zürich, London, New York, Calcutta and Moscow. Even the First World War did not interrupt this development. In 1918–19 Dr Anton von Freund (Budapest) founded the International Psychoanalytic Press, which published the journals and books that served psychoanalysis; in 1920 the first Psychoanalytic Outpatients' Clinic for the treatment of impoverished neurotics was opened by Dr M. Eitingen in Berlin. Translations of the present writer's main works into French, Italian and Spanish, which are in preparation at present, testify to the awakening of interest in psychoanalysis in the Latin world as well. Between 1911 and 1913 two trends branched off from psychoanalysis, clearly seeking to mitigate its offensive aspects. One, adopted by C. G. Jung, sought to do justice to ethical claims, stripped the Oedipus complex of its real significance through symbolic re-evaluation, and in its practice neglected the revelation of the forgotten, 'prehistoric' period of childhood. The other, initiated by Alfred Adler in Vienna, reproduced certain elements of psychoanalysis under a different name, for example repression in a sexualized version, as 'masculine protest', but otherwise ignored the unconscious and the sexual drives and attempted to trace characteristics such as the development of neuroses back to the will to power, which strives to restrain the dangers arising out of organic inferiority by means of over-compensation. These two systematically constructed trends have had no lasting influence on the development of psychoanalysis; as regards the Adlerian, it soon became clear that it had too little in common with the psychoanalysis that it wanted to replace.

*Recent Developments in Psychoanalysis.* Since psychoanalysis became the field of work of such a great number of researchers, it has been enriched and reinforced in ways that can unfortunately receive only the briefest of mentions in this essay.

*Narcissism.* Its most important theoretical development was probably the application of the libido theory to the repressing ego. One came to imagine the ego itself as a store-house of the libido – called narcissistic – from which the libido investments of the objects flow, and into which they can be absorbed again. With the help of this idea it became possible to approach the analysis of the ego and undertake the clinical division of the psychoneuroses into *transference neuroses* and *narcissistic* illnesses. In the first (hysteria and compulsive neurosis), a quantity of libido striving for transference to foreign objects is available, and is used to carry out the analytic treatment; narcissistic disorders (dementia praecox, paranoia, melancholia) are on the contrary characterized by the withdrawal of the libido from its objects, and consequently hardly accessible to analytic therapy. But this therapeutic inadequacy has not kept analysis from making the most substantial approaches towards a deeper understanding of those illnesses that are classed as psychoses.

*Change in the Technique.* After the formation of the technique of interpretation had, so to speak, satisfied the analyst's curiosity, interest had to turn to the problem of the ways in which the patient might be most usefully influenced. It soon turned out that the doctor's next task was to help the patient to recognize and later to overcome the *resistances* which appeared within him during treatment, and which were not at first conscious to him. At the same time it was acknowledged that the essential part of the healing work consists in the overcoming of those resistances, and if that was not accomplished, a lasting psychical change in the patient cannot be accomplished. Since the analyst's work has been adjusted towards the patient's resistance in this way, the analytic technique has gained a precision and delicacy to rival the technique of the surgeon. Consequently, one should be urgently advised against undertaking psychoanalytic treatment without strict training, and the doctor who risks undertaking this, trusting to his state-recognized diploma, is no better than a layman.

*Psychoanalysis as a Therapeutic Method.* Psychoanalysis has never presented itself as a panacea or claimed to perform miracles. In one of the most difficult areas of medical activity, it is the only possible method for dealing with individual illnesses, and for others it is the method that provides the best or most lasting results, never without a corresponding expenditure of time and work. To the doctor not entirely absorbed in the task of helping people, it richly rewards the effort with unimagined insights into the complications of the psychical life and the connections between the psychical and the physical. Where it cannot at present offer a remedy, but only theoretical understanding, it may clear the way for later and more direct ways of influencing neurotic disorders. Its area of work is above all the two transference neuroses, hysteria and compulsive neuroses, in which it has contributed to the revelation of the internal structure and the effective mechanisms, but also all kinds of phobias, inhibitions, character deformations, sexual perversions and difficulties with the erotic life. According to some analysts, even the analytic treatment of organic disorders is not hopeless (Jelliffe, Groddeck, Felix Deutsch), since in many cases a psychical factor is also involved in the origin and maintenance of these illnesses. As psychoanalysis takes advantage of a degree of psychical plasticity in its patients, it must keep to certain age-boundaries in selecting them, and as it involves a long and intensive engagement with the individual patient, it would be uneconomical to waste such expenditure on completely worthless individuals who are also neurotic. What modifications are required to make the psychoanalytic healing process accessible to wider layers of the population, and adapt it to lower levels of intelligence, only the experience of material from out-patient clinics will teach us.

*Its Comparison with Hypnotic and Suggestive Methods.* The psychoanalytic process differs from all those which are suggestive, persuasive, etc., in that it does not seek to suppress any psychical phenomena in the patient by means of authority. It seeks to explain the cause of the phenomenon and abolish it through lasting alteration of the conditions of its origin. In psychoanalysis, the unavoidable suggestive influence of the doctor is directed towards the task assigned to the patient, to overcome his resistances, that is, to effect the work of healing. One protects oneself against the danger of suggestively falsifying the patient's accounts of his memory by careful implementation of the technique. But in general one is protected precisely by the awakening of resistances against misleading effects of the suggestive influence. The goal of the treatment may be identified as follows: to bring about, by means of the abolition of the patient's resistances and examination of his repressions, the most extensive unification and strengthening of his ego, to spare him the psychical expenditure for inner conflicts, to form from him the best that he can be according to his temperaments and abilities, and to render him as efficient and capable of enjoyment as possible. The removal of the symptoms of illness is not striven for as a particular goal, but is produced, when the analysis is properly carried out, as what we might call an added bonus. The analyst respects the uniqueness of the patient, does not try to remodel him according to his – the doctor's – personal ideals, and is pleased when he can spare himself the issuing of advice and can instead awaken the initiative of the analysand.

*Its Relationship to Psychiatry.* Psychiatry is at present a significantly descriptive and classificatory science which is still more somatically than psychologically oriented, and which lacks possibilities for explaining observed phenomena. But psychoanalysis is not in opposition to psychiatry, as one might be led to believe by the almost unanimous behaviour of psychiatrists. Rather, as *depth psychology*, the psychology of processes in the psychical life withdrawn from consciousness, its task is to provide psychiatry with its indispensable foundation and help it out of its present limitations. It is anticipated that the future will create a scientific psychiatry for which psychoanalysis will have served as an introduction.

*Criticisms and Misunderstandings of Psychoanalysis.* Most of the arguments directed against psychoanalysis in scientific works are based on inadequate information, which in turn seem to be explained by affective resistances. So it would be wrong to accuse psychoanalysis of '*pansexualism*' and say that it derives all psychical events from sexuality and traces them back to it. It would be more true to say that psychoanalysis has, from the very beginning, distinguished the sexual drives from others that it has provisionally called 'ego-drives'. It has never occurred to it to want to explain 'everything', and it has not even derived the neuroses from sexuality alone, but from the conflict between the sexual strivings and the ego. In psychoanalysis (except in the work of C. G. Jung), the term *libido* refers not to psychical energy as such, but to the driveforce of the sexual drives. Some claims, such as that every dream is a sexual wish-fulfilment, have never actually been made. The accusation of one-sidedness is levelled just as inappropriately against psychoanalysis, which as a science takes its particular and limited field of work from the *psychical unconscious*, as it would be if levelled against chemistry. It is a bad misunderstanding, justified only by ignorance, to say that psychoanalysis expects the healing of neurotic complaints to result from the 'free expression' of sexuality. Rather, the bringing of repressed sexual desires to consciousness through analysis makes it possible to control them in a way that could not be achieved through the earlier repression. It would be more correct to say that analysis frees the neurotic from the fetters of his sexuality. Furthermore, it is entirely unscientific to judge psychoanalysis according to whether it is suited to undermining religion, authority and morality, since it is, like all science, entirely non-tendentious and knows only one intention, to grasp a piece of reality without contradiction. Finally, one may describe as practically guileless the fear that one sometimes encounters, that the so-called highest blessings of mankind, research, art, love, moral and social feelings, stand to lose their value or their dignity because psychoanalysis is in the position to demonstrate their descent from elemental, animal drive-impulses.

*The Non-medical Applications and Connections of Psychoanalysis.* The appraisal of psychoanalysis would be incomplete if one neglected to mention that it alone among the medical disciplines has the broadest connections with the humanities, and that it is about to gain an importance for the history of religion and culture, mythology and literary study similar to that which it has for psychiatry. This might come as some surprise, if we bear in mind that its original goal was only the understanding and influencing of neurotic symptoms. But it is easy to show at which point the bridge to the humanities was built. When the analysis of dreams provided insight into the unconscious psychical processes and demonstrated that the mechanisms which create the pathological symptoms are also active in normal psychical life, psychoanalysis became *depth psychology*, and as such capable of application to the humanities, and was able to solve a large number of questions before which traditional conscious psychology was forced to come helplessly to a standstill. The connections with human *phylogeny* were formed early on. It was recognized how frequently the pathological function is nothing other than a *regression* to an earlier stage of normal development. C. G. Jung was the first expressly to indicate the surprising agreement between the bleak fantasies of patients suffering from dementia praecox with the mythical formations of primitive peoples; the present writer pointed out that the two wishful impulses which make up the Oedipus complex coincide entirely in their content with the two chief prohibitions of *totemism* (not to kill the ancestors and not to wed a woman from one's own clan), and drew extensive conclusions from this. The significance of the Oedipus complex began to grow to an enormous degree, one began to sense that state order, morality, law and religion in the primeval age of humanity had come into being as a reactive formation to the Oedipus complex. Otto Rank has thrown a great deal of light on mythology and literary history by applying psychoanalytic insights to them, just as Theodor Reik has on the history of morals and religions, and the Revd O. Pfister (Zürich) has aroused the interest of pastors and teachers and provided an understanding of the value of psychoanalytic viewpoints for educational theory. This is not the place for further accounts of these applications of psychoanalysis; let us content ourselves with remarking that their scope cannot yet be predicted.

*Characteristic of Psychoanalysis as an Empirical Science*. Psychoanalysis is not a system like those found in philosophy; it does not, as they do, proceed from a few sharply defined fundamental concepts, attempt on the basis of these to grasp the world as a whole and then, once it has done its job, have no room left for new discoveries and improved insights. Rather, it keeps to the facts of its field of work, attempts to solve the next problems of observation, continues to feel its way around experience, is always incomplete, always prepared to adjust or alter its theories. Like physics or chemistry, it endures the fact that its chief concepts are unclear, its premises are provisional, and awaits a clearer definition of them from future work.

## 11  *Libido Theory*

*Libido* is a term from drive theory, used in this sense by A. Moll to designate the dynamic expression of sexuality (*Investigations into the Libido sexualis*, 1898), and introduced into psychoanalysis by the present writer. The paper below is only intended to show the developments, as yet unfinished, that drive theory has experienced in psychoanalysis.

*Opposition of Sexual Drive and Ego-drives.* Psychoanalysis, which soon recognized that it would have to construct all psychical events above the play of forces of the elemental drives, found itself in an extremely poor position, as there was no drive theory in psychology, and no one could say what a drive actually was. It was entirely arbitrary, each psychologist tended to assume the existence of whichever and however many drives he saw fit. The first area of phenomena studied was the so-called transference neuroses (hysteria and compulsive neurosis). Their symptoms arose out of the fact that sexual drive impulses had been dismissed (repressed) by the personality (the ego) and had created an expression for themselves along detours through the unconscious. So one was able to cope with this by opposing ego-drives (*self-preservation drives*) to the sexual drives, and then found oneself in accord with the poet's statement, popular at the time, that the business of the world is kept going 'through hunger and through love'. The libido was the expression of the force of love, just as hunger was the expression of the self-preservation drive. The nature of the ego-drives remained at first vague and inaccessible to analysis, like all the other features of the ego. Whether we may assume qualitative difference between the two kinds of drive, and if so which, could not be said.

*The Primal Libido.* C. G. Jung attempted to overcome this darkness in a speculative way, by assuming only a single primal libido that could be sexualized and desexualized, and which thus essentially coincided with psychical energy as such. This innovation was methodically disputable, it prompted a great deal of confusion, reduced the term 'libido' to a superficial synonym and yet, in practice, still had to distinguish between the sexual and the asexual libido. The difference between the sexual drives and the drives with other goals could not be abolished by means of this new definition.

*Sublimation.* The deliberate study of sexual strivings accessible only through analysis had, in the meantime, produced remarkable individual insights. What was called the sexual drive was a compound of many things, and could break down again into its partial drives. Each partial drive was unalterably characterized by its *source*, namely the region or zone in the body from which it drew its excitation. Apart from that, an *object* and a *goal* could be distinguished in it. The goal was always the discharge of satisfaction, but it could undergo a transformation from activity to passivity. The object was less firmly attached to the drive than one might at first have imagined; it was easily exchanged for another; and the drive that had had an external object could also be turned against the subject's own person. The individual drives could remain independent of one another or – in a way that is still impossible to imagine – combine with one another, merge in order to work together. They could also support one another, transfer their libido investment to one another, so that the satisfaction of one supplanted the satisfaction of the other. Of the greatest significance seemed to be the drive-fate of *sublimation*, in which object and goal were switched, so that the originally sexual drive now finds satisfaction in an accomplishment that is no longer sexual, but socially or ethically more highly valued. These are all traits that still do not combine into a whole.

*Narcissism.* One crucial advance occurred when we approached the analysis of dementia praecox and other psychotic diseases, and thus began to study the ego itself, which we had previously known only as a repressing and resisting agency. It was recognized that the pathogenic process of dementia occurred when the libido was withdrawn from its objects and introduced into the ego, while the noisy phenomena of the illness derived from the vain attempts of the libido to find a way back to the objects. So it was possible for object-libido to turn into ego-investment and vice versa. Further considerations showed that this process could be assumed to occur on a very large scale, that the ego was rather to be seen as a large storehouse of the libido from which libido was despatched to the objects, and which was always prepared to receive the libido flowing back from the objects. The self-preservation drives, then, were also libidinous in nature, they were sexual drives which, rather than external objects, had taken as their object the subject's own ego. From clinical experience we knew individuals who behaved strikingly as though they were in love with themselves, and had called this perversion *narcissism*. Now the libido of the self-preservation drives was termed the *narcissistic libido*, and a high level of such self-love was acknowledged as the primal and normal state. The earlier formula for the transference neuroses now needed not correction, but modification; rather than speaking of a conflict between sexual drives and ego-drives, it was more correct to speak of a conflict between object-libido and ego-libido, or, since the nature of the drives was the same, between the object-investments and the ego.

*Apparent Approach Towards the Jungian View.* In this way it came to appear that the slow psychoanalytic research of Jungian speculation was descended from the primal libido, particularly since the transformation of the object-libido into narcissism inevitably involved a certain desexualization, a relinquishment of the special sexual goals. In the meantime the consideration arises that even if the self-preservation drive of the ego is acknowledged as libidinous it is not yet proven that no other drives come into effect in the ego.

*The Herd Drive.* Many people claim that there is a particular and innate 'herd drive' that cannot be broken down any further, which determines people's social behaviour and compels individuals to unite. Psychoanalysis must contradict this hypothesis. While the social drive may be innate, it can be traced back without difficulty to originally libidinous object-investments and develops in the individual child as a reactive formation to hostile attitudes of rivalry. It is based on a particular kind of identification with the other.

*Goal-inhibited Sexual Strivings.* The social drives belong to a class of drive-impulses that do not yet need to be called sublimated, although they are close to being so. They have not abandoned their directly sexual goals, but they are kept from accomplishing them by internal resistances, and content themselves with coming close to satisfaction in various ways, and for that reason they produce particularly firm and lasting bonds between people. Particular examples of this kind are the relationships of tenderness between parents and children, which are entirely sexual in origin, the emotions of friendship and the emotional bonds of marriage which arise out of sexual affection.

*Acknowledgement of Two Kinds of Drive in the Life of the Psyche.* While psychoanalytic work is otherwise concerned to develop its theories as independently as possible from those of other sciences, it is still obliged to seek support for drive-theory in biology. On the basis of extensive consideration about the processes that constitute life and lead to death, it becomes likely that two kinds of drive must be acknowledged, in line with the contradictory processes of construction and dissolution within the organism. According to this theory some drives, which fundamentally work in silence, pursue the goal of guiding the living being to death, for that reason merit the name of the '*death-drive*' and are, through the combined effects of the many cellular elemental organisms, turned outwards, and appear in the form of *destructive* or *aggressive* tendencies. The others are the libidinous sexual or life drives, more familiar to us from analytic work, best summarized as Eros, the intention of which is to form ever larger units, in this way to preserve the continuation of life and guide it towards higher developments. In living creatures, the erotic and the death-drives regularly form blends and alloys; but it is also possible to unmake these combinations. Life consists in the manifestations of the conflict or interference of the two kinds of drive, and brings the individual the triumph of the destructive drive in death, but also the victory of Eros through reproduction.

*The Nature of Drives.* The characteristics of drives can be identified on the basis of this conception: they are the innate tendencies within the living substance to re-establish an earlier state, historically conditioned and conservative in nature and, so to speak, the expression of an organic inertia or elasticity. Both kinds of drive, the Eros and the death-drive, work together and come into conflict with one another from the very beginning of life.

(1925)

# Beyond the Pleasure Principle

## I

In psychoanalytic theory we assume without further ado that the evolution of psychic processes is automatically regulated by the pleasure principle; that is to say, we believe that these processes are invariably triggered by an unpleasurable tension, and then follow a path such that their ultimate outcome represents a diminution of this tension, and hence a propensity to avoid unpleasure or to generate pleasure. When, in our study of psychic processes, we look at them with specific reference to this manner in which they evolve, we introduce the 'economic' perspective into our work. An account that pays due attention to this economic factor, as well as to the topical and dynamic aspects, seems to us to be the most complete kind that is presently conceivable, and to merit special distinction by use of the term *metapsychological*.[1]

It is of no interest to us in any of this to investigate the extent to which, in postulating the pleasure principle, we have echoed or embraced any particular, historically established philosophical system. We have arrived at such speculative assumptions simply as a result of our efforts to give a description and account of the facts that we observe on a daily basis in our field of study. Being original or getting there first do not figure among the aims laid down for psychoanalytic inquiry, and the impressions on which the postulation of this principle is based are so obvious that it is scarcely possible to overlook them. On the other hand, we would gladly acknowledge our gratitude to any philosophical or psychological theory capable of revealing to us the *meaning* of these sensations of pleasure and unpleasure that are so imperative for us. In this respect, unfortunately, nothing of any use is available to us. This is the darkest and most impenetrable area of the psyche, and whilst we cannot possibly avoid touching upon it, it seems to me that we do best to offer only the most tentative of suppositions on the subject. After much consideration we are minded to posit a connection between pleasure/unpleasure and the quantity of excitation present – yet not annexed[2] in any way – within the psyche; a connection whereby unpleasure corresponds to an *increase* in that quantity, and pleasure to a *decrease*. We are not thinking here in terms of a simple relationship between the strength of the sensations and the quantitative changes that we are linking them to; least of all – in view of everything that psycho-physiology has taught us – are we thinking in terms of a directly proportional relationship. The key determining factor so far as the sensation is concerned is probably the intensity of the decrease or increase over a particular period of time. Experimentation may well have a part to play here: we analysts would certainly be well advised not to venture any more deeply into these problems until such time as we can be guided by very specific observations.

However, we cannot help but feel a certain excitement when we discover that such a penetrating scientist as G. T. Fechner advocated an interpretation of pleasure and unpleasure that accords in all essential respects with the one so forcefully suggested to us by our psychoanalytic work. Fechner's statement on the matter is contained in his brief study *Einige Ideen zur Schöpfungs- und Entwicklungs-geschichte der Organismen* [*Some Ideas on the Origin and Evolution of Organisms*] of 1873 (Section XI, supplementary note, p. 94), and reads as follows: 'Inasmuch as conscious impulses are always associated with pleasure or unpleasure, we may suppose that pleasure and unpleasure, too, are linked psycho-physically to conditions of stability and instability; and this gives grounds for a hypothesis that I shall develop in more detail elsewhere, namely that every psycho-physical motion that passes the threshold of consciousness involves pleasure to the degree that it moves beyond a certain point *towards* complete stability, and unpleasure to the degree that it moves beyond a certain point *away from* that stability; whilst *between* these two points – which may be defined as the qualitative thresholds of pleasure and unpleasure – there is a certain margin of aesthetic indifference . . .'

The facts that have caused us to believe in the dominion of the pleasure principle within the psyche also inform our assumption that one aspiration of the psychic apparatus is to keep the quantity of excitation present within it at the lowest possible level, or at least to keep it constant. The latter postulate is the same as the former, albeit expressed in different terms, for if the psychic apparatus is geared to minimizing the quantity of excitation, then anything tending to *increase* that quantity is bound to be experienced as counter-functional, and hence unpleasurable. The pleasure principle arose out of the constancy principle; in reality, however, the constancy principle was inferred from the same facts that compelled us to postulate the pleasure principle. We shall also discover on deeper consideration that the particular aspiration we attribute to the psychic apparatus is subsumable as a special case under Fechner's principle of 'the tendency to stability', to which he linked the sensations of pleasure and unpleasure.

That being so, however, we have to acknowledge that it is strictly speaking incorrect to say that the pleasure principle has dominion over the way in which psychic processes evolve. If this were the case, then the vast majority of our psychic processes would need to be accompanied by pleasure or lead to pleasure, whereas all common experience contradicts such a conclusion. The true situation, therefore, can only be that the pleasure principle exists as a strong *tendency* within the psyche, but is opposed by certain other forces or circumstances, so that the final outcome cannot possibly always accord with the said tendency in favour of pleasure. Compare Fechner's remark in a similar context (op. cit., p. 90) that 'the tendency to achieve a particular goal does not imply the actual achievement of that goal, and the goal may not be achievable at all except in approximate terms'. If we now turn to the question as to which circumstances are capable of preventing the pleasure principle from being carried into effect, we find ourselves back on safe and familiar ground, and in seeking an answer we are able to draw on a rich profusion of psychoanalytical experience.

The primary example of the pleasure principle being thus inhibited is already familiar to us as a spontaneous and automatic process. We know that the pleasure principle belongs to a *primary* operational level of the psychic apparatus, and that so far as self-preservation is concerned it is never anything but useless, indeed highly dangerous, given the challenges posed by the external world. Thanks to the influence of the ego's self-preservation drive it is displaced by the *reality principle*,[3] which, without abandoning the aim of ultimately achieving pleasure, none the less demands and procures the postponement of gratification, the rejection of sundry opportunities for such gratification, and the temporary toleration of unpleasure on the long and circuitous road to pleasure. This notwithstanding, the pleasure principle remains for a long period of time the vehicle of the much less 'educable' sexual drives, and there are countless occasions – be it on the basis of these latter drives, be it within the ego itself – where the pleasure principle overwhelms the reality principle, to the detriment of the entire organism.

There is no doubt, however, that displacement of the pleasure principle by the reality principle can be held responsible for only a very few experiences of unpleasure, and for none whatever of the most intense ones. Another source of unpleasure, no less spontaneous and automatic, arises from the conflicts and divisions that occur within the psychic apparatus during the course of the ego's development to more highly composite forms of organization.[4] Almost all the energy that fills the psychic apparatus stems from its innate drive-impulses, but not all of these are granted access to the same phases of development. As things evolve, so there are numerous occasions where individual drives, or elements of individual drives, prove to be incompatible in their aims and demands with all those others that are capable of joining together to yield the all-embracing unity of the ego. They are therefore separated off from this unified whole through the process of repression; they are restricted to lower levels of psychic development and, for the time being at least, cut off from any possibility of gratification. If they subsequently manage by circuitous means to fight their way to some form of direct or surrogate gratification – as so easily happens in the case of repressed sexual drives – this success, which otherwise would have offered an opportunity for pleasure, is experienced by the ego as unpleasure. Because of the earlier conflict with its outcome in repression, the pleasure principle is once again confuted, right at the very time when various other drives are busy giving effect to it by occasioning new pleasure. The details of the process whereby repression converts an opportunity for pleasure into a source of unpleasure are not yet clearly understood, and cannot be described with any precision, but it is doubtless the case that *all* neurotic unpleasure is of this kind, that is to say, pleasure that cannot be experienced as such.[5]

The two sources of unpleasure identified here by no means account for the majority of our experiences of unpleasure, but of the remainder one can say with some semblance of justification that their existence does not contradict the dominion of the pleasure principle. After all, most of the unpleasure that we feel is *perceptual* unpleasure, involving perception of the turbid pressure of ungratified inner drives, or perception of *external* things; this latter perception may be unpleasant in itself, or it may provoke unpleasurable expectations within the psychic apparatus, and hence be recognized by the latter as a 'danger'. The reaction to these demands of the drives within and dangers posed from without – a reaction that manifests the proper activity of the psychic apparatus – may thus quite correctly be regarded as deriving from the pleasure principle or from its modifier,[6] the reality principle. This being so, it might seem otiose to grant the existence of any further constraints upon the pleasure principle; yet it is precisely an investigation of the psyche's response to external dangers that affords new material and raises new questions concerning the problem at issue here.

## Notes

1. [The terms 'economic', 'dynamic' and 'topical' are all used by Freud in a special sense within the context of his 'metapsychological' system. Cf. the opening paragraphs of Chapters II and IV of *The Unconscious*, New Penguin Freud, 2005]

2. [See below, Section IV, note 5.]

3. [The 'reality principle' – one of Freud's central notions – may be defined as 'the regulatory mechanism that represents the demands of the external world, and requires us to forgo or modify gratification or postpone it to a more appropriate time. In contrast to the pleasure principle, which . . . represents the id or instinctual impulses, the reality principle represents the ego, which controls our impulses and enables us to deal rationally and effectively with the situations of life.' (*The Longman Dictionary of Psychology and Psychiatry*)]

4. [Before acquiring its more modern senses, the word 'organization' (*Organisation* in Freud's German) related chiefly to 'organ', 'organism', etc.; cf. the *OED* entry for 'Organization': 'The action of organizing, or condition of being organized, as a living being'; 'An organized structure, body, or being; an organism' (etc.).]

5. [*Addition 1925*:] The essence of the matter is presumably that pleasure and unpleasure, being conscious sensations, are tied to the ego. [See the first few paragraphs of Chapter II of *Inhibition, Symptom, and Fear* in *Beyond the Pleasure Principle and Other Writings* (New Penguin Freud, 2003) – which Freud wrote in the same year in which he added this footnote.]

6. [Freud uses the word *modifizieren*, and clearly intends the less common meaning that occurs in both languages, and which in the case of English 'modify' is defined thus in the *OED*: 'To alter in the direction of moderation or lenity; to make less severe, rigorous, or decided; to qualify, tone down, moderate'.]

## II

A condition consequent upon severe mechanical shock, train crashes, and other life-threatening accidents has long since been identified and described – a condition that has come to be known as 'traumatic neurosis'. The terrible war that has only just ended[1] gave rise to a great many such disorders, and did at least put an end to the temptation to attribute them to organic impairment of the nervous system brought about by mechanical force.[2] The clinical picture presented by traumatic neurosis is not unlike that of hysteria in its plethora of similar motor symptoms, but generally goes well beyond it in the very marked signs of subjective suffering that it displays – not unlike those in hypochondria or melancholia – and in the clear evidence it affords of a far more comprehensive and generalized enfeeblement and attrition of the individual's psychic capabilities. As yet, no one has managed to attain to a full understanding of either the neuroses of war or the traumatic neuroses of peacetime. In the case of the war neuroses, it seemed on the one hand illuminating, yet simultaneously baffling, that the selfsame clinical picture occasionally arose *without* the involvement of any raw mechanical force. In the case of ordinary traumatic neurosis, two features stand out very clearly, and have proved a useful starting point for further thought: first, the fact that the key causative element appeared to lie in the surprise factor, the *fright* experienced by the victim; and second, the fact that if any physical wound or injury was suffered at the same time, this generally inhibited the development of the neurosis. The words 'fright', 'dread' and 'fear' are wrongly used as interchangeable synonyms, for they can be easily differentiated from each other in their relationship to danger.[3] 'Fear' represents a certain kind of inner state amounting to expectation of, and preparation for, danger of some kind, even though the nature of the danger may well be unknown. 'Dread' requires a specific object of which we are afraid. 'Fright', however, emphasizes the element of surprise; it describes the state that possesses us when we find ourselves plunged into danger without being prepared for it. I do not believe that fear can engender a traumatic neurosis; there is an element within fear that protects us against fright, and hence also against fright-induced neurosis. We shall return to this proposition later on.

The study of dreams may be regarded as the most reliable approach route for those seeking to understand the deep-level processes of the psyche. Now it is a distinctive feature of the dream-life of patients with traumatic neurosis that it repeatedly takes them back to the situation of their original misadventure, from which they awake with a renewed sense of fright. People have shown far too little surprise at this phenomenon. The fact that the traumatic experience repeatedly forces itself on the patient even during sleep is assumed to be proof indeed of just how deep an impression it made. The patient is assumed to be, so to speak, psychically fixated[4] on the trauma. Such fixations on the experience that first triggered the illness have long been familiar to us in the context of hysteria. Breuer and Freud expressed the view in 1893 that hysterics suffer mainly from reminiscences. In the case of war neuroses, too, observers such as Ferenczi and Simmel have been able to explain various motor symptoms as arising from a fixation on the moment of trauma.

On the other hand, however, I am not aware that those suffering from traumatic neurosis are very much preoccupied in their *waking* life with memories of their misadventure. Perhaps, rather, they are at pains *not* to think of it. To take it for granted that night-time dreams automatically thrust them back into the situation that provoked their illness would be to misunderstand the nature of dreams. It would be rather more in the nature of dreams to conjure up pictures from the time when the patient was healthy, or else pictures of the return to health that is hoped for in the future. If the dreams of those with accident-induced neurosis are not to make us start doubting the wish-fulfilling tendency of dreams in general, then we might have recourse to the explanation that in this disorder the dream-function, like so much else, is thrown into disarray and distracted from its proper purposes; or we might have to turn our minds to the mysterious *masochistic* tendencies of the ego.[5]

I should now like to suggest that we leave the dark and dismal topic of traumatic neurosis and study the workings of the psychic apparatus by reference to one of its earliest forms of *normal* activity. I mean the play of children.

The various theories of children's play have only recently been collated and psychoanalytically evaluated by S[igmund] Pfeifer in *Imago* (vol. V, no. 4), and I would refer readers to this paper. These theories seek to divine the motive forces behind children's play, but they do so without paying sufficient attention to the *economic* perspective: the concern of the individual to gain pleasure. Without wishing to embrace the whole gamut of these phenomena, I took advantage of an opportunity that happened to present itself to me in order to elucidate a game played by a one-and-a-half-year-old boy, the first that he had ever invented for himself. It was more than a fleeting observation, as I lived under the same roof as the child and his parents for several weeks, and it was quite some time before the puzzling and constantly repeated behaviour of the child yielded up its meaning to me.

The child was by no means precocious in his intellectual development; at one and a half he spoke only a few intelligible words, and in addition had a small repertoire of expressive sounds comprehensible to those around him. But he had a good rapport with his parents and the family's one maid, and was praised for being a 'good boy'. He didn't disturb his parents during the night; he conscientiously heeded injunctions not to touch certain things and not to enter certain rooms; above all, he never cried when his mother left him for hours at a time, even though he was fondly attached to her, she having not only fed him herself, but also cared for him and looked after him without any outside help. However, this good little boy had the sometimes irritating habit of flinging all the small objects he could get hold of far away from himself into a remote corner of the room, under a bed, etc., so that gathering up his toys was often no easy task. While doing this he beamed with an expression of interest and gratification, and uttered a loud, long-drawn-out 'o-o-o-o' sound, which in the unanimous opinion of both his mother and myself as observer was not simply an exclamation but stood for *fort* ('gone'). I eventually realized that this was probably a game, and that the child was using all his toys for the sole purpose of playing 'gone' with them. Then one day I made an observation that confirmed my interpretation. The child had a wooden reel with some string tied around it. It never crossed his mind to drag it along the floor behind him, for instance, in other words to play toy cars with it; instead, keeping hold of the string, he very skilfully threw the reel over the edge of his curtained cot so that it disappeared inside, all the while making his expressive 'o-o-o-o' sound, then used the string to pull the reel out of the cot again, but this time greeting its reappearance with a joyful *Da!* ('Here!'). That, then, was the entire game – disappearing and coming back – only the first act of which one normally got to see; and this first act was tirelessly repeated on its own, even though the greater pleasure undoubtedly attached to the second.[6]

The interpretation of the game readily presented itself. It was associated with the child's immense cultural achievement in successfully abnegating his drives (that is, abnegating the gratification thereof) by allowing his mother to go away without his making a great fuss. He compensated for it, so to speak, by *himself* re-enacting this same disappearance–reappearance scenario with whatever objects fell to hand. So far as the affective evaluation of this game is concerned, it is of course immaterial whether the child invented it himself or adopted it in response to a cue from someone else. What interests us is a different point altogether. The going away of the mother cannot possibly have been pleasant for the child, nor even a matter of indifference. How then does his repetition of this painful experience in his play fit in with the pleasure principle? One might wish to reply that the mother's departure would need to be re-enacted in the game as the precondition of her happy return, and that this latter event was its real purpose. Such a view would be contradicted by the evident fact that Act One, the departure, was played as a game all on its own, indeed vastly more often than the full performance with its happy conclusion.

The analysis of a single case such as this cannot resolve the issue with any certainty; but the impression gained by an unprejudiced observer is that the child had a different motive in turning the experience into a game. The experience affected him, but his own role in it was passive, and he therefore gave himself an active one by repeating it as a game, even though it had been unpleasurable.

This endeavour could be attributed to an instinctive urge to assert control that operates quite independently of whether or not the memory as such was pleasurable. But we can also try another interpretation. The act of flinging away the object to make it 'gone' may be the gratification of an impulse on the child's part – which in the ordinary way of things remains suppressed – to take revenge on his mother for having gone away from him; and it may thus be a defiant statement meaning 'Alright, go away! I don't need you; I'm sending you away myself!' This same child whose game I had observed when he was one and a half had the habit a year later of flinging down any toy that had made him cross and saying 'Go in war!' At the time he had been told that his absent father was away in the war, and he didn't miss his father in the least, instead giving out the clearest indications that he did not want his exclusive possession of his mother to be disrupted.[7] We know from other children, too, that they are capable of expressing similar hostile impulses by flinging away objects in place of people.[8] One accordingly begins to have one's doubts as to whether the urge to psychically process powerful experiences, to achieve full control over them, is capable of manifesting itself on a primary level, independently of the pleasure principle. After all, in the case discussed here the child may well only have been able to repeat an unpleasant experience in his play because the repetition was associated with a different but direct gain in pleasure.

Even if we proceed further with our examination of children's play, this does not resolve our uncertainty as to which of the two postulates to adopt. It is plainly the case that children repeat everything in their play that has made a powerful impression on them, and that in so doing they abreact the intensity of the experience and make themselves so to speak master of the situation. On the other hand, however, it is equally clear that all their play is influenced by the one wish that is dominant at that particular age: the wish to be grown up, and to be able to do the things that grownups do. It is also an observable fact that the unpleasurable nature of an experience does not always render it unusable for play purposes. If a doctor examines a child's throat or performs some minor operation on him, we can be quite sure that this frightening experience will become the content of his next game – but the gain in pleasure from a different source is plain to see. Exchanging his passive role in the actual experience for an active role within the game, he inflicts on his playmate whatever nasty things were inflicted on him, and thus takes his revenge by proxy.

One thing that *does* emerge from this discussion is that there is no need to posit a specific imitative drive as the motive force behind children's play. We might also bear in mind that the form of play and imitation practised by adults, which in contradistinction to that of children is directed at an audience, does not spare its spectators the most painful of experiences, for instance in the performance of tragedies, and yet may none the less be regarded by them as something supremely enjoyable. This encourages us in the conviction that even under the dominion of the pleasure principle there are ways and means enough for turning what is essentially unpleasurable into something to be remembered and to be processed in the psyche. Some economically oriented aesthetic theory may wish to concern itself with these cases and situations where unpleasure leads ultimately to a gain in pleasure; for our particular purposes, however, they are of no value at all, for they presuppose both the existence and the dominion of the pleasure principle, and offer no evidence for the prevalence of tendencies *beyond* the pleasure principle; tendencies, that is, that are arguably more primal than the pleasure principle, and quite independent of it.

### Notes

1. [First World War.]
2. Cf. *Zur Psychoanalyse der Kriegsneurosen* [*Psycho-Analysis and the War Neuroses*]. With contributions by Ferenczi, Abraham, Simmel and E. Jones (1919). [Freud wrote the Introduction to this volume.]
3. [The original words are respectively *Schreck*, *Furcht* and *Angst*. The distinctions that Freud draws are lexically somewhat specious – particularly

the purported distinction between *Furcht* and *Angst* – and this speciousness is duly reflected in the translation. See also *Inhibition, Symptom, and Fear*, Chapter XI, Addendum B: 'Fear: Supplementary Remarks'.]

4. [*fixate* . . . to cause (a person) to react automatically to stimuli in terms which relate to a previous strong emotional experience; to establish (a response) in this way.' (*OED*).]

5. [The final clause of this sentence (from 'or' to 'ego') was added by Freud in 1921.]

6. This interpretation was then fully confirmed by a further observation. One day when the child's mother had been absent for many hours, she was greeted on her return with the announcement 'Bebi o-o-o-o!', which at first remained incomprehensible. It soon turned out, however, that while on his own for this long period of time the child had found a way of making himself disappear. He had discovered his reflection in the full-length mirror reaching almost to the floor, and had then crouched down so that his reflection was 'gone'.

7. When the child was five and three-quarters his mother died. Now that she was really and truly 'gone' (o-o-o), the boy showed no signs of grief. However, a second child had been born in the meantime, provoking the most intense jealousy in him.

8. Cf. 'Eine Kindheitserinnerung aus *Dichtung und Wahrheit*' (1917) ['A Childhood Recollection from [Goethe's] *Dichtung und Wahrheit*'].

## III

Twenty-five years of intensive work have meant that the immediate aims of psychoanalytic practice are completely different today from what they were at the beginning. At first, the analysing physician could hope to do no more than construe the unconscious of which the patient himself was quite unaware, put the various elements together into a coherent picture, and communicate this to the patient at the appropriate time. Psychoanalysis was above all an art of interpretation. As the therapeutic need was not met by this process, the next task that immediately arose was to compel the patient to confirm the analyst's interpretation on the basis of his own memory. In this enterprise the emphasis lay chiefly on the patient's resistances. The art at this juncture was to uncover these resistances as rapidly as possible, make them clear to the patient, and then induce him to relinquish them by bringing one's influence to bear on a directly human level (this being the point where suggestion[1] plays its part, operating in the form of 'transference').

It then became increasingly clear, however, that the intended aim of making the patient conscious of his unconscious could not be fully achieved even by this means. The patient is unable to remember all that is repressed within him, especially perhaps its most essential elements, and thus fails to be convinced that the interpretation presented to him is the correct one. Instead he is driven to *repeat* the repressed matter as an experience in the present, instead of *remembering* it as something belonging to the past, which is what the physician would much rather see happen.[2] The content of these all-too-accurate reproductions of the past is always a particular element of infantile sexual life, namely the Oedipus complex and its offshoots, and they always take place within the ambit of the transference process, that is to say of the relationship with the physician. Once the treatment has reached this point, one may reasonably say that the original neurosis has been replaced by a brand-new transference neurosis – the physician having done his best to limit the scope of this transference neurosis as much as possible, to force as much as possible into the realm of memory, to allow as little as possible to come out in the form of repetition. The ratio as between remembrance and repetition varies from case to case. As a rule the physician cannot spare the patient this phase of the treatment; he must necessarily make him re-experience a certain portion of his past life, and must see to it that he remains to some degree above it all so that he remains cognizant at every turn that what appears to be reality is in truth the refracted image of a forgotten past. If the physician manages to achieve this, then the battle is won: the patient accepts the validity of the interpretation, and the therapy – which wholly depends on this acceptance – can be successfully concluded.

If we are to stand a better chance of understanding this 'compulsion to repeat' that manifests itself during the psychoanalytic treatment of neurotics, we must above all free ourselves of the mistaken idea that in combating the resistances within a patient we are dealing with resistance on the part of the 'unconscious'. The unconscious, that is, the 'repressed',[3] offers no resistance whatever to the endeavours of the therapy; indeed it has but a single aim itself, and that is to escape the oppressive forces bearing down on it, and either break through to consciousness, or else find release in some form of real action. The resistance that manifests itself in the course of treatment derives from the same higher levels and systems of the psyche that effected the repression in the first place. However, since experience tells us that patients undergoing treatment are initially not conscious of the motive forces behind the resistances, or indeed of the resistances themselves, we would do well to amend our inappropriate terminology. We make things much clearer if we posit an antithesis not between the conscious and the unconscious, but between the coherent *ego* and the *repressed*. Much of the ego is itself no doubt unconscious – especially the part we may term its nucleus[4] – and only a small portion of that is covered by the term 'pre-conscious'. Once we have thus substituted a systematic or dynamic definition for what was merely a descriptive one, we can say that the patient's resistance stems from his *ego*,[5] and we then immediately realize that the compulsion to repeat is attributable to the unconscious *repressed* within him. It seems likely that this compulsion to repeat can only manifest itself once the patient's treatment has had the necessary benign effect of loosening the grip of the repression.[6]

There can be no doubt that the resistance of the conscious and pre-conscious ego serves the interests of the pleasure principle; it seeks after all to forestall the unpleasure that would be caused if the repressed part of the psyche were to break free – whereas our own efforts are all directed at opening the way to just such unpleasure by calling upon the reality principle. But what of the compulsion to repeat, the show of strength put on by the repressed part of the psyche: how does *that* stand in relation to the pleasure principle? It is plain that most of what the compulsion to repeat makes the patient relive necessarily causes the ego unpleasure, since it brings out into the open the workings of repressed drive-impulses; but, as we have already seen, this is unpleasure of a kind that does not conflict with the pleasure principle, for though it constitutes unpleasure for the one system, it simultaneously constitutes gratification for the other. The new and remarkable fact that we now have to report, however, is that the compulsion to repeat *also* brings back experiences from the past that contain no potential for pleasure whatever, and which even at the time cannot have constituted gratification, not even in respect of drive-impulses that were only subsequently repressed.

The early florescence of infantile sexuality is doomed to come to nothing because a child's desires are incompatible with reality, and its physical development insufficiently advanced. Its demise is brought about in the most harrowing circumstances, and accompanied by intensely painful emotions. The loss of love and the failure that this represents leave an enduring legacy of diminished self-feeling amounting to a narcissistic scar; in my experience, as also corroborated by the findings of Marcinowski (1918), this contributes more than any other factor to the 'feeling of inferiority' so common in neurotics. Sexual exploration, necessarily circumscribed by the child's state of physical development, cannot be brought to any gratifying conclusion; hence the lament later on that 'I can't accomplish anything, I can't succeed in anything'. The child's bond of intimacy, usually with the parent of the opposite sex, is killed off by disappointment, by the vain wait for gratification, by jealousy at the birth of a sibling – an event that unambiguously demonstrates the infidelity of the loved one. The child's attempt – undertaken with tragic solemnity – to produce such a baby himself is a humiliating failure. The ever-diminishing affection shown to the child, the ever-increasing demands of his upbringing, the reprimands, the occasional punishments – all ultimately reveal to him the full measure of the rejection that it has fallen to him to suffer. There is a fairly small and regularly recurring range of ways in which the love so typical of this phase of childhood is brought to an end.

All these unwelcome circumstances and painful layers of emotion

147

are accordingly repeated by neurotic patients in the transference process, and are brought back to life with immense ingenuity. They seek to break off the treatment in mid-stream; they contrive to rekindle their vivid sense of rejection, and to goad the physician to harsh words and a cold demeanour; they find suitable objects for their jealousy; in place of the passionately desired child of yore they offer the prospect or promise of some grandiose gift, the latter mostly just as unreal as the former had been. None of this was capable of bringing pleasure in the past – and one might reasonably suppose that it would bring less unpleasure in the present if it were to emerge in memories or dreams, rather than reconstituting itself as a lived experience. It is a question, of course, of the action of drives that were supposed to lead to gratification. However, the patient's experience of the fact that then, too, they brought unpleasure instead of gratification makes not a scrap of difference: the action is repeated regardless. The patient is driven to this by a compulsion.

The same thing that psychoanalysis makes manifest in the transference phenomena exhibited by neurotic patients can also be found in the lives of people who are *not* neurotic. In their case it takes the guise of an ineluctable fate dogging their every step, a daemonic current running through their whole existence, and from its earliest beginnings psychoanalysis has regarded such semblances of fate as being largely self-engendered, and determined by experiences in early infancy. The compulsion that reveals itself in these cases is no different from the neurotic's compulsion to repeat, even though such people have never shown the telltale signs of a neurotic conflict resolved as a result of symptom-formation. Thus we all know people whose human relationships invariably end in the same manner: benefactors who are angrily abandoned after a certain period by each of their protégés in turn, no matter how much these may otherwise differ from one another, and who thus seem destined to drink the cup of ingratitude to its bitter dregs; men whose every friendship ends in betrayal; others who in the course of their lives repeatedly elevate some individual to the status of Great Authority for themselves or even for society at large, and then in due course bring them crashing down in order to replace them by someone else; lovers whose every intimate relationship with a woman goes through the selfsame phases and leads to the selfsame outcome. We are never particularly surprised at this 'eternal recurrence of the same' when it involves *active* behaviour on the part of the individual concerned, and when we recognize the unchanging character trait that defines his being, and that necessarily finds expression in the repetition of similar experiences. We are much more strongly affected by cases where people appear to be the *passive* victim of something which they are powerless to influence, and yet which they suffer again and again in an endless repetition of the same fate. One need only think, for instance, of the story of the woman who married three men in succession, each one of whom soon fell ill and had to be nursed until finally he died.[7] The most moving poetical depiction of such a predisposition to fate is given by Tasso in his romantic epic *Gerusalemme liberata*. The hero Tancred unwittingly kills his beloved Clorinda, she having done battle with him in the armour of an enemy knight. After her burial he penetrates the strange charmed forest that so frightens the army of crusaders. There he smites a tall tree with his sword, but blood gushes from the wound, and the voice of Clorinda, whose spirit has magically entered into that very tree, accuses him of yet again doing harm to his beloved.

Taking due account of such observations of the way patients behave in the transference process and of the kinds of fate that befall people in ordinary life, we shall dare to postulate that within the psyche there really is a compulsion to repeat that pays no heed to the pleasure principle. We shall accordingly also be disposed to relate both the dreams of patients with accident-induced neurosis and the play-urge of children to this same compulsion. At the same time, though, we do need to bear in mind that only on rare occasions will we be able to catch the compulsion to repeat operating purely on its own, without the interaction of other motive forces. In the case of children's play we have already emphasized that its emergence lends itself to a variety of different interpretations. The compulsion to repeat, and the direct and pleasurable gratification of drives, seem here to interconnect with each other in an intimate mutuality. The phenomena of transference clearly serve the interests of the resistance offered by the ego, which remains bent on repression; the compulsion to repeat, which the therapy sought to divert to its own ends, is so to speak enlisted by the ego in its determination to hold fast to the pleasure principle. As for what one might term the 'fate compulsion', much of it seems on rational consideration to be comprehensible, so that we see no need to posit some new and mystical motive force behind it. The case that least arouses our suspicions is perhaps that of dreams recalling accidents; but on closer reflection one really does have to admit that in the other examples, too, the facts of the matter are not fully accounted for by the effect of the motive forces currently known to us.[8] Sufficient evidence remains to justify the hypothesis of a compulsion to repeat; and this compulsion appears to us to be more primal, more elemental, more deeply instinctual than the pleasure principle, which it simply thrusts aside. But if there is indeed such a compulsion to repeat in the psyche, then we should like to know something about it. We should like to know what function it corresponds to, what circumstances it can arise in, and what relationship it bears to the pleasure principle – to which, after all, we have hitherto attributed sole dominion over the manner in which excitational processes develop within the psyche.

## Notes

1. [See Freud's footnote below, note 6.]
2. See *Remembering, Repeating, and Working Through* (1914) [for example, pp. 394ff. in this volume].
3. ['*das Verdrängte*'; the inverted commas are Freud's.]
4. [Freud radically altered his view on this matter. In this context, it might be noted that this phrase ('especially the part we may term its nucleus') did not figure at all in the original edition of the essay. The rest of the sentence *did* appear, but in somewhat different terms: 'Much of the ego may itself be unconscious, and probably only part of that is covered by the term "pre-conscious".']

5. [Freud will explicitly modify his position in *Inhibition, Symptom, and Fear*; see Chapter XI, Section A, Sub-section (a): 'Resistance and counter-cathexis'.]

6. [*Addition 1923*:] I have made the point elsewhere that the compulsion to repeat is aided here by the 'suggestion effect' in psychoanalytic therapy, that is, by that amenability to the physician that has its roots deep in the patient's unconscious parent-complex. [Compare 'Remarks on the Theory and Practice of Dream-Interpretation' (1923), Chapter VII and (especially) VIII.]

7. Cf. the apt remarks of C. G. Jung in his essay 'Die Bedeutung des Vaters für das Schicksal des Einzelnen' ['The Significance of the Father in the Destiny of the Individual'] (1909).

8. [This sentence is faithful to the original in its less than perfect clarity and logic!]


IV


What now follows is speculation, often quite extravagant speculation, which readers will regard or disregard according to their own particular standpoint. For the rest, it is an attempt to follow an idea right through to its logical conclusion, undertaken out of sheer curiosity as to where this will lead.

Psychoanalytic speculation takes its impetus from the strong impression conveyed by the study of unconscious processes, that consciousness surely cannot constitute the universal character of psychic processes, but can only be one particular function of them. To express it in metapsychological terms: such speculation asserts that consciousness is the product of a particular system that it terms *Cs*. Since consciousness chiefly delivers perceptions of excitations emanating from the external world, and feelings of pleasure and unpleasure that can come only from within the psychic apparatus, a specific locus can be attributed to the *Pcpt-Cs* system:[1] it must lie at the border between the external and the internal; it must face out towards the external world, and simultaneously embrace the other psychic systems. We might note at this point that in making these suppositions we are not taking some bold new step, but are aligning ourselves with the locational hypotheses of cerebral anatomy, which places the 'seat' of consciousness in the cerebral cortex, the outermost, enveloping layer of the central organ. Cerebral anatomy has no need to devote any thought to the question of why – anatomically speaking – consciousness is located on the surface of the brain, instead of being safely lodged somewhere in its innermost recesses. Perhaps we shall help to clarify the issue by explaining this location in terms of our *Pcpt-Cs* system.

Consciousness is not the only distinctive characteristic that we are disposed to ascribe to the processes in this system. We are basing ourselves on the evidence garnered in our psychoanalytic experience when we postulate that all excitation processes occurring in the *other* systems leave lasting traces within them which form the basis of memory – residual memories, in other words, that have nothing to do with consciousness. These traces are often strongest and most enduring when the process that brought them into being never entered consciousness at all. We find it difficult to believe, however, that such lasting traces of excitation also arise in the *Pcpt-Cs* system. Were they to remain conscious, they would very soon limit the ability of the system to absorb new excitations;[2] if on the other hand they were *un*conscious, they would land us with the problem of explaining the presence of unconscious processes in a system the operation of which is otherwise characterized by the phenomenon of consciousness. We would, so to speak, have changed nothing and gained nothing by putting forward our hypothesis that consciousness belongs within a specific system. While this may not be an absolutely binding consideration, it may none the less lead us to the supposition that it is not possible within a given system for something both to enter consciousness and also to leave a memory trace. We would accordingly be able to argue that excitation processes do indeed enter consciousness within the *Cs* system, but leave no lasting trace there; and that all the traces of these processes that memory depends upon arise in the proximate inner systems to which the excitations migrate. It is in precisely these terms that I conceived the diagram included in the speculative section of my

*Interpretation of Dreams* in 1900.[3] When one considers how little we know from other sources about the origins of consciousness, one is bound to give at least *some* credence to the proposition that 'consciousness arises *instead of* a memory trace'.

One might thus say that the *Cs* system has the particular distin-guishing feature that excitation processes do not leave a mark in the form of an enduring alteration of its elements, as they do in all the other psychic systems, but simply evaporate, as it were, in the process of entering consciousness. Such a departure from the general rule can only be explained by some factor relevant solely to this one system, and this exclusive factor, not found in any of the other systems, could easily be the exposed location of the *Cs* system, its direct contiguity with the external world.

Let us imagine living organisms in their simplest possible form as an undifferentiated vesicle of irritable matter; its *surface*, inas-much as it faces out towards the external world, is thus differen-tiated by its very position, and serves as the vesicle's receptor organ. Embryology *qua* recapitulation of evolution really does show, more-over, that the central nervous system develops from the ectoderm; and the grey cerebral cortex remains a derivative of the primor-dial outer surface, and may well have inherited some of its essen-tial attributes. It is therefore easily conceivable that by dint of constant bombardment of the vesicle's outer surface by external stimuli, the substance of the cell becomes permanently altered down to a certain depth, with the result that excitation occurs differently in this surface layer from the way it occurs in the deeper layers. A cortex would thus form that ultimately becomes so tempered by the effect of the stimuli that it becomes perfectly adapted to their reception and becomes incapable of further modi-fication. Applying this analogy to the *Cs* system, it would mean that the latter's elements cannot undergo any enduring change as a result of the excitation passing through it, since they are already modified to the fullest possible extent in terms of this particular process. But they *do* now have the capability to allow conscious-ness to come into being. What exactly constitutes this modification of both the matter itself and the excitation process taking place within it, is open to a variety of conjectures, none of which is currently susceptible of being properly tested. We can suppose that in passing from one element to the other the excitation has to overcome a resistance, and that it is precisely in dissipating this resistance that the excitation lays down an enduring trace ('path-making'[4]); and we can further suppose that in the *Cs* system there no longer exists any such resistance to the transition from one element to another. We can link this notion to Breuer's distinction between *quiescent* (i.e. already annexed[5]) and *free-moving* cathectic energy within the elements of psychic systems;[6] on this basis, the elements of the *Cs* system would not carry any energy that is already annexed, but only such as is readily available for release. But I rather think that for the time being it is better to speak of these things only in the most general terms. In speculating thus we have at least perhaps established some kind of connection between the origins of consciousness and both the location of the *Cs* system, and the particular characteristics of the excitation process that are attributable to that system.

There are other matters that we still need to discuss with regard to the above-mentioned living vesicle with its stimulus-receiving cortical layer. This tiny piece of living matter floats around in an external world charged with energies of the most powerful kind, and would be destroyed by their stimulative effect if it were not equipped with some form of *protection* against stimulation. It acquires this protection by virtue of the fact that its outermost surface abandons the structure proper to living things, becomes to all intents and purposes inorganic, and in consequence operates as a special covering or membrane impeding the stimuli; that is to say, it allows only a fraction of the external energies' intensity to pass through it to the layers immediately beyond, which remain fully organic. These latter, safe behind their protective screen, can now devote themselves to receiving the reduced levels of stimuli that are thus allowed through. The outer layer becomes necrotic – but by doing so it protects all the deeper-lying ones from suffering a similar fate, at any rate so long as the stimuli do not bombard it with such force that they break through the protective barrier.

For the living organism, the process *protecting* it against stimuli is almost more important than the process whereby it *receives* stimuli; the protective barrier is equipped with its own store of energy, and must above all seek to defend the particular transformations of energy at work within it against the assimilative and hence destructive influence of the enormously powerful energies at work outside it. The process of receiving stimuli chiefly serves the purpose of determining the direction and nature of the external stimuli, and for that it must clearly be sufficient to take small specimens from the external world, to sample it in tiny quantities. In highly developed organisms the stimulus-receiving cortical layer of the erstwhile vesicle has long since retreated into the inner depths of the body, but parts of it have remained on the surface immediately beneath the general protective barrier. These are the sense organs, which essentially are equipped to register the effects of specific stimuli, but also include special devices to provide additional protection against excessively high levels of stimulation, and to exclude unsuitable types of stimulus. It is characteristic of them that they process only very small quantities of the external stimulus; they merely take samples of the external world. One can perhaps compare them to feelers that reach out tentatively towards the external world and then repeatedly draw back.

At this point I shall venture to touch very briefly on a topic that would merit the most thorough consideration. As a result of certain insights afforded to us by psychoanalysis, Kant's dictum that time and space are necessary forms of human thought is today very much open to debate. We have come to appreciate that unconscious psychic processes are in themselves 'timeless'. This primarily means that they are not temporally ordered; that time does not alter them in any way; and that the notion of time cannot be applied to them. These are negative attributes that we can only clearly discern by means of a comparison with *conscious* psychic processes. Indeed, our abstract notion of time seems to be altogether derived from the *modus operandi* of the *Pcpt-Cs* system, and to be equivalent to its perception of itself. Given that the system functions in this way, the protection process may well follow a quite different path. I realize that the ensuing propositions sound very obscure, but I must confine myself here to mere suggestions of this sort.

We argued just now that the living vesicle is equipped with a barrier protecting it against stimuli in the external world. Prior to that we established that the cortical layer immediately beneath this barrier must be differentiated in such a way as to receive stimuli from the outside. However, this sensitive cortical layer, which later becomes the *Cs* system, also receives excitation from within. The location of this system between the outside and the inside, and the difference between the conditions determining the penetration achieved by the one side and those determining the penetration achieved by the other, become decisive for the performance of the system and indeed of the entire psychic apparatus. There is a protective barrier *vis-à-vis* the *outside*, so that any quanta of excitation arriving from that quarter can exert their effect only on a much reduced scale. But no such protection is possible *vis-à-vis* the *inside*: the excitations that come from the deeper layers carry over into the system directly and without diminution, whereby certain features of their mode of progression generate successive sensations of pleasure and/or unpleasure. It is true that, given their type of intensity and other qualitative characteristics (possibly also their amplitude), the excitations coming from within are going to be better suited to the *modus operandi* of the system than the barrage of stimuli coming from the external world. But two things are decisively determined by these circumstances; first, the fact that the sensations of pleasure and unpleasure – which are an index of processes going on *within* the psychic apparatus – take precedence over all *external* stimuli; second, a response-pattern tending to counter those inner excitations that bring about an excessive increase in unpleasure. A tendency inevitably emerges to treat them as if they came from without rather than from within, in order to be able to deploy the protective barrier's defensive capabilities against them. This is the origin of *projection*, which plays such a major role in the causation of pathological processes.

I have the sense that while these latter reflections may have given us a clearer understanding of the dominant role of the pleasure principle, we have not managed to cast any light on those cases that defy it. Let us therefore go a step further. We may use the term *traumatic* to describe those excitations from outside that are strong enough to break through the protective barrier; in my view the notion of 'trauma' cries out to be applied to such a case given that the resistance to stimuli is normally so effective. An event such as external trauma will doubtless provoke a massive disturbance in the organism's energy system, and mobilize all available defence mechanisms. In the process, however, the pleasure principle is put into abeyance. It is no longer possible to prevent the psychic apparatus from being flooded by large quanta of stimulation; instead a quite different challenge presents itself: to assert control over the stimuli; to psychically annex the quanta of stimulation that have burst in, and then proceed to dispose of them.

The *specific* unpleasure of the physical pain experienced probably results from the fact that the protective barrier has been penetrated over a very small area. From this one point on the periphery a continuous stream of excitations floods into the central apparatus of the psyche, such as can normally come only from *within* the apparatus itself.[7] And how can we expect the psyche to react to this invasion? Cathectic energy is summoned up from all sides in order to create appropriately large cathexes in the area where the breach occurred. A massive 'counter-cathexis' is brought into being, for the sake of which all the other psychic systems are deprived of their energy, with the result that general psychic activity is extensively paralysed or diminished. We aim to learn from such examples, we aim to use them as models on which to base our metapsychological suppositions. We therefore conclude from this particular response-pattern that a system that is itself highly cathected is capable of taking in a whole stream of new energy and converting it into quiescent cathexis, thus psychically 'annexing' it. The more powerful the system's own quiescent cathexis, the greater its annexative power would seem to be; and conversely, the less powerful the cathexis, the less the system is going to be capable of taking in a stream of energy from outside, and the more violent the consequences of such a breach of the protective barrier must necessarily be. It would not be a valid objection to this hypothesis to argue that the increase in cathexis around the point of entry could far more easily be explained in terms of a direct dispersal of the incoming quanta of excitation. If that were the case, then of course the psychic apparatus would simply experience an increase in its energy-cathexes, and both the paralysing nature of the pain and the depletion of all the other systems would remain unexplained. The very powerful release effects of pain do not detract from our explanation either, for they occur reflexively, that is to say, they happen without any prompting from the psychic apparatus.

Needless to say, the haziness of all these deliberations of ours, which we term metapsychological, derives from the fact that we know absolutely nothing about the nature of the excitation process within the elements of the various psychic systems, and do not feel justified in forming any hypothesis on the matter; we thus constantly operate with a massive unknown quantity 'x', which we carry with us into every new formula that we propose. It is reasonable to assume that this process takes place with energies that differ *quantitatively* from each other, and it seems probable that there are also *qualitative* differences (for instance in the *type* of a given amplitude). A new possibility that we have taken into consideration is Breuer's proposition that *two* kinds of energy charge are involved, such that a distinction may be drawn between two different forms of cathexis of the psychic systems (or their elements): a quiescent form, and one that is free-flowing and constantly pressing for release. We might reasonably suspect that the 'annexing' of the energy flooding into the psychic apparatus consists in its being transferred from the free-flowing to the quiescent state.

I believe we can reasonably venture to regard ordinary traumatic neurosis as resulting from an extensive breach of the protective barrier. This would appear to reinstate the old, naïve 'shock' theory, seemingly at the expense of a later and psychologically more sophisticated one that sees the key aetiological factor not in the direct impact of the mechanical violence itself, but in the element of fright and in the threat to life. These contrasting perspectives are not irreconcilable, however, and the psychoanalytic view of traumatic neurosis is not identical to the shock theory in its crudest form. Whereas for the latter the essential thing about the shock is that it directly damages the molecular or even the histological structure of the nerve elements, we for our part seek to understand its effects in terms of the breaching of the protective barrier around the psyche, and the new challenges that this gives rise to. For us, too, fright remains an important factor. Fright can occur only in the absence of a state of apprehensiveness,[8] a state that would bring with it a hypercathexis of the systems that initially receive the extra stimulation. Because of the lower level of cathexis that this absence entails, the systems are not adequately primed to annex the quanta of excitation that now supervene, and so the consequences of the breaching of the protective barrier make themselves felt that much more easily. We thus find that apprehensiveness, together with the attendant hypercathexis of the receiving systems, constitutes the last line of defence of the protective barrier. Across quite a broad range of traumas, the outcome may well depend on whether the relevant systems are primed (by virtue of hypercathexis) or unprimed; though this factor is probably no longer of any importance once the trauma has reached a certain level of intensity. Under the dominion of the pleasure principle, it is the function of dreams to make a reality of wish-fulfilment, albeit on a hallucinatory basis; but the purposes of wish-fulfilment are certainly not being served by the dreams of patients with accident-induced neurosis when they thrust them back – as they so regularly do – into the original trauma situation. We may reasonably assume, however, that such dreams are thereby contributing to a quite different task that has to be completed before the pleasure principle can begin to prevail. These dreams seek to assert control over the stimuli *retrospectively* by generating fear – the absence of which was the cause of the traumatic neurosis in the first place. They thus afford us a clear view of a function of the psyche which, without contradicting the pleasure principle, is none the less independent of it, and appears to be more primal than the objective of gaining pleasure and avoiding unpleasure.

This might be an appropriate point, therefore, to acknowledge for the first time that there is an exception to the proposition that dreams are a form of wish-fulfilment. Fear-based dreams[9] do *not* constitute such an exception, as I have repeatedly and exhaustively demonstrated, and nor do 'punishment dreams', for these simply replace the forbidden wish-fulfilment with the punishment appropriate to it, and thus represent the wish-fulfilment of the individual's guilty conscience in its reaction to the drive that has been rejected. But the above-mentioned dreams of patients with accident-induced neurosis can no longer be viewed in terms of wish-fulfilment, and nor can those dreams, familiar to us from psychoanalysis, that bring back memories of the psychic traumas of childhood. Instead they obey the compulsion to repeat, though of course this is reinforced in analysis by the wish – itself strongly encouraged by 'suggestion' – to summon up all that has been forgotten and repressed. We might therefore also suppose that it was not the *original* function of dreams to dispel the forces tending to interrupt sleep by fulfilling the wishes of the impulses causing the disruption; dreams were able to acquire this function only *after* the entire psyche had accepted the dominion of the pleasure principle. If there is indeed a prior realm 'beyond the pleasure principle', then it is only logical to allow that there must likewise have been a prior era before dreams developed their predisposition to wish-fulfilment. This is not to gainsay their subsequent function. But as soon as we accept that this predisposition is capable of being breached, a further question arises: dreams such as these that enact the compulsion to repeat in furtherance of the psychic annexing of traumatic experiences – can they not also occur *outside* analysis? The answer to this question is emphatically 'yes'.

With regard to 'war neuroses', in so far as this term signifies more than simply a reference to the circumstances in which the condition arose, I have already argued elsewhere that they could very well be traumatic neuroses facilitated by an ego conflict.[10] The aforementioned fact that the chances of a neurosis arising are less when the trauma simultaneously causes a gross physical injury (see above, pp. 37–8) no longer seems incomprehensible when we bear in mind two circumstances highlighted by psycho-analytic research: first, the fact that mechanical jolts and vibrations have to be acknowledged as one of the sources of sexual excitation (cf. the remarks on the effects of swings and of railway travel in *Three Essays on Sexual Theory*, 1905); and second, the fact that throughout their duration, painful and feverish illnesses exert a powerful effect on the distribution of the libido. Thus it may well be the case that while the mechanical violence of the trauma unleashes a quantum of sexual excitation which in the absence of a state of apprehensiveness is potentially traumatic in its effect, the simultaneous physical injury annexes the excessive excitation by making use of a narcissistic hypercathexis of the affected organ (see *On the Introduction of Narcissism*, pp. 367–8). It is also a well-known fact – though one insufficiently taken into account in the development of the libido theory – that even such severe disruption of libido distribution as occurs in melancholia is put into abeyance by intercurrent organic illness; indeed, under the same conditions even a fully developed dementia praecox is capable of temporary regression.

### Notes

1. [*Pcpt* represents the 'perceptual system', first proposed by Freud in *The Interpretation of Dreams* (1900).]

2. This is based entirely on J[osef] Breuer's discussion of the topic in the theoretical section of *Studien über Hysterie* [*Studies in Hysteria* by Sigmund Freud and Josef Breuer (New Penguin Freud, 2004)], 1895.

3. [See *The Interpretation of Dreams* (in the Penguin Freud Library, vol. 4, p. 687).]

4. [*Bahnung* (without inverted commas in Freud's original). The verb *bahnen* (cognate with English 'bane' in its etymological sense of 'strike' or 'wound') means 'to strike a path through (snow, the jungle, a press of people, etc.)'. The *Standard Edition* bizarrely renders the word as 'facilitation'.]

5. [*gebunden*. The verb *binden* (past participle *gebunden*) is a key term in Freud's theory of the psyche – but it is not clear precisely how he visualized the metaphor, and it is therefore difficult to render it in English

with any certainty; 'annex' seems the likeliest equivalent, and is generally used throughout this volume (the *Standard Edition* opts for 'bind' and 'attach'). It is notable that in the course of the essay Freud twice feels obliged to enclose the word in inverted commas, suggesting that he himself did not regard the concept as either self-evident or self-explanatory.]

6. *Studien über Hysterie* [*Studies in Hysteria*], by Josef Breuer and Sigmund Freud (1895).

7. Cf. 'Triebe und Triebschicksale' ['Drives and Their Fates'] (1915).

8. [*Angstbereitschaft* – literally 'fear-preparedness'.]

9. [*Angstträume*.]

10. Introduction to *Zur Psychoanalyse der Kriegsneurosen* [*Psycho-analysis and the War Neuroses*] (1919) [see above, Section II, note 2].

## V

The fact that the stimulus-receiving cortical layer lacks any shield protecting it against excitations from within must presumably mean that these stimuli acquire greater economic importance, and often give rise to economic dysfunctions, which are equatable with traumatic neuroses. The most abundant sources of such excitation from within are the organism's so-called drives, which represent all those manifestations of energy that originate in the inner depths of the body and are transmitted to the psychic apparatus – and which are themselves the most important and the most inscrutable element of psychological research.

We shall perhaps not think it too bold to suppose that the impulses deriving from the drives adhere not to the 'annexed' type of nervous process, but rather to the type that is free-flowing and constantly pressing for release. The best information we possess concerning these processes comes from our study of dream-work. We found that the processes in the unconscious systems are fundamentally different from those in the (pre-)conscious ones; that within the unconscious, cathexes can easily be completely transferred, displaced, compressed – something that could only produce flawed results if applied to pre-conscious material, and indeed for that very reason produces the familiar peculiarities of manifest dreams, the pre-conscious residua of the preceding day having been processed according to the laws of the unconscious. I termed this kind of process in the unconscious the 'primary' psychic process, in contradistinction to the 'secondary' process that obtains in our normal waking life. As the drive-impulses all act on our *unconscious* systems, it is scarcely a new departure to assert that they follow the primary process, and it is also no very great step to identify the primary psychic process with Breuer's 'free-flowing' cathexis, and the secondary one with his 'annexed' or 'tonic' cathexis.[1] This would then mean that it was the task of the higher echelons of the psychic apparatus to annex excitations originating from the drives and reaching it via the primary process. Any failure of this annexion process would bring about a dysfunction analogous to traumatic neurosis. Only when the annexation has taken place would the pleasure principle (or, once the latter has been duly modified, the reality principle)[2] be able to assert its dominion unhindered. In the meantime, however, the psychic apparatus's other task of controlling or annexing the excitation would be very much to the fore – not, it is true, in opposition to the pleasure principle, but independently of it, and to some extent quite heedless of it.

The manifestations of a compulsion to repeat that we have described with respect to the early activities of the infant psyche, and also with respect to our experiences in the course of psycho-analytic practice, plainly bear the stamp of drives, and wherever they are in opposition to the pleasure principle they equally plainly exhibit their daemonic character.[3] In the case of children's play it seems readily comprehensible to us that the child also repeats *un*pleasurable experiences, because by thus being active he gains far more thorough-going control of the relevant powerful experience than was possible when he was merely its passive recipient. Each new repetition seems to add to the sense of command that the child strives for; and in the case of pleasurable experiences, too, the child never tires of repeating them, and will be implacable in insisting that every experience is identical to the first. This trait is destined to disappear later on: a joke will fall flat at the second time of hearing; a play will never again make the same impression that it did on first viewing; indeed it would be difficult to get an adult to re-read a much-enjoyed book until considerable time had elapsed. Novelty will always be the precondition of enjoyment. The child, however, will never tire of requiring adults to repeat a game that they showed him or played with him, until they refuse out of sheer exhaustion. And once anyone has told him a nice story, he wants to hear the same story again and again rather than a new one; he implacably insists that every repetition be exactly the same; and he corrects every least change that the story-teller misguidedly incorporates, perhaps fondly imagining it will gain him extra kudos. In this, the pleasure principle is not being contradicted; it is evident that the repetition, the replication of the original experience in identical terms, itself represents a source of pleasure. In the case of analysis, on the other hand, it becomes clear that the compulsion to repeat the events of infancy in the transference process flouts the pleasure principle in *every* way. The patient behaves in a completely infantile manner, and thus shows us that the repressed memory traces of his primal experiences are not in an annexed state, indeed are to all intents and purposes incapable of secondary processing. It is this non-annexed state, moreover, that accounts for their ability to form a wish-fantasy[4] by latching on to the residua of the day, a fantasy that finds expression in dreams. The same compulsion to repeat very often confronts us as an obstacle to therapy when at the end of a patient's course of treatment we seek to bring about his complete disattachment from the physician; and we may reasonably suppose that the turbid fear of patients unfamiliar with analysis, who shrink from reawakening something that in their view is best left dormant, essentially reflects their dread of seeing this daemonic compulsion make its appearance.[5]

But what is the nature of the connection between the realm of the drives and the compulsion to repeat? At this point we cannot help thinking that we have managed to identify a universal attribute of drives – and perhaps of *all* organic life – that has not hitherto been clearly recognized, or at any rate not explicitly emphasized. A drive might accordingly be seen as *a powerful tendency inherent in every living organism to restore a prior state*, which prior state the organism was compelled to relinquish due to the disruptive influence of external forces; we can see it as a kind of organic elasticity, or, if we prefer, as a manifestation of inertia in organic life.[6]

This conception of drives sounds strange, for we have become accustomed to seeing drives as the key factor pressing for change and development, and now we are supposed to see them as the direct opposite: as the expression of the *conservative* nature of organic life. On the other hand it doesn't take us very long to think of examples in the animal world that seem to confirm that drives are indeed historically determined. When certain kinds of fish undertake arduous journeys at spawning time in order to lay their eggs in particular waters, far from their normal habitat, then in the view of numerous biologists they are simply returning to the previous domain of their species, which, in the course of time, they have exchanged for others. The same is said to apply to the migration of birds; but we have no need to search around for further examples once we remember that the phenomena of heritability and the facts of embryology offer us the most spectacular proofs of the existence of an organic compulsion to repeat. We see how in the course of its development the embryo of any existing animal is compelled to repeat – albeit in the most fleeting and abbreviated way – the structures of all the forms from which the animal is descended, instead of hurrying by the shortest route to its definitive shape; and given that we can explain this behaviour scarcely at all in *mechanical* terms, we have no call to disregard the *historical* explanation. And we similarly find a reproductive faculty extending far into the higher echelons of the animal kingdom whereby a lost organ is replaced through the creation of a new one altogether identical to it.

Some consideration must doubtless be given to the evident objection that as well as the conservative drives that compel repetition, there may also be others that press for new forms and for progress;

indeed, we shall take account of this objection later in our discussions. But in the meantime we may find it enticing to pursue the hypothesis that 'all drives seek to restore a prior state' right through to its logical conclusion. While the outcome of this might seem airy-fairy or reminiscent of the mystical, we are none the less confident in the knowledge that no one can accuse us of *intending* such an outcome. We seek the sober results of research or of reflections founded on research, and we seek to impart to these results no other quality but that of reliability.[7]

If, then, all organic drives are conservative, historically acquired, and predisposed to regression and the restoration of prior states, we must accordingly ascribe the achievements of organic development to external influences and their disruptive and distracting effects. On this view, the elementary organism did not start out with any desire to change, and given the continuance of the same circumstances would have constantly repeated the selfsame life-cycle; but in the final analysis, so the argument goes, it must be the developmental history of our planet and its relationship to the sun that has left its imprint for us to behold in the development of organisms. The conservative organic drives have assimilated every one of these externally imposed modifications of the organism's life-cycle and duly preserved them in order to repeat them, and therefore inevitably give the misleading impression of being forces bent on change and progress, whereas they merely seek to achieve an old goal by new means as well as old. And this ultimate goal of all organic striving may be equally susceptible of definition. It would contradict the conservative nature of drives if it were the goal of life to achieve a state never previously attained to. Rather, it must aspire to an *old* state, a primordial state from which it once departed, and to which via all the circuitous byways of development it strives to return. If we may reasonably suppose, on the basis of all our experience without exception, that every living thing dies – reverts to the inorganic – for *intrinsic* reasons, then we can only say that *the goal of all life is death*, or to express it retro-spectively: *the inanimate existed before the animate*.

At some point or other, the attributes of life were aroused in non-living matter by the operation upon it of a force that we are still quite incapable of imagining. Perhaps it was a process similar in essence to the one that later, at a certain level of living matter, gave rise to consciousness. The tension generated at that point in previously inanimate matter sought to achieve equilibrium; thus the first drive came into existence: the drive to return to the inanimate. At that stage death was still easy for living matter; the course of life that had to be gone through was probably short, its direction determined by the newly created organism's chemical structure. In this way living matter may have experienced a long period of continual re-creation and easy death, until decisive external factors changed in such a way that they compelled still-surviving matter to take ever greater diversions from its original course of life and ever more complex detours in achieving its death-goal. These detours on the path to death, all faithfully preserved by the conservative drives, may well be what gives us our present picture of the phenomena of life. If one holds fast to the notion that the drives are exclusively conservative in nature, one cannot arrive at any other logical postulates concerning the origin and goal of life.

These conclusions may seem disturbing, but so too is the picture that emerges in respect of the great groups of drives that we posit behind the vital phenomena of organisms. The theory that there are drives directed at self-preservation, drives that we ascribe to all living beings, stands in striking opposition to the hypothesis that the entire life of the drives serves to procure death. Considered in this light, the theoretical significance of the drives concerned with self-preservation, self-assertion and dominance diminishes greatly. They are indeed 'partial' drives,[8] charged with the task of safeguarding the organism's own particular path to death and barring all possible means of return to the inorganic other than those already immanent; but the baffling notion of the organism striving to endure in defiance of the entire world – a notion incapable of being fitted into any sensible nexus – simply evaporates. The fact that remains is that the organism wants only to die in its own particular way; and so these guardians of life, too, were originally myrmidons of death.[9] Thus arises the paradox that the living organism resists in the most energetic way external influences ('dangers') that could help it to take a short cut to its life's goal (to short-circuit the system, as it were); but it is precisely this sort of behaviour that characterizes purely drive-engendered strivings as against those of intelligence.

But if we really think about it, this cannot be true! Things take on a quite different aspect in the light of the sexual drives, to which neurosis theory has attached particular importance. Not *all* organisms have yielded to the external pressure impelling them to ever greater development. Many have succeeded in remaining at their own lowly level right into the present time; indeed, there are many living things still in existence today that must resemble, if not all, then at least many of the early stages in the development of the higher animals and plants. And by the same token, not *all* the individual organic elements that make up the complex body of a higher organism stay with it throughout the entire course of its development to the point of natural death. Some of them, the germ-cells, probably retain the original structure of living matter, and after a certain period they separate off from the organism, carrying with them the full gamut of inherited and newly acquired drives. It is perhaps precisely these two characteristics that enable these cells to have an independent life. Given favourable circumstances, they begin to develop, i.e. they repeat the game to which they owe their own existence, and the outcome of this is that one portion of their matter continues its development right through to the end, while another reverts once more to the beginnings of the development process as a new germ particle. These germ-cells thus work in opposition to the death of living matter, and succeed in giving it what in our eyes must seem like potential immortality, while in reality perhaps signifying merely an extension of the dying process. We attach the greatest possible significance to the fact that the germ-cell acquires the strength, not to say the actual ability to achieve this feat only by merging with another germ-cell similar to it and yet different.

The drives that take charge of the destiny of these organic elements that outlive the larger entity, keep them safe while they are vulnerable to the stimuli of the external world, and bring about their encounter with the other germ-cells – these constitute the group termed 'sexual drives'. They are conservative in the same sense that the others are in that they reincorporate previous states of the relevant living matter, only to a more marked degree inasmuch as they show themselves to be particularly resistant to external influences; and they are also conservative in a further sense, since they preserve life itself for longer periods.[10] They constitute the true life-drives; and the fact that they act *against* the intent of the other drives, an intent that by its very nature conduces to death, points to a conflict between them and the rest, the importance of which was recognized very early on by neurosis theory. It amounts to a kind of fluctuating rhythm within the life of organisms: one group of drives goes storming ahead in order to attain the ultimate goal of life at the earliest possible moment, another goes rushing back at a certain point along the way in order to do part of it all over again and thus prolong the journey. But even though sexuality and gender differentiation were assuredly not present when life began, it none the less remains possible that the drives that subsequently merited the term 'sexual' were active from the very beginning, and that it was *not* only at some later stage that they began to counter the antics of the 'ego drives'.[11]

Let us go back for a moment ourselves and ask whether all these speculations are not perhaps entirely baseless. Are there really no other drives *apart from the sexual drives* that seek to restore a prior state, nor others again that strive for a state never previously attained to? I know of no reliable example in the organic world that contradicts the picture that we have suggested. There seems to be no clear evidence of a universal drive favouring higher development within the animal and plant worlds, even though it remains an undisputed fact that developments do in fact proceed in that direction. But for one thing, it is in many cases merely a matter of subjective judgement when we declare one level of development to be 'higher' than some other; and for another thing, biology shows us that higher development in one particular respect is very often paid for or balanced out by regression in another. Moreover, there are plenty of animal forms whose early stages clearly reveal that they have developed regressively rather than progressively. Higher development and regression might both be the result of the pressure to adapt exerted by external forces, and the role of the drives might be limited in both cases to the task of assimilating the imposed change as an inner source of pleasure.[12]

Many of us, too, may find it difficult to abandon the belief that there is in mankind itself an inherent drive towards perfection that has brought human beings to their present high level of intellectual attainment and ethical sublimation, and that can be relied on to ensure their further development to the status of *Übermensch*. For my own part, however, I do not believe in any such inner drive, and can see no way of salvaging this agreeable illusion. The development of mankind thus far appears to me to call for no other explanation than that applicable to animals; and the restless urge for ever greater perfection that we observe in a minority of individual human beings can readily be understood as resulting from the repression of drives – the foundation on which all that is most precious in human civilization is built. The repressed drive never abandons its struggle to achieve full gratification, which would consist in the repetition of a primary gratification experience. All the sublimations and reaction-formations and surrogate-formations in the world are never enough to resolve the abiding tension; and the gulf between the level of gratificatory pleasure *demanded* and the level actually *achieved* produces that driving force that prevents the individual from resting content with any situation he ever contrives, and instead – as the poet says – he 'presses ever onward unbridled, untamed' (Mephisto in *Faust* I, 'Faust's Study'). The way back, the way to full gratification, is usually blocked by the resistances that keep the repressions fully active, and there is accordingly no alternative but to proceed in the one direction still available, namely that of development – though without any prospect of bringing the process to a conclusion and attaining the desired goal. The pattern of events during the formation of a neurotic phobia (which is nothing other than an attempt to evade the gratification of a drive) offers us a model exemplifying the genesis of this seeming 'drive for perfection', which, however, we cannot possibly attribute to *all* individual human beings. The dynamic conditions for the phenomenon are indeed universally present, but the economic circumstances appear to favour it only in rare cases.

However, we would draw attention here, albeit very briefly, to the fact that, having rejected the 'perfection drive', we can probably find a replacement in the striving of Eros to concentrate organic matter in ever larger units.[13] Taken in conjunction with the effects of repression, it could well account for the phenomena attributed to the 'perfection drive'.

## Notes

1. Cf. Chapter VII, 'The Psychology of Dream Processes', in my *Interpretation of Dreams*.
2. [Freud's grammar is quite often slapdash, but in the case of this parenthesis it is garbled to the point of complete obscurity. The translation is therefore conjectural, and has been derived by reference to the penultimate sentence of Chapter II (see also the associated note concerning Freud's use of 'modify').]
3. [This phrase directly renders Freud's mercifully unambiguous German (*zeigen . . . den dämonischen Charakter*); the *Standard Edition*, however, bowdlerizes this into 'give the appearance of some "daemonic" force at work'. See also below, note 5.]
4. [*Wunschphantasie* – yet another example, like 'dream-work' (*Traumarbeit*) in the second paragraph of this chapter, of Freud's zest for creating new words by shunting together two seemingly ill-assorted ones.]
5. [The *Standard Edition* offers another revealing bowdlerization here: Freud uses the plain, no-nonsense words *dieser dämonische Zwang* – but James Strachey felt obliged to render the phrase as 'this compulsion with its hint of possession by some "daemonic" power'.]
6. I have no doubt that similar suppositions as to the nature of 'drives' have already been expressed on numerous occasions.
7. [*Addition 1925:*] The reader is asked to bear in mind that what follows is the elaboration of an extreme line of thought, which will be qualified and amended later on when the sex drives are taken into consideration.
8. [*Partialtrieb*. The *Standard Edition* routinely renders the *Partial*-element

of this term as 'component . . .', but there is no good reason to depart from the straightforward translation 'partial . . .' (cf. such standard technical terms as *Partialbruch, Partialdruck* – 'partial fraction', 'partial pressure').]

9. [The phrase 'these guardians of life' presumably refers back to 'the drives' – but this is left unclear by Freud.]

10. [*Addition* 1923:] And yet it is to these alone that we can attribute an inner tendency towards 'progress' and higher development!

11. [*Addition* 1925:] It should be clear from the whole context that the term 'ego drives' is intended here only as a provisional one that harks back to the original nomenclature of psychoanalysis.

12. Ferenczi arrived at the same potential interpretation, but via a different route: 'If we follow this line of thought to its logical conclusion, we must accustom ourselves to the idea that a tendency to stasis or regression also prevails in organic life, while the tendency to development, adaptation, etc. is aroused only by external stimuli.' (*Entwicklungsstufen des Wirklichkeitssinnes* [*Stages in the Development of the Sense of Reality*], 1913, p. 137.)

13. [See below, pp. 181ff.]


VI


There are no doubt many respects in which we ourselves are going to feel dissatisfied with our conclusions thus far, which posit a sharp contrast between the 'ego drives' and the sexual drives, and argue that the former are bent on death, the latter on the continuation of life. Furthermore, it was really only the *former* that we could claim showed the conservative character of drives or – better – their regressive character, corresponding to the compulsion to repeat. For according to our hypothesis, the ego drives arise when inanimate matter becomes animate, and set out to restore the inanimate state. In the case of the sexual drives, on the other hand, they clearly *do* reproduce the primitive states of the organism – but the goal they strive for with all the means at their disposal is the merging of two germ-cells that are differentiated in a particular way. If this union does not come about, then the germ-cell dies, just like all the other elements of multicellular organisms. Only in this one circumstance can the sexual function extend life and confer upon it a semblance of immortality. But what important event in the developmental history of living matter is being repeated by sexual reproduction or by its precursor, the conjugation of two individual organisms amongst the protista? We do not know the answer to this question, and would therefore find it a considerable relief if our entire theory were to prove wrong. The antithesis of ego drives (death drives) and sexual drives (life drives) would then lose all validity, and at the same time the compulsion to repeat would lose the significance that we have attached to it.

Let us therefore go back to one of the postulates woven into our argument, in the confident expectation that it will lend itself to complete rebuttal. We based a whole variety of conclusions on the presupposition that all living matter dies for reasons that are *intrinsic* to it. We made this assumption so blithely because it does not appear to us to *be* an assumption. It is our habit of mind to think in these terms, and the habit is reinforced by our poets and playwrights. Perhaps we have decided to embrace this belief because it brings us comfort. If we are to die ourselves, having first lost to death all those most dear to us, then we prefer to succumb to an implacable law of nature, the majestic 'Ανάγχη ['necessity'], rather than to a chance event that might well have proved avoidable. But perhaps this belief that death has its own intrinsic logic is simply one of the illusions we have created for ourselves in order to be able to 'bear the heavy burden of existence'.[1] It is certainly not primal: the idea of 'natural death' is alien to primitive peoples, who attribute every death that occurs amongst them to the influence of an enemy or an evil spirit. To investigate this belief, therefore, let us turn without further ado to biological science.

Once we do so, however, we are entitled to feel astonished at how little agreement there is amongst biologists on the question of 'natural death', indeed at the way the whole concept of death loses all substance the moment they touch it. The fact that, in the case of the higher animals at least, there is a distinct average lifespan does, of course, tend to support the notion that death occurs for intrinsic reasons; but this impression is cancelled out again by the circumstance that individual large animals and giant trees reach a very great age that we are as yet unable to calculate. According to Wilhelm Fliess's grand conception, all the vital phenomena of an organism – and doubtless its death as well – are tied to the fulfilling of a specific timescale that expresses the dependence of two living substances, one male, one female, on the solar year. But when we look at how easily and how extensively external factors can influence the timing of physiological events in plants in particular, accelerating or delaying them, we see a picture that is sharply at variance with the rigidity of Fliess's formulae, and at the very least raises doubts as to whether the laws he postulates do indeed reign supreme.

In our view, the most interesting treatment of the topic of the lifespan and death of organisms is to be found in the publications of August Weismann (1882, 1884, 1892, etc.). It was Weismann who proposed the differentiation of living matter into two parts: the mortal and the immortal. The mortal part is the body in the narrower sense of the word, the 'soma'; it alone is subject to natural death. The germ-cells, however, are potentially immortal inasmuch as they are capable under certain favourable conditions of developing into a new individual, or – to put it another way – of enveloping themselves with a new soma.[2]

What is truly fascinating here is the unexpected similarity of this to the view that we ourselves arrived at by such a very different route. Weismann, who looks at living matter in morphological terms, discerns in it one part that is doomed to die – the soma, the entire body *except* the element concerned with sexuality and heredity – and another that is immortal, precisely this latter element, the germ-plasm, that serves to preserve the species by reproducing it. We for our part focused not on living matter itself but on the forces at work within it, and this led us to identify two different kinds of drives: those that seek to guide life towards death; and others, the sexual drives, that continually seek and achieve the *renewal* of life. This sounds very much like a dynamic corollary to Weismann's morphological theory.

However, all sense of a basic concurrence of views immediately evaporates once we take note of Weismann's position on the problem of death. For in Weismann's view the distinction between mortal soma and immortal germ-plasm is applicable only to multicellular organisms, while in unicellular organisms the specific individual and the reproductive cell remain one and the same.[3] He therefore declares unicellular organisms to be potentially immortal, death only entering the picture with the metazoa, i.e. multicellular organisms. While the death of these higher organisms is indeed a natural one in his view, that is to say a death arising from inherent factors, it does not rest upon a primal attribute of living matter,[4] and therefore cannot be regarded as an absolute necessity grounded in the very essence of organic life.[5] He sees it instead as a purely functional device, a phenomenon reflecting adaptation to the external conditions of life: once the body-cells separated into soma and germ-cells, it would have been a functionally quite inappropriate luxury if the individual had carried on having an unlimited life-span. As soon as this differentiation took place in multicellular organisms, death became possible and functionally appropriate. Ever since then the soma of higher organisms has died after a certain span of time due to inherent factors, whereas the protista have remained immortal. Reproduction, on the other hand, did not appear only when death did, but instead is for Weismann a primal attribute of living matter, just like growth, out of which indeed it arose, and life has accordingly been continuous right from its very beginnings on earth.[6]

It will be readily appreciated that our own argument gains very little from the fact that Weismann grants that the higher organisms die a natural death. If death is a late acquisition on the part of living beings, then there can no longer be any question of death drives that date from the very beginning of organic life. In this scenario, multicellular organisms may well still die due to inherent factors, be it shortcomings in their differentiation or imperfections in their metabolism – but this is wholly irrelevant to the question that concerns us. It is surely the case, too, that this sort of view, and this sort of explanation of the origins of death, are much closer to people's customary way of seeing things than the discomfiting theory of 'death drives'.

The debate prompted by Weismann's propositions did not in my judgement decide the issue either one way or the other.[7] Some authors reverted to the position taken by Goette (1883), who regarded death as the direct consequence of reproduction. Hartmann does not characterize death in terms of the supervention of a 'corpse', of a portion of living matter that has become dead, but instead defines death as the 'conclusion of individual development'. In this sense, the protozoa are mortal too; in their case death is always coincident with reproduction, but is masked as it were by the latter, in that the entire substance of the parent organism can be transferred directly into the individual offspring.[8]

Researchers soon turned their attention to testing the alleged immortality of living matter by means of experiments on unicellular organisms. An American, Woodruff, started to breed a ciliate infusorium, a 'slipper animalcule', which reproduces by dividing into two new individual organisms, and followed it right through to the 3,029th generation before breaking off the experiment, each time isolating one of the two products of the division process and putting it into fresh fluid. The remote descendant of the first animalcule was just as vigorous as its ancestor, without any signs of ageing or degeneration; the hypothesis of the immortality of the protista thus appeared to be susceptible of experimental proof, assuming that figures of this order can be deemed conclusive.[9]

Other researchers came to other conclusions. In contradistinction to Woodruff, it was found by Maupas, Calkins and others that after a certain number of divisions these infusoria, too, become weaker, diminish in size, lose part of their organic structure, and ultimately die, unless they are revitalized by certain influences acting upon them. According to this view, the protozoa die after a period of senile decay just as the higher animals do – which directly contradicts the assertions of Weismann, who sees death as an attribute acquired by living organisms only relatively late in their evolution.

From this whole body of research we would single out for

special emphasis two particular facts which appear to support our argument.

First: if, at a point before they exhibit signs of senescence, two animalcules are able to coalesce with each other, to 'conjugate' – after which in due course they separate again – then they remain unaffected by age; they have become 'rejuvenated'. This conjugation is surely the precursor of sexual reproduction in the higher animals; at this stage, however, it has nothing to do with propagation, but is limited simply to the merging of the respective individuals' living matter (Weismann's 'amphimixis'). But the rejuvenating effect of conjugation can also be achieved by other means: use of certain stimulative agents, changes in the composition of the nutrient fluid, increase in temperature, or shaking. One is reminded of the famous experiment undertaken by J[acques] Loeb, who by the use of certain chemical stimuli induced segmentation in the eggs of sea-urchins – a process that normally occurs only after fertilization.

Second: it *does* seem altogether probable that the infusoria proceed via their own life-processes to a natural death, for the contradiction between Woodruff's results and those of others derives from the fact that Woodruff put each new generation in fresh nutrient fluid. When he tried *not* doing so, he observed the same senescence across the generations as the other researchers did. He concluded that the animalcules must be damaged by the metabolic products given off into the surrounding fluid, and was then able to demonstrate convincingly that it is only the products of their *own* metabolism that have this lethal effect. For when placed in a solution supersaturated with the waste products of a less closely related species, these same animalcules that would surely have perished if massed in their own nutrient fluid flourished in a quite remarkable way. Left to itself, therefore, an infusorium dies a natural death because it does not satisfactorily dispose of the products of its own metabolism; but perhaps all the higher animals also die essentially because of the same deficiency.

We might begin to doubt at this point whether it was at all helpful to try to resolve the question of 'natural death' by reference to the study of protozoa. The primitive structure of these organisms may conceal from us certain features which, though present in them too, are actually *observable* only in the higher animals, where they have found morphological expression. If we shift from a morphological to a dynamic standpoint, then we can regard it as a matter of complete indifference whether or not the protozoa can be said to die a natural death. In their case the matter identified as being immortal at some later point has not yet separated off in any way whatever from the part that is mortal. The drives that seek to convert life into death could easily be at work from the very beginning in them too, and yet their effect could be so well masked by the effect of the life-preserving forces that it becomes extremely difficult to demonstrate their presence. As we have discovered, the biologists' observations *do* allow us to suppose that such inner processes conducing to death may be present in the protista as well. Even if the protista prove to be immortal in Weismann's sense, however, his assertion that death is an attribute acquired at a relatively late stage applies only to the physical *manifestations* of death, and does not rule out hypotheses about *processes* doing all they can to bring about death.

Our expectation that biology would simply scupper the notion of death drives thus turns out to be unfounded. We can continue to entertain the possibility of such drives, assuming we have other grounds for doing so. Furthermore, the striking similarity between Weismann's soma/germ-plasm distinction and our own differentiation of death drives and life drives not only still exists, but has regained all its relevance.

Let us dwell for a moment on this exquisitely dualistic conception of the life of the drives. According to Ewald Hering's theory of what happens in living matter, two processes are ceaselessly at work within it that run in opposite directions to each other: one that is anabolic or 'assimilative', and another that is catabolic or 'dissimilative'. We are surely not presuming too much if we see in these two contrary directions taken by the vital processes the workings of our two sets of drive-impulses, the life drives and the death drives. One thing we cannot close our eyes to, however, is the fact that we have unwittingly fetched up in the philosophical domain of Schopenhauer, for whom, of course, death is the 'proper result' of life and hence its purpose,[10] whereas the sexual drive is the embodiment of the will to life.

Let us boldly attempt to take the argument a step further. It is generally accepted that the coming together of numerous cells to form a single animate unit – the multicellularity of organisms – became a means of extending their lifespan. Each cell helps to preserve the life of the others, and the community of cells can survive even if individual cells have to die off. We have already heard that even conjugation, the temporary coalescence of two unicellular organisms, has a life-preserving and rejuvenating effect on both of them. All of this being so, we might try to take the libido theory evolved through psychoanalysis and apply it to the cells' relationship to each other. We might then try to imagine that it is the life drives or sexual drives active within each cell that make the other cells their object, partially neutralizing their death drives (or rather the processes that the latter instigate) and thereby keeping them alive, while other drives do exactly the same for them, and others again sacrifice their whole existence by performing this libidinal function. The germ-cells themselves could be said to behave in a totally 'narcissistic' fashion – to apply the term we are accustomed to use in neurosis theory when an individual retains his libido entirely within his own ego and expends none of it on object-cathexes. The germ-cells need their libido, the activity of their life drives, entirely for themselves by way of reserves for their later, magnificently anabolic activity. (Perhaps we may also use the term 'narcissistic' in the same sense to describe the cells of malignant neoplasms that destroy the organism. After all, pathologists are prepared to accept that the seeds of these growths are present at birth, and to concede that they display features characteristic of embryos.)[11] All of this being so, it would appear that the libido of our sexual drives is one and the same thing as the Eros evoked by poets and philosophers, the binding force within each and every living thing.

This seems an opportune moment for us to review the slow

evolution of the libido theory. The psychoanalysis of transference neuroses initially compelled us to postulate an antithesis between 'sexual drives' directed outwards at an object, and other drives that we only very imperfectly understood, and that we provisionally termed 'ego drives'. Amongst the latter, the drives that were inevitably recognized first were those that contribute to the individual's self-preservation; for the rest, no one was in a position to know what other drives might be identified. In order to establish psychology on a sound footing, nothing could have been more important than some kind of insight, however approximate, into the general nature of drives and the particular characteristics they might prove to have; but there was no other field of psychology in which people were groping so completely in the dark. Everyone posited as many drives or 'basic drives' as they liked, and played around with them rather as the ancient Greek philosophers did with their four elements: earth, air, fire and water. Psychoanalysis, which couldn't escape having *some* kind of theory on the subject, stuck initially to the distinction popularly made between drives, exemplified in the phrase 'hunger and love'. At least this was no new arbitrary act. And it enabled us to progress quite a long way in the analysis of neuroses. The concept of 'sexuality' – and with it the concept of a sexual drive – did of course have to be considerably extended, to the point where it included much that could not be classed as having a reproductive function, and this caused quite a stir in the world of the puritanical, the posh and the purely hypocritical.

The next step came about when psychoanalysis was able to feel its way a bit closer to the psychological ego, which initially it had known only as an entity given to repression and censorship, and adept at reaction-formation and the construction of protective mechanisms.[12] It is true that critical spirits and others of a far-sighted disposition had long since objected to the libido concept being restricted solely to the energy manifested by *object-oriented* sexual drives; but they neglected to tell us the source of this superior knowledge, and they had no idea how to turn it to advantage in the actual practice of psychoanalysis. Things then began to progress in a more considered way when practitioners of psychoanalysis observed how regular an occurrence it was for libido to be withdrawn from the object and directed onto the ego (introversion); and in the process of studying the earliest phases of libido development in children, they came to the conclusion that the ego is the true and original reservoir of the libido, and that it is from *there* that the libido is first extended to objects.[13] The ego thus took its place amongst the sexual objects, and was immediately recognized as the most sophisticated of them all. When the libido resided in the ego in this way, it was termed 'narcissistic'.[14] This narcissistic libido was of course also in psychoanalytical terms a manifestation of energy on the part of *sexual* drives, which one had no choice but to identify with the 'self-preservation drives' that had been acknowledged from the outset. This meant that the original antithesis of ego drives and sexual drives was no longer adequate. A part of the ego drives was now recognized as being libidinal; within the ego there were – in addition to others no doubt – sexual drives at work as well. None the less, it can justifiably be said that the old principle that psychoneurosis[15] rests upon a conflict between the ego drives and the sexual drives contains nothing that we would nowadays reject. The distinction between the two kinds of drives, which was originally thought of as being *qualitative* in some way, now simply has to be differently defined, namely as being *topical* in nature.[16] The transference neuroses in particular – the real object of study in psychoanalysis – are still the result of a conflict between the ego and a libidinal object-cathexis.

It is all the more necessary that we stress the libidinal character of the self-preservation drives at this point since we want to take the argument a step further by venturing to see in the sexual drive the all-preserving force that is Eros, and to suggest that the ego's narcissistic libido derives from the quotas of libido that enable the soma cells to adhere to each other. But we now find ourselves suddenly confronted by a challenging question: if the self-preservation drives are *also* libidinal in nature, then perhaps we have no drives whatever *except* libidinal ones? There are certainly no others in evidence. But if this is so, then we are going to have to concede the point after all to those critics who suspected from the outset that psychoanalysis would explain *everything* in terms of sexuality, or to those innovators like Jung who opted without further ado to use 'libido' for 'drive-energy' in general. Is this not the case?

This would certainly not be the outcome we intended. On the contrary, the starting point of our whole argument was the sharp distinction that we drew between ego drives – death drives – on the one hand, and sexual drives – life drives – on the other. (We were of course prepared at one stage to include amongst the death drives the self-preservation drives attributed to the ego, but we have since decided that this view was incorrect and withdrawn it.[17]) Our conception has been a *dualistic* one right from the outset, and remains so today more emphatically than ever, particularly since we started classifying the two opposites as 'life drives and death drives' rather than 'ego drives and sexual drives'. Jung's theory, on the other hand, is *monistic*; the fact that he used the term 'libido' for what he saw as a single drive-energy was bound to cause confusion, but need not concern us any further.[18] We strongly suspect that other drives are active within the ego besides the libidinal self-preservation drives; we just need to be able to produce evidence of them. It is regrettable that analysis of the ego has made so little progress that we find it exceedingly difficult to provide this proof. The libidinal ego drives may of course be tied in some very particular way to the other ego drives that are as yet unknown to us. Even before we had fully recognized the phenomenon of narcissism, it was suspected within psychoanalysis that the 'ego drives' had acquired libidinal components. But these are distinctly shaky notions that will hardly do much to convince our opponents. It really is most unfortunate that analysis has thus far only ever enabled us to demonstrate the presence of *libidinal* drives.[19] None the less, the conclusion that there simply aren't any others is not one that we are minded to share.

Given that so much is obscure at present in the theory of drives, it would surely not be sensible of us to reject any idea that promises to cast light on the matter. Our departure point was the great antithesis of life drives and death drives. Object-love itself shows us a second such polarity – that of love (affection) and hate (aggression). What if we succeeded in connecting these two polarities, what if we succeeded in tracing one back to the other! We have always acknowledged a sadistic component in the sexual drive;[20] as we know, this component can develop a life of its own and turn into a perversion that dominates a person's entire sexual life. It also occurs as a dominant partial drive in one of those forms of organization of sexual life that I have termed 'pre-genital'. But how could we possibly suppose that the sadistic drive, which aims to harm its object, derives from Eros, the preserver of life? Isn't it altogether plausible to suppose that this sadism is actually a death drive that has been ousted from the ego at the instance of the narcissistic libido, and as a result only becomes apparent in conjunction with the object? It then becomes an ancillary of the sexual function. In the oral stage of the organization of the libido, 'taking possession of the love object' and 'destroying the object' are still coterminous; later, the sadistic drive separates off, and ultimately, in the phase of genital primacy, it serves the purposes of reproduction by taking on the role of subjugating the sexual object to the extent necessary for the fulfilment of the sexual act. Indeed, one could say that, following its expulsion from the ego, the sadistic element shows the libidinal components of the sexual drive which direction to take; in due course they follow its example and strive to reach the object. Where the primal sadism element does not undergo any mitigation or dilution, the outcome is an erotic life marked by the familiar ambivalence of love and hate.[21]

If such a supposition is indeed permissible, then we might be said to have met the requirement that we produce an example of a death drive, albeit a displaced one. The only problem is that this conception is altogether impalpable, and indeed has a positively mystical air. We will be suspected of having resorted to desperate measures in an effort to escape from a gravely embarrassing situation. In that case we may reasonably point to the fact that such a supposition is by no means new, that we have indeed already put it forward at an earlier stage, before there was ever any mention of an 'embarrassing' situation. At that particular time, clinical observations compelled us to form the view that masochism, the partial drive complementary to sadism, has to be understood as the sadism within an individual turning back upon his own ego. But a drive turning from object to ego is in principle no different from a drive turning from ego to object – the latter phenomenon being the new contention at issue here. That being so, then masochism – an individual's drive turning back upon his own ego – is in reality a return to an earlier stage of the drive, a regression. The account of masochism given at that time may need correcting in one particular, on the grounds that it was altogether too restrictive: masochism could also very possibly be a primary phenomenon – a notion I then sought to dispute.[22]

But let us return to the life-preserving sexual drives. As we have already learnt from the research carried out on protista, the coalescence of two individuals *without* subsequent [cell-]division (i.e. conjugation) has a strengthening and rejuvenating effect on both individuals, assuming that they separate from each other soon afterwards (see above, p. 177; cf. also Lipschütz). In later generations they display no symptoms of degeneration, and appear to be capable of withstanding the injurious effects of their own metabolism for a longer period. I believe that this particular observation may *also* be regarded as exemplifying the effect of sexual union. But in what way does the coalescence of two cells that differ very little from one another bring about such a revitalization? The experiment in which the action of chemical and even of mechanical stimuli[23] is substituted for conjugation in protozoa surely allows us to answer this question with complete confidence: it happens because of the supply of new quanta of stimulation. This in turn accords well with the hypothesis that the life process of the individual leads for intrinsic reasons to the equilibration of chemical tensions, that is to death, whereas union with the living matter of a different individual *increases* these tensions, introduces new *vital differentiae* as it were, which must then be 'lived out'. Needless to say, this differentness must be subject to one or more optima. One of our strongest motives for believing in the existence of death drives is indeed the fact that we have perceived the dominant tendency of the psyche, and perhaps of nervous life in general, to be the constant endeavour – as manifested in the pleasure principle – to reduce inner stimulative tension, to maintain it at a steady level, to resolve it completely (the *Nirvana principle*, as Barbara Low has called it).[24]

However, we still see it as a major drawback in our argument that in the case of the sexual drive, of all things, we remain unable to demonstrate a compulsion to repeat, the very attribute that put us on the trail of the death drives in the first place. It is true that the realm of embryonal development processes exhibits a plethora of such repetition phenomena; indeed the two germ-cells involved in sexual reproduction, together with their whole life-history, are themselves but repetitions of the very beginnings of organic life. But the fact remains that the essence of the processes that fall within the purview of the sexual drive is the coalescence of two cell bodies. In the case of the higher organisms, it is this coalescence alone that ensures the living matter's immortality.

In other words, we would really need to attain to a full understanding of the genesis of sexual reproduction and the origins of the sexual drives in general – a task that non-specialists are bound to shrink from, and one that the specialists themselves have so far been unable to accomplish. Let us therefore focus – in the most compressed and concentrated manner possible – on those elements amidst the mass of conflicting assertions and opinions that will permit us to pick up the thread of our argument.

One particular interpretation takes the teasing mystery out of the problem of reproduction by treating it as a manifestation of just one aspect of growth (fissiparation, gemmation, blastogenesis). Taking a sober Darwinian view of how reproduction through sexually differentiated germ-cells came about, we might envisage a scenario in which the advantage of amphimixis[25] that arose from the chance conjugation of two protista at some point in the past was retained and exploited in the subsequent development process.[26] On this premiss, therefore, 'sex' is not all that old, and the extraordinarily fierce drives that seek to bring about sexual union are thereby merely repeating something that happened by chance at a random moment in time and subsequently became firmly established because of the advantages it brought.

The same question arises here as arose earlier in respect of death, namely whether we should rely solely on the characteristics that the protista actually exhibit, and whether we should assume that forces and processes that only become *manifest* in the higher organisms also only began to *exist* in those organisms. For our particular purposes, the above-mentioned interpretation of sexuality has very little to offer. One can reasonably object that it presupposes the existence of life drives that were already active in the simplest organisms, for otherwise conjugation – which runs counter to the course of life and makes it more difficult to live life out and then die – would obviously have been avoided, not seized on and elaborated. Therefore if we do not want to abandon the hypothesis of death drives, we have to see them as having been accompanied from the very beginning by life drives. But we then have to admit that we are working on an equation with two unknowns.

When we look to see what else science can tell us about the origins of sexuality, we find so very little that we can liken the problem to a Stygian darkness that remains unrelieved by even the faintest glimmer of a hypothesis. We *do* come upon such a hypothesis in a very different sort of place, but one that is so fantastic – unquestionably more myth than scientific explanation – that I would not dare to mention it here but for the fact that it meets precisely that particular condition that we are so keen to see met. For it traces a drive back to *the need to restore a prior state*.

Needless to say, I mean the theory that Plato has Aristophanes expound in the *Symposium*, and which deals with the origins not only of the sexual drive, but also of its most important variation in relation to the object: 'Long ago, our nature was not the same as it is now but quite different. For one thing, there were three human genders, not just the present two, male and female. There was also a third one, a combination of these two . . . [the] "androgynous".' In these human beings, however, everything was double; they therefore had four hands and four feet, two faces, two sets of genitalia, etc. Zeus then decided to 'cut humans into two, as people cut sorb-apples in half before they preserve them . . . Since their original nature had been cut in two, each one longed for its own other half and stayed with it. They threw their arms round each other, weaving themselves together, *wanting to form a single living thing*.'²⁷

Shall we follow the poet-philosopher's hint and venture the hypothesis that when living matter *became* living matter it was sundered into tiny particles that ever since have endeavoured by means of the sexual drives to become reunited? That in the course of the protistan era these drives, in which the chemical affinity of inanimate matter still subsists, gradually overcame the difficulties put in the way of such an endeavour by an environment charged with life-threatening stimuli, and developed a cortical layer as a necessary protection against that environment? That in this way the scattered fragments of living matter achieved multicellularity and ultimately transferred the reunificatory drive to the germ-cells in the most intensely concentrated form? – But this, I think, is the appropriate point at which to stop.

Not, however, before adding a few words of critical reflection. People might ask me whether and to what extent I myself am convinced by the hypotheses set out here. My answer would be that I am not convinced myself, nor am I trying to persuade others to believe in them. Or to put it more accurately: I do not know how far I believe in them. It seems to me that the emotional factor of 'conviction' need not enter into it at all. One can certainly give oneself over completely to a particular line of thought, and follow it through to wherever it leads, out of sheer scientific curiosity, or out of a desire to act as devil's advocate – without signing oneself over to the devil. I am well aware that this third step in the theory of drives that I have undertaken here cannot lay claim to the same degree of certainty as the previous two, namely the broadening of the concept of sexuality, and the postulate of narcissism. These latter innovations were a direct translation of actual observations into theory, and were susceptible to sources of error no greater than those that inevitably pertain in all such cases. To be sure, the assertion that drives are *regressive* in nature is also based on the observation of facts, namely those manifest in the compulsion to repeat – but I have perhaps overestimated their importance. In any event, it is only possible to carry this idea through by repeatedly combining the factual with the purely notional, and thereby moving far away from empirical observation. One knows very well that the more often one does this in elaborating a theory, the more unreliable the end result becomes, but the degree of uncertainty cannot be calculated. One might have made a lucky guess, or one might have gone horribly wrong. In work of this kind I put little trust in so-called intuition, which, whenever I have encountered it, has always seemed to me more the fruit of a certain impartiality of mind – except that people are unfortunately seldom impartial when it comes to the ultimate questions, the great problems of science and of life. Here, I think, we are all ruled by proclivities that go to the very root of our being, and in our speculations we unwittingly play into their hands. Given such good grounds for mistrust, the only way for us to approach the results of our own intellectual endeavours is probably to regard them with cool benevolence. I hasten to add, however, that a self-critical stance of this kind entails absolutely no obligation to show particular tolerance to discrepant opinions. One can pitilessly reject theories that even the briefest analysis of empirical evidence serves to refute, while at the same time recognizing that the validity of one's own theory is merely provisional.

In judging our speculations about life drives and death drives we would be little bothered by the fact that so many strange and impalpable processes figure within them, such as one drive being ousted by others, or a drive turning from the ego to the object, and so on. All of this simply arises from the fact that we must necessarily operate with the given scientific terminology, i.e. the *figurative* language specific to psychology (or, more precisely, depth psychology). Otherwise we couldn't describe the relevant processes at all, indeed we wouldn't even have realized that they were there. The shortcomings in our account of things would probably disappear if, instead of using psychological terminology, we were already in a position to use that of physiology or chemistry. It is true that this terminology, too, belongs to a merely figurative language – but a perhaps simpler one, and one that we have known for a longer period of time.

On the other hand we need to be fully aware that the uncertainty of our speculations has been greatly increased by the need to borrow repeatedly from the science of biology. Biology is truly a realm of infinite possibilities; we can expect it to yield the most astonishing insights, and we cannot begin to guess what answers it might give to our questions in a few decades' time. Perhaps such as will sweep our carefully contrived edifice of hypotheses entirely away. 'If that is the case', someone might ask, 'then what is the point of writing papers like this, and why on earth bother to make them public?' Well, I just have to admit that some of the analogies, correlations and connections contained therein have seemed to me to be worthy of attention.[28]

### Notes

1. [Freud is quoting from Schiller's dire tragedy, *The Bride of Messina* (I, 8).]
2. Weismann (1884) [August Weismann, *Über Leben und Tod* (*On Life and Death*)].
3. Weismann (1882, p. 38) [August Weismann, *Über die Dauer des Lebens* (*On the Duration of Life*)].
4. Weismann (1884, p. 84).
5. Weismann (1882, p. 33).
6. Weismann (1884, pp. 84ff.).
7. Cf. Max Hartmann (1906) [*Tod und Fortpflanzung* (*Death and Reproduction*)], Alex[ander] Lipschütz (1914) [*Warum wir sterben* (*Why We Die*)], Franz Doflein (1919) [*Das Problem des Todes und der Unsterblichkeit bei den Pflanzen und Tieren* (*The Problem of Death and Immortality in Plants and Animals*)].
8. Hartmann (1906, p. 29).
9. For this and what follows, cf. Lipschütz (1914, pp. 26 and 52ff.).
10. *Über die anscheinende Absichtlichkeit im Schicksale des Einzelnen* [*On Apparent Intentionality in the Destiny of the Individual*].
11. [These two sentences were added by Freud in 1921.]

**12.** [See *On the Introduction of Narcissism*, pp. 381ff.]

**13.** [See *On the Introduction of Narcissism*, p. 366, note 10.]

**14.** *On the Introduction of Narcissism* (1914).

**15.** [See below, *On the Introduction of Narcissism*, p. 377, note 3.]

**16.** [See above, *Beyond the Pleasure Principle*, p. 137, Section I, note 1.]

**17.** [See above, pp. 167 and 181.]

**18.** [This sentence and the one preceding it were added by Freud in 1921.]

**19.** [Although he does not say so, Freud clearly means *ego* drives here.]

**20.** *Drei Abhandlungen zur Sexualtheorie* [*Three Essays on Sexual Theory*], from the first edition onwards (1905).

**21.** Cf. *Sexualtheorie* [*Sexual Theory*] and 'Triebe und Triebschicksale' ['Drives and Their Fates'] (1915).

**22.** These speculations have been anticipated to a very considerable extent by Sabina Spielrein in a paper that is rich in substance and ideas but not, to my mind, entirely lucid. Her term for the sadistic component of the sexual drive is 'destructive' (1912). Using yet another approach, A[ugust] Stärcke (1914) identified the libido concept itself with the theoretically supposable biological concept of an *impulsion to death*. (Cf. also Rank, 1907.) All these efforts, like those in the present text, bear witness to the urgent need to bring to the theory of drives the clarity that has so far proved elusive.

**23.** Lipschütz (1914).

**24.** [Barbara Low, *Psycho-Analysis*, (London and New York, 1920), p. 75.]

**25.** [See above, p. 177.]

**26.** However, Weismann (1892) denies this advantage too: 'Fertilization does not by any means signify a rejuvenation or renewal of life; it would not be in the least necessary for the continuation of life; it is solely and simply *a device for enabling two different heredity streams to merge.*' But he *does* consider increased variability in the organism to be an outcome of such merging.

**27.** [Plato, the *Symposium*, trans. by Christopher Gill (London, Penguin, 1999), pp. 22–4.] [*Addition 1921:*] I am indebted to Professor Heinrich Gomperz (Vienna) for the following suggestions regarding the origins of Plato's myth, which are reproduced here partly in his own words:

I should like to point out that essentially the same theory already occurs in the *Upanishads*. For in the *Brihad-aranyaka Upanishad*, I,4,3, where the emergence of the world from the Atman (the self or ego) is described, we read: 'He, verily, had no delight. Therefore he who is alone has no delight. He desired a second. He became as large as a woman and a man in close embrace. He caused that self to fall into two parts. From that arose husband and wife. Therefore, as Yājñvalkya used to say, this (body) is one half of oneself, like one of the two halves of a split pea. Therefore this space is filled by a wife' [trans. by S. Radhakrishnan, *The Principal Upanishads*, (London, 1953), p. 164]. The *Brihad-aranyaka Upanishad* is the oldest of all the *upanishads*, and no competent scholar is likely to date it later than *c.* 800 BC. As to the question whether Plato could possibly have drawn on these Indian ideas, even if only indirectly: contrary to current opinion I should not want to dismiss the idea completely, given that in the case of the metempsychosis theory, too, such a possibility cannot really be disputed. If there *were* indeed such a link, mediated in the first instance by the Pythagoreans, it would scarcely detract from the significance of the congruity of ideas, since if any such story *had* somehow percolated through to Plato from the oriental tradition, he would not have made it his own, let alone given it such a prominent role, if it had not seemed to him replete with truth.

In his essay *Menschen und Weltenwerden* [*The Coming into Being of Man and World*] (1913), K[onrat] Ziegler systematically explores the history of this particular notion *prior* to Plato, and traces it back to Babylonian conceptions.

28. We would like to add a few words here in order to clarify our nomenclature, which has undergone a certain degree of evolution in the course of this discussion. We derived our knowledge of 'sexual drives' from their relationship to the sexes and to the reproductive function. We still retained this term when the findings of psychoanalysis obliged us to recognize that their relationship to reproduction was more slender than we had supposed. With our postulation of narcissistic libido and our extension of the libido concept to the individual cell, the sexual drive transformed itself in our scheme of things into Eros, the force that seeks to push the various parts of living matter into direct association with each other and then keep them together, and the sexual drives – to use the common appellation – appeared to be the portion of this Eros that is turned towards the object. We then speculated that this Eros was active from the beginning of life, and, as the 'life drive', pitted itself against the 'death drive', which came into being when the inorganic became animate. We sought to solve the riddle of life by supposing these two drives, and supposing them to have been locked in battle with each other right from the very beginning. [*Addition 1921:*] The changes undergone by the concept of the 'ego drives' are perhaps less clear. Originally we used this term for all those drives about which we knew nothing except that their *direction* made them distinguishable from the sexual drives directed at the object; and we represented the ego

drives as being in opposition to the sexual drives, the manifestation of which is the libido. Later we began to analyse the ego, and realized that one part of the ego drives, too, is libidinal in nature, having taken the ego itself as its object. These narcissistic self-preservation drives therefore now had to be reckoned as belonging to the libidinal sexual drives. The opposition between ego drives and sexual drives changed into an opposition between ego drives and object drives, both libidinal in nature. This, however, was replaced by a new opposition between libidinal (ego and object) drives and others that may be posited in the ego, and which are perhaps evincible in the destruction drives. In the course of our speculations, this opposition changes into the antithesis of life drives (Eros) and death drives.

## VII

If it really is such a universal characteristic of drives to seek to restore a prior state, we should not be surprised that so many processes in the psyche take place quite independently of the pleasure principle. This characteristic would automatically be transmitted to each and every partial drive, and in the case of such drives would involve the retrieval of a particular stage of the development process. But while the pleasure principle may not as yet have gained command of these things, this does not necessarily mean that they are in conflict with it; in fact the problem of determining the relationship of the drives' repetition processes to the dominion of the pleasure principle still remains unsolved.

We have found it to be one of the earliest and most important functions of the psychic apparatus to 'annex' newly arriving drive-impulses, replace the primary process prevailing within them by a secondary process, and change their free-moving cathectic energy into a largely quiescent (tonic) cathexis. While this transformation is taking place no attention can be paid to any unpleasure that may arise – but that does not mean that the pleasure principle is thereby nullified. On the contrary, the transformation occurs on *behalf* of the pleasure principle: the annexion is a preparative act that both heralds and ensures the dominion of the pleasure principle.

Let us distinguish more sharply than we have done hitherto between 'function' and 'tendency'.[1] The pleasure principle can then be seen as a tendency serving the interests of a specific function whose responsibility it is *either* to render the psychic apparatus completely free of excitation, *or* to keep the quantum of excitation within it constant, *or* to keep it at the lowest possible level. We cannot yet decide for certain which of these alternatives is the correct one, but we note that this function as here defined would partake in that most universal endeavour in all living matter to revert to the quiescence of the inorganic world. We have all experienced how the greatest pleasure we can ever achieve, namely that of the sexual act, is accompanied by the momentary vanishment of a supremely intense excitation. The annexing of the drive-impulse, however, might be seen as a preparative function intended to make the excitation ready for its final dissolution in the pleasure of release.

This same context gives rise to the question whether sensations of pleasure and unpleasure can be produced equally by both annexed and non-annexed excitation processes. Now it does appear to be clear beyond all doubt that the non-annexed, primary processes result in far more intensive sensations in both directions (pleasure and unpleasure) than do the annexed, secondary ones. The primary processes are also the ones that occur first; they are the only ones operative at the start of the psyche's life; and we can reasonably infer that if the pleasure principle were not already active within these earlier processes, it would not be able to materialize at all for the later ones. We thus arrive at the basically rather convoluted conclusion that at the beginning of the psyche's life the striving for pleasure manifests itself far more intensively than it does later on, but enjoys less of a free run, in that it has to put up with frequent irruptions. Once the psyche is more developed the dominion of the pleasure principle is very much more secure, but the pleasure principle itself has no more escaped the taming process than any of the other drives have. In any event, the element within the excitation process that gives rise to the sensations of pleasure and unpleasure must be present in the secondary process just as much as in the primary one.

This would be the appropriate starting-point for further research. Our consciousness transmits to us from within ourselves sensations not only of pleasure and unpleasure, but also of a peculiar tension that again can be either pleasurable or unpleasurable. Are we then, on the basis of these sensations, to differentiate annexed and non-annexed energy processes from one another? Or does the sensation of tension relate to the *absolute* quantum, or perhaps level, of cathexis, whilst the incidence of pleasure/unpleasure reflects *changes* in the quantum of cathexis within a particular period of time? We also cannot fail to be struck by the fact that the life drives have so much more to do with our inner perception, since they behave as troublemakers and constantly bring tensions, the resolving of which is perceived as pleasurable, whereas the death drives appear to do their work unobtrusively. The pleasure principle seems to be positively subservient to the death drives; but it *does* also watch for any stimuli from without that are adjudged by both kinds of drives to be dangerous, and more particularly for any increases in stimulation emanating from within that make the task of living more difficult.

This all leads on to countless other questions to which at present we have no answers. We have to be patient and wait for new means and opportunities for research. And we must also be prepared to abandon any path that appears to be going nowhere, even though we may have followed it for quite some time. Only those fond believers who demand of science that it take the place of the catechism they have forsaken will object to a scientist developing or even changing his ideas. For the rest, let us take consolation for the slow progress of our scientific knowledge from the words of a poet (Rückert in his *Makamen des Hariri*):

Was man nicht erfliegen kann, muss man erhinken.

. . .

Die Schrift sagt, es ist keine Sünde zu hinken.

(Whatever we cannot achieve on the wing, we have to achieve at a patient limp ... Scripture tells us clear enough: it never was a sin to limp.)

(1920)

*Notes*

1. [See above, pp. 133–4.]

# From the History of an Infantile Neurosis [The 'Wolfman']

## 1 Preliminary Remarks

The case of illness that I shall document in the following pages[1] – once again only in fragmentary form – has a number of distinguishing peculiarities which demand some special comment before I embark on my account. The case concerns a young man who suffered a physical collapse in his eighteenth year following a gonorrhoeal infection; when, several years later, he came to me for psychoanalytic treatment he was completely dependent and incapable of autonomous existence. He had lived more or less normally during the decade of his youth which preceded the illness and had completed his secondary school studies without undue disruption. His earlier years, however, had been dominated by a serious neurotic disorder which began shortly before his fourth birthday as anxiety hysteria (animal phobia) and then turned into an obsessive-compulsive neurosis [Zwangsneurose], religious in content, the ramifications of which persisted into his tenth year.

I shall document only this infantile neurosis. Despite a direct demand to this effect on the part of my patient I have declined to write a complete history of his illness, treatment and recovery because I regard the exercise as technically impracticable and socially unacceptable. This deprives me of the possibility of demonstrating the connection between his childhood illness and the later, definitive episode. Of the latter I can say only that it caused our patient to spend long periods of time in German sanatoria where his case was classified by the highest authorities as 'manic-depressive psychosis'. This was an accurate diagnosis of the patient's father, whose life, rich in interests and activities, had regularly been disrupted by severe attacks of depression. As far as the son is concerned, however, I have been unable to observe, in the course of several years, any mood swings that go beyond what is consonant with the obvious psychic situation in terms of intensity and conditions of appearance. I have formed the impression that this case, like many others on which clinical psychiatry imposes a variety of changing diagnoses, is to be understood as a residual condition resulting from a case of obsessive-compulsive neurosis which has spontaneously run its course but where recovery has been incomplete.

My account will thus deal with an infantile neurosis analysed not during the course of the illness but fifteen years after it had come to an end. This situation has both advantages and disadvantages in comparison with the other. Analysis of the neurotic child himself will appear fundamentally more reliable but is unlikely to contain much by way of content; we have to put too many words and thoughts into the child's mouth and may perhaps find nevertheless that the deepest strata cannot be penetrated by consciousnes. Analysis of a childhood illness via the medium of adult memory, where the individual is now intellectually mature, is free of such limitations; but we must take into account the distortion and adjustment that takes place when, at a later date, we look back at our own past. The former situation brings more convincing results, perhaps, but the latter is by far the more instructive.

In any case it is fair to say that the analysis of childhood neuroses can lay claim to a particularly high degree of theoretical interest. Such analyses do about the same for the proper understanding of adult neurosis as children's dreams do for the dreams of adults. Not that they can be seen through more easily or are composed of fewer elements; the difficulty of empathizing with the inner life [*Seelenleben*] of the child in fact makes such dreams particularly hard work for the physician. However, they dispense with so many of the subsequent layers that the essential elements of the neurosis emerge with unmistakable clarity. It is well known that resistance to the results of psychoanalysis has taken a new form in the present phase of the battle over psychoanalysis. Previously it was enough to challenge the reality of the facts asserted by analysis and to this end the best technique appeared to be to avoid any kind of verification. Apparently, this procedure is gradually being exhausted and opposition now takes a different route, acknowledging the facts but disposing of the resulting conclusions by means of re-interpretation so that it is possible, after all, to fend off such offensive conclusions. The study of childhood neurosis shows that these attempts at reinterpretation, which are either shallow or forced, are entirely inadequate. It demonstrates that the libidinal drives which my opponents would so like to deny are of paramount importance in the formation of neurosis, while revealing the absence of any pursuit of distant cultural goals, about which the child knows nothing and which can therefore have no meaning for him.

Another feature that commends the analysis described here to the reader's attention relates to the severity of the illness and the length of treatment required. Those analyses that lead quickly to a favourable outcome are valuable for the therapist's self-confidence and demonstrate the medical significance of psychoanalysis; but they remain of scant importance in promoting our scientific understanding. We learn nothing new from them. They lead so quickly to success only because we already knew everything that was necessary to deal with them. We can only learn something new from analyses that present us with particular difficulties, which can only be surmounted after some considerable time. In these cases alone do we succeed in descending to the deepest and most primitive strata of inner development in order to retrieve solutions to problems which are posed by the forms assumed subsequently by that very development. Strictly speaking we might then say that only an analysis that has penetrated thus far is worthy of the name. Of course, a single case cannot enlighten us with regard to everything we should like to know. Or, more precisely, it could tell us everything if we were only in a position to comprehend it all and if the unpractised nature of our own perceptions did not oblige us to be content with just a little.

The case of illness that I shall describe in the following pages left nothing to be desired in terms of productive difficulties of this kind. The first years of treatment produced very little change. A fortunate constellation decreed that external circumstances made it possible, nevertheless, to continue with the therapeutic attempt. I can easily imagine that in less favourable circumstances the treatment would have been abandoned after a certain period of time. I can only say in favour of the physician's standpoint that he must be as 'timeless' in his approach as the unconscious itself if he wants to learn or achieve anything. In the end this can only happen if he is prepared to renounce any short-sighted therapeutic ambitions. There are few other cases in which one can expect the degree of patience, submissiveness, insight and trust that were required on the part of this patient and those closest to him. The analyst can tell himself, however, that the results achieved in one case by such lengthy endeavours will now help significantly to reduce the treatment time in another, equally severe case, and that in this way the timeless nature of the unconscious can progressively be overcome, once one has yielded to it on the first occasion.

The patient I am concerned with here maintained an unassailable position for a long time, entrenched behind an attitude of submissive indifference. He listened and understood but would allow nothing to come anywhere near him. One could not fault his intelligence, but it was as if it had been cut off by those involuntary [*triebhaft*] forces that determined his behaviour in the few human relationships left to him. He had to be educated for a long time before he could be persuaded to take an independent interest in our work and when, as a result of his efforts, the first moments of release occurred, he suspended the work immediately to prevent any further possibility of change and to maintain the comfortableness of the former situation. His timidity at the prospect of an independent existence was so great that it outweighed all the hardships of being ill. There was only one way of overcoming it. I had to wait until his attachment to me had grown strong enough to counterbalance it, and then I played off the one factor against the other. I decided – not without allowing myself to be guided by reliable signs that the timing was right – that the treatment would have to end by a certain date, no matter what progress had been made. I was determined to keep to this deadline; in the end my patient recognized that I was serious. Under the inexorable pressure of the deadline that I had set, his resistance, his fixed determination [*Fixierung*] to remain ill gave way, after which the analysis delivered up all the material which made it possible, within a disproportionately short length of time, to dissolve his inhibitions and eliminate his symptoms. It is from this last period of therapeutic work, during which the patient's resistance had at times completely disappeared and he gave an impression of the kind of lucidity normally only to be attained through hypnosis, that I derived all the explanations which enabled me to understand his infantile neurosis.

In this way the course of the treatment illustrated the dictum, long held to be true by the analytic technique, that the length of the road that the analysis must travel with the patient and the wealth of material that must be mastered on that road are as nothing compared to the resistance encountered during the work, and are only worthy of consideration in that they are necessarily proportional to that resistance. It is the same process as when a hostile army takes weeks and months to cross a stretch of land that an express train could cover in a few hours in peace time, and that one's own army had crossed in a matter of days a short time before.

A third peculiarity of the analysis in question only compounded the difficulty of deciding whether to write about it. On the whole the results are satisfactorily congruent with what we already knew, or else a clear connection can be established. However, many details appear so curious and incredible, even to me, that I hesitate to ask others to give them credence. I exhorted my patient to subject his memories to the most rigorous criticism but he found nothing improbable in what he had said and maintained that he was telling the truth. My readers can at least be sure that I am merely reporting something that arose as an independent experience and was not influenced in any way by my expectations. I could not do otherwise than recall those wise words that tell us there are more things in heaven and earth than are dreamt of in our philosophy. Anyone capable of screening out his acquired convictions even more thoroughly than I could no doubt discover still more of such matters.

### Note

1. This case history was written up shortly after conclusion of the treatment in winter 1914/15, in the light of the recent attempts to re-interpret psychoanalytic material undertaken by C. G. Jung and Adolf Adler. It is to be taken in conjunction with the essay published in the *Jahrbuch der Psychoanalyse* [*Yearbook of Psychoanalysis*], vol. VI (1916), 'Zur Geschichte der psychoanalytischen Bewegung' ['On the History of the Psycho-Analytic Movement', 1914] and supplements the essentially personal polemic which that essay contains with an objective evaluation of the analytic material. It was originally intended for the subsequent volume of the *Yearbook* but since its appearance in that journal was postponed indefinitely as a result of the retarding effects of the Great War, I decided to include it in this collection, organized by a new publisher. I had meanwhile been obliged to discuss much that should have found its first expression here in my *Vorlesungen zur Einführung in die Psychoanalyse* [*Introductory Lectures on Psychoanalysis*], given in 1916/17. There are no modifications of any note to the text of the first version; additional material is indicated in square brackets.

## II  *Survey of the Patient's Milieu and Medical History*

I can write neither a purely historical nor a purely pragmatic history of my patient; I can provide neither a treatment history nor a case history, but shall find myself obliged to combine the two approaches.

It is well known that no way has yet been found to embed the convictions that are gained through analysis within any account of the analysis itself. Certainly nothing would be gained by providing exhaustive minutes of what took place during analytic sessions; moreover, the techniques of the treatment preclude the production of any such minutes. An analysis of this kind is not published, then, to command the conviction of those who have hitherto shown themselves to be dismissive and incredulous. We expect to offer something new only to those researchers whose experiences with patients have already sown the seeds of conviction.

I shall begin by describing the child's world and relating those aspects of his childhood story that I learned without any particular effort; essentially nothing was added to this material over several years, and it remained just as opaque during the whole of this time.

His parents married young; it was a happy marriage, but the first shadows were soon to be cast by illness on both sides, his mother suffering from gynaecological complaints, his father from attacks of moroseness which resulted in his absence from the family home. Only much later did our patient develop some understanding of his father's illness, of course, but his mother's ill-health was known to him from his earliest years. For this reason she had relatively little to do with her children. One day, certainly before the age of four, holding his mother's hand, he listens to his mother complaining to the doctor whom she is accompanying on his way, and commits her words to memory, later using them of himself. He is not the only child, but has a sister some two years older, lively, gifted and impetuously naughty, who is to play an important role in his life.

He is cared for by an old children's nurse as far back as he can remember, working-class, uneducated and untiringly affectionate towards him. For her he is a substitute for her own son, who died young. The family lives on a country estate which in the summer they exchange for another country estate. Neither is far from the city. It marks a turning-point in his childhood when his parents sell the estates and move to the city. Close relatives often come to stay on one or other estate for long periods of time, his father's brothers, his mother's sisters and their children, his maternal grandparents. In the summer, his parents used to go away for several weeks. In a cover-memory [*Deckerinnerung*] he sees himself standing with his nurse, watching his father, mother and sister being driven away in a carriage, and then going calmly back into the house. He must have been very small at the time.[1] The next summer his sister was left at home and an English governess appointed, whose responsibility it was to supervise the children.

In later years he was told a great many things about his childhood.[2] Much of it he knew himself but without being able to make connections, of course, in terms of chronology or content. One story handed down in this way, which had been repeated in his presence on countless occasions because of his later illness, introduces the problem to whose solution we shall devote our attention. He is said to have been a very gentle, obedient and rather quiet child at first, so that people used to say he should have been the girl and his sister the boy. But once when his parents came back from their summer holiday they found him transformed. He had become discontented and irritable, was constantly flying into a passion, and would take offence at the slightest thing, raging and yelling like a savage, so that when this condition persisted, his parents expressed concern that it would not be possible to send him to school later on. It was the summer when the English governess was there; she had turned out to be a silly, cantankerous woman, and, incidentally, a slave to drink. His mother was thus inclined to see a connection between the boy's changed character and the English woman's influence, and assumed that he had been provoked by her treatment of him. His grandmother, a shrewd woman who had also spent the summer with the children, was of the opinion that the boy's touchiness was the result of constant quarrelling between the English governess and the children's nurse. The governess had repeatedly called the nurse a witch and obliged her to leave the room; the little boy had openly taken the part of his beloved 'Nanja' and made clear his hatred of the governess. Whatever the case, the English woman was sent away soon after the parents' return, without the child's disagreeable behaviour changing one whit.

The patient has retained his own memories of this difficult time.[3] He thinks he made the first scenes when he did not receive two lots of presents at Christmas time, as he had a right to expect, Christmas Day being also his birthday. His beloved Nanja was not exempt from his demands or his touchiness, indeed she was perhaps the most relentlessly tormented of all. But this phase of character change is indissolubly linked in his memory to many other strange and morbid phenomena, which he is unable to bring into any kind of chronological order. He bundles together everything I shall be describing here, things that cannot possibly have occurred at the same time and that are full of internal contradictions, attributing them all to one and the same period of time, which he calls 'when we were still living on the first estate'. They left this estate, he thinks, when he was five years old. He is thus able to tell me that he suffered from an anxiety that his sister exploited in order to torment him. There was a particular picture book, which showed a picture of a wolf standing on its hind legs and stepping out. Whenever he set eyes on this picture he would start to scream furiously, fearing that the wolf would come and gobble him up. His sister, however, always managed to arrange matters so that he would have to see this picture and took great delight in his terror. At the same time he was also afraid of other animals, both large and small. On one occasion he was chasing after a lovely big butterfly with yellow-striped wings that had pointed tips, trying to catch it. (Probably a 'swallowtail'.) Suddenly he was seized by a dreadful fear of the creature and gave up his pursuit, screaming. He also experienced fear and disgust at the sight of beetles and caterpillars. And yet he was able to recall that at the same period he had tortured beetles and cut up caterpillars; horses also gave him an uncanny feeling. He would scream if a horse was beaten and once had to leave a circus for this reason. On other occasions he enjoyed beating horses himself. Whether these two conflicting attitudes to animals really held sway simultaneously, or whether one had not in fact supplanted the other – though if that were the case, in what order and when – his memory would not allow him to decide. He was also unable to say whether the difficult period was replaced by a period of illness or whether it had persisted throughout. In any case, in the light of what he went on to say, one was justified in making the assumption that in those childhood years he had gone through what could clearly be recognized as an episode of obsessive-compulsive neurosis. He told me that for a long period of time he had been very pious. He had had to pray at great length and cross himself endlessly before he could go to sleep at night. Every evening he would do the rounds of the holy pictures hanging in his room, using a chair to stand on, and bestow a reverent kiss on each one. It was somewhat out of keeping, then – or actually perhaps entirely in keeping – with this pious ritual that he recalled blasphemous thoughts coming into his mind, as if planted there by the devil. He was obliged to think: 'God – swine' or 'God – crud'. Once, journeying to a German spa, he was tortured by a compulsion to think of the Holy Trinity when he saw three piles of horse dung or other excrement lying on the road. At this time he used also to adhere to a peculiar ritual if he saw people who inspired pity in him, beggars, cripples, old men. He had to breathe out noisily in order not to become like one of them, and under certain conditions also had to inhale deeply. I was naturally inclined to assume that these clear symptoms of obsessive-compulsive neurosis belonged to a somewhat later period of time and a later stage of development than the signs of anxiety and the cruel behaviour towards animals.

Our patient's more mature years were characterized by a very unpromising relationship with his father, who after repeated depressive episodes could now no longer conceal the morbid aspects of his character. In the early years of his childhood it had been a most affectionate relationship, and this was how his son remembered him. His father was very fond of him and enjoyed playing with him. Even as a little boy he was proud of his father and would only ever say that he wanted to grow up to be a gentleman just like him. His Nanja had told him that his sister was his mother's child, but he was his father's, and this pleased him greatly. As his childhood came to an end he became estranged from his father. His father undoubtedly preferred his sister and he was very hurt by this. Later, fear of his father became the dominant emotion.

When he was getting on for eight all the symptoms the patient ascribed to the phase of existence which had begun with the difficult period disappeared. They did not disappear all at once but returned a few more times, finally ceding, in the patient's opinion, to the influence of the teachers and tutors who replaced his female carers. Put very briefly, then, the enigmas which yielded up their solutions in the course of the analysis are as follows: where did the boy's sudden change of character come from, what was the meaning of his phobia and his perversions, how did he acquire his compulsive [*Zwangs-*] piety and what was the connection between all these phenomena? Let me remind the reader once again that our therapeutic work was directed towards a later neurotic episode of recent occurrence and that information about those earlier problems could only emerge if the course of the analysis led us away from the present for a while, obliging us to take a detour through the prehistory of the patient's childhood.

### Notes

1. 2½ years old. It later became possible to say quite definitely when most things had taken place.
2. As a general rule information of this kind can be regarded as material whose credibility is beyond question. An obvious possibility, requiring no effort, is therefore to fill in the gaps in a patient's memory by making inquiry of older family members; however I cannot warn strongly enough against such techniques. The stories told by the patient's relatives when invited and exhorted to provide such information are open to all the critical misgivings that could possibly apply. One regularly regrets having made oneself dependent on such information, and in asking for it one has undermined the relationship of trust in the analysis and invoked a different authority. Everything that it is possible to remember will eventually emerge in the course of the analysis.

3. [The phrase used by Freud, *'schlimme Zeit'*, refers both to the boy's naughtiness and to the fact that it was a painful period for him. I have attempted to convey this ambiguity by using the adjective 'difficult'.]

## III  *Seduction and its Immediate Consequences*

Understandably my suspicions fell first on the English governess, whose presence in the house had coincided with the change in the boy. He had retained two cover-memories relating to her, which in themselves were incomprehensible. Once, as she was walking ahead of them, she said to the children following behind: 'Look at my little tail!' On another occasion her hat blew away when they were out on a trip, to the great satisfaction of brother and sister. These pointed towards the castration complex and might allow us to reconstruct, say, a threat made by her against the boy, contributing significantly to the development of abnormal behaviour. It is not in the least dangerous to put such reconstructions [*Konstruktionen*] to the analysand: they do no harm to the analysis if they are erroneous and in any case one does not give voice to them if there is not some prospect of coming closer to the truth in the process. The immediate effect of putting forward these ideas was the appearance of dreams that it was not possible to interpret completely but which always seemed to play around with the same content. The subject of the dreams, as far as one could tell, was aggressive action on the boy's part towards his sister or the governess, which resulted in energetic rebuke and punishment. As if he had tried . . . after a bath . . . to expose his sister's nakedness . . . to tear off layers of clothing . . . or her veil . . . and the like. It was not possible, however, to arrive by means of interpretation at any definite content, and, once we had formed the impression that the same material was being processed in these dreams in ever-changing ways, it was clear how we were to understand what were apparently involuntary memories [*Reminiszenzen*]. It could only be a question of fantasies that the dreamer had once entertained about his childhood, probably during puberty, and which had now emerged again in a form so difficult to recognize.

We learnt what they meant in one fell swoop when the patient suddenly recalled the fact that his sister had seduced him 'when he was still very little, when they were living on the first estate' into sexual pursuits. First came the memory that on the lavatory, which the children often used together, she had issued the invitation: 'Shall we show each other our bottoms?' and had then suited the action to the word. Later we arrived at the more essential elements of the seduction and all the accompanying details of time and locality. It was in the spring, at a time when the father was away from home; the children were playing on the floor in one room while their mother was working in the next room. His sister had reached for his penis and played with it, saying incomprehensible things about Nanja all the while, as if by way of explanation. She said that Nanja did this all the time with everyone, the gardener, for example, she would turn him upside down and then take hold of his genitals.

This made it possible to understand the fantasies we had guessed at earlier. They were intended to erase the memory of an event which later offended the patient's sense of masculine pride, achieving this goal by replacing historical truth with its wished-for opposite. According to these fantasies he had not taken the passive role towards his sister, but on the contrary had been aggressive, had wanted to see his sister without her clothes on, had been rejected and punished, and had thus fallen into the rage recounted so insistently by domestic tradition. It was also expedient to weave the governess into this story, since his mother and his grandmother attributed most of the blame to her, after all, for his bouts of rage. His fantasies thus corresponded exactly to the creation of sagas, by means of which a nation which later becomes great and proud seeks to conceal the insignificance and misadventure of its origins.

In reality the governess could have played only the most remote part in the seduction and its consequences. The scenes with his sister took place in the spring of that same year in which the

English governess arrived to take the parents' place during the midsummer months. The boy's hostility to the governess in fact came about in a different way. By calumniating the children's nurse and saying she was a witch the governess was following in his sister's footsteps, since it was she who had first told him those dreadful things about their nurse, and this gave him the opportunity to express the repugnance that, as we shall learn, he had come to feel for his sister after she had seduced him.

That his sister had seduced him was certainly no fantasy, however. Its credibility was strengthened by a piece of information he received in later, more mature years and had never forgotten. In a conversation about his sister, a cousin, more than a decade older, had told him that he could remember very well what a forward, sensual little thing she had been. As a child of four or five she had once sat down on his lap and unfastened his trousers to take hold of his penis.

I shall interrupt the story of my patient's childhood for a moment in order to speak of this sister, her development, her subsequent fate and the influence she had over him. She was two years older and always ahead of him. Boisterous and tomboyish as a child, she underwent a dazzling intellectual development distinguished by an acute and realistic understanding; she favoured the natural sciences as an avenue of study yet at the same time produced poems of which their father had a very high opinion. She was intellectually far superior to her numerous early suitors and used to make fun of them. In her early twenties, however, she grew morose, complained that she was not pretty enough and withdrew from all social contact. Sent away on a tour in the company of an older lady, a friend of the family, she told the most improbable stories on her return of how her companion had ill-treated her, yet her inward attention remained obviously fixed on the woman who had allegedly tormented her. On a second journey, which took place soon afterwards, she poisoned herself and died a long way from home. Her state of mind probably corresponded to the onset of dementia praecox. Her case was among those testifying to a considerable inherited tendency to neuropathic affliction in the family, but it was by no means the only one. An uncle on the father's side, who lived for many years as an eccentric, died with every indication of having suffered from severe obsessive-compulsive neurosis; among the more distant relatives a considerable number have been and are afflicted by more minor nervous disorders.

In childhood our patient saw his sister – leaving aside for a moment the matter of the seduction – as an uncomfortable rival for their parents' approval and found the superiority that she so ruthlessly demonstrated highly oppressive. He particularly envied her the respect that their father demonstrated for her mental capabilities and her intellectual achievements, while he, inhibited intellectually since the episode of obsessive-compulsive neurosis, had to accept being held in lesser regard. From the age of thirteen onwards his relationship with his sister began to improve; similar intellectual aptitudes and shared opposition to their parents brought them so close that they were on the best and friendliest of terms. In the turbulent sexual agitation of puberty he ventured to approach her with a view to physical intimacy. When she rejected him with as much determination as skill he immediately turned from her to a young peasant girl, a servant in the house who bore the same name as his sister. In doing so he took a decisive step as far as his choice of heterosexual object was concerned, for all the girls he later fell in love with, often with the clearest signs of compulsion, were also servant girls, whose education and intelligence necessarily lagged far behind his own. We cannot deny that if all these objects of his love were substitutes for the sister who had refused him, then a tendency to demean his sister, to neutralize the intellectual superiority which had once so oppressed him, played a crucial part in his choice of object.

Alfred Adler subordinates everything, including the individual's sexual attitudes, to motives of this kind, arising from the will to power and the drive to assert oneself [*Behauptungstrieb*]. Without for a moment wishing to deny the validity of such motives of power and prerogative, I have never been convinced that they are able to support the dominant, exclusive role he attributes to them. If I had not seen the analysis of my patient through to the end, my observation of this case would have obliged me to modify my prejudice in the direction of Adler's theories. The concluding stages of the analysis provided unexpected new material, however, from which it became evident that these power motives (in this case, the tendency to demean) had only governed the patient's choice of object in the sense that they had contributed to it, rationalized it, while the real, more profoundly determining element allowed me to hold fast to my earlier convictions.[1]

When news of his sister's death reached him, our patient told me that he felt barely a trace of pain. He forced himself into an outward show of mourning and was able coolly to rejoice in the fact that he was now the sole heir to the family fortunes. He had already been suffering from his more recent illness for some years when this occurred. I must admit, however, that this one statement made me hesitate in my diagnostic judgement of the case for some considerable time. True, it was to be supposed that his pain at the loss of the most beloved member of his family would be inhibited in its expression by continued jealousy towards her and the intrusion of his now unconsciously felt incestuous love, but I needed to find some kind of substitute for the outburst of pain that had failed to take place. I eventually found one in another expression of strong feeling, which had remained incomprehensible to him. A few months after his sister's death he had himself made a journey to the region where she had died; there he sought out the grave of a great poet whom at that time he idealized, and shed hot tears over the grave. He himself was perplexed by his reaction, for he knew that more than two generations had passed since the death of the poet he so admired. He understood what had happened only when he remembered that their father used to compare his dead sister's poems to those of the great poet. An error in his narrative had given me another indication as to the true meaning of this homage apparently paid to the poet, which I was able to draw his attention to at this point. He had repeatedly told me earlier that his sister had shot herself and then been obliged to correct himself, since she had taken poison. The poet, however, had been shot, in a duel.

I shall now take up the brother's story again, and for a while I must describe what actually took place. It turned out that at the time when his sister set about seducing him the boy was $3\frac{1}{4}$ years old. It happened, as I have said, in the spring of that same year in which his parents found him so radically changed on their return home in the autumn. It seems obvious, then, to assume that there was some connection between this transformation and the awakening of sexual activity that had taken place in the intervening period.

How did the boy react to his older sister's enticements? The answer is that he rejected her, but he rejected the person, not the thing. His sister was not acceptable to him as a sexual object, probably because rivalry for their parents' love had already determined his relationship with her as a hostile one. He avoided her and her advances soon ceased. In her place, however, he sought to win for himself another, more beloved person, and the things his sister herself had said, invoking Nanja as her model, guided his choice towards Nanja. He thus began to play with his penis in front of Nanja, something that must be taken, as in so many other cases where children do not conceal masturbation, as an attempt at seduction. Nanja disappointed him, telling him with a serious expression that that was a naughty thing to do. Children who did that would get a 'wound' there.

We can trace the effect of this remark, which was to all intents and purposes a threat, in various directions. His attachment to Nanja became less strong. He could have been angry with her; later, when the tantrums began, it became clear that she had indeed enraged him. Yet it was characteristic of him that initially he would stubbornly defend against anything new, whatever libido position he was having to give up. When the governess took the stage and insulted Nanja, driving her out of the room and trying to destroy her authority, he in fact exaggerated his love for the person under threat and behaved negatively and defiantly towards the attacking governess. Nevertheless he began secretly to look for another sexual object. The seduction had given him the passive sexual objective of having his genitals touched; we shall learn in due course the person with whom he hoped to achieve this and the paths that led to his choice.

It is entirely in accordance with our expectations to learn that his sexual inquiries began with his first experiences of genital arousal and that he soon came up against the problem of castration. At this time he had the opportunity to watch two girls urinate, his sister and her friend. He was bright enough to have been able to grasp the true state of affairs from this alone but instead behaved in the same way as we know other male children to behave. He rejected the idea that he was seeing confirmation here of the wound with which Nanja had threatened him, and explained it to himself as the girls' 'front bottom'. This decision did not mark the end of the subject of castration, however; he found new indications of it in everything he heard. Once, when sticks of barley sugar were handed out to the children, the governess, who was inclined to lurid fantasies, declared that they were chopped-up pieces of snake. This caused him to remember that his father had once come upon a snake when out for a walk and had chopped it into pieces with his walking-stick. He had been told the story (from *Reineke Fuchs* [*Reynard the Fox*]) where the wolf tried to catch fish in winter and used his tail as bait, whereupon his tail froze in the ice and broke off. He learnt the different names used for horses depending on the intactness of their sex. He was thus preoccupied with the thought of castration without believing in it or being frightened by it. Other problems relating to sexuality were posed by the fairy tales with which he became acquainted at this time. In 'Little Red Riding Hood' and 'The Seven Little Kids' children were pulled out of the body of the wolf. Was the wolf female, then, or could men also carry children in their bodies? At this time he had not yet decided on the answer to that question. He had no fear of wolves as yet, incidentally, at the time of these investigations.

One remark made by our patient will clear the way to an understanding of the change in character that manifested itself during his parents' absence and that was distantly connected with his sister's seduction. He relates that soon after Nanja had rejected and threatened him he gave up masturbation. *The sexual life directed by the genital zone, which was beginning to stir, had succumbed to external inhibition, and this influence had flung it back into an earlier phase of pre-genital organization.* As a result of the suppression of masturbation, the boy's sexual life became anal-sadistic in character. He became irritable and took pleasure in tormenting animals and people, using this to achieve satisfaction. The principal object of torment was his beloved Nanja, whom he knew how to torture until she burst into tears. In this way he took his revenge for the rejection he had received at her hands, and at the same time satisfied his sexual desires in a form corresponding to this regressive phase. He started to be cruel to tiny creatures, catching flies so that he could pull off their wings, stamping on beetles; in his imagination he also enjoyed beating large animals, horses. These were entirely active, sadistic pursuits; we shall hear something of his anal impulses during this period in another context.

It is valuable to learn that fantasies of a quite different kind, contemporaneous with these, also surfaced in the patient's memory, the content of which was that boys were being punished and beaten, beaten in particular on the penis; and we can easily guess for whom these anonymous objects served as whipping-boys by looking at other fantasies, which took the form of the heir-apparent being locked in a narrow room and beaten. He himself was obviously the heir-apparent; in his imagination his sadism was turned against himself, veering into masochism. The detail of the sexual organ itself taking its punishment allows us to conclude that a sense of guilt, directed at his masturbation, was already at work in this transformation.

In analysis there could be no doubt that these passive aspirations [*Strebungen*] emerged at the same time as, or very soon after, the active, sadistic ones.[2] This is in keeping with an uncommonly distinct, intense and persistent *ambivalence* on the part of the patient, expressing itself here for the first time in the symmetrical development of contradictory pairs of partial drives. This behaviour was in future to remain as characteristic of him as the further trait that none of the libido positions which he achieved was ever in fact fully superseded by a later one. Each would exist alongside all the others, allowing him to vacillate unceasingly in a way that proved incompatible with the acquisition of a fixed character.

The boy's masochistic tendencies bring us to another point, which I have not mentioned up until now because it can only be firmly established through analysis of the subsequent phase of development. I have already mentioned the fact that, after Nanja rejected him, he broke away from her and focused his libidinal expectations on a different sexual object. This person was his father, then absent from home. He was guided towards this choice, no doubt, by the coincidence of various factors, including chance ones such as his memory of the dismembered snake; above all, however, he was renewing his first, original choice of object, which had been made, in accordance with the narcissism of the small child, by way of identification. We have already heard that his father had been a much-admired example to him, and that when asked what he wanted to be he used to answer: 'A gentleman like my father.' The object of identification in his active current [*Strömung*] now became the sexual object of a passive current in the anal-sadistic phase. We gain the impression that his sister's seduction of him had forced him into a passive role and given him a passive sexual objective. Under the continuing influence of this experience, he followed a path from sister to Nanja to father, from the passive attitude towards a woman to the same towards a man, and yet in doing so he was able to connect up with an earlier, spontaneous stage of development. The father was once again his object, identification having been succeeded by object-choice, as is appropriate at a higher stage of development; transformation of an active attitude into a passive one was both outcome and sign of the seduction that had taken place in the intervening period. Taking an active attitude towards the excessively powerful figure of the father during the sadistic phase would of course have been much less feasible. On his father's return, in late summer or autumn, his tantrums and furious scenes were put to a different use. They had served an active, sadistic purpose towards Nanja; now, towards his father, their purpose was masochistic. By parading his difficult behaviour he wanted to compel his father to punish and beat him and in this way gain from him the masochistic sexual satisfaction he desired. His screaming fits were nothing other than attempts at seduction. In accordance with the motivation behind masochism, he would also have found satisfaction for his sense of guilt in being punished. One memory had stored up a recollection for him of how, during one such exhibition of difficult behaviour, his screaming gets louder as soon as his father comes in; yet his father does not beat him but attempts to calm him down by throwing the cushions from the bed up in the air and catching them again.

I do not know how many times, in the face of a child's inexplicable naughtiness, parents and mentors would have occasion to recall this typical connection. The child who is behaving so wildly makes a confession, intending to provoke punishment. In being punished the child is seeking both the appeasement of its sense of guilt and the satisfaction of its masochistic sexual aspirations.

We owe the further clarification of this case to a memory, which came to the patient with great certainty, that the symptoms of anxiety had only joined the other signs of character change once a certain incident had occurred. Before then there had been no anxiety; immediately after this occurrence he found himself tormented by anxiety. We can state with certainty that the point at which this transformation took place was just before his fourth birthday. Thanks to this clue, the period of childhood with which we are particularly concerned can be divided into two phases, a first phase of difficult behaviour and perversity which lasted from his seduction at the age of $3\frac{1}{4}$ until his fourth birthday, and a longer, subsequent phase dominated by the signs of neurosis. The incident that permits us to draw the dividing line was no external trauma, however, but a dream, from which he awoke beset with anxiety.

*Notes*

1. See below, p. 281.
2. By passive aspirations I mean those with a passive sexual objective, but what I have in mind is not a transformation of the drives but a transformation of their objective.


## IV  *The Dream and the Primal Scene*

I have already published this dream elsewhere[1] because of the fairy-tale elements it contains and so I shall begin by reproducing what I wrote at that time:

'I dreamed that it is night and I am lying in my bed (the foot of my bed was under the window, and outside the window there was a row of old walnut trees. I know that it was winter in my dream, and night-time). Suddenly the window opens of its own accord and terrified, I see that there are a number of white wolves sitting in the big walnut tree outside the window. There were six or seven of them. The wolves were white all over and looked more like foxes or sheepdogs because they had big tails like foxes and their ears were pricked up like dogs watching something. Obviously fearful that the wolves were going to gobble me up I screamed and woke up. My nurse hurried to my bedside to see what had happened. It was some time before I could be convinced that it had only been a dream, because the image of the window opening and the wolves sitting in the tree was so clear and lifelike. Eventually I calmed down, feeling as if I had been liberated from danger, and went back to sleep.

'The only action in the dream was the opening of the window, for the wolves were sitting quite still in the branches of the tree, to the right and left of the tree trunk, not moving at all, and looking right at me. It looked as if they had turned their full attention on me. I think that was my first anxiety-dream. I was three or four at the time, certainly no more than five. From then on until I was ten or eleven I was always afraid of seeing something terrible in my dreams.'

He then drew a picture of the tree with the wolves sitting in it, too, which confirms the description he gave [Fig. 1]. Analysis of the dream brought the following material to light.

He always related this dream to the memory that in those childhood years he would express a quite monstrous anxiety at the picture of a wolf that was to be found in his book of fairy tales. His elder sister, highly superior, would tease him by showing him this very picture on some pretext or other, at which he would begin to scream in horror. In this picture the

Fig. 1

wolf was standing on his back paws, about to take a step forward, paws outstretched and ears pricked. He thought this picture was there as an illustration to the fairy tale 'Little Red Riding Hood'.

Why are the wolves white? That makes him think of the sheep which were kept in large flocks quite near the estate. His father sometimes took him to visit the flocks of sheep and he was always very proud and happy when this happened. Later on – inquiries suggest that it could easily have been shortly before this dream took place – an epidemic broke out among the sheep. His father sent for one of Pasteur's disciples, who inoculated the sheep, but after the inoculation they died in even greater numbers than before.

How did the wolves get up in the tree? A story occurs to him that he had heard his grandfather tell. He cannot remember whether it was before or after the dream, but the content of the story strongly supports the first possibility. The story goes as follows: a tailor is sitting in his room working when the window opens and in leaps a wolf. The tailor hits out at him with his measuring stick – no, he corrects himself, he grabs him by the tail and pulls it off, so that the wolf runs away, terrified. Some time later the tailor goes into the woods and suddenly sees a pack of wolves coming towards him, and so he escapes from them by climbing up a tree. At first the wolves do not know what to do, but the maimed one, who is also there and wants his revenge on the tailor, suggests that one should climb on another's back until the last one can reach the tailor. He himself – a powerful old wolf – will form the base of this pyramid. The wolves do as he says, but the tailor recognizes the wolf who visited him, the one he punished, and he calls out suddenly, as he did before: 'Grab the grey fellow by the tail.' The wolf who has lost his tail remembers what happened, and runs away, terrified, while the others all tumble down in a heap.

In this story we find the tree that the wolves are sitting on in the dream. There is also an unambiguous link with the castration complex, however. It is the *old* wolf who loses his tail to the tailor. The foxtails which the wolves have in the dream are no doubt compensation for the absence of a tail.

Why are there six or seven wolves? It seemed that we could not answer this question, until I expressed some doubt as to whether his anxiety-image could in fact have referred to the tale of Little Red Riding Hood. That fairy tale gives rise to only two illustrations, the meeting of Little Red Riding Hood and the wolf in the forest, and the scene where the wolf is lying in bed wearing Grandmother's nightcap. Another fairy tale must therefore be concealed behind his memory of that picture. He soon found that it could only be the story of 'The Wolf and the Seven Little Kids'. Here we find the number seven, and also the number six, for the wolf gobbles up only six of the little kids while the seventh hides in the clock-case. We also find white in this story, for the wolf has the baker whiten his paws after the little kids recognize him on his first visit by his grey paw. The two fairy tales have a great deal in common, incidentally. In both we find people being eaten up, the stomach being cut open, the people who have been eaten taken out again, heavy stones being put back in their place and finally the big bad wolf being killed in both cases. In the story of the little kids we find the tree as well. After he has eaten his fill the wolf lies down under a tree and snores.

I shall have a particular reason to concern myself with this dream in another context, where I shall evaluate it and consider its possible meaning in greater depth. It is a first anxiety-dream, remembered from childhood, the content of which gives rise to a very particular sort of interest in the context of other dreams which followed soon after, and certain incidents in the dreamer's childhood. Here we shall confine ourselves to the dream's relationship to two fairy tales which have a great deal in common, 'Little Red Riding Hood' and 'The Wolf and the Seven Little Kids'. The impression left on the child dreamer by these fairy tales found expression in a veritable phobia about animals, distinguished from other similar cases only by the fact that the animal that gave rise to the anxiety was not a readily accessible object (such as a horse or a dog) but one familiar only from stories and picture books.

I shall look at the explanation for these animal phobias and the significance that we should attribute to them on another occasion. Here, I shall anticipate myself only by remarking that this explanation is entirely in keeping with the main characteristic which the dreamer's neurosis reveals in later life. Fear of the father was the most powerful motive for his illness and an ambivalent attitude towards any father-substitute dominated his life, just as it dominated his behaviour in the consulting room.

If, in my patient's case, the wolf was merely the first father-substitute, the question arises as to whether the secret content of the tale of the wolf who gobbled up the little kids or the tale of Red Riding Hood is anything other than infantile fear of the father.[2] My patient's father, incidentally, had a characteristic tendency to *'affectionate scolding'*, of the kind used by many people in dealing with their children, and the teasing threat 'I'll gobble you up' may have been uttered more than once when the father, later so strict, used to cuddle and play with his little son. One of my patients told me that her two children were never able to feel really fond of their grandfather because he used to frighten them, in the course of his affectionate games, by telling them he would cut open their tummies.

Leaving aside everything in this essay that anticipates how we might apply the dream, let us return to the immediate issue of how we should interpret it. I should point out that to arrive at an interpretation was an exercise that took several years. The patient told me about the dream very early on, and quickly embraced my conviction that it concealed the cause of his infantile neurosis. In the course of the treatment we often came back to the dream but only arrived at a complete understanding of it during the last months of the therapy, thanks to spontaneous work on the part of my patient. He had always emphasized that two moments in the dream had made the most powerful impression on him, first, the utter calm of the wolves, their motionless stance, and second, the tense attentiveness with which they all stared at him. The sense of reality as the dream came to an end, which persisted after he had woken up, also seemed noteworthy to him.

Let us take up this last point. Experience of the interpretation of dreams tells us that there is a particular meaning to this sense of reality. It assures us that something in the latent material of the dream lays claim to reality in the dreamer's memory, and thus that the dream refers to an incident that actually took place and has not merely been fantasized. I am referring, of course, only to the reality of something unknown; the conviction, for example, that his grandfather really told him the story of the tailor and the wolf, or that the tale of 'Little Red Riding Hood' or 'The Seven Little Kids' had really been read to him could never be replaced by that sense of reality which outlasts the dream. The dream appeared to point to an incident the reality of which is emphasized by its very contrast with the unreality of the fairy tales.

If we were to assume the existence of an unknown scene of this kind, concealed behind the content of the dream, i.e. a scene which had already been forgotten at the time of the dream, it must have occurred at a very early age. The dreamer tells us after all that 'when I had the dream I was three or four, certainly no more than five'. We might add, 'And the dream reminded me of something that must have taken place even earlier.'

Those aspects of the manifest dream-content singled out by the dreamer, the moments of attentive watching and motionlessness, had to lead us to the content of that scene. We naturally expect this material to be distorted in some way, perhaps even to be distorted into its opposite, as it reproduces the unknown material of the scene.

It was possible to draw a number of conclusions from the raw material provided by the first analysis, conclusions that could be fitted into the context we were seeking. Concealed behind the mention of sheep-breeding we could find evidence for his exploration of sexuality, interests that could be satisfied in the course of the visits he made together with his father; but there must also have been hints of a fear of death, since for the most part the sheep died in the epidemic. What stands out most in the dream, that is, the wolves in the tree, led directly to the grandfather's story, the most gripping aspect of which could hardly have been anything other than its connection with the topic of castration, the stimulus for the dream.

The first, incomplete analysis of the dream had further led us to infer that the wolf was a father-substitute, so that this first anxiety-dream had brought to light the fear of his father, which was to dominate his life from then on. It is true that even this conclusion was not yet a definite one. However, if we assemble the elements that can be deduced from the material provided by the dreamer, the results of the preliminary analysis, we find the following fragments, which could be used as the basis of a reconstruction:

*An actual event – occurring at a very early age – watching – motionlessness – sexual problems – castration – the father – something terrible.*

One day our patient took up the interpretation of the dream once again. He thought that the part of the dream in which 'suddenly the window opens of its own accord' is not entirely explained by its relation to the window at which the tailor is sitting and through which the wolf comes into the room. He thought it must mean: my eyes are suddenly opened. I am asleep then, and suddenly wake up, and then I see something: the tree with the wolves. There was nothing to object to here, but we could take it further. He had woken up, and had seen something. The attentive gaze, which in the dream he attributes to the wolves, is actually to be ascribed to him. At a decisive point a reversal [*Verkehrung*] had taken place, indicated, incidentally, by another reversal in the manifest content of the dream. For it is a reversal for the wolves to be sitting in the tree, whereas in the grandfather's story they are down below and are unable to climb up into the tree.

Now, what if the other moment emphasized by the dreamer had also been distorted by reversal or inversion [*Umkehrung*]? Instead of absence of motion (the wolves sit there motionless, gazing at him but not moving) we should have: violent movement. He woke up suddenly, then, and saw a scene of violent excitement which he watched with tense attentiveness. In the one case distortion consists in the exchange of subject and object, active and passive modes, being watched instead of watching; in the other case it consists in transformation into the opposite: calm instead of excitement.

Further progress in understanding the dream was made on another occasion by the abruptly surfacing notion that the tree was the Christmas tree. And now he knew that he had dreamed the dream shortly before Christmas, in anticipation of Christmas itself. Since Christmas Day was also his birthday it was now possible to establish a definite time for the dream and the transformation which it brought in its wake. It was shortly before his fourth birthday. He had fallen asleep in excited anticipation of the day that was to bring him two lots of presents. We know that, in circumstances like these, the child readily anticipates the satisfaction of his wishes in dreams. And so in the dream it was already Christmas, and the content of the dream showed him his presents, the gifts that were intended for him hanging on the tree.

But instead of presents they had turned into – wolves, and the dream ended with his fear that the wolf (probably his father) would gobble him up, so that he sought refuge with his nurse. Our knowledge of his sexual development before the dream took place makes it possible for us to fill in the gap in the dream and explain the way in which satisfaction was transformed into fear. Among the wishes that informed his dreams, the strongest one that stirred must have been for the sexual satisfaction he longed to receive from his father. The strength of that wish succeeded in refreshing the long-forgotten memory trace [*Erinnerungsspur*] of a scene that could show him what sexual satisfaction from his father looked like, and the result was fright, horror at the satisfaction of his wish, repression of the impulse represented by the wish and therefore flight from the father towards the less dangerous figure of the nurse.

The significance of this Christmas date had been preserved in the alleged memory that his first tantrum had occurred because he had not been satisfied by his Christmas presents. This memory draws together true and false elements: it could not hold true without some modification since his parents had frequently repeated their assurance that his difficult behaviour had already been apparent after their return in the autumn and not just at Christmas, but the crucial aspect, the relationship between tantrums, Christmas and a lack of sexual satisfaction, had been established in this memory.

What was the image, however, conjured up by those sexual yearnings at work in the night, an image capable of scaring him away so powerfully from the fulfilment he desired? According to the material provided by the analysis there was one condition it had to fulfil: it had to be of a kind which would convince him of the existence of castration. Castration anxiety then became the driving force behind the transformation of his feelings.

We are now approaching the point at which I must abandon my attempt to draw on the actual course of the analysis. I fear that it will also be the point at which the reader will abandon his faith in what I have to say.

What was activated that night out of the chaos of unconscious traces left by a memory imprint [*Eindruck*] was the image of coitus between the boy's parents in conditions which were not entirely usual and which lent themselves to observation. It gradually became possible to find satisfactory answers to all the questions that might be prompted by this scene, given that that first dream was reproduced endlessly in countless variations during the therapy, and on each occasion the analysis provided the wished-for explanations. In this way we were first able to establish the child's age when he observed his parents, some 18 months.[3] At the time he was suffering from malaria, and the attacks recurred at a certain time each day.[4] From the age of nine onwards he was periodically subject to depressive moods, which would set in during the afternoon, reaching their lowest point at around five o'clock. This symptom was still present during the analytic treatment. The recurrent depression replaced the previous attacks of fever or lassitude; five o'clock was either the time when the fever reached its height or the time when he observed the coitus, supposing that the two did not coincide.[5] He was probably in his parents' bedroom precisely because he was ill. This episode of illness, which is also directly corroborated by tradition, suggests that the incident took place in the summer, so that we can assume an age of n + 1½ for the boy born on Christmas Day. He had thus been asleep in his cot in his parents' room and woke up, possibly as a result of mounting fever, in the afternoon, perhaps at five o'clock, the hour that was later to be marked by depression. It would be in accordance with our assumption that it was a hot summer's day if his parents had retired for an afternoon siesta, only half dressed.[6] On waking, he witnessed 'coitus a tergo' [from behind], repeated three times;[7] he could see his mother's genitals as well as his father's penis and understood what was happening as well as what it meant.[8] Eventually he disturbed his parents' intercourse in a way that will be discussed later.

Fundamentally, there is nothing out of the ordinary, nothing that gives the impression that we are dealing here with the product of wild imaginings, in the fact of a young married couple, married only a few years, allowing a siesta on a hot summer's day to evolve into tender relations, ignoring as they did so the presence of the 18-month-old boy asleep in his cot. I would say rather that it is entirely banal, an everyday occurrence, and even the coital position that we must infer does not alter this judgement in any way. Particularly since there is nothing in the evidence to suggest that coitus took place each time from behind. A single occasion would have sufficed, after all, to allow the spectator the opportunity to make observations that would have been rendered more difficult, impossible even, if the lovers had assumed a different position. The content of the scene itself is thus no argument against its credibility. The suspicion of improbability will be raised on three other counts: that at the tender age of 18 months a child should be capable of perceiving such a complicated event and retaining it so accurately in the unconscious; second, that it is possible at the age of 4 to process the memory imprints received in this way, belatedly advancing to an understanding of what was seen; and, finally, that the child should succeed by whatever method in making conscious the details of such a scene, witnessed and understood in such circumstances, in a way that is both coherent and convincing.[9]

Later I shall subject these and other misgivings to careful scrutiny; let me assure the reader that I am no less critical than he in my acceptance of the child's observation, and would ask him to join me in resolving to believe *provisionally* in the reality of this scene. Let us first continue to study the way in which this 'primal scene' [*Urszene*] is related to the patient's dream, his symptoms and his life history. We shall then consider separately the effects proceeding from the essential content of the scene and from one of the visual imprints contained in it.

By this last I mean the positions he saw his parents assume, the man upright and the woman bent over, rather like an animal. We have already heard how his sister used to scare him during his period of great anxiety by showing him the picture in his fairy-tale book in which the wolf is depicted standing on his hind legs with one foot forward, paws outstretched and ears pricked. While in therapy with me he never tired of searching in antiquarian book-shops until he found his childhood picture-book and recognized in one of the illustrations to 'The Tale of the Seven Little Kids' the image that had so terrified him. He thought that the position assumed by the wolf in this picture might have reminded him of the position taken by his father in the primal scene we had reconstructed. At any rate, this picture was the starting-point for a further backwash of fear. On one occasion, at the age of six or seven, when he learned that he was to have a new teacher the next day, he dreamed the following night that this teacher was a lion and was approaching his bed, roaring loudly, in the stance taken by the wolf in the picture, and once again awoke in terror. By then he had already overcome the wolf phobia and so was free to choose another animal as the object of his anxiety; in this later dream he recognized that the teacher was a father-substitute. Each of his teachers played this same paternal role in the later years of his childhood and was vested with the influence wielded by his father for good and ill.

Fate gave him strange cause to renew his wolf phobia during his grammar school years, and to make the relationship underlying it a channel for serious inhibitions. The name of the teacher responsible for Latin instruction in his class was *Wolf*. He was intimidated by this man right from the start and was once resoundingly told off by him for making a stupid mistake in a Latin translation, after which he could not shake off the paralysing anxiety this teacher induced in him, soon transferred on to other teachers as well. The occasion on which he came to grief in his translation is not without significance, however. He had to translate the Latin word 'filius' and did so using the French word 'fils' instead of the corresponding word in his own tongue. The wolf was indeed still the father.[10]

The first of the 'transitory symptoms'[11] that the patient produced during treatment in fact went back to the wolf phobia and the tale of 'The Seven Little Kids'. In the room where the first sessions took place there was a large grandfather clock opposite the patient, who lay on a divan with his head turned away from me. I was struck by the fact that, from time to time, he would turn his face towards me, look at me in a very friendly way, as if to placate me, and then turn his gaze away from me towards the clock. At the time I thought this was an indication that he was longing for the end of the session. A long time afterwards the patient reminded me of this dumb-show and gave me the explanation, reminding me that the youngest of the seven little kids found a hiding-place in the case of the wall-clock while his six brothers were gobbled up by the wolf. And so what he wanted to say was: Be kind to me. Must I be afraid of you? Are you going to gobble me up? Should I hide from you in the clock-case, like the youngest of the seven little kids?

The wolf whom he feared was undoubtedly the father, but his fear of the wolf was conditional upon its being in an upright position. His memory told him quite definitely that pictures of the wolf where he was on all fours or, as in the story of 'Little Red Riding Hood', lying in bed, did not frighten him. No less significant was the position that, according to our reconstruction of the primal scene, he had seen assumed by the female; this significance was restricted, however, to the sexual sphere. Once he had reached maturity the most striking phenomenon in his erotic life were attacks of compulsive physical infatuation that occurred and disappeared again in mysterious succession, releasing enormous energy in him even at times where he was otherwise inhibited, and which were quite beyond his control. An especially valuable connection obliges me to delay a full evaluation of these compulsive love episodes a little longer, but I can state here that they were linked to a particular condition, hidden from his conscious mind, which we were first able to recognize during the therapy. The woman must have taken up the position attributed to his mother in the primal scene. From puberty onwards he felt a woman's greatest charm to be the possession of large, conspicuous buttocks; coitus in any position other than from behind gave him scarcely any pleasure at all. There is every justification, it is true, for the critical objection that a sexual preference of this kind for the rear parts of the body is a general characteristic of individuals inclined to obsessive-compulsive neurosis and that we are not justified in deriving this from any particular memory imprint from childhood. It is part of the structure of a disposition to anal eroticism and of the archaic features which distinguish such a constitution. Copulation from behind – *more ferarum* [in the manner of beasts] – is after all certainly to be regarded as the phylogenetically older form. We shall return to this point, too, in later discussion, once we have noted down the material relating to his unconscious condition for sexual relations.

Let us now return to our discussion of the connections between the dream and the primal scene. According to our previous expectations, the dream should present the child, who is looking forward to having his wishes fulfilled on Christmas Day, with the image of sexual satisfaction received from his father, as seen in the primal scene, providing a model for the satisfaction which he himself longs to receive from his father. Instead of this image, however, there appears material from the story which his grandfather had told him a short time before: the tree, the wolves, the loss of the tail in the form of over-compensation, in the bushy tails of the creatures that are apparently wolves. A connection is missing, an associative bridge that would lead us from the content of the primal story to that of the wolf story. This connection is again provided by the position, and by the position alone. The tail-less wolf in the grandfather's story tells the others to *climb on top of him*. The memory of the image of the primal scene was awakened by means of this detail; in this way material from the primal scene could be represented by material from the wolf story and at the same time the number 2, denoting his parents, could be replaced in the desired manner by the larger number of wolves. The content of the dream underwent a further transformation as the material from the wolf story adapted itself to the content of the tale of 'The Seven Little Kids', borrowing from here the number 7.[12]

The transformation of the material – primal scene, wolf story, tale of 'The Seven Little Kids' – mirrors thought progression as the dream takes shape: longing for sexual satisfaction received from the father – understanding of the condition of castration attached to it – fear of the father. Only now, I think, have we arrived at a full explanation of the four-year-old boy's anxiety dream.[13]

As to the pathogenic effect of the primal scene and the alteration in sexual development that its resurrection produced: after all we have already touched on, I shall be brief in my remarks. We shall only follow up the particular effect to which the dream gives expression. At a later stage, we must make it clear to ourselves that the primal scene does not give rise to a single sexual current, but to a whole series of them, a positive splintering of the libido. We must keep in view, moreover, the fact that the activation of this scene (I am deliberately avoiding the word 'memory' here) has the same effect as if it were a recent experience. The effectiveness of the scene has been postponed [*nachträglich*], and loses none of its freshness in the interval that has elapsed between the ages of 18 months and 4 years. In what follows we may perhaps find grounds for supposing that it had certain effects even at the time when it was witnessed, from the age of 18 months on.

When the patient submerged himself in the situation of the primal scene, he brought the following perceptions to light from his own experience: he had previously assumed that the process he had observed was an act of violence, but this did not accord with the expression of pleasure he saw on his mother's face; he had to acknowledge that what was at issue here was satisfaction.[14] The essentially new fact that observation of his parents' intercourse brought him was the conviction that castration was a reality, a possibility which had already preoccupied his thoughts before then. (The sight of the two girls urinating, Nanja's threat, the governess's interpretation of the sticks of barley sugar, the memory of his father cutting a snake into pieces.) For now he could see with his own eyes the wound that Nanja had spoken of and understood that its presence was a condition of intercourse with his father. He could no longer confuse it, as he had done when watching the little girls, with the girls' bottoms.[15]

The dream ended in fear, which was only allayed once he had his Nanja with him. He thus sought refuge from his father with her. His fear was a rejection of his wish for sexual satisfaction from his father, the aspiration that had implanted the dream. The expression of that fear – being gobbled up by the wolf – was simply the reversal – a regressive one, as we shall hear – of the wish for coitus with the father, that is, for satisfaction such as his mother had experienced. His latest sexual objective, the passive attitude towards his father, had succumbed to repression; fear of his father, in the form of the wolf-phobia, had taken its place.

And the force which drove this repression? All the facts of the case suggest that it could only be narcissistic genital libido, which, in the form of concern for his male member, resisted a satisfaction that appeared to be conditional upon the sacrifice of that member. He drew from his threatened narcissism the masculinity to defend himself against the passive attitude towards his father.

At this point in our account we recognize the need to modify our terminology. During his dream he had reached a new phase of sexual organization. Up until then the sexual opposites for him had been *active* and *passive*. Since the seduction, his sexual objective had been a passive one, that of having his genitals touched, which regression to the previous stage of anal-sadistic organization then transformed into the masochistic objective of being disciplined, punished. It was a matter of indifference to him whether he achieved this objective with a man or a woman. He had moved on from Nanja to his father regardless of the difference in sex, asking Nanja to touch his penis, hoping to provoke his father into beating him. In this way the genital aspect was disregarded; in his fantasy of being struck on the penis this connection, which had been concealed by regression, was able to find expression. But now the activation of the primal scene in his dream led him back to the genital mode of organization. He discovered the vagina and the biological meaning of male and female. He now understood that active equalled male, passive female. His passive sexual objective would have had to be transformed into a female one, expressed as being taken in intercourse by the father instead of having his father strike him on the penis or the bottom. This feminine objective now fell forfeit to repression, and had to be replaced by fear of the wolf.

Here, we must break off discussion of his sexual development until new light can be shed back on to this earlier stage from later stages of his history. In evaluating the wolf phobia we might add that his mother and father were both turned into wolves. His mother played the castrated wolf, which let the others climb on to its back, his father the wolf who did so. We have heard him say, however, that his fear related to the wolf only when it was in a standing position, that is, to the father. We are also struck by the fact that the fear in which the dream ends is foreshadowed in the grandfather's story. In that story the castrated wolf who let the others climb on to its back is overcome by anxiety as soon as he is reminded of the absence of his tail. It would seem, then, that during the dreaming process he identified with his castrated mother and is now struggling to resist this outcome. Translated, I hope accurately, it is as if he is saying: if you want to be satisfied by your father you must accept castration as your mother has done; but I do not want that. A distinct protest in favour of masculinity! Let us be clear, incidentally, that the great disadvantage of the sexual development in this particular case is that it is not an undisrupted one. It was first crucially influenced by the seduction and is now sent off course by the observation of coitus, the postponed effect of which is like a second seduction.

### Notes

1. 'Märchenstoffe in Träumen' ['Fairy-tale Material in Dreams'] (1913).
2. Cf. the similarity perceived by O. Rank between these two fairy tales and the myth of Kronos (1912) [Völkerpsychologische Parallelen zu den infantilen Sexualtheorien' ('Parallels with Infantile Sexual Theories in the Psychology of Peoples'), *Zentbl. Psychoanal.*].
3. A less likely possibility, virtually untenable in fact, is an age of 6 months.
4. Cf. the way in which this element was later reworked in the obsessive-compulsive neurosis. In dreams during the therapy it was replaced by a strong wind. [*Addition 1924:*] ('Aria' = air).
5. We should recall in this context that the patient only drew *five* wolves to illustrate his dream, although the text of the dream refers to 6 or 7.

**6**. In white underclothes, hence the *white* wolves.

**7**. Why three times? He once asserted quite suddenly that I had reconstructed this detail by means of interpretation. This was not the case. It was a spontaneous notion, eluding further criticism, which, as was his wont, he attributed to me, ensuring its reliability by means of this projection.

**8**. I mean that he understood it at the time of his dream, when he was 4 years old, not at the time he observed it. At the age of 18 months he acquired the memory imprints that he was able to understand later, at the time of his dream, thanks to his subsequent development, his sexual excitement and his sexual exploration.

**9**. The first of these problems is not resolved if we assume that the child was in fact probably a year older when he observed his parents, that is, $2\frac{1}{2}$, so that he might have been entirely capable of speech. As far as my patient was concerned, the possibility of re-scheduling the event in this way was virtually excluded by the accompanying circumstances of the case. We should, incidentally, take into account the fact that it is not rare in analysis to uncover such scenes in which parental coitus is observed. The condition of doing so is precisely, however, that they take place in earliest childhood. The older the child, the greater the pains taken by the parents, at a certain social level, to deny the child any such opportunity for observation.

**10**. After he had been told off by the teacher-wolf, he discovered that his chums were all of the opinion that the teacher was expecting to be appeased with – money. We shall return to this point later. – I can imagine what a relief it would be to any rationalistic consideration of this childhood tale if we could assume that in reality all the boy's fear of the wolf could be attributed to the Latin teacher of the same name, projected back into childhood and giving rise, in conjunction with the illustration from the fairy-tale book, to this fantasy of the primal scene. Yet this is untenable; the evidence for the prior occurrence of the wolf phobia and its attribution to the childhood years on the first estate is all too certain. And the boy's dream at the age of 4?

**11**. Ferenczi (1912) ['Über passagère Symptombildungen während der Analyse' (On Transitory Symptom Formations during Analysis') *Zentbl. Psychoanal.*].

**12**. In the dream, 6 or 7. Six is the number of children who were eaten up, the seventh takes refuge in the clock case. It remains one of the strictest laws of dream interpretation that an explanation can be found for every detail.

**13**. Now that we have succeeded in producing a synthesis of the dream

I shall attempt to provide an overview of the relationship between the manifest dream-content and the latent dream-thoughts.

*It is night and I am lying in my bed.* This last is the beginning of the reproduction of the primal scene. 'It is night': a distortion of 'I was asleep'. The remark: 'I know that it was winter in my dream, and night-time' refers to the memory of the dream and does not form part of its content. The remark is correct: it was on a night before his birthday, or more precisely before Christmas Day.

*Suddenly the window opens of its own accord.* To be translated: suddenly I awake for no reason, memory of the primal scene. The influence of the wolf story, in which the wolf leaps in through the window, here acts to modify the material and transforms direct expression into metaphorical expression. At the same time, the introduction of the window serves to locate the dream content that follows in the present time. On Christmas Eve the doors are suddenly opened and there before our eyes is the tree with all the presents on it. Thus the influence of the boy's anticipation of Christmas asserts itself here, including the element of sexual satisfaction.

*The big walnut tree.* Represents the Christmas tree, thus topical; also the tree from the wolf story, where the tailor seeks refuge when chased by the wolves, and under which the wolves lie in wait. Experience has convinced me that the tall tree is also a symbol of observation and voyeurism. When sitting at the top of a tree one can see everything going on below without being seen oneself. Cf. the well-known story by Boccaccio and similar farcical stories.

*The wolves.* Their number: six or seven. In the wolf story, a pack of no particular number. The designated number shows the influence of the tale of 'The Seven Little Kids', six of whom were eaten. Replacing the number two found in the primal scene with a larger number, which would be absurd in the primal scene, provides a welcome means of distortion, which serves the purposes of resistance. In the drawing that the dreamer produced to illustrate the dream, he gives expression to the number 5 which is probably intended to correct his assertion that 'it was night'.

*They are sitting in the tree.* Initially they replace the Christmas presents hanging on the tree. They have also been transferred on to the tree because that could mean that they are watching. In the grandfather's story they are lying all around the bottom of the tree. In the dream, their relationship to the tree has thus been reversed, from which we may conclude that other reversals of the latent material are also present in the dream-content.

*They are watching him with tense attentiveness.* This aspect has come into the dream from the primal scene entire, at the cost of complete reversal.

*They are completely white.* A trivial feature in itself, strongly emphasized in the dreamer's narration, it owes its intensity to the way in which it fuses a considerable number of elements from every level of the dream and unites secondary details from the other dream sources with a more important element from the primal scene. The determining factor here is doubtless derived from the white of the bedlinen and the parents' underclothes; in addition there is the white of the flocks of sheep and the sheepdogs as an allusion to the sexual exploration carried out in the animal kingdom and the white in the tale of 'The Seven Little Kids', where the mother is recognized by the whiteness of her hand. Later we shall also have cause to see the white underclothes as an allusion to death.

*They are sitting there motionless.* A contradiction of the most conspicuous content of the scene observed by the boy: the violent excitement which, by virtue of the position to which it leads, forms the connection between the primal scene and the wolf story.

*They have tails like foxes.* This is intended to contradict a conclusion derived from the permeation of the wolf story by the primal scene, a conclusion which is to be recognized as the most important outcome of his sexual exploration, namely that there really is such a thing as castration. The sense of fright that accompanies the results of his musings finally forces its way out in his dream and generates its conclusion.

*Fear of being eaten up by the wolves.* This appeared to the dreamer not to have been motivated by the dream-content. He said: there was no need to be afraid, since the wolves looked more like foxes or dogs and they were not flying at me as if they were going to bite me, on the contrary they were quite calm and not at all terrifying. Here we recognize that the dream-work [*Traumarbeit*] has endeavoured for a while to render painful contents harmless by transforming them into their opposite. (They are not moving, they have the finest of tails.) Until eventually this device fails to be effective and fear breaks through. It finds expression by means of the fairy-tale in which the goat-children are eaten up by the wolf-father. It is possible that this fairy-tale content even recalled the father's teasing threats when playing with the child, so that the fear of being eaten up by the wolf could just as well be an involuntary memory as a displacement-substitute.

The wish-motifs in this dream are blatantly obvious; the superficial daytime wishing that Christmas and all its presents would come (dream of impatience) is reinforced by the more deep-seated wish, permanently present during this period, for sexual satisfaction from his father, which is initially replaced by the wish to re-experience what was so absorbing on the first occasion. The psychic process then runs all the way from the fulfilment of that wish in the primal scene conjured up out of the unconscious, to rejection of the wish, which has now become unavoidable, and hence to repression.

The scope and detail of this account, imposed upon me by the endeavour to offer the reader some sort of equivalent for the evidential value of an analysis that one has seen through to its conclusion oneself, may at the same time discourage the reader from demanding the publication of analyses which extend over several years.

14. We can most easily make sense of the patient's remark if we assume that what he observed was initially coitus in the normal position, which must create the impression of a sadistic act. Only after this was the position changed, so that he had the opportunity of making other observations and forming other judgements. But there is no evidence for this assumption and it does not seem absolutely necessary to me. Even though my textual account presents it in abbreviated form, we must not lose sight of the actual situation, namely that the patient in analysis, more than 25 years old, expresses the impressions and impulses of his four-year-old self in words that he could not have used at the time. If we overlook this observation we can easily find it comical and incredible that a four-year-old should be capable of such technical judgements and erudite thoughts. This is simply another case of *postponed understanding*. At the age of 18 months the child receives a memory imprint to which he cannot react adequately, and only understands it, is only overcome by it when what has been imprinted is re-awakened at the age of four; only in analysis two decades later can he grasp in conscious intellectual activity what it was that took place inside him at that time. The analysand is then right to override these three phases of time, putting his present self in the long-forgotten situation. We follow him in doing so for, given correct self-scrutiny and interpretation, the effect must be such that one overlooks the distance between the second and third phases. We have no other means, moreover, of describing the processes of the second phase.

15. We shall find out later, when considering the matter of his anal eroticism, how he subsequently dealt with this part of the problem.

## v  *Some Matters for Discussion*

The polar bear and the whale cannot wage war, so they say, because each is confined within his own element and is unable to make contact with the other. It is equally impossible for me to hold a discussion with workers in the field of psychology or neurosis who do not recognize the premises of psychoanalysis and regard its conclusions as mere artefacts. In the last few years, however, a further form of opposition has arisen, voiced by others who, in their own opinion at least, are practitioners of analysis, have no quarrel with its techniques and results, and simply consider themselves justified in drawing different conclusions from the same material and subjecting it to other interpretations.

Theoretical contradictions are for the most part fruitless, however. As soon as we begin to move away from the material that should be our source, we run the risk of becoming intoxicated by our own assertions, and we end up putting forward views that a moment's observation would have contradicted. It seems very much more to the purpose, then, to combat divergent views by testing them against individual cases and problems.

I have argued above that it would no doubt be considered improbable that 'at the tender age of 18 months a child should be capable of perceiving such a complicated event and retaining it so accurately in the unconscious; second, that it is possible at the age of four to process the memory prints received in this way, belatedly advancing to an understanding of what was seen; and finally, that the child should succeed by whatever method in making conscious the details of such a scene, witnessed and understood in such circumstances, in a way that is both coherent and convincing'.

This last question is purely a matter of fact. Anyone who takes the trouble to go to these kinds of depths in analysis, according to the techniques I have mapped out, will be readily convinced that it is indeed possible; those who do not do so, breaking off the analysis at some more superficial level, have renounced the right to pass judgement in this matter. But this does not settle the question of how we are to interpret what we encounter in depth analysis.

The two other reservations are based on a disparaging attitude towards impressions formed in early infancy, and a reluctance to ascribe such lasting effects to them. They prefer to seek the cause of neuroses almost exclusively in the serious conflicts of later life, and assume that the significance of childhood is simply a sham created in analysis by the neurotic's tendency to express present interests by means of involuntary memories and symbols drawn from his infant past. If we were to evaluate the significant moments of infancy in this way we would lose a great deal that goes to form the most intrinsic characteristics of analysis, as well as much, admittedly, that creates resistance to it and discourages outsiders from placing their trust in it.

Let us hold up for discussion, then, the view that scenes from early infancy such as are provided by the exhaustive analysis of neurotic individuals, of which the present case is an example, do not reproduce real events to which we may attribute some influence on the structuring of later life and on symptom formation, but are on the contrary fantasy-formations, drawing their inspiration from riper years, intended as a symbolic representation, so to speak, of real wishes and interests, and owing their emergence to a regressive tendency, a turning-away from the tasks of the present moment. If this is indeed the case, we need not bring such disconcerting expectations to bear on the inner life and the intellectual achievements of children still far from the age of discretion.

Quite apart from the wish to rationalize and simplify the difficult task, common to us all, there are various matters of fact that tend to support this view. At the very outset, moreover, one can clear up a particular misgiving that the practising analyst above all might harbour. It is true that if the interpretation of these scenes from infancy that we have put forward is the correct one, then nothing changes in the first instance in the way the analysis is carried out. If a neurotic individual does indeed have the unfortunate characteristic of turning his interest away from the present day in order to attach it to regressive fantasy substitute-formations of this kind, then there is nothing for it but to follow him along these paths and help him to bring these unconscious productions to consciousness for, leaving aside their lack of real value, they are extremely valuable to us as carriers and possessors in the present moment of the interest that we want to set free so that we can direct it towards the tasks of the present day. The analysis would have to follow exactly the same course as it would if, naively credulous, we took such fantasies for truth. The difference would be seen only at the end of the analysis, once these fantasies had been uncovered. One would then have to say to the patient: 'Good; the course taken by your neurosis has been as if, in your childhood years, you received memory imprints such as these and continued to weave stories around them. You realize, of course, that that is not possible. They were products of imaginative activity intended to divert you from the real-life tasks which confronted you. Now let us attempt to discover what these tasks were, and what connecting pathways existed between them and your fantasies.' It would be possible to implement a second phase of treatment, more closely concerned with real life, once these infantile fantasies had been dealt with.

To shorten this route, that is, to alter psychoanalytic therapy as it has been practised up to now, would be technically inadmissible. If we do not make the full extent of these fantasies conscious to the patient we cannot make available to him the interest that attaches to them. If we divert his attention from them as soon as we sense their existence and their general outlines, we are merely giving support to the work of repression that has rendered them inviolable, immune to the patient's best efforts. If we devalue them at too early a stage, perhaps by disclosing that we shall be dealing only with fantasies and that these are without any real significance, we shall never be able to enlist the patient's cooperation in leading them towards consciousness. Correctly practised, the analytic technique should remain unaltered, regardless of the value we ascribe to these scenes from infancy.

I have already mentioned that in interpreting these scenes as regressive fantasies one can appeal for support to a number of matters of fact. Above all to the fact that in therapy – in my experience to date – these scenes from infancy are not reproduced as memories but are the results of reconstruction. For many people, no doubt, this admission alone will appear to settle the dispute.

I do not wish to be misunderstood. Every analyst knows and has experienced on numerous occasions the way in which, when therapy has been successful, the patient will relate any number of spontaneous memories from childhood, and the physician will feel that he is completely innocent of the fact that they have surfaced – perhaps surfaced for the first time – since he has not suggested any content of this kind to the patient through some attempt at reconstruction. These previously unconscious memories do not even have to be true; they may be true, but their truth is often distorted and interspersed with fantasized elements in a very similar way to so-called cover-memories that have been spontaneously retained. I will say only that scenes such as we find in my patient's case, from such an early age and with such content, which then lay claim to such extraordinary significance for the history of the case, are not as a rule reproduced as memories but must be guessed at – reconstructed – from the sum total of indications, step by step and with considerable effort. This is sufficient for the purposes of my argument, whether I acknowledge that in cases of obsessive-compulsive neurosis such scenes are not conscious as memories, or whether I limit my remarks simply to the case which we are considering here.

Now I am not of the opinion that these scenes must necessarily be fantasies simply because they do not come back as memories. It seems to me that they are completely on a par with memory in that – as in the present case – they find a substitute in dreams, analysis of which regularly leads back to the same scene, reproducing every element of its content in tireless variation. To dream is, after all, to remember, even under the night-time conditions of dream-formation. It is through this recurrence in dreams that I would explain the fact that patients themselves gradually become firmly convinced of the reality of these primal scenes, with a conviction every bit as strong as that based on memory.[1]

My opponents need not regard opposition to these arguments as a lost cause, and give up the fight. It is well known that dreams can be influenced.[2] And the conviction of the analysand can be the outcome of suggestion, for which we are still seeking a role in the play of forces released in analytic treatment. A psychotherapist of the old school would suggest to his patient that he is healthy and has overcome his inhibitions, etc. etc.; the psychoanalyst, on the other hand, suggests that as a child he underwent this or that experience, which he must now recall in order to regain his health. Therein lies the difference between the two approaches.

Let us be clear that this last attempt at explanation on the part of my opponents amounts to a far more sweeping dismissal of scenes experienced in infancy than was first suggested. They were not to be realities, but fantasies. Now the demand is obviously that they should not be the patient's fantasies, but the analyst's, imposed on the analysand as a result of some personal complex or other. In response to this reproach the analyst will of course reassure himself by demonstrating how gradually the reconstruction of this fantasy – which he apparently implanted – came about, how, as it was built up, the process continued quite independently, on many counts, of any stimulus offered by the physician, how, from a certain phase of treatment onward, it appeared to be the point on which everything converged, and how, now that a synthesis has been achieved, the most diverse and remarkable results radiate out from it, how the problems and peculiarities of the patient's medical history, from the large to the very small, find their solution in this one single assumption; and he will assert that he does not see himself as possessing the astuteness necessary to concoct an event that could fulfil all these requirements at a single stroke. Even this plea, however, will have no effect on the part of the population that has not itself had the experience of analysis. Sophisticated self-deception, some will say; others: an absence of discernment; and no verdict will be reached.

We may now consider another factor that supports a hostile

reading of these reconstructed scenes from infancy. It is as follows: all the processes which are brought into play in order to explain away these questionable formations as fantasies exist in reality and are to be acknowledged as significant. The averting of interest from the tasks of real life,[3] the existence of fantasies as substitute-formations for actions that have not been performed, the regressive tendency expressed through these creations – regressive in more than one sense, inasmuch as there is a simultaneous shrinking back from life and a falling back on the past – this is all to the point and is regularly confirmed by analysis. We might well suppose that this would also be sufficient to account for what are apparently involuntary memories from early infancy such as we are discussing here, and according to the economic principles of scholarship this explanation is to be preferred over the other one, which cannot manage without bringing in new and unsympathetic assumptions.

I shall permit myself at this point to draw the reader's attention to the fact that the dissenting views to be found in current psychoanalytic literature are usually based on the principle of *pars pro toto*. From a whole which has been carefully pieced together and built up one removes just one or two of the effective factors, proclaims them to be the truth and denies the importance of the other parts and of the whole in favour of these. If we examine the group for which a preference is expressed, we find that it is the one containing material already familiar from elsewhere or whatever can most readily be connected with it. Thus for Jung we find it is actuality and regression, for Adler egoistic motives. The very things that are new about psychoanalysis and are most characteristic of it are the ones that are neglected, dismissed as a mistake. In this way the revolutionary advances of psychoanalysis, that uncomfortable notion, can most easily be repelled.

It is far from futile to emphasize that there was no need for Jung to present a single one of the factors that were invoked by the opposing point of view, to facilitate understanding of those scenes from childhood, as a new discovery. Present conflict, turning-away from reality, substitute satisfaction in fantasy, regression to material from the past, all of this has always been an integral part of my own theories, similarly structured although perhaps with minor modifications in terminology. It was not the whole of it, but only the part concerned with causality, which permeates down from reality to the formation of neuroses in a regressive direction. Alongside this I left room for a second, *pro*gressive [progredient] influence, which works forward from childhood impressions, showing the way to the libido that shrinks back from life, and providing an explanation for that regression to childhood that would otherwise be incomprehensible. In my view, therefore, both these factors work together in symptom-formation, but an earlier instance of their working together seems to me equally significant. I would maintain that *childhood influence already makes itself felt in the initial situation of neurosis-formation, since its intervention is crucial in helping to determine whether, and at what point, the individual fails in his attempts to master the problems of real life*.

What is at issue, then, is the significance of the infantile factor. What is needed is to find a case that can prove its significance beyond all doubt. The case that is the subject of this detailed account is one such, since its distinguishing characteristic is the way in which neurosis in later life has been preceded by neurosis in the early years of childhood. It is for this very reason that I have chosen to write about this case. If anyone were to reject it on the grounds that animal phobia does not seem important enough to be regarded as an independent neurosis, let me point out that the phobia was immediately succeeded by compulsive ritual, and by compulsive actions and thoughts that will form the subject of the next section of this essay.

Neurotic illness in the fourth or fifth year of childhood proves most importantly that the experiences of infancy are enough in themselves to produce neurosis, and that it does not require flight from a task with which life confronts the individual. We might object that even the child constantly encounters tasks that he would perhaps like to evade. This is true, but it is easy to gain an overall sense of the life of a child before he starts school, and it is possible to investigate whether it contains a 'task' responsible for causing the neurosis. However, all that we discover are involuntary impulses [*Triebregungen*], which the child finds it impossible to satisfy and which he is not yet able to master, together with the sources from which they flow.

As we might expect, the tremendous shortening of the interval between the outbreak of the neurosis and the occurrence of the childhood experiences in question massively reduces the regressive element in the causation of neurosis, and gives us a clearer glimpse of the '*progressive*' element, the influence exercised by earlier impressions. The present case history will, I hope, provide a clear image of this relationship. For other reasons, too, childhood neurosis will provide a decisive answer to our question as to the nature of primal scenes and those earliest childhood experiences traced in analysis.

If we start from the uncontradicted premiss that we were technically correct in formulating a primal scene of this kind, and that a comprehensive solution to all the riddles posed by the complex of symptoms produced by that childhood illness demands that all the effects radiate out from it just as all the threads of analysis lead back to it, then as far as its content is concerned it is impossible that it could be anything but the reproduction of a reality experienced by the child. For the child, just like the adult, can only produce fantasies with material that he has acquired from somewhere; and the ways in which he might acquire it are in part closed to the child (reading, for example), while the period of time available for such acquisition is short and can easily be scrutinized for sources of this kind.

In our case, the primal scene contains the image of sexual intercourse between the child's parents in a position that is particularly favourable to observation of a certain kind. Now, it would give us no proof of the reality of this scene if we encountered it in a patient whose symptoms, that is, the effects of such a scene, had emerged some time in later life. Such a patient could have acquired impressions, ideas and knowledge at a wide variety of points in that long interval of time, which are then transformed into a fantasy image, projected back into his childhood and attached to his parents. But when the effects of such a scene emerge in the child's fourth or fifth year, he must have been present to witness it at an even earlier age. In that case, however, all the disconcerting conclusions remain in place that were produced by the analysis of infantile neurosis. Unless, of course, someone wished to conclude that the patient had not only unconsciously fantasized that primal scene, but had also dreamed up the change in his character, his fear of the wolf and his religious compulsion, an excuse, however, that is contradicted by his otherwise sober manner and the tradition of straightforwardness in his family. We must stick to our guns – there is nothing else for it – either the analysis based on his childhood neurosis is a delusion from start to finish, or else the way in which I have portrayed it above is the correct one.

We have already acknowledged ambiguity in the fact that the patient's predilection for the female 'nates' [buttocks] and for coitus in the position where these are particularly in evidence apparently invites connection with his observation of his parents' intercourse, whereas a preference of this kind is a general characteristic of those archaic constitutions that are disposed to obsessive-compulsive neurosis. There is a possible explanation to hand, namely that we resolve the contradiction as over-determination. The person whom he observed in this coital position was after all his very own father, from whom he might also have inherited the same constitutional predilection. Neither his father's later illness nor the family history are against it; as I have already mentioned, an uncle on his father's side died in a condition which must be construed as the last stage of a severe compulsive disorder.

In this context let us recall that when seducing the $3\frac{1}{4}$-year-old boy, his sister uttered a strange calumny against their dear old nurse, saying that she turned everyone upside down and took hold of their genitals. It is an unavoidable notion that at a similarly tender age his sister might have witnessed the same scene as her brother did later, and that this is where she derived the suggestion of people being turned upside down in the sexual act. Such an assumption would also indicate one possible source for her own sexual impetuosity.

[⁴It was not my original intention to enter into any further discussion here of the real value of 'primal scenes', but since in the meantime I have been obliged to treat the topic in a broader context and without any polemical intention in my *Introductory Lectures on Psychoanalysis*, it would be misleading if I failed to apply to the present case points of view that I present there as decisive. In the interests of completeness and to correct any mistakes let me therefore add the following remarks: there is indeed another possible interpretation of the primal scene that forms the basis for my patient's dream, which diverts us a good way from the verdict that we reached earlier and relieves us of a number of difficulties. Admittedly, the theoretical approach, which seeks to reduce such scenes from infancy to mere regressive symbols, will not gain anything by this modification either; in fact it seems to me that this – or indeed any other – analysis of childhood neurosis puts an end to the matter once and for all.

In my opinion, it is also possible to interpret the facts of the case as follows: we cannot forgo our assumption that the child observes coitus and in doing so acquires the conviction that castration might be more than an empty threat; the significance adhering to the positions of man and woman, in the first place for the development of his fears, and subsequently as a condition of intercourse, leaves us no choice, moreover, but to conclude that it must have been *coitus a tergo* [from behind], *more ferarum* [in the manner of the beasts]. Another factor is less crucial, however, and could be left aside. The child might have observed coitus between animals, rather than between his parents, and then imputed it to his parents, as if he had decided that his parents would not do it any other way.

This interpretation is supported above all by the fact that the wolves in the dream are actually sheepdogs and appear as such in my patient's drawing. Shortly before the dream, the boy had repeatedly been taken to see the herds of sheep, and there he could have seen big white dogs like this and probably watched them copulating. I would also cite in this context the number three which the dreamer produced without any obvious motivation for doing so, and would assume that he retained a memory of the sheep dogs doing so on three occasions. On the night of his dream we find, in addition to expectant excitement, the transference on to his parents of *every detail* of the recently acquired memory-image; and it is only this that made possible those powerful emotional effects. There then came a belated understanding of those impressions received perhaps a few weeks or months before, a process which every one of us may perhaps have experienced for himself. Now, the transference from the copulating dogs to his parents was not brought about by a final stage in the procedure, which was dependent on words, but by seeking out the memory of a real scene where his parents were enjoying intimacy, which he could fuse with the situation of coitus. All the details of the scene that were claimed in the analysis of the dream might have been reproduced exactly. It really was a summer afternoon, during the time when the child was suffering from malaria, the parents were both present, dressed in white, as the child awoke from sleep, but – the scene was harmless. In his eagerness to learn, the remaining details were supplied later, on the basis of what he had learned from the dogs, by the child's wish to spy on his parents while they were making love, so that now the fantasy scene unfolded with all the effects we have attributed to it, just as if it had been entirely real and had not been glued together from two components, an earlier one without any real significance and a later one which had left a deep impression.

It is immediately apparent how much this eases the effort of credulity that we are called upon to make. We need no longer assume that the parents completed their act of coitus in the presence of their child, an idea that many of us find repugnant, even if he was indeed very small at the time. The part played by postponed response is considerably reduced, since it now applies only to a few months in the child's fourth year and does not draw at all on those first dim years of childhood. There is now almost nothing that might take us aback in the child's behaviour as he effects a transference from dogs to parents and replaces fear of the father with fear of the wolf. The child is, after all, at that stage of developing his view of the world that is characterized in *Totem and Taboo* as the return of totemism. The theory that seeks to explain the primal scene of neurosis as a retrospective fantasy that takes place in later life would appear to find considerable support in this observation, despite the fact that this particular neurotic individual is at the tender age of four. Young as he is, he has succeeded in replacing an impression acquired at the age of four with a fantasized trauma occurring at the age of 18 months, a regression, however, that appears neither mysterious nor tendentious. The scene that he needed to produce had to fulfil certain conditions, which could only be found, precisely because of the circumstances of the dreamer's life, in this early time, such as the fact, for example, that his bed was in his parents' room.

Most readers will find what I can add here, drawing on the results of analysis in other cases, a decisive factor in making up their mind as to whether the interpretation I suggest is correct. It is not at all rare in the analysis of neurotic mortals to find that in very early childhood they have observed a scene – whether a real memory or a fantasy – in which the parents engage in sexual intercourse. It may perhaps be an equally frequent occurrence in individuals who do not go on to suffer from neurosis. It may perhaps form a regular part of their treasure chest of – conscious or unconscious – memories. Every time I was able to unravel such a scene through analysis, however, it demonstrated the same peculiarity that made us suspicious in the case of this particular patient, namely that it referred to *coitus a tergo,* the only position which makes an inspection of the genitals possible to the observer. We need surely doubt no longer that we are simply dealing with a fantasy that is perhaps regularly inspired by observation of the sexual intercourse of animals. Indeed, there is more: I indicated that my description of the 'primal scene' remained incomplete, since I was leaving it until later to relate the way in which the child disturbed his parents' act of intercourse. I must now add that the way in which this disturbance takes place is also the same in every case.

I can imagine that I have now made myself vulnerable to

suspicions of a serious kind on the part of the reader of this case history. If I had these arguments in favour of such an interpretation of the 'primal scene' at my disposal, how could I begin to justify having first put forward a different view, one that was apparently so absurd? Or had I perhaps accumulated new evidence in the interval between writing the first draft of this case history and formulating the present additional material that obliged me to modify my original interpretation, and was yet unwilling for some reason to admit to this? Instead I shall make a different admission: it is my intention to close discussion as to the real value of the primal scene this time with a *non liquet* [deferred judgement]. We have not yet reached the end of this case history, and in due course a moment will arise that will undermine the certainty that at present we believe we enjoy. Then there will be nothing for it but to refer the reader to those passages in my *Lectures* where I discuss the problem of primal fantasies, or primal scenes.]

### Notes

1. A passage from the first edition of *Die Traumdeutung* [*The Interpretation of Dreams*] (1900) will prove at what an early stage I became concerned with this problem. On p. 126, analysing speech occurring in a dream, I wrote: *that is no longer available to us*, these words are my own; some days earlier I had explained to her 'that the earliest childhood experiences *are no longer available to us* as such, but are replaced in analysis by "transferences" and dreams'.

2. The mechanism of the dream cannot be influenced, but to some extent one can be in command of the dream-material.

3. I have good reasons for preferring to say: the averting of the *libido* from the *conflicts* of the present moment.

4. [This square bracket and the final closing square bracket on p. 249 above are Freud's.]

## VI  *Obsessive-compulsive Neurosis*

Now, for the third time, he was influenced in a way that decisively altered his development. At the age of 4½, when there was still no improvement in his state of irritability and anxiety, his mother decided to acquaint him with the stories of the Bible in the hope of distracting and uplifting him. She succeeded in doing so, for his introduction to religion put an end to the previous phase, but as a result the symptoms of anxiety were succeeded by symptoms of compulsive behaviour. He had previously found it difficult to fall asleep because he was afraid of having bad dreams such as he had had the night before Christmas: now, before he went to bed, he had to kiss every single holy picture in the room, recite prayers and make the sign of the cross countless times over himself and the place where he slept.

An overall view suggests that his childhood can be divided into the following epochs: first, the period of pre-history lasting up until the seduction (at age 3¼) and including the primal scene; second, the period of altered character, lasting until the anxiety dream (at age 4); third, the period of animal phobia lasting until his introduction to religion (at age 4½); and after this the period of obsessive-compulsive neurosis, lasting until after his tenth year. That there should be a smooth transition at a given moment from one phase to the next is neither in the nature of things, nor in our patient's nature: it was characteristic of him, on the contrary, to hold on to what had gone before and to allow the most diverse currents to coexist. His difficult behaviour did not disappear when his anxiety appeared but continued, slowly diminishing, into his pious period. In this last phase, however, there is no further mention of the wolf phobia. The course of his obsessive-compulsive neurosis was discontinuous; the first attack was the longest and the most intense, with others occurring at the age of eight and ten, the cause each time being visibly connected with the content of the neurosis. His mother told him the sacred story herself and also made Nanja read it aloud to him from an illustrated book. The principal emphasis of their account fell naturally on the Passion narrative. Nanja, who was very pious and superstitious, provided her own commentary, but also had to listen to the objections and doubts expressed by the young critic. If the struggles which now began to shake him eventually concluded in the victory of faith this was not least as a result of Nanja's contribution.

What he claimed to remember of his reactions when introduced to religion met at first with definite incredulity on my part. These, I maintained, could not be the thoughts of a child of $4\frac{1}{2}$ or 5; he was probably attributing to his early past ideas which had grown out of the reflections of an adult of nearly 30.[1] But the patient would not hear of any such correction; I was unsuccessful in my attempts to win him over, as I had been able to do on many other occasions when we had differed in our judgements; eventually, in fact, I was obliged to believe him because of the coherence between his remembered thoughts and the symptoms he reported, as well as the way they fitted into his sexual development. I then told myself, moreover, that only a diminishing minority of adults can rise to a critique of religious doctrines such as this, a critique which I doubted this child to be capable of.

I shall now present the material which his memories supplied, and only afterwards shall I seek out the path which will lead us to understand it.

The impression that he received from narration of the sacred story, he told me, was not at first a pleasant one. He struggled to come to terms, first, with the suffering nature of the person of Christ, and then with the whole way in which his story fitted together. His dissatisfaction and criticism were directed towards God the Father. If he was omnipotent, it was his fault that people were bad and tormented other people, and then went to Hell for it. He should have made them good; he himself was responsible for everything evil and for all torments. He took exception to the commandment to offer the other cheek when someone strikes us, as he did to Christ's wish, when hanging on the cross, that the cup should pass from him, but also to the fact that a miracle did not take place to prove that he was the Son of God. In this way his critical faculties were awakened and he was rigorous and unrelenting in sniffing out the weaknesses in the sacred narrative.

Rationalistic criticism was very quickly accompanied by brooding and doubts, which may reveal that secret impulses were also at work. One of the first questions he addressed to Nanja was whether Christ also had a backside. Nanja told him that he was a God, but also a man. As a man he had everything and did everything that other men did. He found this reply most unsatisfactory but comforted himself by saying that someone's bottom was just the continuation of their legs, after all. His fear of having to demean the sacred person of God, barely calmed by this, flared up again when the question surfaced in his mind as to whether Christ also shat. He did not dare put this question to the pious Nanja, but extricated himself in a way which she could not have bettered, by telling himself that since Christ made wine out of nothing, he could also make nothing out of food and was thus able to spare himself the need to defecate.

We shall come closer to understanding such brooding thoughts if we make the connection with an aspect of his sexual development that we discussed earlier. We know that since Nanja had rejected him and he had suppressed the beginnings of genital activity as a result, his sexual life had developed in the direction of sadism and masochism. He tormented and mistreated small creatures, and fantasized about beating horses; but on the other hand he also fantasized about the heir to the throne being beaten.[2] In sadism he was able to maintain the ancient identification with his father, in masochism he had chosen that same father as his sexual object. He was thus right in the middle of a phase of pre-genital organization in which I perceive the disposition to obsessive-compulsive neurosis to lie. The gradual effect of the dream, which brought him under the influence of the primal scene, could have been to enable him to progress to the genital mode of organization, transforming his masochism towards his father into a feminine attitude towards him, into homosexuality. But the dream did not bring progress of this kind with it; it ended in fear. His relationship with his father, which should have led from the sexual objective of being punished by him to the next objective, that of being taken in sexual intercourse by his father, like a woman, was thrown back on to a more primitive level still by the protest of his narcissistic masculinity, and having been displaced on to a father-substitute was split off as fear of being gobbled up by the wolf, but was not by any means dealt with. Indeed, we can only do justice to these apparently complicated facts by maintaining our belief in the coexistence of three sexual aspirations, all focused on the father. From the time of the dream onwards he was unconsciously homosexual; during his neurosis he was at the level of cannibalism; the earlier masochistic attitude remained the dominant one. All three aspirations had passive sexual objectives; we find the same object and the same sexual impulse, but a split had occurred which caused them to evolve towards three different levels.

His knowledge of sacred history now gave him the opportunity to sublimate the dominant masochistic attitude towards his father. He became Christ, an identification that was facilitated, in particular, by the fact that they shared a birthday. This made him something great and also made him – though insufficient emphasis was put on the fact initially – a man. In his doubt as to whether Christ could have a backside we catch a glimmer of his repressed homosexual attitude, for the significance of this brooding thought can only be the question as to whether he can be used by his father as if he were a woman, as his mother was used in the primal scene. When we come to the solution of other compulsive ideas we shall find confirmation of this interpretation. The repression of his passive homosexuality corresponds to his misgivings that it is insulting to make a connection between the sacred person of Christ and outrageous ideas of this kind. We might note that he made considerable efforts to keep this new sublimation clear of additional material drawn from the sources of repression. But he did not succeed in doing so.

We do not yet understand why he now also struggled to come to terms with the passive character of Christ and his ill-treatment at his father's hands, and thus also began to deny his previous masochistic ideal, even in its sublimated form. We can assume that this second conflict was particularly favourable to the emergence of humiliating compulsive thoughts from the first conflict (between the dominant masochistic current and the repressed homosexual one), for it is only natural that in inner conflict all counter-tendencies are added together, even if they come from the most diverse sources. New material that he related will allow us to discover the motive for his struggle and for his critical attitude towards religion.

His sexual exploration had also benefited from what he had been told of sacred history. Up until then, he had had no reason to assume that only women have children. On the contrary, Nanja had led him to believe that he was his father's child and his sister their mother's, and he had particularly valued this close relationship with his father. Now he learnt that Mary was called the Mother of God. So it was women who had children, and what Nanja said was no longer tenable. Furthermore, he was confused by the stories and was no longer sure who Christ's father was. He was inclined to think it was Joseph, since he had been told that they had always lived together, but Nanja said that Joseph was only *like* his father and that his real father was God. He could make nothing of this. All he understood was, that if it was possible to talk about it at all, the relationship between father and son was nothing like as intimate as he had always imagined it to be.

The boy sensed something of the ambivalence of feeling towards the father that is enshrined in all religions, and attacked his religion because it weakened that paternal relationship. Of course his opposition soon ceased to be doubt as to the truth of the doctrine and was instead turned directly against the person of God. God had been harsh and cruel in his treatment of his son, yet he behaved no better towards human beings. He had sacrificed his son and demanded the same of Abraham. He began to be afraid of God.

If he was Christ, then his father was God. But the God that religion sought to impose on him was no real substitute for the father he had loved and of whom he did not want to be deprived. His love for his father gave him his critical sharpness. He put up a fight against God so that he could hold on to his father, and in doing so was actually defending the old father against the new one.

Here he had a difficult stage in the process of detaching himself from his father to complete.

Thus it was the old love for his father, revealed in earliest days, on which he drew for the energy to combat God and for the sharpness to criticize religion. On the other hand, this hostility towards the new God was not an original act but was modelled on a hostile impulse towards his father that had come into being under the influence of the anxiety-dream, and was fundamentally only the resurgence of the same impulse. The two opposing emotional impulses that were later to rule his whole life met here in a battle of ambivalence over the issue of religion. What this struggle yielded in the form of symptoms, his blasphemous ideas, the compulsion which came over him to think 'God – crud', 'God – swine' was also for this reason a genuine compromise outcome, as we shall see from the analysis of these ideas in the context of anal eroticism.

Some other compulsive symptoms of a less typical kind lead us with equal certainty to the father, but also reveal the connection between the obsessive-compulsive neurosis and the earlier chance occurrences.

One element in the ceremonial piety that he eventually used to expiate his blasphemies was the requirement that under certain conditions he should breathe in a ritual manner. When making the sign of the cross he had to breathe in deeply each time or exhale loudly. In his language breath is the same as spirit. This, therefore, was the role of the Holy Spirit. He had either to breathe in the Holy Spirit or else to breathe out the evil spirits which he had heard and read about.[3] He also ascribed to these evil spirits the blasphemous thoughts for which he imposed such great penance on himself. He was obliged to exhale, however, whenever he saw beggars, cripples, or ugly, old and wretched people and he could not see how to connect this compulsion with the spirits. The only way he could account for it to himself was that he did it so as not to become like them.

Then, in connection with a dream, analysis brought the explanation that it was only after the age of five that he had begun to breathe out when he saw pitiful individuals, and that this was connected with his father. He had not seen his father for many long months when one day his mother said that she would take the children to the city and show them something that would make them very happy. She then took them to a sanatorium where they saw their father again; he looked ill and his son felt very sorry for him. His father, then, was the archetype of all those cripples, beggars and poor people, the sight of whom obliged him to breathe out, just as the father is normally the archetype of the grimaces seen in anxiety states and of the caricatures drawn to express contempt. We shall discover elsewhere that this pitying attitude goes back to a particular detail of the primal scene, which took effect at this late stage in the obsessive-compulsive neurosis.

The resolution not to become like them, which was the motivation for his breathing out in front of cripples, was thus the old identification with the father transformed into a negative. And yet he was also copying his father in a positive sense, for his noisy breathing was an imitation of the sounds he had heard his father make during intercourse.[4] The Holy Spirit owed its origins to this sign of erotic excitement in a man. Repression turned this breathing into an evil spirit, for which there also existed a second genealogy, that of the malaria from which he had been suffering at the time of the primal scene.

The rejection of these evil spirits corresponded to an unmistakably ascetic aspect of his character, which was also expressed in other reactions. When he heard that Christ had once driven out evil spirits into pigs, which then plunged into an abyss, he thought of the way his sister, in the earliest years of her childhood, before he could remember, had rolled down from the harbour cliff-path on to the beach. She too was one of those evil spirits and pigs; it was only a short step from this to 'God – swine'. Even his father had turned out to be dominated by sensuality in just the same way. When he was told the story of the first man, he was struck by the similarity between Adam's fate and his own. He expressed hypocritical astonishment when talking to Nanja that Adam had allowed himself to be plunged into misery by a woman, and promised Nanja that he would never get married. Around this time, as a result of his sister's seduction, his feelings of enmity towards womankind found powerful expression. They were later to trouble him often enough in his erotic life. His sister became the permanent embodiment, to him, of temptation and sin. When he had been to confession he would feel pure and free from sin. But then it would seem as if his sister was watching for an opportunity to plunge him into sin once more, and before he was aware of it he would have provoked a quarrel with his sister, which made him sinful again. In this way he was obliged to reproduce the fact of seduction over and over again. He never, incidentally, divulged his blasphemous thoughts in the confessional, even though they weighed heavily on him.

We have unexpectedly progressed to a discussion of symptoms manifested in the later years of obsessive-compulsive neurosis; let us therefore skip the very great deal that occurred in the meantime and relate how the condition came to an end. We already know that, as well as being a permanent condition, it was subject to periodic intensification, such as on one occasion, which we are unable as yet to understand, when a boy in the same street died, with whom he was able to identify. When he was ten he acquired a German tutor who quickly came to have considerable influence over him. It is most instructive to find that the whole heavy weight of piety disappeared, never to return, once he had noticed, and learnt from his teacher's didactic conversation, that this father-substitute set no store by piety and did not believe in the truth of religion. His piety fell away, along with his dependence on his father, who was now being superseded by a new, more affable father. It must be said that this did not occur without one last flaring-up of his obsessive-compulsive neurosis; he had a particularly strong memory of the compulsion to think of the Holy Trinity every time he saw three piles of dung lying together on the street. He simply never gave in to one stimulus without making a final attempt to keep hold of what no longer had any value for him. When his teacher talked him out of his cruelty towards small creatures he put a stop to his misdeeds, but not before he had had one last orgy of cutting up caterpillars. He behaved in exactly the same way in analytic treatment by developing a transitory 'negative reaction'; whenever something important had been resolved he would try to negate the effects for a while, in that there would be a worsening of symptoms that had been resolved. We know that in general children behave in a similar way in the face of prohibitions. When they have been told off, for example for making a disagreeable noise, they will repeat it once more after they have been told not to, before stopping. In doing so they make it look as if they have stopped voluntarily, thus defying the prohibition.

Under the German teacher's influence he found a new and better way to sublimate his sadism, which, as befitted his approaching puberty, had then gained the upper hand over his masochism. He developed a passion for military life, for uniforms, weapons and horses, and used this to feed his constant daydreaming. Under a man's influence he had thus got away from his passive attitudes and was initially on a fairly normal track. One after-effect of his attachment to his teacher, who left soon afterwards, was that in later life he preferred the German element (doctors, clinics, women) to the native one (representing the father), which was of great benefit for the therapeutic transference.

Another dream belongs in the period before his liberation by the teacher, which I mention here because it had been forgotten up until the moment when it surfaced in therapy. He saw himself riding a horse, pursued by a giant caterpillar. He recognized a reference here to a still earlier dream from the period before the teacher came, which we had interpreted long before. In this earlier dream he saw the devil in black robes, assuming the upright stance which had previously so terrified him in the wolf and the lion. With his outstretched finger he was pointing to a giant snail. He had quickly guessed that this devil was the demon who features in a well-known poem, and the dream itself a reworking of a widely disseminated picture showing the demon in a love-scene with a young girl. The snail, an exquisite symbol of female sexuality, stood for the woman. Guided by the demon's pointing gesture, we were quickly able to declare the meaning of the dream to be his longing for someone who could give him the final instruction he lacked in the mysteries of sexual intercourse, just as his father had first enlightened him long ago in the primal scene.

In amplification of the later dream, where the female symbol was replaced by the male one, he remembered a particular experience that had taken place a little while before. Riding on the estate one day he passed a peasant, asleep with his son lying next to him. The boy woke his father and said something to him, whereupon the father began to shout at the rider and ran after him, until he and his horse quickly moved off. This was in conjunction with a second memory that on that same estate there were trees that were completely white, completely covered in caterpillar cocoons. We see that he took flight from realization of the fantasy that the son was sleeping with his father, and that he brought in the white trees to create a reference to the anxiety-dream, to the white wolves in the walnut tree. It was thus a positive eruption of fear expressed at the feminine attitude towards men, which initially he had defended himself against by means of religious sublimation; soon after that he was to defend himself against it even more effectively, by means of military sublimation.

It would be a major error, however, to assume that, once the compulsive symptoms had been eliminated, no permanent effects of the obsessive-compulsive neurosis remained. The process had led to the victory of pious belief over critical inquiry and rebellion, and was predicated upon repression of the homosexual attitude. Both factors resulted in permanent disadvantages. After this first great defeat his intellectual activity remained seriously impaired. He developed no particular eagerness to learn and demonstrated nothing of the critical acuity with which, at the tender age of five, he had subverted religious doctrine. The repression of his excessively strong homosexuality, which took place during the anxiety-dream, meant that this significant impulse was reserved for the unconscious mind, thus maintaining its original attitude towards its objective and eluding all the sublimations to which it would normally lend itself. For this reason, the patient lacked all the social interests which give content to life. Only as we succeeded through analytic therapy in releasing his homosexuality from its fetters was there a turn for the better in this state of affairs, and it was a remarkable thing to watch the way in which – without any urging on the part of the physician – each liberated element of his homo-sexual libido was eager to be brought to bear on life and attached to the great common concerns of humanity.

### Notes

1. I also attempted repeatedly to bring the patient's story forward by at least a year, putting the seduction at $4^1/_4$ and the dream on his fifth birth-day, etc. There was nothing to be gained by these intervals, after all, but the patient was not to be moved, although he was, incidentally, unable to dispel the last vestiges of my scepticism. To postpone everything by a year in this way clearly had no significance for the impression made by his story, nor for the discussions and arguments arising from it.
2. And especially about blows to the penis.
3. This symptom had developed, as we shall learn, at the age of five, when he learned to read.
4. Provided we accept the reality of the primal scene!

## VII *Anal Eroticism and the Castration Complex*

I must ask the reader to remember that this history of an infan-tile neurosis was recovered as a by-product, so to speak, of the analysis of a patient who had fallen ill in more mature years. I was thus obliged to piece it together out of even tinier fragments than those that are normally available when any kind of synthesis is attempted. Such work, which is otherwise not difficult, finds its natural limit at the point where it becomes a question of captur-ing a multidimensional structure in the two-dimensionality of description. I must therefore content myself with offering individ-ual limbs which the reader can join together into a living whole.

The obsessive-compulsive neurosis I have described developed, as I have emphasized repeatedly, out of an anal-sadistic constitution. Up until now, however, we have only considered one of these two principal factors, sadism and its transformations. Anything concerned with anal eroticism I have deliberately left on one side in order to give a full account of it here.

Analysts have long agreed that the many involuntary impulses [*Triebregungen*] that can be summed up as anal eroticism are extraordinarily and inestimably important to the development of the individual's sexual life and to inner activity as a whole. And equally, that one of the most important expressions of eroticism derived from this source and recast in a different mould is to be found in the treatment of money, a valuable substance which, in the course of the individual's life, attracts the psychic interest which properly belongs to that product of the anal zone, faeces.[1] We have grown accustomed to tracing interest in money, where its nature is libidinal rather than rational, back to excremental pleasure, and to expect of any normal person that his relationship to money should be kept free of libidinal influences and controlled by realistic considerations.

In our patient's case this relationship was particularly badly disrupted at the time of his later illness, this being not the least important reason for his lack of independence and his inability to cope with life. Having inherited money from both his father and his uncle, he was now very rich and it was manifestly of great importance to him that people should know that he was a rich man; he could be greatly offended if he was underestimated in this regard. And yet he did not know how much he possessed, what his expenditure was, nor how much was left. It was difficult to know whether to call him a miser or a spendthrift. Sometimes he behaved one way, sometimes another, but never in a way that suggested consistent intentions. Certain striking traits of character, which I shall describe later, might lead one to conclude that he was an unrepentant swank who regarded his wealth as his greatest personal asset and who would never even begin to put feelings on a par with money. But he did not judge other people according to their wealth and there were many occasions when he actually turned out to be modest, sympathetic and ready to help. It was simply that money eluded his conscious control and held another meaning for him.

I mentioned earlier that I regarded with deep suspicion the way in which he consoled himself for the loss of his sister – who in the later years of her life had become his best friend – with the thought that now he would not need to share their parents' inheritance with her. More striking still, perhaps, was the calm way in which he could tell me this, as if he had no comprehension of the coarseness of feeling to which he was admitting. Analysis rehabilitated him to some extent by demonstrating that his pain at his sister's death had merely been displaced, but now it seemed more incomprehensible than ever that he should have thought he could find a substitute for his sister in his increased wealth.

His behaviour in another instance seemed to be a mystery even to him. After his father's death, the fortune he had left was divided between himself and his mother. It was administered by his mother, who responded to his requests for money, as he himself acknowledged, with irreproachable generosity. And yet any discussion of money matters between them would end with the most violent reproaches on his part: that she did not love him, that her only thought was to save money by keeping him short, and that she would probably prefer it if he were dead, so that she could have all the money for herself. In tears his mother would then protest her unselfish motives and he would be ashamed, assuring her quite truthfully that he really did not think of her in that way, and yet sure that the same scene would be repeated on the next occasion.

That faeces signified money to him long before he entered analysis can be seen from many chance occurrences, two of which I shall relate here. At a time when his bowels were still unconnected with his illness, he once visited a poor cousin living in a large town. As he left he reproached himself for not giving his cousin financial support, whereupon he immediately had 'perhaps the strongest urge to defecate he had ever felt in his life'. Two years later he did indeed offer to pay his cousin an allowance. And the other instance: at the age of 18, while preparing for his final examinations at school, he visited a fellow-student and came to an agreement with him which seemed advisable in the light of the fear they both felt of failing the examination.[2] They had decided to bribe the school janitor, and his share of the money they needed to find was of course the larger one. On the way home he was thinking that he would willingly pay even more if he could only pass, if only nothing would go wrong in the examination, and he did indeed have a little accident[3] before he could reach his own front door.

All this prepares us for the fact that during his later illness he suffered from extremely persistent disturbance of the bowel function, though one that fluctuated with different causes. When he entered treatment with me he had become accustomed to receiving enemas, administered by a companion; he might not experience spontaneous emptying of the bowels for months at a time, unless there was sudden stimulus from a particular quarter, following which normal bowel activity would be resumed for a few days. His principal complaint was that he felt the world to be shrouded in a veil, or that there was a veil dividing him from the world. This veil was torn open only at the moment when the content of the bowel left the bowel after an enema, whereupon he would feel healthy again, and normal.[4]

The colleague to whom I referred my patient for an assessment of his bowel condition was sufficiently perceptive to declare it to be determined by functional or even psychic factors, and to eschew medical intervention. Neither this, incidentally, nor the diet he ordered my patient to follow, were of any use. During the years in which he was in analysis he never had any spontaneous bowel movements (except under the influence of those sudden stimuli). The patient allowed himself to be persuaded that any more intensive treatment of the refractory organ would simply make the condition worse, and was content to bring about a forced evacuation of the bowels once or twice a week by means of an enema or laxative.

In discussing these disruptions to the function of the bowel I have allowed my patient's later state of illness to take up more space than I had intended in a piece of work devoted to his childhood neurosis. There were two reasons for my decision: first, the fact that the bowel symptoms had remained virtually unchanged from the period of childhood neurosis to the later one, and, second, that they were enormously significant in bringing the treatment to an end.

We know how important doubt is to the physician analysing a case of obsessive-compulsive neurosis. It is the patient's most powerful weapon, his preferred means of resistance. For years, thanks to this doubt, our patient too was able to let the efforts made in therapy bounce off him, safe behind a barricade of respectful indifference. Nothing changed, and there was no way of convincing him. Finally I recognized the significance of his bowel disorder for my intentions: it represented the touch of hysteria that is regularly found to underlie any obsessive-compulsive neurosis. I promised the patient that his bowel activity would be fully restored; my undertaking forced his disbelief into the open, so that I then had the satisfaction of watching his doubt disappear as his bowel began to 'add its voice' to the work, as if it were an hysterically affected organ, regaining its normal function, which had for so long been impaired, in the course of a few weeks.

I shall now return to the patient's childhood, to a time when faeces cannot possibly have signified money to him.

He experienced bowel disorders at a very early age, especially the most common kind, entirely normal in children, namely incontinence. We would undoubtedly be correct, however, in rejecting any kind of pathological explanation for these earliest incidents and seeing in them merely proof of his intention not to be disturbed in or held back from the pleasure accompanying the function of evacuation. He continued to be greatly amused, well into his later illness, by anal jokes and exhibitions of the kind that appeal to the natural coarseness of many sections of society.

During the era of the English governess it repeatedly came about that he and Nanja were obliged to share a bedroom with the woman they loathed. Nanja noted sympathetically that it was always on these nights that he soiled the sheets, something that he normally no longer did. He was not at all ashamed of this: it was an expression of his defiance towards the governess.

A year later (at the age of $4\frac{1}{2}$), during his period of great anxiety, it so happened that he once soiled his trousers during the day. He was dreadfully ashamed, wailing as he was cleaned up that he could not go on living like this. Something had changed in the meantime, then, and by turning our attention to his lament we can track down what it was. It turned out that the words 'he could not go on living like this' were spoken in imitation of someone else. On some occasion or other[5] his mother had taken him along when she accompanied the doctor who had come to visit her to the railway station. As they walked she was lamenting her pains and bleeding and exclaimed, in those selfsame words, 'I cannot go on living like this', without imagining that the child whose hand she was holding would retain them in his memory. The lament, which he was incidentally to repeat on countless occasions in his later illness, thus signified his identification with his mother.

Soon a missing link between the two incidents, as regards both time and content, came into his memory. Once, at the beginning of his period of anxiety, it came about that his mother, greatly concerned, issued warnings that the children were to be guarded against the dysentery that had made an appearance in the vicinity of their estate. He enquired what that might be and, when he heard that one symptom of dysentery is blood in the stools, he became very anxious and claimed to have found blood in his own stools; he was afraid of dying of dysentery, but allowed himself to be examined and persuaded that he had made a mistake and that there was no need to be afraid. We can understand that his anxiety was an attempt to carry through the identification with his mother, about whose bleeding he had heard in the conversation with the doctor. In his later attempt to identify with his mother (at the age of $4\frac{1}{2}$) he had dispensed with the blood; he no longer understood what it was he was feeling, thought that he was ashamed of himself and did not know that he was seized with mortal fear; yet this is what his lament quite unambiguously reveals.

At that time his mother, suffering as she did from gynaecological complaints, was generally fearful for herself and her children, and it is perfectly probable that his anxiety was founded on identification with his mother, as well as the other motives which fuelled it.

Now, what is the significance of his identification with his mother?

Between his impudent exploitation of incontinence at the age of $3\frac{1}{2}$ and his horror of it at the age of $4\frac{1}{2}$ there lies the dream that inaugurated the period of anxiety, bringing a belated understanding of the scene[6] he experienced at the age of 18 months and enlightenment as to a woman's role in the sexual act. The obvious explanation is that the change in his attitude towards defecation is also connected with that great upheaval. Dysentery was clearly the name of the illness he had heard his mother complaining about, the one you could not go on living with; his understanding was that his mother's illness was not gynaecological in nature, but an illness of the bowel. Under the influence of the primal scene he inferred that the connection ran as follows: his mother's illness was due to the thing his father had done with her,[7] and his fear of finding blood in his stools, that is, of being as ill as his mother, was the rejection of his identification with his mother in that sexual scene, the same rejection that awakened him from his dream. His fear was also proof, however, that in his later processing of the primal scene he had put himself in his mother's place and envied her this relationship with his father. The organ through which he could express his identification with the female and his passive homosexual attitude towards the male was the anal zone. Dysfunction in this zone had acquired the significance of the stirrings of feminine tenderness, which it retained also during his later illness.

At this point we must air an objection, discussion of which could contribute greatly to clarification of an apparently confused state of affairs. We have had to assume that during the dreaming process he understood women to be castrated, having a wound in the place of the male member which serves the purposes of sexual intercourse, and that castration was thus the condition of female identity; under the threat of this loss he repressed the feminine attitude towards the male and awoke in fear from his homosexual raptures. How is this understanding of sexual intercourse, this acknowledgement of the vagina, to be reconciled with his choice of the bowel as a means of identification with the female? Are his bowel symptoms not founded on what is probably a more ancient conception, which entirely contradicts castration anxiety, that of the anus as the site of sexual intercourse?

It is true that this contradiction exists and that the two conceptions are inconsistent with one another. The question is merely whether they need to be consistent. We are disconcerted because we are always inclined to treat unconscious inner processes as if they were conscious ones, forgetting the profound differences between the two psychic systems.

When in excited anticipation the Christmas dream conjured up the image of his parents' sexual intercourse, once observed (or reconstructed), the old view of it no doubt occurred to him first, according to which that part of the woman's body receiving the penis was the anus. What else could he have thought when he watched this scene at the age of 18 months?[8] But now, at the age of 4, came the new event. His previous experiences, the hints he had received as to the possibility of castration, now awoke and cast doubt on his 'cloaca theory', prompting recognition of the difference between the sexes and the sexual role of the female. He then behaved as children generally do when they are given an explanation they do not want – whether of sexual matters or of anything else. He rejected the new one – in this case, motivated by castration anxiety – and held on to the old one. He decided in favour of the bowel and against the vagina in the same way as he did later, and for similar motives, when he took his father's part against God. The new explanation was rejected, and he held fast to the old theory, which probably provided the material for his identification with the female, later appearing as the fear of a death brought on by bowel infection, and for his first religious scruples, such as whether Christ had a backside. Yet it is not as if his new insight had failed to have any effect; on the contrary, it took effect in a remarkably powerful way, providing the motivation for keeping the whole dream process in a state of repression and excluding it from later, conscious assimilation. But this was the full extent of the effect it had, for it had no influence in deciding the sexual problem. It was indeed a contradiction that, from that point onward, castration anxiety could exist alongside identification with the female by means of the bowel, but it was only a logical contradiction, which does not mean very much. Rather, the whole process is characteristic of the workings of the unconscious. Repression is a different thing from out-of-hand dismissal.

In studying the genesis of the wolf phobia we were tracing the effects of the new insight into the sexual act; now, investigating disorderly bowel activity, we find ourselves in the realm of the ancient cloaca theory. The two standpoints remain separated from each other by a stage of repression. The female attitude towards the male, dismissed through the act of repression, withdraws, so to speak, into bowel symptoms and expresses itself through the frequent episodes of diarrhoea, constipation and bowel pain of the patient's childhood years. His later sexual fantasies, constructed on the basis of correct sexual knowledge, can now be expressed regressively as bowel disorder. We cannot understand them, however, until we have uncovered the change in meaning that faeces have undergone since the patient's earliest childhood.[9]

I hinted earlier that I had kept back a part of the content of the primal scene, which I can now fill in. The child eventually interrupted his parents' intimacy by evacuating his bowels, thus providing a motive for his crying. As far as criticism of this additional information is concerned, the same holds true here as for my previous discussion of the content of this scene. The patient accepted this reconstructed concluding action and appeared to confirm it by means of 'transitory symptoms'. A further additional detail that I had suggested, namely that the father had been annoyed by the disturbance and given vent to his displeasure by shouting at the child, had to be dropped. There was no reaction to it in the material of the analysis.

The detail which I have just supplied is not, of course, all of a piece with the rest of the scene's content. Here it is not a question of something imprinted on the memory from outside, which we can expect to encounter again in any number of later indications, but rather of the child's own reaction. Not a single detail of the story would change if this manifestation had not occurred, or if it had been inserted into the sequence of events later on. There is no doubt as to how we are to understand it, however. It signifies excitement in the anal zone (in the broadest sense of the word). In other cases of a similar type the observation of sexual intercourse ended in urination; in the same circumstances an adult male would be aware of an erection. The fact that the little boy produces a stool as a sign of his sexual excitement is to be judged as characteristic of the sexual constitution that is already in place. He immediately takes up a passive attitude and shows a greater inclination towards later identification with the female than with the male.

Here he uses the contents of the bowels in the same way as any other child, in one of its first and earliest senses. Faeces are the first *gift*, the child's first loving sacrifice, a part of his own body that is relinquished, but only in favour of a beloved person.[10] Its use as an act of defiance, as in this case towards the governess at the age of $3\frac{1}{2}$, is merely to give its earlier meaning as a gift a negative slant. The *grumus merdae* left by burglars at the scene of the crime appears to have both meanings: both scorn and a regressive way of offering compensation. When a higher level has been reached, the earlier one can always be put to use in a negative, debased sense. Repression finds expression in the coexistence of antithetical impulses.[11]

At a later stage of sexual development, faeces assume the meaning of *babies*. Babies are born through the anus, after all, just like stools. The meaning of faeces as a gift readily permits this transformation. Linguistic usage refers to babies as 'gifts'; we hear more frequently of the woman 'presenting her husband with a baby', but in unconscious usage equal weight is quite rightly given to the other side of the relationship, with the woman 'receiving' the baby from her husband as a gift.

The meaning of faeces as money arises from its meaning as a gift, but branches off in another direction.

The deeper meaning behind our patient's early cover-memory of producing his first tantrum because he did not get enough Christmas presents is now revealed. What was missing was sexual satisfaction, which he had taken in an anal sense. His sexual exploration before the dream had prepared him for the fact, grasped during the dreaming process, that the sexual act solves the mystery of where babies come from. Even before the dream he did not like tiny children. Once he found a little bird, still naked, which had fallen out of the nest and, taking it for a tiny human being, had been filled with dread. Analysis demonstrated that all the tiny creatures, caterpillars and insects he had raged against had signified tiny children in his mind.[12] His own relationship with his elder sister had given him cause to think a great deal about how older children relate to younger ones; and when on one occasion Nanja told him that his mother loved him so much because he was the youngest he acquired an understandable motive for wishing that there should be no younger child to follow him. His fear of this youngest child was then reactivated under the influence of the dream that brought his parents' intercourse to his attention.

We ought therefore to add a new sexual current to those we already know about; like the others it stems from the primal scene reproduced in the dream. In his identification with the female (the mother) he is ready to give his father a child and is jealous of the mother who has already done so, and may perhaps do so again.

By way of this detour demonstrating a common point of departure in their significance as gifts, money can now attract to itself the meaning of children, and in this way take over the expression of feminine (homosexual) satisfaction. In our patient's case this process occurred once at a time when brother and sister were both staying in a German sanatorium, and he saw his father give his sister two large banknotes. In fantasy he had always harboured suspicions about his father and his sister; now his jealousy was awakened and he fell on his sister as soon as they were alone, demanding his share of the money with such violence and heaping such reproaches on her that his sister, weeping, threw the whole amount at him. It was not just the real matter of the money that had upset him, but rather the baby, the anal sexual satisfaction he desired from his father. This, then, was his source of comfort when his sister died – during their father's lifetime. The scandalous thought which occurred to him when he heard the news of her death in fact meant simply: now I am the only child and my father must love me and me alone. Yet while the thought in itself was entirely capable of becoming conscious, its homosexual background was so unbearable that it was easier to disguise it as filthy greed, for this no doubt came as a great relief.

It was the same story when, after his father's death, he reproached his mother so unjustly for wanting to cheat him out of his money, for loving money more than she loved him. His old jealous feelings that she might love a child other than himself, and the possibility that she might have hoped for another child after him, compelled him to make accusations which he himself acknowledged to be groundless.

This analysis of the meaning of faeces makes it clear that the compulsive thoughts obliging him to make a connection between God and faeces had another meaning besides the abuse he thought them to be. They were in fact a true compromise outcome in which a current of tender devotion played just as much of a part as that of hostile invective. 'God – crud' was probably an abbreviated form of an offer which sometimes comes to one's ears in unabbreviated form. 'To shit on God' or 'to give a shit for God' can also mean to give him a baby, to be presented by him with a baby. The old meaning of 'gift', negatively debased, and the meaning of 'baby' which later developed out of this are combined in the patient's compulsive phrase. The latter expresses a feminine tenderness, a readiness to renounce manliness if in return one can be loved as a woman. Precisely that impulse towards God, then, articulated so unambiguously in the delusive system devised by the paranoid president of the Senate, Schreber.

When, later, I come to describe the resolution of the patient's last symptoms, we shall see once again how his bowel disorder had placed itself at the service of the homosexual current, expressing the feminine attitude towards the father. A new meaning of faeces will now clear the ground for a discussion of the castration complex.

Given that the column of faeces stimulates the erogenous mucous membrane of the bowel, it functions as an active organ, behaving as the penis does towards the mucous membrane of the vagina and acting as a precursor of the penis, so to speak, in the cloacal phase. The surrender of faeces in favour of (out of love for) another person, for its part, becomes the model of castration and is the first case in which a part of one's own body[13] is renounced in the hope of winning favour from a beloved other. What is otherwise narcissistic love for one's own penis is thus not without some trace of anal eroticism. And so faeces, baby, penis, all come together to form a single entity, one unconscious concept – *sit venia verbo* [if you will excuse the expression] – that of something small that can be separated from the body. Along these connecting pathways displacements and reinforcements of libido-charge [*Libidobesetzung*] can take place that are significant to a patient's pathology and can be uncovered in analysis.

We now know what our patient's initial attitude towards the problem of castration was. He dismissed it out of hand, maintaining that intercourse took place in the anus. When I say 'dismissed', I mean by this primarily that he refused to know anything about it, in the sense of repressing it. He did not actually pass judgement as to whether it existed or not, but effectively it did not. This attitude cannot have remained the definitive one, however, even during the years of childhood neurosis. Later on we can produce good evidence to show that he acknowledged castration as a fact. On this point, too, he behaved in that characteristic way that certainly makes both description and empathetic response so extraordinarily difficult. At first he expressed resistance, then gave in, but the one reaction did not cancel out the other. In the end two contradictory currents existed alongside one another, one of which abhorred the very idea of castration, while the other was prepared to accept it, consoling itself with femaleness as a substitute. The third current, the oldest and deepest, which had simply dismissed castration out of hand, without entertaining even the possibility of judging whether it was real or not, could no doubt also still be activated. Elsewhere[14] I have recounted an hallucination that occurred to this selfsame patient at the age of five, which in this context requires only the addition of a short commentary:

'When I was five I was playing in the garden near my nurse, using my penknife to carve the bark of one of those walnut trees[15] which also came up in my dream.[16] Suddenly I was inexpressibly terrified to discover that I had cut right through the little finger of my (right or left?) hand, so that it was only attached by the skin. I felt no pain, only great fear. I did not dare say anything to my nurse, who was only a few steps away, but sank down on to the nearest bench and just sat there, incapable of even glancing at my finger. In the end I calmed down, took a long look at my finger and, lo and behold, it wasn't damaged at all.'

We know that after he had been introduced to sacred history at the age of $4\frac{1}{2}$, intense intellectual activity set in, which later turned into compulsive piety. We may therefore assume that this hallucination occurred around the time when he was making up his mind to acknowledge the reality of castration, and that it was perhaps intended to mark precisely that step. Even the patient's little correction is not without interest. If he hallucinated the same horrific experience which Tasso relates of his hero Tancred in *Gerusalemme Liberata*, we are justified in suggesting that, for my young patient too, the tree represented a woman. He was thus playing the role of the father, bringing together his mother's bleeding, which he knew about, and the castration of women, the 'wound', which he now acknowledged.

The stimulus to hallucinate about cutting off a finger was provided, he told me later, by the story of one of his relatives who was born with six toes, the superfluous member being hacked off immediately with an axe. Thus women had no penis because it had been removed at birth. In this way he came to accept, at the time when he was suffering from obsessive-compulsive neurosis, what he had learned in the dream process and rejected at that time by means of repression. The ritual circumcision of Christ, and of the Jews in general, could not, moreover, have remained unknown to him at a time when he was reading and discussing the sacred story.

It was undoubtedly at this time that his father became the terrifying figure who threatens castration. The cruel God with whom he was wrestling, who allowed people to become guilty so that he could then punish them, who sacrificed his own son and the sons of men, threw the shadow of his character back on to the father – whom the boy sought to defend, on the other hand, against that same God. He has a phylogenetic schema to fulfil here and manages to do so even though his own personal experiences do not seem to square with it. The threats, or hints, of castration he had received had actually emanated from women,[17] but this did not delay the end result for long. In the end it was his father at whose hands he feared castration. On this point heredity triumphed over accidental experience; in the pre-history of the human race it was certainly the father who carried out castration as a punishment, subsequently reducing it to the practice of circumcision. The more he repressed his sensuality as the process of obsessive-compulsive neurosis went on[18] the more natural it seemed to him to endow his father, that true representative of sensual activity, with evil intentions of this kind.

The identification of his father with the castrator[19] was significant in that it was the source of an intense unconscious hostility towards him – which went as far as wishing him dead – as well as of the guilt he felt in response to this. To this extent he was, however, behaving normally, that is, like any other neurotic individual possessed by a positive Oedipal complex. What was remarkable was that in him a counter-current existed for this too, according to which his father was in fact the castrated figure, and as such demanded his sympathy.

In my analysis of the breathing rituals prompted by the sight of cripples, beggars, etc., I was able to show that this symptom could also be traced back to the father, whom he had felt sorry for when he visited him in the clinic during his illness. Analysis permitted us to trace this thread back still further. Very early on, probably even before the seduction (at the age of $3\frac{1}{4}$), there was a poor day-labourer on the estate whose job it was to carry water into the house. He was unable to speak, supposedly because his tongue had been cut out. He was probably a deaf mute. The little boy was very fond of him and pitied him with all his heart. When he died, he looked for him in the heavens.[20] This man was thus the first of the cripples for whom he felt such sympathy and, judging by the context and the point at which he was mentioned in analysis, undoubtedly a father-substitute.

In analysis other memories followed on from this of servants whom he liked; in each case he dwelt on the fact that they were in poor health or Jewish (circumcision!). The lackey who helped clean him up after his little accident at the age of $4\frac{1}{2}$ was Jewish too, as well as consumptive, and enjoyed his sympathy. All these figures can be placed in the period before he visited his father in the sanatorium, that is, before formation of the symptom, which was really intended to keep identification with the person pitied at a distance by means of exhalation. Then suddenly, in connection with a dream, the analysis turned back to the patient's very early life, giving him the opportunity to assert that he had observed the disappearance of the penis in coitus during the primal scene, pitied his father on this account and rejoiced at the reappearance of what he had thought to be lost. Another new feeling, then, inspired by this scene. Incidentally, we cannot fail to recognize the narcissistic roots of such sympathy, underlined by the word itself.[21]

### Notes

1. [Throughout this chapter Freud uses the word *Kot* to denote faeces. This word can be translated into a variety of linguistic registers. It may be used coarsely, as in the verbal association of God and crud (p. 255), or more politely, as a circumlocution. Freud normally uses it in a doctorly sense, as here.]
2. The patient told me that in his mother tongue it is not possible to use the familiar German word '*Durchfall*' to designate a disturbance of the bowel. [*Durchfall* can mean both 'failure' and 'diarrhoea'.]
3. This expression means the same in the patient's mother tongue as it does in German. [And in English!]

4. The same effect was achieved whether someone else administered the enema, or whether he saw to it himself.

5. We cannot say for certain when this was, but it was in any case before the anxiety-dream that occurred at the age of four, and probably before his parents went away.

6. See above p. 229.

7. He was probably not mistaken in this assumption.

8. Or as long as he had no understanding of canine coitus.

9. Cf. 'Über Triebumsetzungen insbesondere der Analerotik' ['On the Transformations of Instinct [Drive]' 1917] etc.

10. It could easily be confirmed, I think, that infants only use their excrement to soil people they know and love; strangers are not considered worthy of such an honour. In *Three Essays on the Theory of Sexuality* I mention the very first use of faeces as a means of auto-erotic stimulation of the mucous membrane of the bowel; from this we progress to the fact that a defecation object is a crucial consideration for the child, who thereby expresses obedience or compliance towards that person. This relation persists in the fact that the older child, too, will only allow certain special people to put him on the pot or help him to urinate; here other purposes of satisfaction must also be taken into account.

11. It is known that the unconscious does not recognize the word 'no'; opposites coincide here. Negation is only introduced through the process of repression.

12. Likewise vermin, which frequently stand for little children in dreams and phobias.

13. This is entirely the sense in which faeces are treated by the child.

14. 'Über fausse reconaissance ("déjà raconté") während der psychoanalytischen Arbeit' ['On *fausse reconaissance ("déjà raconté")* in Psychoanalytical Work', 1914].

15. Corrected on a later retelling to: 'I don't think I was actually digging the knife into the tree. I am getting confused with another memory which must also have been an hallucinatory forgery; I cut into the tree with my knife and then *blood* came out of the tree.'

16. Cf. 'Märchenstoffe in Träumen' ['Fairy-tale Matter in Dreams'].

17. We know this is true of Nanja; the same thing will turn out to be true of another woman.

18. See the evidence for this on pp. 256–7.

19. Among the most excruciating and at the same time most grotesque symptoms of his later suffering was his relationship to a tailor, from whom he had ordered an item of apparel: his respect and timidity in the face of

this exalted person, his attempts to win him over with excessively large tips and his despair at the outcome of the work, whatever it might have been.

20. In this context I might mention dreams that occurred later than the anxiety-dream, but still while they were living on the first estate, which depicted the scene of coitus as an event taking place between heavenly bodies.

21. [The German word *Mitleid* (sympathy) quite explicitly means 'suffering with'.]

## VIII *Supplementary Material from Earliest Childhood – Solution*

It is often the case in analysis that new material surfaces in the memory once the end is in sight, material which up until then has been kept carefully hidden. Or else an inconspicuous remark will be tossed casually into the conversation, in an indifferent tone of voice, as if it were something quite superfluous, and then something else added on another occasion which makes the physician prick up his ears, until we finally recognize that these passed-over scraps of memory hold the key to the most important of secrets, glossed over by the patient's neurosis.

At an early stage my patient had recounted a memory dating from the time when his difficult behaviour would suddenly veer over into anxiety. He was chasing a lovely big butterfly with yellow stripes, whose large wings had pointed tips – a swallow-tail, in fact. Suddenly, as the butterfly settled on a flower, he was overcome by a terrible fear of the creature and ran away screaming.

This memory recurred from time to time in the analysis and demanded some sort of explanation, which for a long time was not forthcoming. We could assume from the outset that a detail of this kind had not retained a place in his memory for its own sake, but was a cover-memory representing something more important which was somehow bound up with it. One day he said that in his language the word for a butterfly was Babuschka, or little granny; butterflies in general made him think of women and girls, while beetles and caterpillars were like boys. It must surely have been the memory of a female, then, which had been awakened in that scene of anxiety. I will not conceal the fact that at the time I suggested as a possibility that the yellow stripes of the butterfly reminded him of similar stripes on an item of clothing worn by a woman. I do so only in order to show by example how inadequate the physician's conjectures are as a general rule in solving questions that have been raised, and how wrong it is to attribute responsibility for the outcome of the analysis to the physician's fantasies and suggestions.

Many months later, in an entirely different context, the patient remarked that it was the way the butterfly's wings opened and closed once it had settled that had given him such an uncanny feeling. It had been like a woman opening her legs, and the legs then made the shape of a Roman V, which as we know was the hour at which he used to experience a darkening of his mood, both in his boyhood and in the present day.

This was a notion that would never have occurred to me and that I was the more inclined to value when I considered that the process of association it revealed was genuinely infantile in character. I have often noticed that a child's attention is drawn by movement far more often than by forms that are at rest, and he will often produce associations on the ground of a similar kind of movement, which we adults neglect to notice or overlook altogether.

For a long time afterwards this little problem was left on one side. I will mention only the commonplace conjecture that the butterfly's pointed, protruding wing tips might have had some significance as genital symbols.

One day a memory of a kind came to the surface, hazy and diffident: very early on, even before the time of his nurse, he must have had a nursery-maid who was very fond of him. She had had the same name as his mother. He was sure he had returned her affection. A first love, then, which had vanished without trace. We agreed, however, that something must have happened then that was to be of importance later.

Then he revised his memory once more. She could not have had the same name as his mother, that was a mistake on his part, proving of course that in his memory she had merged with his mother. Her real name had come back to him by a circuitous route. He suddenly found himself thinking of a store-room on the first estate where fruit was kept after it had been picked, and of a particular sort of pear with an excellent flavour, a large pear with yellow-striped skin. In his language the word for pear was 'Gruscha', and this had also been the name of the nursery-maid.

It thus became clear that behind the cover-memory of the butterfly he had chased there lay concealed the memory of this nursery-maid. The yellow stripes were not on her dress, however, but on the pear whose name she shared. Yet where did his anxiety come from when this memory was activated? The most obvious, crass conjecture might have been that as a small child it was this nursery-maid whom he had first seen perform movements of the legs which he had fixed in his mind with the Roman symbol V, movements which allowed access to the genitals. We spared ourselves such conjectures and waited for new material to emerge.

Soon afterwards came the memory of a scene, incomplete but, as far as it went, distinct. Gruscha was kneeling on the ground, beside her a pail and a short broom made of birch twigs tied together; he was there and she was teasing him or scolding him.

We could easily supply the missing information from elsewhere. In the first months of therapy he had told me about his compulsive infatuation with a peasant girl from whom at the age of 18 he had caught the infection which led to his later illness. At the time he had been conspicuously unwilling to give the girl's name. It was an isolated instance of resistance; normally he gave unqualified obedience to the ground rules of analysis. He claimed, however, that he was so very ashamed to say the name out loud because it could only belong to a peasant; a girl of better breeding would never have been given such a name. Eventually we learned that this name was *Matrona*. It had a motherly ring to it. His shame was obviously displaced. He was not ashamed of the fact that he felt these infatuations exclusively for girls of the most lowly birth, he was ashamed only of the name. If the affair with Matrona had anything in common with the Gruscha episode, then we could locate his feelings of shame back in that earlier incident.

On another occasion he told me how very moved he was when he heard the story of Johannes Huss; his attention was caught by the bundles of twigs that were dragged to the place where he was burned at the stake. His sympathy for Huss awoke a particular suspicion in me; I have often encountered it in younger patients and have always found the same explanation to hold true. One of them had even produced a dramatic version of Huss's story; he began to write his drama on the very day the object of his secret infatuation was taken away from him. Huss is burned to death, and, like others who fulfil the same condition, he is a hero to those who formerly suffered from enuresis. The patient himself made a connection between the bundles of twigs around Huss's funeral pyre and the nursery-maid's broom (made of birch twigs).

This material fitted together effortlessly to fill in the gaps in his memory of the scene with Gruscha. As he was watching the girl cleaning the floor he had urinated into the room; at this she had threatened him, no doubt playfully, with castration.[1] I do not know if my readers are already able to guess why I have described this episode from early infancy in such detail.[2] It establishes an important link between the primal scene and the compulsive eroticism that was later to have such a decisive effect on his fortunes, and introduces moreover, a sexual condition which throws some light on that compulsion.

When he saw the girl crouched down cleaning the floor, on her knees with her buttocks projecting and her back horizontal, he recognized the position that his mother had assumed in the scene of coitus he had observed. In his mind she became his mother, he was overcome by sexual excitement as that image was activated,[3] and behaved in a manly fashion towards her like his father, whose actions he could then only have understood as urination. His urinating on the floor was actually an attempt at seduction, to which the girl responded with a threat of castration as if she had understood what he was doing.

The compulsion derived from the primal scene was transferred to this scene with Gruscha and its continued effect was mediated through it. The sexual condition underwent a modification, however, which testifies to the influence of the second scene; it was transferred from the woman's position to what she was doing in that position. This became evident, for example, in his experience with Matrona. He was walking through the village attached to their (later) estate when he saw a peasant girl kneeling at the edge of the pond, washing dirty linen in the water. He fell violently and irresistibly in love with the girl on the instant, although he could not even see her face. By virtue of her posture and her activity she had taken Gruscha's place. We can now understand how feelings of shame applying to the scene with Gruscha could be linked to the name Matrona.

We can see the compulsive influence of the scene with Gruscha at work in another attack of infatuation some years earlier. For a long time he had been attracted to a young peasant girl who was in service in the household, but had not allowed himself to approach her. One day he was seized with infatuation when he came across her alone in the room. He found her crouched down, cleaning the floor with pail and broom beside her, exactly like the other girl in his childhood.

Even his definitive choice of object, so significant in his life, turned out to be dependent in its circumstantial details, which are not our concern here, on that same sexual condition, an offshoot of the compulsion that governed his sexual choice from the primal scene onwards, via the scene with Gruscha. I remarked earlier that I am well aware of the way in which my patient attempts to demean the object of his love. We can trace this back to a reaction against the pressure of his sister's superiority. I promised at the time, however, to demonstrate that this arrogant motive was not the only one determining his behaviour, but concealed purely erotic motives, which constituted a more profound determining force. His memory of the nursery-maid cleaning the floor, her position admittedly a demeaning one, brought this motivation to light. All the later objects of his love were substitutes for this one woman, whom a chance situation had made the first substitute for his mother. In retrospect we can easily recognize our patient's first response to the problem of his fear of the butterfly as a distant allusion to the primal scene (the fifth hour). The relationship between the scene with Gruscha and the threat of castration was confirmed by a particularly suggestive dream, which he was able to translate on his own. He said: 'I dreamed that *a man was tearing the wings off an asp [Espe]*'. 'Asp?' I naturally asked, 'What do you mean by that?' – 'Well, the insect with yellow stripes on its body, the one that can sting you. It must be a reference to Gruscha, the yellow-striped pear.' – Now I was able to correct him: 'You mean a *wasp*, then [*Wespe*].' – 'Is the word wasp? I really thought it was asp.' (Like so many others, he used his unfamiliarity with German to conceal his symptomatic actions.) But an asp, that must be me, S. P. (his initials). An asp is of course a mutilated wasp. The dream tells us clearly that he is taking his revenge on Gruscha for having threatened to castrate him.

The action of the 2½-year-old boy in the scene with Gruscha is the first known effect of the primal scene, one in which he appears as a copy of his father, revealing a tendency to develop in the direction that will later merit the name 'masculine'. The seduction forces him into passivity, although we were admittedly already prepared for this by his behaviour as an onlooker during his parents' intercourse.

One aspect of the treatment history, which I must emphasize, is that in dealing with the Gruscha scene, the first experience that he could truly remember and indeed did remember without any contribution or conjecture on my part, one had the strong impression that the problem of the therapy had been solved. After this there was no more resistance; all that was needed was to gather material and piece it together. Suddenly the old trauma theory, which was after all constructed on the basis of impressions formed in the course of psychoanalytic therapy, came into its own again. Out of critical interest I made one further attempt to impose a different interpretation of his story upon my patient, one more welcome to sober common sense. I suggested that there was no reason to doubt that the scene with Gruscha had taken place, but that it meant nothing in itself; regression had caused it to seem more substantial in retrospect because of the events surrounding his choice of object, which had been diverted from his sister because of his inclination to demean and had fallen on servant-girls instead. The observation of coitus, on the other hand, might simply be a fantasy of later life, the historical kernel of which might perhaps have been the observation or experience of a harmless enema. Many readers will perhaps be of the opinion that only in making assumptions such as these had I reached a true understanding of the case; the patient looked at me uncomprehendingly and with a certain contempt as I presented this view, and never once reacted to it. I have expounded my own arguments against rationalizations of this kind above in the appropriate context.

[⁴Not only does the Gruscha scene contain the conditions of object-choice that were to be crucial for the patient's life, however, thus guarding us against the error of over-estimating the significance of his inclination to demean women. It also enables me to justify my former refusal to trace the primal scene back to animal behaviour observed shortly before the dream, and to regard this without hesitation as the only possible solution. It surfaced spontaneously in the patient's memory without my having said or done anything. The fear of the yellow-striped butterfly, which could be traced back to it, proved that its content had been significant, or that it had subsequently become possible to invest its content with significance. We could quite confidently supply those significant elements that were no longer present to memory, by means of the accompanying associations and the conclusions suggested by them. It then transpired that his fear of the butterfly was entirely analogous to his fear of the wolf, and in both cases was a fear of castration, initially directed towards the person who had first voiced the castration threat but then transferred on to the person to whom it must adhere according to the phylogenetic model. The scene with Gruscha occurred when he was $2\frac{1}{2}$; the anxiety he experienced at the sight of the yellow butterfly must have been after the anxiety-dream, however. It would be readily comprehensible if his later sense of the possibility of castration had latched on to the scene with Gruscha and generated anxiety from it; but the scene itself contains nothing offensive or improbable, only details of an entirely banal nature that there was no reason to doubt. There is nothing to encourage us to trace them back to the child's fantasy; indeed, it would hardly seem possible to do so.

The question now arises as to whether we are justified in seeing proof of his sexual excitement in the fact that the boy urinated in a standing position while the girl was kneeling on the floor, cleaning it. If so, his excitement would testify to the influence of an earlier impression, which could just as easily be the actual occurrence of the primal scene as something he watched animals do before the age of $2\frac{1}{2}$. Or was the situation entirely harmless, the child emptying his bladder purely a matter of accident, and the whole scene imbued with sexuality only later on, in his memory, once he had recognized the significance of similar situations?

I do not think I am able to come to any conclusion here. I must say that I think it greatly to the credit of psychoanalysis that it can even ask questions such as these. But I cannot deny that the scene with Gruscha, the role it played in analysis and the effects it had on my patient's life can be explained most naturally and fully if we affirm the reality of the primal scene, which at other times might be seen as the product of fantasy. There is nothing fundamentally impossible in what it asserts, and the assumption that it was a reality is entirely in keeping with the stimulating influence of his observations of animals, to which the sheepdogs in the dream-image allude.

I shall turn from this unsatisfying conclusion to a question I explore in my *Introductory Lectures on Psychoanalysis*. I should very much like to know myself whether my patient's primal scene was a fantasy or a real experience, but taking other, similar cases into consideration we are obliged to conclude that it is not actually very important to reach a verdict on this matter. Scenes where parental intercourse is observed, scenes of childhood seduction and the threat of castration are undoubtedly inherited property, a phylogenetic inheritance, but they could just as well have been acquired by personal experience. The seduction of my patient by his older sister was an indisputable reality; why not the observation of his parents' coitus, too?

In the primal history of neurosis we see that the child resorts to this phylogenetic experience when his own experience is not enough. He fills out the gaps in individual truth with prehistoric truth, putting ancestral experience in the place of his own. In acknowledging this phylogenetic inheritance I am in complete agreement with Jung (*Die Psychologie der unbewußten Prozesse* [*The Psychology of Unconscious Processes*], 1917, a work published too late to influence my own *Lectures*), but I consider it methodologically incorrect to resort to a phylogenetic explanation before one has exhausted the possibilities of ontogenesis; I do not see why we should obstinately deny the pre-history of childhood a significance that we readily concede to ancestral pre-history; I cannot overlook the fact that phylogenetic motives and products are themselves in need of the light that can be shed on them in a whole series of instances drawn from individual childhoods; and finally, it does not surprise me to find that when the same conditions remain in force they again cause the same things to come about organically in the individual as they had done in ancient times, and which they then passed down in the form of a disposition to re-acquire them over and over again.

The interval between the primal scene and the seduction (18 months – 3¼ years) is also where we must place the mute water-carrier, who was a father-substitute for my patient just as Gruscha was a mother-substitute. I do not think we are justified in referring here to an inclination to demean, even though both parents are represented by members of the servant class. The child takes no notice of social distinctions, which mean very little to him as yet, putting even quite lowly people on a level with his parents if they respond to him lovingly in the same way that his parents do. Equally, this inclination is of little significance when it comes to using animals as substitutes for his parents, for nothing could be further from the child's mind than to hold animals in low esteem. There is no thought of demeaning them when uncles and aunts are enlisted as parent-substitutes, a procedure attested by many of our patient's memories.

In the same period there are vague tidings of a phase during which he only wanted to eat sweets, so that concern was expressed for his physical well-being. He was told of an uncle who had not wanted to eat anything either and who wasted away at an early age. He also heard that he had been so seriously ill when he was three months old that they had made his shroud in readiness. They succeeded in making him so fearful that he started to eat again; later in his childhood he even took this obligation to extremes, as if to shield himself against the threat of death. His fear of dying, summoned up for his own protection, came into evidence again later, when his mother issued a warning about the danger of dysentery; later still it provoked an attack of obsessive-compulsive neurosis (p. 256). At a later stage we shall attempt to look into its origins and significance.

I would wish to claim that the eating disorder is significant as the very first instance of neurotic illness in my patient; thus the eating disorder, the wolf phobia and the compulsive piety represent the full range of infantile illnesses that predispose the individual to neurotic breakdown in the years after puberty. It will be objected that few children altogether avoid disorders such as a passing unwillingness to eat or an animal phobia. This is an argument I welcome, however. I am prepared to assert that every adult neurosis builds on childhood neurosis, but that the latter is not always powerful enough to attract attention and to be recognized as such. The objection only enhances the theoretical significance of the infantile neuroses for our understanding of those illnesses that we treat as neuroses and believe to be derived only from what affects us in later life. If our patient had not picked up compulsive piety in addition to his eating disorder and his animal phobia, his story would not be noticeably different from that of any other living soul and we would have missed out on valuable material that could keep us from making obvious mistakes.

The analysis would be unsatisfactory if it did not enable us to understand the lament in which our patient summed up his sense of suffering. He said that for him the world was shrouded in a veil, and psychoanalytic training leads us to dismiss any expectation that these words might be meaningless or accidental. The veil was only torn apart – oddly enough – in one situation, namely when, after the application of an enema, stools were passed through the anus. He would then feel well again and for a very short while would see the world clearly. Understanding the meaning of this 'veil' was as difficult as understanding his fear of the butterfly. He did not insist on its being a veil, moreover, and it became even more elusive to him, a feeling of twilight, *ténèbres*, and other such intangibles.

It was only shortly before leaving therapy that he recalled having heard that he had been born with a caul.[5] For this reason he had always considered himself to be particularly lucky, a child whom no ill could befall. This confidence only left him when he was obliged to acknowledge that his gonorrhoeal illness had done serious damage to his body. He broke down in the face of this insult to his narcissism. We might say that this was the repetition of a mechanism that had come into play once before. The wolf phobia, too, had broken out when he was forced to confront the fact that castration was indeed possible, and for him gonorrhoea was clearly on a par with castration.

The veil shrouding him from the world and shrouding the world from him was thus the caul. His lament is in fact the fulfilment of a wish-fantasy in which he is shown as having returned to the womb: a wish-fantasy, admittedly, of flight from the world. We might translate it thus: my life is so unhappy that I must go back to my mother's womb.

What is the meaning of the fact that this symbolic veil, once a real veil, is torn apart, however, at the very moment when the bowels are evacuated after a clyster [enema] and that his illness abates under these conditions? The context permits us to reply: when the birth veil is torn apart, he sees the world and is reborn. The stool is the baby, and as that baby he is born a second time to a happier life. This is the fantasy of rebirth to which Jung recently drew our attention and to which he attributed such a dominant position in the wishful fantasies of the neurotic individual.

That would be all very well, if it were a complete response. Certain details of the situation, together with the consideration that there should be a connection with the particular facts of our patient's life history, require us to take our interpretation further. The condition of rebirth is that a man administers a clyster (only later, when absolutely necessary, did he perform this function himself). This can only mean that he has identified himself with the mother, the man plays the role of his father, the clyster reproduces the act of copulation, which bears fruit in the birth of the stool-baby – that is, of himself. The fantasy of rebirth is thus intimately bound up with the condition of sexual satisfaction received from a man. Our translation now runs as follows: only when he is allowed to take the woman's place, to substitute himself for his mother in order to gain satisfaction from his father and bear a child for him, does his illness abate. Here the fantasy of rebirth is merely the mutilated, censored reproduction of his homosexual wish-fantasy.

If we look more closely, we must in fact recognize that, by setting this condition for his cure, the patient is simply reproducing the situation found in the so-called primal scene: at the time he wanted to take on his mother's attributes and in that scene he himself produced the stool-baby, as we had long ago supposed. As if spell-bound, his inner gaze is fixed on the scene that was to be decisive for his sexual life, the recurrence of which, that night of the dream, inaugurated his illness. The veil tearing is analogous to his eyes unclosing, to the window opening. The primal scene has been remodelled as the condition imposed for his cure.

We can easily take what is represented in the patient's lament, and what is represented by the exception to the condition he laments, and draw them together to form a single entity whose full meaning is then revealed. He wishes he were back in his mother's womb not simply in order to be reborn, but so as to be reached by his father during coitus, to gain satisfaction from him, to bear him a child.

To be born of his father, as he at first supposed, to gain sexual satisfaction from him, to give him a child, even if that means surrendering his manhood, and to express all this in the language of anal eroticism: with these wishes the wheel of his fixed obsession with his father comes full circle, in them his homosexuality finds its highest and most intimate expression.[6]

In my opinion this example sheds some light on the meaning and origin of fantasies of the womb and of rebirth. The former frequently stems from an attachment to the father, as in our case. There is a desire to be in the mother's womb so as to act as her substitute during coitus, to take her place with the father. As a rule the fantasy of rebirth probably constitutes a euphemism, so to speak, a toning-down of the fantasy of incestuous intercourse with the mother, an *anagogic* abbreviation of it, to borrow H. Silberer's expression. There is a desire to return to the situation in which one was in the mother's genitals; here the man identifies himself with his penis and uses it to represent his whole self. Thus it is revealed that each of the two fantasies is the counterpart of the other, expressing the wish for sexual intercourse with the mother or the father, depending on whether the individual concerned adopts a male or female attitude. We cannot discount the possibility that both fantasies, and hence both incestuous wishes, are united in our patient's lament and in the condition set for his cure.

Once again I shall attempt to reinterpret the latest results of the analysis according to the model preferred by my opponents: the patient laments his flight from the world in a typical womb-fantasy, glimpses the possibility of cure only in rebirth, as typically understood. He expresses the latter through anal symptoms appropriate to his dominant predisposition. According to the model of anal fantasies of rebirth he constructs a childhood scene that recapitulates his wishes using archaic symbols as the medium of expression. His symptoms are then interlinked in such a way that they appear to proceed from a primal scene of this kind. He was forced to embark on this whole line of retreat because he came up against a task in real life that he was too lazy to solve, or because he had every reason to mistrust his inferior attributes and thought this the best way of protecting himself against being passed over.

This would be all well and good if the unhappy man had not been only four years old at the time of the dream with which his neurosis began, the stimulus for which was his grandfather's story about the tailor and the wolf, and the interpretation of which necessitates the assumption of a primal scene of this kind. The relief that Jung's and Adler's theories might have afforded us comes to grief in the face of these petty but inviolable facts. As things are, it seems to me more likely that the fantasy of rebirth issues from the primal scene than the other way round, that the primal scene reflects the fantasy of rebirth. Perhaps we may also assume that four years after his birth the patient was just a little too young to be wishing for rebirth already. Yet I must withdraw this last argument, for my own observations prove that we have under-estimated children and are no longer able to say just what they are capable of.[7]

## Notes

1. It is most remarkable that the reaction of shame is so intimately bound up with involuntary emptying of the bladder (by day or night) and not to the same extent with faecal incontinence, as one might expect. Experience leaves us in no doubt on this point. The connection regularly found between urinary incontinence and fire also gives us pause for thought. It is possible that a precipitate of the cultural history of mankind is to be found in these reactions and connections, which reach down further than any of the traces retained in myth and folklore.

2. It took place around the age of $2\frac{1}{2}$, between the supposed observation of coitus and the seduction.

3. Before the dream!

4. [Freud's square bracket.]

5. The German word for a 'caul', '*Glückshaube*', means literally a 'lucky bonnet'.]

6. A possible secondary sense, in which the veil represents the hymen that is torn in intercourse with the man, does not exactly coincide with the condition set for the patient's cure and has no application in his life, as virginity was without significance for him.

7. I admit that this is one of the most tricky questions in the whole of psychoanalytic theory. It did not take Adler's pronouncements or Jung's to make me look critically at the possibility that those forgotten childhood

experiences – experienced at such an incredibly early stage of childhood! – which analysis claims actually took place, are in fact rooted in fantasies created in response to some later occurrence, and that anywhere in analysis where we think we find the after-effects of an infantile memory imprint of this kind we must assume that it is actually the expression of a significant constitutional moment or a disposition that has been phylogenetically preserved. On the contrary: no cause for doubt has so preoccupied me, no other uncertainty more decisively held me back from publication. None of my opponents refers to the fact that I was the first to draw attention not only to the role of fantasy in symptom-formation but also to the way in which an individual may be prompted, later in life, to 'fantasize back' to his childhood and to sexualize it retrospectively. (See *Die Traumdeutung* [*The Interpretation of Dreams*], 1st edition, p. 49, and 'Bemerkungen über einen Fall von Zwangsneurose' ['Some Remarks on a Case of Obsessive-compulsive Neurosis'].) If I nevertheless hold fast to the more problematic and less probable view and claim it as my own, I do so in the light of arguments that force themselves upon the attention of anyone investigating the case I have described here or that of any other infantile neurosis, arguments that I now present to my readers once again to enable them to make up their own minds on this matter.

## IX  *Recapitulations and Problems*

I do not know whether my readers will have succeeded in forming a clear picture of the genesis and development of my patient's state of illness from the report of the analysis given above. Indeed, I fear that this will not be the case. However, whereas I never normally boast of my own narrative skills, on this occasion I should like to plead mitigating circumstances. To initiate the reader into a description of such early phases and such profound strata of a patient's inner life is a problem which has never before been tackled, and it is better to solve it badly than to take to one's heels, particularly since losing heart presents certain dangers in itself. Better, then, to make a bold show of not having been put off by consciousness of one's own deficiencies.

The case itself was not a particularly auspicious one. The very thing that made it possible to gain such a wealth of information about the patient's childhood, the fact that we could study the child through the medium of the adult, was bought at the price of the most dreadful fragmentation of the analysis and a corresponding incompleteness in my account of it. Aspects of personality, a national character which is alien to our own, made it difficult to empathize with him. The contrast between the patient's charming and responsive personality, his sharp intelligence and refined way of thinking, and his complete lack of restraint at the level of the drives made it necessary to spend an excessively long time on the work of preparation and education, thus rendering any kind of overview more difficult. Though it may have posed the hardest descriptive problems, however, the patient himself cannot be held responsible for the nature of the case. In adult psychology we have happily succeeded in separating the processes of the inner life into conscious and unconscious, and describing both in clear language. As far as the child is concerned, however, this distinction almost gives way. We are often at a loss to decide what we would describe as conscious, and what unconscious. Processes that have become dominant and that, given their later behaviour, we must treat in the same way as conscious ones, were nevertheless not conscious in the child. We can easily understand why this is so: consciousness in the child has not yet developed its full range of characteristics and is not yet entirely capable of being converted into language-pictures. The way in which we are regularly guilty of confusing the phenomenon of something appearing in consciousness in the form of a perception, and something belonging to an accepted psychic system that we ought to call by some conventional name but for which we also use the term 'consciousness' (System *Cs*), such confusion is harmless in the psychological description of an adult, but misleading in the case of a small child. To introduce the concept of the 'pre-conscious' does not help much here, for there is no reason why the child's pre-consciousness should be congruent with the adult's. We must therefore be content with having clearly recognized the obscurity which confronts us.

A case such as the one described here could obviously create an opportunity to embark on a discussion of all the results and problems of psychoanalysis. It would be an endless undertaking, and one quite without justification. We have to tell ourselves that we cannot discover everything, cannot decide everything on the basis of a single case and that we must be content to use it for what it can show us most clearly. The task of explanation in psycho-analysis is in any case narrowly circumscribed. What we need to explain are conspicuous symptom-formations, by revealing how they have come about; what we are not to explain, only describe, are the psychic mechanisms and drive processes that we encounter in doing so. Formulation of new general statements on the basis of what we have learned about these last-named aspects requires numerous cases of this kind, analysed accurately and in depth. They are not easy to come by, for each individual case requires years of work. Thus progress in these areas will only take place very slowly. There is an obvious temptation, of course, to content oneself with 'scratching the psychic surface' of a number of individuals and replacing neglected effort with speculation advanced under the patronage of some philosophical school of thought or other. There are also practical necessities that can be urged in favour of such a procedure, but the necessities of scholarship cannot be satisfied by any surrogate.

I want to attempt to sketch out a synthesis, an overall view of my patient's sexual development, beginning with the earliest indi-cations. The first thing we hear about him is of a loss of pleasure in eating that I would interpret on the basis of other experiences, but nevertheless with circumspection, as the outcome of an occur-rence in the sexual sphere. I had thus to consider the first recog-nizable mode of sexual organization to be the so-called *cannibal* or *oral* mode of organization, in which the scene is dominated by the original dependence of sexual excitement on the drive to eat. We cannot expect to find any direct expression of this phase, but may find some indications in the appearance of disorders. The impairment of the drive to eat – which may of course have other causes as well – draws our attention to the fact that the organism has not succeeded in controlling sexual excitement. The sexual objective in this phase could only be cannibalism, eating; in our patient's case this comes to the fore as a result of regression from a higher level, in his fear of being gobbled up by the wolf. We had to translate this fear as that of being taken in coitus by the father. It is well known that at a much later stage, in girls going through puberty or slightly older, we encounter a neurosis that expresses the rejection of sexuality through anorexia; a connection may be drawn with the oral phase of sexuality. We encounter the erotic objective of the oral mode of organization once again at the height of paroxysms of love ('I love you so much I could eat you') and in affectionate contact with small children, in which the adult himself behaves in an infantile fashion. Elsewhere I have expressed the suspicion that our patient's father himself inclined to 'affectionate scolding', and when playing at wolves or dogs with the little boy had threatened in jest to gobble him up (p. 220). The patient only provided confirmation of this view through his striking behaviour in the transference. Whenever he retreated from difficulties in the therapy and sought refuge in transference, he would threaten to gobble me up, and later to subject me to every possible form of ill-treatment, all of which was merely a way of expressing his affection.

His linguistic usage has been permanently coloured in certain ways by this oral phase of sexuality: he refers to 'luscious' love-objects, describes his beloved as 'sweet'. We recall that as a child our patient only wanted sweet things to eat. When they occur in dreams, sweeties and bonbons generally stand for caresses and sexual satisfaction.

It appears that there is also an anxiety that belongs in this phase (where there is a disorder, of course), which manifests itself in the form of generalized anxiety and may adhere to anything that is suggested to the child as appropriate. In our patient's case it was used to teach him to overcome his reluctance to eat, to overcompensate for it, indeed. We are led to the possible source of his eating disorder when we recall – basing ourselves on the assumption we have discussed in such detail – that his observation of coitus, which was belatedly to cast so many ripples, took place at the age of 18 months, certainly before the period at which he experienced eating difficulties. We may perhaps assume that it speeded-up the processes of sexual maturity, so that it also took effect directly, if inconspicuously.

I know, of course, that we can also explain the symptoms manifested during this period, his fear of the wolf, his eating disorder, in a different, more straightforward way that takes no account of sexuality or of a pre-genital stage of sexual organization. Anyone who likes to ignore the signs of neurosis and the logical connections between phenomena will prefer this other explanation, and I shall not be able to prevent him from doing so. It is difficult to find out anything compelling about these initial stages of sexuality other than by taking the roundabout routes I have indicated.

The scene with Gruscha (at the age of 2½) shows our young patient embarking on a development that merits recognition as a normal one, except perhaps that it is somewhat premature: identification with the father, eroticism of the bladder as a substitute for virility. It too is very strongly influenced by the primal scene. Up until now we have interpreted the identification with the father as a narcissistic one, but bearing in mind the content of the primal scene we cannot deny that it already corresponds to the stage of genital organization. The male genitals have begun to play their part and will continue to do so under the influence of his sister's seduction.

We gain the impression, however, that the seduction not only encourages this development but also, to a greater extent, disrupts and diverts it. It results in a passive sexual objective that is fundamentally irreconcilable with the action of the male genitals. The first external impediment, Nanja's suggestion of castration, leads to the breakdown (at the age of 3½) of the still precarious mode of genital organization, and regression to the previous stage of anal-sadistic organization, which he might perhaps otherwise have passed through with only the same slight symptoms as those found in other children.

It is easy to recognize that the anal-sadistic mode of organization is a continuation of the oral one. The violent muscular activity towards its object by which it is characterized falls into place as an act preparatory to eating, but eating is no longer present as a sexual objective. The preparatory act becomes an objective in its own right. What is new about it in comparison with the previous stage is the fact that the receptive, passive organ has now been separated off from the oral zone, and developed in the anal zone instead. Biological parallels suggest themselves, as does the interpretation of pre-genital human modes of organization as the residue of arrangements that have been permanently retained in many classes of animal. Equally characteristic of this stage is the way in which the exploratory drive constitutes itself from its component elements.

Anal eroticism is not conspicuously in evidence. Under the influence of sadism faeces have exchanged their affectionate meaning for an aggressive one. A feeling of guilt, which indicates, moreover, that developments are taking place in areas other than the sexual sphere, plays its part in the transformation of sadism into masochism.

The seduction continues to exert an influence, in that it maintains the passivity of the sexual objective. It now transforms sadism to a great extent into its passive counterpart, masochism. It is doubtful whether we can put the boy's characteristic passivity entirely down to the seduction, for his reaction to the observation of coitus at the age of 18 months was already predominantly a passive one. The sexual excitement that he felt in observation was expressed in a bowel movement, in which we must admittedly recognize an active element. Sadism, which finds active expression in tormenting small creatures, continues to exist alongside the masochism that dominates his sexual aspirations and is expressed in his fantasies. From the time of the seduction onwards his sexual curiosity has been stirred, and is essentially directed towards two problems, namely where babies come from and whether loss of the genitals is possible; it becomes bound up with the expression of his drives. It is this that focuses his sadistic tendencies on those tiny creatures, which he sees as representing tiny children.

Our description has taken us almost up to his fourth birthday, at which point the dream causes the observation of coitus at the age of 18 months to come belatedly into effect. We can neither completely grasp nor adequately describe the processes that are now set in motion. The activation of that image, which thanks to advances in his intellectual development can now be understood, has the effect of a newly occurring event, but is also like a fresh trauma, an alien intrusion analogous to the seduction. The genital mode of organization, which had been suspended, is resumed at a stroke, but the progress made in the dream cannot be maintained. Rather, a process that can only be compared to a kind of repression causes him to reject this new knowledge and replace it with a phobia.

Thus the anal-sadistic mode of organization continues in existence, even during the animal phobia phase that now begins, but with some manifestations of anxiety mixed in. The child still pursues both sadistic and masochistic activities, while reacting fearfully against one component; the reversal of sadism into its opposite probably fares somewhat better.

We can see from the analysis of the anxiety dream that repression follows immediately after the knowledge of castration. The new knowledge is rejected because to accept it would cost the boy his penis. More careful consideration reveals something like the following: what has been repressed is the homosexual attitude in the genital sense, which had been formed under the influence of the new knowledge. This attitude remains preserved in the unconscious, however, constituted as a deeper, closed-off stratum. The driving force behind this repression appears to be the narcissistic masculinity of the genitals that comes into conflict with the passivity of the homosexual objective, a conflict for which the ground was laid long before. Repression is thus one of the outcomes of masculinity.

This might lead us into the temptation to revise one small aspect of psychoanalytic theory. It seems patently obvious, after all, that repression and the formation of neuroses proceed from the conflict between masculine and feminine aspirations, that is, from bisexuality. But such a view has its shortcomings. Of these two conflicting sexual impulses one is acceptable to the I [*ichgerecht*], the other offends against narcissistic interests and thus falls prey to repression. In this case, too, it is the I [*Ich*] who sets repression in motion in favour of one of the two sexual aspirations. In other cases, such a conflict between masculinity and femininity does not exist; there is a single sexual aspiration present, which sues for acceptance but runs counter to certain powers of the I and is therefore banished. Far more frequent than conflicts within sexuality itself are those conflicts that arise between sexuality and the moral inclinations of the I. There is an absence of moral conflict of this kind in our case. To emphasize bisexuality as the motivation for repression would be too restrictive, whereas conflict between the I and the sexual aspirations (the libido) covers all eventualities.

Against the theory of 'masculine protest' as developed by Adler, it must be objected that repression by no means always upholds masculinity against femininity; in many whole categories of cases it is masculinity that is obliged to accept repression by the I.

A more balanced evaluation of the process of repression in our particular case, incidentally, would challenge whether narcissistic masculinity is significant as the only motivating factor. The homosexual attitude that comes into being in the course of the dream is so powerful that the little boy's I fails to control it and fends it off through the process of repression. To achieve this end the I enlists the help of the narcissistic masculinity of the genitals that is in opposition to the homosexual attitude. Simply in order to avoid any misunderstanding let me state that all narcissistic impulses work out from the I and remain in the I's domain, while repression is directed towards those objects carrying a libidinal charge.

Let us now turn from the process of repression a notion we have perhaps not succeeded in mastering entirely, to the boy's state when he awakened from the dream. If it had indeed been masculinity that had triumphed over homosexuality (femininity) during the dream process we should now find an active sexual aspiration, already explicitly masculine in character, to be the dominant one. There is no question of this, however: the essential nature of the mode of sexual organization is unchanged, the anal-sadistic phase still continues in existence and remains dominant. The triumph of masculinity can only be seen in the fact that the boy reacts fearfully to the passive sexual objectives of the dominant mode of organization (which are masochistic, but not feminine). There is no triumphant masculine sexual impulse present, but only a passive one, and an unwillingness to accept it.

I can imagine the difficulties that this sharp distinction between the active/masculine and passive/feminine will cause the reader, a distinction that is unfamiliar but essential to our purpose, and so I shall not hesitate to repeat myself. We can describe the state of affairs after the dream, then, as follows: the patient's sexual aspirations have been split, the genital mode of organization having been achieved in the unconscious and a highly intensive homosexuality constituted; above this (virtually at the level of consciousness) the earlier sadistic and predominantly masochistic sexual current continues to exist, while the I has altered its position, by and large, towards sexuality, anxiously rejecting the dominant masochistic objectives just as it reacted towards the deeper homosexual ones with the formation of a phobia. Thus the outcome of the dream was not so much the victory of a masculine current as reaction against a feminine, passive one. We would do violence to the facts if we ascribed masculine characteristics to this reaction. For the I does not have sexual aspirations, only an interest in self-protection and the preservation of its narcissism.

Let us now look closely at the phobia. It came into existence at the level of genital organization and demonstrates the relatively simple mechanism of an anxiety-hysteria. The I protects itself from something it judges to be excessively dangerous, that is, homosexual satisfaction, by developing anxiety. However, the process of repression leaves a trace that we cannot miss. The object to which the dreaded sexual objective has become attached must find representation in conscious thought by means of another. It is not fear of the *father* that comes to consciousness, but fear of the *wolf*. Once it has been formed, the phobia is not restricted to a single content. Some considerable time later the wolf is replaced by a lion. Sadistic impulses towards tiny creatures compete with a phobic response towards them, inasmuch as they represent the boy's rivals,

the babies whose arrival is still possible. The genesis of the butterfly phobia is particularly interesting. It is like a repetition of the
mechanism that generated the wolf phobia in the dream. A chance
stimulus activates an old experience, the scene with Gruscha, whose
castration threat belatedly comes into effect, whereas at the time
it appeared to have left no impression.[1]

We can say that the fear that goes into the formation of these
phobias is fear of castration. This statement in no way contradicts
the view that the fear arises from the repression of homosexual
libido. Both modes of expression refer to the same process, in
which the I withdraws libido from the homosexual wish-impulse,
which is converted into free-floating anxiety and then allows itself
to be bound up in phobias. It is merely that the first mode of
expression also indicates the motive that drives the I to act in this
way.

Looking more carefully, we then find that the random choice of
a single phobia does not represent the full extent of this first
episode of illness (not counting the eating disorder) in our patient,
but that it must be understood as a genuine case of hysteria, compris-
ing both anxiety symptoms and conversation phenomena. An
element of the homosexual impulse is retained by the organ
involved, for henceforward, and in later years too, the bowel behaves
like an organ that has been hysterically affected. The unconscious,
repressed homosexuality withdraws into the bowel. It was this particular bit of hysteria that served us so well when it came to resolving
the patient's later illness.

Now we should steel ourselves to tackle the still more complicated circumstances of the obsessive-compulsive neurosis. Let us
examine the situation once again: a dominant masochistic sexual
current and a repressed homosexual one, opposed to an I that is
caught up in hysterical refusal; what processes could transform this
state into one of obsessive-compulsive neurosis?

The transformation is not the spontaneous result of internal
developments, but arises from an external, alien influence. Its visible
outcome is that the boy's relationship to his father, still very much
to the fore, and expressed up until then through the wolf phobia,

now finds expression in compulsive piety. I cannot let this opportunity pass without pointing out that the process that our patient undergoes provides unambiguous confirmation of a claim I put forward in *Totem and Taboo* concerning the relationship of the totemic animal to the deity.[2] There I concluded that the idea of God does not develop out of the totem but arises independently from common roots to supersede it. The totem is the first father-substitute, the god a later one in which the father regains human form. We find the same thing in our patient's case. He goes through the stage of the totemic father-substitute, as represented by the wolf phobia, which is then broken off and, after a new relationship has been forged between the boy and his father, is replaced by a phase of religious piety.

The influence behind this transformation is his acquaintance with religious doctrine and sacred history, arranged by his mother. The result is exactly the one that education aspires to. The sadomasochistic mode of sexual organization draws gradually to a close, the wolf phobia quickly disappears and in the place of his frightened rejection of sexuality we find a higher form of sexual suppression. Piety becomes the dominant power in the child's life. These efforts of will are not achieved without a struggle, however: its signs are the appearance of blasphemous thoughts and its consequence the onset of a compulsive exaggeration of religious ritual.

Leaving aside these pathological phenomena, we can say that, in this case, religion has achieved everything it is employed to do in the education of the individual. It has curbed his sexual aspirations by offering sublimation and a safe anchor, and undermined his family relationships, thus preventing the isolation that threatens him by giving him access to the wider human community. The unruly, apprehensive child has become socially conscious, civilized and educable.

The principal driving force behind the religious influence was his identification with the figure of Christ, which readily suggested itself given the coincidence of his date of birth. The excessive love for his father that had made repression necessary could finally be channelled into an ideal sublimation. It was possible as Christ to love the father, now called God, with an intensity that he had striven in vain to vent on his own earthly father. The ways in which this love could be attested were clearly indicated by religion and no guilt adhered to them, whereas there was no way of separating guilt from the erotic aspirations of the individual. While the patient's deepest sexual current, already laid down as unconscious homosexuality, could still be drained off in this way, his more superficial masochistic aspirations lost very little in finding a sublimation without parallel in the passion of Christ, who had allowed himself to be mistreated and sacrificed on behalf of the divine father and to his greater glory. And so religion did its work in this boy who had gone off the rails, through the mixture of satisfaction, sublimation, diversion from sensual processes to purely spiritual ones, and the opening up of social relationships which it offers the believer.

His initial reluctance to accept religion was derived from three different sources. First, it was simply his way to ward off anything new: we have already seen a number of examples of this. Once he had taken up a given libido position he would defend it every time against the new one he was to occupy, fearful of what he would lose in giving it up and mistrusting the likelihood of finding a fully satisfactory substitute. This is an important and fundamental psychological particularity, which I put forward in *Three Essays on Sexual Theory* as the capacity to become *fixed*. Referring to it as psychic 'lassitude', Jung sees it as the principal cause of all neurotic failure. I believe he is wrong to do so, for it is more far-reaching than this and has a significant part to play even in the lives of those untouched by neurosis. The fluidity or viscosity of libidinal energy charges, and of other types as well, is a particular characteristic found in many normal individuals and not even in all those of a neurotic disposition, and up until now no connection has been made between it and anything else, as if it were a prime number which cannot be divided any further. We know only one thing: the mobility of psychic charges is a property which dwindles noticeably with age. This provides us with one of the indicators for the limits of psychoanalytic influence. There are people, however, whose psychic plasticity is maintained far beyond the usual limits of age and others who lose it very early on. If these are neurotic individuals then we discover to our discomfort that in their case, under what are apparently the same conditions, it is impossible to reverse changes that can readily be controlled in others. In examining conversion in psychic processes we must therefore give consideration to the concept of an *entropy*, which is in proportional opposition to the undoing of what has already taken place.

A second target was provided by the fact that there is no single, clear relationship to God the Father underlying religious doctrine, on the contrary it is shot through with signs of the ambivalent attitude that prevailed at its inception. His own highly developed ambivalence enabled him to sniff this out and use it as a starting point for the penetrating criticism that so astonished us in a four-year-old child. Most significant of all, however, was undoubtedly a third factor to which we may ascribe the pathological effects of his battle against religion. The current of energy pressing him towards manhood, for which religion was to provide a form of sublimation, was no longer free, as part of it had been separated off by the process of repression and thus eluded sublimation, remaining bound to its original sexual objective. On the strength of their connection the repressed part strove either to break through to the sublimated part or else to drag it down to its own level. Those first brooding thoughts circling around the person of Christ already contained the question as to whether this sublime son could also fulfil the sexual relationship to his father that the patient had retained in his unconscious. Repudiation of this endeavour resulted only in the emergence of apparently blasphemous compulsive thoughts in which physical tenderness for God continued to assert itself in a form intended to demean Him. A violent struggle [*Abwehrkampf*] to parry these compromise formations led inevitably to compulsive exaggeration of all those activities in which piety and the pure love of God found expression through the prescribed channels. The victory eventually fell to religion, but the way in which it was rooted in the drives proved incomparably stronger than the durability of what was produced by sublimation. As soon as life provided a new father-substitute whose influence was directed against religion, it was dropped and replaced by other things. We should also bear in mind the interesting complication that piety came about under the influence of women (mother and nurse) whereas masculine influence liberated him from it.

The fact that obsessive-compulsive neurosis came about at the anal-sadistic stage of sexual organization on the whole confirms the views presented elsewhere in 'Die Disposition zur Zwangsneurose' ['The Disposition to Obsessional Neurosis'] (1913). However, the pre-existence of a powerful state of hysteria makes the case more obscure in that respect. I shall conclude my survey of our patient's sexual development by highlighting the transformations it underwent in later life. In puberty the strongly sensual male current that we refer to as normal made its appearance, its sexual objective that of the genital mode of organization, and its vicissitudes fill up the time until his later episode of illness. It was directly connected with the Gruscha scene and derived from it the character of a compulsive infatuation, coming and going like an attack; it also had to struggle with the inhibitions created by the residue of the infantile neurosis. Violent breakthrough to the female meant that he finally won his full masculinity; from now on he held fast to this sexual object, but its possession brought him little joy, for a strong and now completely unconscious inclination towards the male, the sum of all the energies generated in earlier phases, was constantly drawing him away from a female object, obliging him to exaggerate his dependence on women in the interstices. His complaint in therapy was that he could not endure being with women, and all our work was directed towards the task of uncovering his unconscious relationship to the male. We could say, in a formulaic way, that the hallmark of his childhood was vacillation between the active and the passive, that of puberty the struggle for manhood, and that of the period following his illness, the fight for the object of male aspirations. The cause of his illness does not come into any of the categories of 'neurotic illness' that I might refer to collectively as special cases of 'refusal' [*Versagung*][3] and so draws our attention to a gap in this series. He broke down when an organic infection of the genitals reawakened his fear of castration, damaged his narcissism and forced him to put away any expectation that Fate had a personal preference for him. The cause of his illness was thus a narcissistic 'refusal'. His excessively strong narcissism was in complete accord with the other indications of inhibited sexual development: with the fact that his choice of heterosexuality, however energetic, was the focus for so few of his psychic aspirations, and also that the homosexual attitude, which is so much closer to narcissism, asserted its unconscious power over him with such tenacity. In the face of such disorders, psychoanalytic therapy obviously cannot bring about an instantaneous change of direction nor parity with normal development; it can only remove obstacles and clear the paths so that life's influences can opt for better directions in which to push through the individual's development.

Let me list those peculiarities of his psyche that were uncovered in psychoanalytic therapy but on which it was not possible to throw further light nor exert any direct influence: the tenacity with which his energies became fixed, as already discussed, the extraordinary extent to which his tendency to ambivalence had been developed, and, a third feature of what we might term an archaic constitution, his ability to maintain a wide variety of violently conflicting libidinal charges, all potentially functioning alongside one another. His constant wavering between them, which for a long time seemed to exclude the possibility of settlement and progress, dominated the profile of his later illness, which we have touched on only briefly here. There is no doubt that this was a character trait of the unconscious, carried over into processes that had become conscious; it was only apparent, however, in the results of emotional [*affektiv*] impulses, whereas in matters of pure logic he demonstrated particular skill in detecting contradictions and inconsistencies. The impression left by his inner life was rather like that of the ancient Egyptian religion, which is inconceivable to us because it conserves all the developmental stages alongside the end-products, keeping the oldest deities and what they signified as well as the most recent, spreading them out two-dimensionally where other developing cultures create a three-dimensional image.

This concludes what I wished to say about this case. Only two of the numerous problems to which it gives rise seem to me to deserve particular emphasis. The first concerns those phylogenetically transmitted patterns that, like philosophical 'categories', enable us to accommodate our impressions of life. I should like to suggest that they are the precipitates of human cultural history. The Oedipus complex, a complete account of the child's relationship to his parents, is one example, indeed the best known. When experiences cannot be fitted into this hereditary schema, they are reworked in the imagination, work that it would undoubtedly be profitable to examine in detail. For it is precisely these cases that are best suited to demonstrate the independent existence of the schema. We are often in a position to note how the schema takes precedence over individual experience, as for example in our case when the father becomes the castrator who threatens childhood sexuality, despite the fact that the Oedipus complex is reversed in every other respect. Another effect of this is seen when the children's nurse takes the place of the mother or the two become merged. The way in which experience contradicts the schema supplies the conflicts of infancy with a wealth of material.

The second problem is not far removed from the first, but its significance is far greater. If we consider the way in which the four-year-old child responds to the reactivated primal scene[4] – indeed, we have only to think of the far simpler reactions of the 18-month-old child to the original experience – it is difficult to dismiss the notion that some kind of knowledge that resists definition, a sort of preparation for understanding, is at work in the child.[5] What this might consist in defies the imagination; the only analogy available to us is the excellent analogy with the largely *instinctive* knowledge found in animals.

If human beings were also in possession of instinctive knowledge of this kind, it would hardly be surprising if it were directed in particular towards the processes of sexuality, although it cannot possibly be restricted to these alone. This instinctive knowledge would form the core of the unconscious, a primitive intellectual activity later dethroned by human reason when this is acquired and overlaid by it, but often, perhaps always, retaining the strength to drag higher inner processes down to its own level. Repression would be the return to this instinctive stage; in this way man would pay for his splendid new acquisition with the capacity for neurosis, while the possibility of neurosis would testify to the existence of the earlier, preliminary stage, instinctive in nature. The significance of early childhood traumas would then lie in the fact that they supply this unconscious part of the psyche with material that prevents it from being sapped by the subsequent process of development.

I know that similar thoughts have been expressed in various quarters, emphasizing the hereditary, phylogenetically acquired factor in the individual's inner life; indeed, I think we are all too ready to make room for them in our psychoanalytic evaluations. It seems to me that they are only admissible when psychoanalysis correctly observes the prescribed stages, and only starts looking for traces of what has been inherited once it has penetrated the layers of what has been acquired by the individual.[6]

(1918 [1914])

## Notes

1. As I have already mentioned, the Gruscha scene was a spontaneous feat of memory on my patient's part, to which reconstruction or suggestion on the part of the doctor made no contribution; the gaps in this memory were filled in by analysis in what we can only call an impeccable manner, if we set any store by working methods in analysis. A rationalistic explanation of this phobia could only say that there is nothing unusual in the fact that a child with a predisposition to anxiety might one day suffer an attack of anxiety even on seeing a yellow-striped butterfly, probably as a result of an inherited tendency to anxiety. (Cf. Stanley Hall, 'A Synthetic Genetic Study of Fear', 1914.) Ignorant of the cause, it might then look for a childhood event to which this fear might be connected, and then use the chance similarity of names and the recurrence of the stripes to construct the fantasy of an amorous adventure with the nursery-maid, still dimly remembered. If, however, in later life those secondary details of an occurrence

that was harmless in itself, the floor-cleaning, the pail and the broom, show that they have the power to determine an individual's object-choice, to permanent and compulsive effect, then the butterfly phobia acquires incomprehensible significance. The facts of the case become at least as remarkable as those asserted in my interpretation, and any gain made from a rationalistic interpretation of the scene simply melts away. The Gruscha scene is thus of particular value to us, since we can use it to prepare the ground for our judgement in the matter of the primal scene, where the situation is less secure.

2. *Totem und Tabu* [*Totem and Taboo*].

3. 'Über neurotische Erkrankungstypen' ['Types of Onset of Neurosis'] (1912).

4. We may overlook the fact that this response could only be put into words two decades later, for all the effects which we attribute to this scene had already been expressed in childhood, and long before the analysis, in the form of symptoms, compulsions, etc. In this respect it is a matter of no importance whether we regard it as a primal scene or as a primal fantasy.

5. Once again I must emphasize that these reflections would be irrelevant if the dream and the neurosis had not themselves taken place in childhood.

6. [*Addition 1923:*] Here, once again, the events mentioned in this case history, in chronological order:

Born on Christmas Day.

18 months: malaria. Observes parents engaging in coitus, or intimacy between them into which he later introduced a fantasy of coitus.

Shortly before the age of $2\frac{1}{2}$: scene with Gruscha.

$2\frac{1}{2}$: cover-memory of parents' departure with sister. This shows him alone with Nanja, thus denying the presence of Gruscha and his sister.

Before the age of $3\frac{1}{4}$: his mother complains to the doctor.

$3\frac{1}{4}$: beginning of his sister's attempts to seduce him; soon after this, threat of castration by Nanja.

$3\frac{1}{2}$: English governess, onset of character change.

4: wolf dream, origin of phobia.

$4\frac{1}{2}$: influence of biblical history. Compulsive symptoms appear.

Shortly before the age of 5: hallucinates loss of finger.

5: the family leaves the first estate.

After the age of 6: visits sick father.

$\left.\begin{array}{l} 8 \\ 10 \end{array}\right\}$ Final outbreaks of obsessive-compulsive neurosis.

My account makes it easy to guess that my patient was a Russian. I discharged him, believing him to be cured, a few weeks before the unexpected outbreak of the Great War and only saw him again after the vicissitudes of war had given the Central Powers access to southern Russia. He then came back to Vienna and told me that immediately after leaving treatment he had found himself endeavouring to break free from the influence of his physician. A few months of work enabled us to deal with an element of the transference that had not yet been mastered, and since then the patient, deprived by the war of his home, his fortune and all his family relations, had felt normal and conducted himself impeccably. Perhaps the very misery he felt had contributed to the stability of his recovery by providing some satisfaction for his sense of guilt.

# Mourning and Melancholia

Dreams having served us as the normal model for narcissistic mental disorders, we shall now attempt to cast some light on the nature of melancholia by comparing it to the normal affect of mourning. This time, though, we must begin our account with an admission which should warn us against overestimating our conclusions. Melancholia, the definition of which fluctuates even in descriptive psychiatry, appears in various different clinical forms; these do not seem amenable to being grouped together into a single entity, and some of them suggest somatic rather than psychogenetic diseases. Apart from those impressions that are available to any observer, our material is restricted to a small number of cases whose psychogenetic nature was beyond a doubt. We shall therefore relinquish all claim to the universal validity of our results, and console ourselves by reflecting that with the means of investigation presently at our disposal we could hardly find something that was not typical, if not of a whole class of illnesses, then at least of a smaller group.

The correlation between melancholia and mourning seems justified by the overall picture of the two conditions.[1] Further, the causes of both in terms of environmental influences are, where we can identify them at all, also the same. Mourning is commonly the reaction to the loss of a beloved person or an abstraction taking the place of the person, such as fatherland, freedom, an ideal and so on. In some people, whom we for this reason suspect of having a pathological disposition, melancholia appears in place of mourning. It is also most remarkable that it never occurs to us to consider mourning as a pathological condition and present it to the doctor for treatment, despite the fact that it produces severe deviations from normal behaviour. We rely on it being overcome after a certain period of time, and consider interfering with it to be pointless, or even damaging.

Melancholia is mentally characterized by a profoundly painful depression, a loss of interest in the outside world, the loss of the ability to love, the inhibition of any kind of performance and a reduction in the sense of self, expressed in self-recrimination and self-directed insults, intensifying into the delusory expectation of punishment. We have a better understanding of this when we bear in mind that mourning displays the same traits, apart from one: the disorder of self-esteem is absent. In all other respects, however, it is the same. Serious mourning, the reaction to the loss of a loved one, contains the same painful mood, the loss of interest in the outside world – except as it recalls the deceased – the loss of ability to choose any new love-object – which would mean replacing the mourned one – turning away from any task that is not related to the memory of the deceased. We can easily understand that this inhibition and restriction of the ego is a manifestation of exclusive devotion to mourning, leaving nothing over for other interests and intentions. The only reason, in fact, why this behaviour does not strike us as pathological is that we are so easily able to explain it.

We also endorse the comparison that identifies the mood of mourning as a 'painful' one. Its justification will probably be clear to us when we are capable of providing an economical characterization of pain.

So what is the work that mourning performs? I do not think I am stretching a point if I present it in the following manner: realitytesting has revealed that the beloved object no longer exists, and demands that the libido as a whole sever its bonds with that object. An understandable tendency arises to counter this – it may be generally observed that people are reluctant to abandon a libido position, even if a substitute is already beckoning. This tendency can become so intense that it leads to a person turning away from reality and holding on to the object through a hallucinatory wish-psychosis (see the essay ['Metapsychological Complement to Dream Theory']).[2] Normally, respect for reality carries the day. But its task cannot be accomplished immediately. It is now carried out piecemeal at great expenditure of time and investment energy, and the lost object persists in the psyche. Each individual memory and expectation in which the libido was connected to the object is adjusted and hyper-invested, leading to its detachment from the libido. Why this compromise enforcement of the reality commandment, which is carried out piece by piece, should be so extraordinarily painful is not at all easy to explain in economic terms. It is curious that this pain-unpleasure strikes us as natural. In fact, the ego is left free and uninhibited once again after the mourning-work is completed.

Let us now apply to melancholia what we have learned from mourning. In a large number of cases it is clear that it too may be a reaction to the loss of a beloved object; when other causes are present, it may be possible to recognize that the loss is more notional in nature. The object may not really have died, for example, but may instead have been lost as a love-object (as, for example, in the case of an abandoned bride). In yet other cases we think that we should cling to our assumption of such a loss, but it is difficult to see what has been lost, so we may rather assume that the patient cannot consciously grasp what he has lost. Indeed, this might also be the case when the loss that is the cause of the melancholia is known to the subject, when he knows *who* it is, but not *what* it is about that person that he has lost. So the obvious thing is for us somehow to relate melancholia to the loss of an object that is withdrawn from consciousness, unlike mourning, in which no aspect of the loss is unconscious.

In the case of mourning, we found that inhibition and apathy were fully explained by the absorption of the ego in the mourning-work. The unknown loss in the case of melancholia will also lead to similar internal work, and will consequently be responsible for the inhibition of melancholia. But melancholic inhibition seems puzzling to us because we are unable to see what it is that so completely absorbs the patient. There is one other aspect of melancholia that is absent from mourning: an extraordinary reduction in self-esteem, a great impoverishment of the ego. In mourning, the world has become poor and empty, in melancholia it is the ego that has become so. The patient describes his ego to us as being worthless, incapable of functioning and morally reprehensible, he is filled with self-reproach, he levels insults against himself and expects ostracism and punishment. He abases himself before everyone else, he feels sorry for those close to him for being connected to such an unworthy person. He does not sense that a change has taken place in him, but extends his self-criticism to cover the past; he asserts that he has never been any better. The image of this – predominantly moral – sense of inferiority is complemented by sleeplessness, rejection of food, and an overcoming of the drive – most curious from the psychological point of view – which compels everything that lives to cling to life.

It would be fruitless both from the scientific and the therapeutic point of view to contradict the patient who levels such reproaches against his ego in this way. In all likelihood he must in some way be right, and must be describing a state of affairs as it appears to him. Indeed, we must immediately confirm some of his information straight away. He really is as apathetic, as incapable of love and achievement as he says he is. But that, as we know, is secondary; it is the consequence of the internal work, unknown to us and comparable to mourning, that is devouring his ego. He also seems to us to be right in some of his other self-reproaches, and only to be grasping the truth more keenly than others who are not melancholic. If, intensifying his self-criticism, he describes himself as a petty, egoistic, insincere and dependent person, who has only ever striven to conceal the weaknesses of his nature, he may as far as we know have come quite close to self-knowledge, and we can only wonder why one must become ill in order to have access to such truth. For there can be no doubt that anyone who has reached such an assessment of himself, and expresses it to others – an assessment like that which Prince Hamlet has ready for himself and everyone else[3] – is sick, whether he is telling the truth or treating himself more or less unjustly. And it is not difficult to observe that there is, in our judgement, no correspondence between the extent of self-abasement and its justification in reality. A hitherto well-behaved, efficient and dutiful woman will not speak of herself more favourably in melancholia than a woman who is really negligent of her household; in fact the former is more likely to fall ill with melancholia than the latter, a person about whom we ourselves would be unable to find anything good to say. Finally, we must be struck by the fact that the melancholic does not behave just as someone contrite with remorse and self-reproach would normally do. The shame before others that characterizes the latter state is missing, or at least not conspicuously present. In the melancholic one might almost stress the opposite trait of an insistent talkativeness, taking satisfaction from self-exposure.

It is not, then, crucially important whether the melancholic is being accurate in his painful self-disparagement when this criticism coincides with the judgement of others. It is more a question of him providing an accurate description of his psychological situation. He has lost his self-esteem, and must have good reason for doing so. Then we find ourselves facing a contradiction which presents us with a mystery that is difficult to solve. Following the analogy with mourning, we were obliged to conclude that he has suffered a loss of object; his statements suggest a loss of his ego.

Before we address ourselves to this contradiction, let us linger for a while over the insight that the emotion of the melancholic gives us into the constitution of the human ego. In him, we see how one part of the ego presents itself to the other, critically assesses it and, so to speak, takes it as its object. Our suspicion that the critical agency which has split off from the ego in this case might also be able to demonstrate its autonomy under other circumstances is confirmed by all further observations. We will actually find a reason for separating this agency from the rest of the ego. What we are seeing here is the agency that is commonly called conscience; we will count it among the great institutions of the ego, along with censorship of consciousness and reality-testing, and somewhere we will find the proofs that it can become ill on its own account. The clinical picture of melancholia stresses moral disapproval of the patient's own ego over other manifestations: the subject will far more rarely judge himself in terms of physical affliction, ugliness, weakness and social inferiority; only impoverishment assumes a privileged position among the patient's anxieties or assertions.

One observation, and one that is not even difficult to make, leads to an explanation of the contradiction set out above. If we listen patiently to the many and various self-reproaches of the melancholic, we will be unable to avoid a sense that the most intense among them often have little to do with the patient himself, but may with slight modifications be adapted to another person whom the patient loves, has loved or is supposed to love. Each time we look into the facts, the patient confirms this supposition. This means that we have in our hands the key to the clinical picture, recognizing self-reproaches as accusations against a love-object which have taken this route and transferred themselves to the patient's own ego.

The woman who loudly pities her husband for being bound to such a useless woman is actually seeking to accuse her husband of uselessness, in whatever sense the term may be used. We should not be too surprised that some authentic self-reproaches are scattered among those applied to the speaker; they may come to the fore because they help to conceal the others and to impede knowledge of the actual facts, since they emerge from the pros and cons of the conflict of love that has led to the loss of love. Now the behaviour of the patients also becomes much more comprehensible. Their laments [*Klagen*] are accusations [*Anklagen*], in the old sense of the German word; they are not ashamed, they do not conceal themselves, because everything disparaging that they express about themselves is basically being said about someone else; and they are a long way away from communicating to those around them the humility and submissiveness that would befit such unworthy people; rather they are aggravating to a very high degree, they always seem as though they have been slighted, and as though a great wrong has been done to them. All of this is possible only because their reactions, as seen in their behaviour, still emanate from the mental constellation of rejection, which has, as the result of a certain process, been transferred to melancholic remorse.

There is then no difficulty in reconstructing this process. An object-choice had occurred, a bond had been formed between the libido and a particular person; through the influence of a real slight or disappointment on the part of the beloved person, that object-relation had been subjected to a shock. The result of this was not the normal one of the withdrawal of the libido from this object and its displacement on to a new one, but another, which seems to require a number of different conditions in order to come into being. Investment in objects proved not to be very resistant, and was suspended. The free libido was not, however, displaced on to another object, but instead drawn back into the ego. But it did not find any application there, but served to produce an identification of the ego with the abandoned object. In this way the shadow of the object fell upon the ego, which could now be condemned by a particular agency as an object, as the abandoned object. Thus the loss of object had been transformed into a loss of ego, and the conflict between the ego and the beloved person into a dichotomy between ego-criticism and the ego as modified by identification.

Some things may immediately be guessed about the preconditions and results of such a process. On the one hand a strong fixation on the love object must be present, but on the other hand, and in contradiction to that fixation, there must be minimal resistance in the form of object-investment. This contradiction seems to require the object-choice, in accordance with a telling observation by Otto Rank, to have occurred on a narcissistic foundation, so that the object-investment, if it encounters difficulties, is able to regress to narcissism. The narcissistic identification with the object then becomes the substitute for the love-investment, with the result that the love relationship, despite the conflict with the loved one, must not be abandoned. This substitution of identification for object-love is a significant mechanism for the narcissistic illnesses. K. Landauer recently uncovered it in the treatment of a case of schizophrenia.[4] It naturally corresponds to the regression of a type of object-choice to original narcissism. Elsewhere we have explained that identification is the preliminary stage of object-choice, and the first way, ambivalent in its manifestation, in which the ego selects an object. It may assimilate this object, and, in accordance with the oral or cannibalistic phase of libido development, may do so by eating it. Abraham is probably right in tracing the rejection of nourishment, which is apparent in severe forms of the melancholic state, back to this connection.

The conclusion which the theory calls for, and which would transfer the predisposition to melancholic illness, or a part of it, to the predominance of the narcissistic type of object-choice, has unfortunately not been confirmed by investigation. In the introductory sentences of this paper I have confessed that the empirical material on which this study is based is inadequate for our claims. Were we able to assume an agreement between observation and our deductions, we should not hesitate in seeing the oral phase of the libido, which still belongs to narcissism, as one of the characteristics of melancholia. Identifications with the object are by no means rare, even in transference neuroses, and are indeed a well-known mechanism of symptom-formation, particularly in hysteria. But we may see the difference between narcissistic and hysterical identification as lying in the fact that in the former the object-investment is relinquished, while in the latter it continues to exist and manifests an effect that is usually restricted to certain individual actions and innervations. Even in the case of transference neuroses, identification is the manifestation of something held in common that may signify love. Narcissistic identification is the older of the two, and grants us access to an understanding of the less well-studied hysterical form.

So melancholia derives some of its characteristics from mourning, and the rest from the process of regression from the narcissistic object-choice to narcissism. On the one hand it is, like mourning, a reaction to the real loss of the love-object, but it also has a condition which either is absent from normal mourning or, where it is present, transforms it into pathological mourning. The loss of the love-object is an excellent opportunity for the ambivalence of love relationships to come to the fore. Consequently, where the predisposition to obsessive neurosis is present, the conflict of ambivalence gives mourning a pathological shape and forces it to manifest itself in the form of self-reproaches for having been oneself responsible for the loss of the love-object, for having wanted that loss. In such obsessive neurotic depressions after the death of loved ones we are shown what the conflict of ambivalence can achieve on its own when the regressive pull of the libido is not involved. For the most part, the causes of melancholia go beyond the clear case of loss through death, and include all the situations of insult, slight, setback and disappointment through which an opposition of love and hate can be introduced to the relationship, or an ambivalence already present can be intensified. This conflict of ambivalence, now more real, now more constitutive in origin, should not be neglected among the preconditions of melancholia. If the love of the object, which cannot be abandoned while the object itself is abandoned, has fled into narcissistic identification, hatred goes to work on this substitute object, insulting it, humiliating it, making it suffer and deriving a sadistic satisfaction from that suffering. The indubitably pleasurable self-torment of melancholia, like the corresponding phenomenon of obsessive neurosis, signifies the satisfaction of tendencies of sadism and hatred,[5] which are applied to an object and are thus turned back against the patient's own person. In both of these illnesses, patients manage to avenge themselves on the original objects along the detour of self-punishment, and to torment their loved ones by means of being ill, having taken to illness in order to avoid showing their hostility directly. The person who provoked in the patient the emotional disturbance from which his form of illness took its orientation will generally be found in the patient's immediate milieu. Thus the melancholic's love-investment in his object has undergone a second fate; in part it has regressed to identification, but it has also been moved back, under the influence of the conflict of ambivalence, to the sadistic stage to which it is closer.

It is this sadism that solves the mystery of the inclination to suicide which makes melancholia both so interesting and so dangerous. We have acknowledged this great self-love of the ego as the primal state from which the life of the drives emanates, and we see in the anxiety that appears when our lives are endangered the liberation of so much narcissistic libido that we cannot grasp how the ego could ever consent to self-destruction. Certainly, we have known for a long time that no neurotic nurtures suicidal intentions who does not turn them back from an impulse to murder others, but we have achieved no understanding of the play of forces that could turn such an intention into action. Now the analysis of melancholia teaches us that the ego can only kill itself when it is able to treat itself as an object because of the return of object-investment, if it is able to direct the hostility that applies to the object back against itself and represents the original reaction of the ego against objects in the outside world. (See 'Drives and Their Fates'.) Thus, in the regression of the narcissistic object-choice the object may have been abolished, but it has proved more potent than the ego itself. In the two contrasting situations of extreme passion and suicide the ego, although in entirely different ways, is overwhelmed by the object.

Hence, as regards the one particularly striking characteristic of melancholia, the emergence of the fear of impoverishment, it seems natural to trace it back to anal eroticism, torn from its context and regressively transformed.

Melancholia confronts us with other questions which to some extent it fails to answer. The fact that it passes after a certain amount of time, without leaving any broad or demonstrable changes, is a characteristic that it shares with mourning. It was there that we observed that time is required for the detailed implementation of the reality-testing command, after which the ego's libido is freed from the lost object. We may consider the ego busy with an analogous task during melancholia; in neither case do we have an economic understanding of its origin. The sleeplessness of melancholia testifies to the inflexibility of the condition, the impossibility of implementing the general drawing-in of investments required for sleep. The complex of melancholia behaves like an open wound, drawing investment energies to itself from all sides (energies which we have, in the case of transference neuroses, called 'counter-investments'), and draining the ego to the point of complete impoverishment; it can easily prove to be resistant to the ego's desire to sleep.

One element which is probably somatic, and which cannot be explained psychogenetically, becomes apparent in the regular allev-iation of the condition that occurs in the evening. These considera-tions raise the question of whether the loss of the ego, regardless of the object (purely narcissistic injury to the ego) is enough to produce the image of melancholia, and whether an impoverish-ment of the ego-libido by the consumption of toxins can produce certain forms of the illness.

The most curious property of melancholia, and the one most in need of explanation, lies in its tendency to turn into the sympto-matically opposite state of mania. As we know, this is not the fate of all cases of melancholia. Some cases develop in periodic relapses, the intervals between which reveal either no hint of mania at all, or only a very slight degree of it. Others demonstrate the regular alternation of melancholic and manic phases that has found expres-sion in the formulation of cyclical insanity. One would be tempted to exclude these cases as being psychogenetic, had psychoanalytic treatment not brought about a therapeutic solution in several cases of this kind. So it is not only permissible, but actually imperative, to extend an analytic explanation of melancholia to mania as well.

I cannot promise that this attempt will be entirely satisfactory. In fact it does not go far beyond the possibility of an initial orien-tation. We have two clues at our disposal here, the first a psycho-analytical impression, the second what we might call a universal economic experience. The impression already expressed by a number of psychoanalytical researchers suggests that mania is not different in content from melancholia, that both illnesses battle with the same 'complex' to which the ego probably succumbs in melancholia, while in mania it has overcome it or pushed it aside. The other clue comes from the experience that in all states of joy, jubilation and triumph shown by the normal model of mania, the same economic conditions are apparent. As the result of a particular influence, a large expenditure of psychical energy, maintained over a long period or frequently recurring, finally becomes superfluous, and thus becomes available for many different applications and possibilities of discharge. Thus, for example: if a poor devil is suddenly relieved of his chronic concern about his daily bread by winning a large amount of money, if a long and strenuous struggle is finally crowned by success, if a person suddenly becomes capable of abandoning some pressing compulsion, a false position that he has had to maintain for a long time, and so on. All such situations are marked by a lightened mood, the signs of discharge of joyful emotion, and the intensified readiness for all kinds of actions, just like mania, and in complete contrast to the depression and inhibition of melancholia. One might dare to say that mania is in fact just such a triumph, except that what it has overcome, the source of its triumph, is hidden from the ego. Alcoholic intoxication, which belongs in the same series of states – albeit a more cheerful one – can be explained in much the same way; here there is probably a suggestion, accomplished by toxins, of the expenditure of repression. Lay opinion likes to assume that one is so keen on movement and activity in such a manic state because one is in 'such a cheerful mood'. Of course we will have to unmake this false connection. The economic state within the mental life which we mentioned above has been fulfilled, and that is why we are on the one hand so cheerful, and on the other so uninhibited in our actions.

If we combine these two suggestions, what we find is this: in mania, the ego must have overcome the loss of the object (or mourning over the loss, or perhaps the object itself), and now the total amount of counter-investment that the painful suffering of melancholia had drawn and bound to itself from the ego has become available. The manic person also unmistakably demonstrates his liberation from the object from which he had been suffering by pouncing on his new object-investments like a ravenous man.

This explanation may sound plausible, but first of all it is too vague, and secondly it throws up more new questions and doubts than we can answer. We do not wish to avoid discussing it, even though we cannot expect to find our way to clarity as a result.

In the first place, normal mourning also overcomes the loss of the object while at the same time absorbing all the energies of the ego during the period of its existence. Why, then, once it has run its course, is there not so much as a hint of the economic condition required for a phase of triumph? I cannot give a simple answer to this objection. It also draws our attention to the fact that we cannot even identify the economic means through which mourning accomplishes its task. However, a conjecture might come to our assistance here. To each individual memory and situation of expectation that shows the libido to be connected to the lost object, reality delivers its verdict that the object no longer exists, and the ego, presented with the question, so to speak, of whether it wishes to share this fate, is persuaded by the sum of narcissistic satisfactions that it derives from being alive to loosen its bonds with the object that has been destroyed. We might perhaps imagine that this process of dissolution takes place so slowly and gradually that by the time it is over the expenditure of energy required for its accomplishment has been dispersed.[6]

It is tempting to try to proceed from conjecture about the work of mourning to an account of the work of melancholia. Here, at the outset, we encounter an uncertainty. Hitherto, we have hardly considered melancholia from the topographical point of view, and neither have we asked in and between which psychical systems the work of melancholia occurs. What part of the psychical processes of the disorder is still taking place in relation to the abandoned unconscious object-investments, and what part in relation to their substitute through identification, in the ego?

The quick and easy answer to this is that the 'unconscious (thing-)representation of the object by the libido is abandoned'. But in fact this representation consists of countless individual impressions (or their unconscious traces), and this withdrawal of the libido cannot be a matter of a moment, but must certainly, as in mourning, be a long drawn-out and gradual process. It is not easy to tell whether it begins simultaneously in many different places, or whether it contains some kind of sequence; in analytic treatment one can often observe that now this, now that memory is activated, and that the identical-sounding laments, tiresome in their monotony, have a different unconscious explanation each time. If the object does not have such a great significance for the ego, one that is intensified by thousands of connections, its loss is not apt to lead to mourning or melancholia. The characteristic of detaching the libido piecemeal can thus be attributed equally to melancholia and mourning; it is probably based on the same economic relations and serves the same tendencies in both.

But melancholia, as we have heard, contains more than normal mourning does. In melancholia, the relationship with the object is not a simple one, it is complicated by the conflict of ambivalence. That ambivalence is either constitutional, that is, it is attached to every love relationship of this particular ego, or else it emerges straight out of experiences that imply the threat of the loss of the object. In its causes, then, melancholia can go far beyond mourning, which is as a rule unleashed only by real loss, the death of the object. Thus in melancholia a series of individual battles for the object begins, in which love and hatred struggle with one another, one to free the libido from the object, the other to maintain the existing libido position against the onslaught. These individual battles cannot be transferred to a system other than the unconscious, the realm of memory traces of things (as against verbal investments). It is in this very place that attempts at solution are played out in mourning, but here they face no obstacle, since these processes continue on their normal way to consciousness through the preconscious. This path is closed to the work of melancholia, perhaps because of the large number of causes or because of the fact that they are all working together. Constitutional ambivalence essentially belongs to the repressed, and the traumatic experiences with the object may have activated other repressed material. Thus, everything about these battles of ambivalence remains withdrawn from consciousness until the characteristic outcome of melancholia has been reached. As we know, this consists in the threatened libido-investment finally leaving the object, only to return to the place in the ego from which it had emerged. So it is by taking flight into the ego that love escapes abolition. After this regression of the libido, the process can become conscious, and represents itself to consciousness as a conflict between one part of the ego and the critical agency.

So what consciousness learns about in the work of melancholia is not the essential part of it, nor is it the part to which we may attribute an influence to the solution of suffering. We see the ego debasing itself and raging against itself, and have as little understanding as the patient about where that can lead and how it can change. We can more readily attribute such an accomplishment to the unconscious part of the work, because it is not difficult to discover a significant analogy between the work of melancholia and that of mourning. Just as mourning impels the ego to renounce the object by declaring its death, and offers the ego the reward of staying alive, each individual battle of ambivalence loosens the fixation of the libido upon the object by devaluing, disparaging and, so to speak, even killing it. There is a possibility of the process in the unconscious coming to an end, either once the fury has played itself out or after the object has been abandoned as worthless. We cannot tell which of these two possibilities brings melancholia to an end, either in all cases or in most, and what influence this termination has upon the further development of the case. The ego may enjoy the satisfaction of acknowledging itself to be the better of the two, and superior to the object.

Even if we accept this view of the work of melancholia, there is still one point upon which we were seeking enlightenment that it does not help to explain. We expected that an explanation of the economic condition for the emergence of mania with the passing of melancholia might be found in the ambivalence that dominates the disorder; this might find support in analogies drawn from various other areas. But there is one fact before which that expectation must bow. Of the three preconditions for melancholia: the loss of the object, ambivalence and the regression of the libido into the ego, we find the first two once more in the obsessive reproaches that we encounter after someone has died. There, it is beyond a doubt ambivalence that represents the main driving force of the conflict, and observation shows that once it has passed, nothing of the triumph of a manic constitution remains. This leads us to the third element as the sole factor responsible. The accumulation of investment, which is freed once the work of melancholia is concluded, and which makes mania possible, must be linked to the regression of the libido to narcissism. The conflict within the ego which melancholia exchanges for the battle over the object must behave like a painful wound requiring an extraordinarily high counter-investment. But here, once again, it makes sense for us to come to a halt and put off any further explanation of mania until we have gained an insight into the economic nature first of physical pain and then of the mental pain analogous to it. We know already that the interdependence of the complex problems of the psyche requires us to break off each investigation before it is completed – until the results of some other investigation can come to its aid.[7]

(1917)

## Notes

1. Abraham, to whom we owe the most significant of the few analytic studies of the subject at hand, also took this as his starting point (*Zentralblatt für Psychoanalyse*, II, 6, 1912).
2. ['Metapsychologische Ergänzung der Traumlehre' (1917), which preceded 'Mourning and Melancholia' in the volume *Das Ich und das Es (The Ego and the Id)*.]
3. 'Use every man after his desert, and who shall 'scape whipping?' *Hamlet*, II, 2.
4. [K. Landauer, 'Spontanheilung einer Katatonie'] *Intern. Zeitschr. für ärztl, Psychoanalyse*, II, 1914.
5. On the difference between them, see the paper on 'Drives and Their Fates'.
6. Hitherto, little attention has been paid to the economic viewpoint in psychoanalytical works. As an exception to this we might mention the essay

by V. Tausk, 'Entwertung des Verdrängungsmotivs durch Rekompense' ['Devaluation of the motive of repression through recompense'] (*Intern. Zeitschr. für ärztl. Psychoanalyse*, I, 1913).

7.[*Addition 1925:*] See further discussion of the problem of mania in *Mass Psychology and Analysis to the 'I' (Ges. Werke.*, vol. XIII).

# Lapses

Ladies and gentlemen! We shall begin not with premises, but with
an investigation. We are choosing as its object certain phenomena
that are very frequent, very familiar and very little appreciated, and
which have nothing to do with illnesses in so far as they can be
observed in any healthy person. These are the so-called *lapses* of
mankind, as when someone wants to say one thing and instead says
a different word, *misspeaking* (slips of the tongue), or the same
thing happens to him when writing, whether he notices it or not;
or when someone reads something in print or handwriting other
than what is supposed to be read, *misreading*; and equally when
he hears something wrongly that is said to him, *mishearing*, there
being, of course, no organic disorder of his hearing ability involved.
Another series of such phenomena is based on *forgetting*, not lasting but only temporary, as, for example, when someone cannot find
a *name* that he in fact knows and regularly recognizes, or when he
forgets to carry out an *intention* that he then later remembers, and
has thus forgotten only for a certain point of time. In a third series,
this condition ceases to be merely temporary, as, for example, in
*mislaying*, when someone puts an object somewhere and is unable
to find it, or in the very similar case of *losing*. This is a kind of
forgetting that is treated in a different way from other types of
forgetting, about which one is surprised or annoyed rather than
finding it comprehensible. To this there may be added certain
*errors* in which the temporary nature of the forgetfulness becomes
apparent once again, in that one for a while believes something
that one knows both before and later to be other than the case,
and a number of similar phenomena that go by different names.

These are all occurrences whose profound affinity is expressed for the most part by the prefix 'mis-'. They are almost all unimportant by nature, generally of very fleeting existence, and without a great deal of importance in the person's life. Only seldom does one of them, like the losing of objects, assume a certain practical importance. For that reason, too, they do not attract a great deal of attention, they arouse only faint affects, etc.

It is to these phenomena, then, that I wish to draw your attention. But you will irritably object: 'there are so many great mysteries in the world and in the smaller confines of the psyche, so many wonders in the sphere of the psychical disorders that require and merit illumination, that it appears truly wilful to squander work and interest on such trivial matters. If you could help us to understand why a human being with healthy eyes and ears can, in broad daylight, see and hear things that do not exist, why someone else suddenly believes himself to be persecuted by the people who were previously dearest to him, or provides the most astute explanation for delusions that would appear nonsensical to any child, then we will think something of psychoanalysis, but if it can do nothing but occupy itself with the question of why an after-dinner speaker says one word instead of another at some point, or why a housewife has mislaid her keys and similarly petty things, then we, too, will find better things to do with our time and our interest.'

I would reply: patience, ladies and gentlemen! I do not think that your criticism is on the right track here. True, psychoanalysis cannot claim that it has never dealt with trivia. On the contrary, the material that it studies usually consists of those inconspicuous events that are rejected by the other sciences as unworthy of attention, what we might call the dregs of the phenomenal world. But are you not, in your criticism, confusing the extent of the problems with the conspicuousness of the clues? Are there not very significant things that can reveal themselves only through quite faint clues, under certain conditions and at certain times? I could easily present you with several such situations. From what clues do you, the young men among you, conclude that you have won the affection of a young lady? Do you wait until you have had an express declaration of love, a stormy embrace, or are you not satisfied with a glance barely noticed by anyone else, a fleeting movement, a second's prolongation of a handshake? And if, as a criminal investigator, you are involved in a murder case, do you really expect to find that the murderer has left his photograph along with his address at the scene of the crime, or are you not out of necessity satisfied with fainter and less distinct traces of the character you are seeking? Let us not now, then, underestimate small clues; perhaps they are capable of leading us to something greater. And I should add that I think as you do that the big problems in the world and in science have the first claim upon our interest. But generally speaking it is of very little use merely to form the intention to attend to some big problem or another. Often in such cases one does not know where to go next. In scientific work it is more fruitful to address the matter in front of one, which one has the opportunity to investigate. If one does that very thoroughly, without prejudice or expectation, and one is lucky, because of the great connection that links everything with everything else, including small things with big ones, even such undemanding work may allow access to the study of big problems.

I would speak in those terms in order to hold your interest in the treatment of such apparently trivial slips among healthy subjects. Let us now bring in someone who is a stranger to psychoanalysis and ask him how he might explain the occurrence of such things.

His first answer is sure to be: 'Oh, that isn't worth explaining; those things are mere coincidences. What does he mean by that? Is he claiming that there are happenings so small that they fall out of the concatenation of global occurrences, and which could equally well be other than they are? If, in this way, someone breaks through the law of natural determinism at one single place, he has toppled the whole of the scientific view of the world. One can then point out to him how much more consistently even the religious view of the world behaves in emphatically assuring us that not a single sparrow falls from the roof without God's particular will. I believe that our friend will not wish to draw the conclusion from his first reply, he will make a concession and say that if he studied these things he would find some kind of explanation for them. They are small derailments, inexactitudes in the psychical function, the conditions for which could be identified. A person who can otherwise speak correctly may slip, 1) if he is slightly unwell and tired, 2) if he is worked up, 3) if excessive claims are being made on his attention by other things. It is easy to confirm these data. Slips of the tongue occur particularly frequently if one is tired, or if one has a headache or a migraine. In the same circumstances it is easy to forget proper names. Some people are used to recognizing the approach of a migraine from the fact that proper names escape them. When one is worked up, too, one often mixes up words, but also things, one 'misuses' things, and the forgetting of intentions as well as a large number of other unintended actions becomes striking if one is distracted, that is, if one is actually concentrating on something else. One famous example of such distractedness is the professor from the *Fliegende Blätter*, who leaves his umbrella behind and picks up the wrong hat because he is thinking about the problems he is going to deal with in his next book. We are all familiar, from our own experience, with examples of the way in which we can forget intentions that we have formed and promises that we have made because in the meantime we have experienced something that has firmly claimed our attention.

Put like that it sounds entirely comprehensible, and seems also immune to contradiction. It is perhaps not very interesting, not as we had expected. Let us take a closer look at these explanations of lapses. The conditions given for the occurrence of the phenomena are not identical to one another. Feeling unwell and suffering from blood disorders provide a physiological explanation for impairment of the normal function; excitement, fatigue and distraction are elements of another kind, which we might call psychophysiological. The latter are easily translated into theory. Both fatigue and distraction, and perhaps, too, general excitement, prompt a distribution of attention that cause one to pay too little attention to the task at hand. That task can then be particularly easily disturbed, imprecisely performed. Feeling unwell and suffering changes in the blood supply to the nervous central organ can have the same effect, by influencing the crucial element, the distribution of attention, in a similar manner. According to this theory, then, these are the effects of a disturbance of the attention, as a result either of organic or of psychical causes.

There seems to be little of interest here to us psychoanalysts. We might feel tempted to abandon the subject again. However, if we take a closer look at our observations, not everything accords with this attention theory of lapses, or at least not everything derives naturally from it. We are aware that such lapses and forgetfulness also occur among people who are not tired, distracted or excited, but who are in a state that is normal in every way, unless one were retrospectively to attribute a state of excitement to the subjects precisely because of the slip, excitement which they themselves would not admit. Nor can it simply be the case that a function guaranteed by the intensification of the attention directed towards it will be threatened by a reduction in that attention. There are many tasks that are carried out purely automatically, with a very low degree of attention, and yet with great assurance. The stroller who barely knows where he is going still keeps to the right path and stops at his destination without having *miswalked*. At least he gets there as a rule. The practised pianist strikes the right keys without thinking about it. He can also, of course, misstrike, but if automatic playing intensified the danger of misstriking, the virtuoso whose playing has become entirely automatic through a great deal of practice would be the one most exposed to that danger. On the contrary, we see that many tasks are performed with particular assurance when they are not the object of a particularly high level of attention, and that the misfortune of the lapse can occur precisely when the task is particularly important, and a distraction from the required attention thus certainly does not take place. In such cases one might say that this is the effect of 'excitement', but we cannot understand why excitement does not instead intensify the application of attention to the task so keenly intended. If someone has a slip of the tongue in an important speech or in oral negotiations, and says the opposite of what he planned to say, that can hardly be explained by either the psycho-physiological theory or the theory of attention.

Lapses also contain very many minor epiphenomena which are not understood, and which cannot be brought closer to us by the explanations we have supplied so far. If, for example, one has temporarily forgotten a name, one becomes annoyed, one desperately wants to remember it and cannot abandon the task. Why is the person thus annoyed so very seldom successful in guiding his attention, as he wishes to do, to the word which is, as he says, 'on the tip of his tongue', and which he immediately recognizes when it is uttered in his presence? And then there are also those cases in which slips multiply, link up with one another, replace one another. The first time one had forgotten an appointment; the next time, for which one had deliberately intended not to forget, one ended up writing down the wrong time. One tries to use detours to remember a forgotten word, and in the process one finds oneself unable to remember a second name that could have been useful in searching for the first. When one goes in search of that second name, a third name escapes, and so on. The same thing, as we all know, can occur with misprints, which can be seen as lapses on the part of the typesetter. One such stubborn misprint is once supposed to have crept into a Social Democrat newspaper. The report on a certain festivity included the following: 'Among those present was his highness, the *Kornprinz* ["Corn Prince", for Kronprinz, "Crown Prince"].' The next day a correction was attempted. The newspaper apologized and wrote: 'That should of course have read: the *Knor*prinz [approximately: "Knot Prince"].' In such cases people are happy to talk of gremlins, printers' devils and so on, expressions that go beyond a psycho-physiological theory of the misprint.

Neither do I know whether you are aware that slips of the tongue can be provoked, prompted, so to speak, by suggestion. An anecdote gives an account of this: once a novice actor was given the important role, in Schiller's play *The Maid of Orleans*, of telling the king that the Constable was sending his sword back. One of the heroic actors played a joke on him during the rehearsal, repeatedly whispering to the shy beginner the phrase 'the comfortable is sending his horse back', and succeeded in his intention. During the performance the unfortunate actor really did begin with this modified announcement, despite the fact that he had had sufficient warning, or perhaps for that very reason.

These small characteristics of lapses are far from being explained by the theory of the withdrawal of attention. But that does not yet mean that the theory must be false. It may lack something, a complement that would make it fully satisfactory. But some lapses themselves can also be considered from a different angle.

Let us single out 'slips of the tongue' as being the most suitable of the lapses for our purposes. We could equally well choose miswriting or misreading. Now we must say that we have so far asked only when, under what conditions one makes a slip of the tongue, and have had an answer only to that question. But one can also direct one's interest in another direction and wish to know why one makes the slip in precisely that way rather than any other; one can take into account what comes out when one makes a slip. You can see that as long as one does not answer this question, and elucidate the effect of the slip, the phenomenon remains something random in psychological terms, even if it has been physiologically explained. If I happen to make a slip of the tongue, I could clearly slip in an infinite number of ways, say one word out of a thousand others for the right one, undertake countless distortions of the correct word. So is there anything that, in a particular case, out of all possibilities, urges me to misspeak in one particular way, or is that a matter of chance and arbitrariness, and perhaps there is nothing sensible to be said on the subject?

In 1895 two authors, Meringer and Mayer (a philologist and a psychiatrist), also performed the experiment of approaching the question of misspeaking from this direction. They collected examples and initially gave their account in purely descriptive terms. That, of course, does not in itself provide an explanation, but it may help to lead in the direction of one. They distinguish the distortions that the intended speech undergoes in the process of misspeaking as follows: transposition, presonance, resonance, contamination and substitution. I will give you examples of these main groups by the two authors. It is a case of transposition if someone says 'the Milo de Venus' instead of 'the Venus de Milo' (transposition in the sequence of the words); a presonance: 'Es war mir *auf der Schwest* . . . auf der Brust so schwer' [literally: 'It was so *chev* . . . so heavy on my chest']; resonance would be the familiar mixed-up toast: 'Ich fordere Sie *auf, auf* das Wohl unseres Chefs *aufzustossen*' [literally: 'I ask you to *burp* – rather than raise – your glasses to the health of our boss']. These three forms of misspeaking are not exactly frequent. Much more numerous, you will find, are those observations in which a slip arises out of a contraction or contamination, for example when a gentleman addresses a lady on the street with the words: 'Wenn Sie gestatten, mein Fräulein, möchte ich Sie gerne *begleit-digen*.' The compound word clearly contains both *begleiten* (accompany) and *beleidigen* (insult), so that the phrase means, literally: 'If you will permit me, I should like to *accompany/insult* you.' (Incidentally, one assumes that the young man did not have much success with the lady.) As an example of a substitution, M. and M. give the instance of someone saying he is putting the preparations in the *Briefkasten* [letterbox] rather than the *Brutkasten* [incubator], and so on.

The attempted explanation that the two authors base their collection of examples on is particularly inadequate. They think that the sounds and syllables of a word are different in value, and that innervation of the more valuable element can have a disturbing influence on the less valuable. The slips they choose are clearly based on presonance and resonance, although these are by no means all that frequent; other results of these verbal preferences, if they exist at all, are of absolutely no consequence. But one most often slips by saying instead of one word another very similar one, and that similarity is for many people sufficient explanation of slips of the tongue. For example, a professor in his inaugural speech: 'I am not *geneigt* (for *geeignet*) [inclined/worthy] to appreciate the merits of my highly esteemed predecessor.' Or another professor: 'Beim weiblichen Genitale hat man trotz vieler *Versuchungen* . . . Pardon:

*Versuche . . .'* ['In the female`genitals one has, despite many *temp-tations* . . . Excuse me: *experiments* . . .']

But the most common and also the most striking kind of slip is when one says precisely the opposite of what one intended to say. In this, of course, we are moving a long way away from relations between the sounds and the effects of similarity, and can instead refer to the fact that opposites have a strong conceptual affinity with one another, and are particularly close to one another in terms of psychological association. There are historical examples of this kind: a President in our Parliament once opened the session with the words: 'Gentlemen, I note the presence of . . . members and thus declare the session *closed.'*

Similarly seductive to the relationship between opposites, then, is some other current association that may under some circumstances arise in a very unsuitable manner. Thus, for example, it is said that on the occasion of the celebration of the marriage of a child of H. Helmholtz to a child of the famous inventor and industrialist W. Siemens, the famous physiologist Du Bois-Reymond delivered the speech. He concluded his doubtless brilliant toast with the words: 'So long live the new company: *Siemens* – and – *Halske!*' That was, of course, the name of the old company. The juxtaposition of the two names must have been as familiar to a Berliner as the names Riedel and Beutel would be to someone from Vienna.

So to relations between sound and verbal similarity we must add the influence of word associations. But that is not enough. In a series of cases the elucidation of the slip observed seems to be successful only once we have taken into consideration what was said or even only thought a sentence previously. So here again we have a case of resonance, like the one put forward by Meringer, only at a greater distance. I must admit that I have the overall impression that we are now further away from an understanding of slips of the tongue than ever!

However, I hope I am not mistaken in saying that during the investigation that we have just carried out, we have all formed a new impression of examples of slips of the tongue, and one which it might be worth lingering over. We have examined the conditions under which a slip can occur in the first place, then the influences that determine the kind of distortion through that slip, but we have not yet considered the effect of the slip itself, regardless of its source. If we decide to do so, we must finally drum up the courage to say that in some of the examples the words produced through slips also had a meaning of their own. What does it mean to say that something has a meaning? Well, it means that the effect of slips perhaps has a right to be considered as a fully valid psychical action that is also pursuing a goal of its own, as an expression of content and meaning. Hitherto we have spoken only in terms of lapses, but now it appears as if the lapse itself is quite a respectable action that has only taken the place of the other, expected or intended action.

This meaning that the lapse possesses seems in individual cases to be tangible and unmistakable. If the President closes, rather than opens, the session of Parliament with his first words, we are inclined, because of our knowledge of the conditions under which his slip occurred, to find it meaningful. He expects no good to come out of the session, and would be happy if he could immediately break it off again. The revelation of this meaning, the interpretation of this slip, causes us no difficulties whatsoever. Or if one lady says to another with apparent admiration: 'Diesen reizenden neuen Hut haben Sie sich wohl selbst *aufgepatzt*?' ['What a charming new hat – did you *botch it up* yourself?'], no amount of scientific thinking in the world will be able to keep us from hearing the expression: 'This hat is a *Patzerei*, a botched job.' Or if a lady known for her energy says: 'My husband asked the doctor what diet he should follow. But the doctor said he doesn't need a diet, he can eat and drink what *I like*,' the slip of the tongue is the unmistakable expression of a consistent programme.

Ladies and gentlemen, if it should prove that it is not only a few cases of slips of the tongue and lapses that generally have a *meaning*, but the majority of them, the meaning of lapses, which we have not yet mentioned, will become the most interesting thing for us and rightly push all other viewpoints into the background. We can then leave aside all physiological or psycho-physiological elements, and may devote ourselves to purely psychological investigations into the meaning, that is, the significance, the intention of the slip. So we will first of all take care to test a large amount of observed material in terms of this expectation.

But before we carry out this intention, I should like to invite you to pursue another trail with me. On many occasions a poet has used slips of the tongue or another lapse as a means of poetic representation. This fact must, on its own, prove to us that he considers the lapse, the slip of the tongue, for example, to be something meaningful, because he produces it deliberately. It is not that the poet miswrites something by accident and then allows his miswriting to persist in his character as a slip. He wishes to make us understand something through the slip, and we are able to see what that may be, whether, for example, he wants to indicate to us that the character in question is distracted and tired or should shortly expect a migraine. Of course we do not wish to overestimate the meaningful use of slips by poets. The slip might, in fact, be meaningless, a random psychical event, or meaningful only in very rare cases, and the poet might reserve the right to lend it a spiritual dimension by furnishing it with a meaning, in order to use it for his own purposes. But neither should it come as a surprise if poets had more to teach us about slips of the tongue than philologists and psychiatrists.

One such example of a slip of the tongue occurs in Schiller's *Wallenstein* (*Piccolomini*, Act I, scene 5). In the previous scene, Max Piccolomini has most passionately taken the side of the Duke, enthusing about the blessings of peace revealed to him on his journey as he accompanied Wallenstein's daughter to the camp. He leaves his father and the court envoy behind in utter dismay. And now the fifth act continues:

QUESTENBERG: O woe to us! Is it so?
    What, friend! and are we letting him go there
    In this madness, not making him come
    Straight back so that we may open his eyes
    On the spot?

OCTAVIO: (*emerging from deep reflection*) My eyes he has opened now,
   And I see more than pleases me.
QUESTENBERG: What is it, friend?
OCTAVIO:                         A curse upon this journey!
QUESTENBERG: Why? What is it?
OCTAVIO:                         Come – I must pursue the unhappy trail,
   See with my own eyes – come. (*Tries to lead him away*)
QUESTENBERG: What, then? Where?
OCTAVIO: (*pressed*) To her!
QUESTENBERG: To –
OCTAVIO: (*corrects himself*): To the Duke! Let us go
   etc.

Octavio meant to say 'to him', to the Duke, but makes a slip of
the tongue and, with his words '*to her*', betrays, at least to us, that
he has very clearly recognized the influence that makes the young
war hero enthuse about peace.

Otto Rank has discovered an even more impressive example in
Shakespeare. It occurs in *The Merchant of Venice*, in the famous
scene in which the fortunate lover chooses between the three
caskets, and I can perhaps do nothing better than to read you
Rank's brief account.

'A *slip of the tongue*, most elegantly motivated and employed
with technical brilliance, which, like the one pointed out by Freud
in *Wallenstein*, reveals that poets are very familiar with the mechanism and meaning of this slip, and also assume that it is understood
by the listeners, occurs in Shakespeare's *The Merchant of Venice*
(Act III, scene 2). Portia, bound by her father's will to the choice
of a husband by the drawing of lots, has so far escaped all her
unlovely suitors by sheer good fortune. As she has finally, in Bassanio,
found the suitor to whom she is really drawn, she finds herself fearing that he too will draw the wrong lot. She would now best like
to tell him that even in that case he could be sure of her love, but
she is kept from doing so by her oath. In this inner conflict, the
poet has her say to the welcome suitor:

> I pray you, tarry: pause a day or two
> Before you hazard; for, in choosing wrong,
> I lose your company: therefore, forbear awhile.
> There's something tells me, but it is not love,
> I would not lose you; [. . .] I could teach you
> How to choose right, but then I am forsworn;
> So will I never be: so may you miss me;
> But if you do, you'll make me wish a sin,
> That I had been forsworn. Beshrew your eyes,
> They have o'erlooked me and divided me:
> *One half of me is yours, the other half yours,*
> *Mine own, I would say;* but if mine, then yours,
> And so all yours.

The very thing, then, that she only sought to hint at quietly because she was really supposed to conceal it from him completely, that she is actually *all* his before the choice is made, and that she loves him, all this the poet allows to emerge into the open with admirable psychological sensitivity in the slip of the tongue, and by so doing he is able to assuage the unbearable uncertainty of the lover as well as the similar excitement of the audience about the outcome of the choice.'

I would also ask you to notice how delicately Portia finally conveys the two statements contained in the slip of the tongue, the way she abolishes the contradiction that exists between them, and finally agrees with the slip:

> but if mine, then yours,
And so all yours.

Sometimes, thinkers remote from medicine have also revealed the meaning of a slip with a remark, anticipating our efforts to elucidate it. You are all familiar with the clever satirist Lichtenberg (1742–99), of whom Goethe said: 'Wherever he makes a joke, a problem lurks.' Now, sometimes, the solution of the problem is revealed by the joke. Amongst his witty and satirical ideas,

Lichtenberg jots down the sentence: 'He had read so much Homer that he always read *Agamemnon* rather than *"angenommen"* [assumed].' That is the theory of misreading in a nutshell.

Next time we shall examine whether we can agree with the poets in their conception of lapses.

(1916 [1915])

# Observations on Love in Transference

Anyone practising analysis for the first time no doubt worries about the difficulties he will face in interpreting the patient's associations and the task of re-creating the repressed. What he will learn in due course, however, is that while he need not take these particular difficulties too seriously, he will instead have really serious problems coping with transference.

From among the situations of this kind that arise, I am going to select a single, very sharply delineated one, chosen both because of its frequent recurrence and its significance in reality, and because of its interest to theory. The case I have in mind is that of the female patient who lets it be known, either by dropping hints or by direct confession, that, like any other woman, she is only human and has fallen in love with the analyst. This situation has its embarrassing and its comic sides as well as its serious one. It is also so complex and determined by so many factors, so unavoidable and so difficult to resolve that discussion of it has for some time been a vital need of analytical technique. But as we who mock others' mistakes are not always free of them ourselves, we have not exactly pushed ourselves to meet this challenge. Time and again here we come up against the obligation to medical discretion, indispensable in life but of no use in our science. Since writing about psychoanalysis is also a part of real life, there is a genuine contradiction here. I recently took up a position beyond discretion and suggested that this precise situation of transference held back the progress of psychoanalysis for its first decade.[1]

For a cultivated layman – the ideal civilized interlocutor for psychoanalysis – affairs of the heart are of a different order of magnitude from everything else; they are, so to speak, inscribed on a special parchment unsuitable for any other form of inscription. Thus, when a female patient falls in love with the doctor, our layman will assume that there can only be two outcomes: the rare one where circumstances permit the legitimate and lasting union of the two, and the commoner one where doctor and patient go their own ways and the work that has been initiated, meant to lead to her recovery, has to be abandoned as though spoilt by an elemental event. Of course, a third outcome is conceivable, apparently even compatible with continuing the therapy: that of starting an illicit love affair not destined to be permanent. But this is surely ruled out as much by bourgeois morality as by the dignity of the medical profession. All the same, our layman would want to be reassured as plainly as possible that the analyst excludes this third option.

Clearly, the psychoanalyst's standpoint has to be different.

Let us take the case of the second outcome of the situation we are discussing: doctor and patient part after the woman has fallen in love with the doctor, and the course of therapy is abandoned. But the condition of the patient necessitates a second attempt at analysis, with a different doctor. It then transpires that the woman feels she has fallen in love with this second doctor, too, and likewise with a third, after she has once again terminated the treatment and then started afresh, and so on. This commonly occurring state of affairs is well known as one of the bases of psychoanalytical theory, and it can be put to use in two ways: one by the doctor conducting the analysis, the other by the patient in need of analysis.

For the doctor it represents a valuable lesson and a good warning about any temptation to counter-transference on his side. He has to be clear that the patient's infatuation is induced by the analytical situation and is not due to his personal attractions, and that he therefore has no reason to be proud of his 'conquest', as it would be called outside the analytical context. And it is always good to be reminded of this. The patient, however, is faced with a choice of alternatives: either she has to renounce psychoanalytical treatment, or she has to accept falling in love with the doctor as her inevitable fate.[2]

I have no doubt that the patient's closest family will declare as decisively in favour of the first of these options as the analysing doctor will for the second. But I think this is a case where the tender – or rather self-centredly jealous – concern of the family should not be allowed to decide. Only the interests of the patient should be conclusive. And her relations' love cannot cure a neurosis. The psychoanalyst does not need to impose himself, but he can put himself forward as indispensable for certain purposes. Any close family member who adopts Tolstoy's position on this problem can continue to enjoy undisturbed possession of his wife or daughter, but will have to try to learn to live with her continuing neurosis and the accompanying problems concerning her ability to love. In the end the case is similar to that of gynaecological treatment. At any rate, the jealous father or husband is greatly mistaken in thinking that the patient can escape falling in love with the doctor if he elects for her to take a non-analytical course of treatment. Rather, the only difference will be that such an infatuation, destined to go unspoken and unanalysed, will never make the contribution to her recovery that analysis would have extracted from it.

It has come to my attention that there are a few doctors practising analysis who often prepare a female patient for the occurrence of love in transference, or even encourage them 'only to fall in love with the doctor in order to move the analysis forward'. I find it hard to think of a more absurd approach. The analyst thereby robs the phenomenon of its convincing spontaneous character and creates for himself many problems that will be hard to overcome.

At first sight, infatuation in transference seems unlikely to bring anything of benefit to the course of therapy. Even the most co-operative patient suddenly no longer understands the treatment and takes no further interest in it, and does not want to talk or hear about anything apart from her love, to which she demands a response. Having given up her symptoms or neglected them, she even declares herself healthy. The scene changes completely, as though a game has suddenly been replaced by the sudden eruption of reality, or the fire alarm sounded in the middle of a theatre performance. When you experience this for the first time as a doctor, it is hard to hold on to the analytical situation and escape the delusion that the treatment really is over.

After some reflection you get your bearings. First and foremost you remember the suspicion that everything that interferes with the progress of the treatment may be an expression of resistance. Resistance undoubtedly has a good deal to do with the outbreak of tempestuous demands for love. For some time you had noticed that the patient was showing signs of an affectionate transference, and you were surely justified in thinking that her feelings for the doctor were responsible for her cooperativeness, her receptiveness to his analytical explanations, and the high level of intelligence she displayed at the time. But now it is as though all of that has been swept away; the patient completely lacks insight; she seems to be lost in her infatuation. And this change happens, with some regularity, just at the point where you had to require her to admit or recall a particularly painful and heavily repressed part of her life. She had thus been in love for some time, but now the resistance begins to make use of her love to prevent the therapy from continuing, completely distracting her interest from the task in hand and causing the medical analyst some painful embarrassment.

On closer inspection it is possible to recognize the influence of complicating motives on the situation; some connected with being in love, but others particularly expressing the resistance. The first type includes the efforts of the patient to convince herself she is irresistible, to destroy the authority of the doctor by reducing him to a mere lover, and whatever else promises to result as a by-product of gratifying her love. You can surmise that the resistance occasionally uses professions of love as a means of putting the strait-laced analyst to the test; should he succumb, his advances would then be turned down. But above all you have the impression that the resistance, acting like an *agent provocateur*, intensifies the state of being in love and exaggerates her willingness to surrender sexually, just in order to vindicate all the more emphatically the effect of the repression by invoking the dangers of such loose behaviour.

It is well known that Alfred Adler saw all this by-play, often absent altogether from purer examples of the phenomenon, as the essence of the whole process.

How should the analyst behave in order to avert failure in this situation, if he is still convinced that the therapy ought to continue right through the effects of the love-transference and in spite of it?

It would be easy for me to lay heavy stress on conventional morality and insist that the analyst should never accept or respond to the affection held out to him. I could say that he should consider that the time has come to represent to the infatuated woman the demands of morality and the need for self-denial, to persuade her to renounce her desires and overcome the animal part of her nature so as to continue the work of analysis.

But I am not going to fulfil these expectations, neither the first nor the second part of them. Not the first, because I am not writing for our clientele, but for doctors who have serious problems to wrestle with, and because I can trace the moral prescription here back to its origins, that is to say, to expediency. On this occasion I am in the happy position of being able to substitute the requirements of analytical technique for a moral dictate, without altering the result.

I am going to reject even more decisively the second part of the expectation I mentioned. It would be pointless, and not the action of an analyst, to demand that the patient should repress, renounce and sublimate her instinct as soon as she confesses her love-transference. It would be like elaborately summoning up a spirit from the underworld only in order to send him away to the depths again without asking him any questions. This would amount to calling the repressed up to the conscious level and then repressing it again out of fright. And you need not delude yourself about the prospects of success from this procedure. Elevated rhetoric notoriously achieves little against passion. The patient will simply feel she has been spurned, and will not waste any time before seeking vengeance.

Neither am I prepared to recommend a middle course – though it would appeal to many people as being particularly clever – which consists of claiming to reciprocate the patient's affection but avoiding all physical expression of this affection, until you can steer the relationship into calmer waters and raise it to a higher level. My objection to this expedient is that psychoanalytical treatment is built on truthfulness. That is the basis of a fair amount of its educational effect and its ethical value. It is dangerous to abandon these fundamentals. If you have become well used to analytical techniques, you no longer encounter the lies and deceptions that doctors otherwise find indispensable, and when, with the best of intentions, you try to make use of them just for once, you tend to give yourself away. Since you demand that the patient should be strictly truthful, you risk forfeiting the whole of your authority if you yourself are caught out departing from the truth. Moreover, there are dangers in the attempt to let yourself drift into feelings of affection for the patient. Self-control is never so good that you might not find yourself going further than you intended. So I believe you should stay true to the disinterest you have acquired, by suppressing any counter-transference.

I have already indicated that analytical technique commands the doctor to deny the infatuated patient the satisfaction she desires. The course of therapy must be conducted on terms of abstinence. By this I do not just mean physical self-denial, nor do I mean blocking all desire, which might be more than any unwell person could bear. What I want to do is to establish the principle that you tolerate the existence of needs and longings on the patient's part as dynamic factors in treatment and change, and you should be careful not to appease these feelings by means of surrogates. And you could not offer anything but surrogates, since the patient's condition makes her incapable of genuine satisfaction, until her repressions have been removed.

We must admit that the principle of conducting therapy abstemiously takes us far beyond the present individual case, and needs more detailed discussion to map out the limits of its feasibility. But we do not propose to have this discussion here, preferring to keep as close as possible to the situation we began with. What would happen if the doctor acted differently and exploited what freedom there was on both sides to requite the patient's love and satisfy her need for affection?

If he did so as a result of calculating that such compliance would secure him control over the patient and so induce her to bring the business of the therapy to a resolution by achieving lasting freedom from her neurosis, then experience would show him to have miscalculated. The patient would achieve her aims, but the same would not apply to him. All you would have is a recapitulation of the amusing story about the pastor and the insurance agent. At the behest of his relatives, a priest is brought in to convert this seriously ill unbeliever before he dies. The conversation goes on for so long that the waiting relatives begin to be hopeful. Finally, the door of the sickroom opens. The atheist has not been converted, but the pastor goes away insured.

It would be a great triumph for the patient to have her offer of love requited, and a total defeat for the therapy. She would have achieved what all patients strive for in analysis: activating and acting out in actual life something that she ought simply to remember, reproduce as mental content and confine within the mental sphere.[3] In the course of the love affair she would display all the inhibitions and unhealthy reactions of her erotic life, with no chance of correcting them, and it would end in regret and a greatly reinforced tendency to repression. The love relationship simply closes off any chance of influencing her through therapy. Any thought of uniting the two is ridiculous.

Satisfying the patient's craving for love is therefore just as disastrous for the analysis as repressing it. The analyst's path is a different one, and there is no pattern for it in real life. You take care not to distract her from the love-transference, to frighten it away, or ruin it for the patient; but just as steadfastly you refrain from reciprocating. You hold on to the love-transference, but you treat it as something unreal, as a situation that has to be worked through in the therapy, taken back to its unconscious origins and made to help bring the most deeply buried aspects of her erotic life up into the patient's consciousness, and therefore under her control. The more you give the impression of being immune to all temptation, the more easily will you be able to extract the psychoanalytical content from the situation. The patient whose sexual repression has not yet been removed, but merely thrust into the background, will then feel confident enough to display all the conditions she attaches to love, all the fantasies of her sexual longing, all the characterstics of her infatuation, and, via all this, open up her own way back to the infantile basis of her love.

However, for one type of woman this attempt to preserve the love-transference for use in the analytical task, but without satisfying it, is doomed to failure. These are women of elemental passion, who will not put up with any surrogates, children of nature who will not accept the mental in place of the material, who in the words of the poet can only be reached 'by soup-logic with dumpling-reasoning'.[4] With this type you have a choice to make: either return her love or suffer the full hostility of a woman scorned. Neither case furthers the cause of the therapy. All you can do is retire defeated and perhaps contemplate the problem of how the capacity for neurosis can be combined with such an implacable need for love.

The question of how to make other women, less violently in love, evolve an understanding of analytical thinking is one that has no doubt similarly preoccupied many analysts. Above all you have to bring out the unmistakable part played by resistance in this 'love'. Really falling in love would make the patient cooperative and increase her willingness to solve the problems of her case, just because the man she loves demands it. Real love would make her want to get to the end of the cure, in order to prove herself worthy in the eyes of the doctor and prepare for a reality in which there was room for the inclination to love. Instead of this the patient, you would say, behaves obstinately and rebelliously, has thrown off all interest in the treatment, and clearly has no respect for the extremely well-founded convictions of the doctor. She thus produces a resistance in the guise of infatuation, and, furthermore, she has no scruples about placing him on the proverbial horns of a dilemma. For if he were to decline, as his duty and his understanding oblige him to do, she would be able to play the part of the woman scorned, and by way of revenge deny herself recovery at his hands, just as she is doing at this moment through her supposed infatuation.

The second argument against the authenticity of this love is the assertion that it bears not a single new trait arising out of the present situation, but is composed entirely of repetitions and pale imitations of earlier reactions, including infantile ones. You will undertake to demonstrate this to the patient through a detailed analysis of her stance in love.

Add to these arguments the requisite measure of patience, and you will usually succeed in overcoming this difficult situation and proceed to work – the infatuation having been either modified or 'knocked on the head' – towards exposing the infantile choice of love-objects and the fantasy that was woven around it. However, I would like to cast a critical light on the arguments in question, and ask whether we are telling the patient the truth when we use them, or in our serious difficulties taking refuge in concealment and misrepresentations. In other words: can the love that manifests itself in therapy really not be seen as genuine?

I believe we have told the patient the truth, but not the whole truth we would tell if we had no regard for the outcome. Of our two arguments, the first is the stronger. The role of resistance in love-transference is beyond dispute and very considerable. But the resistance did not create this love; it finds it ready-made, makes use of it and exaggerates its self-expression. And the resistance does not invalidate the authenticity of the phenomenon. Our second argument is much weaker; it is true that this infatuation consists of reissuing old components and repeating infantile reactions. But that is always the essence of falling in love. Everybody repeats childhood patterns. It is precisely what stems from its conditioning in childhood that lends infatuation its compulsive character, with its overtones of the pathological. Perhaps love in transference has slightly less freedom than the love that occurs ordinarily in life and is called normal; it shows more clearly its dependence on its infantile predecessor, and it proves to be less adaptable and flexible, but that is all – the differences are not essential.

What other ways are there to tell if love is genuine? By its productivity, its usefulness in achieving love's goals? In this respect love in transference does not seem inferior to any other; you have the impression you could achieve anything by its means.

To sum up: you have no right to deny the title of 'genuine' love to an infatuation that makes its appearance during analytical treatment. If it appears so far from normal, this is easily explained by the circumstance that falling in love even outside analytical therapy is more reminiscent of abnormal than normal mental phenomena. All the same, it has a few outstanding characteristics that assure it of a special place. It is 1. provoked by the situation; 2. it is highly intensified by the resistance that dominates this situation; and 3. it manages to pay little regard to reality. It is less astute, less concerned about the consequences, more blind in its estimate of the loved one, than we are willing to concede to a normal state of love. But we must not forget that it is precisely these departures from the norm that constitute the essence of falling in love.

It is the first of these three qualities of transference-love that decisively affects the doctor's course of action. He has coaxed this infatuation into life by initiating an analytical treatment to cure the neurosis; for him it is the inevitable result of a medical situation, similar to physically laying bare a sick person, or having some life-and-death secret confided to him. For him, the medical situation dictates that he must not gain any personal advantage from the infatuation. The willingness of the patient makes no difference to this; it simply throws all the responsibility back upon himself. As he must know, this was precisely the healing mechanism anticipated by the patient. After successfully surmounting all the difficulties, she will often confess what she imagined when she embarked on the course of therapy: if she behaved well, in the end she would be rewarded with the doctor's affection.

For the doctor, ethical motives now combine with technical ones to restrain him from offering the patient any loving relationship. He must keep his objective in mind; the woman must have her capacity for love, which is invaluable to her but has been impeded by childhood fixations, placed freely at her disposal. But instead of depleting it during therapy she should save it for the real-life demands it will make on her when her treatment is over. He must not repeat with her the scene at the dog-racing stadium where a string of sausages is held up as a prize, and some joker ruins the race by throwing a single sausage on to the track. The dogs all fall upon it and forget the race and the enticing string of sausages in the distance awaiting the winner. I do not want to claim that it is always easy for the doctor to stay within the bounds that ethics and technique prescribe for him. Particularly for a younger and still unattached man it may be a difficult assignment. Sexual love undoubtedly has a prime place among life's experiences, and the uniting of mental and physical satisfaction in the act of love is one of its high points. Everybody knows this, apart from a few weird fanatics, and arranges his life accordingly; only in scientific circles does anyone make a fuss about admitting it. On the other hand, it is difficult for the man to play the part of the one who rejects and refuses the woman when she makes advances to him, and a fine woman who confesses her passion radiates a magic beyond compare, for all her neurosis and resistances. It is not the crudely sensual desire of a patient that presents the temptation. On the contrary, that will tend to have an off-putting effect, and all your reserves of tolerance will be required for you to accept it as a natural phenomenon. The more refined stirrings of desire in the female, inhibited in its aims, are perhaps the ones that pose the danger of making you forget your clinical methodology and responsibility, for the sake of a wonderful experience.

And yet it is out of the question for the analyst to give way. However highly he prizes love, he must value more highly still his opportunity to lift the patient over a decisive stage in her life. She has to learn from him how to subdue the pleasure principle, to renounce immediate but socially unsuitable satisfaction in favour of the kind that is more distant, perhaps altogether less certain, but psychologically and socially irreproachable. To achieve this self-conquest she has to be taken through the primordial age of her mental development and by this means acquire that enhanced mental freedom that distinguishes conscious mental activity – in the systematic sense – from unconscious.

The analytical psychotherapist thus has to conduct a threefold struggle: the one in his own mind against the forces that would like to pull him down below the analytical level; the external one against the opponents who question the importance he ascribes to the sexual drives and refuse to let him make use of them in his scientific technique; and in analysis, the struggle against his patients, who initially behave like his opponents, but then make clear that an overestimation of sexual life has them in its grip, and would like to make the doctor captive to their socially ungovernable passions.

The lay people whose attitude to psychoanalysis I mentioned at the beginning will no doubt seize upon this discussion as a further opportunity to draw the world's attention to the dangers of this therapeutic method. Psychoanalysts know that they are working with the most explosive forces, and that they need to deploy the same care and conscientiousness as the chemist. But when has a chemist ever been banned on account of danger from dealing with the explosive materials whose reactive properties make them indispensable to him? It is strange that psychoanalysis is obliged to fight afresh for all the privileges long since granted to other medical procedures. I am not in favour of giving up harmless methods of treatment. They are adequate for treating many cases, and after all human society has no more need of the *furor sanandi* [mania for healing] than of any other kind of fanaticism. But to believe that these disorders ought to be conquerable by operating innocuous little mechanisms would be to underestimate very badly the origins and practical significance of the psycho-neuroses. No, in medical practice there will always be room for the *ferrum* and the *ignis* alongside the *medicina* [iron, fire, medicine], and so the professional, unabated practice of psychoanalysis, not afraid to handle the most dangerous mental impulses and harness them for the patient's benefit, will continue to be indispensable.

(1915)

*Notes*

1. 'Zur Geschichte der psychoanalytischen Bewegung' ['On the History of the Psychoanalytical Movement'] (1914), *Gesammelte Werke*, Vol. X.
2. It is well known that transference can be expressed in other, less tender ways, but this aspect will not be dealt with in this essay.
3. See the essay 'Erinnern, Wiederholen und Durcharbeiten' ['Remembering, Repeating and Working Through'], *Gesammelte Werke*, Vol. X, pp. 126–36.
4. [This is a quotation from Heinrich Heine's poem 'Die Wanderratten' (The Wandering Rats): townspeople plagued by an influx of rats attempt to repel them with weapons and with reasoning. Both fail, the latter because:

> *Im hungrigen Magen Eingang finden*
> *Nur Suppenlogik mit Knödelgründen,*
> *Nur Argumente von Rinderbraten,*
> *Begleitet mit Göttinger Wurstzitaten*

(A hungry stomach is open to access only by soup logic with dumpling reasons, only roast-beef arguments, accompanied by quotes from Göttingen sausages.)]

# On the Psychology of the Grammar-school Boy

It is a strange feeling, having reached such an advanced age, to be asked once again to write a 'German essay' for grammar school. But one obeys automatically, like the old soldier who must, at the command 'attention!', align his hands with the seams of his trousers and let his pack fall to the ground. It is curious how readily one agreed, as though nothing in particular had changed over the last half-century. But one has grown old since then, one is about to turn sixty, and both bodily sensations and the mirror unambiguously demonstrate how much of life's candle has already burned down.

Even as little as ten years ago there were still moments when one suddenly felt quite young again. Walking through the streets of one's home town, already wearing a grey beard and weighed down with all the burdens of bourgeois existence, one would unexpectedly meet some well-preserved elderly gentleman whom one would greet almost with humility, recognizing him as one of one's old grammar-school teachers. But then one would stop and look dreamily after him, wondering: is that really him, or just someone who looks deceptively like him? How youthful he looks, and you yourself have grown so old! How old would he be now? Could it be that those men who once represented the adult world to us, were so little older than we were ourselves?

It was then as though the present had darkened, and the years of one's life between the ages of ten and eighteen rose up from the recesses of memory with their presentiments and vagaries, their painful transformations and inspiring consequences, the first glimpses of a vanished world of civilization which would, to me at least, be a peerless consolation in the face of life's struggles, one's initial encounter with the sciences, from which one believed one could choose which to devote one's – undoubtedly indispensable – services. And I thought I remembered that the whole period was pervaded by the sense of a task that suggested itself only very quietly at first, until I was able to express it, in my graduation essay, by stating firmly that during my life I wanted to make a contribution to the sum of our human knowledge.

I then became a doctor, or rather more of a psychologist, and I was able to establish a new psychological discipline by the name of 'psychoanalysis', which currently holds the attention of doctors and researchers in foreign countries both near and far – but less so, of course, those in our own homeland.

As a psychoanalyst I must take a greater interest in affective than in intellectual processes, more in the unconscious than in the conscious life of the psyche. The emotion that seized me upon encountering my former grammar-school teacher leads me to make one first admission: I do not know which it was that made the greater claim upon us and held more significance, the study of the sciences being presented to us, or the study of the personalities of our teachers. At any rate there was an unceasing undercurrent of the latter, and in many cases the path towards the sciences led only via the figures of the teachers; some remained stuck on this path, and for some it was – why not admit it? – endlessly deferred.

We wooed them or turned away from them, we imagined sympathies or antipathies in them that probably did not exist, studied their characters and formed or distorted our own on the basis of theirs. They provoked our greatest levels of rebelliousness and forced us into complete submission; we sought out their foibles, and were proud of their preferences, their knowledge and their justice. Basically we loved them very much if they gave us any reason to; I do not know whether all our teachers noticed that. But it cannot be denied that we faced them in a very special way, a way that might in some respects have been uncomfortable for them. From the outset we were equally disposed to love and to hatred, to criticism and to worship of them. Psychoanalysis calls such willingness to engage in contradictory behaviour 'ambivalent'; and it does not shy from revealing the source of such an emotional ambivalence.

It has, in fact, taught us that the affective attitudes towards other people, so hugely important for the individual's later behaviour, are completed at an unthinkably early age. Even during the first six years of childhood the little human being has established the manner and affective tone of his relationships with people of the same and the opposite sex. From that point onwards he is able to develop them and transform them in particular directions, but not erase them. The people upon whom he fixates in this way are his parents and siblings. All the people he meets later on become substitutes for those first emotional objects (his carers as well as his parents) and arrange themselves in series with their sources in the 'imagoes', as we call them, of the father, the mother, the siblings and so on. These later acquaintances must thus bear a kind of emotional inheritance, they encounter sympathies and antipathies to the acquisition of which they themselves have contributed very little; all later choices in terms of friendship and love take place on the basis of memory traces that those first models have left behind.

Among the imagoes of a childhood not usually stored in the memory, however, none is more significant for the youth and the man than that of his father. Organic necessity has introduced into this relationship an emotional ambivalence, the most moving expression of which we can grasp in the Greek myth of King Oedipus. The little boy must love and admire his father, he seems to him to be the strongest, the kindest and wisest of all creatures; God himself is only an intensification of this image of the father as the infant psyche depicts it. But soon the other side of this emotional relationship emerges. The father is also recognized as a powerful trouble-maker where the child's own drives are concerned, he becomes the model that one seeks not only to imitate but also to remove in order to assume his place oneself. The affectionate and the hostile impulse towards the father now continue to exist side by side, often throughout the person's whole life, the one unable to abolish the other. In such a juxtaposition of opposites lies the characteristic of that which we call 'emotional ambivalence'.

In the second half of childhood a change in this relationship towards the father is prepared for, the importance of which cannot be overstated. The boy begins to look out of his nursery into the real world, and now he must make the discoveries that undermine the high esteem in which he originally held his father, and encourage him to break away from that first ideal. He finds that his father is no longer the most powerful, the wisest, the wealthiest; he becomes dissatisfied with him, learns to criticize him and classify him in social terms, and then usually makes him pay heavily for the disappointment that he has given him. Everything hopeful, but also everything repellent that distinguishes the new generation, is shaped by this break with the father.

With this phase of the development of the young person coincides his encounter with teachers. We now understand our relationship to our grammar-school teachers. These men, who were not even all fathers themselves, became father-substitutes for us. It was for that reason that they seemed so mature to us, so unreachably adult, even if they were still very young. We transferred to them the respect and expectations of the omniscient father of our childhood years, and then we began to treat them like our fathers at home. We brought to them the ambivalence that we had acquired in the family, and with the help of that attitude we fought with them as we were used to fighting with our physical fathers. Without reference to the nursery and the family home we would not be able to understand our attitude towards our teachers, or to excuse it.

As grammar-school boys we had other, hardly less important experiences with the descendants of our siblings, our schoolmates, but those will need to be written down elsewhere. The school anniversary celebrations keep our thoughts firmly with our teachers.

(1914)

# On the Introduction of Narcissism[1]

## I

'Narcissism' originated as a term of clinical description, having been chosen by Paul Näcke in 1899 to define that form of behaviour whereby an individual treats his own body in the same way in which he might treat that of any other sexual object, by looking at it, stroking it and caressing it with sexual pleasure[2] until by these acts he achieves full gratification. In this formulation the term 'narcissism' means a perversion that has swallowed up the entire sexual life of the individual, and consequently entails the same expectations that we would bring to the study of any other perversion.

Psychoanalysts were then struck in the course of their observations by the fact that individual elements of narcissistic behaviour are encountered in many people suffering from other disorders, for instance – according to Sadger – in homosexuals, and finally the supposition inescapably presented itself that a form of libido lodgement[3] definable as narcissism may occur on a far larger scale, and may well be able to lay claim to a role in the normal sexual development of human beings.[4] The difficulties encountered in the psychoanalytical treatment of neurotics led to the same supposition, for it looked as if just such a narcissistic pattern of behaviour on their part was one of the factors limiting their amenability to influence. One might say that narcissism in this sense is not a perversion, but the libidinal correlative of the egoism of the self-preservation instinct, an element of which is rightly attributed to every living creature.

358

Compelling grounds for entertaining the notion of a primary and normal form of narcissism arose when the attempt was made to apply the libido theory to our understanding of dementia praecox (Kraepelin) or schizophrenia (Bleuler). Those suffering from this condition, for whom I have proposed the term paraphrenics, display two fundamental characteristics: megalomania, and withdrawal of interest from the external world (people and things). The latter development makes them unamenable to psychoanalysis, it makes them incurable no matter how hard we try. The paraphrenic's withdrawal from the external world, however, needs to be more precisely characterized. The hysteric and the obsessional neurotic likewise abandon their relationship to reality, assuming their illness develops to that point. But analysis shows that they by no means forsake their erotic relationship to people and things. They hold fast to it in their imagination, on the one hand replacing or mingling real objects with imaginary ones drawn from their memory, whilst on the other not initiating in respect of those objects any of the motor activities needed for the attainment of their goals. For this condition of the libido alone, and for no other, should one use the term indiscriminately applied by Jung, namely *introversion* of the libido. With the paraphrenic, however, the position is quite different. He really does seem to have withdrawn his libido from the people and things of the external world without replacing them with any others in his imagination. In cases where he *does* so replace them, this appears to be a secondary process, and to form part of an attempt at recovery that seeks to lead the libido back to the object world.[5]

The question then arises as to the subsequent fate of the libido in schizophrenia once it has been withdrawn from objects. The megalomania characteristic of this condition points the way. We can assume that it arose at the expense of object-libido. The libido, having been withdrawn from the external world, is channelled into the ego, giving rise to a form of behaviour that we can call narcissism. However, the megalomania itself is not a new entity, but, as we know, only a magnified and more distinct form of a pre-existing state. This is turn leads us to think that the form of narcissism that arises as a result of the incorporation of object-cathexes[6] is a second-ary one that develops on top of a primary one rendered obscure by a variety of different influences.

Let me stress once again that I am not seeking here either to resolve or further to complicate the schizophrenia problem, but am merely bringing together what has already been said in other contexts, in order to justify introducing the concept of narcissism.

A third factor contributing to this, in my view legitimate, exten-sion of the libido theory arises from our observations and inter-pretations of the inner life of children and primitive peoples. In the latter we find traits which, if they were to occur individually, could be classed as megalomania: an overestimation of the power of their wishes and psychic acts – the 'omnipotence of thoughts'; a belief in the magical power[7] of words; a technique for dealing with the external world, namely 'magic', which appears as the logi-cal application of these megalomaniac premisses.[8] We expect to encounter an entirely analogous attitude to the external world in the child of our own day and age, whose development is far less clear to us.[9] We thus find the notion taking shape in our mind that it was the *ego* that originally underwent libido-cathexis;[10] some of this libido is later transferred to objects, but essentially it stays put, and relates to the object-cathexes rather as the body of an amoeba relates to the pseudopodia that it sends forth. This aspect of libido lodgement inevitably remained hidden from us to begin with, given the symptom-based nature of our researches. The only things apparent to us were the emanations of this libido, namely object-cathexes, which can be sent forth and then retracted again. We can also discern what in broad terms we can call an antagonism between the ego-libido and the object-libido – the more replete the one becomes, the more the other is depleted. The highest phase of development achievable by the latter appears to us to be the state of being in love, which presents itself to us as an abandonment by the individual of his own personality in favour of an object-cathexis, and which has its antithesis in the paranoiac's fantasy (or self-perception) regarding the 'end of the world'.[11] What we ultimately conclude regarding the differentiation of psychic energies is that initially, in the state of narcissism, they remain clustered together, and hence undifferentiable in terms of our crude analysis, and that only the supervention of object-cathexis makes it possible to differentiate sexual energy, the libido, from the energy of the ego drives.

Before I go any further, I must touch on two questions that take us to the heart of the difficulties entailed by this topic. First, how does narcissism as we are here proposing it relate to auto-eroticism, which we have elsewhere described as an early form of libido? Second, if we attribute a primary libido-cathexis to the ego, why is there any need to differentiate sexual libido from non-sexual energy in the ego drives? Wouldn't the supposition of a single, unified psychic energy spare us all the difficulties associated with trying to distinguish between ego-drive energy and ego-libido, between ego-libido and object-libido?

As to the first question, I say this: it is a necessary hypothesis that there is no entity present in the individual from the very beginning that is equatable with the ego; the ego has to be developed. Auto-erotic drives, however, are primal; therefore something else must supervene in addition to auto-eroticism, a new psychic process, in order to produce narcissism.

Any psychoanalyst called upon to give a definitive answer to the second question is bound to feel distinctly uncomfortable. One balks at the idea of abandoning empirical observation for the sake of sterile theoretical disputes, but none the less we cannot shirk the obligation to try to resolve the issue. Notions such as that of an ego-libido or an ego-drive energy etc. are undoubtedly neither particularly easy to grasp nor sufficiently weighty in content; a speculative theory of the relevant relationships would want above all to establish a sharply defined concept as a basis for everything else. But in my view that is precisely the difference between a speculative theory and a science founded on the interpretation of empirical facts. The latter will not envy speculation its privilege of resting upon neat and tidy foundations of unassailable logic, but will gladly make do with nebulously evanescent, scarcely conceivable basic ideas, hoping to grasp them more clearly as they develop, and willing if need be to exchange them for others. For these ideas are not the foundation upon which the entire science rests; instead, it rests solely upon observation. They are not the substructure but the superstructure of the whole edifice, and can be replaced or discarded without harm. We are currently seeing the same sort of thing happen in physics, moreover, whose fundamental ideas about matter, centres of force, attraction and such like are scarcely less precarious than their counterparts in psychoanalysis.

The value of the concepts 'ego-libido' and 'object-libido' resides in the fact that they derive from thorough study of the intimate characteristics of neurotic and psychotic processes. The separation of the libido into one that pertains to the ego, and one that becomes attached to objects, is a necessary corollary of a primary hypothesis that differentiated between sexual drives and ego drives. This, at any rate, was the conclusion that I was driven to by analysis of both of the pure forms of transference neurosis (hysteria and obsessional neurosis), and I know only that all attempts to account for these phenomena by other means have utterly failed.

Given the complete lack of any guiding theory of drives, it is legitimate, not to say imperative, first to take a hypothesis of some kind and test it thoroughly and rigorously until it either fails, or proves valid. Now, quite a number of things tend to support the hypothesis of a primal separation of sexual drives and other kinds of drives, i.e. ego drives, not least its efficacy in the analysis of transference neuroses. I admit that this factor on its own would not be unambiguous, for it might well be a question here of indifferent psychic energy that turns into libido only through the process of object-cathexis. For one thing, however, this conceptual distinction corresponds to the distinction so commonly encountered in ordinary life between hunger and love. For another thing, *biological* considerations lend support to the hypothesis. The individual really does lead a double existence both as an end in himself, and as a link in a chain that he serves against his will, or at any rate regardless of his will. He even supposes sexuality to be one of his own designs – whereas on an alternative view he appears as a mere appendage of his germ-plasm,[12] to whose purposes he devotes all

his energies in return for the reward of a mere sensation of pleasure. On this view, he is but the mortal vehicle of a – perhaps –
immortal essence; like the lord of an entailed estate, he is but the
temporary occupant of an institution that will outlast him. The
separation of the sexual drives from the ego drives would simply
mirror this dual function of the individual. Thirdly, one has to bear
in mind that all our tentative psychological theories will need to
be grounded at some point in organic systems. It will then very
likely transpire that it is particular substances and chemical
processes that are responsible for the workings of sexuality, and
which make it possible for the life of the individual to carry over
into the life of the species. We take full account of this likelihood
by substituting particular psychological forces for particular chemical substances.

Precisely because I am normally at pains to keep psychology
separate from all that is alien to it, including the mode of thinking characteristic of biology, I wish to concede quite explicitly at
this point that the hypothesis of separate ego drives and sexual
drives, i.e. the libido theory, is essentially biologically based, and
is grounded scarcely at all in psychology. I shall therefore also be
consistent enough to drop this hypothesis if a better and more ser-
viceable theory of drives were to emerge from psychoanalytical
work itself – though this has not so far proved to be the case. It
might then turn out that – at the deepest possible level and at the
remotest possible distance – sexual energy, the libido, originated
as a part of the energy inherently active in the psyche that then
separated-off through differentiation. But such a proposition is of
little relevance. It concerns things that are so far removed from
the problems raised by our clinical observations, and so limited in
their contribution to our knowledge, that it is no more worth contest-
ing than it is worth applying in practice. Any such primal oneness
is perhaps just as irrelevant to our analytical interests as the primal
kinship of all the races of man is to the Probate Officer seeking
proof of kinship between an heir and a testator. All these speculations get us nowhere. And as we cannot wait until the definitive
theory of drives is handed to us on a plate by some other science,

it is far more expedient to try to see what light can be thrown on these fundamental biological puzzles by a synthesis of *psychological* phenomena. By all means let us acquaint ourselves with the possibility of error, but let us not be deterred from rigorously following-up the first hypothesis we mentioned,[13] viz. that of an antagonism between ego drives and sexual drives thrust upon us by our analysis of the transference neuroses, and thereby discovering whether it can be developed in a fruitful and consistent way, and whether it can be applied to other disorders as well, e.g. schizophrenia.

Things would be different, of course, if it were proven that the libido theory had already come to grief in failing to explain this latter disorder. C. G. Jung has made precisely this claim (1912) and has thereby forced me to set out the considerations above, which I would much rather have been spared. I should have preferred to follow through to its conclusion the path already taken in my analysis of the Schreber case, without going into its underlying assumptions. Jung's claim, however, is premature at the very least. His reasoning is scant. He bases his argument in the first place on my own supposed admission that in the face of the difficulties of the Schreber analysis I felt driven to modify the libido concept, that is to say, to abandon the notion of its having a sexual content and to regard the libido as being part and parcel of psychic interest[14] in general. As to rectifying this misconception, Ferenczi (1913) has already said all that needs to be said in his thorough critique of Jung's book.[15] I can only agree with Ferenczi, and repeat that I have never voiced any such renunciation of the libido theory. A further argument of Jung's, asserting that there was no reason to think that the loss of the normal reality-function[16] could be caused solely by withdrawal of the libido, is not an argument at all, but an assertion of dogma; it 'begs the question'[17] and pre-empts debate, whereas the question whether and how such a thing might be possible really does need to be explored. In his next major work (1913), Jung touches briefly on the solution that I pointed to quite some time ago: 'Now in all this we admittedly also need to take account of the fact – something incidentally that Freud refers to in his account of the Schreber case – that introversion of the *Libido sexualis* leads to a cathexis of the "ego", which is conceivably what causes this reality-loss effect to appear. The possibility that the psychology of reality-loss might be explained in this way is indeed an enticing one.' Unfortunately, however, Jung does not explore this possibility very far. Only a few lines later he dismisses it with the comment that on such a basis 'the psychology of an ascetic anchorite would emerge successfully, but not a dementia praecox'. To show how little this inapt analogy can contribute to a resolution of the issue, we need only remark that such an anchorite in his 'eagerness to eradicate every trace of sexual interest' (though only in the popular sense of the word 'sexual') does not even need to exhibit any pathogenic libido lodgement. Though he may have completely averted his sexual interest from human beings, he can easily have sublimated it into a heightened interest in the divine or natural or animal realm without falling victim to an introversion of his libido on to his fantasies, or a reversion of his libido to his ego. This analogy appears to disregard from the very outset any possibility of differentiating between interest arising from erotic sources, and that arising from others. If we also bear in mind that the researches of the Swiss school, however commendable, have elucidated only two features of dementia praecox – the existence of complexes familiar to the healthy as well as to neurotics, and the similarity between patients' fantasies and folk myths – whilst for the rest proving unable to throw any light on the actual mechanism of the disorder, then we can readily reject Jung's claim that the libido theory has been proved a 'failure' by its inability to solve the problem of dementia praecox, and is therefore finished in respect of other neuroses too.

### Notes

1. [The title given in the *Standard Edition* is *On Narcissism: an Introduction* – but this is a startling mistranslation of Freud's wording (*Zur Einführung des Narzissmus*). Far from introducing us to an apparently well-recognized

phenomenon, as the *Standard Edition* mis-title implies, Freud is signalling the introduction of a whole new theory of narcissism (cf. the fifth paragraph of the essay!).]

2. [It is at once striking and instructive that the phrase 'with sexual pleasure' (*mit sexuellem Wohlgefallen*) is simply omitted from the *Standard Edition*.]

3. [Freud's term *Unterbringung der Libido* (in other contexts *Libidounterbringung*) is a metaphor that cannot be adequately replicated in English. The relevant verb (*unterbringen*) means 'house', 'accommodate', 'find an appropriate niche for'. The *Standard Edition* has 'allocation', but this suggests something quite different from Freud's original.]

4. Otto Rank (1911) ['Ein Beitrag zum Narzissismus' ('A Contribution on Narcissism')].

5. Regarding these propositions, cf. the discussion of the 'end of the world' in the analysis of Senate President Schreber (1911); cf. also Abraham (1908) [Freud deals with the Schreber case in 'Psychoanalytic Remarks on an Autobiographically Described Case of Paranoia (Dementia Paranoides)'; an English version of Abraham's treatise may be found in K. Abraham, *Selected Papers* (London 1927; New York 1953), Ch. 11].

6. ['Cathexis' is an ugly and opaque term – coined by James Strachey – that has nothing of the apparent simplicity of Freud's metaphor *Besetzung*. Unfortunately, however, Freud's word has no direct or uncontentious equivalent in English, and Strachey's well-established Hellenism is therefore reluctantly retained throughout this present volume (together with the associated verb 'cathect').]

7. [The obfuscatory tendencies of the *Standard Edition* are epitomized by the fact that it renders Freud's *Zauberkraft* – a word that any child would instantly understand – as 'thaumaturgic force'!]

8. See the relevant sections of my book *Totem und Tabu* [*Totem and Taboo*] (1912–13). [See Chapter III.]

9. See Ferenczi (1913) [Sándor Ferenczi, 'Entwicklungsstufen des Wirklichkeitssinnes' ('Stages in the Development of the Sense of Reality', *First Contributions to Psycho-Analysis*, London, 1952, Ch. VIII)].

10. [See also *Beyond the Pleasure Principle*, above, p. 181. This idea will be revised later on, once Freud has evolved the notion of the 'id'. The *Standard Edition* carries a lengthy Appendix by the editors on the 'considerable difficulty' attaching to this particular metaphor of Freud's.]

11. There are two mechanisms involved in this 'end of the world' scenario: when the entire libido-cathexis streams out on to the love-object, and when it all floods back into the ego.

**12**. [Cf. *OED*: 'The germ-plasm is the essential part of the germ-cell, and determines the nature of the individual that arises from it' (sample quotation dated 1890).]

**13**. [The first two German editions of the essay printed *ersterwählte* – the first hypothesis *chosen* – whereas subsequent editions printed *ersterwähnte* – the first hypothesis *mentioned*. The *Standard Edition* opts for the original version – but there seems little logic in this, given that Freud did indeed 'mention' this hypothesis just a few paragraphs earlier.]

**14**. [This curious term is Freud's own (*psychisches Interesse*).]

**15**. [Freud is referring to Ferenczi's review of Jung's *Wandlungen und Symbole der Libido* (published in English under the title *Psychology of the Unconscious*).]

**16**. [Freud's term is *Realfunktion*, derived from Pierre Janet's *la fonction du réel*.]

**17**. [Freud gives this phrase in English.]

## II

Any *direct* study of narcissism seems to me to be prevented by a number of special difficulties. The principal means of approaching the matter is likely to remain the analysis of paraphrenias. Just as the transference neuroses have enabled us to trace the libidinal drive-impulses, so, too, dementia praecox and paranoia will afford us insight into the psychology of the ego. Once again, our understanding of the normal in all its seeming simplicity has to be derived from the pathological with all its warped and coarsened features. All the same, a few other paths to a better understanding of narcissism do remain open to us: the study of organic illness, of hypochondria, and of the love-life of the sexes; and I shall now discuss each of these in turn.

In considering the influence of organic illness on the distribution of the libido, I am following a suggestion made to me in conversation by Sándor Ferenczi. It is universally known, indeed it seems self-evident to us, that anyone tormented by organic pain and dire discomfort abandons all interest in the things of the external world, except in so far as they bear on his suffering. Closer observation shows us that he also withdraws all libidinal interest from his love-objects; that so long as he suffers, he ceases loving. The banality of this fact need not prevent us from translating it into the language of the libido theory. We would then say: the patient retracts his libido-cathexes into his ego, and redeploys them once he is well. 'The sole abode of his soul forsooth', says Wilhelm Busch of a toothache-stricken poet, 'is the small black hole in his molar tooth.' Libido and ego-interest share the same fate in this regard, and are once again indistinguishable from each other. The notorious egoism of the ill covers both. We find this egoism so self-evident because we know for certain that in similar circumstances we would behave in exactly the same way. In its own way, comedy, too, exploits this phenomenon whereby physical ailments sweep away even the most passionate inclinations, and replace them with utter indifference.

Like illness, the sleep state, too, involves a narcissistic process whereby the libido is withdrawn from its various positions[1] and focused on the self or, to be more precise, on the sole desire for sleep. The egoism of dreams probably fits in very well in this context. If nothing else, we see examples in both cases of alterations in libido distribution as a result of ego-alteration.[2]

Hypochondria, like organic illness, expresses itself in painful and distressing physical sensations, and matches it, too, in the effect it has on libido distribution. The hypochondriac withdraws both his interest and – particularly markedly – his libido from the objects of the external world, and concentrates both of them on the organ that concerns him. But a disparity between hypochondria and organic illness forces itself on our attention here: in the latter case the painful sensations are grounded in demonstrable physical changes, whereas in the former they seem not to be. However, it would be fully in accord with our conception of neurotic processes as a whole if we were to venture the view that the message given out by hypochondria must indeed be quite right, and that it, too, must surely involve organic changes. But what would these changes consist in?

We are going to let ourselves be guided here by our knowledge that physical sensations of an unpleasant kind, comparable to those encountered in hypochondria, are also present in the other neuroses. I have already on an earlier occasion mentioned my inclination to regard hypochondria as the third 'actual' neurosis[3] alongside neurasthenia and anxiety neurosis.[4] It is probably not going too far to suppose that an element of hypochondria may also routinely be present in the other neuroses; the finest example of this is probably to be seen in anxiety neurosis and its overlying hysteria. It is of course the genital organ in its various states of excitation that constitutes the most familiar exemplar of an organ at once painfully sensitive and physically changed in some way, yet not in any ordinary sense of the word morbid. In such circumstances it becomes engorged with blood, swollen, moist, and the locus of manifold sensations. Let us use the term *erogeneity* to describe the process whereby a part of the body transmits sexual stimuli to the psyche; let us also bring to mind that our reflections on the theory of sexuality have long since accustomed us to the view that certain other parts of the body – the *erogenous* zones – might be able to substitute for the genitals and behave in a similar way to them: there is then just one further step that we must dare to take at this point. We can venture to regard erogeneity as a general property of *all* the organs, and we can then speak of it as increasing or diminishing in intensity in any particular part of the body. Any such variation in the erogeneity of the organs might be paralleled by a change in libido-cathexis within the ego. It is in such factors perhaps that we need to search for whatever it is that we might consider the basis of hypochondria, and that is capable of having the same effect on libido distribution as when the organs are affected by physical illness.

We note that if we continue thinking along these lines we shall come face to face with the problem not only of hypochondria, but also of the other 'actual' neuroses, neurasthenia and anxiety neurosis. Let us therefore call a halt at this juncture: the purposes of a purely psychological study are not served by straying so far into the realm of physiological research. We might simply mention that on the available evidence it seems reasonable to suppose that hypochondria stands in a similar relationship to paraphrenia as the other 'actual' neuroses do to hysteria and obsessional neurosis, that is to say that it depends on ego-libido just as the others depend on object-libido; on this supposition, hypochondriac fear is the counterpart on the ego-libido side to neurotic fear. Furthermore, given that in the case of the transference neuroses we are already familiar with the idea that the mechanism of the onset of illness and of symptom-formation – the progression from introversion to regression – can be linked to a heavy build-up of object-libido,[5] then we may also feel more inclined to embrace the idea of a heavy build-up of ego-libido, and relate it to the phenomena of hypochondria and paraphrenia.

Naturally enough, our thirst for knowledge prompts us at this point to ask why such a build-up of libido in the ego has to be experienced as unpleasurable. I should like to make do here with the reply that unpleasure is routinely the form in which increased tension expresses itself, and that therefore what happens here, as elsewhere, is that a certain quantity of the physical process transmutes into the psychic quality of unpleasure; though it may then well be the case that what determines the degree of unpleasure is not the absolute magnitude of that physical process, but rather some particular function of it. From this vantage point one may even dare to approach the question as to *where* the compulsion comes from in the first place that makes the psyche transcend the boundaries of narcissism and invest the libido in objects. Again, the logical answer in terms of our overall train of thought would be that the compulsion arises when the libidinal cathexis of the ego has exceeded a certain level. A strong ego affords some protection against falling ill; but in the end we must necessarily start loving if we are not to fall ill, and we must necessarily fall ill if refusal[6] makes us incapable of loving – rather along the lines of the model offered by Heinrich Heine when he envisions the psychogenesis of Creation:

Krankheit ist wohl der letzte Grund
Des ganzen Schöpferdrangs gewesen;
Erschaffend konnte ich genesen,
Erschaffend wurde ich gesund.

(Sickness no doubt was the ultimate cause of my urge to become the Creator; by dint of creation I was able to recover, by dint of creation I regained my health.[7])

We have identified our psychic apparatus as being above all an instrument charged with asserting control over excitations that would otherwise prove distressingly uncomfortable or pathogenic. This psychic processing activity achieves extraordinary things with regard to the inner discharge of excitations that are incapable of direct external release,[8] or for which such release would be undesirable at that particular moment. With inner processing of this kind, however, it is initially irrelevant whether it operates with real objects or imaginary ones. The difference only becomes apparent later on, if there is a heavy build-up of libido as a result of the latter turning to non-real objects (introversion). In the case of the paraphrenias, megalomania permits a similar inner processing of the libido once it has retreated into the ego; it is perhaps only when the megalomania has failed that the build-up of libido within the ego becomes pathogenic and triggers the healing process that strikes us so forcibly as illness.

Trying as I am at this point to penetrate just a little way into the mechanism of paraphrenia, I shall rehearse those concepts that seem to me at the present time to be worthy of attention. In my view, what makes these disorders different from the transference neuroses is the fact that when libido is freed up as a result of refusal, it does not resort with objects in the imagination, but withdraws to the ego; that being so, megalomania corresponds to the process in the transference neuroses whereby the psyche asserts control over this quantum of libido, i.e. introverts it on to products of the imagination; any failure of this psychic control-process gives rise to the hypochondria characteristic of paraphrenia, which is homologous to the fear characteristic of transference neuroses. We know that this latter fear can be dislodged by other forms of psychic processing too, namely conversion,[9] reaction-formation, and the formation of protection mechanisms (phobias). In the case of the paraphrenias, this role is played by the phase of attempted restitution, to which we owe the conspicuous symptoms of morbidity. Given that paraphrenia in many – if not most – cases involves only a partial dislodgement of the libido from objects, the clinical picture may be divided into three distinct groups of symptoms: 1) those reflecting what the subject retains of his normal state or neurosis (residual symptoms); 2) those reflecting the illness process itself (dislodgement of the libido from objects, and also megalomania, hypochondria, affective disorder, regression in all its various forms); 3) those reflecting the restitution process which, after the manner of hysteria (in the case of dementia praecox and paraphrenia proper) or obsessional neurosis (in the case of paranoia), re-attaches the libido to objects. This new libido-cathexis takes place on a different level and under different conditions from the primary one. The difference between the transference neuroses created by this secondary cathexis, and their counterparts as formed by the normal ego, would surely afford us the deepest possible insight into the structure of our psychic apparatus.

A third point of access to the study of narcissism is provided by the love-life of human beings, given the different forms that it takes in men and women. Just as the object-libido initially hid the ego-libido from our inquiring eye, so too in the case of object-choice on the part of the child (and developing individual) we initially focused our attention on the fact that they derive their sexual objects from their gratification experiences. A child's first experiences of autoerotic sexual gratification occur in the context of vital functions conducing to self-preservation. Sexual drives initially develop by imitating the ego drives and their gratification, and only subsequently make themselves independent of them – though the imitative process remains evident in the fact that it is the people concerned with the child's feeding, care and protection who become its first sexual objects, hence primarily the mother or mother-surrogate. But alongside this type and its associated source of object-choice, which we can term the *imitative* type,[10] a second and quite unexpected one has been revealed to us by our psychoanalytical researches. We have found – and this has been particularly clear in the case of people whose libidinal development has been disturbed in some way, such as perverts and homosexuals – that they model their subsequent love-object not on their mother, but on their own person. They quite clearly seek *themselves* as love-object, thereby exhibiting what we can call the *narcissistic* type of object-choice. It is this observation above all that has driven us to our narcissism hypothesis.

Now we have not concluded from all this that human beings fall into two sharply differentiated groups, one predisposed to the imitative type of object-choice and the other to the narcissistic, but instead prefer the hypothesis that both paths are open to each and every individual, and that either is equally capable of being preferred. We are arguing that every human being originally has two sexual objects: himself, and the woman who cares for him; and concomitantly we postulate a primary narcissism in all human beings, which in certain circumstances can prove dominant in their object-choice.

A comparison of males and females then shows that there are fundamental – though not of course universal – differences between them in their relationship to the two types of object-choice. Full object-love as per the imitative type really does seem to be characteristic of males. It displays conspicuous sexual over-valuation, which probably derives from the original narcissism present in childhood, and accordingly represents its transference on to the sexual object. This sexual over-valuation gives rise to the curious condition of being in love, reminiscent of neurotic obsession, and amounting as such to a transfer of libido that depletes the ego for the benefit of the object. Things develop in a quite different way in the commonest, probably purest and most authentic type of female. Here, the onset of puberty manifest in the development of the previously latent female sexual organs appears to be accompanied by an intensification of her original narcissism unfavourable to the forming of any proper object-love with its due complement of sexual over-valuation. Particularly where she develops the attributes of beauty, a woman comes to feel sufficient unto herself, which compensates her for the greatly reduced freedom of object-choice imposed on her by society. Strictly speaking, such women love only themselves, and with the same intensity as men display in loving them. Their need, furthermore, is not to love, but to *be* loved, and they deign to tolerate any man who fulfils this condition. The importance of this type of woman for the love-life of human beings is very great. Such women hold the greatest possible fascination for men, not only for aesthetic reasons, since they are usually the most beautiful, but also because of an interesting combination of psychological factors. For it seems clearly apparent that narcissism in an individual becomes magnetically attractive to those who have altogether relinquished their own narcissism,[11] and who are casting around for object-love. The fascination of the child rests to a great extent on its narcissism, on the fact that it is sufficient to itself and impervious to others; so too does the fascination of certain animals that appear to show no interest in us, such as cats and the great beasts of prey; indeed, even dire criminals and comic heroes captivate us within the context of the arts by dint of the narcissistic rigour with which they keep at bay anything tending to diminish their ego. It is as though we envied them their retention of a blissful psychic state, of an unassailable libido position, that we ourselves have since relinquished. However, the powerful fascination of the narcissistic woman is not without its darker side; the lovelorn male's frustration, his doubts about the woman's love, his lamentations on her enigmatic nature, are largely rooted in this incongruence of the two types of object-choice involved.

It is perhaps not entirely superfluous for me to emphasize that in describing women's love-life in these terms I am not remotely animated by any bias inclining me to disparage women. Quite apart from the fact that bias of any kind is alien to me, I am also well aware that these different patterns of development reflect the differentiation of functions within an extremely complex biological nexus; furthermore, I am quite ready to concede that there are innumerable women who love on the male pattern and also develop the sexual over-valuation characteristic of it.

Even for those women who remain narcissistic, and cool in their response to men, there is a path that can lead them to full object-love. In the child that they bear, they encounter a part of their own body as a distinct and separate object upon which, on the basis of their narcissism, they can now bestow full object-love. Then there are other women who do not need to wait for a child in order to progress from (secondary) narcissism to object-love. These are women who, prior to puberty, feel themselves to be male and manage up to a certain point to develop in a male way; their efforts in this direction are abandoned once female sexual maturity comes upon them – but they thereafter remain capable of yearning for a male ideal, which really amounts to a perpetuation of the boy-like being that they themselves once were.

A brief summary of the various paths to object-choice may serve to bring these adumbrations to a close.

We love one or other of the following:

1) *Narcissistic type*:
   a) what we ourselves are,
   b) what we ourselves were,
   c) what we would like to become,
   d) a person who was once part of our own self.
2) *Imitative type*:
   a) the woman who feeds us,
   b) the man who protects us,
   and the many surrogates who take their place.

Category c) of the first type can only be substantiated at a later stage in the argument.

The significance of narcissistic object-choice in the case of male homosexuality remains to be discussed in a separate context.

❊

The primary narcissism of the child that we have postulated, and that constitutes one of the premises of our libido theories, can be more easily inferred from other factors than captured by direct observation. When one looks at the attitude of affectionate parents towards their children, one cannot but recognize it as a resurgence and repetition of their own long-abandoned narcissism. The trusty characteristic of 'over-valuation', which we have already discussed as a distinctive marker of narcissism in the context of object-choice, predominates in this affective relationship, as is universally known. There is accordingly a compulsion to ascribe to the child all conceivable perfections, something for which dispassionate observation would find no cause, and to conceal and forget all its faults – indeed it is in this context that denial of child sexuality has its place. However, there is also a tendency when faced by the child to suspend all the cultural accretions that we ourselves came to accept only in the teeth of opposition from our narcissism, and to reassert through the child our long-abandoned claims to rights and privileges. Things are to be better for the child than they were for its parents; it is to be saved from subjection to those imperatives that we have accepted as paramount in life. Disease, death, the forgoing of sensual pleasure, the curbing of one's own will – none of this is to apply to the child; the laws of nature and of society are to stop at its door; it really is to become the very core and centre of creation once again: *His Majesty the Baby*,[12] as we once thought ourselves to be. The child is to fulfil all the wishful dreams that its parents dreamed but never realized; it is to become a great man and great hero as proxy for the father, or get a prince for a husband as belated compensation for the mother. That most precarious aspiration of the narcissist scheme of things – immortality of the ego, so gravely threatened by sheer reality – is rendered secure by finding refuge in the child. Parental love, so touching yet essentially so childlike, is nothing other than the resurgent narcissism of the parents, which in its transformation into object-love unmistakably reveals its original nature.

Notes

1. [*Positionen*. This is a recurrent term of Freud's in connection with the libido, especially with regard to the loci that it comes to occupy as a result of cathexis.]

2. [*Ichveränderung*.]

3. [See the *Longman Dictionary of Psychology and Psychiatry*, ed. Robert M. Goldenson, New York and London, 1985: '*actual neurosis* – a neurosis which, according to Freud, stems from current sexual frustrations, such as coitus interruptus, forced abstinence, or incomplete gratification, as contrasted with psychoneurosis, which stems from experiences in infancy or childhood. The term was applied primarily to anxiety neurosis, hypochondriasis, and neurasthenia, but is rarely used today.']

4. [*Angstneurose*. The long-established term 'anxiety neurosis' is reluctantly retained here but it should be noted that *Angst* means 'fear', and is normally used in precisely that sense by Freud.]

5. Cf. 'Über neurotische Erkrankungstypen' (1912) ['Types of Onset of Neurosis'].

6. [Freud's important but challenging term is *Versagung*, from the verb *versagen*, itself cognate with English 'forsake' – one now-obsolete meaning of which is 'To decline or refuse (something offered)' (*OED*). What he means by the term is rather more clearly shown by the opening sentences of 'Die am Erfolge scheitern' ('Those who Founder on Success'): 'Our work in psychoanalysis has presented us with the following proposition: People incur neurotic illness as a result of *refusal*. What is meant by this is that their libidinal desires are refused gratification' – i.e. by the savagely censorious entity within that oversees their every thought and deed. See also the penultimate sentence of this present essay: 'We can thus more readily understand the fact that paranoia is frequently caused by the ego being wounded, by gratification being refused within the domain of the ego-ideal.' The *Standard Edition* routinely and astonishingly mistranslates the term as 'frustration'.]

7. [The voice here is God's; the lines are from Heine's *Neue Gedichte* ('Schöpfungslieder', vii).]

8. ['Release' is used throughout this volume to render Freud's important but not readily translatable metaphor *Abfuhr* (the *Standard Edition* prefers 'discharge').]

9. [*Konversion*. See also below, *Remembering, Repeating, and Working Through*, note 3.]

10. [Freud's term – used here for the first time in his *œuvre* – is

*Anlehnungstypus*. Alas, it cannot be rendered directly into English, and so 'imitative type' is necessarily an approximate rather than a precise translation (as are the two immediately preceding instances of 'imitate', both rendering words derived from the verb *sich anlehnen*). However, this is a considerable improvement on the *Standard Edition*, which goes seriously awry when it translates Freud's term as 'the "anaclitic" or "attachment" type'. 'Anaclitic' is a specially concocted word – but concocted on the basis of a startling misunderstanding of the German expression *sich anlehnen an*, as the footnote in the *Standard Edition* makes embarrassingly clear: the expression does *not* imply 'attach' or 'attachment'; it simply means that A 'is modelled on', 'is based on', 'follows the example of' B; thus one might typically say that Beethoven's early symphonies *lehnen sich an* the mature work of Mozart, or that Freud's theories *lehnen sich an* the ideas and visions of nineteenth-century German literature (in the *Introductory Lectures on Psychoanalysis: New Series* Freud himself notes that the term 'id' (*das Es*) was devised on the model of Nietzsche's linguistic practice – *in Anlehnung an den Sprachgebrauch bei Nietzsche*).]

11. [Freud's German is somewhat ambiguous; his wording is such that it could be understood to mean 'who have *partly* relinquished their own narcissism' (this is the interpretation preferred by the *Standard Edition*).]

12. [Freud cites the phrase in English, and is probably quoting the title of a painting exhibited in the Royal Academy, which depicted a baby being wheeled grandly across a busy London street while two policemen hold up the traffic.]

### III

There are certain questions that I should like to leave to one side for the time being since they represent an important area of study that has still not been fully dealt with: questions as to what disruptions the primal narcissism in children is prey to, what reactions it displays in resisting them, and what paths it is forced along in the process. The most significant part of all this can be identified as 'castration complex' (penis-fear in the boy, penis-envy in the girl), and can be dealt with in conjunction with the effects of sexual intimidation during infancy. Psychoanalytical research, which normally serves as the means for us to track the various fates of the libidinal drives when they have become isolated from the ego drives and then find themselves in conflict with them, allows us in this present context to draw inferences as to the nature of an earlier stage and psychic situation in which both sets of drives manifest themselves in harmonious interaction and indissoluble combination with each other as narcissistic interests. It was on the basis of this nexus that Alfred Adler arrived at his 'masculine protest', which he elevates to the status of being almost the sole driving force behind the formation of personality and neuroses alike, whilst grounding it not in a narcissistic, i.e. still libidinal impulse, but in a social value-judgement. The standpoint of psychoanalytical research has been to acknowledge from the outset both the existence and the importance of the 'masculine protest', but to argue, in opposition to Adler, that it is narcissistic in nature, and has its origins in the castration complex. It pertains to character-formation, to the genesis of which it contributes along with many other factors, and as such is wholly irrelevant to the elucidation of problems concerning neuroses, the only noteworthy aspect of which for Adler is the way they serve the ego-interest. I find it quite impossible to suppose that the genesis of neurosis rests solely on the slender basis of the castration complex, no matter how powerfully the latter may manifest itself amongst the resistances displayed by men to treatment of their neuroses. I might add, too, that cases of neurosis are known to me in which the 'masculine protest' or, in our terms, the castration complex, plays no pathogenic role, or indeed is entirely absent.

Observation of the normal adult shows his erstwhile megalomania to be much reduced, whilst the psychic characteristics from which we inferred his infantile narcissism are scarcely distinguishable. What then has become of his ego-libido? Are we to suppose that it was entirely absorbed by object-cathexes? Such a possibility clearly contradicts the entire thrust of our argument. But we can find pointers to a quite different answer to this question in the psychology of repression.

We have learned that libidinal drive-impulses are subject to the fate of pathogenic repression when they come into conflict with the individual's cultural and ethical notions. What we understand by this is *not* that the individual has a merely intellectual awareness that these notions exist, but rather that he fully accepts them as his own yardstick and fully submits to the demands that they entail. As we have said, repression emanates from the ego; or, to put it more precisely, from the self-respect of the ego. The same impressions, experiences, impulses, desires that one human being will readily entertain, or at least consciously process, will be rejected by another with utter indignation, or be stifled before they even enter consciousness. However, the difference between the two, which reflects the conditions in which repression takes place, can easily be expressed in terms enabling us to resolve the issue by means of the libido theory. We can postulate that the one individual has set up an *ideal* within himself against which he measures his actual ego,[1] whereas the other has formed no such ideal. On this view, the formation of an ideal[2] constitutes the necessary condition on the part of the ego for repression to take place.

It is this ideal ego that is now the recipient of the self-love enjoyed during childhood by the real ego. The individual's narcissism appears to be transferred onto this new ideal ego which, like the infantile one, finds itself possessed of every estimable perfection. Here too, as is ever the case in matters of the libido, human beings have proved incapable of forgoing gratification once they have enjoyed it. They are unwilling to forsake the narcissistic perfection of their childhood, and when – discomfited by the admonitions raining down on them while they are developing, and with their powers of judgement duly awakened – they fail to retain that perfection, they seek to retrieve it in the new guise of the ego-ideal. What they project as their ideal for the future is a surrogate for the lost narcissism of their childhood, during which they were their own ideal.

It is appropriate at this point to explore the ways in which this forming of an ideal relates to sublimation. *Sublimation* is a process involving object-libido, and consists in a drive latching on to a different goal far removed from sexual gratification, the main aim here being to divert attention away from the sexual. *Idealization* is a process involving the object itself, whereby the object is magnified and exalted in the individual's mind without itself changing in nature. This idealization can occur within the domains of both ego-libido and object-libido. Thus, for example, sexual over-valuation of an object constitutes an idealization of that object. To the extent, therefore, that sublimation has to do with drives whereas idealization has to do with objects, the two concepts need to be clearly distinguished from each other.

The formation of ego-ideals is frequently confused with the sublimation of drives, to the considerable detriment of our understanding. Just because someone has traded his narcissism for veneration of an exalted ego-ideal does not necessarily mean that he has managed to sublimate his libidinal drives. The ego-ideal certainly demands such sublimation, but cannot force it to happen; sublimation remains a separate process that may be triggered by the ideal, but then runs its course entirely independently of any such trigger. It is precisely in the case of neurotics that one finds the most electric disparities between the sophistication of their ego-ideal and the degree of sublimation of their primitive libidinal drives; and it is generally much harder to convince an idealist that his libido is inappropriately located than it is to convince the uncomplicated sort who has remained modest in his expectations. Sublimation and the formation of ideals also play completely different roles in the causation of neurosis. As we have seen, the formation of ideals intensifies the demands of the ego, and is the strongest single factor favouring repression; sublimation represents the let-out whereby such demands can be met *without* recourse to repression.

It would not be surprising were we to come across a special entity[3] in the psyche charged with ensuring that narcissistic gratification is indeed achieved in accordance with the ego-ideal, and to this end incessantly scrutinizes the actual ego and measures it against the ideal. If indeed such an entity exists, there can be no question of our discovering it as such; all we can do is to assume that it exists, and we may reasonably suppose that the thing we call our *conscience* matches the description. By acknowledging this entity we are better able to understand the so-called object-of-attention delusion or, more correctly, object-of-*scrutiny* delusion, that crops up so conspicuously in the symptomatology of paranoid illnesses, and which may perhaps also occur as a separate illness or as a random element in a transference neurosis. Patients then complain that all their thoughts are known, their actions watched and monitored. They are informed of the workings of this entity by voices, which characteristically speak to them in the third person ('Now she's thinking about that again', 'Now he's going away'). The complaint is justified, it depicts the true situation: such a power really does exist, and it exists in all of us in normal life, registering, scrutinizing, criticizing our every intention. Object-of-scrutiny delusions reflect it in a regressive form, thereby revealing both its genesis and the reason why the patient rebels against it. For what first triggered the formation of the ego-ideal – the duly appointed keeper of which is the conscience – was the critical influence of the individual's parents, communicated by voice, who were joined in the course of time by others involved in his upbringing, by his teachers, by the vast and indeterminate mass of all the other people in his milieu (people in general, public opinion).

Large quantities of essentially homosexual libido are drawn on for the purposes of forming the narcissistic ego-ideal, and achieve discharge and gratification through keeping it going thereafter. Conscience is instituted basically as an embodiment first of parental criticism, and subsequently of criticism by society at large, a process that more or less repeats itself in the emergence of repressive tendencies stemming from prohibitions and obstacles initially encountered in the external world. Neurosis then brings to light both the inner voices and the indeterminate mass, and the whole developmental history of the person's conscience is thereby regressively reproduced. However, his recalcitrance against this *censorial entity* derives from the fact that – in full accord with the fundamental nature of his illness – he wants to free himself from all these influences, starting with that of his parents, and withdraws his homosexual libido from them. He then sees his conscience in regressive refraction as a hostile force bearing down on him from outside.

The bitter complaining characteristic of paranoia also demonstrates that the self-criticism expressed via the conscience is essentially all of a piece with the self-scrutiny upon which it is based. The same mental process that has taken on the function of conscience has thus also lent itself to the exploration of the inner self, which is what provides philosophy with the material for its cerebrations. This may well have considerable bearing on the urge to construct speculative systems that is characteristic of paranoia.[4]

It will doubtless be a significant step for us when we are able to find evidence in other realms, too, of the activity of this entity dedicated to critical scrutiny – duly elevated to its role as both conscience and agent of philosophical introspection. I would like to draw here on what Herbert Silberer has termed the 'functional phenomenon', one of the few incontestably valuable additions to the theory of dreams. As is well known, Silberer has demonstrated that in states between sleeping and waking one can directly observe the conversion of thoughts into visual images, but that often in such circumstances what is actually represented is not the thought content but the *state* (of willingness, tiredness, etc.) that the person fighting sleep finds himself in. He has also shown that dream closures and breaks within dreams in some cases signify nothing but the dreamer's own perception of sleeping and waking. He has thus proved that self-scrutiny – in the sense of paranoid object-of-scrutiny delusion – plays a role in dream-formation. This role is not a constant one; I probably overlooked it because it plays no great part in my own dreams; it may well become very marked in the case of people who are philosophically gifted and accustomed to introspection.

We might remind ourselves at this point that we have argued elsewhere that the formation of dreams takes place under the sway of a censorial process that forces dream-thoughts to become distorted. In positing this censorship, however, we did not envisage any special power at work, but chose the term to describe that portion of the repressive tendencies governing the ego that is directed at dream-thoughts. If we go more deeply into the structure of the ego, then we may reasonably see in the ego-ideal and the dynamic utterances of the conscience the *dream censor*[5] as well. Supposing that this censor also remains alert to some extent during sleep, then we can readily comprehend that the prerequisite of its activity, namely self-scrutiny and self-criticism, helps to shape the content of dreams with contributions like 'now he's too sleepy to think', 'now he's waking up'.[6]

We can now attempt a discussion of self-feeling[7] in normal individuals and in neurotics.

Self-feeling seems to us in the first place to be an expression of the ego in its totality, without further regard being paid to its essentially composite nature. Everything one possesses or has achieved, every remnant of one's primitive sense of omnipotence that has been borne out by experience, helps to enhance this self-feeling.

If we are going to introduce our distinction between sexual drives and ego drives, then we must also acknowledge that self-feeling is particularly intimately dependent on narcissistic libido. We base this contention on the two fundamental facts that in the paraphrenias self-feeling is enhanced whereas in the transference neuroses it is diminished; and that in love-relationships an individual's self-feeling is increased by his being loved, and decreased by his *not* being loved. We have already argued that, in the case of narcissistic object-choice, being loved constitutes both the goal and the means of gratification.

It is easy to see, moreover, that the libidinal cathexis of objects does not enhance self-feeling. Dependence on the love-object has a belittling effect; to be in love is to be humble. Loving someone means, so to speak, forfeiting part of our narcissism, and we can make good the deficit only by being loved. In all these respects self-feeling appears to remain directly proportional to the degree of narcissism involved in the subject's love-life.

The realization of impotence, of one's own inability to love, as a result of some psychological or physical disorder, has an extremely debilitating effect on self-feeling. Here, so it seems to me, may lie one of the sources of the feelings of inferiority so readily avouched by those suffering from transference neuroses. The main source of these feelings, however, is the depletion of the ego that occurs when extraordinarily large cathexes of libido are withdrawn from it; in other words, impairment of the ego by sexual urges that are no longer subject to control.

A[lfred] Adler has rightly argued that when people recognize deficiencies in their own organs, this acts as a spur to their psyche (assuming the latter to be functioning adequately), and by means of over-compensation serves to lift their level of achievement. But it would be a gross exaggeration if we were to follow Adler's procedure and regard organ deficiency as the origin and neces- sary condition of every instance of high achievement. Not all painters are afflicted by eye defects, not all orators were origi- nally stutterers. There are abundant examples, too, of excellent things achieved by people blessed with exceptional organs. When it comes to the aetiology of neurosis, organic deficiency and wast- ing play a minor role, perhaps much the same as that played by the perceptual material of the moment in the formation of dreams. The neurosis uses it as a pretext just as it uses every other expe- dient factor. One has no sooner given credence to a neurotic patient's notion that she was bound to become ill because – as she saw it – she was ugly, misshapen and devoid of charm, so that no one could ever conceivably love her, than one is taught a lesson by the very next female neurotic to come along, who doggedly cleaves to her neurosis and rejection of sexuality despite seem- ing more than averagely desirable, and indeed being actively desired. The majority of hysterical women may be numbered among the attractive and even beautiful representatives of their sex; and inversely, the heavy incidence of ugliness, infirmity and wasted organs in the lower classes of our society has no effect whatever on the frequency of neurotic disorders occurring amongst them.

The relationship of self-feeling to the erotic (i.e. to libidinal object-cathexes) may be summed up in the following terms. We need to determine which of two alternatives applies: whether the love-cathexes are *ego-accordant*,[8] or whether on the contrary they have undergone repression. In the former case (i.e. where libido deployment is ego-accordant), the same value attaches to loving as to any other activity of the ego. The process of loving in itself, inasmuch as it entails yearning and going without, diminishes self-feeling; the process of being loved, of finding one's love returned, of gaining possession of the loved object, restores it to its previous level. In the case of repressed libido, the love-cathexis is experienced as a severe depletion of the ego; no gratification of the love is possible; replenishment of the ego can be achieved only by withdrawal of the libido from its objects. The return of object-libido to the ego, and its transformation into narcissism, creates as it were a semblance of love happily achieved, whilst a love happily achieved in actual reality corresponds in turn to the primal state in which object-libido and ego-libido cannot be differentiated from one another.

The importance and complexity of this subject is perhaps sufficient justification for appending a few extra paragraphs here in more or less random order.

The development of the ego consists in an ever-increasing separation from one's primary narcissism, and gives rise to an intense struggle to retrieve it. This separation occurs through the displacement of libido on to an ego-ideal imposed from without; gratification occurs through fulfilment of that ideal.

At the same time, the ego sends forth libidinal object-cathexes. It becomes depleted for the sake of these cathexes and for the sake of the ego-ideal, but replenishes itself through object-gratifications[9] and through fulfilment of the ideal.

One part of self-feeling is primary, the residue of childhood narcissism; another derives from our sense of omnipotence as borne out by experience (fulfilment of the ego-ideal); a third arises out of the gratification of our object-libido.

The ego-ideal puts considerable difficulties in the way of libido gratification through objects by causing some of them to be rejected by its censor[10] as unsuitable. Where no such ideal has developed, the relevant sexual urge enters the individual's personality in unmodified form as a perversion. Becoming our own ideal again in respect of our sexual urges as well as everything else, just as in our childhood: therein lies the happiness that human beings aspire to.

Being in love consists in the ego-libido overflowing abundantly on to the object. It has the power to undo repressions and remedy perversions.[11] It exalts the sexual object into the status of sexual ideal. Given that in the case of the 'object' or 'imitative' type it has its basis in the fulfilment of infantile conditions of love, we may venture the dictum: 'Whatever fulfils this condition of love is consequently idealized.'

The sexual ideal can enter into an interesting support role in relation to the ego-ideal. Where narcissistic gratification encounters real obstacles, the sexual ideal can be used for surrogate gratification. The person then enacts the narcissistic type of object-choice by loving what he once was but has meanwhile forfeited, or by loving whatever possesses the qualities that he himself doesn't have at all (cf. above under *c*) [page 375]). The formula parallel to the one cited above runs as follows: 'Whatever possesses the qualities that the ego lacks *qua* ideal, is consequently loved.' This particular resort holds special significance for the neurotic, whose ego becomes depleted because of his excessive object-cathexes, and who is hence incapable of achieving his ego-ideal. Having squandered his libido on objects, he then seeks a way back to narcissism by adopting the narcissistic type of object-choice and choosing a sexual ideal possessed of the qualities he himself cannot attain. This is healing through love, which as a rule he prefers to the psychoanalytical variety. Indeed, he has no faith in any other healing mechanism; he generally embarks on his therapy in expectation of it, and duly focuses this expectation on the person of the physician treating him. What stands in the way of this curative scheme, of course, is the patient's incapacity for love as a result of his panoply of repressions. If the treatment manages to remedy this to some degree, we often meet with a successful if unintended outcome in that the patient withdraws from treatment in order to make a love-choice, and to entrust his further recovery to his shared life with the loved person. We might be content with this outcome if it did not bring with it all the dangers of a crushing dependence on his helper in adversity.

The ego-ideal opens up a significant new avenue for our under-standing of mass psychology.[12] This ideal has a social element as well as an individual one, for it is also the shared ideal of family, class, nation. Besides narcissistic libido, it also harnesses a large quantum of a person's homosexual libido, which thereby reverts to the ego. Non-gratification resulting from non-fulfilment of this ideal releases homosexual libido, which converts into guilty conscience (social fear). Guilty conscience originates as fear of parental punishment, or rather – to put it more accurately – fear of losing the parents' love; later, the indeterminate mass of fellow human beings takes the parents' place. We can thus more read-ily understand the fact that paranoia is frequently caused by the ego being wounded, by gratification being refused within the domain of the ego-ideal. Also, in the case of the paraphrenic illnesses, we can better understand the concomitance within the ego-ideal of ideal-formation and sublimation, the retrogression of sublimations, and the re-formation[13] of ideals that occurs in certain circumstances.

(1914)

## Notes

1. [*sein aktuelles Ich.*]
2. [*Idealbildung*. Freud is particularly fond of creating compound nouns ending in -*bildung*, the gerund of the verb *bilden*, 'to form' (cognate with

English 'build'), e.g. *Reaktionsbildung, Symptombildung, Traumbildung.*]

**3**. [Freud's word is *Instanz* – a cardinal term in his vocabulary, but one that has no direct linguistic or indeed cultural equivalent in English, with the result that a number of different renderings are deployed in this present translation to match the relevant context. The key feature of the word is that it implies some kind of judicial or quasi-judicial authority making judgements about what is permissible and impermissible, acceptable and unacceptable – and doing so very often in implacably harsh and even sadistic terms involving 'guilt', 'condemnation', 'punishment', etc. This vision of the human psyche as a domain under constant surveillance by draconian but shadowy forces is fascinatingly similar to that of Freud's fellow Jew and Austro-Hungarian near-contemporary, Franz Kafka.]

**4**. Merely by way of conjecture I would add that the development and consolidation of this all-scrutinizing entity might also embrace the ultimate emergence of (subjective) memory and of the phenomenon whereby time holds no validity for unconscious processes.

**5**. [Having thus far used abstract nouns (*Instanz, Zensur*) to convey the policing of the psyche, Freud gives the process a far sharper edge here by suddenly personifying it (*Zensor*).]

**6**. I cannot here resolve the issue whether the differentiation of this censorial entity from the rest of the ego is capable of providing a psychological substantiation of the philosophical distinction between consciousness and self-consciousness.

**7**. [*Selbstgefühl*. The *Standard Edition* bizarrely renders this as 'self-regarding attitude'. For useful definitions and examples of 'self-feeling' as a technical term current in nineteenth- and early twentieth-century thinking, see *OED*.]

**8**. [*Ichgerecht*. The *Standard Edition* has 'ego-syntonic', but this is misleading as well as obfuscatory given that the term *Syntonie* ('syntony') was not introduced into psychiatry (by Eugen Bleuler) until 1925 – more than a decade after Freud's *Narcissism* essay.]

**9**. [*Objektbefriedigungen*. This is one of Freud's more brutalist compounds. As the ensuing paragraphs make clear, it is elliptical for 'gratifications *pertaining to* objects'.]

**10**. [*Zensor*. See above, note 5.]

**11**. [On the face of it, Freud's German (*Perversionen wiederherzustellen*) means 'restore' or 'reinstate' the individual's perversions (the *Standard Edition* duly translates it in this sense); but it is more plausibly an elliptical usage highlighting love's benignly restorative effect on the individuals themselves (*wiederherstellen* is a standard expression for 'restore to health').]

12. [*Massenpsychologie*. In the *Standard Edition* this term is routinely translated as '*group* psychology'.]

13. [*Umbildung*.]

# Remembering, Repeating, and Working Through

It seems to me by no means superfluous to remind the student of psychoanalysis again and again of the profound changes that psycho-analytical technique has undergone since its first beginnings. First of all, in the phase of catharsis as practised by Breuer, the tech-nique was to focus directly on the factor of symptom-formation, and make a rigorously sustained attempt to reproduce the psychic processes of that situation in order to resolve them through conscious activity. Remembering and abreacting[1] were the goals at that stage, to be achieved with the help of hypnosis. Once hypno-sis had been discarded, the task that then demanded our attention was to use the free associations of the patient to work out what he himself was failing to remember. The process of interpretation and the communication of its results to the patient were seen as the means to overcome the resistance within him; there was still the same focus on the situations in which the symptoms first arose, and any others that proved to underlie the onset of the illness, whilst abreaction diminished in importance and appeared to be replaced by the considerable effort that the patient had to expend when forced to overcome his hostility towards his free associations (in accordance with the basic rule of psychoanalysis). Then finally the rigorous technique of the present time evolved whereby the physician no longer focuses on a specific factor or problem, but is quite content to study the prevailing surface-level of the patient's mind, and uses his interpretative skills chiefly for the purpose of identifying the resistances manifest there, and making the patient conscious of them. A new kind of division of labour then comes into being: the physician reveals the resistances that were hitherto unknown to the patient; and once these have been overcome, the patient often recounts without any difficulty the situations and contexts that he had forgotten. The goal of these various techniques has of course remained the same throughout; in descriptive terms, to fill the gaps in the patient's memory; in dynamic terms, to overcome the resistances brought about by repression.

The old technique of hypnosis still deserves our gratitude for having shown us in discrete and schematized form a number of psychic processes that occur in analysis. It was thanks to this alone that we were able to develop the boldness, within psychoanalytic practice itself, to create complex situations and keep them transparent.

'Remembering' took a very simple form in these hypnotic treatments. The patient reverted to an earlier situation, which he appeared never to confuse with his present one, conveyed the psychic processes of that earlier situation in so far as they had remained normal, and in addition conveyed whatever resulted from translating the unconscious processes of that time into conscious ones.

I shall add a few remarks at this point that every analyst has seen confirmed by his own experience.[2] The forgetting of impressions, scenes, experiences comes down in most cases to a process of 'shutting out' such things. When the patient speaks of these 'forgotten' things, he rarely fails to add: 'I've always known that really, I've just never thought about it.' He not uncommonly expresses disappointment that so few things seem to want to come to mind that he can acknowledge as 'forgotten', things that he has never thought about again since the time they happened. Even this yearning, however, is capable of being gratified, particularly in the case of conversion hysterias.[3] The term 'forgetting' becomes even less relevant once there is due appreciation of the extremely widespread phenomenon of screen-memories.[4] In quite a number of cases of childhood amnesia,[5] that familiar condition so important to us in theoretical terms, I have gained the impression that the amnesia is exactly counterbalanced by the patient's screen-memories. These memories contain not merely *some* essential elements of the patient's childhood, but *all* such elements. One simply has to know how to use analysis to retrieve these elements from the memories. The latter represent the forgotten childhood years as completely as the manifest content of dreams represents the dream-thoughts.

The other group of psychic processes which, as purely internal acts, can be contrasted to impressions and experiences – fantasies, relationary processes,[6] emotional impulses, thought-connections[7] – need to be considered separately as regards their relationship to forgetting and remembering. Something that occurs particularly frequently here is that something is 'remembered' that can never have been 'forgotten', since it was never at any point noticed, never conscious; moreover it appears to make no difference whatsoever to the psychic outcome whether such a 'connection' was a conscious one that was then forgotten, or whether it never reached the status of consciousness in the first place. The conviction that the patient arrives at in the course of analysis is entirely independent of this kind of memory.

Particularly in the case of the many forms of obsessional neurosis, forgetting is limited in the main to losing track of connections, misremembering the sequence of events, recalling memories in isolation.

A memory usually cannot be retrieved at all in the case of one particular group of extremely important experiences, namely those occurring at a very early stage of childhood that are experienced at the time without understanding, but are then *subsequently* understood and interpreted. We become aware of them via the patient's dreams, and are compelled to credit their existence by overwhelming evidence within the overall pattern of the neurosis; we are also persuaded by the fact that, once the patient has overcome his resistances, he does not see the absence of a memory or sensation of familiarity as grounds for not accepting that they took place. This topic needs to be approached with so much care, however, and introduces so much that is new and disturbing, that

I shall deal with it quite separately with reference to appropriate material.[8]

Now the introduction of the new technique has meant that very little, and in many instances nothing whatever, has remained of this splendidly smooth progression of events. Here, too, there are cases that initially develop just as they would under the hypnotic technique, only to diverge at a later stage; other cases behave differently right from the outset. If for the purposes of defining the difference we stick to the latter type, then we may say that the patient does not *remember* anything at all of what he has forgotten and repressed, but rather *acts it out*. He reproduces it not as a memory, but as an action; he *repeats* it, without of course being aware of the fact that he is repeating it.

For example, instead of the patient recounting that he remembers having been defiant and refractory *vis-à-vis* his parents' authority, he behaves in just such a manner towards the physician. Instead of remembering that he became hopelessly stuck in his infantile sexual explorations, he presents a mass of confused dreams and associations, wails that he is no good at anything, and sees it as his fate never to bring any undertaking to a successful conclusion. Instead of remembering that he was intensely ashamed of certain sexual activities and fearful of discovery, he exhibits shame regarding the treatment that he has embarked upon, and tries to keep it secret from all and sundry – and so on.

More particularly, he *begins* the treatment with just such a repetition. Often when one has explained the basic rule of psychoanalysis to a patient with an eventful life story and a long history of illness, and asks him to say whatever comes into his mind, and then expects a stream of utterances to come bursting forth, the first thing one discovers is that he has no idea what to say. He remains silent, and maintains that nothing at all has come into his mind. This is of course nothing other than the repetition of a homosexual stance, which manifests itself as a resistance to remembrance of any kind. He remains in the grip of this compulsion to repeat for as long as he remains under treatment; and in the end we realize that this is his way of remembering.

What is chiefly going to interest us, of course, is the relationship that this repetitional compulsion bears to the transference and the resistance exhibited by the patient. We soon realize that the transference is itself merely an instance of repetition, and that this repetition involves transference of the forgotten past not only onto the physician, but onto all other areas of the patient's current situation. We must therefore expect that the patient will yield to the compulsion to repeat – which now takes the place of the impulse to remember – not only in his personal relationship to the physician, but in all other activities and relationships taking place in his life at the same time; for example, if during the course of the treatment he chooses a love-object, takes some task upon himself, involves himself in a project of any sort. The role played by resistance is also easy to recognize. The greater the resistance, the more thoroughly remembering will be replaced by acting out (repetition). After all, in hypnosis the ideal form of remembering corresponds to a condition in which resistance is completely pushed aside. If the treatment begins under the aegis of a mild and tacit regime of positive transference, this initially encourages submersion in the domain of memory (just as happens in hypnosis), during the course of which even the symptoms of the patient's illness are mute; however, if this transference subsequently becomes hostile or unduly intense, and therefore needs to be repressed, then remembering immediately gives way to acting out. From that point onwards it is the resistances that determine the sequence of what is repeated. The patient uses the arsenal of the past to arm himself with weapons to fight against the continuation of the treatment – weapons that we have to wrest from him one by one.

Now having seen that the patient repeats rather than remembers, and does so under conditions of resistance, we may now ask what it really is that he repeats or acts out. The answer is that he repeats everything deriving from the repressed element within himself [9] that has already established itself in his manifest personality – his inhibitions and unproductive attitudes, his pathological characteristics. Indeed, he also repeats all his symptoms during the course of the treatment. And we can now see that in emphasizing the compulsion to repeat we have not discovered a new fact, but merely arrived at a more coherent view. It is now quite plain to us that the start of a patient's analysis does not mean the end of his illness, and that we need to treat the illness not as a matter belonging to the past, but as a force operating in the present. Piece by piece the entire illness is brought within the scope and ambit of the treatment, and while the patient experiences it as something intensely real and immediate, it is our job to do the therapeutic work, which consists to a very great extent in leading the patient back to the past.

Getting the patient to remember, as practised in hypnosis, inevitably had the air of a laboratory experiment. Getting the patient to repeat, as practised under the more modern technique of analysis, means summoning up a chunk of real life, and cannot therefore always be harmless and free of risk. The whole problem arises here of 'deterioration during treatment', a phenomenon that often proves unavoidable.

Most importantly, the very inception of the treatment itself necessarily induces a change in the patient's conscious attitude to his illness. As a rule he has been content up to then to bemoan his illness, to despise it as so much nonsense and to underestimate its significance, whilst for the rest applying the same repressive behaviour, the same head-in-the-sand strategy, to the manifestations of his illness that he applied to its origins. Thus it can happen that he does not properly appreciate the conditions under which his phobia functions, does not listen carefully enough to what his obsessional ideas are saying to him, or does not grasp the real intention of his obsessional impulse. This of course is the last thing his treatment needs. He has to find the courage to focus his attention on the manifestations of his illness. He must no longer regard the illness as something contemptible, but rather as a worthy opponent, a part of his very being that exists for good reasons, and from which he must extract something of real value for his subsequent life. The way is thus prepared from the outset for him to be reconciled with the repressed element within himself, which expresses itself in his symptoms, whilst at the same time allowing for a certain tolerance towards his illness. And if as a result of this new relationship to his illness the patient's conflicts are exacerbated, or if symptoms are forced into the open that had previously remained in the shadows, then one can easily reassure him on this score by pointing out that these merely constitute a necessary but transitory deterioration in his condition, and that one cannot destroy an enemy if he is absent or out of range. However, the resistance can exploit the situation for its own ends and seek to abuse the licence to be ill. It then seems to exclaim: 'Look what happens when I really do let myself become involved in these things! Wasn't I quite right to consign them all to repression?' Juvenile and child patients are particularly prone to use the focus on their illness necessitated by their treatment as an excuse to wallow in their symptoms.

Further dangers arise as treatment progresses, in that new, more deep-seated drive-impulses – still nascent rather than fully established – can emerge as repetition. Lastly, the patient's actions outside the transference process can cause temporary harm in his everyday life, indeed can be so chosen as to permanently undermine that very condition of health that the treatment is meant to achieve.

The tactic that the physician has to adopt in this situation is easily justified. The goal that he holds fast to, even though he knows it to be unattainable under the new technique, remains the old form of remembering, that is, reproducing things within the psychic domain. He prepares himself for a constant battle with the patient, in order to keep within the psychic domain all those impulses that the patient would prefer to divert into the motor domain, and regards it as a therapeutic triumph when he successfully uses the remembering process to resolve an issue that the patient would rather get rid of in the form of an action. If the bond formed through transference is at all effective, then the treatment will successfully prevent any really significant acts of remembering on the part of the patient, and will use the nascent stage of any attempts at such acts as material contributing to the therapeutic process. One can best protect the patient from being damaged through giving rein to his impulses if one puts him under an explicit obligation not to make any decisions during the course of his treatment that vitally affect his life, such as choosing a career or a definitive love-object, but instead to wait until he is fully recovered.

In doing this, however, it is sensible to give scope to such aspects of the patient's personal freedom as are consistent with these precautions, and not to stop him from carrying out intentions which, though foolish, are without consequence, whilst also bearing in mind that people can really only achieve insight through their own hurt and their own experience. There are indeed also cases in which the patient cannot be prevented from entering upon some wholly inappropriate undertaking, and which only later become ripe for psychoanalytical treatment, and responsive to it. Occasionally there are also bound to be cases where one does not have the time to put the bridle of transference on a patient's rampant drives, or where the patient in the course of an act of repetition destroys the bond that ties him to the treatment. As an extreme example of this I might mention the case of an elderly lady who, when afflicted by twilight states,[10] had repeatedly left home and husband and fled somewhere or other without ever becoming conscious of the force impelling her to 'run away' in this manner. On starting her treatment with me she displayed a well-developed form of affectionate transference, this intensified with uncanny rapidity over the first few days, and by the end of the week she had 'run away' from me too, without my having had the time to say anything to her that might have prevented this repetition.

However, the chief means for controlling the patient's compulsion to repeat, and turning it into a means of activating memory,[11] lies in the way that the transference is handled. We render the compulsion harmless, indeed beneficial, by allowing it some sovereignty, by giving it its head within a specific domain. We offer it transference as a playground in which it has licence to express itself with almost total freedom, coupled with an obligation to reveal to us everything in the way of pathogenic drives that have hidden themselves away in the patient's psyche. The patient's cooperation need extend only as far as respect for the conditions of existence of the analysis, and, provided this is the case, we can routinely succeed in giving all the symptoms of his illness a new meaning in terms of transference; in replacing his ordinary neurosis with a transference neurosis, of which he can be cured through the therapeutic process. Transference thus creates an intermediate realm between sickness and a healthy life by means of which the transition from one to the other is accomplished. The new condition has assumed all the characteristics of the illness, but it constitutes an artificial illness that is in all respects amenable to treatment. At the same time it is a real, lived experience, but one made possible by particularly favourable conditions, and purely temporary in nature. The repetition reactions exhibited in transference then lead along familiar paths to the reawakening of memories, which surface without any apparent difficulty once the patient's resistances have been overcome.

I could close here if it were not for the fact that the title of this essay obliges me to demonstrate one further element of psychoanalytical technique. As is well known, what opens the way to the overcoming of resistances is that the physician identifies the resistance that the patient himself had never recognized, and reveals it to him. Now it seems that beginners in the practice of analysis are inclined to think that this purely preliminary phase constitutes the entire task. I have often been asked for advice in cases where the physician complained that he had shown the patient his resistance, yet nothing had changed; indeed, the resistance had merely intensified and the entire situation had become even more impenetrable than before. The treatment seemed to be going nowhere. But this gloomy assessment invariably proved to be wrong. In most cases the treatment could not have been going better, the physician had simply forgotten that identifying the resistance can never result in its immediate cessation. One has to give the patient time to familiarize himself with the resistance now that he is aware of it, to *work his way through it*, to overcome it by defying it and carrying on with the therapy in accordance with the basic rule of analysis. Only when the resistance is at its most intense can one manage in cooperation with the patient to detect the repressed drive-impulses that sustain the resistance; and it is only by directly experiencing it in this way that the patient becomes truly convinced of its existence and power. The physician need do nothing other than wait, and allow things to take their course – a process that cannot be prevented, and cannot always be accelerated. If he bears this steadfastly in mind, he will often save himself from the delusion that he has failed, when in fact he is conducting the treatment along entirely the right lines.

This process of working through the resistances may in practice become an arduous task for the patient and a considerable test of the physician's patience. But it is the phase of treatment that effects the biggest change in the patient, and which distinguishes psychoanalytical treatment from any form of suggestion-based therapy. Theoretically speaking, one can equate it to the 'abreacting'[12] of the emotional quanta pent up through repression that hypnotic treatment entirely depended on for its success.

(1914)

## Notes

1. [*Abreagieren*. The term, together with the attendant therapeutic concept, was introduced by Freud and Breuer in their *Studien über Hysterie* (*Studies in Hysteria*, 1895). 'Abreaction' is defined in the *OED* as follows: 'The liberation by revival and expression of the emotion associated with forgotten or repressed ideas of the event that first caused it. Hence "abreact", to eliminate by abreaction'. In *Inhibition, Symptom, and Fear* (published twelve years after *Remembering, Repeating, and Working Through*), Freud was to comment that he had long since 'abandoned the abreaction theory'.]
2. [This paragraph and the three that follow – all printed in smaller type than the rest of the text when first published in 1914 – amount to an extended parenthesis, interpolated between two paragraphs that essentially belong together.]
3. [*Konversionshysterien*. 'Conversion' in Freud's sense is defined in the *OED* as 'The symbolic manifestation in physical symptoms of a psychic

conflict'; the *OED* entry also includes the following quotation from Freud's disciple Ernest Jones: 'The energy finds an outlet in some somatic manifestation, a process Freud terms "conversion".']

4. [*Deckerinnerungen*. The *deck*-element of the neologism means 'cover', 'conceal'.]

5. [*Kindheitsamnesie*. 'Childhood amnesia' in Freud's sense is amnesia *concerning* childhood – not amnesia *during* childhood.]

6. ['Relationary processes' is more a guess than a translation. Freud's neologism is *Beziehungsvorgänge* – and there is no clue as to which of the various meanings of the word *Beziehung* he had in mind. The *Standard Edition* offers 'processes of reference'.]

7. ['Thought-connections' is also a guess – all the wilder for the fact that in itemizing the various 'psychic processes', Freud chooses a word (*Zusammenhänge*) that cannot by any stretch of the imagination be used to describe a 'process' . . .]

8. [Freud is referring to the case of the 'Wolf-man'.]

9. [*aus den Quellen seines Verdrängten*. Freud's key term *das Verdrängte* is not easy to render in English: the direct translation is 'the repressed', but substantivized past participles tend in English to refer to *people*, not to things or to abstracts ('the damned', 'the defeated', 'the oppressed', etc.). The traditional 'techno'-translations of Freud have long since established 'the repressed' as the English jargon-word, but in many contexts the term would not be readily comprehensible to the non-specialist reader.

10. [*Dämmerzustände*.]

11. [Here – as also in the penultimate sentence of the preceding paragraph, and on numerous other occasions throughout these essays – Freud uses the term *Motiv*. The *Standard Edition* routinely translates this as 'motive', but this is potentially misleading: whereas 'motive' commonly refers to the *purpose* of an act, i.e. the end result envisaged by its perpetrator ('the killer's motive was money'), *Motiv* in Freud's usage almost invariably seems to be a quasi-scientific, not to say mechanistic term meaning 'motive force', thus relating to the *generation* of an act or event, not to any supposed aim or purpose.]

12. [The inverted commas are Freud's.]

# from *Contributions to the Psychology of Erotic Life*

## II *Concerning the Most Universal Debasement in the Erotic Life*

### 1

If the psychoanalyst asks himself for which illness he is most frequently approached for help – apart from the various forms of anxiety – he must reply: psychical impotence. This strange disorder affects men of a highly libidinous nature, and is expressed in the refusal of the executive organs of sexuality to perform the sexual act, despite the fact that they can be demonstrated to be intact and properly functioning both before and after, and that there is a strong psychical inclination to the performance of the act. The patient himself takes his first step towards an understanding of his state when he learns that such a failure only occurs during his attempts with certain people, while with others it is never a problem. Then he knows that the inhibition of his masculine potency arises from some quality of the sexual object, and he will sometimes describe having the sense of an obstacle within himself, the perception of a counter-volition successfully obstructing the conscious intention. But he cannot guess what that internal obstacle is and what property of the sexual object it is that puts it into effect. If he has repeatedly experienced such failure, by making a familiar erroneous connection he will probably conclude that the memory of the first occasion has prompted the repetitions as a disturbing anxiety. As to the first occasion, he will connect it with an impression that he has had 'by chance'.

A number of authors have written and published psychoanalytical studies into psychical impotence. Any analyst can confirm the explanations offered on the basis of his own medical experience.[1] It is really a matter of the inhibiting effect of certain psychical complexes outside the knowledge of the individual. What emerges as the most general content of this pathogenic material is the incestuous fixation on mother and sister which has not been overcome. Otherwise, one should bear in mind the influence of accidental impressions of embarrassment connected with infantile sexual activity, and the elements that generally reduce the libido that is to be directed at the female sexual object.[2]

If one subjects cases of harsh psychical impotence to deep psychoanalytic study, one obtains the following information about the psychosexual processes at work. Once again, the basis of the illness is here – as it is most probably in all neurotic disturbances – an inhibition in the evolution of the libido towards what we would call its normal final formation. Here we have two currents that have failed to coincide, which can be brought together only by a completely normal loving relationship, and which we can identify as the *affectionate* and the *sensual*.

Of these two currents the affectionate is the older. It derives from the earliest years of childhood, was formed on the basis of the interests of the drive to self-preservation and is aimed at the members of the family and those with the responsibility of caring for the child. From the very outset it has admitted contributions from the sexual drives, components of erotic interest that are already more or less clearly apparent in childhood, and which, in neurotics, are revealed in every case by later psychoanalysis. This corresponds to the *primary infantile object-choice*. It tells us that when the sexual drives find their first objects, they are supported by the evaluations of the ego-drives, just as the first sexual satisfactions take their support from the bodily functions necessary for the preservation of life. The 'affection' of parents and carers, which rarely denies its erotic character ('the child is an erotic toy'), does a great deal to increase the contributions of eroticism to the investments of the child's ego-drives, and to take them to a level which one will have to take account of in subsequent development, particularly if certain other conditions lend their assistance.

These affectionate fixations on the part of the child continue through childhood and repeatedly bring with them eroticism which, in consequence, is distracted from its sexual goals. During puberty the powerful 'sensual' current is added to this, and it no longer fails to recognize its goals. It apparently never avoids following earlier paths, and then invests the objects of the primary infantile choice with much stronger libidinal charges. But since it there encounters the obstacle of the barrier against incest that has been erected in the meantime, it will manifest the tendency to find, as soon as possible, the passage away from these objects, which are unsuitable in reality to other, extraneous objects, with which a real sexual life can be led. These extraneous objects will still be chosen according to the model (the imago) of the infantile objects, but over time they will attract the affection that was attached to the earlier objects. The man will leave his father and mother – according to the biblical prescription – and pursue his wife: affection and sensuality will be reunited. The highest levels of sensual passion will imply the highest psychical valuation of the object (the normal over-valuation of the sexual object by the man).

Two factors will be crucial in deciding whether this advance in the development of the libido is to fail. First, the degree of *frustration in reality* that will oppose the new object-choice and devalue it for the individual. There is no sense in setting out to make an object-choice if one is not permitted to choose, or if one has no prospect of being able to choose anything suitable. Secondly, there is the degree of *attraction* that can be manifested by the infantile objects that are about to be abandoned, which is proportional to the erotic investment assigned to them in childhood. If these two factors are strong enough, the general mechanism of neurosis formation comes into play. The libido turns away from reality, is absorbed by fantasy activity (introversion), intensifies the images of the first sexual objects and becomes fixated on those. The prohibition on incest, however, forces the libido turned towards these objects to remain in the unconscious. The masturbatory activity of the sensual current that now belongs to the unconscious plays its own part in the reinforcement of that fixation. If progress that has failed in reality is now accomplished in the fantasy, and if, in fantasy situations leading to masturbatory satisfaction, imaginary sexual objects are replaced by different objects, nothing has been altered in this state of affairs. By virtue of this substitution, fantasies become capable of reaching consciousness, while no progress is made in the real placement of the libido.

Thus it can happen that the whole of a young person's sensuality is bound, in the unconscious, to incestuous objects or, we might say, fixated on unconscious incestuous fantasies. The result is then absolute impotence, which may be further ensured by a real weakening – acquired at the same time – of the organs that perform the sexual act.

For psychical impotence, properly so-called, to come into existence, less severe conditions are required. The whole of the sensual current need not succumb to the fate of having to hide behind the affectionate current; it must have remained strong enough, or resistant enough, to inhibition, to force its way partially out into reality. But the clearest signs show that the sexual activity of such people does not have the complete psychical drive-force behind it. This activity is capricious, easily disturbed, often incorrect in its performance, and provides little enjoyment. Most importantly, however, it must make way for the affectionate current. So a limitation in the object-choice has been generated. The sensual current that has remained active seeks only objects that do not recall the forbidden incestuous people; if a person emanates an impression that might lead to a high psychical valuation, it does not lead to an excitement of sensuality, but to affection without erotic effects. The erotic life of such people remains split in the two directions that are characterized in art as heavenly and earthly (or animal) love. Where they love they do not desire, and where they desire they cannot love. They seek objects that they do not need to love, in order to keep their sensuality far from their beloved objects, and the strange failure of psychical impotence recurs according to the laws of 'complex sensitivity' and the 'return of the repressed', when, in the object chosen to avoid incest, one feature, and usually an inconspicuous one, recalls the object that is to be avoided.

The chief means of protection against such a disturbance that a person can employ in this division of love consists in the psychical *debasement* of the sexual object, while the over-valuation normally applied to the sexual object is reserved for the incestuous object and its substitutes. As the condition of debasement is fulfilled, sensuality can express itself freely, allowing significant sexual achievements and a high degree of pleasure. Another connection contributes to this result. People in whom the affectionate and the sensual currents have not properly converged also generally have a love-life that is not especially refined; perverse sexual goals have been preserved there, the non-fulfilment of which is felt to be a severe deprivation of pleasure, but fulfilment of which appears possible only with the debased, despised sexual object.

We can now understand the motives behind the fantasies of a boy, mentioned in the first of our 'contributions', which reduced his mother to the status of a prostitute. They are efforts to bridge the gulf between the two currents of the love-life, in fantasy at least, and to acquire the mother as an object of sensuality by debasing her.

2

So far we have examined psychical impotence from a medicinal and psychological point of view, which is not justified by the title of this essay. But we shall see that we needed this introduction in order to have access to our actual theme.

We have reduced psychical impotence to the non-convergence of the affectionate and the sensual currents in erotic life, and we have explained this inhibition of development with reference to the influences of powerful childhood fixations and the later frustration that came about with the arrival of the barrier against incest in the meantime. There is one chief objection to this theory: it gives us too much, it explains to us why certain people suffer from psychical impotence, but makes it seem mysterious to us that others are able to escape that illness. Since all manifest elements under consideration – the strong infantile fixation, the prohibition on incest, and frustration in the years of development after puberty – must be acknowledged by almost all civilized people, we would be justified in expecting that psychical impotence was a universal illness of the civilized, and not an illness of certain individuals.

The obvious way to escape this conclusion would be to point to the quantitative factor of the cause of the illness, to the greater or lesser contributions of the individual causal elements responsible for whether or not a recognizably successful illness results from them. But although I must acknowledge this answer to be the correct one, I do not intend to use it to dismiss the conclusion. On the contrary, I wish to posit the assertion that psychical impotence is far more widespread than we imagine, and that a certain degree of it actually characterizes the erotic life of the civilized human being.

If, rather than restricting psychical impotence to the failure of coital action, where the intention of pleasure is present and the genital apparatus is intact, we extend the concept, we may add those men who are described as psychoanaesthetics, in whom the action itself never fails, but is performed without any particular pleasure: a condition that occurs more frequently than one would wish to think. Psychoanalytic examination in such cases reveals the same aetiological elements that we have encountered with psychical impotence in the narrower sense, although the symptomatic differences are not at first explained. From psychoanaesthetic men we are led by an easily justifiable analogy to the very large number of frigid women, whose behaviour in love cannot actually be better described or understood than by being equated with the more conspicuous psychical impotence of the man.[3]

But if, rather than extending the concept of psychical impotence, we consider the nuances of its symptomatology, we cannot rule out the insight that men's behaviour in love in our contemporary civilized world generally bears the stamp of psychical impotence. The affectionate and the sensual currents converge as they should only in a very small minority of civilized people; in almost every case the man almost feels restricted in his sexual activity by respect for the woman, and only develops his full potency if he has a debased sexual object before him. This in turn is partly explained by the fact that his sexual goals include perverse components, which he does not dare satisfy with the women he respects. He can only have complete sexual pleasure if he is able to abandon himself unreservedly to satisfaction, and he does not dare do this with his lawful wife. Hence his need for a debased sexual object, a woman who is ethically inferior to himself, to whom he does not have to ascribe aesthetic considerations, who does not know him, who is not able to judge him with reference to the other circumstances of his life. He is happiest devoting his sexual power to such a woman, even if all of his affection belongs to a superior woman. It may be that the tendency, which we so often observe, of men of the highest social classes to choose a woman of a lower class as a long-term lover or even a wife, is merely the consequence of the need for a debased sexual object, psychologically connected to the possibility of complete satisfaction.

I have no hesitation in holding the elements at work in true psychical impotence – the intense incestuous fixation of childhood and the real frustration of adolescence – responsible for this so frequent attitude of civilized men in their love-life. It is rather unpleasant to say so, and it is also paradoxical, but nevertheless it must be said: in order to feel truly free in one's erotic life, and thus also happy, one must overcome respect for the woman, and become familiar with the idea of incest with one's mother or sister. Anyone who subjects himself to serious self-examination in regard to this demand will doubtless find within himself that he considers the sexual act as basically something debasing, something that stains and sullies, not only in the physical sense. He will only be able to seek the origin of this appreciation, which he will certainly not be happy to admit, during that time of his youth when his sensual current was already strongly developed, but when its satisfaction was forbidden almost equally with an extraneous as with an incestuous object.

In our civilization women also undergo the after-effects of their upbringing and, at the same time, the repercussions of men's behaviour. The damage to the woman is, of course, the same if the man does not come to them with his full potency, as if the initial over-valuation of passionate love dissolves when contempt sets in once he has possessed her. Women show little sign of a need for debasement in the sexual object; this certainly has something to do with the fact that they do not generally display anything resembling the sexual over-valuation that occurs in men. But the fact that the woman spends a long time away from sexuality, and her sensuality lingers in the fantasy, has another significant consequence for her. Often she is then no longer capable of severing the connection between sensual activity and prohibition, and she proves to be psychically impotent, frigid, once such activity is finally permitted to her. This is the source, in many women, of the tendency to keep even permitted relationships a secret for some time, and in others of the capacity to experience normal sensations as soon as the condition of prohibition is reintroduced in a secret love affair.

I think the condition of prohibition in the erotic life of women may be assimilated to the need for the debasement of the sexual object in the man. Both are the consequences of the long delay between sexual maturity and sexual activity that is required, for cultural reasons, by education and upbringing. Both seek to abolish psychical impotence, which results from the non-confluence of the affectionate and the sensual impulses. If the same causes have a very different result in women and men, this may derive from another difference in the behaviour of the two sexes. Civilized women tend not to transgress the prohibition on sexual activity during the period of waiting, and consequently establish an internal connection between prohibition and sexuality. Men usually transgress that prohibition under the condition of the debasement of the object, and thus carry that condition with them into their later erotic life.

In view of such active efforts in the contemporary civilized world to reform the sexual life, it is not superfluous to recall that psycho-analytic research makes no more claims in this direction than any other. It seeks merely to uncover connections by tracing that which is manifest back to that which is hidden. Psychoanalysis will be content if these reforms use its discoveries to replace that which is harmful with that which is more advantageous. But it cannot predict whether other institutions will not have other, perhaps more serious, sacrifices as a result.

3

The fact that the curbs placed by civilization on erotic life lead to the most universal debasement of the sexual object may divert us from the objects to the drives themselves. The harm done by the initial frustration of sexual pleasure is expressed in the fact that when it is later freely given in marriage it is no longer completely satisfying in its effects. But even unlimited sexual freedom from the very first does not produce better results. It is easy to establish that the psychical value of the need for love immediately declines once satisfaction becomes a matter of comfort. An obstacle is required if the libido is to be heightened, and where natural resistance is inadequate to satisfaction, people have in all ages introduced conventional forms of resistance in order to be able to enjoy love. That is equally true of individuals and of whole peoples. In times when no difficulties were placed in the way of the satisfaction of love, as for example during the decline of the ancient civilizations, love became worthless, life became empty, and stronger reaction formations were needed in order to re-establish the indispensable affective values. In this context we might claim that the ascetic current within Christianity created a set of psychical values for love which pagan antiquity could never give it. It assumed its supreme significance among the ascetic monks, whose lives were filled almost entirely with the struggle against libidinous temptation.

At first, of course, one will certainly be tempted to trace back the difficulties outlined here to universal features of our organic drives. In general it is certainly also true to say that the psychical significance of a drive rises in proportion to its frustration. We might imagine exposing a number of very different people to starvation under the same conditions. As the imperious need for nourishment grew, all individual differences would blur and instead make way for the uniform manifestations of a single unsatisfied drive. But is it also true that the psychical value of a drive generally declines to a similar extent with its satisfaction? We might think, for example, of the drinker's relationship to wine. Is it not the case that wine always offers the drinker the same toxic satisfaction that has been so often compared with the erotic in poetry, and which may also stand comparison with it from the scientific point of view? Has anyone ever heard of a drinker being forced to keep changing his drink because if he drinks the same one all the time it loses its flavour for him? On the contrary, habit forges the bond between the man and the sort of wine that he drinks ever more strongly. Are we aware of the drinker needing to go to a country where wine is more expensive, or where the drinking of wine is forbidden, in order to stimulate his declining satisfaction by interposing such difficulties? We are not. If we listen to the statements of our great alcoholics, such as Böcklin, concerning their relationship with wine,[4] it sounds like the purest harmony, a model for a happy marriage. Why is the lover's relationship to his sexual object so very different?

Surprising as it may sound, I think that one would have to deal with the possibility that there is something in the nature of the sexual drive itself that is unfavourable to the achievement of complete satisfaction. Within the long and difficult history of the development of the drive two elements immediately stand out which might be responsible for this difficulty. First, because of the dual-phase beginning of object-choice, with the barrier against incest coming in between, the definitive object of the sexual drive is no longer the original one, merely a surrogate for it. But psychoanalysis has taught us this: if the original object of an impulse of desire has been lost through repression, it is often represented by an infinite series of substitute objects, none of which, however, is completely satisfying. This may explain the inconstancy in the object-choice, the 'hunger for stimuli', which so often characterizes the erotic life of adults.

Secondly, we know that the sexual drive at first breaks down into a large series of components – or rather that it emerges from such a series – not all of which can be absorbed into its later formation, but must first be suppressed or put to some other use. Most important among these are the coprophilic parts of the drive, which have probably proved incompatible with our aesthetic culture since we raised our olfactory organ from ground level by walking upright; and also a high proportion of the sadistic drives belonging to love-life. But all such developmental processes affect only the upper layers of the complex structure. The fundamental processes supplying erotic excitement remain unchanged. The excremental has grown too deeply and inseparably intertwined with the sexual, the position of the genitals – *inter urinas et faeces* – remains the defining and unalterable element. Here, to modify a well-known saying of the great Napoleon, we might say: anatomy is destiny. The genitals themselves did not participate in the development of the forms of the human body as it became beautiful, they remained bestial, and consequently love is basically just as animal as it has always been. The erotic drives are difficult to educate, their education achieves now too much, now too little. That which civilization seeks to turn them into appears impossible to accomplish without a significant loss of pleasure, and the persistence of unused impulses becomes apparent in sexual activity as dissatisfaction.

We should, then, perhaps familiarize ourselves with the notion that it is impossible to balance the demands of the sexual drive with the requirements of civilization, that renunciation and illness, and, more remotely, the threat of the extinction of the human race because of its cultural development cannot be averted. This gloomy prognosis, however, is based only on the supposition that cultural dissatisfaction is the inevitable consequence of certain particularities that the sexual drive has developed under the pressure of civilization. The same incapacity of the sexual drive to yield complete satisfaction once it is subjected to the first demands of civilization becomes the source of the greatest cultural achievements, which are brought about as the result of a sublimation, pushed ever further onwards, of its drive components. For, what reason would people have for putting the sexual drive-forces to other uses if, by some distribution of those forces, they could have provided complete satisfaction of desire? People would be unable to break away from that desire, and would accomplish no further progress. So it seems that it is the irreducible differences between the demands of the two drives – the sexual and the egoistic – that make people capable of ever higher accomplishments, although there is always the constant danger to which weaker individuals are at present subject in the form of neurosis.

The intention of science is neither to frighten nor to console. But I myself am willing to admit that such far-reaching conclusions as those set out above should be established on a broader basis, and that perhaps other modes of development for humanity will be able to correct those that are treated here in isolation.

(1912)

## Notes

1. M. Steiner, 'Die funktionelle Impotenz des Mannes und ihre Behandlung' ['Functional Impotence in Men and its Treatment'], 1907 [*Wiener medizinische Presse*, vol. 48, Sp. 1535]. W. Stekel, in *Nervöse Angstzustände und ihre Behandlung* [*Nervous Anxiety and its Treatment*], [Berlin and] Vienna, 1908 (2nd edition, 1912). – Ferenczi, 'Analytische Deutung und Behandlung der psychosexuellen Impotenz beim Manne' [correctly: des Mannes] ['Analytical Interpretation and Treatment of Psychosexual Impotence in Men'], *Psychiatrische-neurologische Wochenschrift*, 1908.
2. W. Stekel: loc. cit., pp. 191ff.
3. And it should be freely admitted that frigidity in women is a complex subject, and one that is also approachable from another direction.
4. G. Floerke: *Zehn Jahre mit Böcklin* [*Ten Years with Böcklin*], 2nd edition [Munich], 1902, p. 16.

# Formulations on the Two Principles of Psychic Functioning

We have long observed that every neurosis has the effect, and so probably the purpose, of forcing the patient out of real life, of alienating him from reality. Such a fact could not escape Pierre Janet's attention; he spoke of a loss *'de la fonction du réel'* as a specific characteristic of neurotics, although without uncovering the connection between this dysfunction and the basic conditions of neurosis.[1]

We have gained some insight into this connection by introducing the process of repression into the aetiology of neurosis. The neurotic turns away from reality because he finds either the whole or parts of it unbearable. The most extreme type of this turning away from reality is exhibited in certain cases of hallucinatory psychosis where the patient attempts to deny the event that has triggered his insanity (Griesinger). Actually, though, every neurotic does the same thing with some fragment of reality.[2] Thus we are presented with the task of studying the development of the relationship of neurotics – and mankind in general – to reality, and so of assimilating the psychological significance of the real outside world into the framework of our theories.

We psychologists grounded in psychoanalysis have become accustomed to taking as our starting point unconscious psychic processes, the peculiarities of which we have come to know through analysis. We consider these to be the older, primary psychic processes, remnants of a phase of development in which they were the only kind. The highest tendency obeyed by these primary processes is easy to identify; we call it the pleasure-unpleasure principle (or the pleasure principle for short). These processes strive to gain pleasure; our psychic activity draws back from any action that might arouse unpleasure (repression). Our dreams at night, our tendency when awake to recoil from painful impressions, these are vestiges of the rule of this principle and evidence of its power.

I am relying on trains of thought developed elsewhere (in the general section of *The Interpretation of Dreams*) when I postulate that the state of equilibrium in the psyche was originally disrupted by the urgent demands of inner needs. At this stage, whatever was thought of (wished for) was simply hallucinated, as still happens every night with our dream-thoughts.[3] It was due only to the failure of the anticipated satisfaction, the disillusionment as it were, that this attempt at satisfaction by means of hallucination was abandoned. Instead, the psychic apparatus had to resolve to form an idea of the real circumstances in the outside world and to endeavour actually to change them. With this, a new principle of psychic activity was initiated; now ideas were formed no longer of what was pleasant, but of what was real, even if this happened to be unpleasant.[4] This inception of the *reality principle* proved to be a momentous step.

1) First, the new demands necessitated a series of adjustments in the psychic apparatus, which, due to our insufficient or uncertain knowledge, we can deal with only in passing here.

The increased significance of external reality heightened in turn the significance of the sense organs directed towards that outside world, and also of the *consciousness* attached to these, which now learnt how to discern sensory qualities in addition to the qualities of pleasure and unpleasure, previously its only concern. A specific function of *attention* was set up with the task of periodically scanning the outside world in order to assimilate its data in advance, should an urgent inner need arise. This activity seeks out sensory impressions rather than waiting for them to occur. Probably at the same time, a system of *retention* was set up with the task of storing the results of this periodic activity of consciousness, an element of what we call *memory*.

In place of repression, which excluded certain of the emerging ideas – those deemed unpleasurable – from being invested with energy, there arose a process of impartial *judgement*, whose task it was to decide if a particular idea was true or false – that is, corresponded with reality or not – a decision reached via comparisons made with memory traces of reality.

Motor discharge, which under the rule of the pleasure principle had served to relieve the psychic apparatus from increases in stimulation by means of innervations sent inside the body (physical gestures, expressions of emotion), was now given a new function, being deployed to make expedient alterations to external reality. It was transformed into *action*.

It now became necessary to hold motor discharge (action) in check, and this was achieved via the *thought process*, which evolved from basic ideation. Thought became endowed with qualities that enabled the psychic apparatus to tolerate the increase in tension from stimuli while discharge was deferred. A thought process is essentially a trial run of an action, displacing smaller quantities of invested energy and involving a low expenditure (discharge) of these. For this purpose, freely displaceable investments of energy had to be converted into fixed ones, which was achieved by raising the level of the whole process of energy investment. Thought – in so far as it went beyond simple ideation and dealt with the relations between object-impressions – was probably originally unconscious and did not acquire qualities perceptible to consciousness until it became linked to the memory traces of words.

2) A general tendency of our psychic apparatus, which can be traced back to the economic principle of conserving expenditure, seems to manifest itself in the tenacity with which we cling to existing sources of pleasure and the difficulty we have in giving these up. At the inception of the reality principle, one kind of thought activity split away, remaining exempt from reality-testing and continuing to obey only the pleasure principle.[5] This is *fantasizing*, which begins with children's play, then later, as *daydreaming*, ceases to rely on actual objects.

3) The transition from the pleasure principle to the reality principle with all its ensuing ramifications for the psyche, schematically

confined here to a single sentence, is actually achieved neither all at once nor along a uniform front. While the ego drives are undergoing this development, the sexual drives diverge in a highly significant way. The sexual drives initially behave auto-erotically, finding their satisfaction in the subject's own body and therefore never experiencing the state of frustration that necessitated the introduction of the reality principle. Later, when they do begin the process of finding an object, this is promptly interrupted by the long latency period that delays sexual development until puberty. As a result of these two factors – auto-eroticism and latency – the sexual drive is arrested in its psychic development and continues to be ruled for much longer by the pleasure principle, in many people never managing to free itself from this at all.

As a result of these conditions, a closer relationship is established, on the one hand, between the sexual drive and fantasizing and, on the other, between the ego drives and the activities of consciousness. This relationship strikes us, in healthy and neurotic people alike, as a very intimate one, even if the above considerations of developmental psychology show it to be *secondary*. The continuing effects of auto-eroticism make it possible for the easier, instantaneous satisfaction of fantasizing about the sexual object to be retained for so long in place of real satisfaction, which involves making efforts and tolerating delays. Repression remains all-powerful in the realm of fantasy; it is able to inhibit ideas *in statu nascendi* – before they reach consciousness – if their being invested with energy could cause a release of unpleasure. This is the weak spot in our psychic organization that can be used to bring already rational thought processes back under the sway of the pleasure principle. Thus an essential element in the psyche's predisposition to neurosis results from the delay in educating the sexual drive to take account of reality, and from the conditions that make this delay possible.

4) Just as the pleasure-ego can do nothing but *wish*, pursue pleasure and avoid unpleasure, so the reality-ego has no other task than to strive for what is *useful* and to protect itself from what is harmful.[6] By taking over from the pleasure principle, the reality

principle is really just safeguarding it, not deposing it. A momentary pleasure with uncertain consequences is given up, but only in order to obtain, by the new approach, a more secure pleasure later on. Still, the endopsychic impact of this transition has been so powerful that it is reflected in a specific religious myth. The doctrine that the – voluntary or enforced – renunciation of earthly pleasures will be rewarded in the afterlife is simply the mythopoeic projection of this psychic transformation. Following this principle to its logical conclusion, *religions* have been able to bring about the absolute renunciation of pleasure in this life in return for the promise of recompense in a future existence; by so doing they have not conquered the pleasure principle. *Science* comes closest to achieving this conquest, but scientific work, too, provides intellectual pleasure and promises practical gain eventually.

5) *Education* can without question be described as an impetus to overcoming the pleasure principle and replacing it with the reality principle; thus it assists the process of development undergone by the ego. For this purpose, it uses the educators' love as a form of reward, and therefore goes awry when a spoilt child believes it possesses this love anyway and cannot lose it under any circumstances.

6) *Art* brings about a reconciliation of the two principles in a unique way. The artist is originally someone who, unable to come to terms with the renunciation of drive satisfaction initially demanded by reality, turns away from it and gives free rein to erotic and ambitious wishes in his fantasy life. Thanks to special gifts, however, he finds his way back to reality from this fantasy world by shaping his fantasies into new kinds of reality, which are appreciated by people as valid representations of the real world. Thus in a certain way he actually becomes the hero, king, creator, favourite he wanted to be, without having to make the enormous detour of actually changing the outside world. But he can achieve this only because other people feel the same dissatisfaction he does at the renunciations imposed by reality, and this dissatisfaction, a result of the transition from pleasure principle to reality principle, is itself an aspect of reality.[7]

7) As the ego undergoes the transformation from *pleasure-ego* into *reality-ego*, the sexual drives undergo the changes that lead from initial auto-eroticism, through various intermediate phases, to object-love in the service of the reproductive function. If it is true that every stage along each of these two courses of development can become the site of a predisposition towards subsequent neurotic illness, it seems likely that the form this illness takes (the *choice of neurosis*) will depend on which phase of ego or libido development the predisposing arrest occurred in. The – as yet uninvestigated – chronological characteristics of these two developments, the possible variations in their respective rates of progress, thus take on a whole new significance.

8) The strangest characteristic of unconscious (repressed) processes, to which the investigator can become accustomed only by dint of great self-discipline, results from their total disregard for reality-testing; thought-reality is equated with external reality, the wish with its fulfilment, just as occurs spontaneously under the rule of the old pleasure principle. For this reason it is extremely difficult to distinguish between unconscious fantasies and memories that have become unconscious. But we should never be tempted to apply the criteria of reality to repressed psychic formations by, say, underestimating the role played by fantasies in the creation of symptoms just because they are not real, or by attributing a neurotic feeling of guilt to some other source because no actual crime can be ascertained. We have to use the currency that prevails in the country we are exploring – in our case, the *neurotic currency*. Suppose, for example, we try to decipher the following dream. A man, who had looked after his father during his long and agonizing fatal illness, reports having repeatedly dreamt in the months following his death: *his father was alive again and was talking with him as usual. But at the same time he felt extremely distressed that his father was indeed dead and was just unaware of the fact.* The only way to make this absurd-sounding dream comprehensible is to add, after 'that his father was indeed dead', the words 'as he had wished' or 'as a result of his wish', and, at the end, the words 'that he had wished for it'. The dream-thought, then, is as follows: It

distresses him to remember how he was driven to wishing for his father's death (as a release) while he was still alive, and how awful it would be if his father had sensed this. So we are dealing with the familiar case of self-reproach after the loss of a loved one, the reproach in this instance stemming from the significance of the death-wish against the father in infancy.

The shortcomings of this little essay – more introduction than exposition – are perhaps only slightly excused if I insist they were inevitable. In the few sentences on the psychic consequences of adapting to the reality principle, I had to touch on ideas that I would have preferred to hold back for now, and which will certainly require a great deal of effort to substantiate. Still, I hope well-disposed readers will recognize where in this work, too, I have had to bow to the reality principle.

(1911)

## Notes

1. [P.] Janet [*Les névroses*, Paris] (1909).
2. Otto Rank has recently pointed out a remarkably clear intimation of this causality in Schopenhauer's *Die Welt als Wille und Vorstellung*. (See Rank ['Schopenhauer über den Wahnsinn'. *Zentbl. Psychoanal.* 1], 1910.)
3. The state of sleep replicates psychic life as it was before the recognition of reality, a prerequisite of sleep being the deliberate shutting out of reality (the sleep-wish).
4. I shall try to flesh out this schematic account with a few further remarks: It will rightly be objected that any organization devoted entirely to the pleasure principle, neglecting the reality of the outside world, could not survive for even the shortest time and so could not have arisen in the first place. Our recourse to a fiction like this can, however, be justified if we point out that the suckling infant very nearly embodies just such a psychic system, if we just include the maternal care. It probably hallucinates the fulfilment of its inner needs, then betrays its displeasure at the increasing stimulus and continued absence of satisfaction through the motor discharge

of crying and flailing about, upon which it actually receives the satisfaction it had hallucinated. Later as a child it learns to use these discharge outlets as a deliberate means of expression. Since nursing is the prototype of all subsequent child-care, the rule of the pleasure principle can really come to an end only with a complete psychic detachment from the parents. – A nice example of a psychic system cut off from the stimuli of the outside world, able to satisfy even its nutritional requirements autistically (to use Bleuler's term), is offered by the bird embryo with its food supply enclosed within the eggshell, maternal care being restricted to the provision of warmth. – I shall regard it as less a correction than an elaboration of the above scheme if it is required to include devices that enable the system living by the pleasure principle to withdraw from the stimuli of the real world. These devices simply correspond to 'repression', which treats inner unpleasurable stimuli as if they were external, projecting them into the outside world.

5. Just as a nation whose wealth is based on exploiting its natural resources sets aside a specific area, like Yellowstone Park, to be preserved in its wild state and spared from the changes brought about by civilization.

6. The superiority of the reality-ego over the pleasure-ego is aptly expressed in Bernard Shaw's words: 'To be able to choose the line of greatest advantage instead of yielding in the direction of least resistance.' (*Man and Superman: A Comedy and a Philosophy*.)

7. Cf. similar in O. Rank [*Der Künstler, Ansätze zu einer Sexualpsychologie*, Leipzig and Vienna] (1907).

# Family Romances

The separation of the individual, as he grows up, from the authority of his parents is one of the most necessary achievements of his development, yet at the same time one of the most painful. It is absolutely necessary for it to take place, and we may presume that it has been achieved in some measure by everyone who has developed into a normal person. Indeed, the progress of society in general rests upon the opposition between the generations. On the other hand, there is a class of neurotics whose condition is recognizably determined by their having failed in this task.

For a small child his parents are at first his only authority and the source of all he believes in. To become like them – that is to say, like the parent of one's own sex – to grow up and be like one's father or mother, is the most intense desire of these early years, and the one most fraught with consequences. However, as the child develops intellectually he cannot help gradually getting to know the category his parents belong to. He becomes acquainted with other parents, compares them with his own, and so becomes entitled to doubt the incomparable and unique status he once attributed to them. Small events in the child's life may induce in him a mood of dissatisfaction and so provide him with an occasion to start criticizing his parents and to support this critical attitude with the recently acquired knowledge that other parents are in some respects to be preferred to them. From the psychology of neurosis we know that, along with other factors, the most intense feelings of sexual rivalry play a part in this. The reason for such a reaction is obviously a feeling of being slighted. There are all too many occasions when a child is slighted, or at least feels that he has been slighted, that he does not have the whole of his parents' love, and when above all he regrets having to share it with brothers and sisters. The feeling that his own affection is not fully reciprocated then finds expression in the idea, often consciously recollected from early childhood, that he is a stepchild or an adopted child. Many people who have not become victims of neurosis frequently remember such occasions when – usually as a result of something they had read – they interpreted and reacted in this way to hostile behaviour on the part of their parents. But here the influence of sex is already evident, in that a boy is far more inclined to feel hostile impulses towards his father than towards his mother, and has a far more intense desire to free himself from *him* than from *her*. In this respect the imaginative activity of girls may prove much weaker. In these childhood emotions, which are consciously recalled, we find the factor that enables us to understand the nature of myths.

Seldom recalled consciously, but nearly always demonstrable through psychoanalysis, is the next stage in the development of this incipient estrangement from the parents, which may be described as the *family romances of neurotics*. For an essential feature of neurosis, and also of any considerable talent, is a special imaginative activity, which reveals itself first in children's games and then, beginning roughly in the prepubertal period, seizes upon the theme of family relations. A characteristic example of this peculiar imaginative activity is the familiar phenomenon of *daydreaming*[1] which continues long after puberty. Precise observation of daydreams shows that their purpose is wish-fulfilment and the correction of real life, and that they have two principal aims, one of them erotic and the other ambitious (though behind the latter the erotic aim is usually present too). At about this time, then, the child's imagination is occupied with the task of ridding himself of his parents, of whom he now has a low opinion, and replacing them by others, usually of superior social standing. In this connection he makes use of the chance concurrence of these aims with actual experiences, such as an acquaintanceship with the lord of the manor or some landowner in the country, or with some aristocrat in the city. Such fortuitous experiences arouse the child's envy, which then finds expression in a fantasy that replaces both parents by others who are grander. The technique used in developing such fantasies, which at this period are of course conscious, depends on the child's ingenuity and the material he has at his disposal. It is also a question of how much or how little effort has gone into making the fantasies seem probable. This stage is reached at a time when the child still lacks any knowledge of the sexual determinants of procreation.

When the child subsequently learns about the different sexual roles of the father and the mother, when he understands that *pater semper incertus est*, whereas the mother is *certissima*[2] the family romance is subject to a peculiar restriction: it contents itself with raising the status of the father, while no longer casting doubt on descent from the mother, which is something unalterable. This second (sexual) stage of the family romance rests on a second motive, which was not present at the first (asexual) stage. Knowledge of sexual processes gives rise to a tendency on the part of the child to picture to himself various erotic situations and relationships. The motive force behind this is a desire to involve his mother – who is the object of extreme sexual curiosity – in situations of secret infidelity and in secret love affairs. In this way the first (as it were asexual) fantasies are now brought up to the level of the current state of knowledge.

Moreover, the motive of revenge and retaliation, which was in the foreground at the earlier stage, is still present at the later one. And as a rule it is precisely those neurotic children whose parents once punished them for sexual misbehaviour who now take revenge on them by means of fantasies of this kind.

It is in particular the younger children of a marriage who seek above all to deprive their older siblings of their prerogatives by inventing such stories (as in historical intrigues) and often do not recoil from attributing as many fictitious love affairs to their mother as they themselves have competitors. An interesting variant of the family romance arises when the author-hero returns to legitimacy himself, while using this device to eliminate his siblings as illegitimate. Moreover, any other special interest can direct the course of the family romance, which, thanks to its versatility and wide applicability, is adequate to all kinds of endeavour. In this way, for instance, the little fantasist can eliminate his blood-relationship to a sister who happens to attract him sexually.

We would remind anyone who turns away in horror from the depravity we have attributed to the mind of the child, or may even wish to deny that such things are possible, that none of these seemingly hostile fictions are really ill-intended, but preserve, under a slight disguise, the child's original affection for his parents. The infidelity and ingratitude are only apparent. For if one takes a close look at the commonest of these romances – the replacement of both parents or just the father by grander personages – one discovers that these new, distinguished parents are provided with features that derive from the child's actual memories of his real, more humble parents: the child does not really eliminate his father, but exalts him. Indeed, the whole effort to replace the real father by another who is more distinguished is merely an expression of the child's longing for the happy times gone by, when his father seemed to him the strongest and most distinguished of men, and his mother the dearest and loveliest of women. He turns away from the man he now knows as his father to the one he believed in as a child. The fantasy is actually only an expression of regret for the happy times that have vanished. In such fantasies, then, the overestimation of the earliest years of childhood once more comes into its own. An interesting contribution to this theme is supplied by the study of dreams. For the interpretation of dreams tells us that when we dream of the Emperor or the Empress, even late in life, these distinguished personalities represent our father and mother.[3] The child's overestimation of his parents is thus retained in the dreams of the normal adult.

(1909)

## Notes

1. On this cf. Freud, 'Hysterische Phantasien und ihre Beziehung zur Bisexualität' ['Hysterical Phantasies and their Relation to Bisexuality']

(*Gesammelte Werke*, vol. VI), where references to the relevant literature may be found.

2. [An old legal tag: 'The father is always uncertain, (the mother) most certain.']

3. *The Interpretation of Dreams*, 8th edn, p. 242 [VI. E] (*Gesammelte Werke*, vol. II/III).

# Hysterical Phantasies and
# their Relation to Bisexuality

We are all familiar with the delusional writings of paranoiacs whose subject is the greatness and suffering of their own self and which assume quite typical, almost monotonous forms. In addition, numerous accounts have acquainted us with the peculiar performances through which certain perverts stage their sexual satisfaction, whether in their thoughts or in practice. Nevertheless, some readers may be surprised to learn that quite analogous psychical formations occur regularly in all psychoneuroses, in particular hysteria, and that these so-called hysterical phantasies can be seen to have important connections with the development of neurotic symptoms.

What are termed the daydreams of youth are a common source and normal model for all these phantastical creations and they have already received a certain, if as yet insufficient, degree of attention in the literature.[1] It is possible that they occur with equal frequency in both sexes: in girls and women they appear without exception to be erotic and in men to be either erotic or ambitious. But even in men, the significance of the erotic factor should not be relegated to second place. Closer inspection of a man's daydreams usually reveals that all his heroic acts are performed and all his achievements won with the sole purpose of pleasing a woman and of her preferring him to other men.[2] These phantasies are wish-fulfilments that stem from privation and longing. They are rightly called 'daydreams', for they are the key to understanding the dreams we have at night in which the nucleus of dream-formation is established by nothing other than these complicated, distorted day phantasies that are misunderstood by the conscious psychical agency.

These daydreams are invested and charged with great interest, carefully tended and on the whole shyly protected as if they were among the most intimate treasures of one's personality. But it is easy enough to recognize someone in the street who is involved in a daydream from the way they give a sudden smile, as if absent, talk to themselves or quicken their pace as if to a run, all of which mark the peak of the situation that is being dreamt. – Every hysterical attack that I have been able to investigate turned out to be the involuntary onset of a daydream of this kind. Having observed this, one is left in no doubt that phantasies of this kind can just as well be unconscious as conscious, and as soon as the latter have become unconscious they can also become pathogenic, i.e. be expressed in symptoms and attacks. Under favourable conditions an unconscious phantasy like this can still be caught hold of by the conscious. One of my patients, whose attention I had drawn to her phantasies, told me that once in the street she had suddenly found that she was crying, and on rapid reflection as to why she was really crying she got hold of the phantasy that she had begun an affair with a virtuoso pianist who was well known in the town (but with whom she was not personally acquainted), had had a child with him (she had no children), and she and the child had then been abandoned by him and left in poverty. At this point in the romance she burst into tears.

Unconscious phantasies are either those that have always been unconscious and were formed in the unconscious or, as is more frequently the case, those that were once conscious phantasies, daydreams which have then deliberately been forgotten and got into the unconscious through 'repression'. Their content has then either remained the same or undergone distortions such that the phantasy that is now unconscious represents a descendant of the phantasy that was once conscious. The unconscious phantasy now occupies a very important relationship with the person's sexual life, namely that it is identical with the phantasy which gave this person sexual satisfaction during a period of masturbation. The masturbatory act (onanistic in the broadest sense) was at the time composed of two items, the calling up of the phantasy and the active behaviour leading to self-gratification at the height of the phantasy. This compound is itself known to be soldered together.[3] Originally, the action was a purely auto-erotic undertaking to gain pleasure from a specific area of the body which may be called erogenous. Later the action merged with a wishful idea from the sphere of object love and served partially to realize the situation in which this phantasy culminated. If the subject then gives up this kind of satisfaction, which is derived from both phantasy and masturbation, the action is omitted but the phantasy turns from being conscious to unconscious. If no other means of sexual satisfaction appears, if the subject remains abstinent and does not succeed in sublimating the libido, that is, in diverting his or her sexual excitation to higher aims, then the condition is established for the unconscious phantasy to be refreshed and to proliferate and, as regards at least a part of its content, to put itself into effect with the whole force of the need for love, in the form of a pathological symptom.

These kinds of unconscious phantasies are the earliest psychical stages of a large number of hysterical symptoms. Hysterical symptoms are nothing other than unconscious phantasies whose representation has been brought about by 'conversion', and, in as much as they are somatic symptoms, are drawn with reasonable frequency from the sphere of the same sexual sensations and motor innervations that had originally accompanied the phantasies when they were still conscious. In this way the attempt to break the habit of masturbation really is cancelled out, and the ultimate aim of the entire pathological process, the restoration of the original primary sexual satisfaction, is always reached by a kind of approximation – if never completely achieved.

Anyone studying hysteria will quickly turn their interest from its symptoms to the phantasies from which they arise. The technique of psychoanalysis first enables these unconscious phantasies to be guessed from the symptoms and then for them to become conscious in the patient. In this way it has now been found that the unconscious phantasies of hysterics correspond completely in terms of content to the situations in which perverts consciously obtain gratification. And should one be at a loss for examples of this kind one need only recall the world-famous performances of the Roman emperors, the madness of which was of course determined only by the enormous and unrestrained power of the creators of these phantasies. The delusional creations of paranoiacs are similar kinds of phantasy, although they have become directly conscious; they are borne by the sado-masochistic component of the sexual drive and likewise may find their exact counterpart in certain of the unconscious phantasies of hysterics. Moreover, cases are also known – and this is of practical significance – in which hysterics do not express their phantasies as symptoms but as conscious realizations, and in so doing fabricate and stage assassination attempts, and acts of cruelty and of sexual aggression.

This method of psychoanalytic investigation, which leads from symptoms which are conspicuous through to phantasies which are hidden and unconscious, conveys everything that can be discovered about the sexuality of psychoneurotics, including the fact that is the focus of this short preliminary publication.

Probably as a consequence of the difficulties that stand in the way of the unconscious phantasies in their endeavour to find expression, the relationship between phantasies and symptoms is not a simple one, but rather one which is complicated in numerous ways.[4] As a rule, that is, once the neurosis has developed fully and existed for some time, a symptom no longer corresponds to one single unconscious phantasy but to a number of them, and not in an arbitrary way but according to a regular pattern of composition. It is unlikely that all of these complications will be developed at the beginning of the illness.

For the sake of general interest I want at this stage to go beyond the immediate context of this paper and add a series of formulations that attempt to give an increasingly exhaustive description of the nature of hysterical symptoms. They do not contradict each other; rather, they constitute either conceptions that are sharper and more complete, or that are taken from different points of view.

1) Hysterical symptoms are memory-symbols of certain (traumatic) impressions and experiences that are active.

2) Hysterical symptoms are substitutes, engendered by 'conversion', for the associative return of these traumatic experiences.

3) Hysterical symptoms express – as do other psychical formations – the fulfilment of a wish.

4) Hysterical symptoms are the realization of an unconscious phantasy that serves the fulfilment of a wish.

5) Hysterical symptoms serve sexual satisfaction and represent a part of the subject's sexual life (corresponding to one of the components of his or her sexual drive).

6) Hysterical symptoms correspond to the return of a means of sexual satisfaction that was real in infant life and has since been repressed.

7) Hysterical symptoms arise as a compromise between two opposing stirrings of the affects or of the drives, one of which endeavours to express a partial drive or a component of the sexual constitution and the other to suppress it.

8) Hysterical symptoms can stand in for various unconscious non-sexual stirrings, but they cannot be devoid of sexual significance.

Of these various definitions it is the seventh that most exhaustively expresses the nature of hysterical symptoms as the realizations of unconscious phantasies, and with the eighth a proper acknowledgement of the sexual factor is given. Some of the previous formulations are preliminary stages of this formulation and are contained within it.

This relationship between symptoms and phantasies means that it is not difficult to move from the psychoanalysis of these symptoms to a knowledge of the components of the sexual drive which controls the individual, as I have set out in the *Three Essays on Sexual Theory* [*Standard Edition*, vol. VII]. In a number of cases, however, this investigation produces an unexpected result. It shows that many symptoms cannot be resolved by an unconscious sexual phantasy or a series of phantasies of which the most significant and earliest is sexual in nature. To remove the symptom two sexual phantasies are needed, one of which has a masculine and the other a feminine character, so that one of these phantasies arises from a homosexual impulse. This development does not affect the proposition given in formulation 7; in other words, hysterical symptoms necessarily represent a compromise between a libidinous and a repressive impulse, but they may additionally represent a union of two libidinous phantasies of opposite sexual character.

I will refrain from giving examples of this proposition. Experience has taught me that short analyses condensed into extracts can never give the impression of decisive proof which was one's intention in citing them. The report of fully analysed cases will, however, have to be reserved for another occasion.

I will content myself then with putting forward the proposition and elucidating its significance:

9) A hysterical symptom is the expression, on the one hand, of an unconscious sexual phantasy that is masculine and, on the other, of one that is feminine.

I want to draw particular attention to the fact that I cannot attribute the same general validity to this proposition as I have claimed for the other formulations. It applies, as far as I can see, neither to all the symptoms of one case, nor to all cases. On the contrary, it is not difficult to point to cases in which the impulses of the opposite sexes have been expressed as separate symptoms so that the symptoms of hetero- and homosexuality can be as sharply distinguished from one another as the phantasies concealed behind them. Yet the relationship put forward in the ninth formula is common enough and, where it occurs, significant enough to deserve particular emphasis. It seems to me to signify the highest level of complexity that can be attained by the determination of a hysterical symptom, and is therefore only to be expected of a neurosis that has existed for some length of time and within which a great deal of organizational work has gone on.[5]

The bisexual meaning of hysterical symptoms that is, in any event, demonstrable in numerous cases is undoubtedly interesting as evidence for the claim I have advanced,[6] that man's postulated bisexual disposition can be observed with particular clarity in the psychoanalysis of psychoneurotics. A completely analogous process occurs in the same field when someone masturbating tries in their conscious phantasies to empathize with both the man and the woman in the imagined situation. Further counterparts indicate certain hysterical attacks in which the patient plays both parts in the underlying sexual phantasy at once, as, for example, in a case I observed, where the patient holds her gown against her body with one hand (as the woman), and tries to tear it off with the other (as the man). This contradictory simultaneity is to a fair degree responsible for the incomprehensibility of the situation which is otherwise so vividly represented in the attack and is therefore extremely well suited to veiling the unconscious phantasy that is at work.

In psychoanalytic treatment it is very important to be prepared for a symptom to have a bisexual meaning. We need not then be surprised or disconcerted if a symptom seems to persist undiminished even though one of its sexual meanings has been solved; it may be maintained by a meaning that belongs to the opposite sex and that we may not have suspected. During the treatment of cases like this we can also observe that while one sexual meaning is being analysed, the patient finds it convenient constantly to switch the thoughts that come to him into the field of contrary meaning, as if onto a neighbouring track.

(1908)


*Notes*

1. See Breuer and Freud, *Studies in Hysteria*, P. Janet, *Névroses et idées fixes* [*Neuroses and idées fixes*], 1898, vol. 1, Havelock Ellis, *Studies in the Psychology of Sex*, 1899, Freud, *Die Traumdeutung* [*The Interpretation of Dreams*], 1900 [*Standard Edition*, vols IV, V], A. Pick, 'Über pathologische Träumerei und ihre Beziehung zur Hysterie', ['On pathological

daydreaming and its relation to hysteria'], *Jb. Psychiat. Neuröl.*, vol. 14, 1896.

**2.** H. Ellis draws a similar conclusion [*Studies in the Psychology of Sex*, 3rd edn., 1910, pp. 185 ff.].

**3.** See Freud, *Drei Abhandlungen zur Sexualtheorie* [*Three Essays on Sexual Theory*] (1905) [Chapter I, section 1A].

**4.** The same thing applies to the relationship between the 'latent' dream-thoughts and the elements of the 'manifest' dream-content. See the section on 'dream-work' in Chapter VI of *The Interpretation of Dreams*.

**5.** I. Sadger recently discovered the proposition under discussion in his own independent psychoanalytic work. However, he does claim that it has general validity. 'Die Bedeutung der psychoanalytischen Methode nach Freud' ['The significance of the psychoanalytic method according to Freud'], *Zentbl. Nervenheilk. Psychiat.*, 1907, N. F. 18, 41.

**6.** *Three Essays on Sexual Theory* [*Standard Edition*, vol. VII].

# Fragment of an Analysis of Hysteria (Dora)

## Foreword

If, after a considerable interval, I am seeking to substantiate the assertions I made in 1895 and 1896 concerning the pathogenesis of hysterical symptoms and the psychical processes at work in hysteria, by publishing a detailed account of the history of an illness and its treatment, I cannot omit the writing of this foreword, which will justify certain of my actions while at the same time returning the expectations that readers may have of it to an appropriate level.

It was certainly awkward for me to have to publish the results of my research, especially results so surprising and uncompromising, when they had not been subjected to the necessary examination by colleagues in my field. But it is hardly any less awkward for me now to begin to submit to general judgement some of the material from which I gleaned those results. I will not escape that reproach – if it was formerly said that I revealed nothing about my patients, I will now be accused of communicating things about them that should not be communicated. I hope that those who change the pretext for their accusation in this manner will be the same people as before, and from the outset I shall make no attempt to deprive them of their accusation.

I still consider the publication of my case histories a problem that is difficult for me to resolve, even if I am not in the slightest concerned about those uncomprehending and malicious individuals. The difficulties are partly technical in nature, although at the same time they arise out of the very essence of the circumstances. If it is correct to say that the cause of hysterical illnesses is to be located in the intimacies of the patient's psychosexual life, and that hysterical symptoms are the expression of her most secret repressed desires, the elucidation of a case of hysteria will inevitably reveal those intimacies and betray those secrets. It is certain that my patients would never have spoken if they had imagined the possibility that their confessions might be scientifically evaluated, and equally certain that it would be utterly futile to ask their permission to publish. Sensitive people, and probably timid ones, would in such circumstances stress the obligation of medical discretion, and regret that they could not serve science in this respect by providing it with information. But it is my opinion that the doctor has duties not only to the individual patient, but to science as well. To science – essentially this means to the many other patients who suffer from, or who will suffer from, the same illness. Publishing what one believes one knows about the causes and structure of hysteria becomes a matter of duty, while neglecting to do so becomes an act of contemptible cowardice, as long as one can avoid doing direct personal damage to the individual patient. I believe I have done everything I can to avoid damage of this kind. I have chosen a person whose destinies were played out not in Vienna but in a distant small town, and hence someone whose personal relationships must be effectively unknown; I have so carefully preserved the secret of the treatment from the very first that only one entirely trustworthy colleague could know that the girl had been my patient. I waited for four years after the conclusion of the treatment until I heard of another change in my patient's life, which led me to assume that her own interest in the events and mental processes narrated here might have faded by now. Obviously no names have been left in that might have put a reader from lay circles on to the trail; publication in a strictly scientific specialist journal was, incidentally, supposed to be a protection against such unskilled readers. Of course I cannot keep the patient herself from feeling embarrassed if the story of her own illness were to fall into her hands. But she will learn nothing from it that she does not already know, and may wonder who else might be able to learn from it that it is about her.

I know that, in this city at least, there are certain doctors who – repellently enough – would choose to read a case history of this kind not as a contribution to the psychopathology of neuroses, but as a *roman à clef* written for their own amusement. I assure this breed of reader that any future case histories will be protected against their sharp perceptions by similar guarantees of secrecy, although the use of my material will be restricted to a quite extraordinary degree as a result.

In this one case history that I have so far been able to free from the restrictions of medical discretion and the unfavourable circumstances of the situation, sexual relations are discussed freely, the sexual organs and functions are named by their proper names, and the pure-minded reader will be able to come away from my account of events convinced that I have not shied away from talking with a young girl about such subjects in such language. So, should I defend myself against this reproach as well? I simply claim the rights of the gynaecologist – or rather rights much more modest than those. It would be a sign of perverse and strange salaciousness to assume that such conversations were a good way of arousing or satisfying sexual desires. I am also inclined to express my judgement on the matter in someone else's words:

It is lamentable to have to grant space to such claims and assertions in a scientific work, but let no one reproach me for that. Let them rather level their accusations at the spirit of the age, which has brought us to the happy situation whereby no serious book can any longer be certain of surviving.[1]

I shall now reveal how I overcame the technical difficulties involved in the writing of this case history. These difficulties are considerable for a doctor, who has to carry out six or eight such psychotherapeutic treatments every day, and who cannot make notes during the session with the patient himself because in doing so he would arouse the patient's mistrust and obstruct his own understanding of the material being presented to him. The question of how a lengthy course of treatment might be recorded for the purposes of communication is another problem to which I have found no solution. In the present case, two circumstances came to my aid: first, that the duration of the treatment was not longer than three months, secondly, that the elucidations were based around two dreams – related in the middle and at the end of the cure – which were written down verbatim immediately after the session, and which provided a secure foundation for the subsequent web of interpretations and memories. I wrote down the case history itself from memory only after the cure had come to an end, while my memory was still fresh and sharpened by my interest in publication. For that reason the transcript is not absolutely – phonographically – faithful, but it can claim a high level of dependability. Nothing essential has been changed within it, except, in some places, the order of elucidations, a change undertaken for the sake of the context.

I should like to stress what will be found in this account and what will be missed out. The essay originally bore the title 'Dream and Hysteria' because it struck me as especially well suited to showing how dream interpretation weaves its way into the story of the treatment, and how, with its help, gaps in the memory can be filled and symptoms elucidated. In 1900, not without good reason, I published a painstaking and penetrating study of dreams in advance of my planned publications on the psychology of neuroses,[2] although its reception demonstrated how little understanding my colleagues still had for such efforts. In this case the objection, that my observations were not verifiably convincing because I had withheld my material, was not justified, because anyone can subject his own dreams to analytical examination, and the technique of dream interpretation is easy to learn according to the instructions and examples I give. Now, as then, I must stress that immersion in the problems of the dream is an indispensable precondition for an understanding of the psychological processes involved in hysteria and the other psychoneuroses, and that no one who wishes to spare himself that preparatory work will be able to advance even a few steps into this field. So, since this case history assumes a knowledge of dream interpretation, it will make extremely unsatisfactory reading for anyone who does not have that knowledge. Such a reader will be disturbed where he expected to be enlightened, and will surely be inclined to project the cause of his disturbance on to the author, declaring him to be a fantasist. In fact, this capacity to disturb is inherent in the phenomena of the neurosis itself; but it is masked from us by our medical habits, and only reappears when we attempt to explain it. It could only be averted completely if we were able fully to deduce neurosis from elements already known to us. But it appears highly likely that, on the contrary, the study of neurosis will spur us on to accept much that is new, and will then gradually become the object of certain knowledge. Novelty has always provoked confusion and resistance.

It would be wrong for anyone to imagine that dreams and their interpretation occupy such a prominent position in all instances of psychoanalysis as they do in this example.

If the present case history appears to receive preferential treatment in terms of the use of dreams, in other areas it is poorer than I would have wished. But its shortcomings have to do with precisely those conditions that make its publication possible. I said above that I could not fully master the material of a case history lasting about a year. This one, which lasted only three months, can be grasped as a whole and remembered; but its results remained incomplete in more than one respect. The treatment was not continued to its planned goal, but interrupted at the wishes of the patient once a certain point had been reached. By that time some mysteries in the patient's illness had still not been dealt with, and others illuminated only very imperfectly, while the continuation of the work would certainly have advanced in all areas to the final elucidation. So here I can offer only the fragment of an analysis.

Perhaps a reader familiar with the techniques demonstrated in the *Studies in Hysteria* will be surprised that it did not become possible, in three months, to provide a definitive solution at least for those symptoms that had been tackled. But this will become understandable if I mention that psychoanalytic techniques have undergone a fundamental revolution since the *Studies* were written. Back then, the work arose out of the symptoms, and their solution advanced sequentially towards its goal. I have since abandoned that technique, finding it utterly unsuited to the more delicate structure of neurosis. Now I allow the patient to determine the subject of our daily work himself, and take as my starting point whatever surface the unconscious happens to have brought to his attention. Then, though, I obtain what is required for the solution of a symptom in fragments, woven into various different contexts and scattered over very different periods of time. Despite this apparent disadvantage the new technique is far superior to the old, and without fear of contradiction it is the only possible one.

Given the incompleteness of my analytical results I had no other choice but to follow the example of those researchers who are so happy to bring the inestimable, though mutilated, remains of antiquity to light after their long burial. Using the best models known to me from other analyses, I have completed that which was incomplete, but, like a conscientious archaeologist, I have taken care, in each case, to reveal where my construction added to the authentic parts.

I myself have deliberately introduced incompleteness of another kind. I have not generally described the interpretative work that had to be undertaken on the patient's ideas and statements, but only its results. So the technique of analytical work, dreams aside, has only been revealed at a very few points. In this case history I was concerned to demonstrate the determination of symptoms and the intimate construction of neurotic illness; it would only have caused irresolvable confusion had I attempted to carry out the other task at the same time. In order to account for the technical rules, which are generally found empirically, one would have had to bring together material from many different case histories. At the same time, however, it should not be supposed that the abbreviation resulting from the omission of the technique was particularly great in this case. The most difficult piece of technical work did not arise with this patient, as the element of 'transference' that comes into play at the end of a case history did not occur during this brief treatment.

Neither patient nor author is responsible for a third kind of incompleteness in this account. Rather, it is obvious that a single patient's story, even if it were complete and not dubious, cannot provide an answer to all the questions arising out of the problem of hysteria. It cannot teach us about all types of illness, all formations of the internal structure of the neurosis, all possible kinds of connection between the psychic and the somatic. One might not reasonably demand more from a single case than that case is able to provide. A person who has not previously wished to believe in the general and universal validity of the psychosexual aetiology of hysteria will not be convinced of it by a single case history, but will at best defer his judgement until he has won the right, through his own work, of forming his own personal conviction.[3]

### Notes

1. Richard Schmidt, *Beiträge zur indischen Erotik* [*Contributions to Indian Erotica*], [Leipzig], 1902, Foreword.
2. *Die Traumdeutung* [*The Interpretation of Dreams*], Vienna 1900.
3. [*Addition 1923:*] The treatment recounted here was interrupted on 31 December 1899 [in fact: 1900], and the report on it written over the following two weeks, but not published until 1905. We can hardly expect that more than two decades of continued work should have changed nothing in the conception and representation of such a case of illness, but it would obviously be absurd to bring this patient's story 'up to date' and adapt it to the current state of our knowledge. So I have left it broadly untouched, and only corrected certain errors and inexactitudes to which my excellent English translators, Mr and Mrs James Strachey, have drawn my attention. As regards critical observations that have struck me as justified, I have included these in the notes appended to this case history. Consequently the reader will be aware that I continue to maintain the opinions set out in the text to this day, if he finds no contradiction of them in the notes. The problem of medical discretion which preoccupies me in this foreword does not apply to other stories of patients in this volume [Volume VIII of the *Gesammelte Werke,* which contained four further case histories], for three of these have been published with the express permission of the patients, and in the case of little Hans with the permission of his father, and in one case (Schreber) the object of analysis is not actually a person but a book which that person had written. In the case of Dora,

the secret has been kept until this year. I heard recently that the woman in question, of whom I had lost sight for a long time, had recently revealed to her doctor, after falling ill for other reasons, that as a girl she had received analytic treatment from me. That revelation made it easy for my colleague to recognize her as the Dora of 1899. If the three months of that treatment did nothing more than resolve that conflict, if they could not provide protection against illnesses arising subsequently, no fair-minded person would reproach analytic therapy for this.

# I  *The Clinical Picture*

Having shown in my *Interpretation of Dreams*, published in 1900, that dreams can generally be interpreted, and that once the task of interpretation has been accomplished they can be replaced by irreproachable thoughts which can be inserted at a particular place in the psychical context, in the pages below I should like to give an example of the one practical application that the art of dream-interpretation seems to permit. In that book[1] I have mentioned how I came to the problem of dreams. I encountered it along the way as I was attempting to heal psychoneuroses by means of a particular process of psychotherapy, when my patients told me – amongst other events from their mental life – their dreams, which seemed to demand interpolation in the long connection leading from the morbid symptom to the pathogenic idea. Then I learned how to translate, without further assistance, from dream language into the immediately comprehensible language in which we express our thoughts. This knowledge, I should stress, is indispensable for the psychoanalyst, because the dream is one of the ways in which psychical material can reach consciousness when it has, because of the resistance that its content provokes, been excluded from consciousness, and become repressed and thus pathogenic. The dream is, to put it more succinctly, one of the *detours around repression*, one of the chief means of so-called indirect representation in the psychical sphere. This fragment from the history of the treatment of a hysterical girl is intended to show how dream interpretation intervenes in the work of analysis. At the same time it should give me my first public opportunity to represent my views concerning the psychical processes and organic conditions of hysteria in a manner detailed enough to avoid further misunderstanding. I shall not apologize for this degree of detail, since it is now known that one cannot match the great demands that hysteria places upon the doctor and researcher by responding with affected disdain, but only by immersing ourselves affectionately in the subject.

> *Nicht Kunst und Wissenschaft allein,*
> *Geduld will bei dem Werke sein!*

[Art and science alone won't do, a little patience is needed, too!]

To begin with a complete and rounded case history would be to place the reader in quite different conditions from those of the medical observer from the very first. In general, the account provided by the patient's relatives – in this case the eighteen-year-old girl's father – gives a most unrecognizable picture of the course of the illness. I do begin the treatment by asking the patient to tell me the whole story of her life and illness, but what I hear is still not enough to provide the bearings I require. This first story is comparable to an unnavigable river whose bed is now obstructed by masses of rock, now broken and made shallow by sandbanks. I can only marvel at the way in which some authors have managed to achieve precise and consistent case histories of hysterics. Certainly, they can adequately and coherently inform the doctor about one part or other of their lives, but then there will be another occasion when their information dries up, leaving gaps and mysteries, and at yet another time one will come across periods of complete darkness, unilluminated by any usable information. Connections, even obvious ones, are generally fragmented, the sequence of different events uncertain; during the narration itself, the patient will correct a piece of information, a date, perhaps, before, after lengthy vacillation, returning more or less to her original statement. The patient's inability to give an ordered depiction of her life history, in so far as it coincides with the case history, is not only characteristic of neurosis,[2] it is also of great theoretical significance. This lack, in fact, has the following causes: first of all, the patient is consciously and deliberately holding back a part of something that is very well known to her, something that she knows she should tell, for the motives, not yet overcome, of shyness and modesty (discretion when other people are involved); that is the portion of deliberate dishonesty. Secondly, part of the anamnestic knowledge that the patient still has at her disposal is left out when she tells her story, although she does not consciously intend this reticence; that is the portion of unconscious dishonesty. Thirdly, there is never a shortage of genuine amnesias, gaps in the memory into which not only old memories but even quite recent ones have fallen, and of inaccurate memories, which have been formed secondarily to fill those gaps.[3] Where the events themselves have been preserved in the memory, the intention underlying the amnesia will be achieved just as surely by abolishing a connection, and that connection will most certainly be severed if the sequence of the events is altered. That sequence always proves to be the most vulnerable component of the memory hoard, and the one most often subjected to repression. We come across some memories in what we might call a first stage of repression, and they are charged with doubt. Some time later that doubt is replaced by forgetfulness or errors of memory.[4]

Theory requires us to see this state of memories relating to the case history as the necessary correlative of the hysterical symptoms. In the course of treatment, the patient will repeat what he has been holding back, or that which has not occurred to him, despite the fact that he has always known it. His misrememberings prove to be untenable, and the gaps in the memory are filled. Only towards the end of the treatment can one have a general view of an internally consistent, comprehensible and complete case history. If the practical goal of the treatment lies in the abolition of all possible symptoms, and their replacement with conscious thoughts, one other theoretical goal might be the task of healing all the damage done to the patient's memory. The two goals coincide: once the former has been achieved, so has the latter; the same route leads to both.

From the nature of the things that form the material of psycho-analysis, it follows that in our case histories we owe as much to the patient's purely human and social relations as we do to the somatic data and the hysterical symptoms. Above all, we will direct our interest towards the patient's family relationships out of considerations which, as we shall see, do not have to do with the examination of heredity alone.

Apart from herself, the family circle of this eighteen-year-old patient consisted of her parents and a brother one and a half years older. The dominant figure was her father, both because of his intelligence and his character traits and because of the circumstances of his life, which provided the framework for the story of the patient's childhood and her case history. When I began treating the girl he was in his late forties, a man of rather uncommon sensitivity and talent, a well-to-do industrialist. His daughter held him in particularly tender affection, and her prematurely awoken critical sense was all the more repelled by some of his actions and idiosyncrasies.

In addition, the tenderness of her affection was intensified by the many serious illnesses to which her father had succumbed since her sixth year. Then, a tubercular illness had been the reason for the family's move to a small, climatically favourable town in our southern provinces; his pulmonary complaint quickly improved there, but in order to avoid a recurrence of the illness, that place, which I shall refer to as B., became the main home of both the children and the parents for about the next ten years. When the girl's father was well he was often absent, visiting his factories; in high summer he went to a spa in the mountains.

When the girl was about ten years old, her father needed a darkness cure for a detached retina. This illness caused lasting impairment of his vision. The most serious illness occurred about two years later; it consisted of an attack of confusion, accompanied by fits of paralysis and minor psychical disorders. A friend of the sick man, whose role we shall later examine, had persuaded him, when he was still not greatly recovered, to travel with his doctor to Vienna to seek my advice. I hesitated for a while about whether I should assume he was suffering from a tabetic paralysis, but then opted to diagnose diffuse vascular infection and, after a specific infection before the patient's marriage was admitted, to undertake a vigorous anti-syphilitic cure, in consequence of which all those disorders which were still present subsided. It was probably because of this fortunate intervention that four years later the father introduced me to his daughter, who had clearly become neurotic, and another two years after that he handed her over to me for psychothera-peutic treatment.

In Vienna, meanwhile, I had met a slightly older sister of the father, who manifested a serious form of psychoneurosis, without characteristic hysterical symptoms. After an unhappy married life, this woman died of rapidly progressing malnutrition, which was never fully explained.

Another brother of my male patient, whom I met occasionally, was a hypochondriac bachelor.

The girl, who became my patient at the age of eighteen, had always stressed her sympathetic relations with her father's side of the family and, since she had fallen ill, had taken the aforemen-tioned aunt as her model. Neither had I any doubt that she belonged, with her gifts and her intellectual precocity, as well as her innate tendency towards illness, to that family. I never met her mother. Judging by the statements of the father and the girl, I received the impression that she was an ill-educated, but more importantly an unintelligent woman, who had concentrated all her interests on the household since her husband's illness and the estrangement that followed from it, and thus developed what we might call 'house-wife psychosis'. Without any understanding of her children's active interests, she spent the whole day cleaning the apartment, the furniture and appliances, so much so that using and enjoying them became almost impossible. It is hard to avoid comparing this condi-tion, of which I find hints often enough in normal housewives, with compulsive washing and other forms of compulsive cleanliness; but among these women, and indeed in our patient's mother, we note a complete lack of awareness of the illness and thus of a significant characteristic of 'compulsive neurosis'. Relations between mother and daughter had been very unfriendly for years. The daughter ignored her mother, criticized her severely and had fully escaped her influence.[5]

The girl's only brother, one and a half years older than the girl herself, had in her earlier years been the model that her ambition had striven to emulate. Relations between the siblings had become more distant over recent years. The young man tried to stay out of family disputes as best he could; when he had to take sides, he sided with the mother. So the usual sexual attraction had brought both father and daughter and mother and son closer together.

Our patient, whom I shall from now on call Dora, showed nervous symptoms from the age of eight. At that time she had suffered from a chronic respiratory illness with occasional violent aggravations. This illness first appeared after a little trip into the mountains and was therefore put down to over-exertion. The condition slowly subsided over a period of six months, after a rest cure was imposed upon her. The family doctor does not seem to have wavered for a moment from his diagnosis of a purely nervous disorder, ruling out an organic cause of the dyspnoea, but he apparently considered this diagnosis compatible with the aetiology of over-exertion.[6]

The little girl passed through the usual infectious childhood illnesses without suffering any lasting harm. As she told me (with symbolic intent!), it was her brother who usually had the illnesses first, although in a mild form, whereupon she followed with more serious symptoms. She began to suffer unilateral migraine headaches and she had attacks of nervous coughing from the age of about twelve. At first the two symptoms always occurred together, before separating and developing in different ways. The migraine became rarer, and by the age of sixteen it had disappeared. The attacks of tussis nervosa, probably caused by common catarrh, never went away. By the time she came to me for treatment at the age of eighteen, she was coughing again in a characteristic way. The number of these attacks could not be established: they lasted from three to five weeks, and on one occasion several months. At least in recent years, during the first half of one attack, the most irritating painful symptom had been a complete loss of her voice. This had been diagnosed as another nervous attack a considerable time previously. The many usual treatments, including hydrotherapy and local electric shocks, were unsuccessful. The girl, who had, in these circumstances, grown to be mature and independent in her judgements, became used to mocking the efforts of doctors and finally giving up on medical help. She had, incidentally, always been reluctant to ask the doctor for his advice, although she had nothing against her family doctor personally. Any suggestion that she should consult a new doctor encountered resistance on her part, and indeed it was only on her father's orders that she had come to me.

I first saw her in the early summer of her sixteenth year, when she was suffering from coughing and hoarseness. Even at that time I suggested a psychical cure, which was rejected, and this longer-lasting attack passed spontaneously. In the winter of the next year, after the death of her beloved aunt, she had stayed in Vienna at the home of her uncle and his daughters, and had there suffered from a feverish condition which was diagnosed as appendicitis.[7] The following autumn, the family finally left the spa town of B., as the father's health seemed to permit this, and settled first in the town where the father's factory was, and barely a year later in Vienna.

By now Dora had blossomed into a girl with intelligent and agreeable facial features, although she caused her parents grave concern. The main sign of her illness had become mood swings and character changes. By now she was clearly no longer happy either with herself or with her family, she was unfriendly towards her father and could no longer bear the company of her mother, who constantly tried to involve her in the housework. She tried to avoid contact with anyone; in so far as the fatigue and lack of concentration of which she complained allowed, she kept herself busy by attending public lectures, and devoted herself seriously to her studies. One day her parents were shocked by a letter that they found on or in the girl's desk, in which she bade them farewell because her life had become unbearable.[8] Her father's not inconsiderable insight led him to the view that the girl was not seriously planning to commit suicide, but he was horrified none the less, and when one day, after a small exchange between father and daughter, she fell into her first fit of unconsciousness,[9] also involving amnesia, it was decided despite all her protests that she should embark on my treatment.

The case history that I have outlined so far probably does not seem, on the whole, worth communicating. 'Petite hystérie', with the most common somatic and psychical symptoms: dyspnoea, tussis nervosa, aphonia, along with migraines, mood swings, hysterical irascibility and a taedium vitae that is probably not to be taken seriously. Certainly, more interesting case histories of hysterics have been published, and often more carefully recorded, and in what follows the reader will find nothing concerning the stigmata of sensitive skin, restriction of the field of vision and so on. I shall merely allow myself to observe that all the collections of strange and astonishing phenomena arising from hysteria have not advanced us much in our understanding of that still puzzling illness. What we need is precisely the explanation of the most ordinary cases, and the most frequent, typical symptoms of those cases. I should be satisfied if circumstances had enabled me to give a complete explanation of this case of small-scale hysteria. On the basis of my experiences with other patients I have no doubt that my analytical means would have been adequate to the purpose.

In 1896, shortly after the publication of my *Studies in Hysteria* with Dr J. Breuer, I asked an eminent colleague in my field for his assessment of the psychological theory of hysteria put forward in that book. He answered frankly that he considered it to be an unjustified universalization of conclusions, which might apply to a small number of cases. I have seen many cases of hysteria since then; I have devoted days, weeks or years to each case, and in no single case have I failed to find the psychical conditions postulated in the *Studies*, the psychical trauma, conflict of the affects, and as I have added in later publications, a disturbance in the sexual sphere. Where we are dealing with things that have become pathogenic in their effort to conceal themselves, we cannot, of course, expect patients to want to present them to their doctor; neither can one abandon the treatment after the first 'no' in response to examination.[10]

In the case of my patient Dora, it was thanks to her father's intelligence, which I have mentioned several times, that I myself did not need to seek the source, at least of the final form of the illness. The father told me that in the town of B. he and his family had enjoyed a close friendship with a couple who lived there. During his serious illness Frau K. had looked after him and thus made a lasting claim upon his gratitude. Herr K. had always been very kind to his daughter Dora, taking walks with her when he was in B., giving her little presents, but no one had seen any harm in that. Dora had taken the greatest care of Herr and Frau K.'s two little children, almost adopting a maternal role with them. When father and daughter came to see me in the summer two years ago, they had been stopping off on the way to see Herr and Frau K., who had taken a summer residence by one of our alpine lakes. Dora was to spend several weeks in the K. household, and her father planned to travel home after a few days. Herr K. was also present at this time. But when her father prepared to set off, the girl suddenly announced very resolutely that she was going with him, and she had done just that. It was only some days later that she gave an explanation for her curious behaviour, asking her mother to inform her father that while they were walking to the lake to take a boat trip, Herr K. had been so bold as to make a declaration of love to her. The accused man, confronted at their next meeting by the girl's father and uncle, most expressly denied any move on his part that would have merited such an interpretation, and began to suspect the girl, who, according to Frau K., was interested only in sexual matters and who, in their house by the lake, had even been reading Mantegazza's *Physiology of Love*, and similar books. In all likelihood, inflamed by such reading material, she had 'imagined' the whole scene that she had recounted.

'I do not doubt,' said the father, 'that this event was responsible for Dora's moodiness, irritability and notions of suicide. She demands that I sever any contact with Herr K., and, particularly, with Frau K., whom she had practically worshipped until then. But I cannot do this, for in the first place I consider Dora's story of the man's immoral impertinence to be a fantasy that has sprung into her mind, and secondly I am bound to Frau K. by an honest friendship and can do nothing to hurt her. The poor lady is very unhappy with her husband, of whom I do not, incidentally, have the best opinion; she herself has suffered very badly from her nerves, and I am her sole support. In view of my own state of health I probably do not need to assure you that there is nothing forbidden in our relationship. We are two poor human beings comforting one another as best we can with friendship and sympathy. You know that I get nothing from my own wife. But Dora, who has inherited my own stubborn demeanour, cannot be diverted from her hatred for Herr and Frau K. Her last attack followed a conversation in which she demanded the same thing from me once again. Please try now to put her on a better track.'

It does not quite accord with these revelations that in other speeches the father tried to place most of the guilt for his daughter's unbearable character on the shoulders of her mother, whose peculiarities spoiled life in the house for everyone. But I had decided long since to defer my judgement about the true state of affairs until I heard the other side.

The experience with Herr K. – the declaration of love followed by an affront to the girl's honour – was supposed to have caused our patient Dora the psychical trauma which Breuer and I had previously postulated as a necessary precondition for the origin of a hysterical illness. But this new case manifested all the difficulties which have led me since then to go beyond that theory,[11] and also presented a new difficulty of a particular kind. The trauma in Dora's life with which we are familiar is, as so often in the case histories of hysterics, incapable of explaining or determining the peculiarity of the symptoms; equally, we would understand the connections just as much or as little if symptoms other than tussis nervosa, aphonia, moodiness and taedium vitae had been the consequence of the trauma. But now there is the additional fact that some of these symptoms – the coughing and the mood swings – had been manifested by the patient years before the trauma, and that they first appeared during childhood, since they had occurred when the girl was seven years old. So we must, if we are not to abandon the trauma theory, return to her childhood to seek influences or impressions that might work analogously to a trauma; and in that case it is quite remarkable that the investigation of cases whose first symptoms did not begin in childhood has also stimulated me to pursue the patient's life history back into the first years of childhood.[12]

After the first difficulties of the cure had been overcome, Dora told me of an earlier experience with Herr K., which was even more apt to act as a sexual trauma. She was fourteen years old at the time. Herr K. had arranged with Dora and his wife that the ladies should come to his shop in the main square of B. in the afternoon to watch a religious ceremony from the building. But he persuaded his wife to stay at home, dismissed his assistant and was on his own when the girl entered the shop. As the time of the procession approached he asked the girl to wait for him by the door which opened on to the staircase leading to the upper floor, as he lowered the awning. He then came back, and instead of walking through the open door, he suddenly pulled the girl to him and pressed a kiss on her lips. That was surely a situation that should have produced a clear sensation of sexual excitement in a fourteen-year-old girl who had never been touched by a man. But at that moment Dora felt a violent revulsion, pulled away and dashed past him to the stairs and from there to the front door. After this, contact with Herr K. none the less continued; neither of them ever mentioned this little scene, and Dora claims to have kept it a secret even at confession at the spa. After that, incidentally, she avoided any opportunity to be alone with Herr K. Both Herr and Frau K. had at that time arranged to go on an outing lasting several days, and Dora was to go along. After the kiss in the shop she declined to go, giving no reasons.

In this second scene, chronologically the first, the behaviour of the fourteen-year-old child is already thoroughly hysterical. Anyone in whom an occasion for sexual excitement provokes predominantly or exclusively feelings of displeasure I would without hesitation identify as a hysteric, whether or not she is capable of producing somatic symptoms. Explaining the mechanism of this *affective reversal* remains one of the most important and at the same time one of the most difficult tasks of the psychology of neurosis. In my opinion I am still a good way away from having achieved that goal; in the context of this communication, however, I shall only be able to present a part of the small amount that I know.

The case of our patient Dora is not yet sufficiently characterized by the emphasis on emotional reversal; in addition, we would have to say that a *displacement* of sensation has taken place. Rather than the genital sensation that would certainly not have been absent from a healthy girl in such circumstances,[13] she feels the sensation of displeasure proper to the mucous tract at the entrance to the alimentary canal: disgust. Certainly, this localization is influenced by the excitement of the lips by the kiss; but I also think I can see another element at work.[14]

The disgust that Dora felt did not become a lasting symptom, and even during the treatment it was only potentially present, as we might say. She had difficulty eating and admitted a slight aversion to food. On the other hand, that scene had produced another effect, a sensory hallucination, which recurred from time to time even when she was delivering her account. She said she could still feel the pressure of that embrace on her upper body. According to certain rules of symptom formation which I have learned to recognize, along with other, otherwise inexplicable particularities of the patient, who would not, for example, walk past a man whom she saw standing in animated or affectionate conversation with a lady, I have made the following reconstruction of the events involved in this scene. I think that during this passionate embrace she felt not only the kiss on her lips but also the pushing of the erect member against her body. This – to her – repellent perception was excised from memory, repressed and replaced by the harmless sensation of pressure on the thorax, which draws its excessive intensity from its repressed source. A new displacement, then, from the lower to the upper body.[15] The compulsive nature of Dora's behaviour, on the other hand, is formed as though prompted by an unaltered memory. She cannot walk past a man she believes to be in a state of sexual excitement because she does not want to see the somatic sign of that state again.

It is remarkable here how three symptoms – disgust, the sensation of pressure on the upper body and a fear of men in affectionate conversation – have their source in a single experience, and that only the interrelation of these three signs enables us to understand the source of the formation of the symptoms. Disgust corresponds to the symptom of repression of the labial erogenous zone (spoilt by infantile sucking, as we shall see). The pressure of the erect member probably led to an analogous change in the corresponding female organ, the clitoris, and the stimulation of that second erogenous zone has been fixated by displacement on to the simultaneous sensation of pressure on the thorax. The fear of men in what may be a sexually excited state follows the mechanism of a phobia, to secure itself against a revival of the repressed perception.

In order to demonstrate the possibility of this deduction, I asked the patient as delicately as I could whether she knew anything about physical signs of excitement in the male body. The answer for now was: yes, and for then: she didn't think so. From the very outset I took the greatest care not to introduce this patient to any new knowledge from the realm of the sexual life, not for reasons of scruple, but in order to put my hypotheses to a severe test in this case. Accordingly, I only called a thing by its proper name when her own clear references showed that direct translation was hardly daring. Her prompt and honest reply also regularly showed that she knew already, but her memory was unable to solve the mystery of *how* she knew it. She had forgotten where all that knowledge came from.[16]

If I am correct in imagining the scene of the kiss in the shop as I have done, I am able to explain the disgust.[17] The sensation of disgust seems originally to have been a reaction to the smell (and later the sight) of excrement. But the genitals, and particularly the male member, can recall the excremental functions, because apart from the sexual function the male member also serves the function of evacuating urine. Indeed, this purpose is the older, and, during the pre-sexual phase, the only one that is known. In this way disgust enters the emotional expressions of sexual life. It is the *inter urinas et faeces nascimur* [we are born between faeces and urine] of the Church Father [St Augustine], which attaches itself to sexual life and cannot be parted from it, however many attempts at idealization one may undertake. But I wish to stress that my viewpoint is that I do not consider the problem solved by the discovery of this associative path. The fact that this association can be provoked does not explain how it was provoked. It is not provoked in this way under normal conditions. Knowledge of the paths does not render superfluous the knowledge of the forces that travel those paths.[18]

In addition, I did not find it easy to draw my patient's attention to her contact with Herr K. She claimed she had finished with him. The uppermost layer of all that occurred to her during our sessions, all that was readily conscious to her, and all that she remembered as conscious from the previous day, always referred to her father. It was quite correct that she could not forgive her father his continuation of relations with Herr K. and particularly with Frau K. But her interpretation of that contact was quite different from the way her father would have chosen to see it. As far as she was concerned there was no doubt that it was an ordinary love affair that bound her father to the beautiful young woman. Nothing capable of reinforcing that opinion had escaped her relentlessly keen perception about this matter, *no gap was to be found in her memories there*. The acquaintance with Herr and Frau K. had begun even before her father's serious illness; but it only became close when the young woman effectively nursed him during his illness, while Dora's mother stayed away from the sick man's bed. During the first summer holiday after the cure, certain things happened that should have opened everyone's eyes to the true nature of that 'friendship'. The two families had rented a floor in the hotel together, and one day Frau K. announced she could not keep the bedroom that she had been sharing up until that point with one of her children, and a few days later Dora's father gave up his bedroom, and they both moved into new rooms, the end rooms, which were separated only by the corridor, while the rooms which they had abandoned had not provided similar guarantees against possible disturbance. When she later reproached her father on the subject of Frau K., he said that he could not understand her hostility, and that the children in fact had every reason to be grateful to Frau K. Her Mama, to whom she then turned for an explanation of this obscure speech, told her that her Papa had at the time been so unhappy that he had wanted to commit suicide in the forest, but Frau K., who had sensed that this was happening, had come after him and had, with her pleading, persuaded him to stay alive for the sake of his family. Of course Dora didn't believe it; they had probably been seen together in the forest and her Papa had come up with this tale of a suicide in order to justify their rendezvous.[19] Then, when they returned to B., Papa had gone to see Frau K. at a particular time every day while her husband was in the shop. Everyone had talked about it and asked her about it in a significant way. Herr K. himself had often complained bitterly to her Mama, but spared her the object of his complaints by making only veiled allusions, which she appeared to interpret as sensitivity on his part. During their walks together, Papa and Frau K. regularly arranged matters so that he was alone with Frau K. There was no doubt that she took money from him, because she paid for things that she could not have afforded with her own money or her husband's. Her Papa also began to give Frau K. large gifts; in order to conceal them, he had at the same time become particularly generous to her mother and to Dora herself. The young woman, who had until then been sickly, and who had herself had to spend months in a sanatorium because she was unable to walk, had been healthy since that time, and full of life.

Even after leaving B., this contact, which they had maintained for several years, continued: from time to time Dora's father would declare that he could not bear the raw climate, that he had to think about himself, and he would start coughing and groaning until all of a sudden he would set off for B., from where he would write the most cheerful of letters. All these illnesses were merely excuses for seeing his girlfriend again. Then one day he announced that they were moving to Vienna, and she began to suspect a connection. They had actually only been in Vienna for three weeks when she heard that the Ks had moved to Vienna as well. They were here now, in fact, and she often encountered her Papa in the street with Frau K. She met Herr K. often as well; he always stared after her, and on one occasion when he met her walking on her own, he had followed her for a long way, in order to ascertain where she was going, and check that she wasn't on her way to a rendezvous herself.

According to Dora, Papa was insincere; there was a false trait to his character; he thought only of his own satisfaction and had the talent of organizing things in the way that best suited him. I often heard such criticisms, particularly during those days when her father felt that his condition had deteriorated again, and set off for several weeks in B., whereupon the keen-eyed Dora soon guessed that Frau K. had set off for the same destination to visit her relations.

I could not dispute this trait in Dora's father in general, and it was easy to see in what particular respects Dora was right to reproach him. In embittered mood, she found herself thinking that she had been handed over to Herr K. as a prize for his toleration of the relationship between Dora's father and his wife, and behind her affection for her father one could hear her fury at being used in such a way. On other occasions she knew that she had been guilty herself of exaggeration in coming out with such speeches. Of course the two men had never made a formal pact in which she had been used as an object of exchange; her father in particular would have recoiled in horror from such impertinence. But he was one of those men who can take the sting out of a conflict by falsifying his judgement of one of the two opposing arguments. Had his attention been drawn to the possibility that a growing girl might be put in danger by constant and unsupervised contact with a man who was not receiving satisfaction from his wife, her father would certainly have replied that he could rely on his daughter, that a man such as Herr K. could never be a danger to her, and that his friend himself was incapable of such intentions. Or: Dora was still a child, and Herr K. treated her as a child. But the truth was that each man avoided drawing from the behaviour of the other the conclusion unfavourable to his own desires. One year, Herr K. had been able to send Dora flowers on all the days when he had been in town, he had used every opportunity to give her expensive gifts, and spent all his free time in her company, although her parents did not recognize such behaviour as having the character of a declaration of love.

When a correctly founded and unobjectionable sequence of thoughts emerges during psychoanalytic treatment, there is a moment of embarrassment for the doctor, which the patient exploits in order to ask: 'Surely that's all true and accurate? What do you want to change, now that I've told it to you?' But one soon realizes that such thoughts, impervious to analysis, can be used to conceal others that seek to evade criticism and consciousness. A series of accusations levelled against other people makes one suspect a series of self-accusations with the same content. One need only turn each individual reproach back on the person of the speaker. There is something undeniably automatic about this way of defending oneself against self-reproach by directing the same reproach against someone else. It has its model in the ripostes that children give, when they answer without hesitation, 'You're the liar' if they are accused of lying. In striving for counter-insult, the adult would look for a genuine weak spot in his opponent, rather than relying on the repetition of the identical insult. In cases of paranoia, the projection of the accusation on to another, without any alteration of the content, and thus with no reference to reality, becomes manifest as a delusional process.

Without exception, Dora's reproaches against her father were also thoroughly reinforced, 'backed up' by the same content, as we shall show with reference to individual cases: she was correct in believing that her father did not want to understand Herr K.'s behaviour towards his daughter, lest his relationship with Frau K. be disturbed. But she had done exactly the same thing. She had turned herself into one of the guilty parties in that relationship and dismissed any clues that arose concerning its true nature. Her clarity about this had dated only from the adventure by the lake, and the strict demands she had made upon her father. Throughout all those previous years, in every possible respect she had encouraged her father's contact with Frau K. She never went to Frau K.'s if she suspected her father might be there. She knew the children would have been sent out, and arranged her route in such a way that she met the children and went walking with them. There had been one person in the house who wanted to open her eyes early on to her father's relations with Frau K., and to encourage her to take sides against her. It had been her last governess, an elderly, very well-read spinster who was free with her opinions.[20] Teacher and pupil had got on very well together for a while, until Dora had suddenly taken against her and insisted on her dismissal. As long as the governess had influence, she used it to stir Dora and her mother up against Frau K. She told Dora's Mama that it was irreconcilable with her dignity to tolerate such intimacy on her husband's part with a strange woman; she also brought to Dora's attention everything that was strange about that contact. But her efforts were in vain, Dora remained affectionately attached to Frau K. and would not hear of any reason to find her father's contact with her repellent. On the other hand, she was very clear about the motives driving her governess. Blind on one side, Dora was clear-sighted enough on the other. She noticed that her governess was in love with Papa. When Papa was present, she was quite a different person, and she could be amusing and helpful. When the family was staying in the factory town and Frau K. was not on the horizon, the governess had stirred things up against Mama, who was the next rival along. Dora held none of this against her. She was only angered when she noticed that the governess was quite indifferent to her, and that the love she had shown her was actually meant for her Papa. During Papa's absence from the factory town the spinster had had no time for her, would not go for walks with her, took no interest in her homework. Hardly had Papa returned from B. than she showed herself willing to undertake any service or assistance. Then Dora dropped her.

The poor girl had, with undesirable clarity, illuminated an aspect of her own behaviour. Just as the governess had sometimes behaved to Dora, so Dora had behaved towards the children of Herr K. She had acted as their mother, she had taught them, gone out with them, given them a complete substitute for the small amount of interest that their own mother showed them. There had often been talk of divorce between Herr and Frau K.; this did not take place because Herr K., who was an affectionate father, did not want to lose either of the two children. The common interest in the children had, from the start, brought Herr K. and Dora together. For Dora, busying herself with the children had clearly been a pretext designed to conceal something else from herself and others.

Her behaviour towards the children, as it was explained by the governess's behaviour towards her, yielded the same result as her tacit toleration of her father's relations with Frau K., namely that she had been in love with Herr K. for all those years. When I voiced this deduction, Dora disagreed. She immediately said that other people, such as a cousin who had visited B. for a while, had said to her, 'You're wild about that man'; but she herself claimed not to be able to remember such feelings. Later, when the wealth of material coming to light made denial more difficult, she admitted that she might have loved Herr K., but since the scene by the lake that was all over.[21] Be that as it may, it was clear that the reproach of having made herself deaf to unavoidable duties and having arranged things so that her own passionate love was left undisturbed, the very accusation that she levelled against her father rebounded upon herself.[22]

The other reproach against her father, that he turned his illnesses into means and pretexts, in turn conceals a whole part of her own secret history. One day she complained of a supposedly new symptom, acute stomach pains, and when I asked, 'Who are you copying with those?' I hit the nail on the head. The previous day she had paid a visit to her cousins, her late aunt's daughters. The younger of these had become engaged, the elder had in response fallen ill with stomach pains and had to be taken to the hospital in Semmering. She thought it was only envy on the part of the elder daughter, who always fell ill when she wanted to get something, and now she wanted to leave the house so that she would not have to witness her sister's happiness.[23] Her own stomach pains, on the other hand, made it clear that she identified with the cousin she had declared to be a fake, either because she also envied the happier party her love or because she saw her own fate reflected in that of the older sister, who had had an unhappy love affair shortly before.[24] But she had also learned how useful illnesses could be through her observations of Frau K. Herr K. spent part of the year travelling; every time he came back he found his wife indisposed, when, as Dora knew, she had been completely healthy the previous day. Dora understood that the husband's presence had the effect of making his wife ill, and that she found being ill a welcome way of escaping her hated marital duties. A remark concerning her own alternation of illness and health during the early girlhood years in B., suddenly introduced at this juncture, made me suspect that her own conditions should be considered in terms of a similar dependence to those of Frau K. In the technique of psychoanalysis, in fact, it is taken as a rule that an internal, but still hidden connection is announced through contiguity, the temporal proximity of ideas, just as the letters $a$ and $b$ written side by side indicate the formation of the syllable $ab$. Dora had often manifested attacks of coughing and loss of voice; might the presence or absence of her loved one have had an influence on this coming and going of her symptoms? If this was so, a coincidence that would reveal as much was bound to turn up. I asked what the average length of these attacks had been. About three to six weeks. And how long had Herr K.'s absences been? She had to admit, also between three and six weeks. So by being ill she was demonstrating her love for K., just as his wife demonstrated her repulsion. But conversely it might have been assumed that she would have been ill when he was absent and healthy after his return. And indeed that did appear to be the case, at least throughout the first period of these attacks: later on a need arose to cover over the coincidence between the attack of the illness and the absence of the secretly beloved man, so that the secret would not be betrayed by its constancy. Then, all that remained as a mark of its original meaning was the duration of the attack.

From my time in Charcot's clinic I remembered seeing and hearing that among people with hysterical mutism writing vicariously stood in for speech. They wrote more fluently, more quickly and better than other people did, or than they themselves had previously done. The same had been true of Dora. In the first days of her aphonia, 'writing had always flowed easily'. In fact this peculiarity did not, as the manifestation of a physiological substitute function, require any psychological explanation; but it was remarkable that such an explanation was so easy to come by. Herr K. wrote to her a great deal on his travels and sent her postcards; on some occasions she alone was told the date of his return, and his wife was surprised by his arrival. Incidentally, it is hardly less obvious that one should correspond with the absent one, to whom one cannot speak, than that one should seek to make oneself understood in writing if one's voice has failed. So Dora's aphonia allowed the following symbolic interpretation: when the loved one was far away, she did without speech; it had lost its value because she could not speak to *him*. Writing, on the other hand, assumed significance as the only way of making contact with the absent one.

So am I about to conclude that in all cases of periodic aphonia we should diagnose the existence of a temporarily absent loved one? Of course that is not my intention. The determination of the symptom is, in Dora's case, far too specific for us to think in terms of the same accidental aetiology occurring with any great frequency. So what is the value of aphonia in our case? Have we allowed ourselves to be deceived by a *jeu d'esprit*? I think not. Let us remember the question that is posed so often, of whether hysterical symptoms are psychical or somatic in origin, or, if we allow the former, whether they are all necessarily psychically determined. This question is, like so many others which we see researchers struggling repeatedly and unsuccessfully to answer, inadequately framed. The true state of affairs is not covered by the alternatives that it contains. As far as I can see, any hysterical symptom needs input from both sides. It cannot come about without a certain *somatic compliance*, which is achieved by a normal or pathological process in or relating to one of the bodily organs. It does not occur more than once – and it is characteristic of the hysterical symptom that it is capable of repeating itself – unless it has a psychical significance, a *meaning*. The meaning is not inherent within the hysterical symptom, it is conferred upon it; it is, so to speak, soldered to it, and it can be different in each case, according to the nature of the suppressed thought that is struggling for expression. However, a series of elements join forces in order that the connections between the unconscious thought and the somatic processes at its disposal be made less random in form, and approach a number of typical combinations. Where therapy is concerned, the definitions present in the accidental psychical material are more important; symptoms are resolved by an examination of their psychical significance. Once that which can be removed by psychoanalysis has been cleared away one is able to have all manner of probably accurate thoughts about the somatic, generally constitutional and organic foundations of the symptoms. As to the attacks of coughing and aphonia in Dora's case we will not restrict ourselves to psychoanalytic interpretation, but demonstrate the organic element behind it, from which the 'somatic compliance' for the expression of affection for a temporarily absent loved one emerged. And if, in this case, the link between symptomatic expression and unconscious thought-content strikes us as adroit and skilful, we will be happy to hear that it can achieve the same impression in every other case, in every other example.

Now I am prepared to hear it said that it is a very moderate gain if, thanks to psychoanalysis, we no longer seek the problem of hysteria in the 'particular instability of the nerve molecules' or in the possibility of hypnoid states, but in 'somatic compliance'.

In reply, however, I should like to stress that as a result of this process the problem is not only pushed back to some degree, it is also somewhat diminished. What is at issue is now no longer the problem as a whole, but one piece of it, containing the particular character of hysteria *as distinct from* other psychoneuroses. The psychical processes at work in all psychoneuroses remain for a long time identical, and only then does the 'somatic compliance' come into consideration, giving the unconscious psychical processes an escape route into the physical. Where this element is not available, the condition as a whole is no longer a hysterical symptom, but becomes something related to it, a phobia, for example, or a compulsive idea, in short a psychical symptom.

I shall now return to the accusation of the 'simulation' of illnesses that Dora levelled against her father. We soon noticed that this reproach corresponded not only to instances of self-reproach concerning earlier illnesses, but also to some concerning the present. At this point the doctor usually has the task of guessing and completing what the analysis only hints at. I had to draw the patient's attention to the fact that her current illness was just as motivated and tendentious as the illness she saw in Frau K. There was no doubt, I told her, that she had a purpose in mind which she hoped to achieve through her illness. But it could only be to turn her father away from Frau K. She could not achieve this with pleading and arguments; perhaps she hoped to accomplish it by frightening her father (see her suicide note) or arousing his sympathy (with her fainting attacks), and if none of that was of any use, then at least she could avenge herself on him. She knew how fond he was of her, and that tears came to his eyes if anyone asked him how his daughter was. I was quite convinced, I told her, that she would immediately become well if her father declared that he would sacrifice Frau K. for the sake of her health. I hoped he would not allow this to happen, because then she would have learned what power she held in her hands, and would certainly not have neglected to use the opportunities presented by sickness again on any future occasion. But if her father did not give in to her, I was quite sure that she would not relinquish her illness so readily.

I shall pass over the details which proved all these hypotheses completely correct, preferring instead to add some general observations about the role of *motives for illness* in hysteria. The motives for illness should be sharply distinguished from the possible ways of being ill, the material from which symptoms are created. The motives themselves play no part in the formation of symptoms, and neither are they present at the beginning of the illness; they only appear secondarily, but the illness is not fully constituted until they appear.[25] The motives for illness are dependably present in every case that constitutes a genuine illness and lasts for a long time. At first the symptom is an unwelcome guest of the psychical life, it has everything going against it, and that is also why it disappears so easily of its own accord, it would seem, under the influence of time. At first it has no useful application in the psychical economy, but it very often achieves such an application secondarily; some psychical current finds it convenient to use the symptom, and for that reason it has achieved a *secondary function*, effectively anchoring itself in the life of the mind. Anyone wishing to improve the health of the patient will, to his astonishment, encounter a great resistance, which teaches him that the patient is not completely serious about his intentions of relinquishing the illness.[26] Imagine a workman, a roof-builder, for example, who has been crippled and now begs his livelihood on the street corner. Along comes a miracle worker and promises him that he will make his crooked leg straight and fit to walk once more. One should not necessarily prepare oneself to see a particularly joyful expression appearing on his face. Of course he felt extremely unhappy when he suffered the injury, realizing that he would never be able to work again, and would have to starve or live on alms. But since then, the very thing that initially made him unemployable has also become his source of income; he lives off his crippled state. Take that away from him and one may render him completely helpless; he will have forgotten his craft in the meantime, lost his working habits, and become accustomed to idleness, and possibly taken to drink.

The motives for illness often begin to stir in childhood. The love-hungry little girl, unhappy at having to share her parents' affection with her brothers and sisters, realizes that all that tenderness comes flowing back when her parents are made anxious by her illness. The girl now knows a way of calling forth her parents' love, and will use this as soon as she has at her disposal the psychical material necessary to produce a morbid state. Once the child has become a woman and, in contradiction of the demands of childhood, has married an inattentive man who suppresses her will, unstintingly exploits her work and expends neither affection nor money upon her, illness becomes the only weapon with which she can assert herself in life. It gives her the rest she craves, it forces the man to make sacrifices of money and care that he would not have made to the healthy woman, and it requires him to treat her with care if she recovers, because otherwise a relapse would be waiting in the wings. Her illness is apparently objective and involuntary, as even her doctor will be obliged to testify, and it enables her to employ, without conscious self-reproach, this useful application of a means that she found effective during childhood.

And yet the illness is indeed intentionally produced! States of illness are generally directed at a certain person, so that they disappear when that person goes away. The crudest and most banal judgement about the illness of the hysteric, which one may hear from uneducated relatives and nurses, is in a sense correct. It is true that the paralysed and bedridden patient would leap to his feet if fire broke out in his room, that the spoilt woman would forget all her troubles if a child fell seriously ill or the house was threatened with disaster. All those who speak of sick people in these terms are right up to a point, but they are ignoring the psychological difference between the conscious and the unconscious, which the child may still be allowed, but which is no longer acceptable for the adult. For that reason, protestations that it is all to do with the will, and attempts to cheer up or abuse the patient, will be in vain. One must first try to convince her, along the roundabout way of analysis, of the existence of her intention to be ill.

It is in the struggle against motives for illness in hysteria that the weakness of all therapy, psychoanalytic therapy included, generally lies. This makes matters easier for destiny; it does not need to assail either the patient's constitution or her pathogenic material. It removes a motive for illness, and the patient is freed from the illness, temporarily, or perhaps even in the longer term. If we doctors only had a greater insight into our patient's hidden interests in life, how many fewer miracle cures, how many fewer spontaneously disappearing symptoms would we allow in our hysterical cases! In one case, a date has finally arrived, in another, concern for another person has become superfluous, a situation has been fundamentally altered by external events, and all of a sudden the patient's suffering, so stubborn until now, is removed, apparently spontaneously, but in fact because its strongest motive, one of its applications in life, has been withdrawn.

Motives supporting illness will probably be found in all fully developed cases. But there are cases with purely internal motives, such as self-punishment, regret and atonement. In cases such as these the therapeutic task will be easier to resolve than in those in which the illness is related to the achievement of an external goal. Dora's goal was obvious: to win over her father and turn him away from Frau K.

None of his actions seemed, incidentally, to have left her so embittered as his readiness to see the scene by the lake as a product of her imagination. She was beside herself when she reflected that she was supposed to have imagined it all. For a long time I was unable to guess the self-reproach that lay concealed behind the passionate rebuttal of this explanation. One was right to suspect that there was something hidden behind it, for a false accusation is a lasting insult. On the other hand, I reached the conclusion that Dora's story must entirely correspond to the truth. After she had understood Herr K.'s intention, she had not allowed him to have his say, she had slapped his face and run off. Her behaviour at the time probably seemed just as incomprehensible to the man she left behind as it does to us, for he must have deduced long before from countless little signs that he could be sure of the girl's affection. In our discussion of the second dream we will find the solution both to this problem and, at the same time, to the self-reproach that we were searching for at the beginning.

When Dora's accusations against her father recurred with wearying monotony, and the cough refused to go away, I found myself thinking that the symptom might have a significance in relation to her father. Furthermore, the conditions that I am accustomed to imposing on the explanation of a symptom were far from fulfilled. According to a rule that I have seen confirmed time and again, but did not yet have the courage to postulate as being universal, a symptom signifies the representation – the realization – of a fantasy with a sexual content: that is, a sexual situation. I should rather say, at least *one* of the meanings of a symptom corresponds to the representation of a sexual fantasy, while for the other meanings, such restrictions concerning content do not exist. When we embark upon psychoanalytical work, we very quickly learn that a symptom has more than one meaning, and serves to represent several unconscious trains of thought. I should like to add that in my view a single unconscious train of thought or fantasy is hardly ever sufficient for the production of a symptom.

The opportunity to interpret nervous coughing in terms of a fantasized sexual situation arose very soon. When Dora stressed once again that Frau K. only loved Papa because he was 'ein *vermögender* Mann' [a wealthy man], I noticed from certain little details in her expression – which I shall pass over here as I shall most of the purely technical aspects of the work of analysis – that the sentence concealed its opposite: Father was 'ein *unvermögender* Mann' [an incapable, or impotent man]. This, then, could only have a sexual meaning: Father was *'unvermögend'*, impotent, as a man. After she had confirmed this interpretation on the basis of her conscious knowledge, I showed her the contradiction she would fall into if, on the one hand, she maintained that the relationship with Frau K. was an ordinary love affair, and on the other, claimed that her father was impotent, and was thus incapable of exploiting such a relationship. Her answer showed that she did not need to acknowledge the contradiction. She was very well aware, she said, that there was more than one kind of sexual satisfaction. She was, however, unable to identify the source of that knowledge. When I went on to ask whether she meant the application of organs other than the genitals for sexual intercourse, she said yes, and I was able to continue: she was thinking of precisely those body parts which were in an aroused state in her own body (throat, oral cavity). She claimed to know nothing of these thoughts, but then, in order for the symptom to appear, she could not have had a full understanding of them. It was therefore impossible to avoid the deduction that her spasmodic coughing, which usually began with a tickle in the throat, represented a situation of sexual gratification *per os* [oral sexual gratification] between the two people whose amorous relationship was a source of constant preoccupation to her. It was of course very true that the cough had disappeared within a very short time after this elucidation, which was tacitly accepted; none the less we did not want to place too much value on this change, because it had appeared spontaneously so often before.

If this little piece of the analysis has aroused surprise and horror in the medical reader, quite apart from the incredulity that is his prerogative, I am prepared to test the justification of these two reactions at this point. Surprise is, I think, motivated by my audacity in talking to a young girl – or a woman of a sexual age – about such delicate and repellent matters. Horror probably relates to the possibility that a chaste young girl might know about such practices and that her imagination might revolve around them. On both of these points I should recommend reserve and level-headedness. In neither case is there cause for indignation. One can talk to girls and women about all kinds of sexual matters without doing them any harm, first if one adopts a particular way of doing this, and secondly if one can convince them that it is unavoidable. Under the same conditions, after all, a gynaecologist will demand all kinds of exposure. The best way of talking about these things is coolly and directly; at the same time it is the furthest removed from the salaciousness with which the same subjects are dealt with in 'society', and with which both girls and women are very familiar. I give both organs and processes their technical names, and inform the patient of them if they – the names – are unknown to them. *'J'appelle un chat un chat.'* [I call a spade a spade.] I have heard of medical and non-medical people who are scandalized by a form of therapy in which such discussions take place, and who seem to envy both me and the patient the thrill that they believe must occur. However, I am too familiar with the respectability of the gentlemen in question to get annoyed with them. I shall not rise to the temptation of satirizing them. I should only like to mention that I often have the satisfaction of hearing a patient, for whom frankness in sexual matters has not at first been easy, later exclaiming, 'No, your cure is far more respectable than Herr X's conversation!'

One must be convinced of the unavoidability of touching upon sexual themes before undertaking a treatment of hysteria, or else one must be prepared to be convinced by experiences. Then one will say to oneself: *pour faire une omelette il faut casser des oeufs.* [You can't make an omelette without breaking eggs.] The patients themselves are easily persuaded; there are only too many opportunities in the course of the treatment. One does not need to reproach oneself for discussing facts from normal or abnormal sexual life with them. If one is relatively careful, one is simply translating into consciousness what they already know in the unconscious, and the whole effect of the cure is based on the insight that the emotional effects of an unconscious idea are more violent and, because invulnerable to inhibition, more dangerous than the effects of a conscious idea. One never risks corrupting an inexperienced girl; and where there is no knowledge of sexual processes in the unconscious, no hysterical symptom will come into being. Wherever one encounters hysteria one can no longer talk of 'pure thoughts' in the sense used by parents and teachers. Among ten-, twelve- and fourteen-year-old children, both boys and girls, I have convinced myself of the utter dependability of this proposition.

A second emotional reaction occurs, which, if I am correct, is directed not at myself but at the patient: this reaction finds the perverse character of the patient's fantasies horrifying. I should stress that such vehement condemnation is not appropriate in a doctor. I also find it, amongst other things, superfluous that a doctor writing about the confusions of the sexual drives should take every opportunity to express his personal revulsion at such unpleasant things. Here is a fact to which I hope, if we suppress our personal tastes, we shall become accustomed. As regards what we call the sexual perversions, transgressions of the sexual function in terms of area of the body and sexual object, we must be able to discuss them without indignation. The very vagueness of the boundaries of what might be called a normal sexual life in different races and at different periods of time should cool the protesters down. But we must not forget that the perversion most repellent to us, the sensual love of man for man, was not only tolerated by the Greeks, a people culturally far superior to ourselves, but even endowed with important social functions. Each one of us goes a bit too far, either here or there, in transgressing the boundaries that we have drawn up in our own sexual lives. The perversions are neither bestialities nor degeneracies in the dramatic sense of that word. They are the development of germs that are all contained within the undifferentiated sexual predisposition of the child, the suppression of which, or their application to higher, asexual goals – their *sublimation* – is destined to supply the forces behind a large number of our cultural achievements. So if someone has become coarse and manifestly perverse, it would be more accurate to say that he has *remained* so, that he represents a stage of an *arrested development*. Psychoneurotics are all people with inclinations that are strongly formed, but which in the course of their development have been repressed and become perverse. Their unconscious fantasies thus reveal exactly the same content as the authentically established actions of perverts, even if they have not read Krafft-Ebing's *Psychopathia sexualis,* which naïve people hold responsible to some degree for the origins of perverse tendencies. The psychoneuroses are, we might say, the *negative* of the perversions. In neurotics the sexual constitution, which also contains the expression of heredity, works alongside the accidental influences of life, which disturb the development of normal sexuality. Water that encounters an obstacle in one river-bed is driven back into older courses previously destined to be abandoned. The drive-forces for the formation of hysterical symptoms are fed not only by repressed normal sexuality but also by unconscious perverse impulses.[27]

The less repellent so-called sexual perversions are the most widespread among our population, as everyone knows apart from medical authors on the subject. Or rather the authors know it too; they just try to forget they do the moment they pick up their pens to write about them. So it can hardly be surprising if our hysteric, who is shortly to be nineteen years of age, and who has heard of the occurrence of one such form of sexual intercourse (the sucking of the member), should develop an unconscious fantasy of this kind and express it with the sensation of irritation in the throat and with coughing. Neither would it be surprising if she had arrived at such a fantasy without external information, something that I have observed with certainty in other patients. The somatic precondition for such an autonomous creation of a fantasy, which coincides with the actions of a pervert, was, in her case, the result of a remarkable fact. She very clearly remembered that in childhood she had been a *'Lutscherin'*, or 'thumb-sucker'. Her father also remembered that he had weaned her off the habit when it continued into her fourth or fifth year. Dora herself had kept in her memory a distinct image from early childhood, in which she sat in a corner on the floor, sucking on her left thumb, while tugging with her right hand on the earlobe of her brother, who sat peacefully beside her. This is the kind of utter self-gratification through sucking that other – later anaesthetic and hysteric – patients have described to me. One of these patients has given me an account that casts a clear light on the origin of this strange habit. The young woman in question, who had never given up sucking, saw herself in a childhood memory, supposedly from the first half of her second year, drinking at her nurse's breast and at the same time pulling rhythmically on her nurse's earlobe. I do not believe that anyone would wish to dispute that the mucous membrane of the lips and the mouth may be declared to be a primary *erogenous zone*, since it has preserved part of that significance for kissing, which is considered normal. The early and generous activation of this erogenous zone, then, is the condition for the later somatic compliance from the mucous tract that begins with the lips. If then, at a time when the actual sexual object, the male member, is already known, situations arise which cause excitement of the still erogenous zone of the mouth to increase once again, it does not take a great deal of creative imagination to substitute for the original nipple and the fingers standing in for it, the actual sexual object, the penis, in a situation of satisfaction. Thus, the perverse fantasy, so shocking to us, of sucking the penis, has the most harmless of origins; it is the reworking of what we might term a 'prehistoric' impression of sucking at the breast of the mother or nurse, which has been revived later on by seeing children at the breast. In the majority of cases, the cow's udder has served a suitable intermediate notion between the nipple and the penis.

The interpretation of Dora's throat symptoms, which we have just discussed, also prompts another observation. The question arises: to what extent can this fantasized sexual situation coincide with the other explanation: that the coming and going of the symptoms of the illness mirrors the presence and absence of the beloved man? If we take the woman's behaviour into account, the idea expressed is the following: if I were his wife, I would love him quite differently, I would be sick (with longing, for example) if he went away, and healthy (with joy) when he came home again. My experiences in the solution of hysterical symptoms lead me to give the following reply: the various meanings of a symptom need not be compatible with one another, that is, they need not connect into a coherent whole. It is enough that the connection is produced by the theme that has given rise to all of these fantasies. Incidentally, in the case under consideration, compatibility of this kind is not excluded: one meaning is more attached to the cough, the other more to the aphonia and the development of conditions; deeper analysis would probably reveal a much greater psychical determination of the details of the illness. We have already seen that a symptom can regularly correspond to several meanings *at once*; let us now add that it can also express several meanings *in sequence*. The symptom can change one of its meanings or its principal meaning over the years, or else the leading role can pass from one meaning to another. It is like a conservative trait in the character of the neurosis that the symptom, once formed, may be maintained even after the unconscious thought that it expresses has lost its meaning. But this tendency to preserve the symptom can also be easily expressed in mechanical terms; the production of such a symptom is so difficult, the transfer of purely psychical to physical excitement, which I have called *conversion*, is dependent upon so many favourable conditions, the somatic compliance required for conversion is so difficult to attain, that the compulsion to discharge the excitement from the unconscious may mean that it contents itself with the already accessible discharge channel. It would appear much easier to produce associative relations between a new thought that needs discharging and the old one, which no longer needs it, than to create a new conversion. Along a path thus traced, excitement flows from the new source of excitement to the old, and the symptom, as the Gospel puts it, resembles an old skin that has been filled with new wine. If, after these discussions, the somatic portion of the hysterical symptom appears to be the one that is more constant, more difficult to replace, and the psychical to be the one that changes, the element more easily replaced, it would not be correct to deduce from this that there was a differ-ence in rank between them. For psychical therapy, the psychical portion is always the more significant.

Dora's tireless repetition of the same thought about the rela-tionship between her father and Frau K. presented the opportu-nity for another important discovery to be made in her analysis.

Such a train of thought may be called excessively strong, *rein-forced* or *supervalent* in Wernicke's sense [Carl Wernicke in *Grundriss der Psychiatrie (Outline of Psychiatry)*, 1900]. It proves to be pathological, despite the apparent correctness of its content, because of the peculiar fact that despite all conscious and delib-erate efforts it cannot be broken down or removed. One finally comes to terms with a normal train of thought, however intense it may be. Dora felt, quite correctly, that her thoughts about her Papa called for a special assessment. 'I can't think about anything else,' she complained repeatedly. 'My brother tells me that we children have no right to criticize these actions of Papa's. We shouldn't worry about them, and should perhaps even be pleased that he has found a woman to attach himself to, since Mama has so little under-standing of him. I can see that, and I would also like to think as my brother does, but I can't. I can't forgive him.'[28]

What is one to do in the face of such a supervalent thought, having listened both to its conscious explanation and the unsuc-cessful objections to it? One tells oneself *that this excessively strong series of ideas owes its reinforcement to the unconscious*. It cannot be resolved by intellectual work, either because its own roots extend into unconscious, repressed material or because it masks another unconscious thought. This latter is usually its exact opposite. Opposites are always closely linked, and often paired in such a way *that one thought becomes conscious in an excessively strong way, while its opposite number is repressed and becomes unconscious.* This relationship is the result of the process of repression. The repression, in fact, has often been carried out in such a way that the opposite of the thought to be repressed is excessively re-inforced. I call this a *reaction* reinforcement, and the thought which is asserted with excessive strength in the consciousness, and which, like a prejudice, proves impossible to break down, the *reaction thought*. These two thoughts relate to one another more or less after the fashion of a pair of astatic needles. With a certain excess of intensity, the reaction thought keeps the unpleasant thought in the repression; but in the process it is itself 'muffled' and rendered immune to conscious intellectual work. The way to remove the excessive strength from the excessively strong thought, then, is to return the unconscious idea opposed to it into consciousness.

Neither should one rule out the possibility that in certain cases one may be presented not with one of two reasons for super-valence, but with a competition between the two. Other combinations may also arise, but these are easily incorporated into the process.

Let us attempt to do this with the example given to us by Dora, first of all with the first hypothesis: that the roots of her compulsive anxiety about her father's relationship with Frau K. are unknown to her because they lie in the unconscious. It is not hard to guess these roots from the situation, and from the symptoms. Dora's behaviour clearly went far beyond a daughter's sphere of interest, and she felt and acted more like a jealous wife, in a way that might have been understandable if her mother had been acting in the same way. In confronting her father with an alternative: 'Either her or me', in the scenes she made and the threat of suicide which she allowed her parents to glimpse, she was clearly putting herself in her mother's position. If we are correct in guessing that the fantasy of a sexual situation is at the root of her cough, then in that fantasy she took the place of Frau K. So she was identifying with both of the women her father had loved, now and in the past. The obvious conclusion to draw is that her inclination towards her father was stronger than she knew or would have wished to admit, that she was in love with her father.

I have learned to see such unconscious love affairs between father and daughter, mother and son – identifiable by their abnormal consequences – as a revivification of the seeds of certain impressions from infancy. Elsewhere[29] I have explained how early sexual attraction becomes apparent between parents and children, and shown that the Oedipus fable should probably be understood as the poetic treatment of what is typical about such relationships. This precocious inclination of the daughter towards the father, of the son towards the mother, a distinct trace of which is probably to be found in most people, must be seen as having been originally more intense in children constitutionally predisposed towards neurosis, precocious and hungry for love. After this, certain influences which cannot be discussed here come into play, fixating the rudimentary amorous excitement or intensifying it in such a way that from childhood, or only from puberty, it becomes something which might be compared to a sexual attraction and which, like a sexual attraction, monopolizes the libido.[30] The external circumstances in our patient's case certainly do not discourage such an assumption. She had always been temperamentally drawn to her father, and his many illnesses must have heightened her affection for him; in some of his illnesses she herself was entrusted with the minor tasks involved in nursing him; proud of her precocious intelligence, he had chosen her as a confidante even when she was a child. The arrival of Frau K. meant that it was not really her mother but Dora herself who was driven out of more than one job.

When I told Dora I assumed that her inclination towards her father had had the characteristics of passionate love, even early on, she gave her usual answer: 'I can't remember', but then she immediately told me something similar about her seven-year-old cousin (on her mother's side), in whom she often thought she saw something like a reflection of her own childhood. The little girl had once witnessed a heated argument between her parents, and had whispered in Dora's ear, when she had visited shortly afterwards: 'You can't imagine how I hate that (pointing at her mother) person! And when she dies I'm going to marry Papa.' I have become used to seeing such instances, which in some respects accord with what I am asserting, as a confirmation issuing from the unconscious. No other 'yes' can be heard from the unconscious; there is no such thing as an unconscious 'no'.[31]

This passionate love for her father had not manifested itself for years; rather, Dora had enjoyed excellent relations with the very woman who had replaced her in her father's life, and had even, as we know from her instances of self-reproach, favoured that woman's relationship with her father. So that love had recently been revived, and if that was the case, we had cause to wonder why it should have happened. Clearly it was a reaction symptom, its purpose being to suppress something else that was still powerful in the unconscious. As things stood, the first thing that occurred to me was that what had been repressed was Dora's love for Herr K. I had to accept that her passionate love was still there, but since the scene by the lake – for unknown reasons – a violent resistance to it had developed, and the girl had revived and intensified her old inclination towards her father, lest she should retain any conscious thought of the love of her first years of girlhood, which was now embarrassing to her. Then I also gained an insight into a conflict that had the potential to shatter the girl's psychical life. On the one hand, she was filled with regret at having repelled the man's proposal, she was filled with longing for him and the little signs of his affection; on the other hand, powerful motives, pride being one that could easily be guessed, did battle with those affectionate and lovelorn impulses. As a result she had managed to persuade herself that she had finished with Herr K. – that was her gain in this typical process of repression – and yet as a protection against her passion, which was constantly forcing its way into her consciousness, she had to appeal to and exaggerate her infantile inclination towards her father. But the fact that she had been almost incessantly dominated by bitter jealousy seemed capable of a further determination.[32]

The most intense denial that I received when I put this interpretation to Dora certainly did nothing to contradict my expectations. The 'no' that one hears from the patient when one first presents the repressed thought to their conscious perception merely confirms the repression and its intensity; it is a measure of its strength, so to speak. If we do not take this 'no' to be the expression of an objective judgement, of which the patient would not in fact be capable, but instead go beyond it and take the work further, we soon have our first proof that in such cases 'no' means the 'yes' one is hoping for. She admitted that she could not be as angry with Herr K. as he deserved her to be. She said that she had met Herr K. in the street one day when she was with her female cousin, who did not know him. Her cousin suddenly called out, 'Dora, what's wrong with you? You're as white as a ghost!' She had felt nothing of this change in herself, but I had to tell her that facial expressions and affective manifestations obey the unconscious rather than the consciousness, and give the unconscious away.[33] On another occasion, after several days of uniform cheerfulness, she came to see me in the most terrible mood, which she was unable to explain. She felt so dreadful today, she explained; it was her uncle's birthday and she could not bring herself to congratulate him; she didn't know why. As my interpretative art was not working that day, I let her go on speaking, and she suddenly remembered that it was Herr K.'s birthday today as well, which I did not neglect to use against her. Then it became relatively easy to explain why the lovely presents on her own birthday a few days previously had brought her no joy. She was missing the one present from Herr K. that would obviously have been the most precious of all.

Meanwhile, she maintained her denial of my assertion for a long time, until, towards the end of the analysis, the crucial proof of its correctness came to light.

I must now mention a further complication to which I would certainly give no space here if I were inventing, as a writer, such a mental state for a novella, rather than dissecting it as a doctor. The element to which I shall now refer can only dull and blur the beautiful conflict, worthy of poetic treatment, which we may assume in Dora; it would rightly fall victim to the censorship of the writer, who carries out a process of simplification and elimination when he deals with psychological matters. But in the reality that I am attempting to describe here, the rule is the complication of motives, the accumulation and composition of mental stimuli, in short: over-determination. The supervalent train of thought, dealing with her father's relationship with Frau K., concealed an impulse of jealousy whose object was Frau K. herself – an impulse, then, that could only be based on an inclination towards her own sex. It has long been known and often stressed that even normal boys and girls may, during puberty, show clear signs of the existence of same-sex inclinations. Infatuated friendship for a fellow schoolgirl, with sworn oaths, kisses, promises of eternal correspondence, and with all the sensitivity of jealousy, is the usual forerunner of the first more intense passionate love for a man. In favourable circumstances the homosexual current often wins out completely; where happiness in love for a man does not come about, in later years it is often reawakened by the libido and heightened to a particular intensity. If this can be observed without much difficulty in healthy people, following on from earlier observations concerning the stronger formation of the normal germs of perversion in neurotics, we may also expect to find a stronger homosexual predisposition in their constitution. This must be so, because I have never carried out psychoanalytic treatment of a man or a woman without bearing such a highly significant homosexual inclination in mind. Among hysterical women and girls, whose sexual libido as directed towards men has been energetically suppressed, one regularly finds that the libido directed towards women has undergone a vicarious kind of reinforcement, and one that can even be said to be partially conscious.

I shall not go into this important theme, which is particularly indispensable for an understanding of hysteria in men, because Dora's analysis came to an end before it could shed any light on these relations in her own case. But I might recall that governess with whom she at first lived in intellectual intimacy, before she noticed that the governess cherished her and treated her well not for her own sake but for her father's. Then she forced the governess to leave the house. She dwelt with striking frequency and special emphasis on the story of another falling-out that she herself considered mysterious. She had always got on well with her second cousin, the one who later became engaged, and had shared all kinds of secrets with her. Now, when her father returned to B. after the interrupted visit to the lake, and Dora naturally refused to go with him, this cousin was asked to travel with Dora's father and agreed to do so. From that point onwards, Dora felt cold towards her cousin, and was herself startled at how indifferent she had become towards her, although she admitted that she had nothing major to reproach her with. These susceptibilities led me to ask what her relationship with Frau K. had been like before the disagreement. I learned then that the young woman and the barely adult girl had lived for years in the greatest intimacy. When Dora was living with the Ks, she had shared a bedroom with the wife; the husband was moved elsewhere. She had been the wife's confidante and adviser throughout all the problems of her married life; there was nothing that they had not talked about. Medea was perfectly happy for Creusa to draw the two children to herself; she certainly did nothing to obstruct contact between the children's father and the girl. One interesting psychological problem is how Dora managed to love the man about whom her beloved friend had so many bad things to say. We may probably solve this with the insight that thoughts dwell particularly comfortably side by side in the unconscious, that even opposites can bear one another without conflict, and that this state is often perpetuated in the consciousness.

When Dora talked of Frau K., she praised the 'delightful whiteness of her body' in a tone more that of a girl in love than a defeated rival. More melancholic than bitter, on another occasion she told me she was convinced that the presents her Papa had brought back for her had been bought by Frau K.; she recognized her taste. On another occasion she stressed that she had clearly been given a present of some pieces of jewellery through the intercession of Frau K., because they were very similar to the ones that she had seen Frau K. wearing, for which she had, on that occasion, expressed a vociferous desire. Indeed, I must say in general that I never heard her utter a harsh or angry word about the woman, whom she must have seen, from the point of view of her supervalent thoughts, as the source of her unhappiness. Her behaviour seemed inconsistent, but that apparent inconsistency was the expression of a complicated current of emotion. For how had the friend she loved with such infatuation behaved towards her? After Dora had made her accusation against Herr K., and her father had demanded an explanation in writing, he first replied with protestations of respect, and offered to come to the factory town to clear up any misunderstandings. A few weeks later, when her father spoke to him in B., there was no longer any sign of respect. He disparaged the girl and played his trump card: a girl who read such books and took an interest in such things had no claim to a man's respect. So Frau K. had betrayed her and blackened her character; it was only with Frau K. that she had talked of Mantegazza and related subjects. It was the same as with the governess; Frau K., too, had loved her not for her own sake but for her father's. Frau K. had thoughtlessly sacrificed Dora so as not to have her own relationship with Dora's father disturbed. Perhaps this insult was more wounding to Dora, was more pathogenically effective, than the earlier wound that had been inflicted when her father had sacrificed her, and with which she wanted to mask the wound inflicted by Frau K. Did such a stubbornly maintained amnesia concerning the sources of her forbidden knowledge not point directly to the emotional value of the accusation, and thus to her betrayal by her friend?

I believe, then, that I am not mistaken in putting forward the hypothesis that the purpose of Dora's supervalent train of thought about her father's relationship to Frau K. was to suppress not only her formerly conscious love for Herr K., but also her profoundly unconscious love for Frau K. It was directly opposed to the latter current. She told herself incessantly that her Papa had sacrificed her to Frau K., and vociferously demonstrated that she would not grant Frau K. possession of her Papa, and in that way she concealed the opposite, that she could not grant her Papa the love of this woman, and that she had not forgiven this beloved woman the disappointment of her own betrayal. In her unconscious, the feminine impulse of jealousy was coupled with jealousy as it might have been felt by a man. These masculine or, we might say, *gynaecophilic* currents of emotion must be considered typical of the unconscious love-life of hysterical girls.

## Notes

1. *The Interpretation of Dreams*, Chapter II [*Gesammelte Werke*, vol. II/III, p. 104ff.].

2. A colleague once passed his sister to me for psychoanalytic treatment after, he told me, she had been unsuccessfully undergoing treatment for years for hysteria (pains and ambulatory disorders). The brief information seemed to accord well with the diagnosis; in one of the first sessions I had the patient tell me her story herself. When this story, despite the curious details to which she referred, turned out to be perfectly clear and orderly, I told myself that the case could not be one of hysteria, and immediately undertook a careful physical examination. The result was the diagnosis of moderately advanced tabes [a wasting disease], which was then considerably improved with Hg [mercury] injections (Ol. Cinereum, performed by Professor Lang).

3. Amnesias and false memories are complementary to one another. Where large gaps appear in the memory, few errors of memory will be encountered. Conversely, the latter can completely conceal the presence of amnesias at first glance.

4. A rule gained by experience tells us that if an account is given hesitantly, one should learn from this manifestation of the narrator's judgement. In an account hovering between two versions, the first should be taken to be correct, and the second seen as a product of repression.

5. I do not hold the view that the sole aetiology of hysteria is hereditary, but, with reference to earlier publications ('L'hérédité et l'étiologie des névroses' ['The Heredity and Aetiology of Neuroses'], *Revue neurologique*, 1896, in vol. I of the complete edition [of the *Gesammelte Werke*]), in which I dispute the above sentence, I do not wish to give a sense that I underestimate heredity in the aetiology of hysteria, or that I consider it to be utterly dispensable. For our patient's case enough of a taint is present in what I have revealed about the father and his brother and sister; indeed, if one takes the view that illnesses like that of the mother are

impossible without a hereditary disposition, one will be able to declare the heredity of this case to be a convergent one. For the hereditary or, more precisely, the constitutional predisposition of the girl, another element seems to me to be more significant. I have mentioned that her father had suffered a bout of syphilis before his marriage. Now a *strikingly large* percentage of the patients whom I have treated with psychoanalysis are descended from fathers who have suffered from tabes or paralysis. Because my therapeutic procedure is a new one, only *serious* cases come to me, those which have already been treated for years without any success. In accordance with the Erb-Fournier theory, tabes or paralysis in the father can be seen as references to a syphilitic infection in the past, which I too have directly identified in a number of cases with fathers such as these. In the last discussion of the descendants of syphilitics (XIIIth International Conference of Medicine in Paris, 2–9 August 1900, papers by Finger, Tarnowsky, Jullien and others) I find no mention of the fact that my experience as a neuropathologist forces me to acknowledge: that syphilis in the father is certainly worthy of consideration as an aetiology for the neuropathic constitution of the children.

**6.** For the probable cause of this first illness, see below.

**7.** Cf. on the same subject the analysis of the second dream.

**8.** This cure, and consequently my insight into the concatenations of the case, has, as I have already stated, remained fragmentary. For that reason I can provide no information on certain points, or only hints and suspicions. When this letter came to be discussed in one session, the girl asked, as though astonished: 'How did they find the letter in the first place? After all, it was locked in my desk.' But as she knew that her parents had read this draft of a suicide note, I conclude that she had played it into their hands herself.

**9.** I believe that in this attack cramps and deliriums were also apparent. But, as the analysis did not get as far as this event either, I do not have access to any definite memory of it.

**10.** Here is an example of the latter. One of my Viennese colleagues, whose conviction of the lack of importance of sexual elements in hysteria has probably been strongly reinforced by such experiences, forced himself, in the case of a fourteen-year-old girl with dangerous hysterical vomiting, to ask the awkward question of whether she might not even have had a love affair. The child answered, 'No', probably with well-acted astonishment, and in her disrespectful way said to her mother, 'Imagine, the fool even asked me if I was in love.' She then entered my treatment and revealed herself – although not at our first discussion – as a masturbator of long standing with a strong fluor albus (which was closely related to the vomiting). She had finally given up the habit of her own accord. In her abstinence, though, she had been so severely tormented by the most violent sense of guilt that she saw all accidents that befell the family as divine punishment for her sins. She was also influenced by the story of her aunt, whose extramarital pregnancy (providing a second determination for her vomiting) her family thought they had successfully kept secret from her. She was considered to be 'entirely a child', but proved to be initiated in all the essentials of sexual relationships.

11. I have gone beyond this theory without abandoning it, that is, I now declare it not to be incorrect, but incomplete. I have abandoned only my emphasis on the so-called hypnoid state, which is thought to appear in the patient as a result of the trauma, and to serve as an explanation of any psychologically abnormal events that subsequently occurred. If one might be permitted in a collaborative work to undertake a retrospective distribution of property, I should like to state that the hypothesis of the 'hypnoid states', which some people see as the core of our work, is the sole initiative of Breuer. I consider it unnecessary and misleading to interrupt the continuity of the problem in which the psychical process consists in hysterical symptom formation by bestowing this name upon it.

12. Cf. my essay: 'Zur Ätiologie der Hysterie' [On the Aetiology of Hysteria'], *Wiener klinische Rundschau*, 1896, vol. 22–6 (Sammlung kl. Schriften zur Neurosenlehre, I. Folge, 1906. 3. Aufl. 1920. – Contained in vol. I of this complete edition [*Gesammelte Werke*]).

13. The appraisal of these circumstances will be made easier by an explanation later on.

14. Dora's disgust in response to this kiss certainly did not have accidental causes, since these would certainly have been remembered and mentioned. I happen to know Herr K.; he is the same person who accompanied the patient's father when he came to see me, a man who was still young and with appealing looks.

15. Such displacements are not being assumed for the purpose of this single explanation, for example, but arise as an indispensable requirement for a whole series of symptoms. Since writing this I have heard from a fiancée who had previously been very much in love, and who turned to me because of a sudden cooling towards her betrothed, which occurred at the same time as a profound depression. She told me of the same effect of horror as the result of an embrace (without a kiss). In this case the fear was traced back without further difficulty to the man's erection, perceived but removed from consciousness.

16. Cf. the second dream.

17. Here, as at all similar places, one should prepare oneself, not for a single, but for several reasons, for *over-determination*.

18. All these discussions contain much that is typical of hysteria and universally applicable to it. The theme of erection provokes some of the most interesting of hysterical symptoms. Female sensitivity to the outlines of the male genitals perceptible through the clothing often becomes, once repressed, the motive for fear of people and of human society. The broad connection between the sexual and the excremental, whose pathogenic significance can probably not be overstated, is the basis for a very considerable number of hysterical phobias.

19. This is connected to her own suicidal drama, which therefore expresses something like the longing for a similar love.

20. This governess, who read all the books about the sexual life etc., and talked to the girl about them, but candidly asked her to keep everything relating to them secret from her parents, since one could not know what their attitude might be – in this girl, for a while, I sought the source for all of Dora's secret knowledge, and perhaps I was not entirely wrong to do so.

21. Cf. the second dream.

22. Here the question arises: if Dora loved Herr K., how are we to explain her dismissal of him in the scene by the lake, or at least the brutal form of that dismissal, with its suggestion of bitterness? How could a girl in love see an insult in a declaration which – as we shall later hear – was far from brash or repellent?

23. An everyday occurrence between sisters.

24. The further conclusion I drew from the stomach pains will be discussed below.

25. [*Addition* 1923:] This is not entirely correct. We would not be justified in our suggestion that the motives for the illness are not present at the beginning of the illness and are only secondary phenomena. On the next page, in fact, motives for the illness are mentioned which exist before the outbreak of the illness and which contribute to it. Later on in the text I have given a better account of this subject by introducing the distinction between *primary and secondary gain from illness*. The motive for illness is the sole intention of such a gain. What is subsequently said in this section applies to the secondary gain from illness. But a primary gain from illness must be acknowledged for any neurotic illness. Becoming ill first of all spares the patient a psychical task, and presents itself as the most comfortable solution in the case of a psychical conflict (*flight into illness*), although in most cases such an escape proves to be unambiguously pointless. This portion of the primary gain from illness can be described

as the *internal*, psychological part. In addition, external elements such as the example quoted of the situation of the woman oppressed by her husband, can provide motives for becoming ill and thus produce the *external* portion of the primary gain from illness.

**26**. A poet, albeit one who is also a doctor, Arthur Schnitzler gave most correct expression to this idea in his *Paracelsus*.

**27**. These sentences about sexual perversions were written several years before the excellent book by I. Bloch (*Beiträge zur Ätiologie der Psychopathia sexualis* [*Contributions to the Aetiology of Psychopathia Sexualis*], 1902 and 1903). Cf. also in that year (1905) *Drei Abhandlungen zur Sexual-theorie* [*Three Essays on Sexual Theory*] (5th edn, 1922).

**28**. This kind of supervalent thought is, along with profound depression, often the only symptom of a condition that is usually called 'melancholia', but it can be resolved by psychoanalysis like a case of hysteria.

**29**. In the *Interpretation of Dreams*, Chapter V, Section D (ß) [*Gesammelte Werke*, vol. II/III], and in the third of the *Three Essays on Sexual Theory*.

**30**. The crucial element in this is probably the premature appearance of real genital sensations, whether they be spontaneous or provoked by seduction and masturbation (see below).

**31**. [*Addition 1923*:] Another very curious and entirely dependable form of confirmation from the unconscious, with which I was unfamiliar at the time, is the patient's exclamation: 'That's not what I was thinking' or 'I hadn't thought of that'. This statement can be practically translated as: 'Yes, that was unconscious to me.'

**32**. Which we shall [shortly] encounter.

**33**. Cf:

*Ruhig kann* [correctly: *mag*] *ich Euch erscheinen, Ruhig gehen sehn.*
[Quietly can I watch you coming, Quietly watch you go.]

From Schiller, 'Ritter Toggenburg' ('Toggenburg the Knight').

## II *The First Dream*

Just as we had the prospect of shedding some light on a dark corner of Dora's childhood thanks to the material that had thrust its way into the analysis, Dora told me that one night recently she had once again had a dream which she had repeatedly dreamed in exactly the same way. A periodically recurring dream was always particularly apt, by virtue of that very characteristic, to arouse my curiosity; in the interest of the treatment, one could envisage weaving this dream into the analysis as a whole. I therefore decided to examine this dream with especial care.

First dream: '*A house is on fire,*'[1] Dora said, '*Father stands by my bed and wakes me up. I get dressed quickly. Mama wants to rescue her jewellery box, but Papa says: I don't want me and my two children to burn to death because of your jewellery box. We dash downstairs, and as soon as I'm outside I wake up.*'

As this is a recurring dream, I naturally ask when she dreamed it first. – She doesn't know. She does remember, though, that she had the dream in L. (the lakeside town where the scene with Herr K. took place) three nights in a row, and then she had dreamed it again here a few days ago.[2] – The connection, thus established, between the dream and the events in L. naturally raises my expectations about the solution of the dream. But first I should like to learn what prompted its last recurrence, so I ask Dora, who has already been trained in dream interpretation through some small examples which we have analysed before, to break down the dream and tell me what comes to mind.

She says: 'Something that can't have anything to do with it, because it's quite fresh, while I've had the dream before.'

It doesn't matter, just say it; it will be the most recent thing connected with the dream.

'Well, around this time Papa has been arguing with Mama because she locks the dining room at night. My brother's room has no door of its own, and can only be reached through the dining room. Papa doesn't want my brother to be locked in like that at night. He said that wouldn't do; something might happen at night and he would need to get out.'

Did that refer to the danger of fire?

'Yes.'

Please take note of your own expressions. We may need them. You said: That *something might happen* (at night), *and he would need to get out.*[3]

But now Dora has found the link between the recent and the earlier causes for the dream, because she goes on:

'When we arrived in L. that time, Papa and I, without beating about the bush he expressed his fear of a fire. We arrived during a violent thunderstorm and saw the little wooden house with no lightning conductor. So that fear was quite natural.'

I am now concerned to establish the connection between the events in L. and the similar-sounding dreams. So I ask: Did you have the dream during the first nights in L., or the last nights before you left, before or after the scene that we know about in the forest? (I know that the scene did not take place on the first day, and that she subsequently stayed in L. for a few days without mentioning what had happened.)

She first answered: 'I don't know.' After a while: 'Actually I think it was afterwards.'

So now I knew that the dream was a reaction to that experience. But why did it recur three times there? I go on: How long did you stay in L. after that scene?

'Another four days, and on the fifth I left with Papa.'

Now I'm certain that the dream was the immediate effect of the experience with Herr K. You dreamed it there first, and not before then. You only added the uncertainty of your memory in order to blur the connection.[4] But I still can't get the numbers to add up. If you stayed in L. for four nights, you may have repeated the dream four times. Was that perhaps the case?

She no longer denies my claim, but rather than answering my question she continues:[5] 'On the afternoon after our trip on the lake, from which we, Herr K. and I, returned at noon, I had lain down as usual on the sofa in the bedroom to have a quick sleep. I suddenly woke up and saw Herr K. standing in front of me . . .'

Just as you saw Papa standing by your bed in the dream?

'Yes. I asked him what he was doing. He replied that no one could stop him going into his bedroom whenever he felt like it; and anyway he wanted to get something. Having been made uneasy by this, I asked Frau K. if there was no key to the bedroom, and the next morning (on the second day) I locked myself in to make

my toilet. Then, when I was about to lock myself in in the afternoon to lie down on the sofa again, the key was missing. I am
convinced that Herr K. had removed it.'

So that is the theme of locking or not locking the door, which
appears in the first dream associations, and which happened to play
a role in the recent occasion for the dream.[6] Should the phrase: *I
get dressed quickly* be placed in that context as well?

'On that occasion I decided not to stay at the Ks without Papa.
The next morning I was worried that Herr K. might surprise me
while I was at my toilet, and so *I* always *got dressed* very *quickly.*
Papa was staying in the hotel, and Frau K. had gone out very
early for an outing with Papa. But Herr K. didn't bother me
again.'

I understand that on the afternoon of the second day you resolved
to escape these vexations, and now, on the second, third and fourth
night after the scene in the forest, you had time to repeat this
intention in your sleep. You already knew you would not have the
key the next – the third – morning to lock yourself in when you
got dressed on the second afternoon, before the dream, and you
were able to resolve to make your toilet as quickly as possible. But
your dream recurred that night precisely because it corresponded
to an *intention*. An intention exists until it has been carried out.
You told yourself, so to speak: I have no peace, I can't sleep peacefully, until I've left this house. Conversely, you say in the dream:
*Once I'm outside I wake up.*

Here I shall interrupt the account of the analysis to measure parts
of a dream interpretation against my general principles about the
mechanism of dream-formation. In my book[7] I explained that
every dream is a desire represented as fulfilled, and the representation is a disguise if the desire is a repressed one which
belongs to the unconscious; apart from the dreams of children,
only unconscious desires, or those that extend into the unconscious, have the power to form a dream. I think I should have
been more certain of general agreement if I had been content to
claim that every dream had a meaning that could be revealed by

a certain piece of interpretative work. After complete interpretation the dream could be replaced by thoughts, which could be inserted at an easily identifiable point in the waking mental life. I could then have gone on to say that this meaning of the dream proves just as diverse as waking trains of thought. On one occasion it is a fulfilled desire, on another it is a realized fear, or a continued reflection, an intention (as in Dora's dream), a piece of intellectual production during sleep, and so on. This representation would certainly have been distinguished by its comprehensibility, and would have been supported by a good number of well-interpreted examples, such as the dream analysed here.

Instead I put forward a general assertion restricting the meaning of dreams to a single form of thought, the representation of desires, and provoked a general tendency to contradiction. But I must say that I do not believe I have either the right or the duty to simplify a psychological process in order to make things more agreeable for the reader, when that process presented the investigation with a complexity whose solution could generally be found only in other spheres. For that reason it will be particularly valuable for me to show that the apparent exceptions, such as Dora's dream here, which seems first of all to reveal an intention formed during the day and continued in sleep, none the less reinforce this contentious rule.

We still have a large part of the dream to interpret. I continue: What about the jewellery box that Mama wants to save?

'Mama is very fond of jewellery, and got a lot of it from Papa.' And what about you?

'I used to love jewellery too: since my illness I've stopped wearing it. – Four years ago (a year before the dream) Mama and Papa had a big row about a piece of jewellery. Mama wanted to wear something particular, drop pearls, in her ears. But Papa doesn't like that kind of thing, so instead of the drop pearls he brought her a bracelet. She was furious, and told him that if he'd spent so much money on a present that she didn't like then he should give it to someone else.'

And you thought you'd have been happy to have it yourself?

'I don't know,[8] I really don't know how Mama ended up in this dream; she wasn't even in L. at the time.'[9]

I'll explain it to you later. Can't you think of anything else about the jewellery box? So far you've only talked about jewellery and said nothing about a box.

'Yes, Herr K. had given me a valuable jewellery box as a present some time before.'

So there was the gift you received in return. You may not know that 'jewellery box' is a popular expression used to refer to something you recently alluded to when you talked about the handbag,[10] that is to say, the female genitals.

'I knew *you'd* say that.'[11]

That means, *you* knew it. – The meaning of the dream now becomes even clearer. You say to yourself: the man is pursuing me, he wants to get into my room, he's threatening my 'jewellery box' and if something awful happens it will be Papa's fault. For that reason you brought into the dream a situation that expresses the opposite, a danger from which Papa is saving you. In this region of the dream, everything is turned into its opposite; you will soon hear why. The mystery, however, lies with your mother. How did she come to be involved? She is, as you know, your former competitor for Papa's favour. In the incident with the bracelet you would gladly have accepted what your Mama rejected. Now let us replace 'accept' with 'give', 'reject' with 'refuse'. It now means that you would be prepared to give Papa what Mama refused him, and what we're dealing with has something to do with jewellery.[12] Now remember the jewellery box that Herr K. gave you. There you have the beginning of a parallel sequence of thoughts in which, as in the situation in which he stood by your bed, Herr K. replaces Papa. He gave you a jewellery box, in order that you should give him your 'jewellery box'; that's why I was just talking of a 'reciprocal gift'. In this sequence of thoughts your Mama will be replaced by Frau K., who was present at the time. So you're ready to give Herr K. what his wife refuses him. Here you have the thought that must be so strenuously repressed, and which requires the transforma-

491

tion of all elements into their opposite. As I have already told you before we discussed this dream, the dream once again confirms that you are awakening your old love of Papa in order to protect yourself against your love of K. But what do all these efforts prove? Not only that you are afraid of Herr K., but that you are more afraid of yourself, and of your temptation to yield to him. In that way you're confirming the intensity of your love for him.[13]

Of course she would not go along with this piece of interpretation.

However, a continuation of the dream interpretation had also presented itself to me, which seemed equally indispensable to the anamnesis of the case and the theory of dreams. I promised to tell Dora about it at the next session.

I could not, in fact, forget the reference that seemed to arise out of the ambiguous words noted above (*that we had to get out, that there might be a mishap during the night*). I put this down to the fact that the elucidation of the dream seemed incomplete to me without the fulfilment of a certain requirement that I do not wish to set up as a universal principle, but which I none the less wished to see observed. A regular dream stands, so to speak, on two feet, one of which is the actual and essential cause, while the other touches on an important event in childhood. The dream establishes a connection between the two, the childhood experience and the experience in the present day, it seeks to remould the present according to the model of the most distant past. The desire that creates the dream always comes from childhood, it repeatedly seeks to reawaken childhood to reality, to correct the present in terms of childhood. In the dream content, I thought I could already clearly discern the pieces that could be assembled into a reference to an event in childhood.

I began my discussion of this with a little experiment, which was, as usual, successful. A large match-holder happened to be standing on the table. I asked Dora to look around and see if she could see anything in particular on the table that was not usually there. She could not see anything. Then I asked her if she knew why children were forbidden to play with matches.

'Yes, because of the risk of fire. My uncle's children love play-ing with matches.'

Not just because of that. They are warned: 'Don't play with fire', and there's a particular belief associated with that.

She knew nothing of this.

Well: the fear is that they will then wet the bed. That is prob-ably based on the opposition of *water* and *fire*. The idea is more or less that they will dream of fire and then try to put it out with water. I don't know exactly. But I can see that the opposition of water and fire is doing excellent service in your dream. Mama wants to save the jewellery box so that it doesn't *burn*, in the dream thought it's important that the 'jewellery box' shouldn't get *wet*. But fire isn't only used as the opposite of water, it also directly represents love, being in love, being burned. From fire, then, one track leads via this symbolic meaning to thoughts of love, while the other leads off via its opposite, water – after another connection to love, which also makes things *wet*, has branched off – in another direction. Where to now? Think of your expressions: that *there might be a mishap* at night, that you'd have to *get out*. Doesn't that signify a physical need, and if you transfer that 'mishap' to child-hood, could it be anything other than the bed getting wet? But what does one do to protect children against bedwetting? Isn't it the case that you wake them from their sleep during the night, *just as your Papa does with you in the dream*? That, then, would be the real event from which you derive the right to replace Herr K., who wakes you from your sleep, with Papa. I must therefore conclude that you suffered from bedwetting for longer than child-ren usually do. Papa says: *I don't want* [. . .] *my two children . . .* to perish. Your brother has otherwise nothing to do with the current situation at the Ks', and he had not gone to L., either. What do your memories tell you about that?

'I don't know about myself,' she answered, 'but my brother wet the bed until he was six or seven, and sometimes it even happened during the day.'

I was about to draw her attention to how much easier it was to remember such a thing about one's brother than about oneself, when she continued with a memory that had come back to her: 'Yes, it did happen to me for a while, but not until I was seven or eight. It must have been bad, because I know they called the doctor in. It was just before the nervous asthma.'

What did the doctor say?

'He said it was a weakness of the nerves; it would pass, he said, and prescribed a tonic.'[14]

The interpretation of the dream now struck me as complete.[15] She added a supplement to the dream the following day. She had forgotten to mention that after waking up she had always smelled smoke. The smoke accorded well with the fire, and also referred to the fact that the dream had a particular relationship to me, because if she claimed that one thing did not conceal another, I would often say, 'There's no smoke without fire.' But to that exclusively personal interpretation she objected that both Herr K. and Papa were passionate smokers, as, indeed, was I. She herself smoked by the lake, and Herr K. had rolled himself a cigarette before making his unfortunate declaration. She thought she was sure she could remember that the smell of smoke had appeared not only in the last occurrence of the dream, but on the three occasions when she had had the dream in L. As she refused to provide any further information, I had to work out how I was to incorporate this supplement within the fabric of the dream thoughts. One possible clue was that the sensation of smoke had presented itself in the form of a supplement, which meant that it had had to overcome a particular effort of repression. Consequently, it was probably among the most obscurely represented and most repressed ideas: the temptation to appear willing to Herr K. If that was so, it could hardly mean anything but the longing for a kiss, which, from a smoker, would inevitably taste of smoke; but there had been a kiss between them about two years previously, and it would certainly have been repeated more than once if the girl had yielded to Herr K.'s advances. In this way, ideas of temptation seemed to have referred back to the earlier scene, and to have reawoken the memory of that kiss. At that time Dora, the thumb-sucker, had protected herself against its enticement with disgust. If I finally bring together all these clues, which suggest a transference to myself, since I am also a smoker, I come to the view that it probably occurred to her during a session between us that she desired a kiss from me. That, for her, was the cause to repeat the warning dream and resolve to abandon the cure. Everything accords very well if this is so, but because of the characteristics of the 'transference' it cannot be proven.

I might now hesitate about whether I should first tackle the result of this dream as it relates to this particular case history, or whether I should deal with the objection against dream theory that it raises. I shall choose the former of these.

It is worth going in some detail into the meaning of bedwetting in the prehistory of neurotics. For the sake of comprehensibility I shall restrict myself to stressing that Dora's case of bedwetting was not an ordinary case. The disorder had not simply continued beyond the time that is considered normal, but by her own definite account had first gone away and then returned relatively late, after the age of six. Such bedwetting has, to my knowledge, no more probable cause than masturbation, the role of which is still grossly underestimated in the aetiology of bedwetting. In my experience children are well aware of this connection, and all psychical consequences thus follow on from it as though it were something they had never forgotten. Now, at the time when the dream was related, we found ourselves pursuing a line of research that led directly to just such an admission of childhood masturbation. A little while previously Dora had asked why it was she who had fallen ill, and, before I could reply, had placed the responsibility upon her father. She based her explanation not on unconscious thoughts but on conscious knowledge. To my astonishment, the girl knew the nature of her father's illness. She had eavesdropped on a conversation after her father's return from surgery, in which the illness was called by its name. In even earlier years, at the time of his detached retina, an optician who had been called in must have referred to its venereal aetiology, because the curious and concerned girl had heard an old aunt saying to her mother, 'He was sick before the marriage', adding something that she didn't understand, and which she later interpreted as referring to indecent things.

So her father had fallen ill because of his licentious ways, and Dora assumed that he had passed on the illness in hereditary fashion. I was careful not to say that I, as I mentioned above (p. 482–3, note 5), am also of the view that the descendants of syphilitics are particularly prone to serious neuropsychoses. The continuation of this train of thought, in which she levelled accusations against her father, passed through unconscious material. For a few days she identified with her mother, in little symptoms and peculiar habits, and this gave her the opportunity to reach new heights in intolerable behaviour, and then led me to suspect that she was considering a stay in Franzensbad, which she had visited in the company of her mother – I can't remember the year. Her mother had suffered from pains in the lower abdomen, and a discharge (catarrh) that called for a cure in Franzensbad. It was her opinion – probably justified, once again – that the source of this illness was Papa, who had therefore passed on his venereal infection to Dora's mother. It was quite understandable for her, like many non-specialists in general, to lump together gonorrhoea and syphilis, hereditary diseases and those passed on through intercourse. Her insistence on their identification almost made me ask whether she suffered from a venereal disease herself, and now I learned that she suffered from a catarrh (fluor albus) and could not remember when it had started.

Now I understood that the train of thought that vociferously levelled accusations against her father concealed, as usual, a self-reproach, and I met her half-way by telling her that, in my eyes, fluor in young women usually suggested masturbation, and that all the other causes posited for such a condition are relatively unimportant compared to that one.[16] So she was on the way to answering her own question about why she had fallen ill, by admitting masturbation, probably in childhood. She categorically denied being able to remember any such thing. But a few days later she mentioned something that I must take to be a further approach towards confession. On that day, unlike any day before or after, she was wearing a little purse around her neck, in the style that was modern at the time, and played with it as she lay there, opening it up, inserting a finger, closing it again, and so on. I watched her for a while and then explained to her what a *symptomatic action* was.[17] Symptomatic actions are what I call those activities that a person performs automatically, unconsciously, without noticing, as though playing, which the person would dismiss as meaningless and which, if asked, he would describe as unimportant and random. More careful observation then shows that such actions, of which the consciousness knows nothing, or wishes to know nothing, express unconscious thoughts and impulses, which are both valuable and instructive as tolerated expressions of the unconscious. There are two kinds of conscious relation towards symptomatic actions. If an inoffensive motivation can be found for them, one becomes aware of them; if such a pretext is absent from consciousness, one will generally be quite unaware that one is doing them. In Dora's case the motivation was easy: 'Why shouldn't I wear a little bag like this, when it happens to be in fashion?' To such a justification the possibility of an unconscious origin of the action in question does not arise. On the other hand, no compelling proof can be demonstrated for such an origin and the meaning that one assigns to the action. One must content oneself with observing that such a meaning fits very well into the context of the situation in question, into the agenda of the unconscious.

On another occasion I shall present a collection of such symptomatic actions as one can observe among healthy and nervous people. The interpretations are sometimes very easy. Dora's bifoliate bag is nothing other than a representation of the genitals, and her playing with it, opening it and inserting her finger, is an unabashed but unmistakable mimed communication of what she would like to do, the act of masturbation. Recently, a similar case presented itself to me, one which was very cheering. In the middle of a session an elderly lady, supposedly wishing to moisten her throat with a sweet, takes out a small bone box, tries to open it and hands it to me to convince me how hard it is to open. I voice my suspicion that the box must signify something in particular, pointing out that this is the first time I've seen it, despite the fact that its owner has been visiting me for over a year. To which the lady says eagerly: 'I always carry this box with me, I take it with me wherever I go!' She only calms down after I point out to her with a laugh how well her words apply to another meaning. The box – *Dose*, πυξιζ – is, like the little bag, like the jewellery box, once again a representative of the Venus shell, the female genitals!

There is much symbolism of this kind in life that we normally pass by without noticing. When I gave myself the task of bringing to light what people hide, not through the compulsion of hypnosis, but through what they say and show, I thought the task more difficult than it actually is. Anyone with eyes to see and ears to hear will be convinced that mortals cannot hide a secret. If one's lips are silent, one will be voluble with one's finger-tips; betrayal seeps through every pore. And for that reason the task of bringing the most hidden parts of the soul to consciousness is very easy to accomplish.

Dora's symptomatic action with the little bag was not the immediate predecessor of the dream. She introduced the session that brought us the relation of the dream with another symptomatic action. When I walked into the room where she was waiting, she rapidly concealed a letter she was reading. Of course I asked her who the letter was from, and at first she refused to admit it. Then something emerged that was utterly irrelevant and unrelated to our cure. It was a letter from her grandmother, asking her to write more often. I think she just wanted to play 'secrets' with me, and hint that the doctor was now going to wrest her secret from her. I now explain her aversion to any new doctor with reference to her anxiety that he might get to the bottom of her illness through physical examination (catarrh), or questioning (the communication about bedwetting), and guess her masturbation. She always spoke very dismissively of doctors, whom she had evidently overestimated in the past.

Accusations against her father for having made her ill, with the self-accusation behind them – fluor albus – playing with the little bag – bedwetting after the sixth year – secrets that she doesn't want the doctor to wrest from her: I consider the clues about child-hood masturbation to have been definitively proven. In this case I had begun to guess about the masturbation when she had told me about her cousin's stomach cramps (see p. 460) and had then iden-tified with her by complaining for several days about the same painful sensations. It is well known how often stomach cramps occur among those who masturbate. A personal communication from W. Fliess states that precisely such gastralgias can be inter-rupted by a cocaine injection to the 'gastric point' that he found in the nose, and by cauterization of that point. Dora was consciously confirming two things to me: that she herself had often suffered from stomach cramps, and that she had had good reasons for think-ing her cousin was a masturbator. It is very common among patients to recognize in others a connection that they could not, because of their emotional resistance, recognize in themselves. And she no longer denied it, although she did not yet remember it. The tempo-ral definition of the bedwetting 'just before the nervous asthma' I also consider clinically valid. Hysterical symptoms hardly ever arise as long as children are masturbating, but only during abstinence.[18] They express a substitute for masturbatory gratification for which a yearning remains in the unconscious while other, more normal gratification has not yet begun and while masturbation remains a possibility. The latter condition determines the possibility of hyste-ria being cured through marriage and normal sexual intercourse. If gratification in marriage is removed once again, through coitus interruptus, psychical aversion and so on, the libido seeks out its old river bed and expresses itself once more in hysterical symptoms.

I should like to be able to say with certainty when and through what particular influence Dora's masturbation was suppressed, but the fact that the analysis was terminated prematurely requires me to present incomplete material. We have heard that the bedwet-ting lasted almost up to the first case of dyspnoea. Now the only explanation that she was able to suggest for that first condition was that her Papa had then travelled away for the first time since his recovery. I could not help seeing that preserved piece of memory as indicating a connection with the aetiology of the dyspnoea. Now, because of symptomatic actions and other clues, I had good reason to assume that the child, whose bedroom was near her parents' room, had listened to a nocturnal visit of the father to his wife, and had heard the panting of the breathless man during coitus. In such cases children sense the sexual in disturbing sounds. The movements demonstrating sexual excitement are already present as innate mechanisms. I demonstrated years ago that the dyspnoea and rapid heartbeat of hysteria and anxiety neurosis are only isolated fragments of the act of coitus, and in many cases, such as Dora's, I was able to trace the symptom of dyspnoea, or nervous asthma, back to the same cause, that of listening to adults having sexual intercourse. The influence of co-excitement can cause a drastic change in the child's sexuality, replacing the inclination to masturbation with an inclination to anxiety. A while later, when her father had been absent and the child, in love with him, remembered him with longing, she then repeated the impression as an attack of asthma. From the cause of this illness preserved in the memory, we may still guess the anxious train of thought that accompanied the attack. The first time she had such an attack was after over-exerting herself on an outing to the mountains, when she had probably been really short of breath. Along with this came the idea that her father was forbidden to climb mountains, that he was not allowed to over-exert himself because he suffered from breathlessness; then there was the memory of how much he had exerted himself at night in Mama's room, and the worry that he might have injured himself, the worry that she might have over-exerted herself in her masturbation, which also led to sexual orgasm with some dyspnoea; and then the intensified return of that dyspnoea as a symptom. I was still able to draw some of this material from the analysis, and had to supply the rest myself. We have been able to see, with reference to masturbation, that the material relating to a theme is only assembled fragmentarily at various times and in various contexts.[19]

Now a series of extremely important questions arises concerning the aetiology of hysteria: whether Dora's case might be seen as typical of the aetiology, whether it represents the only type of cause, and so on. But I am certainly correct in making the answer to these questions wait for the communication of a larger series of similarly analysed cases. I would have to begin by turning the question on its head. Instead of saying simply yes or no, in response to the question of whether or not the aetiology of this illness lies in childhood masturbation, I would first of all discuss the conception of aetiology in psychoneuroses. The point of view from which I replied would be significantly remote from the point of view from which the question was put. It is enough for us to convince ourselves that childhood masturbation is demonstrably present in this case, that it is not a random factor, and that it cannot be irrelevant to the form of the symptoms.[20] We may more readily understand Dora's symptoms if we consider the meaning of the fluor albus to which she admitted. The word 'catarrh', which she learned to apply to the infection when her mother had to go to Franzensbad for a similar reason, is in turn a 'switch' that opened up access, via the symptom of coughing, to a whole series of thoughts about her Papa's responsibility for his own illness. This cough, which certainly had its origins in an insignificant and real catarrh, was, furthermore, an imitation of her father, who also suffered from a lung condition, and was capable of expressing her sympathy and concern for him. But in a way it also announced to the world something that she might not yet have been aware of: 'I am Papa's daughter. I have catarrh just as he does. He made me ill just as he made Mama ill. It is from him that I have the bad passions that are punished with illness.'[21]

We may now attempt to bring together all the various determinations that we have found for the attacks of coughing and hoarseness. At the very bottom of this stratification is a real, organically caused coughing irritation, the grain of sand around which the mollusc forms the pearl. This irritation may be fixated because it affects a region of the body that has to a large degree preserved the significance of an erogenous zone in the girl. It is also suited to expressing the excited libido. It is fixated by what is probably the first psychical coating – sympathetic imitation of the sick father – and subsequently by self-reproach because of 'catarrh'. The same group of symptoms also proved capable of representing relations with Herr K., regretting his absence and expressing the desire to be a better wife to him. Once a part of the libido has turned back towards the father, the symptom acquires what may be its final meaning: identification with Frau K. I would like to guarantee that this series is by no means complete. Unfortunately this unfinished analysis cannot pursue the change of meaning over chronological time, or reveal the sequence and co-existence of different meanings. One might make such demands upon a complete analysis.

At this point I must not neglect to examine further connections between genital catarrh and Dora's hysterical symptoms. At a time when we were still a long way away from a psychical explanation of hysteria, I heard other, experienced colleagues assert that among hysterical patients with fluor a deterioration in the catarrh generally means an intensification of the hysterical illness, particularly in terms of appetite loss and vomiting. No one knew very much about this connection, but I believe that they were inclined towards the view of the gynaecologists, who, as we know, assume genital infections to have a very great direct and disturbing effect on the nervous functions, although proof of this is generally lacking. As regards the state of our knowledge today, such a direct and organic influence cannot be ruled out, but its psychical form is more easily identifiable. Women take a special pride in the state of their genitals; if these succumb to illnesses which seem likely to prompt distaste or even disgust, women's self-esteem is injured and humiliated to a quite incredible extent. Abnormal secretions of the vaginal mucous membrane are considered disgusting.

Let us recall that Dora had a vivid feeling of disgust after Herr K.'s kiss, and that we found reason to complete her narration of the kissing scene with reference to the fact that she felt the pressure of the erect member against her body during that embrace. Now we learn further that the same governess whom she had rejected because of her disloyalty had told her from the experience of her own life that all men were flighty and unreliable. For Dora this meant that all men were like Papa. She believed her father to be suffering from a venereal disease, and her concept of venereal disease was of course formed from her own personal experience. Suffering from venereal disease, then, meant being afflicted with a disgusting discharge – might this not be a further motivation for the disgust that she felt at the moment of the embrace? That disgust, transposed to the man's touch, would in that case be disgust projected on to the primitive mechanism mentioned above (see pp. 457–8), which finally referred to her own fluor.

I suppose that these may be unconscious thoughts, stretched out over prefigured organic relations like garlands of flowers draped over metal wire, so that in another case one might be able to find different paths of thought leading between the same starting and finishing points. But knowledge of those chains of thought, which have been individually effective, is of indispensable value in terms of resolving symptoms. If we are obliged to fall back on suppositions and deductions in Dora's case, this is only because the analysis was prematurely terminated. Without exception, the material that I have used to fill the gaps is based on other cases in which the analysis was completed.

The dream whose analysis provided us with the above conclusions corresponds, as we found, to an intention of Dora's, which she takes with her into sleep. For that reason the dream is repeated every night until the intention is fulfilled, and it reappears years later when the occasion arises to form an analogous intention. The intention may be consciously expressed more or less in the following terms: from this house, in which, as I have seen, my virginity is threatened, I set off with Papa, and in the morning at my toilet I seek to take precautions not to be disturbed. These ideas find their clear expression in the dream; they belong to a current which has attained consciousness and which dominates the waking state. Behind them we may guess a more obscure train of thought which corresponds to the opposite current, and which has for that reason succumbed to repression. It culminates in Dora's temptation to give herself to the man in thanks for the love and affection he has shown her for the past few years, and perhaps evokes the memory of the only kiss that she has had from him. But according to the theory developed in my *Interpretation of Dreams*, such elements are not sufficient to form a dream. A dream is not an intention represented as accomplished, but a desire represented as fulfilled, and possibly a desire from childhood. We are duty-bound to examine whether this proposition is not contradicted by our dream.

The dream, in fact, contains infantile material that is not at first glance explicably connected with the intention to flee Herr K.'s house and the temptation emanating from him. Why does the memory arise of bedwetting as a child, and of the trouble that her father had taken then to accustom the child to cleanliness? Because, one might reply, only with the help of this train of thought is it possible to suppress the intense thoughts of temptation and allow the intention of defeating them to triumph. The child decides to flee *with* her father; in reality she is fleeing *to* her father, for fear of the man who is propositioning her; she reawakens an infantile inclination towards her father, an inclination that is supposed to protect her against her recent inclination towards a stranger. Her father is himself to some extent guilty of the present danger, having abandoned her to a stranger in the interest of his own love affair. How much nicer it was, though, when the same father loved no one more than her, and made every effort to save her from the dangers that threatened her then. The infantile and now unconscious desire to place her father in the position of the stranger is the power that forms the dream. If there has been a situation resembling this one in all respects except for the person involved, this becomes the main situation of the dream content. Such a situation exists: her father had, like Herr K. the day prior to the dream, once stood by her bed and woken her with a kiss or something similar, as perhaps Herr K. intended to do. So the intention to flee the house is not in itself enough to facilitate a dream, but is made capable of doing so by the fact that it is joined by another intention, based on infantile desires. The desire to substitute her father for Herr K. provides the driving force for the dream. I would remind the reader of the interpretation, imposed upon me by the intensified train of thought referring to her father's relationship with Frau K., that an infantile attachment to her father had been awoken to keep her repressed love for Herr K. in the repressed state; this abrupt change in the patient's mental life is reflected in the dream.

As regards relations between waking thoughts that continue in sleep – the day's residues – and the unconscious dream-forming desires, I have in the *Interpretation of Dreams*, Chapter VII, Section C, set down some observations that I shall quote here in full, because I have nothing to add to them, and because the analysis of this dream of Dora's proves once again that this is an accurate representation of things.

'I am prepared to admit that there is a whole class of dreams whose *stimulus* consists primarily or even exclusively in the residues of daily life, and I think that my own wish finally to be *Professor extraordinarius* (extraordinary professor)[22] would have allowed me to sleep in peace on that night had not my concern for my friend's health the previous day still been active. But that concern had not yet formed a dream; the *driving-force* needed by the dream had to be supplied by a desire; it was up to that concern to create such a desire as a driving force for the dream. To put it metaphorically: it is entirely possible that a diurnal thought should act as the *entrepreneur* for the dream; but the entrepreneur, who, as they say, has the idea and the drive to put it into action, can do nothing without capital; he requires a *capitalist* with the necessary outlay, and that capitalist, who provides the psychical outlay for the dream, is always and inevitably, whatever the diurnal thought may be, *a desire from the unconscious.*'

No one familiar with the delicacy of the structure of such formations as dreams will be surprised to discover that the desire for the father to assume the place of the tempting man calls to memory not random material from childhood, but material most intimately related to the repression of that temptation. For if Dora feels incapable of yielding to her love for that man, if she represses that love rather than giving in to it, that decision is not more intimately connected with any element than with her precocious sexual pleasures and their consequences, bedwetting, catarrh and disgust. Such antecedents can, according to the sum of constitutional conditions, explain two attitudes towards demands made by the erotic life in adulthood: either unresisting abandon to sexuality, bordering on perversion, or, a reaction involving the rejection of sexuality, accompanied by neurotic illness. Our patient's constitution and level of intellectual and moral education had led to the latter outcome.

In particular, I should also like to point out that the analysis of this dream has led us to information concerning pathogenically effective experiences which were not otherwise accessible to memory, let alone to reproduction. The memory of childhood bedwetting had, as it turned out, already been repressed. Dora had never mentioned the details of Herr K.'s pursuit of her, as it had not occurred to her to do so.

A few additional remarks[23] concerning the synthesis of this dream. The dream-work begins on the afternoon of the second day after the scene in the forest, when Dora notices that she can no longer lock the door to her room. Then she says to herself: I'm in serious danger here, and forms the intention not to stay alone in the house, but to leave with her Papa. This intention becomes available for dream-work because it is able to continue into the unconscious. Corresponding to this intention within the unconscious is the fact that it conjures up the infantile love of the father as a protection against the present temptation. The reversal that consequently occurs within her is fixated and leads her to the point of view represented by her supervalent train of thought (jealousy of Frau K. over her father, as though she were in love with him). There is a struggle within her between the temptation to yield to the man who is courting her, and complex resistance to that temptation. The latter is assembled from motives of respectability and good sense, hostile impulses resulting from the governess's revelation (jealousy, wounded pride, see below) and an element of neurosis, the pre-existing sexual repugnance deriving from her childhood history. Dora's love for her father, awakened to protect her against temptation, derives from that childhood history.

The dream transforms the intention, deep within the unconscious, to flee to the father, into a situation that represents the desire for her father to save her from danger as being already fulfilled. For this to be achieved, an obstructive thought must be removed, that it is her father who has put her in that danger. We will encounter the hostile impulse (inclination towards revenge) against her father, which is here suppressed, as one of the motors of the second dream.

According to the conditions of dream-formation, the fantasized situation is selected in such a way that it repeats an infantile situation. It is a most particular triumph if it manages to transform a recent situation, such as that which occasioned the dream, into an infantile situation. This can occur in this case because of a coincidence in the material. Herr K. stood by her bed and woke her, just as her father often did in the years of her childhood. The complete reversal that Dora effected can be accurately symbolized by substituting her father for Herr K. in that situation.

But in those days her father woke her so that she would not wet the bed.

This idea of 'wet' becomes defining for the rest of the dream content, although in that content it is represented only by a remote reference and by its opposite.

The opposite of 'wet', 'water', can easily be 'fire', 'burning'. The coincidental fact that her father voiced a fear of the fire on their arrival at the town [L.] contributes to the danger from which her father saves her: the danger of fire. The chosen situation of the dream image is based on this coincidence and the opposition to 'wet': there is a fire, her father stands by her bed to wake her. Her father's chance remark would not achieve this significance in the dream content if it did not accord so excellently with the victorious emotional current that wishes to see the father as helper and saviour. He sensed the danger immediately upon their arrival, and he was right! (In fact it was he who put the girl in that danger.)

Within the dream thoughts, easily traceable connections give the idea of 'wet' the role of an intersection point for several different circles of representation. 'Wet' belongs not only to bedwetting, but also to the circle of thoughts of sexual temptation, which are suppressed behind this dream content. She knows that there is also a wetness in sexual intercourse, that the man gives the woman something liquid in *the form of drops* in the act of intercourse. She knows that the danger lies there, that she is given the task of protecting the genitals from being made wet.

At the same time, with 'wet' and 'drop', the other circle of associations closes, that of the disgusting catarrh, which in her more mature years has the same shaming significance as bedwetting had in her childhood. Here 'wet' is equated with 'contaminated'. The genitals, which should be kept clean, are contaminated by catarrh, both in her Mama's case and her own (p. 501). She appears to believe that her Mama's addiction to cleanliness is a reaction to this contamination.

The two circles are superimposed here: Mama has had both from Papa, the sexual 'wet' and the contaminating fluor. Dora's jealousy of her Mama is inseparable from the circle of thoughts concerning the infantile love of her father, which is conjured up here as a means of protection. This material is not yet capable of representation. But if a memory can be found which stands in a similar relation to both circles of 'wet', but which manages not to be offensive, that memory will be able to assume the function of representation in the dream content.

One example of this is to be found in the detail of the 'drops' that Mama wanted as a piece of jewellery. Apparently the link between this reminiscence and the two circles of the sexual 'wet' and of contamination is an external and superficial one, conveyed through words, because 'drop' is used as a 'switch', an ambiguous word, and 'jewellery' is used more or less as 'clean', a rather forced opposition to 'contaminated'. In fact very firm underlying associations can be demonstrated. The memory emerges from the material of Dora's jealousy of her Mama, which had infantile roots but continued long after childhood. Through these two verbal associations all significance attached to the ideas of sexual intercourse between the parents, the fluor infection and Mama's irritating habit of cleaning is transferred to a single reminiscence of 'jewellery drops'.

But a further displacement must occur for the purposes of the dream content. What finds its way into the dream is not the 'drops', which are close to the original 'wet', but the more remote 'jewellery'. So, if this element is incorporated into the previous fixated dream situation, it could have meant the following: 'Mama still wants to save her jewellery.' In the new alteration, 'jewellery box', the influence of elements from the underlying circle of temptation on the part of Herr K., assumes belated validity. Herr K. did not give her jewellery, but he did give her a 'little box' for it, the substitute for all the favours and affection for which she should now be grateful. And the resulting composite, 'jewellery box', has another particular representational value. Is 'jewellery box' not a commonplace image for the immaculate, intact female genitals? And, on the other hand, an innocuous word, ideally suited both to suggest the sexual thoughts behind the dream and to conceal them?

Thus we find, at two points in the dream: 'Mama's jewellery box', and this element replaces the mention of infantile jealousy, the drops, and thus the sexual 'wet', at once contamination by fluor and the now current thoughts of temptation, which urge towards a reciprocal love and depict in anticipation the sexual situation, both longed-for and threatening. The element of the 'jewellery box' is, more than any other, the product of condensation and displacement, and a compromise between opposing currents. Its multiple origin – from both an infantile and a contemporary source – is indicated by its twofold appearance in the dream content.

The dream is the reaction to a fresh and stimulating experience, which necessarily awakens the memory of the only analogous experience from earlier years. That is the scene with the kiss in the shop, during which Dora felt disgust. But the same scene can be reached from elsewhere, from the circle of thoughts around catarrh (see pp. 501–2) and from the circle of the current temptation. So it makes a contribution of its own to the dream content, which must adapt to the preformed situation. Something is on fire . . . the kiss probably tasted of smoke, so Dora smells smoke in the dream content, which in this case continues after she has awoken.

Unfortunately, I inadvertently left a gap in the analysis of this dream. The speech is put into the mouth of the father: 'I didn't want my two children to perish' etc. (we may probably add, on the basis of the dream thought: through the consequences of masturbation). Such a speech in a dream is generally assembled from pieces of real speech, whether heard or uttered. I should have inquired into the true origin of this speech. The result of that would have made the construction of the dream more complicated, but it would also certainly have rendered it more transparent.

Should we assume that this dream had exactly the same content in L. as it did when repeated during the cure? That would not seem necessarily to be the case. Experience shows that people often claim to have had the same dream while the individual phenomena of the recurring dream differ in numerous details and other modifications. Thus one of my patients tells me she has had her favourite recurring dream once again, and in the same way: she is swimming in the blue sea, parting the waves with pleasure, and so on. Closer examination shows that against a common background sometimes one detail and sometimes another is applied; on one occasion, indeed, she was swimming in the sea when it was frozen, surrounded by icebergs. Other dreams, which she herself does not try to present as being identical, prove to be intimately connected with this recurring dream. For example, she sees at the same time, from a photograph, the highlands and lowlands of Heligoland in real dimensions, a ship on the sea bearing two friends from her youth, and so on.

It is certain that Dora's dream, which occurred during the cure – perhaps without changing its manifest content – had acquired a new and current significance. Its dream thoughts included a connection with my treatment, and corresponded to a renewal of her intention at the time to escape from a danger. If her memory was not in error, when she claimed to have smelled the smoke after waking up in L., we must acknowledge that she very skilfully incorporated my utterance: 'There's no smoke without fire' into the fully formed dream, where the words appear to be used to over-determine the last element. Incontestably, it was the result of chance that the final cause, her mother's locking of the dining room, which meant that Dora's brother was locked in his bedroom, produced a connection with Herr K.'s pestering of her in L. It was here, when she could not lock her bedroom, that her resolution reached maturity. Perhaps her brother did not appear in her dreams at that time, with the result that the words 'my two children' entered the dream content only after the final cause of the dream.

## Notes

1. There was never a real fire at our house, she said in answer to my question.

2. The content allows us to conclude that the dream was *first* dreamed in L.

3. I emphasize these words because they make me suspicious. They sound ambiguous to me. Does one not use the same words for certain physical needs? But ambiguous words are like switches or points at a railway junction, changing the course of associations. If the switch is changed from the way it appears in the dream content, in all likelihood one ends up on the track on which the thoughts behind the dream sought, and still hidden, are moving.

4. Concerning what was initially said about doubts when remembering, see above pp. 443–4.

5. In fact we must wait for new remembered material before my question can be answered.

6. I assume, although without telling Dora, that she picked up this element because of its symbolic significance. 'Rooms' (*Zimmer*) in dreams often seek to represent women (*Frauenzimmer*), and it can of course not be a matter of indifference whether a woman is 'open' or 'closed'. The 'key' that opens in this case is well known.

7. *The Interpretation of Dreams*, 1900.

8. The usual phrase with which she acknowledged something repressed.

9. This observation, which testifies to a complete misunderstanding of the rules of dream interpretation, with which she was otherwise familiar, as well as the hesitancy and sparse exploitation of her ideas about jewellery boxes, proved to me that this was material that had been most emphatically repressed.

10. About this little bag see below.

11. A very common way of rejecting an item of knowledge arising from the repressed.

12. For the drops we will later also be able to find an interpretation required by the context.

13. To this I add: Incidentally, I must conclude from the recurrence of

the dream over recent days that you consider the same situation to have recurred, and that you have decided to stay away from the cure, to which only your father brings you. – Subsequent events showed how correct my guess had been. Here my interpretation touches upon the theme of 'transference', extremely significant both from the practical and theoretical points of view, to which I will have little opportunity to refer further in this essay.

14. This doctor was the only person in whom she showed any trust, because the experience made her aware that he had not discovered her secret. With anyone else whom she could not yet assess she felt anxiety, now motivated by the possibility that he might guess her secret.

15. The core of the dream, translated, would be more or less as follows: The temptation is so strong. Dear Papa, protect me once again as you did in my childhood days, so that my bed doesn't get wet!

16. [*Addition 1923:*] An extreme view that I would no longer hold today.

17. Cf. my essay *Zur Psychopathologie des Alltagslebens* [*Psychopathology of Everyday Life*], 1901, Chapter IX.

18. The same thing is true in principle of adults, but here, too, relative abstinence, a restriction of masturbation, is enough for a high level of libido-hysteria and masturbation to appear together.

19. In a similar way, proof of infantile masturbation is also produced in other cases. The material for this is generally similar in nature: indications of fluor albus, bedwetting, ceremonial related to the hands (compulsive washing) and so on. One can always tell with certainty by the set of symptoms connected with the case whether or not the habit has been discovered by a carer, or whether a campaign of dissuasion or a sudden volte-face has put an end to the sexual activity. In Dora's case masturbation had remained undiscovered, and had come to an end all of a sudden (secrecy, fear of doctors – substitution of dyspnoea). It is true that patients regularly dispute the capacity of these clues to supply proof, even when the memory of catarrh or their mother's warning ('it'll make you stupid; it's poisonous') has remained in conscious memory. But some time later the memory of this piece of the child's sexual life appears with certainty in all cases – as for instance in a patient with obsessive ideas deriving directly from infantile masturbation. Here the traits of self-prohibition and self-punishment – if they have done one thing, they mustn't do another, they mustn't be disturbed, they insert pauses between one performance (with the hands) and the next, hand-washing, and so on – prove to be pieces of deterrence on the part of their carers, preserved unaltered. The warning: 'Now, that's poisonous!' was the only thing that had been preserved in the memory. On this subject, compare my *Drei Abhandlungen zur Sexualtheorie*

[*Three Essays on Sexual Theory*], 1905, 5th German edition, 1922 [the second essay].

20. The learning of the habit of masturbation must somehow be connected to her brother, for in this context she told me with the emphasis that reveals a 'screen memory' that her brother had regularly passed on all his infections to her. He endured them easily, she with difficulty. In the dream, her brother is also protected against 'perishing'; he himself has suffered from bedwetting, but stopped before his sister did. In a sense it was also a 'screen memory' when she announced that she was able to keep pace with her brother up until her first illness, and from then on she had lagged behind him in her school work. As though she had been a boy until that point, and only then become girlish. She was really a wild thing, but from her 'asthma' onwards she became quiet and well-behaved. This illness formed [in her] the borderline between two phases of sexual life, the first of which was male in character, the second female.

21. The word ['catarrh'] played the same role in the fourteen-year-old girl whose case history I have crammed into a few lines on p. 483–4, note 10. I had placed the child with an intelligent lady, who performed the services of a carer for me, in a pension. The lady told me that her little patient could not bear her presence at bedtime, and that in bed she developed a strikingly bad cough of which there was no sign throughout the day. When she was asked about these symptoms, all the little girl could think was that her grandmother coughed the same way, and she was said to have catarrh. It then became clear that she too had catarrh, and that she did not want to be observed when washing in the evening. The catarrh which had been pushed *from top to bottom* by means of this word even showed an unusual level of intensity.

22. This refers to the analysis of the dream taken as a model at this point [Chapter V, Section D], II/III.

23. [The remainder of this chapter was printed as a footnote in editions earlier than 1924.]

## III  *The Second Dream*

A few weeks after the first dream came the second, and the analysis was terminated after its elucidation was complete. It cannot be rendered as completely transparent as the first, but it brought the desired confirmation of a hypothesis that had become necessary concerning the patient's state of mind, filled a gap in the memory and provided a deep insight into the origin of another of Dora's symptoms.

Dora related her dream: *'I am going for a walk in a town I don't know, I see streets and squares that are strange to me.*[1] *Then I enter a house where I live, go to my room and find a letter from my Mama lying there. She writes: As I am away from home without my parents' knowledge, she was not going to write to tell me that Papa was ill. Now he has died, and if you want*[2] *you can come. Now I make for the station and ask about a hundred times: Where is the station? I keep getting the answer: five minutes away. Then I see a dense forest ahead of me, walk into it and there ask a man I meet. He tells me: Another two and a half hours.*[3] *He offers to come with me. I decline and go on my own. I see the station ahead of me and can't reach it. At the same time there's that habitual feeling of anxiety that you have when you can't get any further in the dream. Then I'm at home, I must have travelled in the meantime, but I can't remember anything about it. – I walk into the porter's lodge and ask about our apartment. The maid opens the door for me and answers: Mama and the others are already at the cemetery.*[4]

The interpretation of this dream was not without its difficulties. Because of the particular circumstances in which we broke up, which related to its content, not everything was explained, and this in turn has something to do with the fact that I have not been able to remember the whole sequence of revelations with equal exactitude. First of all I shall mention the subject that we were analysing when this dream occurred. For some time Dora herself had been asking questions about the connection between her actions and what one took to be the motives for them. One of these questions was: 'Why did I remain silent for the first few days after the scene by the lake?' The second: 'Why did I then suddenly tell my parents about it?' I thought we still needed an explanation of why she had felt so gravely insulted by Herr K.'s advance, particularly as I was beginning to understand that his courtship of Dora had not been a frivolous attempt at seduction on Herr K.'s part either. I interpreted the fact that she had informed her parents about the event as an action already influenced by pathological revenge. A normal girl would, I should have thought, have come to terms with such events on her own.

So I shall set out the material that presented itself to the analysis of this dream in the rather haphazard order in which it comes to mind.

*She is wandering alone in a strange town, and sees streets and squares.* She assures me that it was certainly not B., my first guess, but a town where she had never been. Naturally I continued: You might have seen paintings or photographs from which you have taken these dream-images. It was after this observation that she mentioned a monument in a square, and immediately after that revealed that she knew the source of the idea. She had been given an album of views of a German spa town for Christmas, and had taken it out again the previous day to show the relatives with whom she was staying. It was in a box of pictures that she could not immediately find, and she had asked her Mama: *Where is the box?*[5] One of the pictures showed a square with a monument. But the present had been given to her by a young engineer whom she had once fleetingly known in the factory town. The young man had taken a job in Germany in order to achieve his independence more quickly, and used every opportunity he had to make her remember him, and it was easy to guess that if his position improved he planned to propose to Dora. But that would take time, and he would have to wait.

The idea of wandering around in a strange town was overdetermined. It led back to one of the diurnal causes of the dream. During the holidays a young cousin had come on a visit, and she was to show him the city of Vienna. This external cause was clearly one of extreme indifference. But the cousin reminded her of a brief first stay in Dresden. On that occasion she had wandered around as a stranger, and of course had not neglected to visit the famous gallery. Another cousin, who was with them and knew Dresden, wanted to act as guide in the gallery. *But she turned him away and went on her own*, stopping by paintings that she liked. Before the Sistine Madonna she stopped for *two hours*, in silently dreaming admiration. She had no clear answer to the question of what she had liked so much about the painting. In the end she said: the Madonna.

It is certain that these ideas really are part of the dream-forming material. They incorporate components which we find unaltered in the dream content (she turned him away and went on her own). I make a note that 'pictures' correspond to an intersection in the fabric of the dream thoughts (the pictures in the album – the paintings in Dresden). And I might single out the theme of the *Madonna*, the virgin mother, for further examination. But above all I see that in this first part of the dream she is identifying with a young man. He is wandering around in a strange place, trying to find a goal, but he is held back, he needs patience, he must wait. If she was thinking about the engineer, then that goal would have been the possession of a wife, Dora herself. Instead it was a station, although according to the connection that exists between the question posed in the dream and the one posed in reality, we can substitute a box for this. A box and a woman go better together.

*She asks about a hundred times* . . . That leads to another, less insignificant cause for the dream. The previous evening, after the party, her father had asked her to bring him the brandy; he could not get to sleep without drinking brandy. She had asked her mother for the key to the larder, but her mother was in the middle of a conversation and did not answer, until Dora erupted with the impatient exaggeration: Now I've asked you *a hundred times* where the key is. In fact, of course, she had only repeated the question about *five times*.[6]

*Where is the key?* strikes me as the masculine counterpart to the question: Where is the box? (see the first dream, pp. 490–91). So these are both questions – about the genitals.

At the same family gathering, someone had raised a toast to Papa and expressed the hope that he would long remain in the best of health etc. At that, her father's tired features had twitched in a very strange way, and she had understood the thoughts he had to suppress. The poor, sick man! Who could tell how much life he still had ahead of him?

This brings us to the *content of the letter* in the dream. Her father had died, she had left home of her own volition. When we came to the letter in the dream, I immediately reminded her of the suicide note that she had written to her parents, or had at least left out where her parents could find it. That letter was designed to frighten her father so that he would leave Frau K., or at least to allow Dora to avenge herself on him if he could not be persuaded to do that. We have reached the subject of her death and the death of her father (*cemetery*, later in the dream). Are we mistaken in assuming that the situation which forms the façade of the dream corresponds to a fantasy of revenge against her father? Her thoughts of pity the previous day would have tallied well with that. But according to the fantasy, she went away from home to a strange place, and out of concern for her, out of longing for her, her father's heart had broken. That meant that she would have had her revenge. She understood very well what her father was lacking, if he was unable to get to sleep without cognac.[7]

Let us keep *vengefulness* as a new element for a later synthesis of the dream thoughts.

But the content of the letter must have allowed further determination. Hence the addition: *If you want?*

Then it occurred to her that after the word 'want' there was a question mark, and this reminded her that the words were a quotation from the letter from Frau K., containing the invitation to L. (by the lake). In this letter, after the words: 'if you want to come?' there had been a question mark that looked very odd in the middle of the sentence.

So that takes us back to the scene by the lake and the mysteries connected with it. I asked her to relate that scene to me in detail again. At first she did not introduce much that was new. Herr K. had begun quite seriously; but she would not let him finish. Once she had understood what was happening, she slapped his face and dashed away. I wanted to know what words he had used;

she could only remember his explanation: 'You know, I get nothing from my wife.'[8] Then, lest she bump into him again, she set off walking around the lake towards L., and *asked a man she met how far away she was*. Hearing his answer: 'Two and a half hours', she abandoned that plan and went back to find the boat which would soon be setting off. Herr K. was there, too, and he approached her, asking her to forgive him and to tell no one of what had happened. She did not reply. – Yes, the *forest* in the dream was quite similar to the forest on the shores of the lake, where the scene she had just described again had taken place. She had seen exactly the same dense forest in a painting in the exhibition at the Secession the previous day. In the background of the painting there were *nymphs*.[9]

Now one of my suspicions became a certainty. *'Bahnhof'* ['station'][10] and *'Friedhof'* ['cemetery'], in place of female genitals, was striking enough, but had directed my sharpened attention towards the similarly formed *'Vorhof'* ['vestibule'], an anatomical term for a particular region of the female genitals. But that could be an error conjured by the mind. Now, when the 'nymphs' were added, seen against the background of the 'dense forest', no doubts were permitted any longer. This was symbolic sexual geography! 'Nymphae', as a doctor will know and the layman will not – and not even every doctor will – is the name given to the small labia in the background of the 'dense forest' of pubic hair. But anyone using such technical names as *'Vorhof'* and *'Nymphen'* must have taken their knowledge from books, and not popular books but anatomical textbooks or a dictionary, the usual refuge of young people consumed with sexual curiosity. If this interpretation were correct, behind the first dream there lay a defloration fantasy, in which a man tried to force his way into a woman's genitalia.[11]

I shared my conclusions with her. The impression must have been compelling, because a forgotten fragment of the dream immediately followed: *That she was walking peacefully*[12] *back and forth in her room, reading a big book that lay on her desk.* Here the emphasis is on the two details: peaceful and with a big book. I asked: Was it in dictionary format? She said it was. But children never look up forbidden material in a dictionary *peacefully*. They tremble and quake, and look anxiously around to see if anyone is coming. Parents are very much in the way where such reading is concerned. But the wish-fulfilling power of the dream had fundamentally improved the uncomfortable situation. Dora's father was dead and the others had already gone to the cemetery. So she could go on reading as she pleased. Did that not mean that one of her reasons for revenge had also been her rejection of the constraints imposed by her parents? If her father was dead, she could read or love as she wished. At first she claimed not to remember ever having looked things up in a dictionary, but then she admitted that she did have such a memory, although it was innocuous in content. When her favourite aunt had been so seriously ill, and it was already decided that she should travel to Vienna, her parents received a *letter* from another uncle, saying that they could not travel to Vienna, since a child, a cousin of Dora's, had fallen dangerously ill with appendicitis. Of what she had read, she still remembered the description of the characteristic pain located in the abdomen.

Now I reminded her that she had supposedly had appendicitis shortly after her aunt's death. I had previously not dared to include this illness among her hysterical accomplishments. She told me that for the first few days she had had a high temperature and felt in her abdomen the same pain that she had read about in the dictionary. She had had cold compresses, but had been unable to bear them; on the second day, amidst violent pains, her period had begun, and was very irregular following her illness. At that time she had suffered constantly from constipation.

It would not have been correct to see this condition as purely hysterical. Although hysterical fever does doubtless occur, it seems arbitrary to relate the fever of this questionable illness to hysteria rather than to an organic cause, which was in fact active at the time. I was about to abandon that trail, when she herself helped me, bringing the final supplement to the dream: *She sees herself particularly clearly going up the stairs.*

Of course I demanded a particular determination for that. She objected, probably not in all seriousness, that she had to go upstairs to get to her apartment on that floor. I was easily able to dismiss this by remarking that if she could travel from the strange town to Vienna in her dream, and skip the railway journey, she could also manage to leave out the steps of the stairs in her dream. She then went on with her story: after her appendicitis she had found walking difficult, and her right foot had dragged. That had remained the case for a very long time, and for that reason she had avoided stairs whenever she could. Even now her foot sometimes dragged. The doctors she consulted on her father's orders had been very surprised by this quite unusual leftover from a case of appendicitis, particularly since the pain in her body had not recurred, and did not accompany the dragging foot in any way.[13]

So that was a genuine hysterical symptom. Even if the fever had also been organically caused – one of those cases of influenza without a particular location, for example – it was securely established that the neurosis had appropriated a chance factor in order to use it for one of its manifestations. So Dora had created for herself an illness that she had read about in the dictionary, and had punished herself for reading about it; she then had to tell herself that the punishment could not apply to the reading of an innocent article, but had come about as the result of a displacement, when this act of reading had been followed by another, less innocent one, now concealed in the memory behind the innocent act of reading that had occurred around the same time.[14] Perhaps we could discover what subjects she had been reading about.

What, then, was the significance of the condition that wished to imitate perityphlitis? The leftover from the infection, the dragging of a leg, which did not really accord with a case of perityphlitis, might accord better with the secret, sexual – let us say – meaning of the illness, and might in turn, if explained, shed some light on the meaning that we were looking for. I tried to find a way into this mystery. Times had appeared in the dream: time is far from irrelevant in all biological events. So I asked when that appendicitis had occurred, whether it had been before or after the scene by the lake. The prompt answer, removing all difficulties at a stroke, was: nine months afterwards. This date is characteristic. So the supposed appendicitis could have realized the fantasy of a *child-birth* with the modest means at the patient's disposal: pains and a period.[15] Of course she knew the significance of the date and could not dismiss the likelihood that she had read about pregnancy and birth in the dictionary. But what about the dragging foot? I would have to guess. That's how you walk when you've put a foot wrong. So she really would have 'put a foot wrong' [*einen Fehltritt gemacht*] if she was giving birth nine months after the scene by the lake. But I had to make one additional demand. I am convinced that one can develop such symptoms only if one has an *infantile* model for them. The memories that one has of later impressions do not, as I must maintain on the basis of my own previous experiences, have the power to be realized as symptoms. I barely dared hope that she would deliver the desired material from childhood, because in reality I cannot yet assert the above proposition, in which I should very much like to believe, as a universal principle. But here the confirmation came *immediately*. Yes, she had once put the same foot wrong as a child, she had slipped in B. when going down the *stairs*: her foot – it was even the same one that had later dragged – swelled up and had to be bandaged, and she took to her bed for several weeks. It was a short time before she developed her nervous asthma, in her eighth year.

Now it was time to turn to account our knowledge of this fantasy: if you give birth nine months after the scene by the lake, and then walk around until the present day with the consequences of 'putting a foot wrong', that proves that in your unconscious you regret the outcome of the scene. So you correct it in your unconscious thought. The precondition for your fantasy of childbirth is that something took place on that occasion,[16] that you had experienced everything on that occasion that you later had to read in your dictionary. You see that your love of Herr K. did not end with that scene, that, as I have claimed, it has continued until the present, albeit unconsciously. – She did not contradict that, either.[17]

This work towards the elucidation of the second dream occupied two sessions. When, after the conclusion of the second session, I expressed my satisfaction with what we had achieved, she replied dismissively: 'So what's really come out?' thus preparing me for the approach of further revelations.

She began the third session with the words: 'You do know, doctor, that this is the last time I'll be coming here?'

I couldn't have known, as you haven't said anything to me about it.

'Yes, I've decided to stick it out until the New Year[18] but I'm not going to wait any longer than that for the cure.'

You know you are free to leave at any time. But let us work today. When did you reach this decision?

'Fourteen days ago, I think.'

That sounds like a servant-girl, or a governess: fourteen days' notice.

'A governess who resigned had been at K.'s once when I visited them in L. by the lake.'

Really? You've never mentioned that to me. Please tell me about it.

'Well, there was a young girl in the house acting as governess to the children, who behaved in a very curious way towards Herr K. She didn't greet him, she didn't reply to him, she didn't hand him anything at table if he asked for something; in short, she treated him like so much air. Incidentally, he wasn't much more polite to her. One or two days before the scene by the lake the girl took me to one side; she had something to tell me. She told me then that on one occasion, when his wife had been away for several weeks, he had approached her, had insistently wooed her and asked her to be nice to him; he got nothing from his wife etc.'

Those are the same words that he used in his advances to you, when you slapped his face.

'That's right. She yielded to him, but after a short time he stopped paying her any attention, and since then she had hated him.'

And that governess had handed in her notice?

'No, she wanted to hand it in. She told me that immediately she had felt abandoned she had related what had happened to her parents, who are respectable people and live somewhere in Germany. Her parents demanded that she leave the house immediately, and then wrote to tell her that if she didn't they would have nothing more to do with her, and she couldn't come home again.'

And why didn't she leave?

'She said she would wait a short time and see if things changed with Herr K. She couldn't bear living like that. If she saw no changes she would hand in her notice and leave.'

And what became of the girl?

'I only know that she left.'

And she didn't leave the affair with a child?

'No.'

Here, then, in the middle of the analysis, as is generally the rule, a piece of factual material had come to light that helped to solve problems thrown up earlier. I was able to tell Dora: now I know the reason behind the slap with which you responded to his advances. It wasn't hurt at his impertinence to you, but jealous revenge. When the girl told you her story, you used your skill to sweep aside everything that didn't suit your emotions. The moment Herr K. used the words: I get nothing from my wife, which he also used to the girl, fresh impulses were awoken in you, and the scales tipped over. You said to yourself: so he dares to treat me like a governess, a servant? That injury to self-esteem was associated with jealousy and also with sensible motives: in the end it was all too much.[19] As proof of how profoundly you were influenced by the girl's story, I present you with your repeated identification with her in the dream and in your behaviour. You tell your parents something that we haven't previously understood, just as the girl wrote to her parents. You dismiss me like a governess with fourteen days' notice. The letter in the dream, which enables you to come home, is a pendant to the letter from the girl's parents, who had forbidden her to do the same.

'Why didn't I tell my parents straight away?'

How much time did you allow to pass?

'The scene took place on the last day of June; on 14 July I told my mother.'

So, fourteen days again, the characteristic period for a servant to give her notice! I can now answer your question. You understood the poor girl very well. She didn't want to go because she still had hopes, because she expected that Herr K. would return his affections to her. So that must have been your motive, too. You waited for that date to see if he would repeat his advances, and from that you would have concluded that he was serious, and that he didn't mean to play with you as he had with the governess.

'He sent a postcard a few days after he left.'[20]

Yes, but when nothing more came, you gave your revenge free rein. Maybe you even thought at the back of your mind that you might persuade him, by means of your accusations, to travel to the place where you were staying.

'. . . As he at first proposed doing,' she interjected.

Then your longing for him would have been satisfied – here she nodded her confirmation, which I hadn't expected – and he could have given you the satisfaction you demanded.

'What satisfaction?'

I'm actually starting to sense that you took matters with Herr K. much more seriously than you previously wished to reveal. Wasn't there often talk of divorce between the Ks?

'Of course, at first they didn't want to because of the children, and now she wants to but he no longer does.'

Might you not have thought that he wanted to divorce his wife to marry you? And that he no longer wanted to because he had no one to replace you with? Two years ago, of course, you were very young, but you yourself have even told me that your Mama was engaged at seventeen and then waited a further two years for her husband. The story of the mother's love usually becomes a model for the daughter. So you wanted to wait for him, too, and assumed that he was just waiting until you were mature enough to become his wife.[21] I imagine you had quite a serious plan for your life. You didn't even have the right to claim that such an intention was ruled out where Herr K. was concerned, and you have told me enough about him that directly indicates such an intention.[22] His behaviour in L. doesn't contradict that, either. You didn't let him finish, and you don't know what he was going to tell you. At the same time the plan would not have been so impossible to carry out. Your Papa's relationship with Frau K., which you had probably only supported for so long for this reason, offered you the certainty that his wife might agree to a divorce, and you can get your Papa to do what you want. Indeed, if the temptation in L. had had another outcome, that would have been the sole possible solution for all parties. I also think that was why you so regretted the other outcome, and corrected it in the fantasy which took the form of appendicitis. So it must have been a severe disappointment for you when, instead of renewed advances, your accusation provoked a denial and insults from Herr K. You concede that nothing makes you so furious as when people think you imagined the scene by the lake. I now know what you didn't want to remember, that Herr K.'s declaration was serious and Herr K. would not give up until he married you.

She had been listening, without contradicting as she usually did. She seemed moved, said goodbye as sweetly as anything, with warmest wishes for the New Year and – never came back. Her father, who visited me a few more times, assured me that she could come back if she wished to; one could tell, he said, that she was longing for the treatment to continue. But he was probably never entirely sincere. He had been supporting the cure, as long as he was able to hope that I would 'dissuade' Dora from believing that there was anything but friendship between himself and Frau K. His interest faded away when he realized that this success was not part of my intention. I knew she would not come back. It was undoubtedly an act of revenge on her part, just when my expectations of a happy conclusion to the cure were at their highest point, to interrupt the analysis and dash those hopes in such an unexpected way. Her tendency to harm herself was also accounted for in this process. Anyone who, like myself, awakens the most wicked demons that dwell untamed in the human breast in order to do battle with them must be prepared to suffer some damage in the course of that struggle. Could I have kept the girl in treatment if I had found a part for myself to play, if I had exaggerated the importance of her presence for myself, and shown her a keen interest, which, in spite of the attenuation caused by my position as a doctor, would have resembled a substitute for the tenderness she longed for? I don't know. Since a part of the factors that we encounter as resistance in any case remains unknown to us, I have always avoided acting out roles, and contented myself with a more modest psychological art. In spite of all my theoretical interest and all my attempts to help as a doctor, I tell myself that boundaries are necessarily set on the psychical influence that one may legitimately exert, and in consequence of this I also respect the patient's will and insight.

Neither do I know whether Herr K. would have achieved more if he had been told that that slap in the face did not mean a definitive 'no' on Dora's part, but corresponded to her recently awakened jealousy, while the strongest impulses of her psychical life sided with him. If he had ignored that first 'no' and continued his advances with convincing passion, his love might have conquered all internal problems in order to win the girl's affection. But I believe that she might equally have been impelled to satisfy her vengeance upon him all the more violently. It is never possible to calculate the direction in which the decision will tend to go in a conflict between motives, whether towards the abolition or the intensification of repression. The inability to satisfy the *real* demands of love is one of the most significant character traits of neurosis; neurotics are dominated by the opposition between reality and fantasy. What they long for most intensely in their fantasies they flee from when they encounter it in reality, and they yield most readily to fantasies when there is no longer any need to fear their realization. The barrier erected by repression can, however, fall to the onslaught of violent excitements with real causes; neurosis can still be overcome by reality. But generally speaking we have no way of knowing in which patient and through which event that cure might be possible.[23]

### Notes

1. To this is later added the important supplement: *In one of the squares I see a monument.*

2. With the addition: *By this word there was a question mark: want?*

3. On a second occasion she repeats: *2 hours*.

4. Two additions in the next hour: *I see myself particularly clearly going up the stairs*, and: *After her answer I go to my room, although not the slightest bit sad, and read a big book on my desk.*

5. In the dream she asks: *Where is the station?* From this convergence I drew a conclusion that I shall develop below.

6. In the dream content the number five is present in the statement of time: *five minutes*. In my book on the interpretation of dreams I have shown with reference to several examples how numbers occurring in the dream thoughts are treated by the dream; one often finds them torn from their contexts and inserted into new ones.

7. Without a doubt sexual satisfaction is the best sleeping draught, just as sleeplessness is generally the consequence of the absence of satisfaction. Her father could not sleep because he lacked intercourse with the woman he loved. Cf. what follows below: I get nothing from my wife.

8. These words will lead to the solution of our mystery.

9. Here for the third time: painting [*Bild*] (cityscapes, gallery in Dresden), but in a much more significant connection. What is seen in the painting turns it into a female [*Weibsbild*] (forest, nymphs).

10. The 'station' incidentally facilitates 'Verkehr' ['traffic', or 'intercourse']. The psychical coating of some instances of fear of railways.

11. The defloration fantasy is the second component feature of this situation. The emphasis on the difficulty of going forward, and the anxiety felt in the dream, refer to the readily emphasized virginity that we find suggested elsewhere by the 'Sistine Madonna'. These sexual thoughts produce an unconscious background for the desires, which are perhaps kept secret, that deal with the suitor waiting in Germany. We have encountered the first component of this dream situation in the revenge fantasy. The two are not entirely identical, but only partially so. We will encounter the traces of an even more significant third train of thought below.

12. On another occasion, rather than using the word 'peacefully', she said 'not the slightest bit sad' (note 4 above). I can adduce this dream as a new proof for the correctness of an assertion contained in the *Interpretation of Dreams*, Chapter VII, Section A, II/III that the first forgotten and subsequently remembered fragments of the dream are always the most important for the understanding of the dream. There I draw the conclusion that the forgetting of dreams also demands to be explained with reference to internal psychical resistance. [The first sentence of this footnote was added in 1924.]

13. We may assume a somatic connection between painfulness identified between the 'ovaries' in the abdomen, and locomotor disturbance of the leg on the same side. In Dora's case this has a particularly specialized interpretation, that is, it is subject to psychical overlayering and utilization. Cf. the analogous observation in the analysis of the coughing symptoms and the connection between catarrh and lack of appetite.

14. A very typical example of symptoms arising out of causes that apparently have nothing to do with sexual matters.

15. I have already suggested that most hysterical symptoms, once they have reached their full formation, represent a fantasized situation of sexual life – a scene of sexual intercourse, a pregnancy, childbirth, etc.

16. The defloration fantasy, then, is applied to Herr K., and it becomes clear why the same region of the dream content includes material from the scene by the lake. (Rejection, two and a half hours, the forest, invitation to L.)

17. Some later additions to these interpretations: The 'Madonna' is clearly Dora herself, first because of the 'admirer' who sent her the pictures, then because she won Herr K.'s love above all through her maternal treatment of his children, and finally because as a virgin she had had a child, a direct reference to the fantasy of childbirth. The Madonna, incidentally, is a common oppositional idea when a girl is under pressure of sexual accusations, as is the case with Dora. I first suspected this connection as a doctor in the psychiatric clinic, when I was treating a case of hallucinatory confusion that had followed a very swift course, and which turned out to be a reaction to an accusation by the bridegroom.

Had the analysis continued, it would probably have become possible to demonstrate maternal longing for a child as an obscure but powerful motive for her behaviour. The many questions that she had recently thrown up seem to be belated offspring of the questions of sexual curiosity that she had sought to satisfy from the dictionary. We may assume that she had read about pregnancy, childbirth, virginity and similar themes. In reproducing the dream, she had forgotten one of the questions that could be incorporated within the context of the second dream situation. It could only be the question: Does Herr X live here? or: Where does Herr X live? There must be a reason why she forgot this apparently innocent question after introducing it into the dream. I find the reason in the surname itself, which also has a meaning referring to an object, and can thus be said to be an *'ambiguous'* word. Unfortunately I cannot communicate this name to show how skilfully it has been used to refer to 'ambiguous' and 'indecent' matters. This interpretation is supported in another region of the dream, where the material is drawn from the memories of the death of Dora's aunt, in the sentence, 'They have already gone to the cemetery', which also contains a reference to the aunt's *name*. These indecent words probably indicate to a second, *oral* source, as the words in question would not have been found in a dictionary. I should not be surprised to hear that Frau K. herself, the traducer, was the source. Dora would then have been nobly sparing her, while pursuing everyone else with an almost sly revenge; behind the multitude of displacements arising in this way we might suspect a simple element, her deep-rooted homosexual love for Frau K.

18. It was 31 December.

19. It was perhaps not irrelevant that she could also have heard the same complaint about his wife, the meaning of which she probably understood, from her father, as I heard it from him.

20. This refers to the engineer, concealed behind the 'I' in the first dream situation.

21. Waiting until one has reached one's goal: that is found in the content of the first dream situation. In this fantasy of waiting for the bride, I see part of the third component of this dream. I have alluded to that component above.

22. Particularly a speech with which he had accompanied the Christmas present of a writing-case during the last year of their stay together in B.

23. Some additional remarks on the structure of this dream, which cannot be so thoroughly understood that we might attempt a synthesis of it. Dora's fantasy of revenge against her father stands out like a prominent façade: She has left home of her own volition. Her father has fallen ill, then died . . . Now she goes home, the others are all already at the cemetery. She goes to her room, not at all sad, and peacefully reads the dictionary. This includes two references to the other act of revenge that she actually carries out by allowing her parents to find her farewell letter: the letter (Mama's letter in the dream) and the mention of the funeral of the aunt who had been a model to her. This fantasy conceals ideas of revenge against Herr K., for which she has found an outlet in her behaviour towards me. The maid – the invitation – the forest – the two and a half hours come from the material of events in L. The memory of the governess and her correspondence with Dora's parents, along with the element of her letter of farewell, joins the letter in the dream content which allows her to come home. The refusal to allow herself to be accompanied, the decision to go on her own, can probably be translated as follows: Because you have treated me as a maid, I am going to leave you behind, go my own way alone and stay unmarried. Elsewhere, covered over by these ideas of

revenge, material from affectionate fantasies of unconsciously continued love for Herr K. shines through: I would have waited for you until I had become your wife – the defloration – childbirth. Finally, it is part of the fourth, most deeply hidden circle of thoughts, that of Dora's love for Frau K., that the defloration fantasy is represented from the man's point of view (identification with the admirer, who is now abroad) and that at two points the clearest references to ambiguous words (does Herr X live here) and the non-oral source of her sexual knowledge (the dictionary). Cruel and sadistic impulses find fulfilment in this dream.

## IV  *Afterword*

It is true that I introduced this account as the fragment of an analysis; but the reader will probably have found that it is far more incomplete than its title might lead him to expect. I shall now attempt to explain the reasons for these far from arbitrary omissions.

Some results of the analysis have been left out partly because by the time the analysis was interrupted they had not been identified with sufficient certainty, and partly because they failed to continue through to a general result. In other instances, when it seemed appropriate to me, I have referred to the probable course that individual solutions would have taken. In these passages I have entirely passed over the technique – far from obvious – that is the only way of extracting the raw material from the ideas that occur to the patient. The disadvantage of this is that the reader is unable to confirm the correctness of my working method on the basis of my account. But I found it quite impracticable to deal simultaneously with the technique of an analysis and with the internal structure of a case of hysteria. It would have been an almost impossible task for me, and it would certainly have made a disagreeable experience for the reader. The technique needs to be represented quite separately, and to be explained with reference to examples taken from a wide variety of cases, whereby it would not be necessary to give the results of each individual case. I have not attempted to explain the psychological hypotheses revealed in my descriptions of psychical phenomena. A fleeting explanation would achieve nothing; a thorough explanation would be a task in itself. I can only assure the reader that without being wedded to a particular psychological system, I set about studying phenomena revealed by the observation of psychoneurotics, and that I then adjusted my opinions until they seemed suited to give a full account of all the patient's symptoms. I am not proud to have avoided speculation; but the material for these hypotheses has been gained through the most extensive and exhaustive observation. In particular, the resoluteness of my point of view concerning the unconscious has provoked dissent, since I work with unconscious ideas, trains of thought and impulses as though, as objects of psychological study, they were just as good and as certain as conscious phenomena; but I am sure that anyone setting out to examine the same field using the same method will be unable to avoid reaching the same point of view, in spite of all attempts by philosophers to persuade him otherwise.

Those among my colleagues who have considered my theory of hysteria to be purely psychological, and who have therefore declared it incapable of solving a pathological problem, will probably conclude from this account that in levelling their accusation, they are unfairly transferring a characteristic of the technique to the theory. It is only the therapeutic technique that is purely psychological; the theory does not neglect to refer to the organic basis of neurosis, although it does not seek that basis in pathological and anatomical change, substituting for chemical changes – which cannot currently be grasped – the provisional nature of the organic function. No one will be able to deny that the sexual function, in which I see the cause of hysteria and of psychoneuroses in general, has an organic element. No theory of sexual life will, I suppose, be able to avoid admitting the exciting action of particular sexual materials. Of all the syndromes that clinical practice teaches us about, the intoxications and the kinds of abstinence produced by the chronic use of certain toxins are closest to genuine psychoneuroses.

Neither have I written in this account about what we can say at present on the subject of 'somatic compliance', about the infantile seeds of perversion, about the erogenous zones and the predisposition to bisexuality. I have only emphasized those points at which the analysis comes into contact with these organic foundations of the symptoms. More could not be done on the basis of an individual case, and for the same reasons I also had to avoid a fleeting discussion of those elements. This will provide ample material for other works, based on a large number of analyses.

Nevertheless, in publishing this account, incomplete though it is, I had two aims: first to provide a supplement to my book about the interpretation of dreams, explaining how this otherwise useless art can be applied to the revelation of that which is hidden and repressed within the life of the human soul; in the analysis of the two dreams reported here, the technique of dream interpretation, similar to the technique of psychoanalysis, must be taken into account. Secondly, I wished to awaken interest in a series of connections at present completely unknown to science, because they are only discovered in the application of this particular process. No one has had a proper idea of the complications of the psychical processes at work in hysteria, the juxtaposition of the most diverse impulses, the reciprocal connection of opposites, instances of repression and displacement, and so on. Pierre Janet's emphasis on the *idée fixe*, which metamorphoses into the symptom, amounts to nothing but a pitiful schematization. In addition, it will not be possible to avoid the suspicion that excitements attached to ideas which are not capable of becoming conscious act upon one another in a different way, run a different course and manifest themselves differently from those which we refer to as 'normal', and the ideas attached to which do reach consciousness. Once we have grasped this, nothing stands in the way of our understanding of a therapy which stresses neurotic symptoms by transforming the former kind of ideas into normal ideas.

I was also concerned to show that sexuality does not intervene only once in the working of those processes that are characteristic of hysteria, as a *deus ex machina*, but that it provides the driving force for each individual symptom and each individual manifestation of a symptom. The manifestations of the illness are, to put it bluntly, the *patient's sexual activity*. No individual case will ever be capable of proving such a general principle, but I can only repeat it over and over again, because I never encounter anything else: sexuality is the key to the problem of psychoneuroses and neuroses in general. No one who scorns this idea will ever be in a position to solve this problem. I am still waiting for the research that might contradict or restrict this principle. But all that I have heard said against it so far has been in the form of expressions of personal displeasure or scepticism, which we need only counter with Charcot's phrase: '*Ça n'empêche pas d'exister*' [That doesn't mean it doesn't exist].

Neither is this case of whose history and treatment I have published a fragment here well suited to cast a proper light on the value of psychoanalytic therapy. Not only the brevity of the treatment, barely three months, but also another factor inherent within the case, prevented the cure from concluding with an improvement admitted both by the patient and by her relatives, which would be attainable otherwise, and would have corresponded more or less closely to a complete cure. Gratifying successes of this kind are achieved where symptoms are maintained only by internal conflict between impulses related to sexuality. In such cases one sees the condition of the patient improving to the extent that one has contributed to the solution of their mental difficulties by translating pathogenic into normal material. The cure proceeds differently when symptoms have been placed at the service of external motives concerning the patient's life, as had been the case with Dora over the previous two years. It is surprising, and it could easily be misleading, to learn that the state of the patient has not noticeably altered as a result even of highly advanced work. In fact, things are not as serious as they might appear; the symptoms may not disappear as a result of the work, but may do so a short while afterwards, once relations with the doctor have been severed. The delay of the cure or improvement is really only down to the personality of the doctor.

Let us add something further to our understanding of this state of affairs. We may say that as a general rule the new formation of symptoms is suspended during a psychoanalytical cure. The productivity of the neurosis is, however, by no means extinguished, but activated in the creation of thought formations of a particular kind, generally unconscious, to which we can give the name 'transferences'.

What are transferences? They are new editions, facsimiles of the impulses and fantasies that are to be awakened and rendered conscious as the analysis progresses, whose characteristic trait is the substitution of the person of the doctor for a person previously known to the patient. To put it another way: a whole series of earlier psychical experiences is brought to life not as something in the past, but as a current relationship with the doctor. There are transferences which differ from their model only in this substitution. To remain with the same metaphor, these are simply reprints, unmodified new editions. Others are made with greater skill, they have undergone an attenuation of their content, a *sublimation*, as I put it, and are even capable of reaching consciousness by basing themselves on some skilfully evaluated, real particularity in the person or the circumstances of the doctor. Those are revised and corrected editions, no longer mere reprints.

If one goes into the theory of analytical technique, one comes to the understanding that the transference is something that it necessarily requires. In practical terms, at least, one becomes convinced that one cannot by any means avoid it, and that this final creation of the illness is something to be struggled against, like all the others. Now this piece of work is by far the most difficult. The interpretation of dreams, the extraction of the unconscious thoughts and memories from the ideas that occur to the patient, and similar arts of translation, are easily learned; the patient always supplies the text himself. But the transference one must effectively guess on one's own, from little signs, taking care not to be guilty of arbitrariness. The transference is inescapable, however, because it is used in the production of all the obstacles that render the material of the cure inaccessible to treatment, and because the patient only becomes convinced of the correctness of the reconstructed connections after the transference has been resolved.

One will be inclined to consider it a serious disadvantage of the analytic process – troublesome enough already – that it increases the doctor's work by creating a new kind of pathological psychical product. One might, in fact, be tempted to conclude that the existence of transferences actually harms the patient in the course of the analytical cure. In both instances one would be mistaken. The doctor's work is not increased by the transference; it may be a matter of indifference to him whether he has to overcome the impulses of the patient as regards himself or another. But the cure also requires the patient to accomplish something new that he would not otherwise have been able to do. If the healing of neuroses takes place in institutions where psychoanalytic treatment is excluded, if, as we might say, hysteria is not healed by the method but by the doctor, if the result tends to be a kind of blind dependency and lasting attachment between the patient and the doctor who has freed him from his symptoms by means of hypnotic suggestion, the scientific explanation for all this lies in a 'transference', which the patient generally effects towards the person of the doctor. The psychoanalytic cure does not create the transference, it only reveals it, as it does other phenomena hidden in the mental life. The difference is expressed in the fact that the patient spontaneously calls upon only affectionate and friendly transferences leading towards his cure; where this cannot take place, he breaks off the treatment as quickly as possible, uninfluenced by the doctor, whom he does not find 'sympathetic'. In psychoanalysis, on the other hand, since the play of motives is different, all impulses, even hostile ones, are awoken, and made available to the analysis by being made conscious. The transference, destined to be the greatest obstacle to psychoanalysis, becomes its most powerful aid if one succeeds in guessing it correctly on each occasion and translating it to the patient.[1]

I had to mention the transference, because that factor alone enables me to explain the peculiarities of Dora's analysis. Its quality, which makes it appear suitable for a first, introductory publication, its particular transparency, is most intimately involved with its great shortcoming, which led to its premature interruption.

I did not succeed in mastering the transference in time; the readiness with which Dora put part of the pathogenic material at my disposal meant that I neglected to pay attention to the first signs of the transference, which she prepared with another part of the same material, a part that remained unknown to me. At first it clearly appeared that I was replacing her father in her imagination, which will be readily understood given the difference in our ages. In addition, she always consciously compared me to him, anxiously seeking to reassure herself about whether I was also being quite honest with her, since her father 'always opted for secrecy and a roundabout way'. Then, when she had her first dream, in which she warned herself to abandon the cure as she had abandoned Herr K.'s house, I should have been on my guard, and told her: 'Now you have made a transference from Herr K. to me. Have you noticed anything to make you suspect bad intentions on my part, similar to those of Herr K., either directly or in some sublimated form, or has something struck you about me, or have you discovered something about me that compels your affection, as happened with Herr K.?' Then I would have drawn her attention to some detail from our relationship, in my person or my situation, concealing something analogous but a great deal more important about Herr K., and as a result of the solution of this transference the analysis would have gained access to new material, probably based on real memories. But I ignored that first warning, telling myself that we had plenty of time, since no other signs of transference were apparent, and since the material for the analysis was not yet exhausted. So the transference took me by surprise, and because of whatever unknown factor it was that made me remind her of Herr K., she avenged herself on me, as she wanted to avenge herself on Herr K., and left me, just as she believed herself deceived and abandoned by him. In that way she was *acting out* a significant part of her memories instead of reproducing them in the cure. What that unknown factor was of course I cannot know: I suspect it may have related to money, or it might have been jealousy of another patient who had stayed in contact with my family after her cure. Where a transference can be prematurely incorporated into the analysis, it develops more slowly and obscurely, but it is better equipped against sudden and invincible resistance.

In Dora's second dream the transference is represented by several clear references. When she told me the dream, I did not know, and learned only two days later, that we only had *two hours* of work ahead of us, the same amount of time that she had spent in front of the Sistine Madonna, the same amount of time, after she had corrected herself (two rather than two and a half hours), as the walk that she had not taken back around the lake. The striving and waiting in the dream, both of which referred to the young man in Germany, and to the length of time she would have to wait before Herr K. could marry her, had been manifest in the transference a few days previously. The cure, she said, was taking too long for her, she wouldn't have the patience to wait that long, although, during the first few weeks, she had been sensible enough not to object when I told her that it would be a year before she had effected a complete recovery. The refusal to be accompanied in the dream, along with her insistence on going alone, which also came from the visit to the Dresden gallery: I was only to learn of these on the day appointed by Dora. The meaning was probably this: 'Since all men are so appalling, I would prefer not to marry. This is my revenge.'[2]

In those cases where impulses of cruelty and motives for revenge, which have already been used in life to maintain the symptoms, transfer themselves to the doctor in the course of the cure, before he has had time to free himself of them by returning to their sources, it can hardly come as a surprise if the patient's condition does not demonstrate the influence of his therapeutic efforts. For how better could the patient avenge herself than by demonstrating with her own person the doctor's impotence and incapacity? None the less, I am inclined not to underestimate the therapeutic value even of a fragmentary treatment such as Dora's.

Only a year and three months after the end of the treatment and the writing of this account of it, I received news of my patient's condition and thus of the outcome of the cure. On a date that was not quite indifferent, the 1st of April – we know that times were never insignificant for her – she appeared at my house to conclude the story and once again ask for help; but a glance at her face was enough to tell me that she was not serious in this respect. She had been in 'a confused state', as she put it, for four or five weeks after leaving the treatment. Then a great improvement began, the attacks became rarer, her mood lifted. In May of the past year, one of the K. children had died, the one who had always been sickly. She took this bereavement as an occasion to pay the Ks a visit of condolence, and was received by them as though nothing had happened over the past three years. On this occasion she was reconciled with them, took her revenge on them and brought the matter to a conclusion that was satisfying to her. To the wife she said: I know you have a relationship with Papa; and she did not deny it. She forced the husband to admit to the scene by the lake, and then took this vindicating information to her father. She did not resume contact with the family after that.

After that she was quite well until mid-October, when she lost her voice once again, not regaining it until six weeks later. Surprised by this information, I asked her whether there was any cause for this, and heard that the attack followed a violent shock. She had seen someone being hit by a car. She finally admitted that the victim of the accident had been none other than Herr K. She met him in the street one day; he approached her on a busy street, stopped in front of her as though confused and, in his distraction, was knocked over by a car.[3] She was sure, incidentally, that he had survived without any serious injuries. She said she still had a faint emotional reaction if she heard talk of her Papa's relationship with Frau K., in which she no longer involved herself. She lived for her studies, and did not think of marriage.

She sought my help for a facial neuralgia on the right-hand side, which had persisted day and night. For how long? 'For exactly fourteen days.'[4] – I had to smile, as I was able to show her that she had read a news item about me in the newspaper exactly fourteen days before, and she confirmed this (1902).

So the supposed neuralgia was a self-punishment, regret for the slap in the face that she had given Herr K., and a revenge-transference that she had passed from him to me. I do not know what kind of help she wanted to ask me for, but I promised to forgive her for losing me the satisfaction of freeing her much more thoroughly from her illness.

Years have passed since she visited me. Since then Dora has married, to the very same young man, if the signs do not deceive me, whom she mentioned at the beginning of the analysis of the second dream. Since the first dream indicated her detachment from the man she loved and a return towards her father, the flight from life into illness, this second dream signified that she was breaking away from her father and that life would win her back.

(1905)

## Notes

1. [*Addition 1923*:] What is said here about transference is continued in the technical essay about 'transference love' (in vol. X [of the *Gesammelte Werke*]).

2. The further removed I am in time from the termination of this analysis, the more likely it seems to me that my technical error was the following: I failed to guess in time, and to inform the patient, that her homosexual (gynaecophilic) feelings of love for Frau K. were the strongest of the unconscious currents in her mental life. I should have guessed that no one other than Frau K. could have been the chief source of her knowledge of sexual matters, the same person who had condemned her for her interest in such questions. It was striking, after all, that she knew all manner of improper things and claimed never to know how she knew them. I should have followed up on that mystery, I should have sought the reason for that strange repression. The reckless desire for revenge expressed in this dream was ideally suited to mask the opposite current, magnanimity, with which she forgave her beloved friend's betrayal and concealed from everyone the fact that it was Frau K. who introduced her to knowledge that was later used to cast suspicion upon her. Before I came to acknowledge the significance of the homosexual current among psychoneurotics, I often found

myself getting stuck in my treatment of cases, or else became completely confused.

3. An interesting contribution to the indirect suicide attempt discussed in my *Psychopathology of Everyday Life*.

4. See the significance of this date and its relationship to the theme of revenge in the analysis of the second dream.

# Screen Memories

In connection with my psychoanalytic treatment (of hysteria, obsessional neurosis, etc.) I have often had to deal with fragments of memories that have stayed with individual patients from their earliest childhood years. As I have indicated elsewhere, we must insist on the great pathogenic importance of impressions from this period of our lives. However, psychological interest in the subject of childhood memories is assured in all cases, because here it becomes strikingly evident that the psychical behaviour of children differs fundamentally from that of adults. No one doubts that our earliest childhood experiences have left indelible traces on our inner selves; but when we question our *memory* as to what impressions are destined to influence us till the end of our lives, it comes up with either nothing at all or a relatively small number of isolated recollections, often of questionable or perplexing significance. Not before our sixth or seventh year – and in many cases not until after our tenth – are our lives reproduced by the memory as a coherent chain of events. From then on, however, a constant relation is established between the psychical significance of an experience and its persistence in the memory. What seems important, by virtue of its immediate or almost immediate effects, is remembered; what is deemed of no consequence is forgotten. If I can remember an event over a long period, this very fact proves to me that it made a profound impression on me at the time. I am usually surprised if I have forgotten something *important*, and perhaps even more so if I have remembered something of apparently no consequence.

Only in certain pathological mental states does the relation that obtains in normal adults between the psychical importance of an impression and its retention in the memory once more cease to apply. A hysteric, for instance, will regularly suffer loss of memory with regard to all or some of the experiences that led to the onset of his sufferings, and that have nevertheless become important to him owing to this causal link, or that may be important to him, irrespective of this link, by virtue of their content. I should like to take the analogy between such pathological amnesia and the normal amnesia relating to our earliest years as a valuable pointer to the close connections between the psychical content of neurosis and the lives we led as children.

Being so used to the absence of childhood memories, we usually misunderstand the problem it conceals and are inclined to explain it as a self-evident consequence of the rudimentary way in which the infantile mind functions. Yet the truth is that any child who has developed normally already exhibits, at the age of three to four, a great many highly complex mental acquirements – an ability to make comparisons, to draw conclusions, to express his feelings – and there is no obvious reason why these mental performances, which are no less valuable than those that come later, should be subject to amnesia.

Before we start work on the psychological problems that attach to our earliest childhood memories, it is of course essential to collect material, to find out, by means of a survey, what kinds of memories a fairly large number of normal adults can report from this period of their lives. A first step in this direction was taken by V. and C. Henri in 1895, when they drew up and distributed a questionnaire, then published their highly interesting results – they had 123 respondents – in *L'Année Psychologique* III (1897) under the title 'Enquête sur les premiers souvenirs de l'enfance'. At present, however, I do not intend to treat the subject in its entirety, and shall concentrate on the few points from which I can go on to introduce the notion of what I call 'screen memories'.[1]

The time of life to which the content of our earliest childhood memories is allocated is usually the period between the ages of two and four. (This is true of 88 of the Henris' respondents.) But there are a few individuals whose memories go back further, even to the period before their first birthday. On the other hand there are some whose earliest recollections date only from their sixth, seventh or even eighth year. It is not possible at present to say what else is linked with these individual differences; but according to the Henris it is to be noted that a person whose earliest recollection belongs to a very tender age – to the first year of his life, let us say – also has further isolated memories from subsequent years, and that he begins to reproduce his experiences as a continuous chain of memory earlier than others, say from his fifth year. In individual cases, then, it is not only the appearance of the first recollection that is precocious or retarded, but the whole functioning of the memory.

Particular interest will attach to the question of what constitutes the normal content of these earliest childhood memories. A knowledge of adult psychology would lead us to expect that, from the material of our experience, certain impressions would be selected as worth remembering – namely, those which produced a powerful affective impact or were soon seen to be significant by virtue of their consequences. Indeed, some of the experiences collected by the Henris seem to confirm this expectation, for, as the most frequent content of the earliest childhood memories, they list on the one hand things that gave rise to fear, embarrassment, physical pain and so on, and, on the other, important events such as illnesses, deaths, fires, births of siblings, etc. One would therefore be inclined to assume that the principle of selection was the same for the child as it is for the adult. It should be expressly stated, of course – though it is fairly obvious – that our memories of childhood are bound to testify to the impressions that preoccupied the child, rather than the adult. It is therefore easy to explain why one respondent reports that, from the age of two, she remembers various accidents that befell her dolls, but has no recollection of the sad and serious events that she may have observed at the time.

Now, it is grossly at odds with this expectation, and bound to cause justifiable surprise, when we hear that the content of some people's earliest memories consists of everyday impressions that are of no consequence and could not have affected the child emotionally, but were nevertheless noted in copious detail – with excessive exactitude, one might say – whereas other, roughly contemporaneous, events are not remembered, even though the parents testify that the child was profoundly affected by them at the time. For instance, the Henris recount the story of a professor of philology, whose earliest memory, assigned to the age of three or four, was of a table set for a meal and with a bowl of ice on it. During that period the child's grandmother had died, and according to his parents her death had had a shattering effect on him. Yet the professor of philology, as he now is, knows nothing of this death; all he can recall from that period is a bowl of ice.

Another respondent reports, as his earliest childhood memory, an episode that took place during a walk, when he broke off a branch from a tree. He thinks he can still identify the spot where this happened. Several other people were present, and one of them helped him.

The Henris describe such cases as rare, but in my experience – admittedly mainly with neurotics – they are common enough. One of the Henris' respondents ventured to explain these memory images, whose banality makes them so hard to understand, and I have to say that I find his explanation entirely apposite. He thinks that in such cases the scene in question is retained in the memory in an incomplete form; this is why it seems meaningless. The parts of the impression that have been forgotten probably contained everything that made it memorable. I can confirm that this is really so, but rather than speak of elements of the experience having been 'forgotten', I would say that they had been 'omitted'. By means of psychoanalysis I have often been able to unearth the missing fragments of an infantile experience and so prove that the original impression, of which only the torso has remained in the memory, actually accorded, when restored, with the presumption that the memory holds on to what is most important. Admittedly this does not explain the curious selection it makes from the component parts of an experience. We must first ask ourselves why it suppresses what is significant, but retains what is of no consequence. It is only when we penetrate more deeply into the mechanism of such processes that we arrive at an explanation. We then conceive the idea that two psychical forces are involved in producing these memories. One of them takes the importance of the experience as a motive for wanting it remembered, but the other – the force of resistance – opposes this preferential choice. The two contending forces do not cancel each other out, nor does the one motive overpower the other, with or without loss to itself. Instead, a compromise is reached, rather like the resultant in a parallelogram of forces. The upshot of this compromise is that it is not the experience itself that supplies the memory image – in this respect the resistance carries the day – but another psychical element, which is closely associated with the one that proved objectionable. Here again we see the power of the former principle, which seeks to establish important impressions by creating reproducible memory images. Hence, the result of the conflict is that, instead of the memory image that was justified by the original experience, we are presented with another, which is to some extent associatively *displaced* from it. Since it was the *significant* components of the impression that made it objectionable, these must be absent from the memory that replaces it, and so it may well seem banal. We find it unintelligible because we would like to see the reason for its retention in its intrinsic content, when in fact it resides in the relation between this content and another, which has been suppressed. Echoing a popular phrase, one might say that, if a certain childhood experience asserts itself in the memory, this is not because it is golden, but because it has lain beside gold.

Among the many possible cases in which one psychical content is replaced by another (all of which are realized in various psychological constellations) the one we have been considering in connection with childhood memories – in which the inessential components of an experience stand in for the essential – is obviously one of the simplest. It is a case of displacement along the plane of association by contiguity, or, if one views the process as a whole, a case of repression, accompanied by the replacement of what is repressed by something in its (spatial or temporal) vicinity. I once had occasion to report a very similar case of substitution that occurred in the analysis of a patient suffering from paranoia.[2] This was a woman who heard voices repeating to her long passages from Otto Ludwig's *Heiterethei*, the most trivial and irrelevant passages in the work. Analysis revealed that other passages in the story had actually aroused the most distressing thoughts in the patient. The distress they caused was a motive for putting up a defence, but there was no way of suppressing the motives for pursuing them, and so a compromise was reached in which the innocuous passages emerged in the patient's memory with pathological force and distinctness. The process that is recognized here – *conflict, repression, substitution involving a compromise* – recurs wherever there are psychoneurotic symptoms and supplies the key to our understanding of how they arise. It is not without significance, then, that it can be shown to operate in the mental life of normal individuals too. The fact that in normal people it influences the selection of childhood memories seems to be yet another pointer to the intimate links, already emphasized, between the mental life of the child and the psychical material of neuroses.

The normal and the pathological defence processes, together with the displacements they lead to, are clearly of great importance, but as far as I know they have not been studied at all by psychologists, and it remains to be ascertained in what strata of mental activity they assert themselves, and under what conditions. This neglect may well be due to the fact that our mental life, in so far as it becomes an object of *conscious* internal perception, reveals nothing of these processes, except in those cases that we classify as 'faulty reasoning' or in some mental operations designed to produce a comic effect. When it is claimed that a psychical intensity can be shifted from one idea (which is then abandoned and remains so) to another (which now takes over the psychological role of the former), we find this bewildering, rather like certain features of Greek myth – as, for instance, when the gods clothe a human being with beauty, as with a veil, while the only transfiguration we know of is brought about by a change of facial expression.

Further investigation of these banal childhood memories has

taught me that they can arise in other ways too, and that an unsuspected wealth of meaning usually lies hidden behind their apparent harmlessness. But on this point I shall not confine myself to a mere statement of opinion, but give a detailed account of a particular instance, which seems to me the most instructive among a fairly large number of similar cases, and will undoubtedly be all the more appreciated because it relates to an individual who is not neurotic, or only very slightly so.

This is a man of thirty-eight, with a university education, who has maintained an interest in psychological questions – though they are remote from his professional concerns – ever since I was able to relieve him of a minor phobia by means of psychoanalysis. Last year he drew my attention to his childhood memories, which had already played some part in his analysis. Having become acquainted with the investigation conducted by V. and C. Henri, he gave me the following summary account of his own experience.

'I can draw upon a fair number of childhood memories, which I can date with great certainty. For at the age of three I left the small town where I was born and moved to a large town. Now, all my memories are set in the place where I was born, so they fall in the second or third year of my life. They are mostly short scenes, but they are very well preserved and incorporate every detail of sense perception, by contrast with the memory images from my mature years, which are devoid of any visual element. From my third year onwards the memories become scantier and less distinct, and there are gaps that must cover more than a year. I think it's only from my sixth or seventh year that the stream of memory becomes continuous. I would further divide the memories from the period up to my leaving my first place of residence into three groups. The first comprises those scenes that my parents repeatedly told me about later; where these are concerned, I'm not sure whether I had the memory image from the start, or only created it after hearing one of these accounts. However, I note that there were some occurrences that have no corresponding memory images, even though my parents described them to me more than once. I attach more importance to the second group; this is made up of scenes that – as far as I know – I was not told about, and some that I *couldn't* have been told about, because I haven't seen the participants since – my nursemaid and my playmates. I'll come to the third group later. As far as the content of these scenes – and hence their claim to be retained in the memory – is concerned, I would say that here I'm not wholly at a loss. Admittedly I can't say that the memories I've retained correspond to the most important events of my life at that time, or what I should now regard as the most important. I know nothing of the birth of a sister, who is two-and-a-half years younger than I am; our leaving home, my first sight of the railway, and the long carriage drive that preceded it have left no trace in my memory. On the other hand, I remember two small incidents during the train journey; as you will recall, these came up in the analysis of my phobia. What ought to have made the biggest impression on me was an injury to my face, which caused me to lose a lot of blood and was stitched up by the surgeon. I can still feel the scar, which testifies to the accident, but I have no recollection that would directly or indirectly point to this experience. Incidentally I was probably not yet two at the time.

'So I'm not surprised by the pictures and scenes from the first two groups. They are of course displaced memories, in which the essential element is mostly missing; but in some of them it is at least hinted at, and in others I can easily fill in the gaps by following certain pointers. If I proceed in this way, a sound connection can be established between the separate fragments of memory, and I can see clearly what childish interest recommended these particular events to my memory. But it's different with the content of the third group, which I've refrained from discussing so far. Here I'm faced with material – a longish scene and several small pictures – that I can really make nothing of. The scene seems to me fairly inconsequential, and I can't understand why it should have become fixed in my memory. Let me describe it to you. I see a square, rather steeply sloping meadow, very green and lush; among the greenery there are lots of yellow flowers, clearly common dandelions. At the top end of the meadow is a farmhouse; standing outside the door are two women, engaged in earnest conversation

– the farmer's wife, wearing a head-scarf, and a nursemaid. In the meadow three children are playing; one of them is myself, aged between two and three; the others are a male cousin, a year older than myself, and a female cousin, his sister, who is exactly my age. We are picking the yellow flowers, and each of us has a number of them. The little girl has the nicest bunch, but we two boys, as if by prior agreement, fall upon her and snatch her flowers from her. She runs up the meadow in tears, and the farmer's wife consoles her by giving her a big slice of black bread. No sooner have we seen this than we throw the flowers away, run up to the house, and also ask for bread. And we are given some. The farmer's wife cuts the loaf with a long knife. I remember that this bread tasted absolutely delicious. At this point the scene breaks off.

'What is there about this experience to justify the expenditure of memory that it put me to? I've racked my brains over this, but to no avail. Does the accent lie on our unkindness to the little girl? Am I supposed to have been so greatly attracted then by the yellow of the dandelion, a flower that I naturally don't find the least bit attractive today? Or did the bread taste so much better than usual, after all the romping around in the meadow, that it made an indelible impression on me? I can't find anything to connect this scene with the fairly obvious interest that forms the link between the other childhood scenes. Altogether I have the impression that there's something not quite right about this scene: the yellow of the flowers is far too prominent in the overall picture, and the delicious taste of the bread seems exaggerated, as though it were part of a hallucination. I can't help being reminded of some pictures I once saw in a parodistic exhibition. Certain parts of them were not painted, but applied in relief – naturally the most improper ones, such as the bustles of the painted ladies. Now, can you show me the way to an explanation or an interpretation of this pointless childhood memory?'

I thought it advisable to ask how long he had been exercised by this childhood memory. Did he think it had recurred periodically since childhood, or had it emerged at a later date, prompted by some occasion that he could recall? This question was all I needed to contribute to the solution of the problem: my interlocutor, who was no novice in the field, discovered the rest by himself.

He replied: 'That's something I've never thought about. But now that you ask, I'm almost certain that this memory didn't occupy me at all in my younger years. And I can also recall the occasion that aroused it, along with many other memories of my earliest years. As a schoolboy of seventeen, I went back to my home town for the first time and spent the holidays with a family who had been friends of ours since the early days. I can well remember what a multitude of emotions took hold of me at the time. But I see that I shall now have to tell you a good deal of my life history. It belongs here, and your question has conjured it up. So listen! My parents were originally well-to-do, and I think they lived a comfortable enough life in that little provincial backwater. But when I was about three, disaster struck the branch of industry that my father was concerned with. He lost his fortune, and we were forced to move to a big city. There then followed long years of hardship; I don't think there was anything about them worth remembering. I never felt really at ease in the town. I don't think I ever ceased to long for the glorious woods of my childhood, in which I would escape from my father when I could barely walk; this is confirmed by a memory I still have from that period. This holiday, when I was seventeen, was the first I'd spent in the country, and, as I said, I was staying with friends who had come up in the world since we moved away. I was able to compare the comfort that prevailed there with the life we led in the city. But it's probably no good avoiding the subject any longer: I have to admit that there was something else that greatly excited me. I was seventeen, and in the family I was staying with was a fifteen-year-old daughter, whom I at once fell in love with. It was my first infatuation, and very intense, but I kept it absolutely secret. After a few days the girl went back to her school, which she too had left for the holidays, and our parting, after such a short acquaintance, really brought my longing to a high pitch. I spent hours going for solitary walks in the lovely woods I had rediscovered, and building castles in the air – but these, curiously, were not directed to the future, but sought to improve the past. If only the crash hadn't occurred! If only I'd stayed in my home town, grown up in the country, and become as strong as the young men of the house, the brothers of the girl I loved! I could then have taken up my father's profession and finally married the girl, whom I'd have been bound to get to know intimately over all these years! I naturally didn't doubt for a moment that, in the circumstances created by my imagination, I should have loved her just as ardently as I actually felt I did then. The strange thing is that when I see her occasionally – she happens to have married someone near here – I'm extraordinarily indifferent to her, yet I well remember how long I went on being affected by the yellow colour of the dress she was wearing at our first meeting, whenever I saw the same colour again somewhere.'

That sounds rather like your passing remark that you now no longer like the common dandelion. Don't you suspect a connection between the yellow of the girl's dress and the excessively bright yellow of the flowers in your childhood scene?

'Possibly, but it wasn't the same yellow. The dress was more of a yellowish brown, like the colour of wallflowers. But I can at least supply you with an intermediate idea that would serve your purpose. Later, in the Alps, I saw that some flowers that have light colours in the plain take on darker shades on the high ground. Unless I'm much mistaken, there's a flower one often sees in the mountains that's very much like a dandelion, but it has a dark yellow colour, exactly like the dress worn by the girl I was in love with. But I haven't finished. I now come to a second occasion, from about the same period of my life, that stirred up impressions of my childhood. At seventeen I had revisited my home town. Three years later, again during the holidays, I went to stay with my uncle, and so I saw my first playmates again – my male cousin, who was a year older than myself, and my female cousin, who was my age – both of whom figure in the childhood scene in the field with the dandelions. This family had left my home town at the same time as we had, and had once more become prosperous in the distant city.'

And did you fall in love again, this time with your cousin, and weave fresh fantasies?

'No, this time it turned out differently. I was already at the university, and wedded to my books. I had no time for my cousin. As far as I know, I invented no fantasies of that kind. But I think my father and my uncle, between them, had a plan for me: that I should switch from the abstruse subject I was studying to one that was of more practical use, and that, on completing my studies, I should settle in the town where my uncle lived and marry my cousin. When they realized how much I was absorbed in my own plans, they probably dropped theirs, but I'm sure my guess was right. It was only later, as a young scholar – when the hardships of life closed in on me and I had to wait so long for a post in the city – that I may sometimes have reflected that my father had meant well when he wanted to see me compensated, by this marriage project, for the loss that the earlier catastrophe had brought upon my life.'

So I would place the origin of the childhood scene we are discussing in this period of your life, when you were struggling for your daily bread – that is, if you can confirm that it was during these years that you made your first acquaintance with the Alps.

'That's right. Climbing holidays were the only pleasure I allowed myself in those days. But I still don't quite understand you.'

I'll come to the point right away. As the most intense element in your childhood scene you single out the delicious taste of the country bread. Don't you see that this imagined experience, which you feel to be almost hallucinatory, corresponds with the idea contained in your fantasy: about how comfortable your life would have turned out to be if you'd stayed in your home town and married that girl – or, to put it metaphorically, how tasty you would have found the bread that you later had to struggle hard for? And the yellow of the flowers points to the same girl. Besides, the childhood scene contains elements that can only relate to the second fantasy – that of being married to your cousin. Throwing away the flowers for a piece of bread seems to me not a bad disguise for the plan your father had for you. You were to renounce your unpractical ideals in favour of 'bread-and-butter' studies, weren't you?

'So it seems that I fused the two sets of fantasies about how my life might have been more comfortable; I took the "yellow" and the "country" bread from the one, and the discarding of the flowers and the actual people concerned from the other?'

Yes. You projected the two fantasies on to one another and turned them into a childhood memory. So the feature of the Alpine flowers is, so to speak, the date-mark for its construction. I can assure you that such things are very often constructed unconsciously – almost like works of fiction.

'But then it wouldn't be a childhood memory at all, but a fantasy that I've transposed into my childhood. But I have a feeling that the scene is genuine. How can that be reconciled with what you say?'

There's no guarantee whatever for what our memory tells us. But I'll gladly concede that the scene is genuine; if so, you singled it out from countless others of a similar or differing kind, because it was suited, by virtue of its essentially indifferent content, to the representation of the two fantasies, which were significant enough to you. Such a memory, whose value consists in the fact that it represents thoughts and impressions from a later period and that its content is connected with these by links of a symbolic or similar nature, is what I would call a *screen memory*. In any case you will cease to be surprised by the frequent recurrence of this scene in your memory. It can no longer be called a harmless one if, as we have discovered, it is intended to illustrate the most important turning points in the history of your life, the influence of the two most powerful motive forces – hunger and love.

'Yes, it represented hunger well enough – but love?'

In the yellow of the flowers, I think. But I can't deny that the representation of love in this childhood scene of yours lags far behind what I should have expected from my previous experiences.

'No, it doesn't at all. The representation of love is the main thing about it. At last I understand! Just think: to take away a girl's flower – that means to deflower her. What a contrast between the impudence of this fantasy and my shyness on the first occasion and my indifference on the second!'

I can assure you that such bold fantasies form the regular complement to juvenile shyness.

'But then the fantasy that's transformed itself into these childhood memories wouldn't be a conscious one that I can remember,
would it, but an unconscious one?'

Unconscious thoughts that continue the conscious ones. You
think to yourself, 'If I'd married this girl or that girl,' and behind
the thought there arises an urge to picture what being married
would have been like.

'I can go on from there myself. For the young good-for-nothing
the most enticing thing about this whole topic is the idea of the
wedding night. What does he care about what comes afterwards?
But this idea doesn't venture into the open; the prevailing mood
of modesty and respect for girls keeps it suppressed. So it remains
unconscious . . .'

And *escapes* into a childhood memory. You're right: the coarsely
sensual element in the fantasy is the reason why it doesn't develop
into a conscious fantasy, but has to be satisfied with being taken
up into a childhood scene, as an allusion dressed up in a *flowery*
disguise.

'But why into a childhood scene, I wonder?'

Perhaps because of the innocence of childhood. Can you imagine any greater contrast to such wicked, aggressive sexual designs
than the pranks played by children? In any case there are more
general reasons that determine why repressed thoughts and desires
should escape into childhood memories, for you can quite regularly point to the same reaction in persons suffering from hysteria.
It also seems that the recollection of things long past is in itself
facilitated by some pleasurable motive: *'Forsan et haec olim memi-
nisse juvabit.'*[3] ['Perhaps even this will one day be pleasant to recall.']

'If that is so, I've lost any faith I had in the genuineness of the
scene with the dandelions. I see it like this: on the two occasions
I've mentioned, and supported by very real, palpable motives, the
idea has occurred to me: "If you had married this or that girl your
life would have become much pleasanter." Now, the sensual current
in me repeats the thought contained in the conditional clause in

images that can offer satisfaction to this sensual current. This second version of the same thought remains unconscious owing to its incompatibility with the prevailing sexual disposition, but for this very reason it is able to live on in my mental life when the conscious version has long since been removed by changes in the real situation. In accordance with a general law, you say, the clause that has remained unconscious seeks to transform itself into a childhood scene, which is allowed to become conscious because of its innocence. To this end it has to undergo a fresh transformation, or rather two: one of them removes the objectionable element from the protasis by expressing it in ideal terms, while the second presses the apodosis into a form that is capable of visual representation, using for this purpose the intermediate notions of "bread" and "bread-and-butter studies". I realize that by producing a fantasy like this I have, as it were, achieved a fulfilment of the two suppressed desires – to deflower the girl and to secure material comfort. But now that I can fully account to myself for the motives that led to the emergence of the dandelion fantasy, I have to assume that I'm dealing here with something that never happened at all, but has been illegitimately smuggled in among my childhood memories.'

Now I have to act as counsel for the defence and vindicate its genuineness. You're going too far. You've heard me say that every suppressed fantasy of this kind has a tendency to escape into a childhood scene. Now, add to this the fact that it can't do so unless a memory-trace is present, whose content offers points of contact with the fantasy, which meets it halfway, as it were. Once such a point of contact is found – in the present case it is the deflowering, the taking away of the flower – the remaining content of the fantasy is remodelled by the addition of any admissible intermediate idea – think of the bread! – until new points of contact with the content of the childhood scene have emerged. It is quite possible that during this process even the childhood scene itself will be subject to modifications; I think it is certain that memories can be falsified in this way. In your case the childhood scene appears to have undergone a little extra chasing; think of the over-emphasis on the yellow and the excessively delicious bread. But the raw material was usable. Had this not been so, the memory could not have emerged into consciousness from among all the others. You wouldn't have had such a scene as a childhood memory, or perhaps you would have had a different one, for of course you know how easily the brain can build connecting bridges in all directions. The authenticity of your dandelion memory is incidentally supported not just by your feeling – which I wouldn't want to underrate – but by something else. It contains features that can't be explained by what you've told me and don't fit in with the meanings that derive from the fantasy. For instance, the fact that your male cousin helps you steal the flowers from the little girl. Can you make sense of such cooperation in the act of defloration? Or of the two women, the farmer's wife and the nursemaid, up there in front of the house?

'I don't think I can.'

So the fantasy doesn't coincide entirely with the childhood scene; it only relies on it at certain points. That speaks in favour of the authenticity of the memory.

'Do you think that such an interpretation of seemingly innocent childhood memories is often appropriate?'

Very often, in my experience. Do you want to amuse yourself by trying to see whether the two examples the Henris report can be interpreted as screen memories for later experiences and desires? I mean the memory of the table that's set for a meal and has a dish of ice on it, which is supposed to be connected with the grandmother's death. And the second one, of the child breaking off a branch during a walk and being helped by another person?

He reflected for a while, then said, 'I can't make anything of the first one. It's very probable that a displacement is involved, but there's no way of guessing what the intermediate elements are. For the second I'd venture an interpretation if the person reporting it as his own were not a Frenchman.'

Now I don't understand you. What difference does that make?

'A big difference, since the linguistic expression probably supplies the link between the screen memory and the one being screened. In German the phrase "to tear one out" is a fairly well-known vulgarism for masturbation. The scene would transpose a later seduction into masturbation into early childhood, as someone helps him to do it. But even so it doesn't work, because so many other people are present in the childhood scene.'

Whereas the seduction into masturbation must have taken place in secret, with no one else around. It's this very contradiction that seems to me to support your view; yet again it serves to make the scene innocent. Do you know what it means when we see 'a lot of strangers' in a dream, as so often happens in dreams of nakedness, in which we feel so terribly embarrassed? Nothing other than – secrecy, which is then expressed by its opposite. In any case this interpretation remains a joke, for we really don't know whether a Frenchman would see an allusion to masturbation in the phrase *casser une branche d'un arbre* or in some modified version of it.

The foregoing analysis, which I have reported as faithfully as possible, may to some extent have clarified the notion of a *screen memory* as one that owes its value as a memory not to its intrinsic content, but to the relation obtaining between this content and some other, which has been suppressed. According to the varying nature of this relation it is possible to distinguish different classes of screen memories. We have found examples of two of these classes among our so-called earliest childhood memories – that is, if we allow the incomplete childhood scene, whose incompleteness ensures its harmlessness, to count as a screen memory. It is to be expected that screen memories will also be formed from remnants of memory that date from later periods of our lives. Anyone who bears in mind their main characteristic – a high degree of memorability together with a wholly banal content – will have no difficulty in identifying many examples of this sort in his own memory. Some of these screen memories – those which deal with experiences from later in life – owe their significance to a connection with experiences of early youth that have remained suppressed; this connection is thus the reverse of the one in the case I analysed above, in which a recollection of childhood is accounted for by later experiences. Depending on which of these chronological relations holds between the screen and what it screens off, a screen memory can be described as either *retrogressive* or *anticipatory*. From another point of view we can distinguish between positive and negative screen memories (or *refractory* memories), whose content stands in a contrary relation to the suppressed content. The subject probably deserves more thorough examination, but here I will confine myself to pointing out what complicated processes are involved in producing our store of memories – processes, incidentally, that are wholly analogous to the formation of hysterical symptoms.

Our earliest childhood memories will always be an object of special interest, because the problem that was mentioned at the beginning of this article – why it is that those impressions that have the most powerful effect on our whole future need not leave a memory image behind – leads us to reflect on the emergence of conscious memories in general. We shall no doubt be inclined at first to eliminate the screen memories we have been discussing as foreign bodies among our surviving childhood recollections; as for the remaining images, we shall probably adopt the simple view that they arise simultaneously with the experiences they relate to and as a direct consequence of the effect these produce, and that from then on they recur from time to time in accordance with the known laws that govern the reproduction of such images. Closer observation, however, reveals individual features that accord badly with this view. Foremost among these is the following: in most of the significant and otherwise unimpeachable childhood scenes that one recalls, one sees oneself as a child and knows that one is this child, yet one sees the child as an outside observer would see him. The Henris do not fail to point out that many of their respondents expressly emphasize this peculiarity of childhood scenes. Now, it is clear that this memory image cannot be a faithful replica of the impression that was received at the time. For the subject was then in the middle of the scene, paying attention not to himself, but to the world outside himself.

Wherever one appears in a memory in this way, as an object among other objects, this confrontation of the acting self with the recollecting self can be taken as proof that the original impression has been edited. It seems as though a memory-trace from childhood had here been translated back into a plastic and visual form at a later date, the date at which the memory was aroused. But no reproduction of the original impression has ever entered our consciousness.

In favour of this alternative view there is another fact that carries even greater conviction. Among our childhood memories of significant experiences, all of which appear equally clear and distinct, there are some scenes that turn out, when checked – against the recollections of adults, for instance – to have been falsified. It is not that they have been freely invented; they are incorrect in so far as they transfer an event to a place where it did not happen (as in one example reported by the Henris), merge two people into one, substitute one person for another, or reveal themselves as combinations of two discrete experiences. Simple inaccuracy of recall plays no significant part in this, given the great sensory intensity of the images and the efficient functioning of the memory in the young. Detailed investigation shows rather that such falsifications are of a tendentious nature; that is to say, they serve to repress and replace objectionable or disagreeable impressions. So even these falsified memories must have arisen at a time when such conflicts and the impulse to repression could already assert themselves in a person's mental life – in other words, long after the period to which their content relates. But here too the falsified memory is the first one of which we have any knowledge, since the raw material out of which it was forged – the earliest memory-traces – has remained inaccessible in its original form.

In our estimation, the recognition of this fact diminishes the gap between screen memories and other memories from childhood. It is perhaps altogether questionable whether we have any conscious memories *from* childhood: perhaps we have only memories *of* childhood. These show us the first years of our lives not as they were, but as they appeared to us at later periods, when the memories were aroused. At these times of arousal the memories of childhood did not *emerge*, as one is accustomed to saying, but *were formed*, and a number of motives that were far removed from the aim of historical fidelity had a hand in influencing both the formation and the selection of the memories.

(1899)

### Notes

1. [This is the standard translation of Freud's term *Deckerinnerungen*, a compound of the stem of the verb *decken* ('to cover') and the noun *Erinnerungen* ('memories'); a more literal rendering would be 'cover memories'.]

2. 'Weitere Bemerkungen über die Abwehr-Neuropsychosen', *Neurologisches Zentralblatt*, 1896, no. 10 (to be found in the collected works [*Gesammelte Werke*, vol. I]).

3. [Virgil, *Aeneid*, I.203.]

# *Humour*

In my book *Jokes and their Relation to the Unconscious* (1905), I actually approached humour only from the economic point of view. My concern was to find the source of the pleasure in humour, and I think I have shown that the gain in pleasure through humour arises out of saved emotional expenditure.

The humorous process can occur in two ways: either through one's own person, which adopts the humoristic attitude, while the role of spectator and consumer falls to the second person, or between two people, one of whom plays no part whatsoever in the humoristic process, while the second makes this person the object of his humorous consideration. When, to linger over the crudest of examples, the criminal who is being led to the gallows on Monday observes, 'Well, that's a good start to the week,' he himself is developing humour, the humorous process is accomplished within his person and clearly brings him a certain satisfaction. I myself, the uninvolved listener, in a sense receive a long-distance effect of the offender's humorous accomplishment; I feel, perhaps in a similar way to the man himself, the humorous gain in pleasure.

The second case occurs when, for example, a poet or story-teller describes the behaviour of real or invented people in a humorous fashion. These people need demonstrate no humour themselves, the humorous attitude applies only to the person taking them as his object, and as in the previous case the reader or listener in turn has access to the enjoyment of humour. To sum up, then, one can say that the humorous attitude – whatever it may consist in – can be turned against one's own person or against third parties; we may assume that it brings a gain in pleasure to the person who does this; a similar gain in pleasure falls to the – uninvolved – listener.

We will most clearly understand the genesis of the humorous gain in pleasure if we turn our attention to the process at work in the listener before whom someone else produces humour. He sees that other person in a situation which suggests that he is about to produce the signs of an affect; he will get annoyed, complain, express pain, be startled or frightened, perhaps even show despair, and the viewer or listener is prepared to follow him in this, and to allow the same emotional impulses to arise in himself. But this emotional readiness is disappointed, the other party is not in fact expressing an affect, but making a joke; the saved emotional expenditure on the part of the listener now becomes the pleasure of humour.

It is easy to reach this point, but soon we also say to ourselves that it is the process at work in the other person, in the 'humorist', that merits the greater attention. Without a doubt, the essence of humour consists in the fact that one is saving oneself the affects that the situation would cause in reality, and dismissing the possibility of such emotional expressions with a joke. To this extent the process at work in the humorist must coincide with that of the listener, or more correctly, the process in the listener must have copied the one at work in the humorist. But how does the humorist bring about that psychical attitude that makes the affective bond redundant for him; what is dynamically occurring in him with his 'humorous attitude'? Clearly the solution to the problem is to be sought in the humorist; all we can assume in the listener is an echo, a copy of that unknown process.

It is time for us to familiarize ourselves with some of the characteristics of humour. There is not only something liberating about humour, just as with jokes and comedy, but something grand and uplifting, traits that cannot be found in the other two kinds of gain in pleasure from intellectual activity. The grandeur clearly lies in the triumph of narcissism, in the triumphantly asserted invulnerability of the ego. The ego refuses to be hurt by causes in reality, to be obliged to suffer, it insists that the traumas of the outside world cannot get near it, indeed it shows that it sees them only as occasions for the gain in pleasure. This last trait is entirely essential to humour. If we imagine that the criminal being led to execution on Monday had said: 'I don't care, what does it matter if a chap like me is hanged, the world won't fall apart over it,' we would judge that while the speech may include such a grand superiority over the real situation, and while it may be wise and justified, it does not betray a trace of humour, indeed, it is based on an assessment of reality that runs directly counter to that of humour. Humour is not resigned, it is scornful, it signifies not only the triumph of the ego, but also that of the pleasure principle, which is here able to assert itself against the disfavour of real circumstances.

These two latter traits, the rejection of the claim of reality and the enforcement of the pleasure principle, bring humour closer to the regressive or reactionary processes that concern us so extensively in psychopathology. With its defence against the possibility of suffering, it assumes a place in the great series of those methods created by the life of the human psyche to escape the compulsion of suffering, a series that begins with neurosis, peaks in madness, and which includes intoxication, self-absorption and ecstasy. From this connection humour derives a dignity that is utterly absent from jokes, for example, because jokes either serve the gain in pleasure or place the gain in pleasure at the service of aggression. So in what does this humorous attitude consist, through which one refuses to accept suffering, stresses the invincibility of the ego by the real world and victoriously asserts the pleasure principle, but does all these things without, unlike other processes with the same intention, leaving the terrain of psychical health? Indeed, the two functions seem incompatible with one another.

If we turn to the situation in which someone adopts a humorous attitude towards other people, the view that I have hesitantly put forward in my book about jokes suggests itself, that he is behaving towards them as an adult behaves towards a child, by recognizing the nullity of the interests and sufferings that seem great to the child, and smiling at them. The humorist, then, gains his superiority from the fact that he places himself in the role of the adult, in a sense identifies with the father and reduces other people to children. This hypothesis probably coincides with the facts, but it hardly seems compelling. One might wonder how the humorist comes to assume this role.

But we remember the other, probably more primitive and significant situation of humour, in which someone directs the humorous attitude against his own person, as a way of defending himself against the possibilities of his suffering. Is it meaningful to say that someone is treating himself as a child and at the same time playing the role of the superior adult towards that child?

I think we will give this rather implausible idea strong support if we bear in mind what we have learned from pathological experiences about the structure of our ego. This ego is not something simple, but has as its nucleus a particular agency, the superego, with which it sometimes merges to such an extent that we cannot differentiate the two, while in other cases it is sharply distinguished from it. The superego is genetically the heir to the parental agency, it often holds the ego in strict dependence, and really continues to treat it as in early childhood the parents – or the father – treated the child. So we dynamically elucidate the humorous attitude if we suggest that it may consist in the fact that the person of the humorist has taken the psychical emphasis away from his ego and transferred it to his superego. The ego may now seem minute to a superego that has been swollen in this way, all its interests may seem trivial, and with this new distribution of energy it may be easy for the superego to suppress the possibilities for a reaction on the part of the ego.

Remaining true to our customary terminology, we shall have to speak not of transposition of psychical emphasis, but displacement of large quantities of investment. We might then wonder whether we can imagine such substantial displacements from one agency of the psychical apparatus to another. It appears like a new, ad hoc hypothesis, but we may recall that in our attempts at a metapsychological idea of psychical activity we have repeatedly, although perhaps not often enough, expected to come across such a factor. Thus, for example, we suggested that the difference between an ordinary erotic object-investment and the state of passionate love consists in the fact that in the latter case a disproportionately larger amount of investment passes to the object, and the ego voids itself, so to speak, in the direction of the object. In the study of some cases of paranoia I have been able to establish that the ideas of persecution are formed early on and persist for a long time without manifesting any noticeable effect, until for some particular reason they receive the quantities of investment that allow them to become dominant. The cure of such paranoid attacks might also consist less in a breakdown and revision of delusory ideas than in the withdrawal of the investment bestowed upon them. The alternation of melancholia and mania, of the cruel suppression of the ego by the superego and the liberation of the ego after such pressure, has given us the impression of such a change in investment, which would incidentally also need to be invoked to explain a whole series of phenomena in normal psychical life. This has hitherto occurred to such a small extent because of our rather praiseworthy reticence. The field in which we feel secure is that of the pathology of the psychical life; it is here that we make our observations and acquire our convictions. We provisionally allow ourselves a judgement about normal psychical life to the extent that we can discern the normal in the isolations and distortions of the pathological. Once our hesitancy has been overcome, we will be able to recognize the important role played both by static conditions and dynamic changes in the quantity of energy investment in the understanding of psychical processes.

I think, therefore, that we should retain the possibility suggested here, that in a particular situation the subject suddenly over-invests his superego and then, proceeding from it, alters the reactions of the ego. What I suspect to be true of humour also finds a remarkable analogy in the related field of the joke. As the origin of jokes I had to assume that a preconscious thought is left over for an element of unconscious revision, so that the joke is the contribution of comedy achieved by the unconscious. Quite similarly, *humour is the contribution to comedy through the agency of the superego*.

In other connections, we know the superego to be a strict master. It will be said that it accords ill with such a character that it condescends to allow the ego the possibility of a small gain in pleasure.

It is correct that humorous pleasure never achieves the intensity of pleasure in comedy or in jokes, and never issues in hearty laughter; it is also true that the superego, when it provokes the humorous attitude, actually rejects reality and serves an illusion. But we attribute to this non-intense pleasure – without really knowing why – a character of very high value, we feel it to be particularly liberating and uplifting. In humour, the joke is not the essential thing, it only has the value of a preliminary test; what is crucial is the intention that humour carries out, whether it engages with the speaker himself or with others. It means: 'Look, this is the world that looks so dangerous. It is child's play, it is only right to make a joke about it!'

If it is really the superego that speaks with such loving consolation to the intimidated ego, we should bear in mind that we still have a great deal to learn about the nature of the superego. Incidentally, not all people are capable of the humorous attitude, it is a rare and delightful gift, and many lack even the ability to enjoy the pleasure of humour conveyed to them. And finally, if the superego strives to comfort the ego through humour, and to protect it from suffering, in so doing it has not contradicted its origins in the parental agency.

(1928)

# Publishing Histories
# Copyright Information

# PENGUIN MODERN CLASSICS

---

### CIVILIZATION AND ITS DISCONTENTS
SIGMUND FREUD

Civilization and its Discontents/'Civilized' Sexual Morality and Modern Nervous
Illness

Translated by David McLintock

With an Introduction by Leo Bersani

'Narratives that have the colour and force of fiction' John Updike

In his final years, Freud devoted most of his energies to a series of highly
ambitious works on the broadest issues of religion and society.

As early as 1908, he produced a powerful paper on the repressive hypocrisy of
'civilized sexual morality', and its role in 'modern nervous illness'. Deepening
this analysis in *Civilization and its Discontents*, he argues that 'civilized' values –
and the impossible ideals of Christianity – inevitably distort our natural
aggression and impose a terrible burden of guilt. It is also here that Freud
developed his last great theoretical innovation: the strange and haunting notion of
an innate death drive, locked in a constant struggle with the forces of Eros.

**General Editor: Adam Phillips**

# PENGUIN MODERN CLASSICS

### MASS PSYCHOLOGY AND OTHER WRITINGS
SIGMUND FREUD

Compulsive Actions and Religious Exercises / Mass Psychology and Analysis of the 'I' / A Religious Experience / The Future of an Illusion / Moses the Man and Monotheistic Religion / A Comment on Anti-Semitism

Translated by J. A. Underwood

With an Introduction by Jacqueline Rose

'Freud was an explorer of the mind ... an overturner and a re-mapper of accepted or settled geographies and genealogies' Edward Said

These works reveal Freud at his most iconoclastic, asking challenging questions about the powerful attraction of group identity and how this has the power to bind us and drive us to hatred.

In *Mass Psychology* he explores the psyche as a social force, with a compelling analysis of how institutions such as the Church and army can generate unquestioning loyalty to a leader and provoke us to commit atrocities – Freud's findings would prove all too prophetic in the years that followed. Works such as 'Moses the Man', written at the time of Freud's flight from Nazism in 1938, warn of the dangers of nationalism. Writings like 'The Future of an Illusion' examine religion and ritual in an unrelenting critique of religious faith.

**General Editor: Adam Phillips**

# ENGUIN MODERN CLASSICS

## BEYOND THE PLEASURE PRINCIPLE AND OTHER WRITINGS
SIGMUND FREUD

On the Introduction of Narcissism / Remembering, Repeating and Working Through / Beyond the Pleasure Principle / The Ego and the Id/Inhibition, Symptom and Fear

Translated by John Reddick

With an Introduction by Mark Edmundson

'Freud's great legacy ... brilliantly exposes the state of the psyche' Mark Edmundson

In Freud's view we are driven by the desire for pleasure, as well as by the desire to avoid pain. But the pursuit of pleasure has never been a simple thing. Pleasure can be a form of fear, a form of memory and a way of avoiding reality. Above all, as these essays show with remarkable eloquence, pleasure is a way in which we repeat ourselves.

The essays collected in this volume explore, in Freud's uniquely subtle and accessible style, the puzzles of pleasure and morality – the enigmas of human development.

**General Editor: Adam Phillips**

# PENGUIN MODERN CLASSICS

**STUDIES IN HYSTERIA**
SIGMUND FREUD AND JOSEPH BREUER

Civilization and its Discontents / Civilized Sexual Morality and Modern Nervous Illness

Translated by Nicola Luckhurst

With an Introduction by Rachel Bowlby

'The effect that psychoanalysis has had upon the life of the West is incalculable'
Lionel Trilling

The tormenting of the body by the troubled mind – hysteria – is among the most pervasive of human disorders, yet at the same time it is the most elusive. Freud's recognition that hysteria stemmed from traumas in the patient's past transformed the way we think about sexuality.

*Studies in Hysteria* is one of the founding texts of psychoanalysis, revolutionizing our understanding of love, desire and the human psyche. As full of compassionate human interest as of scientific insight, these case histories are also remarkable, revelatory works of literature.

**General Editor: Adam Phillips**